J. S. Cotman

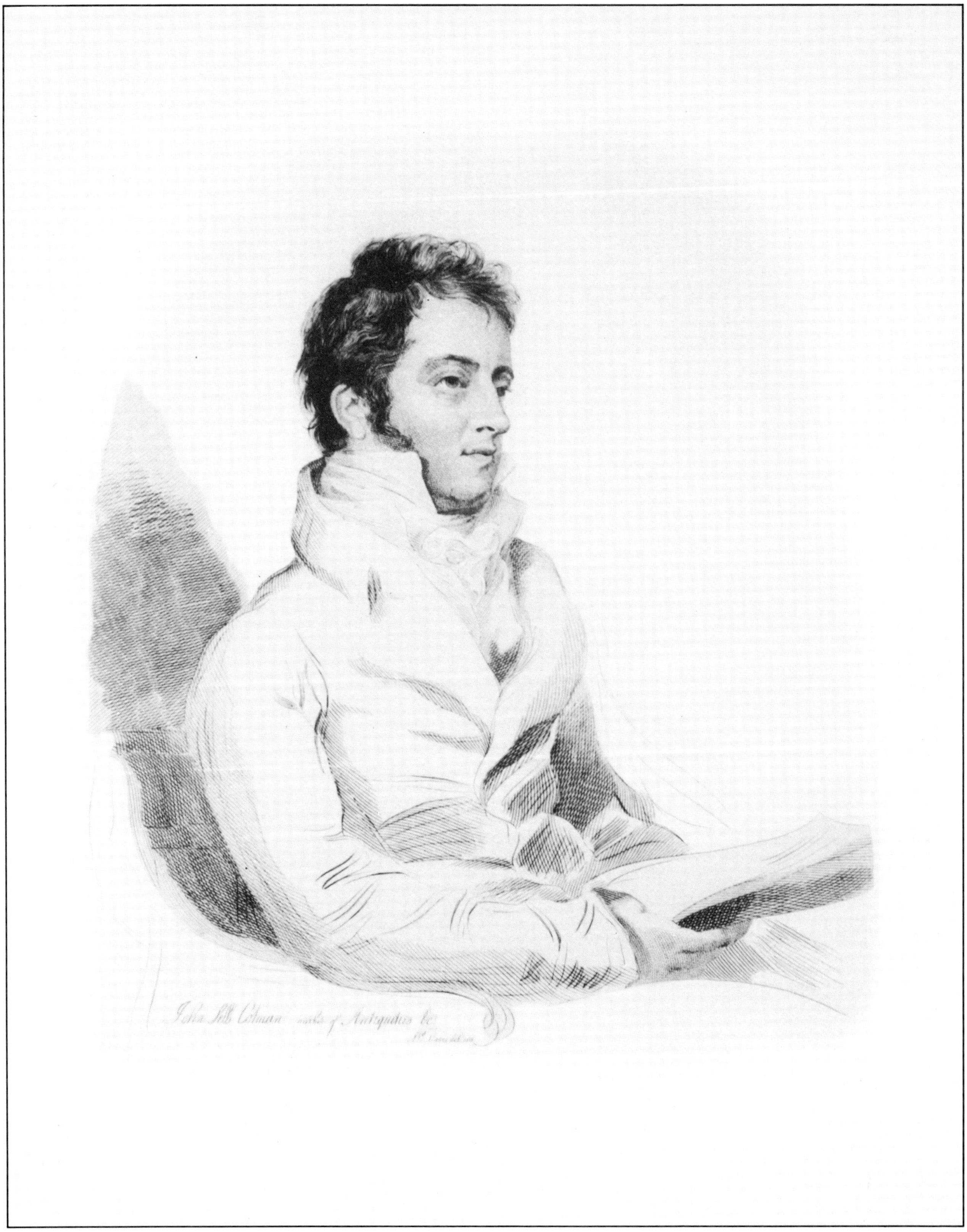
John Sell Cotman

Andrew W Moore

John Sell Cotman

1782 – 1842

Norfolk Museums Service
Director Francis Cheetham OBE BA FMA

Cotman Bicentenary Exhibition

The exhibition was organised in conjunction with the 1982 Norfolk & Norwich Triennial Festival of Music and the Arts which receives financial assistance from the Arts Council of Great Britain, Norfolk County Council and Norwich City Council. An additional welcome grant towards photography was received from the Area Museums Service for South Eastern England.

Grateful acknowledgement is also made to Marks and Spencer p.l.c., for their generous financial support.

Front cover Kett's Castle, Norwich, *c.*1809-10 (No. 58).

Back cover and Frontispiece Mary (Mrs Dawson) Turner, etched portrait of John Sell Cotman after a drawing of 1818 by J. P. Davis

ISBN 0 903101 42 4 (softback)
ISBN 0 903101 41 6 (hardback)

Designed by Richard Malt

Filmset in Bembo and printed by
Witley Press Ltd., Hunstanton, Norfolk

Contents

Colour Illustrations

Foreword

John Sell Cotman is now recognised as one of the leading watercolourists in the history of British and indeed European Art. Born in the parish of St. Mary Coslany, Norwich on 16 May 1782, Cotman developed rapidly as the greatest draughtsman of the local association or 'School' of Painters. Yet his eminence, in his own lifetime and since, has only been celebrated in part.

The bicentenary of Cotman's birth has provided a welcome occasion on which to present a selection of the best of his work as represented in the significant holdings at the Castle Museum, Norwich. Although it is appropriate that the largest and most comprehensive collection of Cotman's work remains in Norwich, in some respects this has limited public knowledge and appreciation of his work. The existence of many copies in the 'Cotman Style' which he himself taught in his rôle as drawing master has contributed to a confusion in the public mind as to the true quality of his genius. This book incorporates a catalogue of the works on show at the bicentenary exhibition held at the Norwich Castle Museum from 9 October to 28 November 1982. The first ten sections trace the development of the artist's personal circumstances and artistic career, while the last two sections survey both the unrivalled collection of the artist's oil paintings at Norwich and his prodigious output as an etcher.

The selection is culled from some 800 works by or attributed to Cotman in the collection of the Castle Museum. Most of the finest examples were bequeathed by two members of a leading Norwich family: Jeremiah James Colman, in 1898, and his son Russell James Colman, in 1946. Under the terms of the latter bequest, the works by Cotman may not be shown outside Norwich Castle Museum. The works selected and illustrated in this volume reveal the splendour and importance of these bequests in both local and national terms.

The celebration of Cotman's bicentenary at Norwich marks the main contribution of the Norfolk Museums Service to the 1982 Norfolk and Norwich Triennnial Festival.

Francis Cheetham
Director, Norfolk Museums Service

Acknowledgements

My greatest debt in the preparation of this publication lies in the published research on John Sell Cotman's early years and Normandy tours by Miklós Rajnai and Marjorie Allthorpe-Guyton. The present text of those entries for drawings previously published by them in 1975 and 1979 is no more than an edited version of their researches. I am equally indebted to the invaluable record systems established within the Art Department of the Castle Museum by Miklós Rajnai and also to the seminal publication by Sydney Kitson in 1937 of his biography of the artist.

A number of people have been of particular help in the preparation of the text. I would like to thank my colleague Norma Watt who has sedulously compiled and checked the provenance, exhibition and reference sections to each previously unresearched catalogue entry as well as compiling the List of Exhibitions and the Bibliography. In this task she was greatly aided by the considerable efforts of Michael Simpson who, often in his own time, collated and checked the archive material for each entry. In addition he compiled a record of critical responses to the work of Cotman from contemporary newspapers and pursued research at the Norfolk Record Office and at the Norwich Reference and Local Studies Libraries, whose help I also acknowledge. Norma Watt also organised photography and cast a critical eye over the text. I would also like to thank my colleague Robin Emmerson for his help in checking the text. I owe an especial debt to my wife Judith Moore who gave generously and selflessly of her own time in reading and commenting upon the manuscript through its progressive stages.

A number of others have also contributed in no small measure. I wish to thank Michael Pidgley for permitting the publication of material from his doctoral thesis on Cotman, completed in 1975; Susan Ashworth for her work in compiling an index of the artist's works sold during his lifetime and since; Gerald Chapman, who has continued to act with habitual efficiency as a volunteer in the Art Department; Richard Malt for undertaking the daunting task of designing the publication and orchestrating its production. I acknowledge also the customary courtesy and help of the staffs of the Print Rooms of the British Museum and the Victoria and Albert Museum and of the Department of Manuscripts of the British Library.

My appreciation is similarly extended to the Director of the Norfolk Museums Service, Francis Cheetham, and to the Deputy Director Brian McWilliams, as well as to colleagues Richard Hubbard, Rosemary O'Donoghue, Jane Alderson, June Santo and finally Julie Hall for her help in typing the final draft. Alan Griffee of GGS Photography undertook both the colour work and black and white photography. Ken Heathcote and his display team, as well as Barry Leveton and his staff contributed to the mounting of the exhibition to accompany the publication.

A.W.M.

Explanations and Abbreviations

Selection

There are 48 oils and 882 drawings and watercolours by or attributed to John Sell Cotman in the collection of Norwich Castle Museum. 43 drawings resulting from Cotman's three Normandy tours were published by the Norfolk Museums Service in 1975. Nos. 81-98, 100-102, 108, 109 in the present selection were fully catalogued by Miklós Rajnai, with the assistance of Marjorie Allthorpe-Guyton, in that publication (see Bibliography). Similarly, a thorough analysis by Rajnai and Allthorpe of 129 early drawings was published by the Norfolk Museums Service in 1979. Nos. 1-71 in the present selection were fully catalogued in that publication (see Bibliography).

The present selection of items includes works whose attribution is considered correct and among the best examples from the collections at Norwich. It includes drawings, watercolours, oils and some etchings.

Arrangement

The drawings are arranged in a broadly chronological order in ten sections. The oils are arranged in a suggested chronology in the eleventh section. The final section is of etchings arranged in order of publication. Related works at Norwich and in other collections are referred to in the main body of the entries or in a note to them. The works in each section are prefaced by a short introduction in an effort to provide an overall view of the artist's career. However, the inclusion of any one item within a section is not intended to imply that that work was of absolute necessity produced within the confines of the period under review. This is particularly the case with works placed at the beginning or end of a section when that work is undated by the artist.

Titles

When it is reasonably certain that a drawing was exhibited by the artist the exhibition title is used. Otherwise the first recorded title is retained unless incorrect.

Dates

Catalogue Numbers 1-71 follow the dates suggested by Rajnai and Allthorpe in 1979. Close dating of a number of the later works, principally oils, has sometimes proved impossible: further suggestions or corrections would be welcome.

Sizes

Height is given before width in centimetres followed by inches in parentheses.

Inscriptions

All inscriptions are in the artist's hand unless stated otherwise. When the inscription of the artist's name is accepted as a signature it is preceded by the word 'signed'. Mounter's notes etc. are not included. To avoid undue emphasis, etched inscriptions appearing in capital letters on Nos. 169-185, are set in upper and lower case type.

Condition

The drawings in the Colman Bequest were treated by S. Kennedy North between 1934 and 1937. Details of the condition and treatment of major works are given in Kennedy North's *Report* published in 1936 (see Bibliography). Some drawings were cut down slightly during restoration and many have since suffered from fading. Nos. 9, 33, 35, 36, 41-43 were treated by D. Lewisohn in March 1979.

Provenance

When a group of drawings has a common provenance, it is given only in one entry and the others are referred to it. Sales are given in full if a copy of the catalogue has been located; otherwise the source referring to the sale is given. Provenance details have been compiled from Colman Collection catalogues and other archive material held by the art department, NCM. Details concerning these are available on application. Details of those drawings previously published in 1975 and 1979 (see above, **Selection**) are given in full in those publications.

Exhibitions

All exhibitions have been abbreviated. Full details may be found on pp. 163, ff.

References

Footnotes to the introductory sections are at the end of those sections. In the catalogue entries to previously published drawings (see above, **Selection**) reference is made only to the publications Rajnai 1975, Rajnai and Allthorpe 1979 and Kitson 1937 (see Bibliography). References to Cotman's published etchings are abbreviated, and given in full on p. 154. Important references only are given in all other entries. Footnotes to all entries refer to both published and unpublished sources, (see also **Manuscript Sources**, below).

Manuscript Sources

Details of manuscript sources are given on p. 165. Where possible, quotations have been checked against the original. In those cases when the writer of a letter underlines his text for emphasis, the relevant words or passages are italicised. All references to correspondence between JSC and the Cholmeley family are from the collection on deposit from Mr. Fairfax Cholmeley, at the North Riding Record Office, published by Adele M. Holcomb and M.Y. Ashcroft in 1980 (see Bibliography), unless stated otherwise. All quotations from the Barker Collection of Cotman letters are from Kitson 1937 or, in preference, from those checked against the original letters and published in Rajnai 1975 and Rajnai and Allthorpe 1979.

Illustrations

All catalogued items are illustrated. Where illustrations do not appear on the same page as the catalogue entry a page reference is given below the title.

Abbreviations

The following list does not include standard abbreviaions which may be found in *The Concise Oxford Dictionary*.

BM	British Museum.
bt.	bought
c.	centre
c.	circa
Cat.	Catalogue
CC	Colman Collection
DT	Dawson Turner
JSC	John Sell Cotman
l.	left or lower
l.l.	lower left
l.r.	lower right
Leeds	Leeds City Art Gallery
NCM	Norwich Castle Museum
n.d.	no date
pub.	published
r.	right
repro.	reproduced
u.	upper
V&A	Victoria & Albert Museum
Witt	London, Courtauld Institute, Witt Library

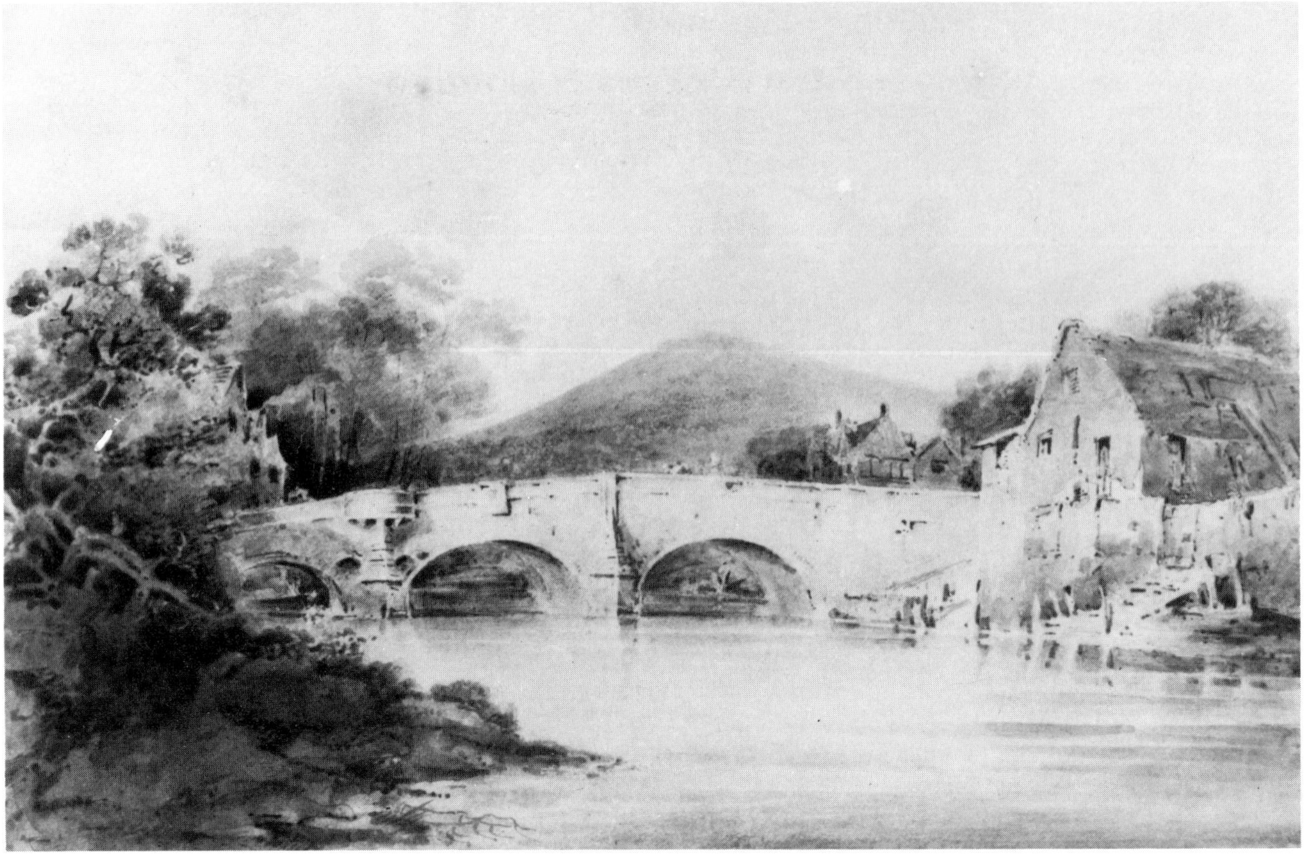

3 Bishopsgate Bridge, Norwich, *c.*1800

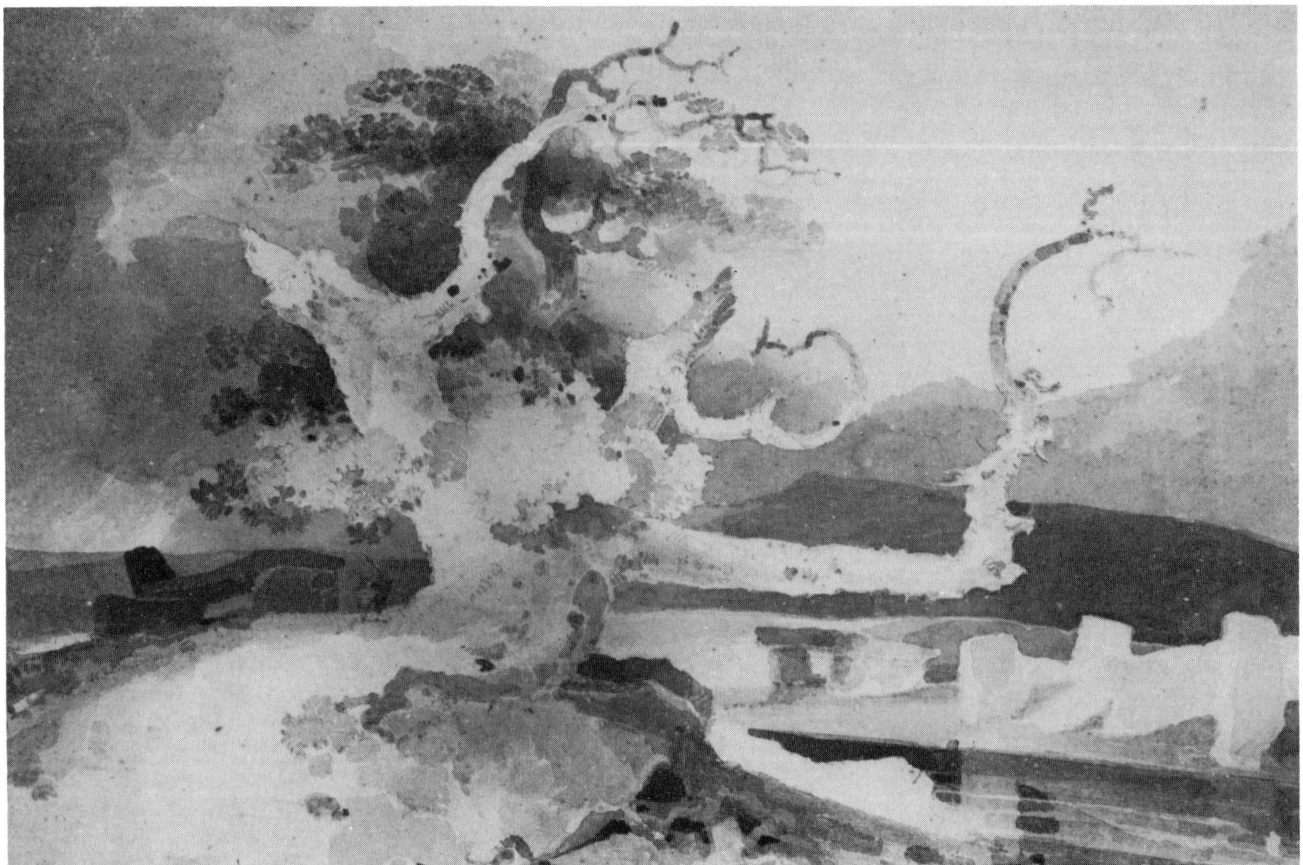

4 Behold Yon Oak, 1804

1
The Early Years & London
1782 - 1806

In the last year of his life John Sell Cotman wrote to his lifelong patron Dawson Turner: 'I was born apparently with a love of my Art, as I never knew the time when I was not fond of drawing, and I have often heard my Mother say I drew "Tips" (ships) long before I could speak.'[1] He had no illusions however as to his earliest attempts at drawing: in his last letter from Norwich before his move to Yarmouth in April 1812 he remarked, 'I by chance picked up two *original drawings* done by myself twenty years since, which must for ever do away with the idea of *original genius*.'[2]

Born in the parish of St. Mary Coslany, Norwich[3] on 16 May 1782, John Sell Cotman gained a free place at Norwich Grammar School on 3 August 1793.[4] Little contemporary evidence survives concerning his early years in Norwich, but a fair amount of information is contained in a letter from his eldest son, Miles Edmund, to Dawson Turner written shortly after Cotman's death.[5] He points out that his father was self-taught whilst at Norwich, and Cotman himself commented to his son John Joseph that at the time of his first move to London 'I did not draw half so well as you do' (see No. 2).

The precise date John Sell Cotman left for London is not known, but tradition and indirect evidence almost certainly suggest the autumn of 1798, when he was sixteen. This was the year of his earliest known drawing (No. 1) and also the time when, reputedly, Edmund Cotman, his father, broached the subject of his son's future as an artist to John Opie, subsequently Professor of Painting at the Royal Academy. He is said to have replied 'let him rather black boots, than follow the profession of an artist'. It was presumably Opie's aim to discourage all potential students in order not to raise their expectations. He meted out similar advice to his students at the Academy during one of his lectures: 'in no profession will [the student] have to labour so hard, and study so intensely—and in no profession is the reward of his talents so precarious and uncertain,—as is lamentably proved by every day's experience, and by every page of history'.[6]

London acted as a focal point for Cotman's aspirations throughout his lifetime. Years later he wrote that 'London, with all its fog and smoke, is the only air for an artist to breathe in'.[7] According to Miles Edmund, 'my father left Norwich in 1798 and went to Ackermann's, but left him—not being treated as he fancied he ought'. As assistant to Rudolph Ackermann, proprietor of the Depository of Arts at 101, The Strand, it is likely that he was employed to colour the establishment's aquatints. Miles Edmund also recalls that his father 'was taken by the late Dr. Monro, with whom he remained some time, studying with Turner and Girtin'. It seems, however, that both Turner and Girtin had left the tutelage of Dr. Monro by at least 1798.

The diary of the artist Joseph Farington provides a telling clue to substantiate these assertions. Farington met Dr. Thomas Monro in 1795 and became a long standing friend, often commenting in his diary on Monro's role as collector, patron and host to an 'academy' of young artists. This academy was held at No. 8 Adelphi Terrace, but also at his country house at Fetcham. Farington's entry for 24 October 1798 gives an account of Monro's method of instruction: 'Turner and Girtin told us that they went to Dr. Monro's house at six and stayed till ten. Girtin drew the outlines and Turner washed in the effects. They were chiefly employed in copying the outlines or unfinished drawings of Cozens etc. of which copies they made finished drawings. Dr. Monro allowed Turner 3/6 each night. Girtin did not say what he had. Turner afterwards told me that Dr. Monro had been a material friend to him as well as to Girtin. He said they worked there for three years'. Among other artists who benefited from Monro's sponsorship were Louis Francia, T. R. Underwood and P. S. Munn all of whom became colleagues of the young Cotman. Farington's entry for 15 December 1799 states that 'Dr. Monro is bringing forward another young man, who comes from Norwich'. Evidence to support the likelihood that the young man was John Sell Cotman exists in early pencil drawings by Cotman from the area around Fetcham, two of which are dated 1799. Formerly in the collection of Sydney Kitson, these are now at Leeds City Art Gallery.[8] After Monro's death in May 1833, his collection was sold through Christie's: Lot 13 contained 'a bundle of very early sketches by J. S. Cotman'.

There is no record of how long Cotman was with Monro, but his address at the time of his first showing at the Royal Academy in May 1800 was 28 Gerrard Street, Soho. Five of his six exhibited works were subjects in Surrey—at Dorking, Leatherhead and Guildford. In the same year, the *Norwich Mercury* reports on 12 July: 'The Society for the Encouragement of Arts, Manufactures and Commerce, held in London, has adjudged the larger Silver Pallette to Mr. John Cotman, son of Mr. Cotman of St. Andrew's, for his drawing of a Mill at Dorking'. Such recognition represented a rapid turn of events for the young artist and must have justified to a great extent his move to London. There is a tradition that the vicissitudes of Cotman's early years in London attempting to survive through the sale of his drawings provided the model for the young Thaddeus, in *Thaddeus of Warsaw,* a novel published in 1803 by Jane Porter, the sister of Robert Ker Porter, a young contemporary of Cotman. However, there is no reason to suggest that Cotman was at this time suffering unduly from lack of recognition. The record of his movements shows rather a hectic schedule of summer tours and regular meetings with his new artistic contacts. Equally, his pursuit of patronage was assiduous. The problems of Thaddeus—early rejection and exploitation by the printsellers of London—would have been the common lot of any young artist of the period. Indeed, Cotman's work was sufficiently well respected by 1802 for Andrew Robertson, the Scottish miniaturist, to single him out in a letter to his brothers in New York, as one of the three leading practitioners in watercolour, along with Turner and Girtin.[9]

Cotman achieved recognition among his contemporaries through his membership of an artistic fraternity which came to call itself *The Brothers.* In 1799 a few of the young artists from Dr. Monro's circle founded a sketching society under the leadership of Thomas Girtin. The first record of the group is inscribed on the reverse of a drawing by Louis Francia.[10] Their first meeting is thus recorded as 20 May at the lodgings of Robert Ker Porter. The group met in each other's rooms, the owner of the rooms being the host for the night: he also set the subject to be drawn and provided the materials. These were essentially those established at Monro's academy, consisting of

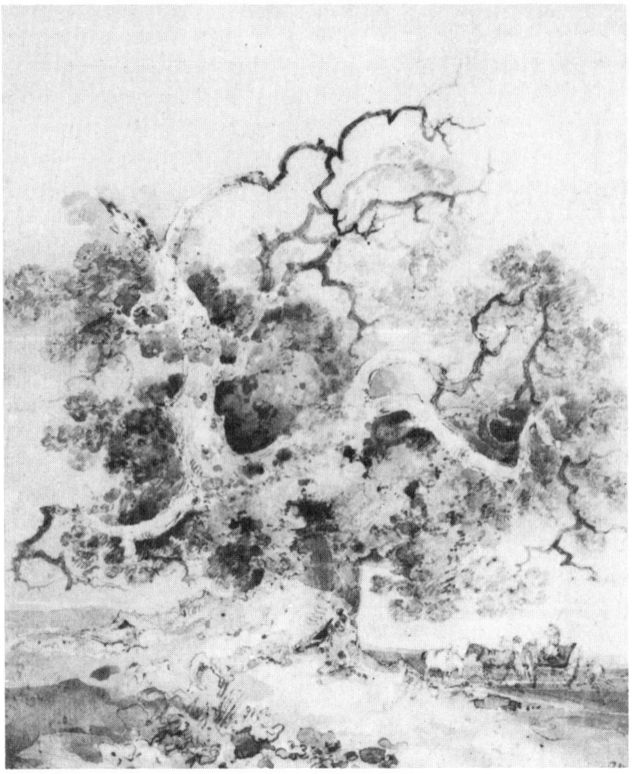

5 The Gnarled Oak, *c.*1804

pencils, paper, indian ink and sepia. It was Francia who coined the cabalistic name of *The Brothers,* 'met for the purpose of establishing by practice a School of Historic Landscape—the subjects being original designs from poetick passages'.[10]

The first dated record of Cotman's membership occurs three years later, although he was probably elected earlier. A record was kept in the Society's minute book for only four months, during which time Paul Sandby Munn joined the group. An undated set of drawings is recorded which provides the strongest evidence that Girtin and Cotman actually met.[11] The set, now dispersed, was of seven drawings by members of the Society when the subject for the evening was *An Ancient Castle.* The contributors were Girtin, Munn, Porter, Samuel, Underwood, Callcott and Cotman. Girtin's contribution denotes that the drawings must date from before his departure from London for Paris in November 1801.

The next recorded date in the Society's history is 5 May 1802, when the subject set was a poem by Cunningham.[12] Again both Cotman and P. S. Munn were present, as was the latter's brother, William. A month later the Society met in Cotman's rooms. A signed drawing by Cotman of a castle on a rock is inscribed on the reverse of the mount with lines by the poet Southey and 'J. S. Cotman, president—T. R. Underwood—W. Alexander—J. Varley—P. S. Munn. Visitors, Green and Webster. June 5, 1802'.[13] Cotman's rooms at the time (as recorded by the Royal Academy Catalogues for 1802-1804)[14] were 107 New Bond Street, over the Stationers' and Printsellers' business belonging to Paul Sandby Munn and his two brothers. It was shortly after this meeting that Cotman and his friend Paul Sandby Munn embarked on their joint sketching tour of North Wales, which is discussed separately in the next section.

By February 1803 Munn was secretary to the group, now called the Drawing Society.[15] On 23 March 1803 they again met in Cotman's rooms. On this occasion, and on 4 November when he was again president, Cotman selected lines from Ossian. The next, and indeed the last, dated drawing of this period with the Drawing Society is *Behold Yon Oak* (No. 4), dated 26 January 1804. The quality of this drawing confirms the assertion that Cotman had established himself as a leader of the group. While they were united in their similar exploitation of graduated washes, it was Cotman who excelled in capturing the tonal qualities inherent in the medium. He was to extend this mastery of monochrome washes in a small group of compositions which he seems to have painted after he had ceased attending Society meetings, but before he finally left London for Norwich in the autumn of 1806 (see Nos. 8, 9, 10). In these works, as in *Behold Yon Oak,* he developed the advances made by Girtin. The eighteenth century method of painting in watercolours depended upon a foundation of underpainting to achieve effects of mass and shadow. It was Girtin who discovered the value of painting in more translucent washes of colour, less muddied in their effect. Cotman developed Girtin's discovery, recognising the tonal values of superimposed washes and discarding the traditional use of underpainting. Flat washes transmuted the patterns of nature into subtle two dimensional forms.

While the following sections recount separately the major tours of Wales and Yorkshire during this period, Cotman also ventured elsewhere in England as opportunity allowed. It must remain speculative as to whether he made a trip to Devon in 1801 or a repeat visit to Bristol the same year. His Devon drawings could well have been based upon the sketches of others, while a drawing of the Bristol bookseller and friend, James Norton, dated 5 November 1801, could have been as easily executed in London as in Bristol.[16] It is probable that his visits to Covehithe and Yarmouth and subsequently Castle Acre, Cambridge, Ely, Croyland (No. 20) and Peterborough in 1804 took place en route for Yorkshire (see p. 24). An important invitation in the summer of 1806 was to Trentham Hall, the seat of the Marquis of Stafford. His good friend Mrs. Cholmeley of Brandsby Hall wrote to Cotman on 14 July 1806 'I think & hope you may find yr. very pleasing invitation to Trentham not only agreeable but beneficial to you . . . apply steadily and vigorously & profit to the utmost of the advantages you may derive from Stafford's invitation and patronage . . .'[17] The only known result of this trip is the magnificent watercolour of the interior of Trentham Church (No. 39), although an excursion to Moreton Hall, Cheshire is also likely during this visit (No. 147).

It appears that Cotman and Munn had gradually drifted apart since their last tour together. The former's successful cultivation of and friendship with the Cholmeleys and their Yorkshire circle may well have rankled with Munn, who had not been back to Brandsby Hall after his first visit. Between the spring of 1804 and 1805 Cotman moved from the Munns' premises to 20 Woodstock Street. A letter of 31 March 1806 from Mrs. Cholmeley to her son reveals she is 'much grieved to find by Cotman's letter this morning that he is *blackballed* by the Brook St. Society'.[18] A month later on 30 April she was 'heartily grieved and vext to find that Munn and so many others were admitted fellows of the Brook Street Association and poor Cotman excluded. I shd fear he must have some personal enemies among them.'[18] This exclusion from the inception of the Old Watercolour Society is indicative perhaps of Cotman's concentration upon his Yorkshire friends to the detriment of his London contacts which he had formerly pursued so assiduously. Nevertheless, Cotman continued to visit his friends in London after his move to Norwich, including a visit to Munn in the spring of 1808.[19] Munn and his former Drawing Society associates, Francia and the Varleys, were all subscribers to his *Miscellaneous Etchings,* issued as a set in 1811.

In the autumn of 1806 he visited his parents at Norwich. On 15 October he wrote to Dawson Turner to inform him of his new experiments in oil painting (see section 11). By 8 December he had written again, this time of his decision to remain in Norwich:

> In consequence of advice from several of my friends in Norwich I have taken a house in Wymer Street, for the purpose of opening a School for Drawing and Design. It will give me the opportunity of turning myself about during my stay, and studying (oil) painting, which of late, I have done but little, having been engaged too much in other things. My reason for troubling you with this, Sir, is this; for the last fortnight after Christmas I shall open my Rooms as an Exhibition for about a fortnight. I am aware of the daring of such a scheme, and I hope the public will consider it with candour, and that it is the effort of but an individual.[20]

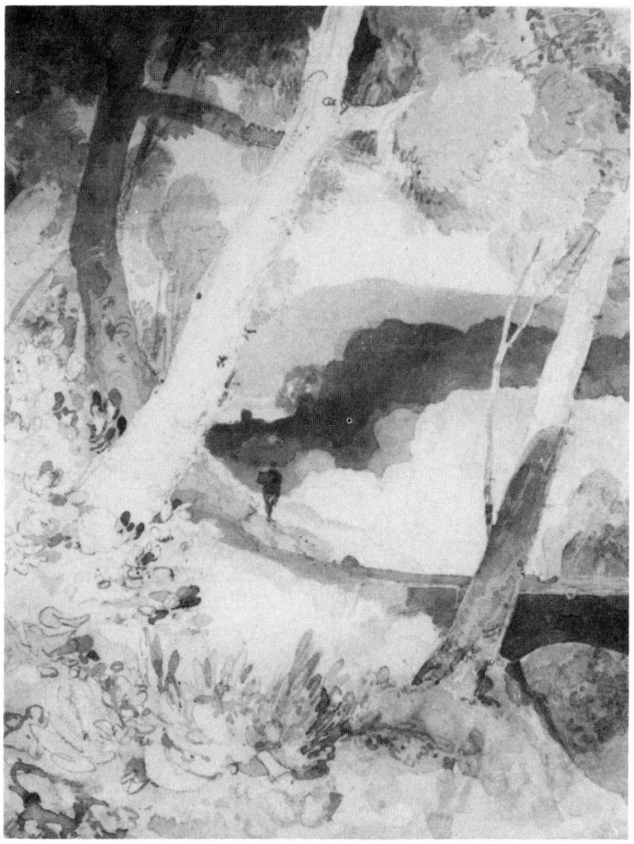

9 Traveller, *c.*1806

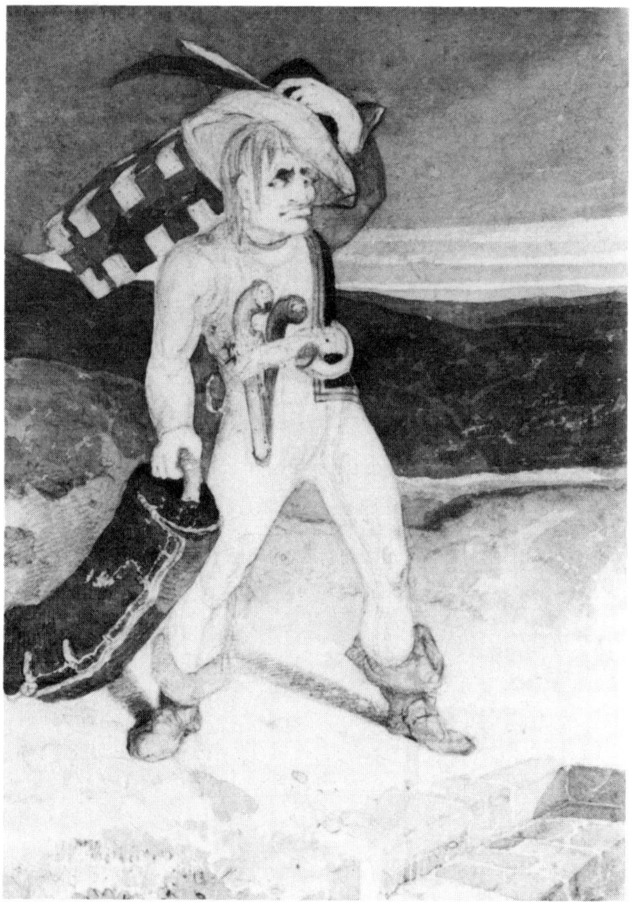

10 Brigand, *c.*1806

Notes

[1]Barker Collection. [2]28 March 1812 (Barker Collection). [3]The Parish Register shows that he was baptized 9 June 1782 (Norfolk Record Office). [4]Court Book No. 36, 1789-1796 (Norfolk Record Office) See Kitson 1937 p. 6. [5]25 August 1842 (Barker Collection). [6]John Opie *Lectures on Painting* 1809 p. 21. [7]JSC to Mrs DT 9 March 1825 (Barker Collection). [8]Leeds 1.9/39; 9.585/49; 9.586/49. [9]Kitson 1937 pp. 45-46. [10]V&A PD 477-1863. [11]Kitson 1937 pp. 31-32. [12]Fitzwilliam Museum, PD 39 and 40-1980. Also Kitson 1937 p. 32. [13]Kitson 1937 pp. 32, 33 (Ashmolean Museum, Oxford). [14]Misprinted as 127 in 1802. [15]Kitson 1937 p. 33 ff. [16]Included in Sotheby's 30 Nov. 1978 lot 50. [17]Reeve Collection, BM. [18]Cholmeley family papers, North Riding Record Office, 1980. All references to correspondence with Francis Cholmeley on subsequent pages refer to this collection, unless stated otherwise. [19]JSC to Francis Cholmeley 22 April 1808. [20]Kitson 1937 p. 99.

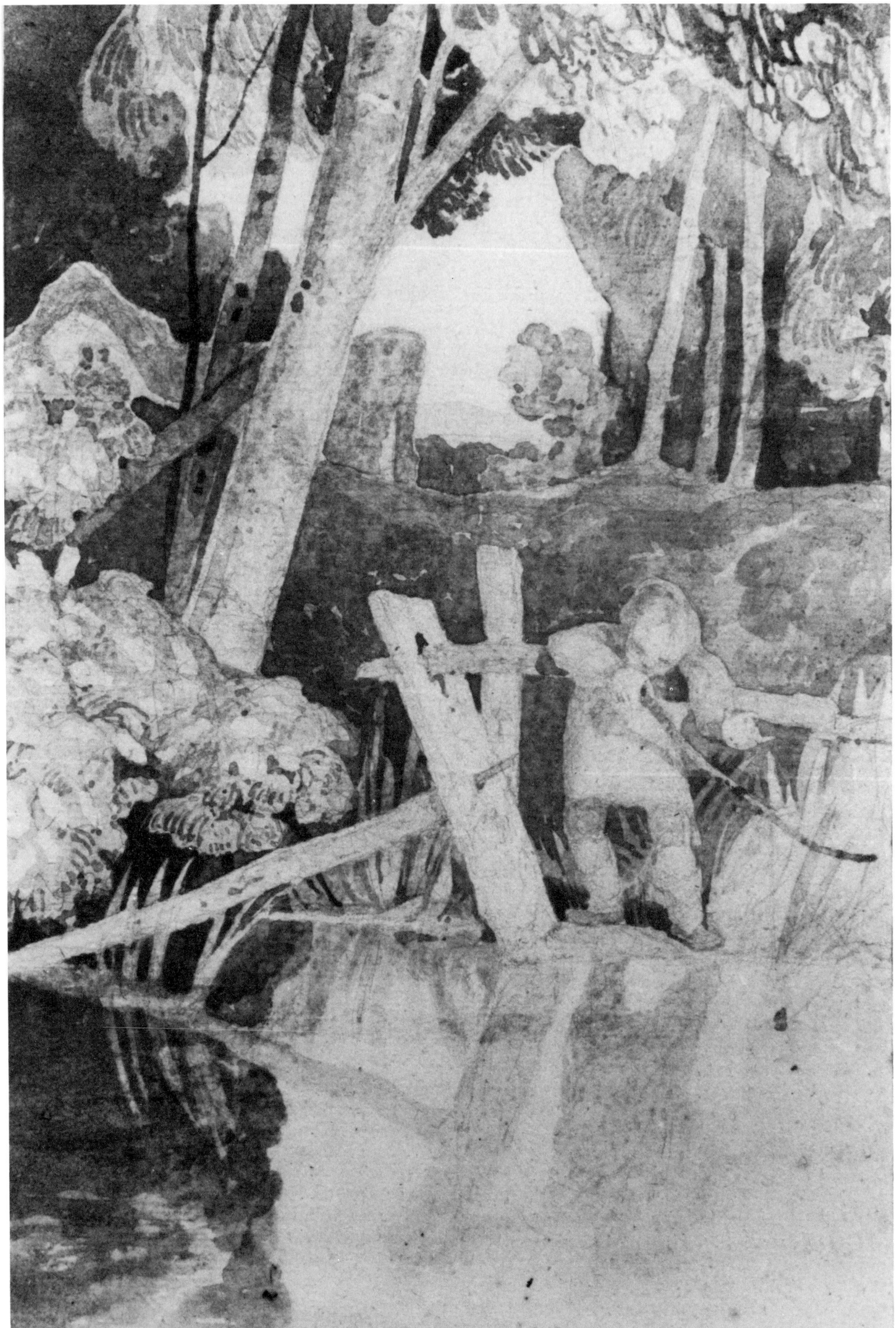

8 Boy Fishing, *c.*1806

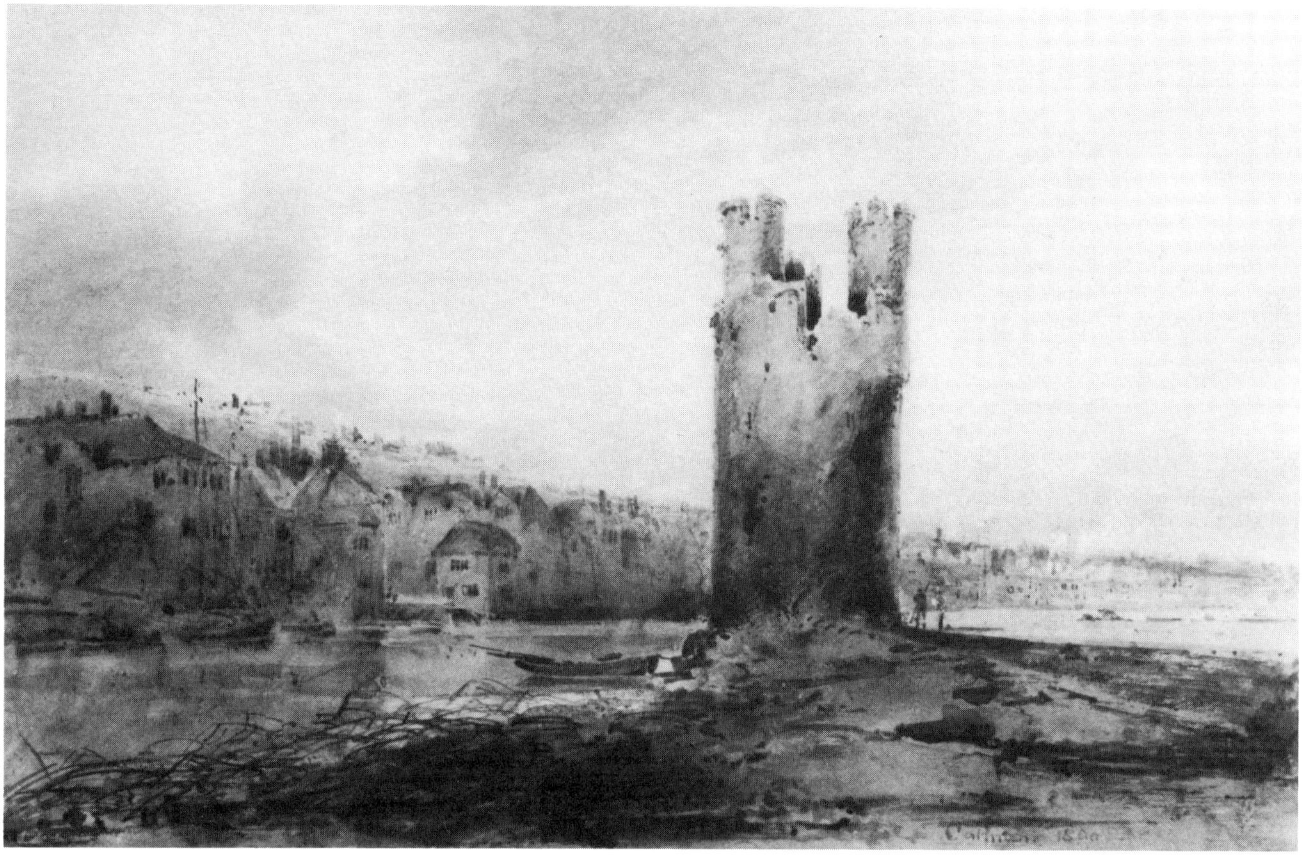

2 The Devil's Tower, Norwich, 1800

1 The Devil's Tower, Norwich, 1798

Pencil on white, laid paper with watermark, a Crown; 10.6 × 20.8 ($4\frac{3}{16}$ × $8\frac{3}{16}$). *Verso,* pencil sketch of a church interior. INSCR: *Recto,* in pencil l.r. *July 3/98.* PROV: Sydney D. Kitson by April 1937; his bequest to Leeds City Art Gallery; presented with fourteen other drawings, under the terms of his bequest 1949. (8.139.949). REF: Kitson 1937 pp. 9, 356; Rajnai & Allthorpe No. 1.

Kitson regards this as the earliest known work of Cotman before he left for London. Rajnai and Allthorpe accept this attribution as a valid one, but emphasise the need for caution in drawing conclusions about such an early work. The naïve character of the drawing would be consistent with the work of a sixteen year old.

The Devil's Tower, on the River Wensum, formed part of the medieval fortifications of Norwich and was a favourite subject with Norwich artists. In 1833 one of its three turrets and much of the western wall fell, since when the fabric has further deteriorated. See No. 134 for a late drawing by Cotman of this subject.[1]

[1]There are two other later drawings of the Devil's Tower by Cotman: NCM 339.235.951 and BM 1902-5-14-101, a similar composition.

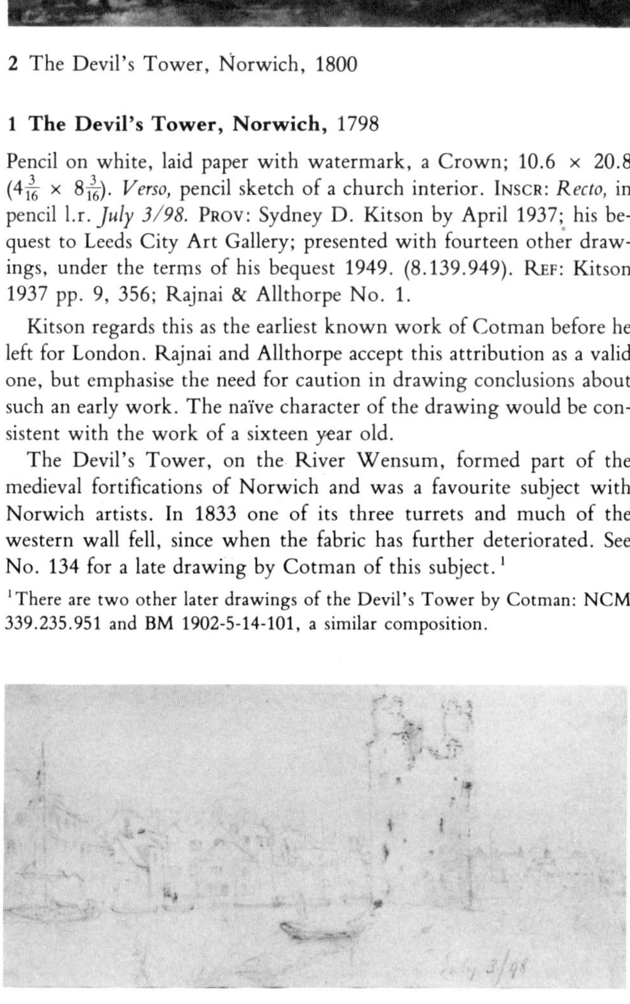

1 The Devil's Tower, Norwich, 1798

2 The Devil's Tower, Norwich, 1800

Pencil and watercolour with slight scraping out, on cream, wove paper; 21.8 × 33.2 ($8\frac{5}{8}$ × $13\frac{1}{16}$). INSCR: *Recto,* signed in watercolour l.r. *Cotman, 1800-.* PROV: ?Thomas Churchyard by 25 June 1844; ?his sale B. Moulton, 28 March 1866, lot 134; H. E. Heyman, Clapham, London by 1909; bt. from him by R. J. Colman, 1909; R. J. Colman Bequest 1946. (122.235.951). EXH: Manchester 1912 (324); Norwich 1930-31. REF: Kitson 1937 pp. 22, 334; Rajnai & Allthorpe No. 2.

The original blue of this watercolour, probably indigo, has flown leaving a predominance of reddish brown. It appears to derive from No. 1 and is presumably the work Cotman mentioned in a letter to John Joseph, his second son, on 12 January 1838:

> I remember for your consolation, that when I first came to London — I did not draw half so well as you do — and for your further consolation I will send you a Drawing of The Devil's Tower, Norwich, executed 1800 which I sold — not half so well as you can now draw.[1]

A larger, slightly later version[2] of this subject is in private hands.

[1]BM [2]Sotheby's, 17 Oct. 1968, lot 50 bt. Beckett.

3 Bishopsgate Bridge, Norwich, *c.*1800

illustrated on p. 10

Pencil and watercolour on cream, wove paper; 22 × 33.4 ($8\frac{5}{8}$ × $13\frac{1}{8}$). PROV: ?W. C. Southwell by 1882; ?Dr. J. Cotman by 1889; ?Daniel Tomkins, his sale Spelman, Gt. Yarmouth, March 1895, 2nd day, lot 786 as *Bishop's Bridge, Norwich, Cotman, 1799;* H. E. Heyman; bt. from him by R. J. Colman, 1909; R. J. Colman Bequest 1946. (124.235.951). EXH: ?Swaffham 1882 (208), lent by W. C. Southwell; ?London, Whitechapel, St. Judes, 1889 (225) lent by Dr. J. Cotman; Manchester 1912 (321); Norwich 1930-31. REF: Rajnai & Allthorpe No. 3.

This representation of Bishop Bridge shows the bridge viewed up river, with the city arms visible over the central arch and Mousehold Hill in the distance. Rajnai and Allthorpe suggests that it derives from a sketch made on a visit to Norwich during Cotman's early years in

London. They point out that the smooth handling of wash and the use of the tip of the brush for linear details relate No. 3 stylistically to *The Devil's Tower,* No. 2, dated 1800. It has similarly faded to leave a hot colouring.

Cotman returned to the subject of Bishop Bridge in a watercolour of *c.*1806-7 (see No. 33) and in a pencil drawing of *c.*1809-10[1]. Built *c.*1340, it is the only remaining medieval bridge in Norwich; it abutted the east side of Bishop's Gate, demolished in 1791. The early gabled buildings to the north of the bridge were demolished in 1878.

[1]NCM 11.139.949: Rajnai & Allthorpe No. 102.

4 Behold Yon Oak, 1804

illustrated on p. 10

Pencil and grey wash on buff, laid paper; 31.2 × 44.7 ($12\frac{1}{4}$ × $17\frac{9}{16}$). INSCR: *Recto,* signed in brown ink l.r. *J S Cotman;* the old mount was inscribed 'Jany. 26 1804 -Thursday / Subject-Behold Yon Oak— / How stern he frowns, and with his broad brown horns [arms] Chills the pale plain beneath him. Mark yon Altar, / The dark stream brawling round its rugged base: / These cliffs, these yawning caverns CARACTACUS. / J. S. Cotman, prest.—P. Munn—J. Varley—J. Powell—Visitor, / Stevens'. PROV: Charles Clowes; bt. from him by James Reeve; bt. from him by H. S. Theobald; bt. from him by R. J. Colman, Feb. 1910; R. J. Colman Bequest 1946. (296.235.951). EXH: Tate 1922 (163). REF: Kitson 1937 p. 35; Rajnai & Allthorpe No. 26.

Cotman had become the leading member of the Sketching Society after Girtin's death in 1802 and the recorded inscription reveals that this drawing was one of his Society contributions. The fact that he was the President for the evening and consequently the host of the meeting, shows that the meeting took place in his lodgings at 107 New Bond Street.

The subject set by Cotman, as President, was from *Caractacus,* a tragedy set in the time of the Roman occupation of Britain during the reign of Claudius, written by William Mason in collaboration with Thomas Gray between 1756 and 1759.[1] The Sketching Society members under Cotman's leadership retained the predilection established under Girtin for historic and fanciful landscape. A more naturalistic version of this composition does appear, however, in a close watercolour version, dated 1804.[2]

Cotman's most sensitive tree studies were made during the period 1803-5 (see No. 21). The gnarled and twisted forms explored in some of them occur in other Sketching Society drawings such as *Woodland Scene.*[3]

[1]*Caractacus. Written on the Model of the ancient Greek Tragedy,* 1759, lines 3-7. [2]Worsley, *Early English water-colours at Hovingham Hall* 1963 (6). [3]Repro. Oppé, note 4 p. 191.

5 The Gnarled Oak, *c.*1804

illustrated on p. 12

Pencil and watercolour on greyish white, laid paper; 31.2 × 25.2 ($12\frac{5}{16}$ × $10\frac{1}{16}$). PROV: The Palser Gallery; bt. from them by Percy Moore Turner, March 1926; bt. from him by R. J. Colman, March 1926; R. J. Colman Bequest 1946. (126.235.951). EXH: Norwich 1945. REF: Rajnai & Allthorpe No. 30.

This drawing, with the weird branches of the oak fantastically twisted against the sky, recalls such Sketching Society subjects as *Behold Yon Oak,* (No. 4). Virtually all the blue of the original drawing has flown, revealing the sensitive assurance of the pencil-work beneath.

6 A Barn with Pigs in foreground, *c.*1804-5

Pencil and greyish brown wash on cream, laid paper with watermark 1.1, ?a Strasburg lily / [1]*800* (paper cut); 20.5 × 15.8 ($8\frac{1}{16}$ × $6\frac{3}{16}$). INSCR: *Recto,* inscribed in pencil u.1. edge *Dark Dark* and colour notes of noughts and crosses; u.r. part of circular stamp; *verso,* inscribed in pencil, in the artist's hand, l.c. *?Mr. Bradbury / 12 Piccadilly / . . . / Mr. Weir / 5 Devonshire Place.* PROV: Included in a volume of 94 drawings by John Sell Cotman presented to the Norwich School of Art by July 1942; on loan since 1967. (23.L1967.9) REF: Rajnai & Allthorpe No. 35.

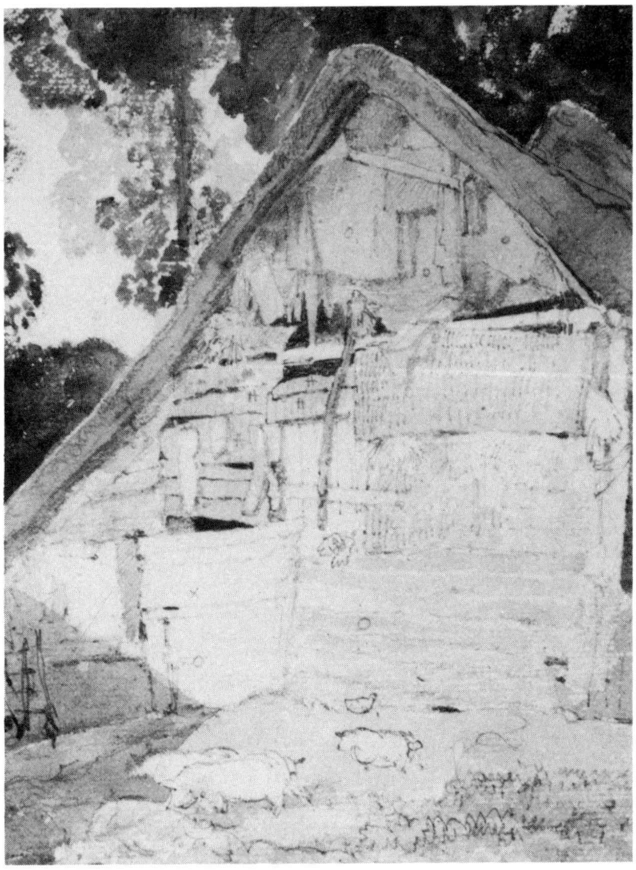

6 A Barn with Pigs in foreground, *c.*1804-5

The subject of this early monochrome is unusual in Cotman's oeuvre at this time in its picturesque affinities. The broken-down barn and the pigs in the foreground recall elements of the picturesque tradition, while the sensitive use of monochrome prefigures the achievement of Cotman's later Normandy drawings. Nevertheless the technique of this drawing is characteristic of Cotman's work at this period. As Rajnai and Allthorpe comment: 'The feathery foliage and use of reserved spaces is close to watercolours of *c.*1804-1805'.

7 St. Botolph's Priory, Colchester, *c.*1804-5

illustrated on opposite page

Pencil and watercolour on cream, wove paper with watermark u.l. *JAMES W* [HATMAN]; 35.7 × 52.1 (14 × $20\frac{1}{2}$). PROV: ?Dawson Turner; his sale, Puttick & Simpson, 16-23 May 1859, 2nd day, lot 811 *Drawings (Original) . . . Cotman, J.S. . . . St. Botolph's Priory, Colchester . . . all in colour;* James Orrock by 1903; his sale, Christie's, 4 June 1904, lot 10, bt. Agnew £189, ?on behalf of R. J. Colman; R. J. Colman Bequest 1946. (128.217.947). EXH: ?Norwich Society 1807 (140); Norwich 1903 (9) lent by James Orrock; Manchester 1912 (362); Norwich 1945; Norwich, Arts Council 1947 (3). REF: Rajnai & Allthorpe No. 36.

Kitson states that Cotman sketched the ruins of St. Botolph's Priory on his way from London to join Dawson Turner and his family at Covehithe on the Suffolk coast in July 1804. However no such visit is documented and it is equally likely that Cotman could have broken any of his journeys between Norwich and London to see the Priory, just south of Colchester Castle.

Much of the blue has flown from No. 7, which is based upon a small sketch[1] now at Leeds. Rajnai and Allthorpe argue that both sketch and watercolour must date from *c.*1804-5 and that the watercolour was that shown by Cotman with the Norwich Society in 1807 (140) as *St. Botolph's Priory, Colchester.* The composition is one of the most harmonious of Cotman's architectural landscapes in watercolour.

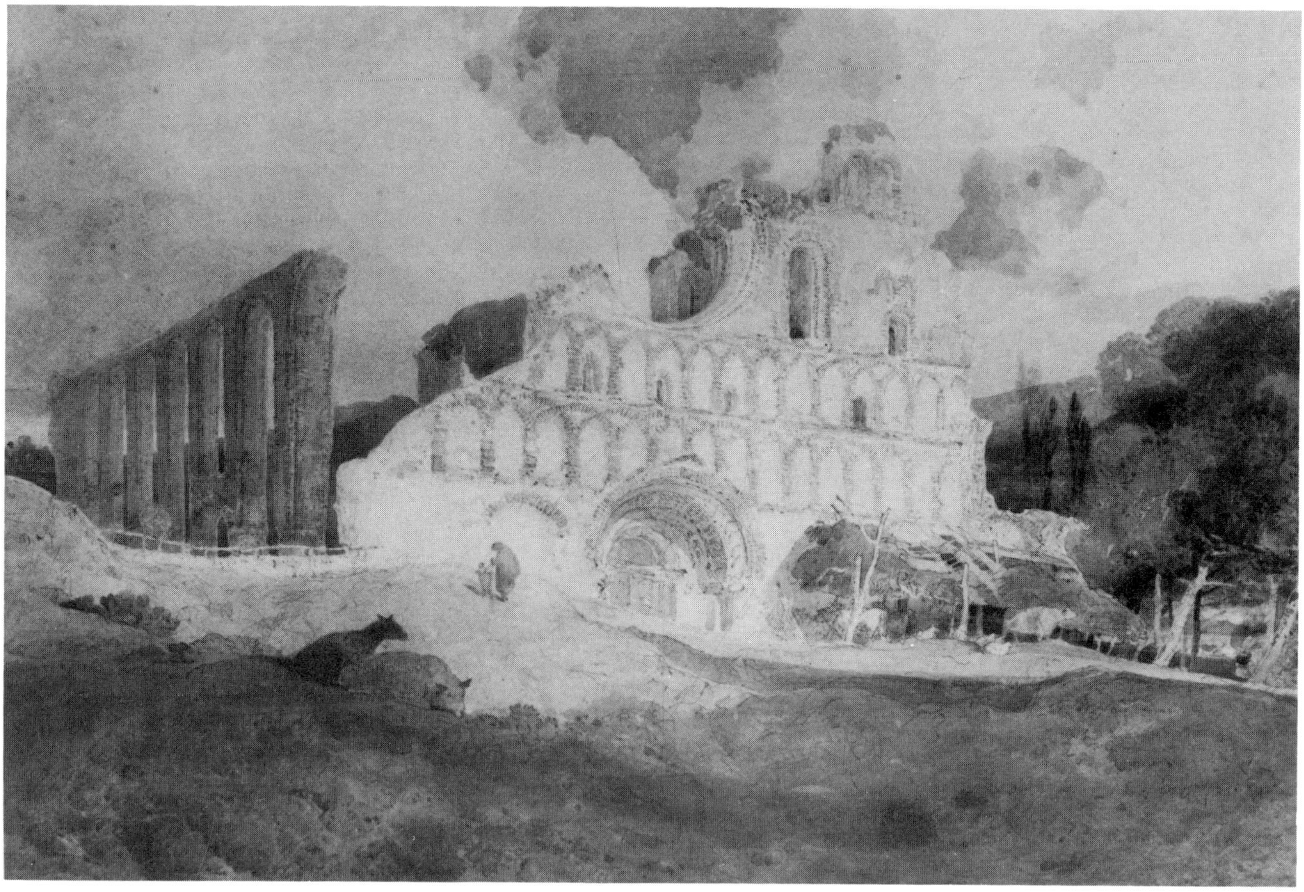

7 St. Botolph's Priory, Colchester, *c.*1804-5

Cotman later etched a version of this subject (see No. 172). There is also a later drawing[2] in the collection at Norwich, which shows a close view of the West Front, signed and dated 1825.

[1]Leeds 5.51/52, Kitson 1937 p.67. [2]NCM 186.235.951. This drawing may not be wholly autograph.

8 Boy Fishing, *c.*1806
illustrated on p. 14

Pencil and brown wash on cream, laid paper; 31.8 × 20.9 ($12\frac{1}{2}$ × $8\frac{1}{4}$). PROV: Cotman sale, Murrell, Norwich, 26-27 Nov. 1862, bt. James Reeve; bt. from him by H. S. Theobald; bt. from him by R. J. Colman, Feb. 1910; R. J. Colman Bequest 1946. (283.235.951). REF: Rajnai & Allthorpe No. 48.

This delicate wash drawing belongs to a small group of monochrome compositions made by Cotman after his Yorkshire tours. This group includes Nos. 9 and 10 as well as *Horses Drinking,*[1] now in the British Museum. All these works display an extraordinary sense of the abstract qualities of the forms and tones of nature. They represent a subtle development of the equally idiosyncratic interpretations of Sketching Society subjects such as *Weird Scene*[2] and *Behold Yon Oak* (No. 4). By this time Cotman had ceased to attend the society meetings.

[1]BM 1902-5-14-41* [2]BM 1902-5-14-39

9 Traveller, *c.*1806
illustrated on p. 13

Pencil and greyish brown wash on buff, wove paper; 35.2 × 26.6 ($13\frac{13}{16}$ × $10\frac{1}{2}$) PROV: ?Cotman sale, Murrell, Norwich, 26-27 Nov. 1862, ? bt. James Reeve; bt. from him by H. S. Theobald; bt. from him by R. J. Colman, Feb. 1910; R. J. Colman Bequest 1946. (308.235.951). REF: Rajnai & Allthorpe No. 49.

This drawing relates to the group of monochromes discussed in the previous entry.

10 Brigand, *c.*1806
illustrated on p. 13

Pencil and brownish grey wash on cream, laid paper; 31 × 21.7 ($12\frac{3}{16}$ × $8\frac{1}{2}$). INSCR: *Recto,* ?signed in pencil l.l. *J Cotman* (only upper half visible, paper cut). PROV: Spelman sale, Norwich, 1880, bt. ? J. J. Colman; his bequest to R. J. Colman 1898; R. J. Colman Bequest 1946 (284.235.951). REF: Rajnai & Allthorpe No. 50.

Brigands were romantic figures that appealed to the early nineteenth century imagination and Cotman's work reveals that he was no exception. In 1808 one of his exhibits with the Norwich Society was *Banditti,* and brigands reappear as subjects in his drawing copies for the pupils of King's College School, London in the late 1830s *Oriental Figure with a Flintlock* (No. 120) is a further example of Cotman's predilection for bandits and soldiery in his costume pieces of the 1830s.

Stylistically, No. 10 can be placed with the imaginary scenes painted by Cotman on his return from his last stay in Yorkshire (see No. 8).

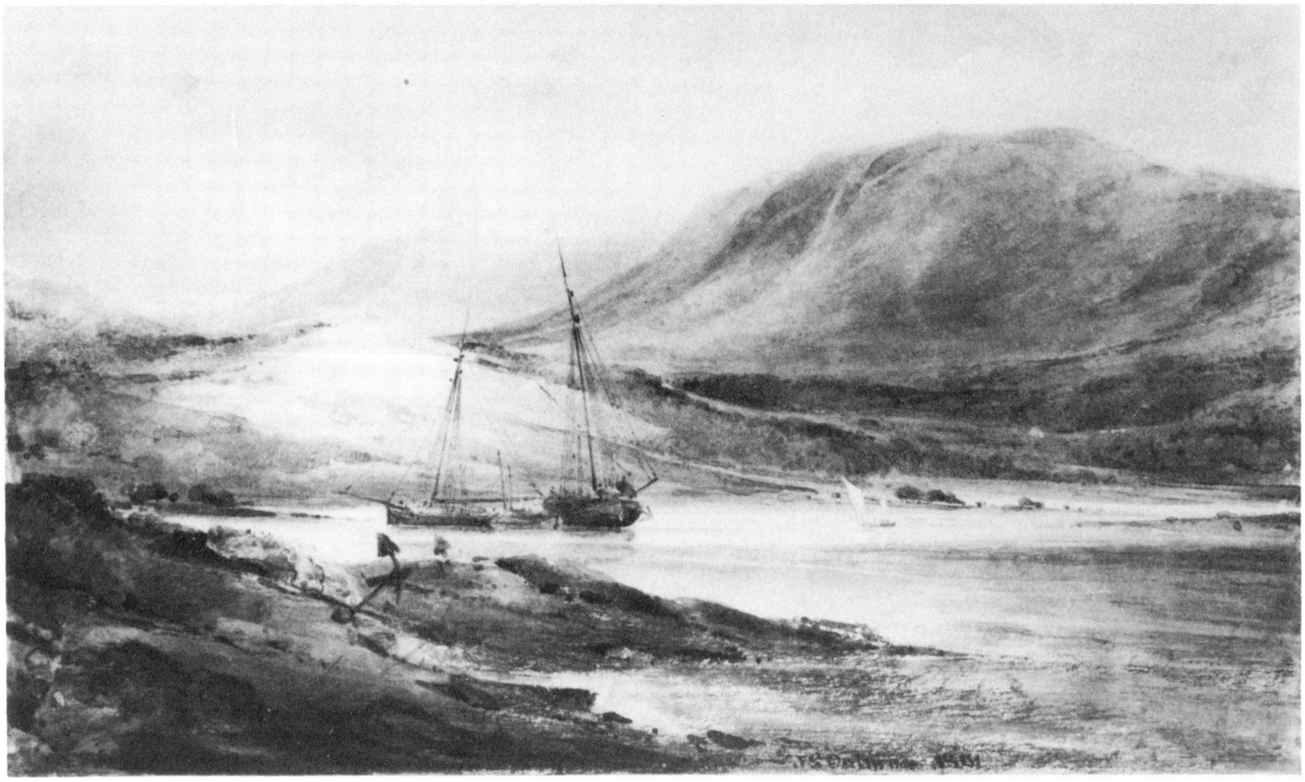

14 Barmouth Estuary, 1801

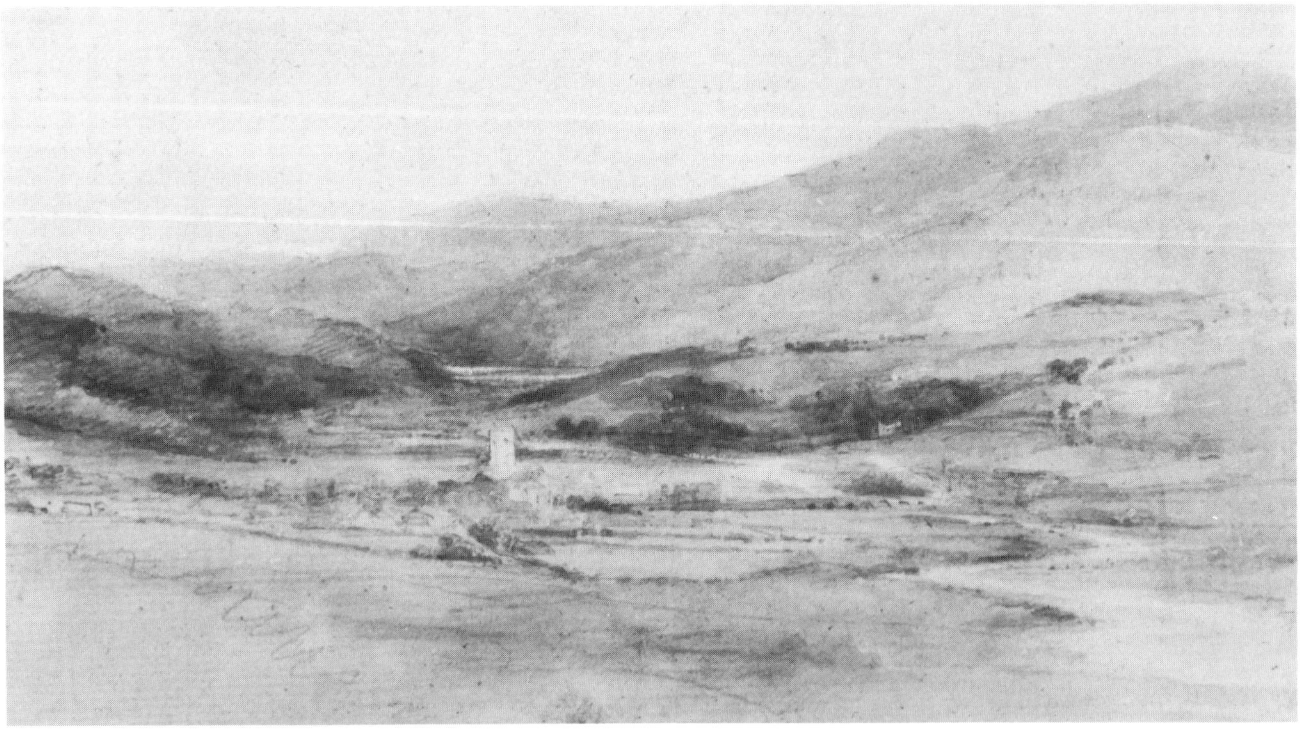

16 Dolgelly, North Wales, *c.*1802

2
The Welsh Tours
1800 & 1802

In June 1800 Cotman journeyed down to Bristol from where, at the end of the month, he set out on his first tour of Wales. At the age of eighteen, the artist was following the example of many of his contemporaries in the current fashion of travelling the length and breadth of the British Isles in search of the Picturesque. A number of surviving dated and inscribed sketches enable one to follow his progress northwards until at least the end of July.

The importance of these few weeks for the future creative output of Cotman's career should not be underestimated. The images of the silhouettes of castles such as Harlech (Nos. 11 and 12) and Conway,[1] the barren heights of Snowdonia and areas such as the Mawddach estuary (Nos. 14, 16, 122, 163) lying low at the foot of distant mountains were to remain with Cotman as a source of pictorial inspiration throughout his lifetime.

Cotman appears to have crossed the Severn and started his tour with a visit to Caldicot Castle on 1 July 1800.[2] The next day he sketched *A House by Water*[3] and proceeded through Chepstow,[4] Tintern[5] and Monmouth[6] en route for Goodrich, where he spent 4 July (No. 13). A drawing survives of Aberystwyth Castle, dated 18 July,[7] while a mountain scene sketched on 23 July probably depicts the Barmouth Estuary.[8] On the last two days of the month he was sketching the impressive form of Harlech Castle (Nos. 11 and 12), gathering material for a subject he was to exhibit three times with the Norwich Society, once in 1807 (129) and twice in 1810 (59 and 161). One of his exhibits at the Royal Academy only that summer had been entitled *Harlech Castle, Wales* (550*), presumably derived from a print or drawing by another artist.

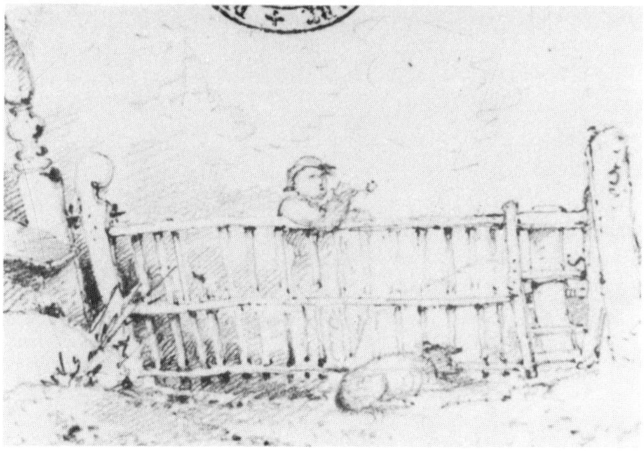

13 Man and Dog beside a Gate at Goodrich Castle, Herefordshire *c.*1800

An indication that Cotman continued his first Welsh tour northwards into the early part of August is to be found on the reverse of a drawing of Snowdon of some nine or ten years later.[9] This bears part of a sketch of Beddgelert, dated August 1800. Similarly, a sketch of Conway Castle,[10] which is undated but in the characteristic hatched pencilwork of this period, suggests a continuation of his tour northwards, to arrive at Conway probably by mid August at the latest. Again this single visit was to provide him with subject-matter for a number of later drawings of the Castle (see also No. 53), and at least three of the Old College House at Conway (see No. 170)—a popular subject with other visiting artists such as Cornelius Varley and David Cox.

One of Cotman's finest finished watercolours resulting from this first tour of Wales is *Barmouth Estuary* (No. 14). Signed and dated the following year, the composition must derive from sketches made in the Barmouth area whilst Cotman was en route for Harlech. The atmospheric quality of its greyish-blue tones, typical of his work at this time, is remarkably Girtinesque and might be thought to add credibility to the theory that Cotman met Thomas Girtin during the summer tour of 1800. However, it has been convincingly established that such a meeting, as suggested by Kitson, has little foundation in fact.[11]

Although there are no further dated sketches for July and August 1800, it is possible to identify other towns and beauty spots through which Cotman passed during the first Welsh tour. It is likely that during July on his progress northwards he gathered material for his subsequent etchings of Monnow Bridge (Monmouth),[12] Raglan Castle,[13] Llanthony Abbey,[14] Devil's Bridge[15] and finally Parson's Bridge,[16] two miles further north, on the way to Aberystwyth. His two exhibition pieces at the Royal Academy in 1801, (311) *Brecknock* and (410) *Llantony Abbey,*[17] confirm that he must have visited both places en route for Aberystwyth the year before. Devil's Bridge, spanning the river Mynach where it enters a deep gorge in a series of waterfalls, was a sight that inspired the young artist to produce one of his most magical watercolours on his return to England.[18]

From this point the evidence for his progress in North Wales becomes more speculative. He was probably in Beddgelert during the first week of August and at Conway by the middle of the month, having journeyed to Conway via Caernarvon. He was to exhibit a picture of *Caernarvon Castle, North Wales*[19] at the Royal Academy in 1802 (420). The return to England was probably made by way of Llangollen[20] and Valle Crucis,[21] to Bridgnorth.[22]

Kitson suggests a second tour of Wales by Cotman in the summer of 1802, but this time in the company of his fellow artist, Paul Sandby Munn.[23] Cotman would have welcomed a companion on a second sketching tour in North Wales and dated sketches by Munn establish an itinerary from 6-30 July. This is substantiated by drawings of related subjects by Cotman.

Although none of Cotman's drawings of subjects similar to those of Munn is dated, there are surviving two dated pencil sketches which corroborate the theory of a second Welsh tour in 1802: *On the Road from Wenlock to Buildwas,* dated 9 July 1802[24] and *Llanberis Pass,* dated 29 July 1802.[25] On the strength of these sketches it is possible to accept the progress of their tour as traced by Kitson. Munn's dated sketches find them at Wolverhampton on 6 July and Bridgnorth on 8 July. They then proceeded to Wenlock[26], Buildwas,[27] Broseley and Ironbridge.[28] It was at this time that Cotman made a pencil drawing of Coalbrookdale, inscribed with the date 1802.[29]

By 19 July, Cotman and Munn appear to have reached the area around Dolgelly where they remained until 23 July, during which time Cotman gathered material that he would use in several future compositions (see No. 16). Certainly this area, dominated to the south of Dolgelly by the mountain ridge of Cader Idris, was to remain in his memory throughout his career (Nos. 122, 163). He then rediscovered familiar territory on the road to Harlech. Beyond Harlech the massive mount of Moelwyn crowning the vale of Tan-y-Bwlch captivated Cotman's eye.[30]

They journeyed on, possibly making a detour via Llyn Ogwen to Llanberis Pass,[31] arriving on 28 July. The next day they sketched again in the Pass, before moving on to Capel Curig, where Cotman made one of his first studies of a church interior.[32] On the last day of the month Munn worked up a sketch of Capel Curig,[33] the arbitrary sweeping grey wash contours of which reveal the influence of his companion's technique. There is no direct evidence for the exact path that their return to England took, but it was probably via Llangollen. It was on this route that Cotman sketched Telford's recently completed aqueduct at Chirk.[34]

By the end of August Cotman had arrived in Norwich, intending to stay for a few weeks in his home town before returning to London. Brimming with self-confidence as a result of his most successful year to date, he issued an advertisement in the *Norwich Mercury* of 4 September:

> J. S. COTMAN RESPECTFULLY informs his Friends that during his Stay in Norwich, which will be three weeks or a month, he proposes giving LESSONS in DRAWING to those Ladies or Gentlemen who may think his SKETCHING from Nature or style of Coloring, beneficial to their improvement. Terms, Half a Guinea an Hour. No. 18, COCKEY-LANE.

Notes

[1]Rajnai & Allthorpe 1979 No. 10. [2]Leeds 9.584/49. [3]Rajnai & Allthorpe 1979 No. 4. [4]*Chepstow Castle and Bridge, c.*1801, watercolour, Private Collection. [5]*Tintern Abbey, c.*1800, watercolour, Bacon Collection No. 682. [6]*Mona Bridge, Monmouth,* watercolour, signed and dated *Cotman 1802,* Christie's 26 Jan. 1971 (54). Also Popham No. 319. [7]BM 1902-5-14-61. [8]Rajnai & Allthorpe 1979 No. 5. For two other dated sketches which presumably relate to this area, see *Ibid.* No. 6. [9]*Ibid.* No. 89. [10]*Ibid.* No. 10. [11]Kitson 1937 pp. 20-21, Rajnai & Allthorpe 1979 p. 13. [12]Popham No. 319. [13]*Ibid.* No. 317. [14]*Ibid.* No. 327. [15]*Ibid.* No. 305. [16]*Ibid.* No. 306. [17]Presumably Tate 970, dated 1801. [18]V & A P29-1939. [19]*Caernarvon Castle,* watercolour, signed *J. S. Cotman, c.*1801, Christie's 14 Feb. 1978 lot 12, could have derived from this visit. [20]*Llangollen,* watercolour, *c.*1803, Oppé Collection. [21]Popham No. 6. [22]BM 1902-5-14-8. [23]Kitson 1937 pp. 39-44. The following account relies upon Kitson's assertions insofar as they relate to the work of Munn. However, it is difficult to believe that he can be entirely correct when he claims that Munn was sketching at Machynlleth on 17 July, at Dolgelly from 19-23 July and yet also on Lincoln Hill, Coalbrooke on 20 July. [24]BM 1902-5-14-62. [25]BM 1902-5-14-63. [26]*Wenlock Abbey,* watercolour, *c.*1804. Worsley Collection. Also Popham No. 328. [27]RA 1803 (446), *Buildwas-abbey, Shropshire.* [28]*Bedlam Furnace near Ironbridge, Shropshire,* watercolour, *c.*1802, Bacon Collection. [29]Leeds 9.651/49. [30]Popham No. 308. [31]*Vale of Llanberis,* dated 28 July 1802, by P. S. Munn is recorded by Kaines Smith as in the Powell Collection; the drawing by Munn mentioned by Kitson as dated 29 July was in the Duke Collection. [32]Popham No. 335. [33]V&A S. Ex. 94-1889. [34]V&A 115.1892. Also Ashmolean Museum, Oxford.

11 Harlech Castle, Wales, 1800

illustrated on opposite page

Pencil on white, wove paper with watermark r. edge *1784/ J WHATMA[N];* 11.5 × 19.1 ($4\frac{1}{2} \times 7\frac{1}{2}$). Inscr: *Recto,* inscribed in pencil l.c. *Harleck* (sic) *July 30th 1800.* Prov: ?Cotman sale, Murrell, Norwich, 26-27 Nov. 1862, bt. James Reeve; bt. from him ?after 1903 by H. S. Theobald; bt. from him by R. J. Colman, Feb. 1910, R. J. Colman Bequest 1946. (494.235.951) Exh: Norwich 1903(1) lent by James Reeve. Ref: Kitson 1937 p. 43; Rajnai & Allthorpe No. 7.

Harlech Castle is a recurring subject in Cotman's work. He exhibited a version of it even before he appears to have visited the castle in the summer of 1800. This early work,[1] exhibited at the Royal Academy in May 1800 (550), was presumably taken second-hand from a print or drawing.

No. 11 and its companion, No. 12, show the castle from the south, with the Weathercock Tower to the left and the Garden Tower to the right. These sketches probably inspired the large watercolour,[2] now in the Tate Gallery, ascribed by Rajnai and Allthorpe to 1804. It is conjectured that this was the version exhibited with the Norwich Society in 1807 (129). Two more versions of the same subject were exhibited with the Society in 1810 (59 and 161). For one of these, see No. 53.

The powerful silhouette of Harlech also appears as the subject of two softground etchings for Cotman's *Liber Studiorum,* plates 25 and 29, the former being based upon Nos. 11 and 12 (see Nos. 186 and 187).

[1]Possibly Ulster Museum 761 [2]Tate T969.

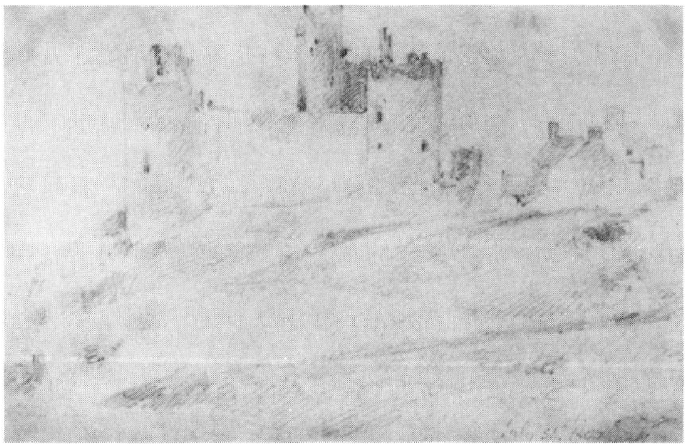

12 Harlech Castle, Wales, 1800

12 Harlech Castle, Wales, 1800

Pencil on white, wove paper; 11.4 × 17.8 ($4\frac{1}{2} \times 7$). Inscr: *Recto,* in pencil l.r. *July 31, 1800.* Prov: See No. 11 (495.235.951). Exh: Norwich 1903 (2) lent by James Reeve. Ref: Kitson 1937 p. 43; Rajnai & Allthorpe No. 8.

This drawing and its pair dated 30 July 1800 are discussed in the previous entry, No. 11. Drawn the next day, this sketch shows the castle from a slightly more south-westerly viewpoint.

13 Man and Dog beside a Gate at Goodrich Castle, Herefordshire, *c.*1800

illustrated on p. 19

Pencil on cream, wove paper; 9.2 × 13.3 ($3\frac{5}{8} \times 5\frac{1}{4}$). Inscr: *Recto,* part of circular stamp u.c.l., see No. 6. Prov: See No. 6. (79.L1967.9). Ref: Rajnai & Allthorpe No. 9.

This sketch must derive from Cotman's visit to Goodrich on 4 July 1800. Three inscribed drawings[1] of that date survive and it is considered by Rajnai and Allthorpe that No. 13 is a studio re-working of such studies.

The scene is identified by a later drawing[2] of the same gate set in a landscape with a castle in the right background and inscribed *Goodrich.*

[1]Leeds 9.1.49, 9.3.49 and another with Stanhope Shelton 1978. [2]BM 1902-5-14-202.

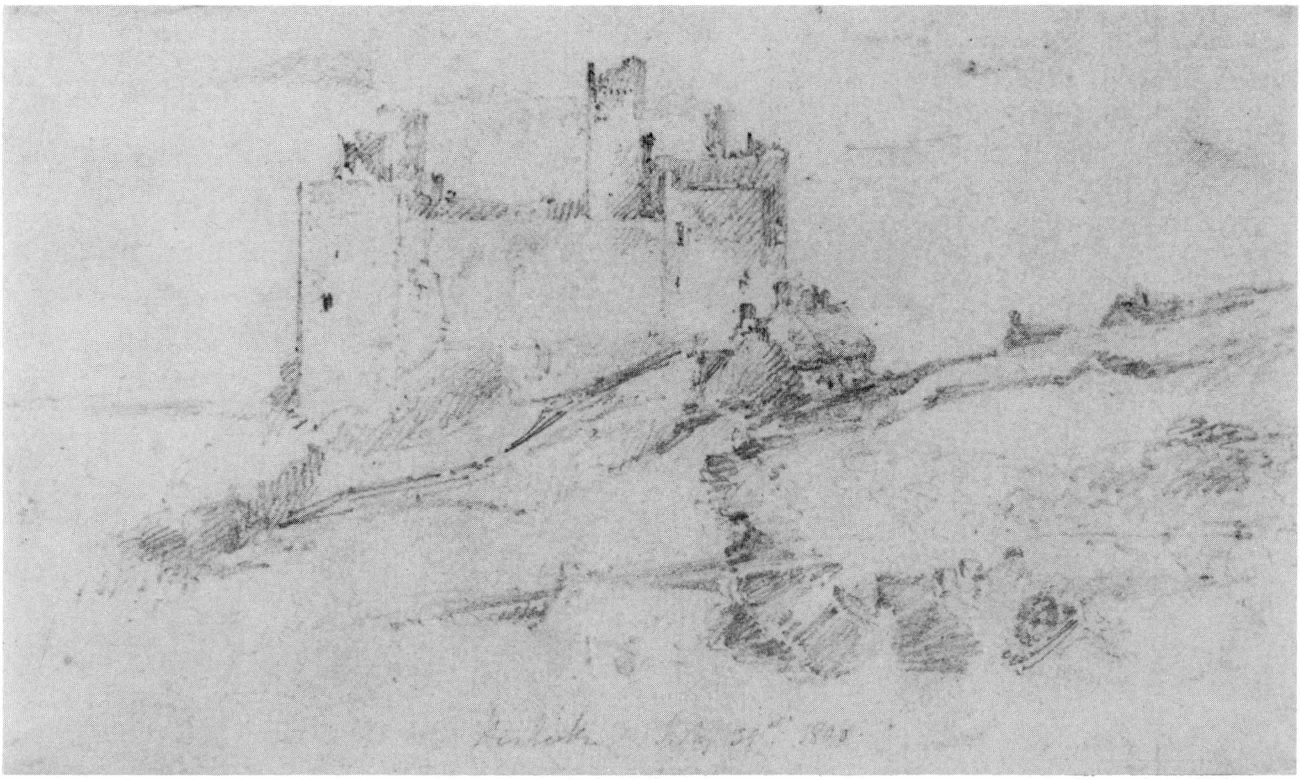

11 Harlech Castle, Wales, 1800

14 Barmouth Estuary, 1801

illustrated on p. 18

Pencil and watercolour with some gum and slight wiping out on sails, on cream, wove paper; 17.4 × 28.8 ($6\frac{13}{16} \times 11\frac{3}{8}$). Inscr: *Recto,* signed and dated in black ink l.r. *J S Cotman 1801; verso,* signed, dated and inscribed in pencil across c. *John S Cotman 1801/Barmouth, N Wales.* Prov: The Palser Gallery; Sotheby's 29 July 1931, lot 110, included in a group of drawings bt. by G. Douglas Thomson; Percy Moore Turner; bt. from him by R. J. Colman 12 Jan. 1934, £150; R. J. Colman Bequest 1946. (125.217.947). Exh: Norwich 1945; Norwich, Arts Council 1947 (1). Ref: Kitson 1937 p. 26; Rajnai & Allthorpe No. 12.

This sketch was made when Cotman was in the Barmouth area some time between 18 and 30 July 1800. It is among the finest and most Girtinesque of his early works[1] and, working from this and other sketches[2] of the same subject, Cotman was to compose several later watercolours.[3] One of these was exhibited at the Royal Academy in 1804 (375),[4] while a later version was shown with the Norwich Society in 1829 as (125) *View near Barmouth, North Wales.* The latter is a view as yet untraced.[5] For a more detailed discussion of the versions of this subject see Rajnai and Allthorpe No. 12.

[1]The earliest version, *c.*1800, is in the Stanford Museum, USA, ex coll. L. G. Duke. [2]Rajnai & Allthorpe No. 5. [3]Two of which are: (a) Somerville & Simpson Ltd., 1977; (b) another version is conjectured through a watercolour copy by Lound, NCM 13.155.938. [4]Royal Watercolour Society, ex. coll. F. J. Nettlefold. [5]A different view, *c.*1801, is at the Yale Center for British Art, New Haven, USA, B 1977.14.4977.

15 A Waterwheel near Harlech, Merionethshire, North Wales, 1802

called *An Overshot Mill*

illustrated in colour on p. 25

Pencil and watercolour on cream, wove paper; 29 × 21.9 ($11\frac{7}{16} \times 8\frac{5}{8}$). Inscr: *Recto,* signed in watercolour l.r. *J. S. Cotman; verso,* the back of the lower backing board was formerly inscribed, signed and dated *A waterwheel near Harlech/Merionethshire North Wales./J. S. Cotman 1802.* Prov: Sir Wyndham Dunstan; Victor Rienaecker; the Palser Gallery; bt. from them by Percy Moore Turner, March 1926; bt. from him by R. J. Colman, March 1926; R. J. Colman Bequest 1946. (123.235.951). Exh: ?RA 1802 (430) as *A grind stone, near Harlech.* Ref: Kitson 1937 p. 17; Rajnai & Allthorpe No. 22.

The inscription on the backing paper, which was removed in 1934, the hilly landscape to the left and the early technique help to identify this drawing as the Royal Academy exhibit of 1802.

The hot colour is again due to the fading of a fugitive blue. The composition shows an early example of Cotman's sense of the monumentality of even the most humble of subjects. The use of zigzag pencilwork and amorphous, reserved spaces amongst the branches, foreshadows his later and more idiosyncratic method of indicating leaf forms.

16 Dolgelly, North Wales, *c.*1802

illustrated on p. 18

Pencil and watercolour on cream, laid paper; 16.8 × 29.5 ($6\frac{5}{8} \times 11\frac{9}{16}$). Inscr: *Verso,* previously inscribed *Dolgelly No. Wales.* Prov: James N. Sherrington; by descent to his widow Mrs. Caleb Rose; her sale Christie's, 30 March 1908, as by John Crome *A View in Cumberland,* one of two items in lot 30 bt. R. J. Colman 16 gns.; R. J. Colman Bequest 1946. (252.235.951). Exh: Norwich, Crome Centenary 1921 (64) as *Dolgelly, N. Wales* by Crome. Ref: Kitson 1937 p. 42; Rajnai & Allthorpe No. 23.

Although this drawing entered the collections at Norwich as by Crome it was later recognised by Percy Moore Turner and Kitson to be Cotman. This attribution is endorsed by Rajnai and Allthorpe.

No. 16 is a view of Dolgelly from the hills to the south-west looking towards the Barmouth Estuary. Kitson suggests that Cotman and Paul Sandby Munn stayed at Dolgelly from 19 to 23 July on the evidence of dated drawings by Munn.[1]

Other early Cotman drawings of Dolgelly survive, in the Cecil Higgins Art Gallery, Bedford[2] and the Fitzwilliam Museum, Cambridge.[3] Two cottage scenes[4] also derive from this visit.

[1]The one dated 19 July is in the British Museum, BM 1889-12018-16, but the drawing dated 23 July is untraced. [2]P.612 [3]Kitson Bequest 1937 No. 2303. [4](a) Pencil, exh. Colnaghi Nov.-Dec. 1973 (17) (b) Bacon Collection (identified by the inscription on a copy by S. C. Edwards, NCM 100.377.965).

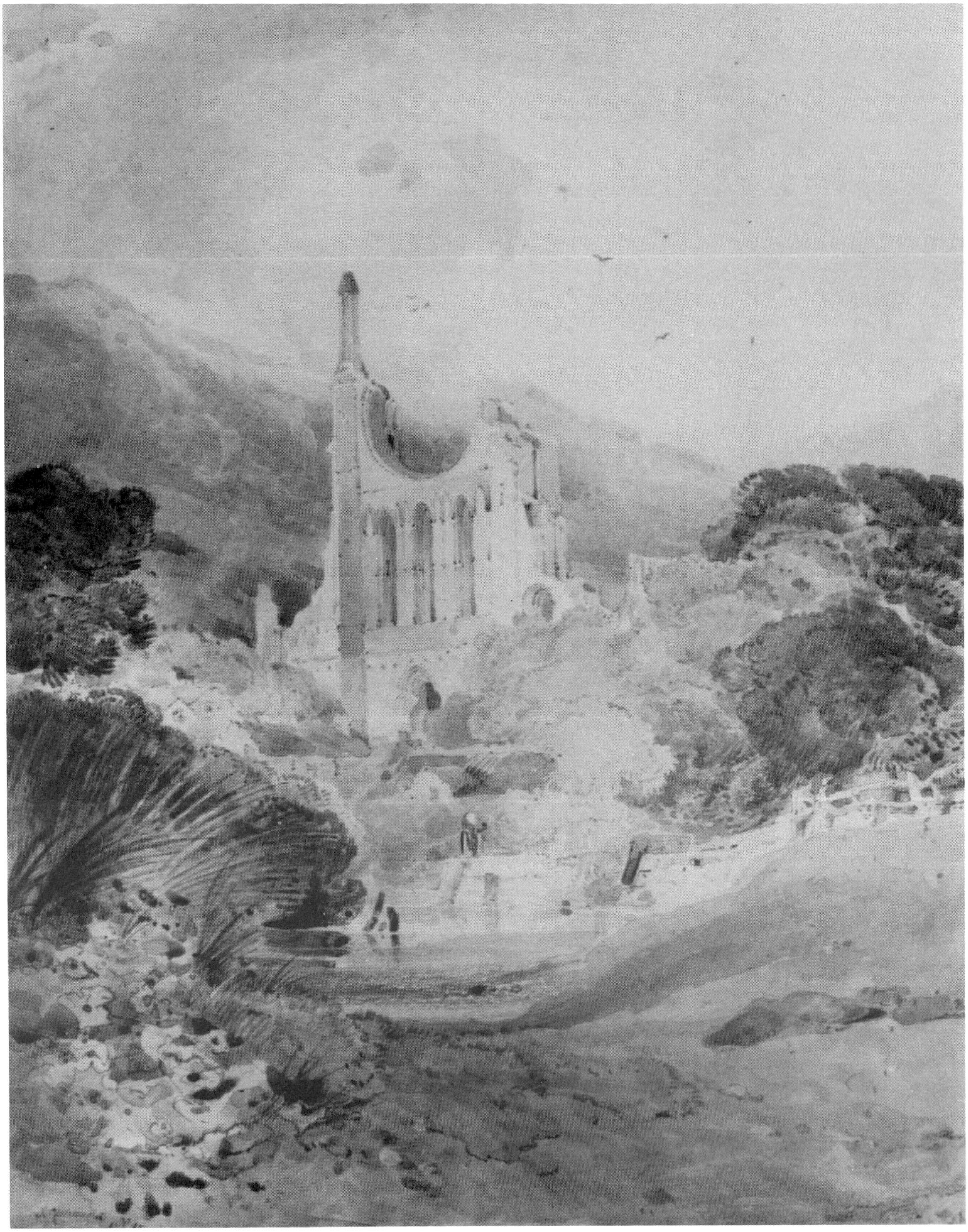

19 Byland Abbey, Yorkshire, 1804

3
The First Visits to Yorkshire 1803 & 1804

The single event of the most outstanding importance for Cotman during 1803 was his first visit to Yorkshire and his befriending by the Cholmeley family. The influence of Yorkshire upon Cotman was as important to him as to Girtin and Turner. Just as Turner was encouraged by Walter Fawkes of Farnley Hall and Girtin by Lord Harewood, so Cotman 'spent the summers of the three most impressionable years of his life at the house of the third Yorkshire country gentleman, that of Francis Cholmeley of Brandsby Hall.'[1]

Brandsby Hall, with its dark grey facade, is some fifteen miles north of York. In 1803 Francis Cholmeley's family consisted of his wife, sister of Sir Henry Englefield, his son, also named Francis, and four daughters. A commonplace book at Brandsby recorded the various activities of the household and this gives a brief account of the visit of the 'two young painters from London, Mr. Munn and Mr. Cotman'.[2] More details of Cotman's visits are provided by a group of letters preserved by the descendants of the Cholmeleys, while further evidence is to be found in surviving dated drawings.

On their way to Brandsby, Cotman and Paul Sandby Munn stayed in York for a few days. Dated sketches by both of them reveal that they were in York by 4 July, when Cotman sketched the sixteenth century bridge spanning the river Ouse.[3] The Brandsby commonplace book records their subsequent arrival there on 7 July. Within their first couple of days they had visited Castle Howard, Rievaulx Abbey ('the finest ruin they had ever seen')[4] and Helmsley,[2] returning on the 10 July. After their return Mrs. Cholmeley wrote to her son Francis, giving her first impressions of the two artists: 'Mr. Munn and Mr. Cottman [sic] are two artists of great merit indeed and both friends of my brother's. I think their sketches superior to any I have ever seen. Cottman is very young, Munn between 30 & 40 and a well establish[e]d artist. He draws with a rapidity and command of his pencil that is quite wonderful. They were delighted with Kirkham and have made some exquisite drawings of it. I wish you c[oul]d see them. Munn is a rough, peculiar manner[e]d man but very shrewd and clever and of course very entertaining. Cottman much more *maniere'd* and gentlemanlike . . .'[2] It is interesting that at this stage Mrs. Cholmeley found Munn's work more impressive on first acquaintance and Cotman's personal manner more courteous. A week later she remembered Munn's company as more congenial, finding him an able raconteur and 'one of the best mimics I ever saw in my life'.[4] By the time they left on the 14 July, they had also visited Byland (see No. 19), Sheriff Hutton and Craike.[4] In the same letter Mrs. Cholmeley mentions how gratified she has been 'by very kind letters from my bro[the]r who seems much obliged and pleased by our kindness to his friends'. Sir Henry Englefield had introduced the artists to the Cholmeleys, an act for which Cotman remained eternally grateful as it enabled him to spend 'the happiest and blith[e]somest Hours of My life' at Brandsby.[5]

Cotman and Munn returned to Brandsby on 2 August, having toured the region. Dated drawings by Munn indicate that they were at Richmond on the 14 July[6] and Gordale Scar, near Malham on the 26 July[7] (see No. 17). A letter from Mrs. Cholmeley to her son, 23 July, reveals that they spent a week based at Ripon to draw Fountains Abbey (No. 8). Munn left Brandsby for the last time on 3 August. The commonplace book records this and the comings and goings of Cotman, the family and their circle, until Cotman himself left after some seven weeks on 22 September. During this period he became a true friend of the family, captivating Mrs. Cholmeley in particular through both his personality and his work: 'Cotman is quite a treasure — only 21 years old and such a draughtsman!!'[8] Katherine wrote on the same day to her brother, informing him that he had 'certainly lost a most pleasant opportunity of enjoying and profiting of Mr. Cotman's drawings', by not joining them at Brandsby. Cotman, meanwhile, divided his time well, acting as drawing coach to the girls in addition to gathering material for his own work. On the 21 August Anne wrote to her brother that both she and Katherine were 'now seriously engaged in sketching from nature w[i]th Mr. Cotman'.

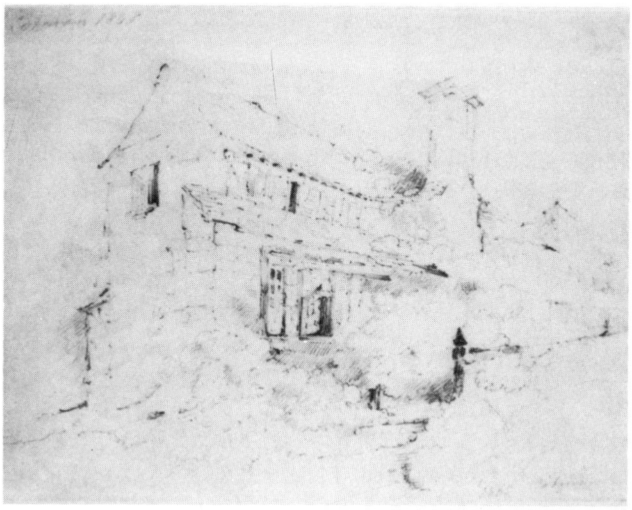

17 House at Bolton, Yorkshire, *c.*1803

Cotman made a number of trips with various members of the Cholmeley family and their circle during his stay in 1803. On Sunday, 7 August he 'went to Helmsley', returning on the Tuesday.[9] This appears to have been the only trip on which he was unaccompanied during these weeks. A drawing dated 7 August 1803 reveals that he visited Rievaulx Abbey, three miles from Helmsley, on that day. The delicate pencilwork traces the forms of the Abbey refectory doorway,[10] while the watercolour washes have a freedom indicative of a new virtuosity in his work. A dated sketch of the inside of the gatehouse of Helmsley Castle indicates that Cotman was there on 8 August.[11] The next day he was sketching briefly at Duncombe Park[12] before returning to Brandsby.

On 13 August Cotman accompanied Mrs. Cholmeley and the four girls to Byland, returning in the evening (see No. 19). His first recorded visit to Gilling Castle was two days later, this time in the company of the Cholmeleys as guests of the Fairfax family for dinner. On the 22 August Mrs. Cholmeley accompanied him to Lake Gormire for the day, a sketching excursion which resulted in the watercolour *Gormire, Yorkshire,* exhibited at the Royal Academy the following year.[13] Two days later they went to York Races with Anne, staying away overnight.

On 29 August they were fishing at Oulston Ponds with Lady Charlotte Belasyse of Newburgh and her husband. The following day they visited Kirkham and on the morning of 1 September were at Easingwold. The commonplace book records a particularly hectic weekend of social upheaval over 4 and 5 September, when visitors included Lady Palmerston and her eldest son, the future Prime Minister, then an undergraduate at Cambridge. On the Saturday afternoon Cotman visited Castle Howard with Mrs. Cholmeley, her son Francis and one Colonel St. George. On the Sunday the household and guests visited Duncombe Park, dining at Rievaulx Terrace. Such excursions would hardly have given Cotman time to make many sketches, if any, but they afforded a social whirl gratifying in its explicit recognition of his courteous and personable character.

Cotman returned to Byland once again on 7 September, this time with Francis Cholmeley, with whom he also visited York the next day. On 9 September he accompanied Mr. and Mrs. Cholmeley and Francis to Newburgh. The commonplace book records that on Wednesday 14 September 'Mr. and Mrs. Cholmeley, Mr. F. Cholmeley & Mr. Cotman left Brandsby on a little tour to Beverley, Hull, Howden, Selby, Leeds & Wakefield'. The family finally parted from Cotman at Wakefield on the morning of 22 September. While no known drawing exists of Beverley or Hull, Cotman evidently had time to sketch the ruined east end of Howden Church, a subject he exhibited the next year at the Royal Academy and subsequently etched.[14] A dated drawing of the West front of the Abbey at Selby confirms that the party had reached Selby by 20 September.[15] It seems that the projected visit to Leeds could only have been cursory, possibly due to poor weather. In 1820 Cotman was to describe a wet day at Falaise in Normandy as 'all haze, rain, smoke & dirt, like Leeds for blackness'.[16] The Cholmeley family correspondence reveals that for the rest of the year Cotman was never far from the thoughts of the Cholmeleys, nor they from his.

During the early part of 1804 Cotman worked up much of the material gathered during the previous summer in Yorkshire. The previous November Sir Henry Englefield had written to Mrs. Cholmeley of a fine drawing then in progress of Newburgh Park.[17] In January Cotman wrote to Mr. Belasyse 'requesting leave to frame and exhibit his two draw[in]gs of Newburgh'[18] and they were indeed included in his contribution of seven drawings at the Royal Academy show that spring. Six of these drawings were of Yorkshire subjects. Besides those of Gormire, Howden and Newburgh, Cotman worked up exhibition pieces of Rievaulx Abbey[19] and Fountains Abbey (see No. 18). Sydney Kitson has also convincingly ascribed two watercolours, *Kirkthorpe Church, Yorkshire* and *View over the Humber From Welton, Yorkshire* to this period, as a result of a possible commission from the Right Hon. J. Smyth M.P. of Heath Hall, Wakefield, from which collection they passed to Kitson.[20] Smyth and his daughter later appear as subscribers to Cotman's *Miscellaneous Etchings* of 1811. It is likely that Cotman's introduction to the Smyth family was effected by Mrs. Cholmeley, a further example of her very practical friendship and patronage of the young artist.

It was in the summer of 1804 that Cotman met for the first time the patron who was to have such a considerable effect upon his future life. It is not clear whether Cotman was specifically en route for Yorkshire at the time but Brandsby Hall was undoubtedly his ultimate goal that summer. The meeting was a mixed blessing, in that Dawson Turner's patronage was not to include the abiding affection which the Cholmeleys fostered. A businessman, botanist and antiquarian, Dawson Turner's eye was attuned to the illustrative record rather than the aesthetic composition. Nevertheless, their initial contact filled Cotman with hopes for the future. It is not clear quite how they came to be acquainted, but Cotman joined the Turner family at Covehithe towards the end of July. Two drawings survive which are presumably of this visit, one of *Covehithe Church,*[21] the other of *Cottages at Cove Hythe.*[22] Both drawings feature a use of flat washes, the style which Cotman was to make fully his own the next year. He accompanied the Turners back to Yarmouth, but had left by 6 August, when Dawson Turner wrote to his fellow botanist, Nathaniel John Winch: 'I have had an eminent artist, Mr. Cotman, at my house lately, who has made sketches of all the fine ruins in Yorkshire. They are done in a most masterly manner . . .'[23]

On 9 August 1804 Cotman wrote the first letter of a lifelong correspondence with Dawson Turner. He describes in graphic terms his visits to both Castle Acre and Croyland Abbey (see No. 20). He was at Castle Acre, just east of King's Lynn, Norfolk by 9 August, a visit which resulted in three etchings.[24] Nine days later he was writing from Croyland, which he reached via Cambridge and Ely. His letter reveals an early fondness for exaggeration and self-deprecating anecdote, as he tells of the trials of 'a paltry inn full of the worst Company I ever heard'. Indeed, he was so 'molested' while sketching the west front of Croyland that he 'was obliged to give one of the ringleaders a sound flogging', which necessitated a somewhat hasty departure for Peterborough.

There is no direct evidence as to Cotman's movements over the next few weeks. The Brandsby commonplace book reveals that the Cholmeley family were holidaying in Scarborough for the late summer and that there they were joined by Cotman, all returning for a late dinner at Brandsby on 25 September. Cotman remained at Brandsby once again for seven weeks, spending his time almost exactly as he had the previous year. His first visit was on 27 September with Mrs. Cholmeley to Newburgh, where he returned with Francis for dinner on 15 October, after a visit to the races. On 4 October he was accompanied by Harriet to Coxwold, which he also visited with Francis on 15 October. This year, Francis was at Brandsby throughout Cotman's stay and their friendship strengthened. The commonplace book records Francis killing his first partridge on 16 October—a success emulated by Cotman only four days before his departure when he shot a woodcock. Mr. and Mrs. Cholmeley accompanied him to York to see him off on 13 November.

Notes:

[1]Kitson 1937 p. 49. [2]Harriet and Mrs. Cholmeley to Francis, 10 July 1803. [3]Rajnai & Allthorpe No. 24. [4]Mrs. Cholmeley to Francis, 17 July 1803. [5]JSC to Francis Cholmeley, 23 July 1822. [6]BM 1889-12-18-10. [7]BM 1889-12-18-17. [8]Mrs. Cholmeley to Francis, 16 Aug. 1803. [9]For this and the following account, see Brandsby Commonplace Book. [10]Oppé Collection. [11]Kitson 1937 p. 54 (New College, Oxford). [12]BM 1902-5-14-313. [13]RA 1804 (928); probably BM 1958-7-12-329. [14]RA 1804 (426); Popham No. 25. [15]Kitson 1937 p. 58. [16]*Cotman's Normandy Letters,* Walpole Society, vol. XV, p. 111. [17]Mrs. Cholmeley to Francis, 12 Nov. 1803. [18]*Ibid.* 22 Jan. 1804. RA 1804 (409 and 418). [19]RA 1804 (498). [20]Kitson 1937 pp. 61-2; Leeds 29.11.38 and 29.12.38. [21]BM 1859.5.28.120. [22]Stanhope Shelton Collection, 1974. [23]Kitson 1937 p. 68. [24]Popham Nos. 90, 91, 92.

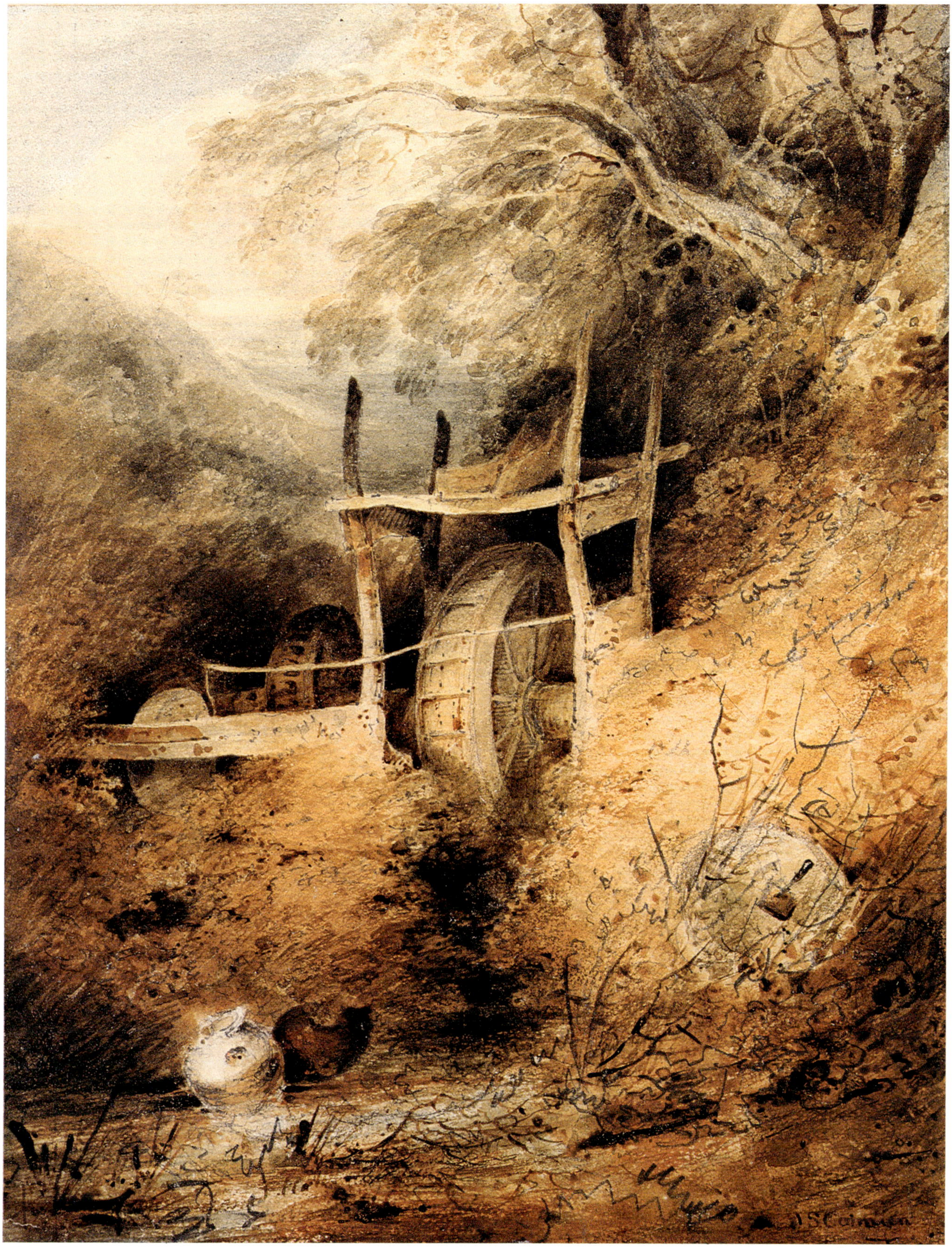

15 A Waterwheel near Harlech, Merionethshire, North Wales, 1802

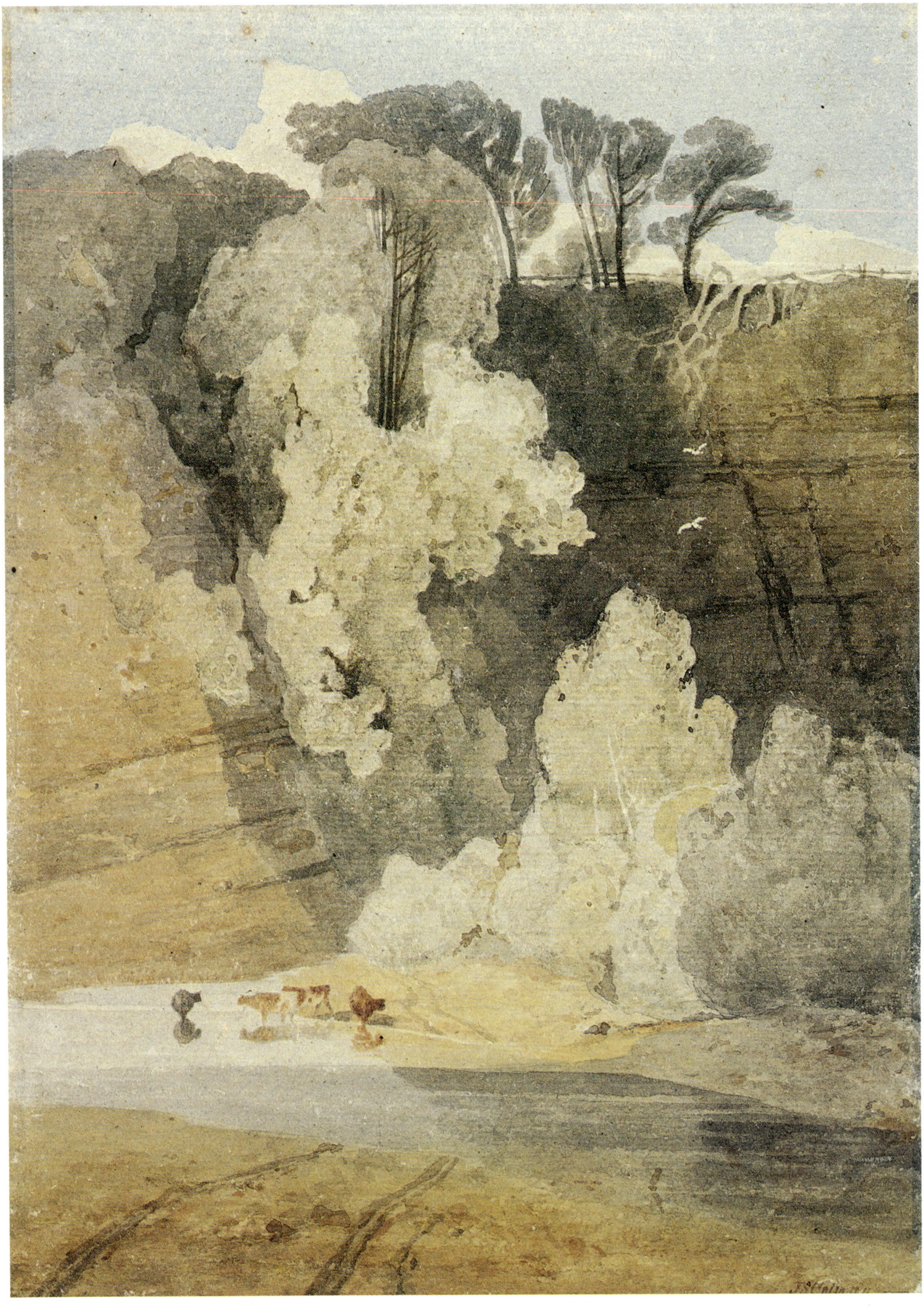

28 On the River Greta, Yorkshire, *c.*1806-7

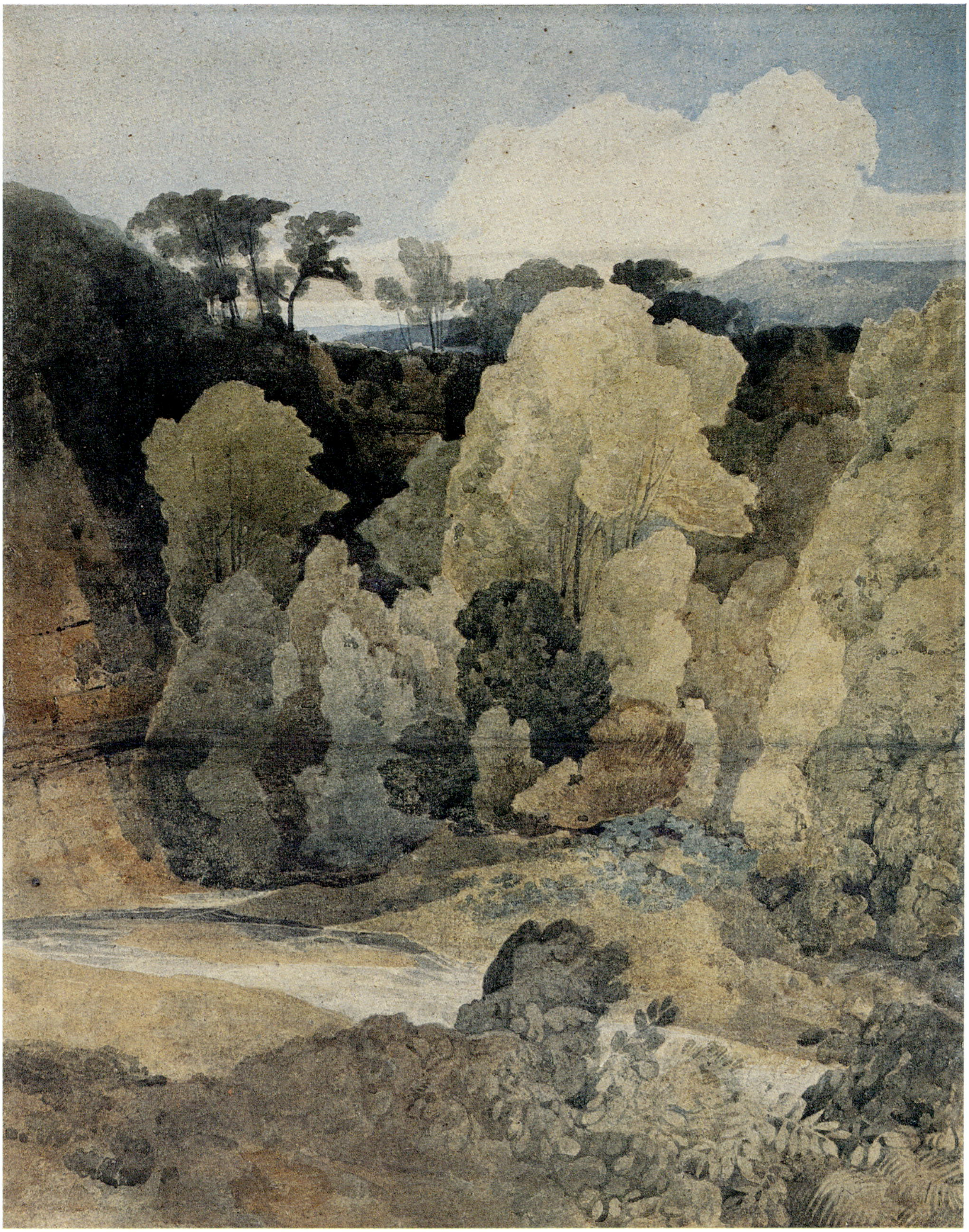

30 'Devil's Elbow, Rokeby Park', *c.*1806-7

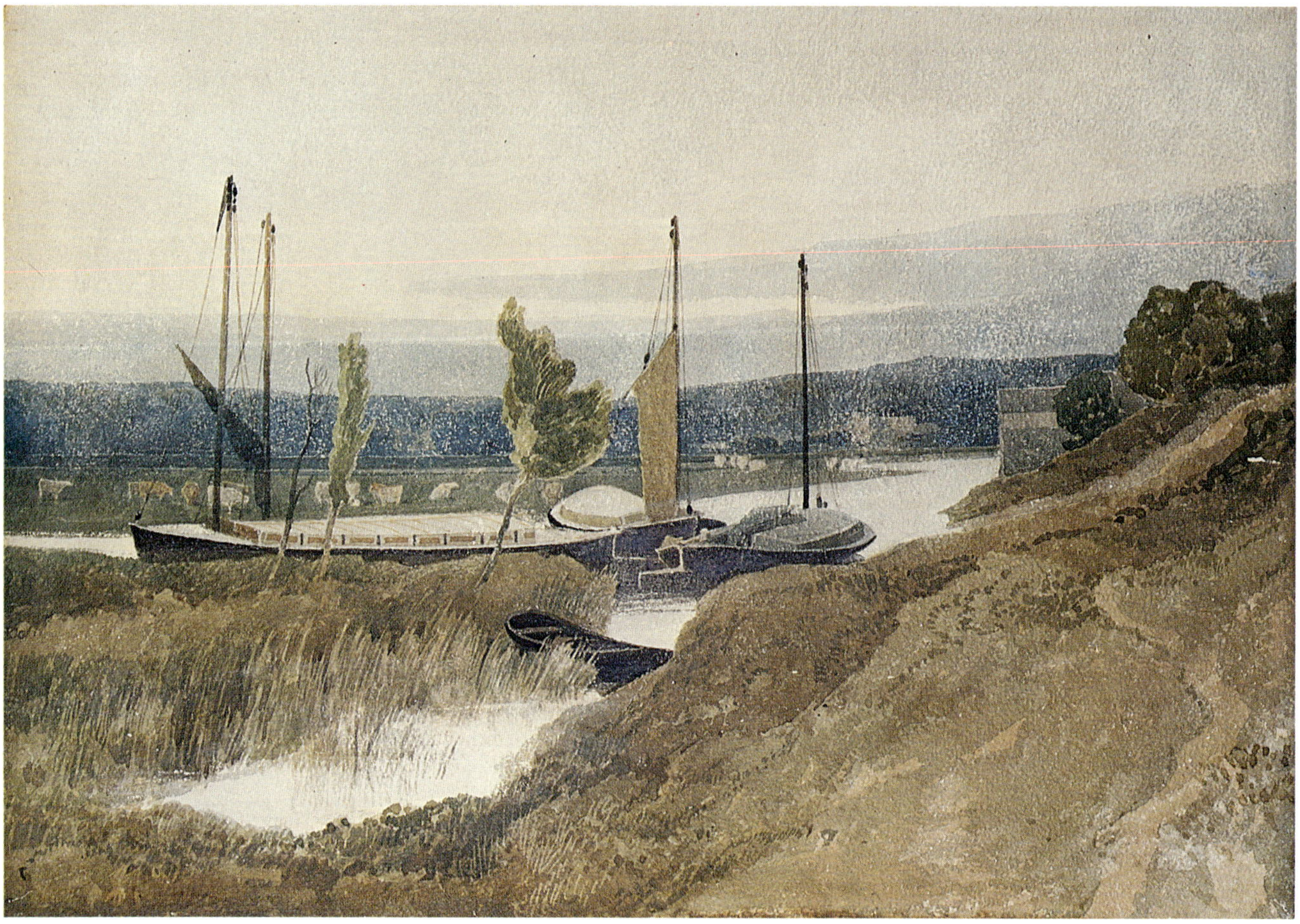

49 'Trowse Hythe, Norwich', *c.* 1809-10

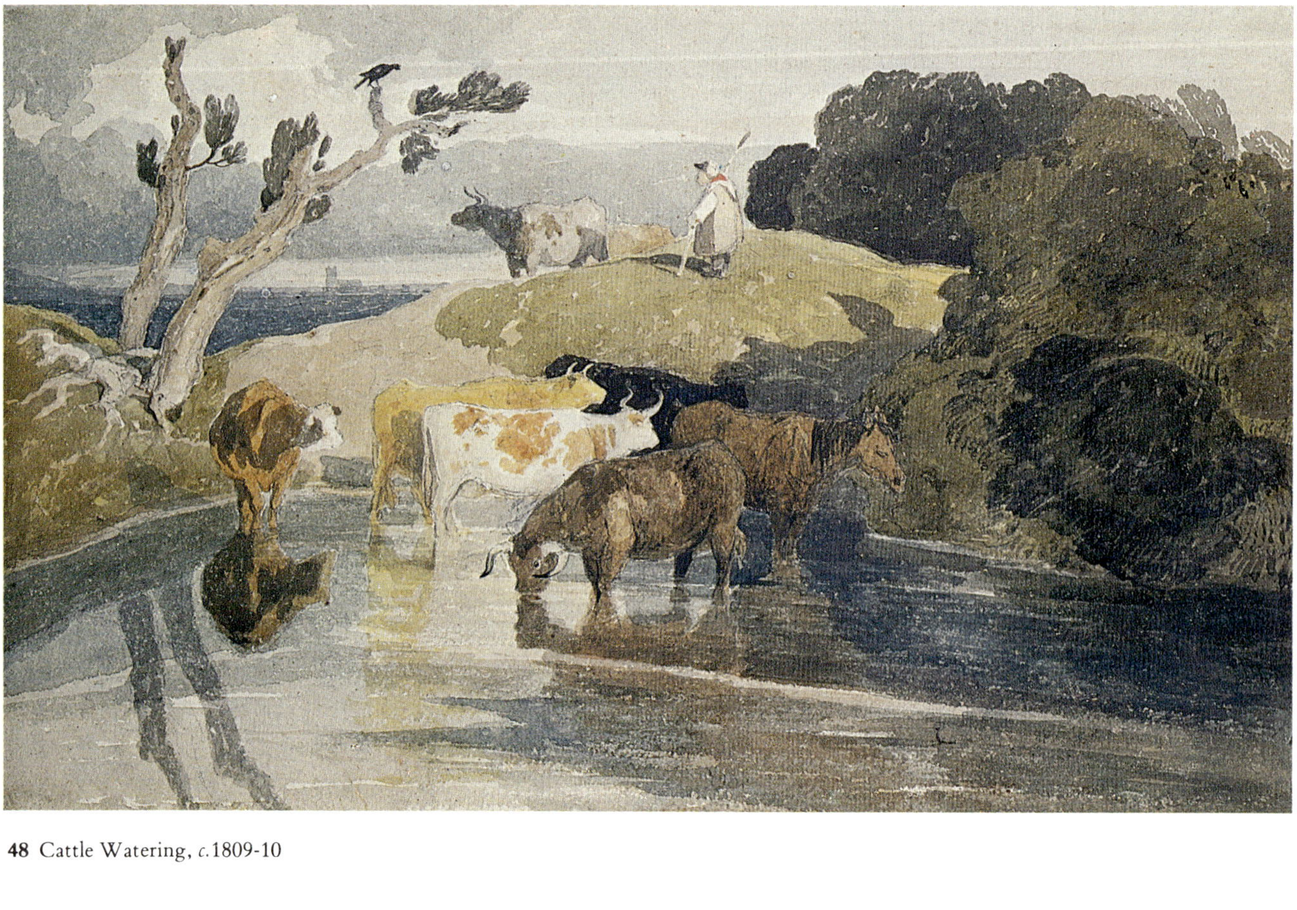

48 Cattle Watering, *c.*1809-10

17 House at Bolton, Yorkshire, *c.*1803
illustrated on p. 23

Pencil and slight grey wash on white, wove paper; 17.1 × 23.3 ($6\frac{3}{4}$ × $8\frac{3}{4}$). INSCR: *Recto,* ?signed and ?dated in pencil u.l. *Cotman 1808,* numbered in pencil u.r. *No. 2,* ?dated and ?signed in pencil l.r. *1808 Cotman; verso,* inscribed in pencil l.r. *J S Cotman.* PROV: Presented by Duncan Cotman with a collection of 43 other drawings by or attributed to Cotman and his family, 1975. (8.474.975). REF: Rajnai & Allthorpe, No. 25.

The subject of this sketch is identified by two inscribed copies[1] by pupils. There is also an inscribed drawing of the same subject dated 1803, by Paul Sandby Munn.[2]

Cotman and Munn probably visited Bolton on 27 July 1803, during their three weeks' tour from Brandsby between 14 July and 2 August. A dated drawing by Cotman shows that they were at Kirkstall, near Leeds,[3] by 28 July.

The twice inscribed date of 1808 is misleading. A drawing of the same subject by Munn is dated 1803 while 'the close hatching, the sharp dark accents and the frilled outlines delineating foliage' discussed by Rajnai and Allthorpe, place it close to dated pencil sketches of 1803. Cotman later executed a watercolour version of this subject, known by a copy.[4]

[1](a) F. A. Martineau, NCM 65.25.964 (b) S. C. Edwards, NCM 135.377.965. [2]V & A E3119-1948. [3]Leeds 9.573/49. [4]NCM 271.235.951.

18 Fountains Abbey, Yorkshire, 1804

Pencil on cream, wove paper; 36.2 × 26.7 ($14\frac{1}{4}$ × $10\frac{1}{2}$). INSCR: *Recto,* signed and dated in pencil l.r. *J S Cotman, 1804.* PROV: Frank Moore; bt. from him by R. J. Colman; R. J. Colman Bequest 1946. (482.235.951). REF: Rajnai & Allthorpe No. 27.

By the 23 July Cotman and Munn were on the southward leg of their tour from Brandsby. They had reached Ripon where they spent a week taking drawings of Fountains Abbey.[1]

Cotman made at least six drawings of the Abbey and exhibited the subject five times: at the RA in 1804 (564), at the Norwich Society in 1811 (71) and 1824 (85 & 90) and at the Norfolk and Suffolk Art Union in 1839 (274).

No. 18 is an interior view of the East End showing the great sanctuary window and the Chapel of the Nine Altars, looking from the south-west. It is a fully worked out studio drawing for an exhibition watercolour of *c.*1804,[2] but it is unlikely that either No. 18 or the watercolour of the same composition could have been the 1804 exhibit which, as Rajnai and Allthorpe argue, must be the exterior view now in the Ashmolean Museum.[3]

Fountains Abbey provided Cotman with material for four other compositions: the Tower Arch, looking from the south-east;[4] part of the Refectory;[5] the 'South Transept';[6] the Chapel of Nine Altars, the same view as the museum's drawing but without the sanctuary arch.[7]

[1]Mrs. Cholmeley to her son Francis, 23 July 1803. [2]Ex coll. Mrs. Worthington; P. M. Turner. [3]Presented to the Ashmolean by the Rev. F. M. T. Palgrave and Miss Annora Palgrave 1941. 4(a) Norwich Society 1824 (90). (b) For a wash drawing of *c.*1803-05, see Kitson 1937 pl. 14. (c) A pencil drawing of the subject was sold Sotheby's, 28 Nov. 1974, lot 115. [5]Popham No. 21. Either the etching, or the drawing for it was Cotman's exhibit with the Norwich Society in 1811 (71). [6]Lot 4 in Cotman's sale, Christie's, 1 May 1824, bt. Taylor £2.7.0. cf. a crude copy, NCM 481.235.951. [7]Known by a drawing, probably a copy, in the V & A, D1909.89, and by a lithograph, in reverse, by Vincent Brooks published before 1862. The east end was the subject of one of Cotman's drawing copies exhibited with the Norwich Society, 1824 (85*).

19 Byland Abbey, Yorkshire, 1804
illustrated on p. 22

Pencil, watercolour and some white bodycolour on cream, wove paper; 34.8 × 27 ($13\frac{11}{16}$ × $10\frac{5}{8}$). INSCR: *Recto,* signed and dated in brown ink l.l. *J. S. Cotman / 1804.; verso,* inscribed in pencil c.*Goo.* PROV: ?Cotman sale, Spelman, Norwich, 16 May 1861; William Wade by 1888; James Reeve by 1889; bt. from him by H. S. Theobald after 1903; bt. from him by R. J. Colman, Feb. 1910; R. J. Colman Bequest 1946. (129.235.951). EXH: Norwich, Art Circle 1888 (33)

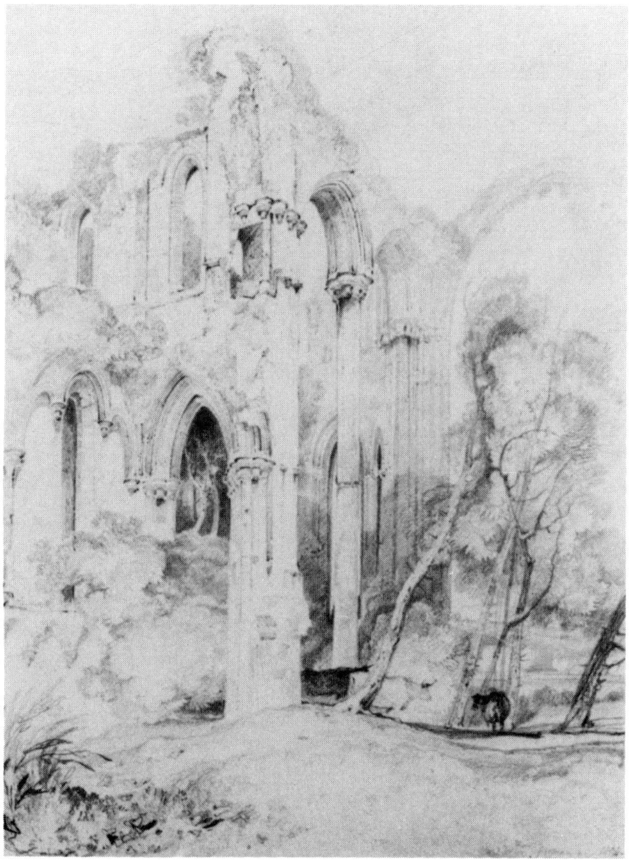

18 Fountains Abbey, Yorkshire, 1804

lent by W. Wade; RA Winter Exhibition 1892 (45) lent by James Reeve; Norwich 1902 (229); Norwich 1903 (5) lent by James Reeve; Manchester 1912 (363); Tate 1922 (11). REF: Kitson 1937 pp. 57, 122, 144, 370; Rajnai & Allthorpe No. 28.

Cotman and Munn had first visited Byland some time between 11 and 13 July 1803. Cotman went there again on Saturday 13 August with Mrs. Cholmeley and her daughters. One of the girls, Katherine, wrote to her brother on 16 August:[1] 'Last Saturday Mama and we four went with him [Cotman] to Byland and spent a very delightful day there indeed . . . Mr. Cotman made some new sketches and tinted one he had taken when there before with Mr. Munn. The Abbey far exceeded our expectations, especially the grand piece with the partial tints of the evening thrown over the wood behind and the most beautiful clouds and dark grey sky'. Cotman made a further visit on 7 September with Francis Cholmeley and Colonel St. George.[2] From sketches taken on these visits he made four watercolours and an etching. He exhibited the subject twice: with the Norwich Society of Artists in 1808 (128) *Byland Abbey; coloured sketch* and 1811 (58) *West Front of Byland Abbey, Yorkshire.*[3]

In No. 19 Cotman has set the ruin, viewed from the south-west, in a greatly romanticised portrayal of the valley of Byland. The drawing, despite the fading of the blues, retains a silvery tonality and is a fine example of this period, incorporating an early use of the idiosyncratic shapes indicating foliage, which were to become a feature of the 1805 Greta drawings. It is closely based on a small watercolour[4] of 1803, inscribed with a record of Cotman's third visit on the 7 September 1803. Another watercolour study is perhaps the 1808 exhibit.[5]

The most magnificent version of this subject is surely that of *c.*1809, No. 47.

[1]Mrs. Cholmeley to her son Francis, 17 July 1803, and Katherine's letter to her brother, 16 August 1803. [2]Brandsby commonplace book. [3]The etching (Popham No. 15) or the drawing for it. [4]National Museum of Wales. [5]Dickes p. 257. There are also two drawing copies of the subject: (a) Spooner Bequest, Courtauld Institute, London; (b) Christie's, 2 Nov. 1976, lot 91.

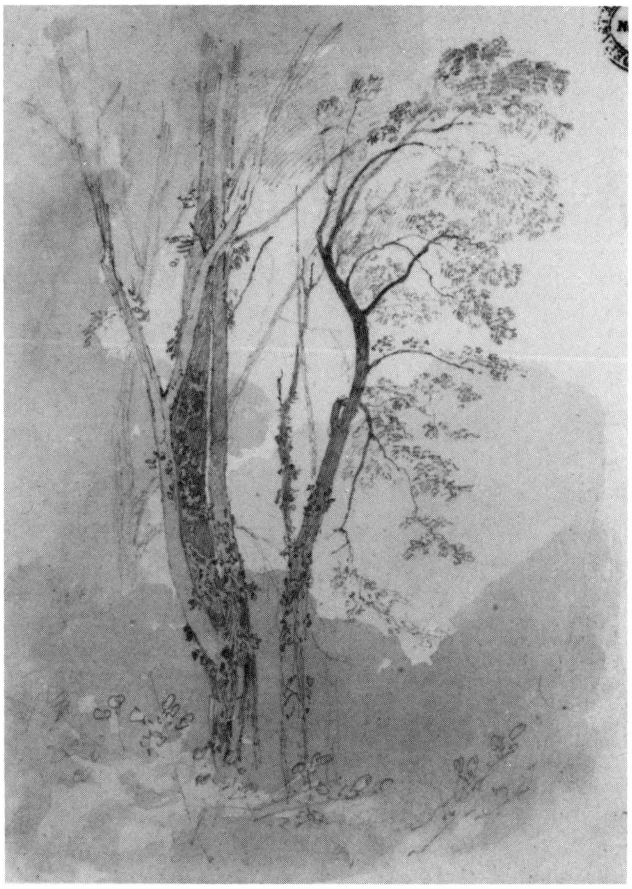

21 Study of Trees *c.*1804-5

20 Croyland Abbey, Lincolnshire, 1804
illustrated on opposite page

Pencil and watercolour on cream, wove paper: 42 × 35.5 ($16\frac{1}{2}$ × 14). INSCR: *Recto,* signed and dated in brown ink l.r. *J S Cotman/1804.* PROV: Christie's sale, 31 July 1936, lot 155 as *Ruins of an Abbey,* bt. Walker's Galleries 66 gns.; R. J. Colman ?after 5 April 1939; R. J. Colman Bequest 1946. (251.235.951). EXH: ?RA 1805 (509). REF: Kitson 1937 pp. 69, 71-73; Rajnai & Allthorpe No. 29.

From a sketch taken on the spot Cotman later made five studio drawings and an etching of Croyland Abbey. He exhibited the subject five times; twice at the RA in 1805 (509, 626) and three times with the Norwich Society, 1807 (45), 1810 (57) and in 1811 (64).[1]

His enthusiasm for the Abbey ruins is revealed in a letter to Dawson Turner written in instalments between Saturday, 18 and Tuesday, 21 August 1804:[1] 'Croyland is most delicious, you know how I esteemed my *Howden.* This Oh this is far, far superior. Castle Acre to it is as Nothing—I am sorry I am obliged to paint this in so brilliant a manner as it precludes all hopes of my ever seeing it now with you, & yet I feel my pen incapable of describing it 'tis so Magnificent, 'tis most magnificent—The old part is full of Nature—the Door, the window in short, the Whole is Wonderful—there is not one upright line in the Composition therefore let not the Botanists criticise when they come to see it & they find me out of the perpendicular—besides, indeed Sir I have found out more *Leaves*—of the kind I *wanted* to represent. (I do not say I have represented them)—& some with the Stalks perpendicular & the Leaf Horizontal.' The same letter details the considerable discomforts Cotman encountered during his stay (see p. 24).

No. 20 is the smaller of two compositions which show the West Front from the south-west. The undulating landscape, peopled here with pigs and cows, is replaced by a more accurate Fenland marsh in the larger watercolour of the same year in the Ferens Art Gallery, Kingston-upon-Hull.[3] Either version could have been either Cotman's exhibit at the RA 1805 (509) *Croyland Abbey, Lincolnshire,* or the watercolour purchased by the Marquis of Stafford to hang in his sitting room at Trentham Park which Cotman visited in 1806.[4] In addition there are two small drawings of this same view, probably of a later date.[5]

The fifth drawing,[6] a distant view also from the south-west, was probably the 1807 Norwich Society exhibit.

[1]See also No. 171. [2]Barker collection. [3]Rienaecker pl. 26 fig. 48. [4]Pidgley p. 49 n.165. [5](a) with Stanhope Shelton 1975; (b) Tate Gallery 3667. [6]BM 2859-5-28-118.

21 Study of Trees, *c.*1804-5

Pencil and grey wash on cream, wove paper; 29.4 × 21 ($11\frac{9}{16}$ × $8\frac{1}{4}$). INSCR: *Recto,* part of circular stamp u.r., see No. 6. PROV: See No. 6. (95.L1967.9). REF: Rajnai & Allthorpe No. 42.

This is the only analytical tree study of this period in the Norwich collection. It relates to the fine series[1] of tree studies referred to in No. 4.

Throughout his career Cotman was to make use of slender tree forms, most notably in the oils of the 1820s such as *Silver Birches* (No. 161). His assured reference to such forms was based upon the delicate studies of this early series.

[1]46 such studies are in the BM, one of which also has an application of grey wash, BM 1902-5-14-298.

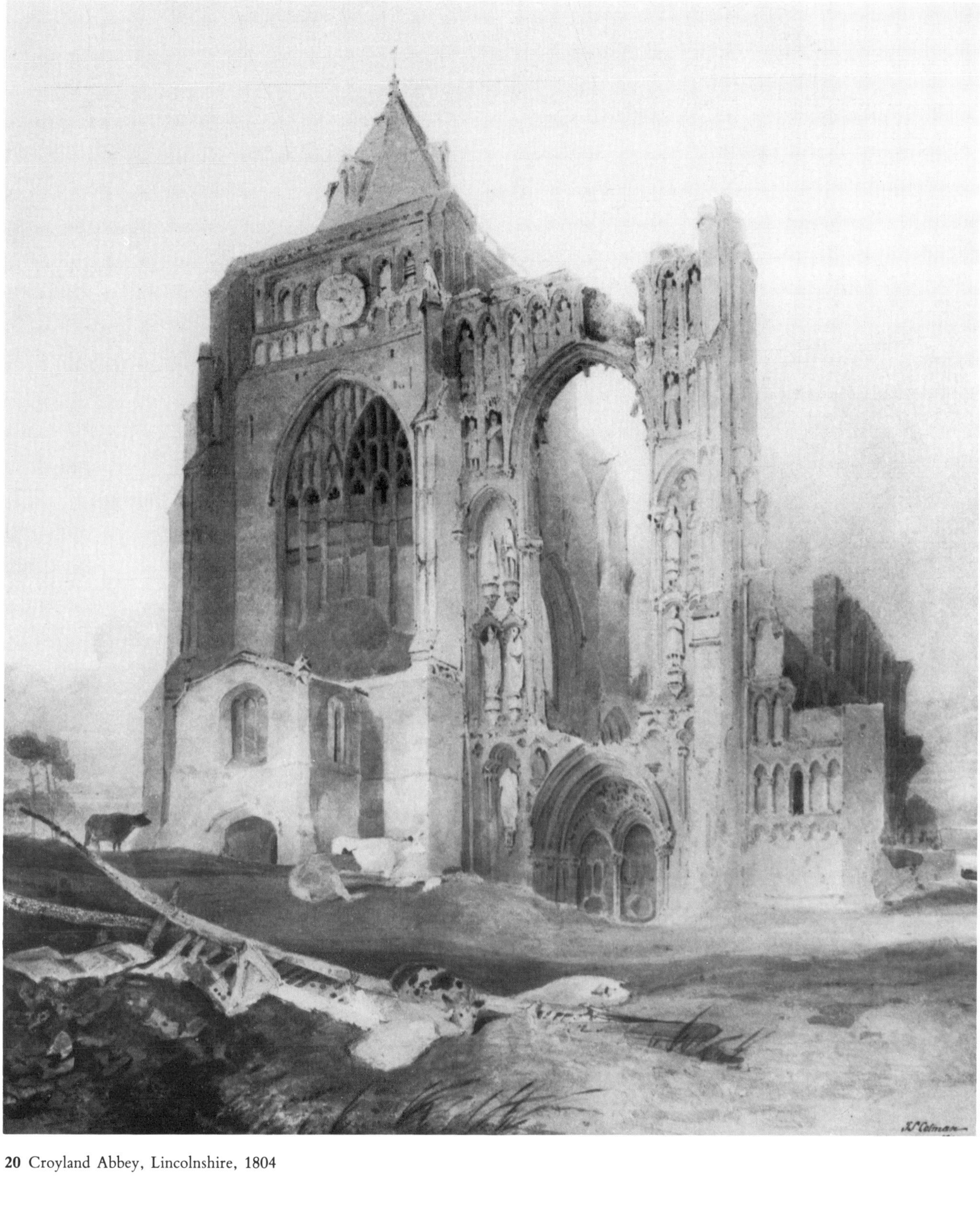

20 Croyland Abbey, Lincolnshire, 1804

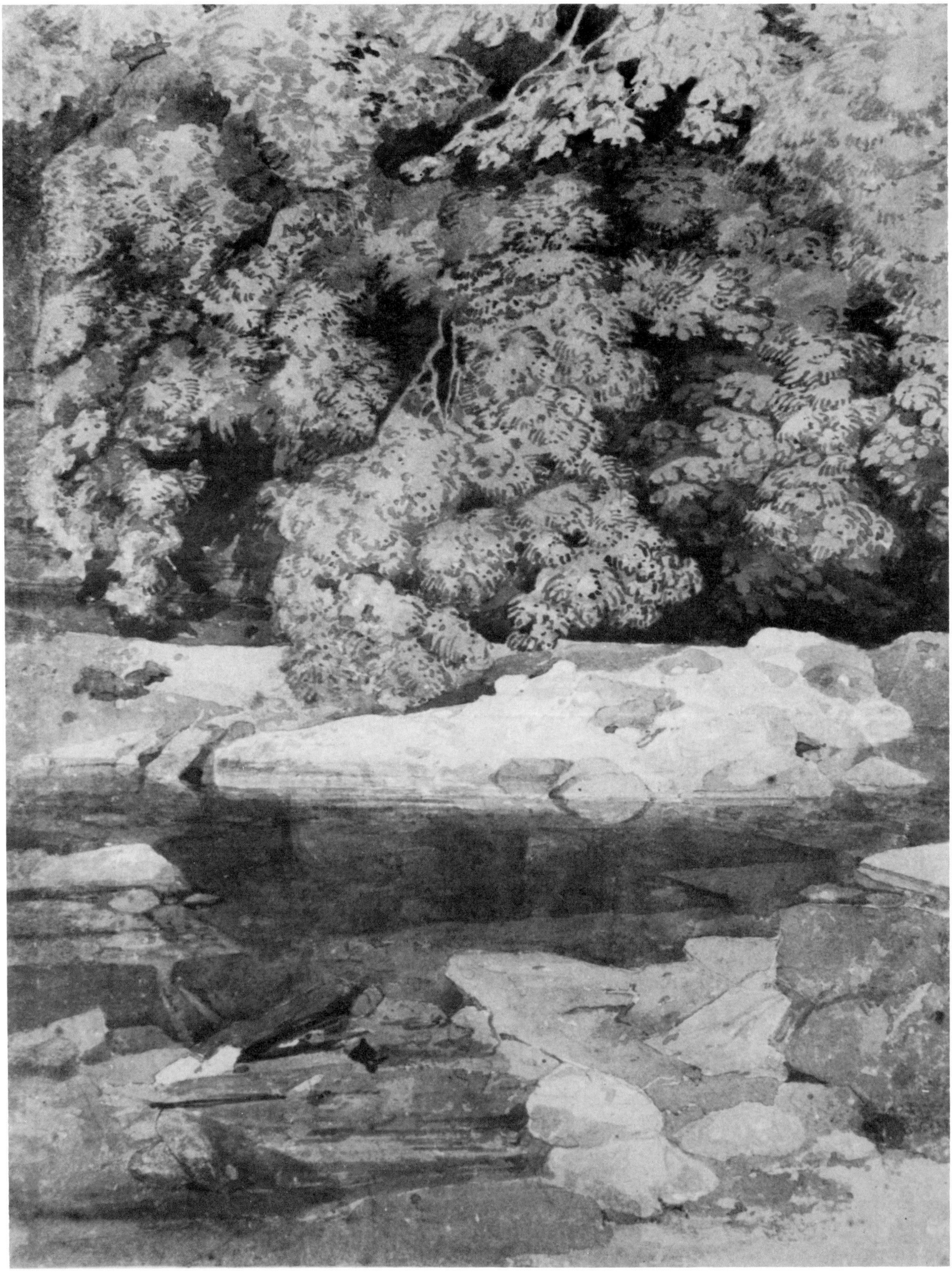

24 Pool *c.*1805-6

4
The Greta
1805

In the spring of 1805 Mrs. Cholmeley was in London, where she visited her brother, Sir Henry Englefield, and took the opportunity to invite Cotman to dine and stay for a weekend of opera and theatre from 8 to 10 March. A letter written by Mrs. Cholmeley to her son the following Tuesday reveals that Cotman was somewhat dispirited over that weekend, having heard nothing further of a projected 'Grecian plan' under the aegis of Lord Aberdeen. He had again dined with Mrs. Cholmeley and her brother on the previous Monday evening, before 'they went together to Fuseli'. By this time Cotman was living at 20 Woodstock Street, the address recorded in the catalogue for the Royal Academy show of that spring, in which he showed four works derived from sketches of the previous summer. [1]

The first surviving dated sketch of this year is a study of trees at Harrow, inscribed and dated 1 July 1805. [2] This, together with *A Study of Trees,* No. 325 at the Royal Academy exhibition, is a first indication of one of Cotman's major preoccupations for this most important year of his personal and creative life. The entry for 13 July in the Brandsby commonplace book records that Cotman arrived there at three in the morning. On 15 July he and Mrs. Cholmeley visited Gilling Castle. A drawing entitled *At Brandsby* is inscribed with the date of 16 July. [3] The watercolour washes of this drawing could arguably have been applied in the open air. If this is so, the composition was to have been completed in studio conditions. In the event, the drawing remains unfinished, but stands as the first true example of Cotman's rapidly developing powers this summer.

The following day Cotman went on a four-day excursion to the area around Whitwell-on-the-Hill. Before leaving, he had discussed with Francis Cholmeley the possibility of visiting Rokeby Hall, the country seat of John Bacon Sawrey Morritt, a good friend of the Cholmeley family. On 22 July Morritt wrote to Francis: 'Your letter and proposed visit gives both Mrs. Morritt and myself the greatest pleasure. We shall also be very happy to see Mr. Cotman, and to shew him a little of the banks of the Tees'. After a three-day visit by Cotman to Helmsley, on the last day of which (27 July) Francis met up with him, they both set off for Rokeby, some fifty miles to the north-west, on Tuesday, 30 July. Two days later, much to Mrs. Cholmeley's concern 'the girls produced Cotty's most important frame and Portfolio' [4] which they had discovered only after the two young men had left. Although she packed it up and sent it off immediately, it does not appear to have arrived until 5 August at the earliest.

According to Sydney Kitson the journey from Brandsby took two days, including an overnight stop at Leeming Bar, the two friends arriving at Rokeby on the evening of Wednesday, 31 July. [5] Rokeby Hall had been built in the Palladio-Burlington style during the late 1720s by the previous owner, Sir Thomas Robinson. He was also mainly responsible for the creation of the park, with which Cotman immediately became enamoured. John Morritt, a traveller and classical scholar, was described by his friend, Sir Walter Scott, whom he first met three years later, as 'a man unequalled in the mixture of sound good sense, high literary cultivation and the kindest and sweetest temper that ever graced a human bosom'. [5] He is perhaps best known today as the purchaser, in 1814, of the famous Rokeby Venus by Velasquez.

Cotman was to remain at Rokeby Park for some three weeks, moving out of the Hall shortly after Francis Cholmeley took his leave to stay with Mr. Charlton at Hesleyside. [6] During this time Cotman relished the beauty of the place which was also to inspire Sir Walter Scott to write the poem *Rokeby,* published in 1813, dedicated to Morritt 'in token of sincere friendship' (see entry for No. 28). The park is situated about half a mile from the village of Rokeby and was described in 1823 as 'an angular area, of the richest soil and shaded by luxuriant woods, bounded by the Tees and the Greta for the space of about a mile upwards from their confluence.' [7]

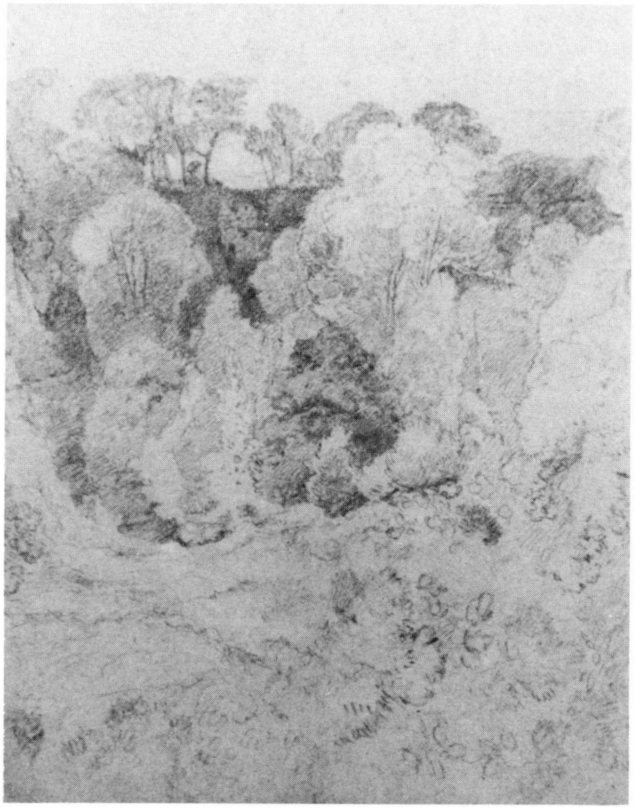

29 'Devils Elbow,' Rokeby Park, *c.*1805-7

The day Francis left, Cotman accompanied him just beyond Raby Castle, about six miles to the north east of Rokeby, and returned via 'Winston Bridge which I think is very fine'. [6] As the Morritts themselves were due to leave he moved out of Rokeby Hall shortly afterwards, to stay at the Inn at Greta Bridge, where he spent the remainder of the month. On 29 August Cotman wrote a long letter to Francis in which he expressed his sadness at having left the hall: 'To be cut off from such a party and to remain on the spot in front of the park gates and when I pass the house I really am quite wretch[e]d. But now I do not pass it. I always avoid it systemmatically . . . They were both very kind to me. I took my pa[r]ting breakfast with them. Mrs. Motts came up and shook me by the hand and wish[e]d me much good weather, goo[d] success and all good things, which I also return[e]d in my first and best manner.' [8]

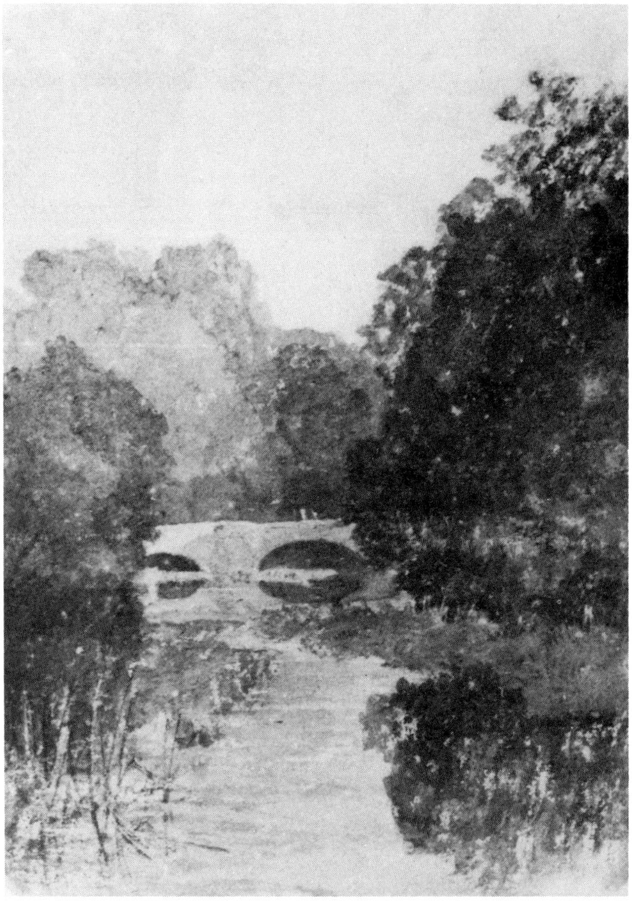

25 Wooded River and Bridge, *c.*1805-6

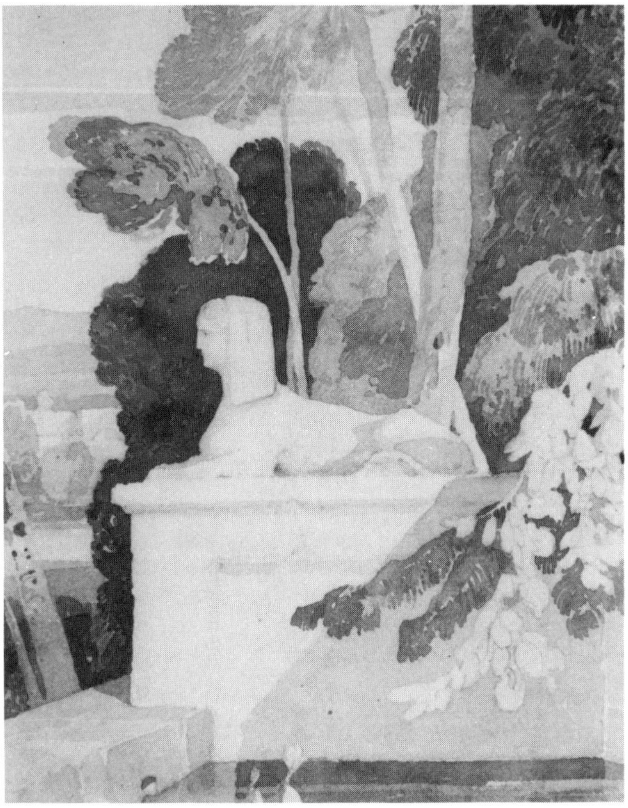

31 Sphinx, *c.*1806-7

Nevertheless, whilst in the area he could not help but be bewitched by it: 'All my studies have been in the wood above the bridge . . . I think it grows upon me in my regard every day, it realy is a delicious spot.' He could not recall being more happily employed than that week, 'industriously employed upon a subject that call[s] forth all my powers.'

Cotman's month in this area resulted in 'one of the finest series of watercolours in the history of European watercolour painting',[9] of which *Devil's Elbow, Rokeby Park* is perhaps the most outstanding and original (No. 30). At least seventeen watercolours survive, including three which can be identified as exhibited works. The *Distant View of Greta Bridge* exhibited at the Royal Academy, 1806 (494) is probably the watercolour now in the Tate Gallery,[10] while *Barnard Castle from Towler Hill,* exhibited at the Royal Academy in the same year (540) could well be the watercolour now at Leeds.[11] *Study of a Rock, Greta River* shown at the Norwich Society Exhibition of 1808 (104) is almost certainly that known as *The Scotsman's Stone* in the British Museum,[12] which shows the great stone that lies at the junction of the Tees and the Greta, near a spot where Cotman would bathe every day.[8] He also exhibited three other Greta subjects, but these are not readily identifiable with exisiting watercolours.[13]

Works such as *Devil's Elbow, Rokeby Park* (No. 30) bear all the finesse of direct observation recollected in the tranquillity of the studio. The subtlety of that experience was poetic in its implications, just as it was for Sir Walter Scott on his subsequent visits to Rokeby:

> The cliffs that rear their haughty head
> High o'er the river's darksome bed
> Were now all naked, wild and grey,
> Now waving all with greenwood spray;
> Here trees to every crevice clung,
> and o'er the dell their branches hung;
> And there, all splinter'd and uneven,
> The shiver'd rocks ascend to heaven
> Oft too, the ivy swath'd their breast
> And wreathed its garland round their crest
> Or from the spires bade loosely flare
> Its tendrils in the middle air . . .[14]

Cotman had planned to remain at the inn by Greta Bridge for a further fortnight, but was persuaded by letters from Mrs. Cholmeley to move on to join them at Durham (see entry for No. 52), where he arrived on Wednesday, 4 September. In the event he just missed the Cholmeleys arriving there 'but a few hours after they left it and within a mile of meeting them'.[15] It seems that in response to the special pleading of Mrs. Cholmeley he also visited Castle Eden Dean at this time. She had begun her summer vacation with a visit to Castle Eden Dean which had far surpassed her expectations. The spot moved her to write to her son on 7 August, describing in glowing terms the scenery of rocks, trees and caverns. The road itself was 'often overhung by embowering trees that cross it in wildest fantastic shapes, and reminded me of the low garden walk at Rokeby by the side of the Greta'. She asked that the letter be given 'to Cotty, who will probably value it more than yourself'. Cotman evidently visited Castle Eden Dean some miles to the south east of Durham, exhibiting the subject at the Royal Academy in 1806 (361).[16] The commonplace book records his return to Brandsby during the night of 14 September.

Cotman was to stay at Brandsby for another two months, making one last major visit, this time to Castle Howard. His

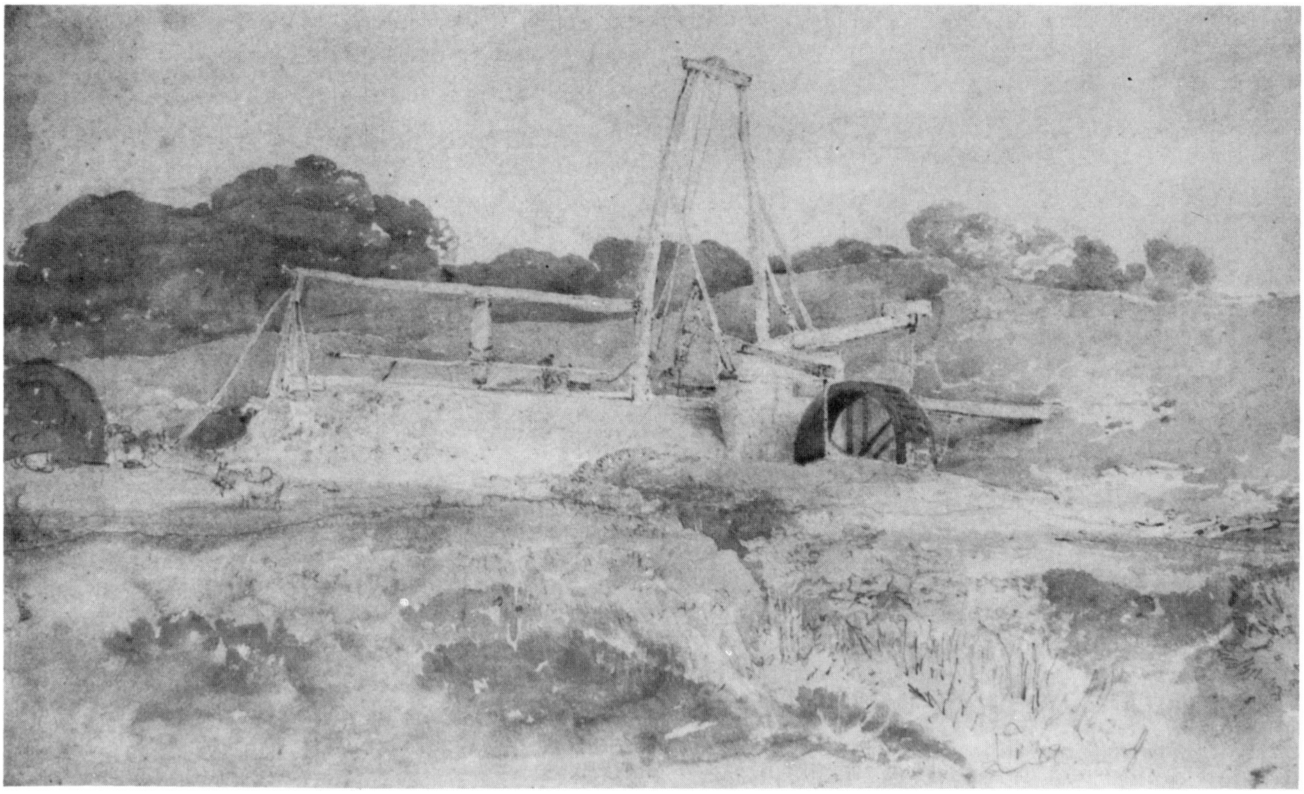

22 Landscape with water driven Tilt Hammer *c.*1805-6

first visit to Castle Howard, in July 1803, was brief, but in 1805 his stay was longer: he left Brandsby on the 4 October and returned on the 11 October. His invitation was presumably to act as drawing master to his hosts, Frederick, the fifth Earl of Carlisle, and Lady Carlisle, the sister of the Marquess of Stafford, of Trentham Hall (see entry for No. 39). Built by Vanburgh and Hawksmoor some eight miles east of Brandsby, Castle Howard prompted Horace Walpole to remark 'I have seen gigantic palaces before but never a sublime one'.[17] Cotman must have spent the best part of a week sketching in the parkland about the Hall, parts of which were ornamented with temples, obelisks and fountains. This was his last visit apart from a short trip with Harriet Cholmeley the day after his return. The Arcadian memory of this great country house and park is perpetuated in a small group of drawings of which No. 31 is a fine example.

After his return from Castle Howard, the Brandsby commonplace book records only two more visits by Cotman. On 1 November he accompanied Francis and another guest, Mr. Ann, to Duncombe Park, while he went for a last trip with Mr. Cholmeley to Gilling Castle on 14 November. On the 19 November Mr. and Mrs. Cholmeley accompanied Cotman to York, where they saw him off on the coach home, before returning the next day. Although Cotman had planned to return to Yorkshire the next summer,[8] events were to overtake him and it was to Norwich he returned the following autumn. He was never to meet Mr. and Mrs. Cholmeley again: Mr. Cholmeley died early in 1808 and Cotman was saddened by Mrs. Cholmeley's request for a portrait drawing by which to remember her late husband. She herself died on 3 October 1810. In his letter informing Cotman Francis Cholmeley wrote; 'Her friendship for you extended beyond the grave, and she left you a bequest of one hundred pounds',[18] to which Cotman responded: 'in her I have lost my kindest and most esteemed friend, one whom it has ever been my pride to acknowledge with the liveliest affection and gratitude . . .'[19]

Since the spring of 1805 Cotman had once again moved to a new London address, this time 71 Charlotte Street, Portland Place. It was from here that he wrote to Dawson Turner on 30 November after his return from Yorkshire.[20] It appears from this letter that Mrs. Turner had, on first meeting, borrowed some of Cotman's sketches, presumably to copy. In addition to requesting their return, he remarks that during the summer his 'chief study has been colouring from Nature many of which are close copies of that fickle Dame, consequently valuable on that account'. This has often been interpreted all too literally as confirming that Cotman's surviving watercolours are the product of a direct interpretation of Nature, painted in the open air. The classical repose and originality of design of works such as *Devil's Elbow, Rokeby Park* (No. 30) and *On the River Greta* (No. 28) belie such interpretation. A number of these works are painted on sizeable sheets of thin and relatively fragile paper, executed with washes of exquisite control. The materials and techniques of the studio combine to recreate his earlier direct response to the forms of Nature.[21]

Notes

[1] RA 1805 (325;448;509;626). [2] Whitworth Art Gallery, Manchester, D.3.1960. [3] Ashmolean Museum, Oxford. [4] Mrs. Cholmeley to Francis, 2 Aug. 1805. [5] Kitson 1937 p. 80. [6] JSC to Francis Cholmeley, 20 Aug. 1805. [7] Baines, *History of the County of York,* vol. 2 1823 p. 512. [8] JSC to Francis Cholmeley, 29 Aug. 1805. [9] Rajnai & Allthorpe 1979 p. 59. [10] Tate 3633, Kitson 1937 pl. 33. [11] Leeds 29.10/38, Kitson 1937 pl. 32. [12] BM 1902.5.14.12; Kitson 1937 p. 83. [13] RA 1806 (524); Norwich Society 1808 (143) & 1824 (78). [14] *Rokeby,* Canto 2 (viii) 1813. [15] JSC to Francis Cholmeley, 6 Sept. 1805. [16] Probably National Gallery of Scotland, D(NG)1025. A study is BM 1902.5.14.43. [17] Pevsner, *Yorkshire: The North Riding* p. 112. [18] BM [19] JSC to Francis Cholmeley, 29 Oct. 1810. [20] Reproduced in facsimile, *Norwich Art Circle Catalogue,* Ninth Exhibition, July 1888 p.3. [21] See Rajnai & Allthorpe 1979 pp. 18-20.

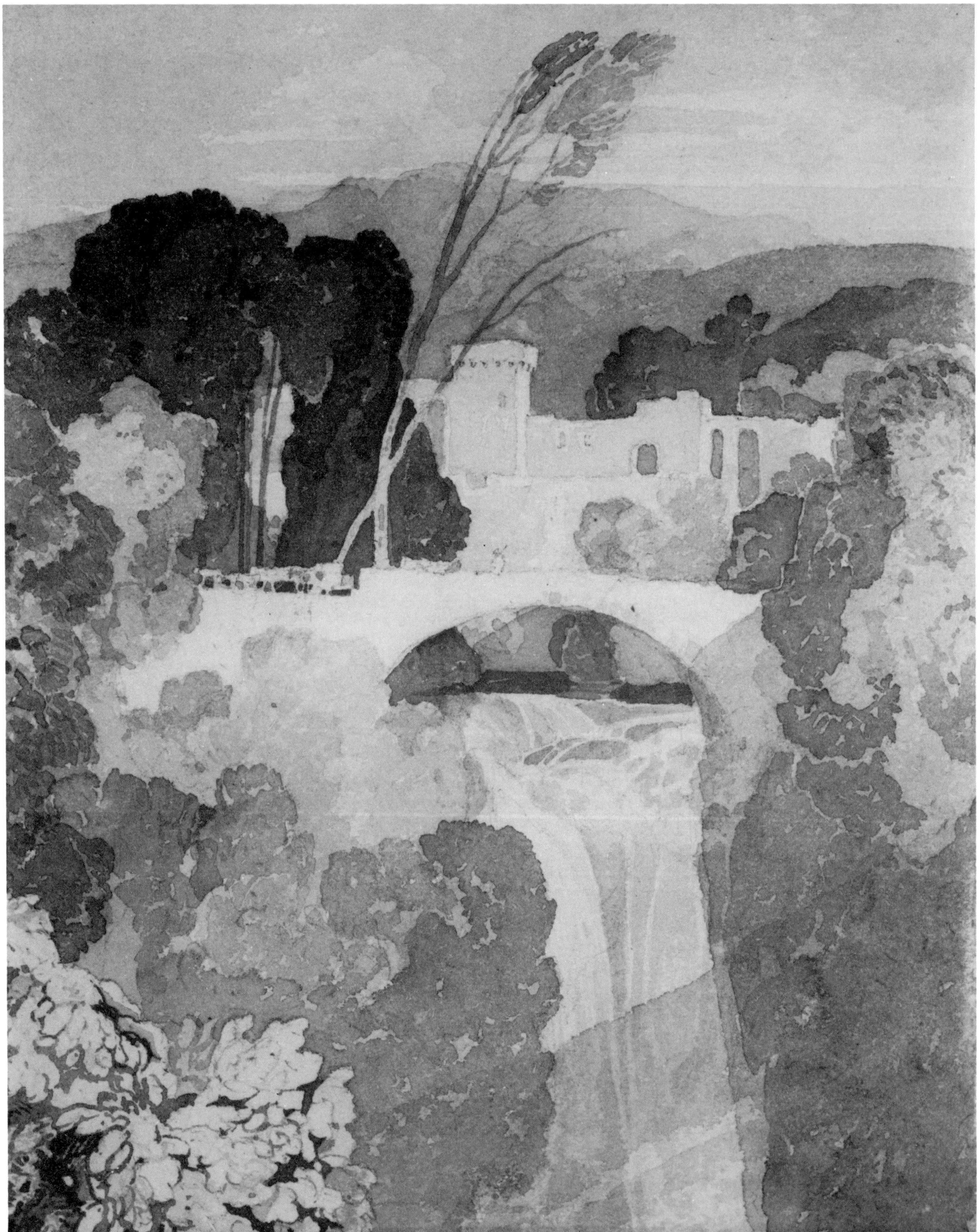

32 The Waterfall, *c.*1806-7

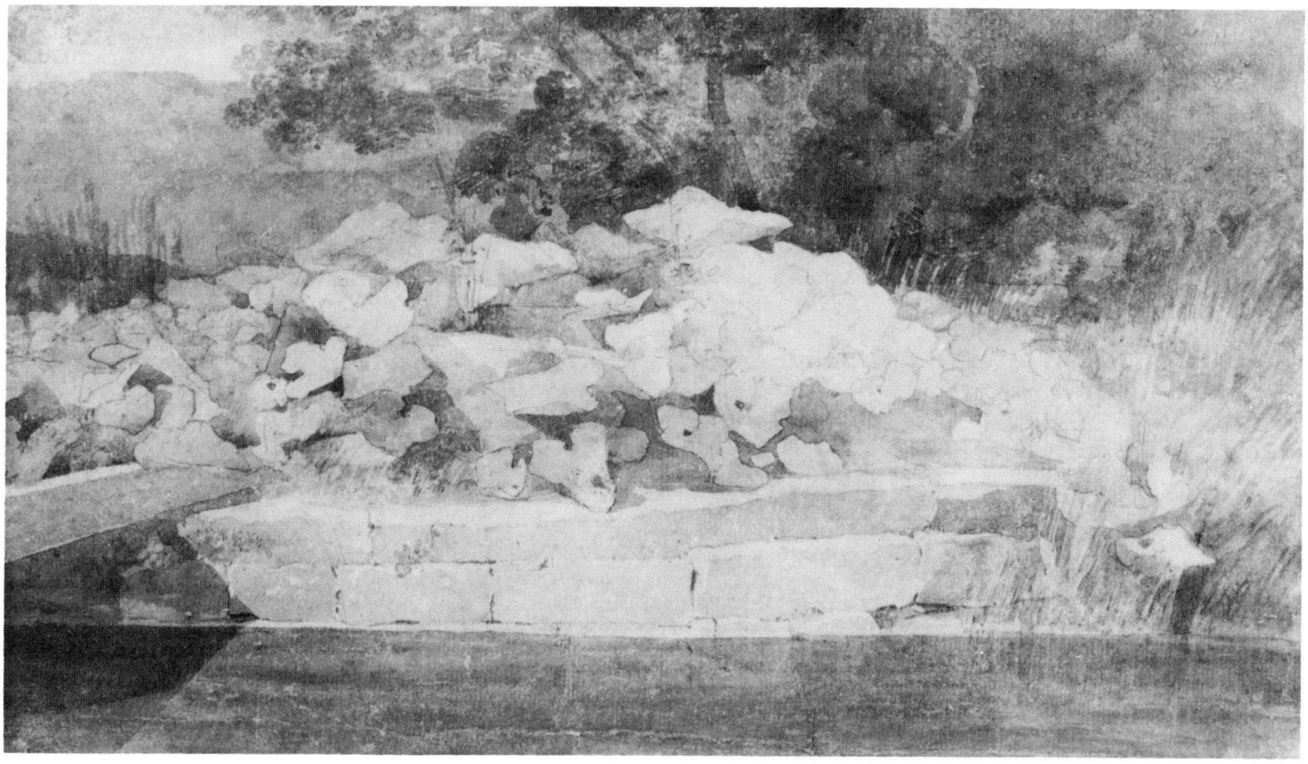

23 Dock Leaves by a Stream *c.*1805-6

22 Landscape with water driven Tilt Hammer, *c.*1805-6
called *Duncombe Park*
illustrated on p. 35

Pencil and watercolour on white, laid paper with a horizontal tear right across, repaired; 26.8 × 43.8 ($10\frac{9}{16}$ × $17\frac{1}{4}$). PROV: Mrs. Arthur Stark; bt. from her by James Reeve by 1888; bt. from him ?after 1903 by H. S. Theobald; bt. from him by R. J. Colman, Feb. 1910; R. J. Colman Bequest 1946. (131.235.951). EXH: Norwich, Art Circle 1888 (44) as *Duncombe Park, Yorkshire,* lent by James Reeve; ?Paris 1906 (14) as *Le Parc de Duncombe;* Tate 1922 (59) as *Duncombe Park;* Norwich 1930-31; Norwich 1945. REF: Rajnai & Allthorpe No. 44.

This watercolour reflects Cotman's fascination with an early industrial scene, of the kind that he explored in the dramatic *Bedlam Furnace* of *c.*1802-3 in the Bacon collection.[1] A small pencil study of a mining structure[2] and a fine watercolour sketch, *c.*1805, of the head of a coal shaft[3] similarly attest to his interest in early industrialisation. His 1808 Norwich Society exhibit (107) *Coal Shaft; coloured Sketch* also reflects this interest.

The quality of the pencil work and the controlled use of wash makes this one of the 'finest of Cotman's watercolours of this date. The curious flat and irregular leaf forms, lower centre right, are found, in closer focus, in drawings such as [No. 23] and in the superb watercolours called *Drop Gate, Duncombe Park* and *On the Greta, Yorkshire* both in the BM'.[4] (Rajnai & Allthorpe).

[1] Watercolour, Kitson 1937 pl. 5 [2] Rajnai & Allthorpe No. 6 [3] Leeds 500/23. [4] BM 1902-5-14-14 and BM 1902-5-14-10.

23 Dock Leaves by a Stream, *c.*1805-6
called *At Kirkham*

Pencil and watercolour on white, laid paper; 25.7 × 43.6 ($10\frac{1}{8}$ × $17\frac{1}{8}$). PROV: Cotman sale, Spelman, Norwich, 16 May 1861, bt. James Reeve; bt. from him ?after 1903 by H. S. Theobald; bt. from him by R. J. Colman, Feb. 1910; R. J. Colman Bequest 1946. (130.235.951). EXH: Norwich, Art Circle 1888 (12) and Norwich 1903 (4) as *At Kirkham, Yorkshire* lent by James Reeve; Tate 1922 (89) as *At Kirkham.* REF: ?Kitson 1937 p. 83; Rajnai & Allthorpe No. 45.

The traditional title of this watercolour is *At Kirkham,* a place Cotman visited and sketched in the summers of both 1803 and 1805. The drawing is not inscribed but it is stylistically related to the superlative watercolours of the Greta period, such as *The Scotsman's Stone, On the Greta* and the *Drop-Gate, Duncombe Park,* all of which are in the British Museum.[1]

Although many of the Greta drawings have been considered by Kitson and others as outdoor works, Rajnai and Allthorpe have convincingly argued that No. 23 is one of a number which must be studio work, presumably based upon on-the-spot pencil studies.[2]

[1] BM 1902-5-14-12; BM 1902-5-14-10; BM 1902-5-14-14. [2] One such study is Rajnai & Allthorpe No. 33.

24 Pool, *c.*1805-6
illustrated on p. 32

Pencil and watercolour with some blue bodycolour on buff, laid paper; 30.6 × 22.6 ($12\frac{1}{16}$ × $8\frac{7}{8}$). PROV: ?Cotman sale, Spelman, Norwich, 16 May 1861, bt. James Reeve; bt. from him by H. S. Theobald; bt. from him by R. J. Colman, Feb. 1910; R. J. Colman Bequest 1946. (270.235.951). EXH: Tate 1922 (27) as *Near Helmsley, Yorkshire;* Tokyo 1929 as *Stream in Yorkshire* repro. pl. XXXVI. REF: Rajnai & Allthorpe No. 46.

This watercolour, originally entitled *Near Helmsley, Yorkshire,* belongs with No. 23 to the close-up views of banks and streams of the Greta series. Rajnai and Allthorpe point out that the touches of blue bodycolour in the lower left corner are uncharacteristic of Cotman's work at this period and may have been added by a later hand.

25 Wooded River and Bridge, *c.*1805-6
called *Conway, North Wales,*
illustrated on p. 34

Black chalk and grey wash, with some scraping out, on bluish grey, wove paper with corners cut; 23.5 × 16.5 ($9\frac{1}{4}$ × $6\frac{1}{2}$). INSCR: *Recto,* previously numbered in pencil l.c. edge ?in the artist's hand *312,* before restoration. PROV: ?Cotman sale, Spelman, Norwich, 16 May 1861; Mr. Christie, Norwich; bt. from him by James Reeve 1862; bt. from him by H. S. Theobald ?after 1903; bt. from him by R. J. Colman, Feb. 1910; R. J. Colman Bequest 1946. (132.235.951). EXH: Norwich, Art Circle 1888 (64) and BFAC 1888 (108) as *North Wales;*

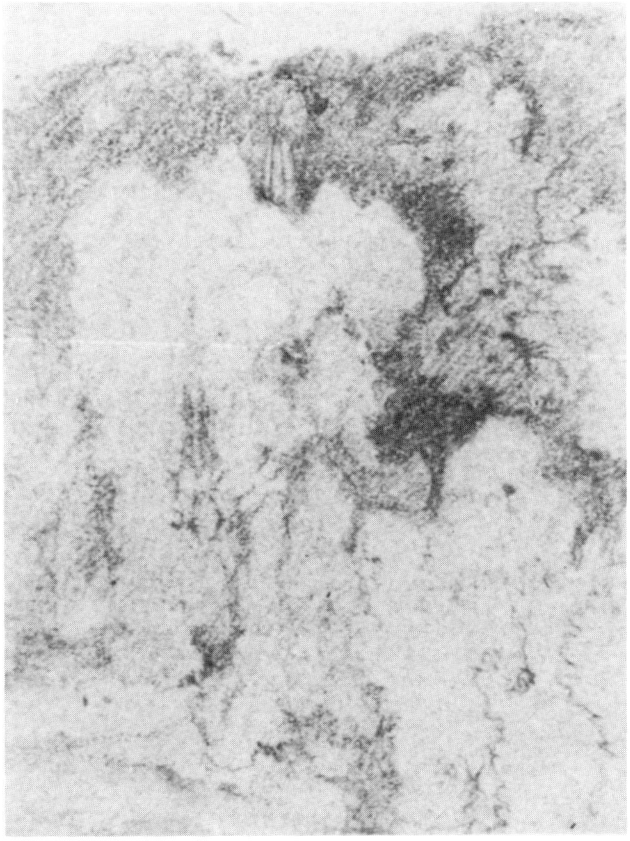

26 On the River Greta, Yorkshire, *c.*1805-7

Norwich 1903 (62) as *North Wales Conway* lent by James Reeve; Manchester, 1912 (354) as *North Wales Conway;* Norwich 1930-1931. REF: Rajnai & Allthorpe, No. 47.

Rajnai and Allthorpe have convincingly argued that this is probably one of the sketches resulting from Cotman's Yorkshire trip of 1805. It compares with other preliminary studies in pencil and grey wash such as *Durham* and *On the Greta* in the Tate Gallery[1] and *Castle Eden Dean* in the British Museum.[2] A similar woodland and bridge study is *New Bridge Durham.*[3]

[1]Tate 3634, 3635. [2]BM 1902-5-14-43. [3]Fitzwilliam, Cambridge, Pd 1-1949 (the watercolour is in the Bacon collection).

26 On the River Greta, Yorkshire, *c.*1805-7

called *Devil's Elbow*

Pencil on bluish grey, wove paper; 15.4 × 11.6 ($6\frac{1}{16} \times 4\frac{9}{16}$). PROV: See No. 27. (337.235.951). REF: Rajnai & Allthorpe No. 52.

This is a study for the watercolour *On the River Greta,* No. 28, showing a detail of the upper centre foliage mass. The drawing represents a first exploration of the shapes on the wall of the gorge through tone, rather than line.

27 On the River Greta, Yorkshire, *c.*1805-7

called *Devil's Elbow*

Pencil with some white chalk on bluish grey, wove paper; 24.8 × 15.4 ($9\frac{13}{16} \times 6\frac{1}{16}$). PROV: Spelman sale, Norwich, 1879, bt. James Reeve; bt. from him by H. S. Theobald; bt. from him by R. J. Colman, Feb. 1910; R. J. Colman Bequest 1946. (336.235.951). REF: Rajnai & Allthorpe No. 53.

This is a pencil study for the composition of *On the River Greta,* No. 28. 'It presents a fully worked out scheme for the arrangement and rendering of the foliage formations but still has a generalised foreground only. In the watercolour this was replaced by a specific one and more sky was let in above the wall of the gorge' (Rajnai & Allthorpe).

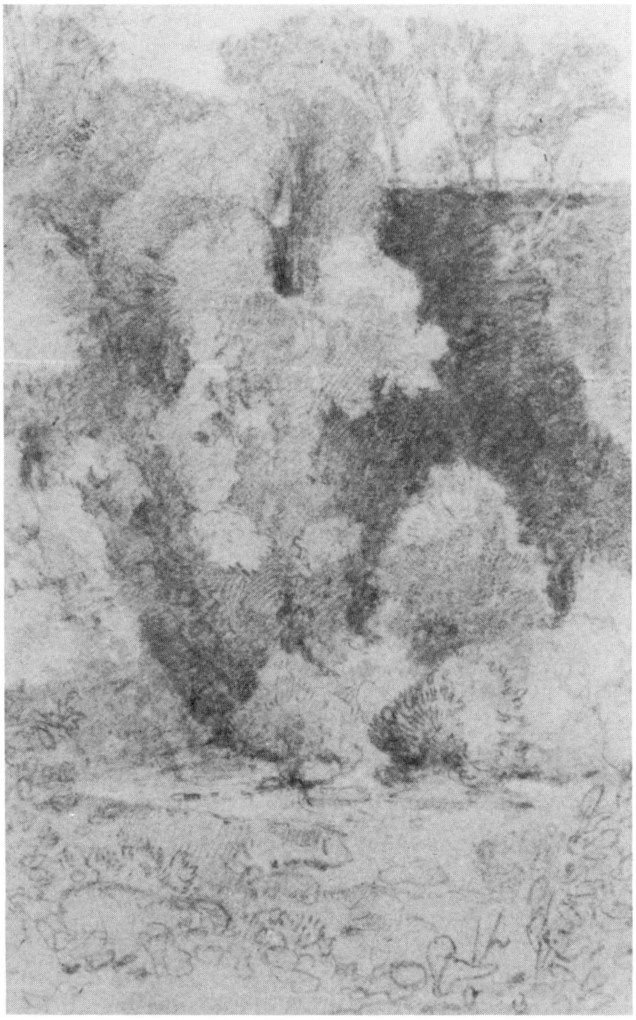

27 On the River Greta, Yorkshire, *c.*1805-7

28 On the River Greta, Yorkshire, *c.*1806-7

illustrated in colour on p. 26

Pencil and watercolour, with birds scraped out, on buff, laid paper; 32.6 × 22.9 ($12\frac{13}{16} \times 9$). INSCR: *Recto,* signed in brown watercolour l.r. *J. S. Cotman—; verso,* backing paper previously numbered, inscribed and signed in brown ink u.c. *No. 68/On the River Greta/Yorkshire/ J. Cotman;* PROV: ?The Palser Gallery; Col. H. Littlewood; his bequest with five other watercolours by or attributed to Cotman, 1961. (84.961). EXH: Aldeburgh, Third Festival 1950 (22); RA 1961-62 (395); China & Berlin 1963-64 (65) repro. pl. 4; Bedford & Cambridge 1966 (9); Rouen 1967 (12); Kenwood 1969 (12); King's Lynn 1970 (4); Japan 1970 (62) repro.; Harlow 1976 (5); The Hague 1977 (8); Ipswich 1978 (3); Koblenz 1980 (8) repro.; Nottingham 1981 (47); China 1982 repro. pl. 32. REF: Rajnai & Allthorpe No. 54.

This fine watercolour, based on the drawings Nos. 26 and 27, is the scene in the left half of *Devil's Elbow, Rokeby Park,* No. 30.

The grandeur of Rokeby was later to inspire Sir Walter Scott who visited the park in 1809 and 1812 and dedicated his long poem *Rokeby* (1813) to his host, Mr. Morritt. Scott speaks of 'the romantic glen, or rather ravine, through which the Greta finds a passage between Rokeby and Mortham; the former situated upon the left bank of Greta, the latter on the right bank, about half a mile nearer to its junction with the Tees . . . [further along] the whole scenery . . . is so much adapted to the ideas of superstition, that it has acquired the name of Blockula, from the place where the Swedish witches were supposed to hold their Sabbath. The dell, however, has superstitions of its own growth, for it is supposed to be haunted by a female spectre, called the Dobie of Mortham'[1]

Although affinities with Scott's 'glen' can be perceived, the precise location of the Cotman scene is unknown. It is likely that the cliffs and bank between Mill Wood and Scotchman's Stone are the spot rather than anywhere within the park itself.[2]

[1]Sir Walter Scott, 'Introduction and Notes to Rokeby', 1830 edition, Note XV, *The Poetical Works of Sir Walter Scott*, ed. J. Logie Robertson, OUP, first published 1904 p. 388. [2]Rajnai & Allthorpe p. 60.

29 'Devil's Elbow, Rokeby Park', *c.*1805-7

illustrated on p. 33

Pencil with some white chalk on bluish grey, wove paper; 28.7 × 22.4 ($11\frac{1}{4}$ × $8\frac{13}{16}$). INSCR: *Verso,* inscription in pencil l.c.r. partly trimmed off and consequently illegible. PROV: James Reeve; bt. from him by H. S. Theobald; bt. from him by R. J. Colman, Feb. 1910; R. J. Colman Bequest 1946. (335.235.951). REF: Rajnai 1978 repro. in colour; Rajnai & Allthorpe No. 55.

This fine drawing is a preliminary compositional sketch for the watercolour, *Devil's Elbow, Rokeby Park,* No. 30. 'It gives the entire composition but before the peculiarities of foliage formation in the crowns of trees were exaggerated and a more elaborate foreground with repoussoir was added'. (Rajnai & Allthorpe).

30 'Devil's Elbow, Rokeby Park', *c.*1806-7

illustrated in colour on p. 27

Pencil and watercolour on buff, laid paper; 45.1 × 35.1 ($17\frac{3}{4}$ × $13\frac{13}{16}$). PROV: The Palser Gallery; Percy Moore Turner; bt. from him with *Mousehold Heath* (see No. 62) by R. J. Colman, 22 April 1926 £3,000; R. J. Colman Bequest 1946. (134.217.947). EXH: Brussels 1929 (39); RA 1934 (725, Commemorative Catalogue 808); Norwich 1945; Norwich, Arts Council 1947 (5). REF: Kitson 1937 pp. 85, 104, pl. 35; Rajnai & Allthorpe No. 56.

This is one of the finest of the inspired Greta drawings. Rajnai and Allthorpe claim that 'It is without doubt one of [Cotman's] greatest drawings and one of the most original contributions to European art of its time.'

Although the scene depicted is characteristic of the Greta in this region, as explained in No. 28, the precise location of Devil's Elbow is unknown. In addition to Nos. 26-29, a further sketch, in pencil and wash, is in the V & A.[1] Cotman also drew at least two other aspects of this wooded gorge as is shown by a pencil drawing in the BM[2] and another at Leeds.[3]

During the month of August 1805 he made other trips beyond Rokeby Park; south-west along the Greta to Brignall Banks and north-west to Barnard Castle.[4] These trips provided Cotman with material for at least seventeen watercolours, six of which he exhibited (see p. 34).

Although Kitson and others following him regard these works as outdoor studies towards fully worked exhibition pieces Rajnai and Allthorpe suggest that the uniform disappearance of all such exhibition work of Greta subjects points to the so-called sketches themselves being the 'missing' exhibits.

Other Greta watercolours, besides Nos. 23, 24 and 32 are in the National Gallery, Edinburgh,[5] Leeds,[6] the Oppé Collection,[7] the British Museum,[8] the Lewis Fry collection,[9] Yale,[10] the Bacon collection,[11] Bedford[12] and lastly the two outstanding views of Greta Bridge one in the British Museum and No. 60.[13]

[1]V&A D353-1888. [2]BM 1902-5-14-110. [3]Leeds 9.654.49. [4]Rajnai & Allthorpe No. 43. [5]Kitson 1937 p. 84. [6]Leeds (a) 16.2/55 and (b) 5.47/52; a pencil study for this composition is also at Leeds, 5.48.52. [7]Photo Witt. [8]BM 1902-5-14-10. [9]Kitson 1937 pp. 84,95, pl. 34. [10]Yale Center of British Art, New Haven, USA. [11]Kitson 1937 p. 83. [12]Cecil Higgins Art Gallery P593. [13]Kitson 1937 p. 83 also refers to a watercolour in which 'a man is creeping up the stream, snaring fish'.

31 Sphinx, *c.*1806-7

illustrated on p. 34

Pencil and grey wash on cream, wove paper; 20.4 × 15.9 (8 × $6\frac{1}{4}$). PROV: John Joseph Cotman; bt. from him by James Reeve 1864; bt. from him by H. S. Theobald; bt. from him by R. J. Colman, Feb. 1910; R. J. Colman Bequest 1946. (306.235.951). EXH: ?London, Paterson Gallery 1913 (40); Tate 1922 (171). REF: Kitson 1937 p. 88, pl. 40; Rajnai & Allthorpe No. 57.

No. 31 relates most closely to two other monochrome drawings, *The Waterfall,* No. 32 and *At Castle Howard, Yorkshire*[1] and it is conjectured by Rajnai and Allthorpe that both *Sphinx* and *At Castle Howard, Yorkshire* are inspired by classical sculptures in the pleasure grounds of Castle Howard, although there is no record of a sphinx actually present there.

Cotman had paid a short visit to Castle Howard in July 1803, but returned in 1805, apparently staying from 4-11 October (see p. 35).

Rajnai and Allthorpe place *Sphinx* and its companions slightly later than the group represented here by the delicately classical *Boy Fishing* (see No. 8). There is also a watercolour version[2] of *Sphinx,* of a similar date, which relates to another watercolour of this period, *Sarcophagus in a Park.*[3]

[1]V & A 9293; a preliminary drawing for this is BM 1902-5-14-323. [2]Kitson 1937 pp. 88, 89. [3]BM 1859-5-28-121.

32 The Waterfall, *c.*1806-7

illustrated on p. 36

Pencil and grey wash on cream, wove paper; 20.9 × 16.2 ($8\frac{1}{4}$ × $6\frac{3}{8}$). PROV: B. Samuel; bt. from him by J. King; bt. from him by James Reeve by 1888; bt. from him by H. S. Theobald after 1905; bt. from him by R. J. Colman, Feb. 1910; R. J. Colman Bequest 1946. (141.235.951). EXH: ? Norwich Society 1808 (221) as *Waterfall, composition;* Norwich, Art Circle 1888 (115) and BFAC 1888 (103) as *Composition* lent by James Reeve; Norwich 1903 (70) lent by James Reeve; ?Paris 1906 (17) as *Composition;* Manchester 1912 (353); Tate 1922 (183); Norwich 1945. REF: Kitson 1937 p. 119, pl. 54; Rajnai & Allthorpe No. 59.

The Waterfall is a monochrome of similar size, medium and date to No. 31. Three more versions of the composition exist: a small studio pencil drawing,[1] the oil No. 148, and a watercolour in a private collection.[2] Cotman exhibited a version of the subject with the Norwich Society in 1808 (221) as *Waterfall, Composition.* This may well have been the oil (see No. 148). Kitson argues that the composition of *The Waterfall* could have been influenced by Cotman's apparently lifelong preoccupation with the French artist Sebastian Bourdon.[3] He also suggests that the composition may be a fantastic elaboration of a remembered scene: 'It may be that it is a dream memory of the scene at the watersmeet of the Tees and Greta, looking up towards the Dairy Bridge at Rokeby, with the Mortham Tower behind; a view which, some years later, Turner drew to serve as a frontispiece for Sir Walter Scott's *Rokeby.*[4]

Although Kitson's speculations may be valid, the composition remains an outstanding example of Cotman's idiosyncratic vision.

[1]Rajnai & Allthorpe No. 58. [2]*Italian Landscape with Waterfall,* repro. *Country Life* 15 June 1967 supplement 51. [3]Cotman's interest in Bourdon is borne out by seven etchings by Bourdon, in Cotman's 1834 sale, lot 48, and by his later purchase of lot 488 *A volume containing 42 engravings by and from Sebastian Bourdon,* at Constable's sale in 1838. A week later, on 19 May 1838, he wrote triumphantly of this buy to his son John Joseph Cotman (BM). [4]Kitson 1937 p. 118.

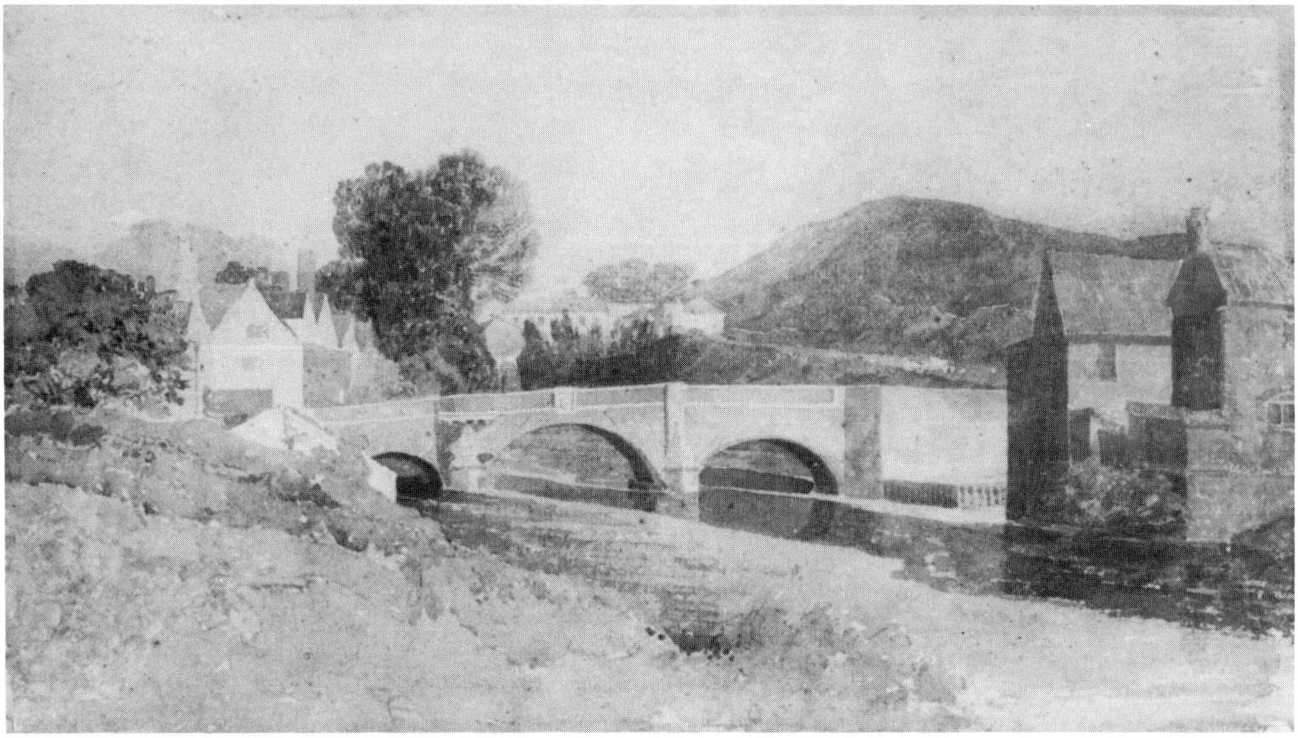

33 Bishopsgate Bridge, Norwich, *c.*1806-7

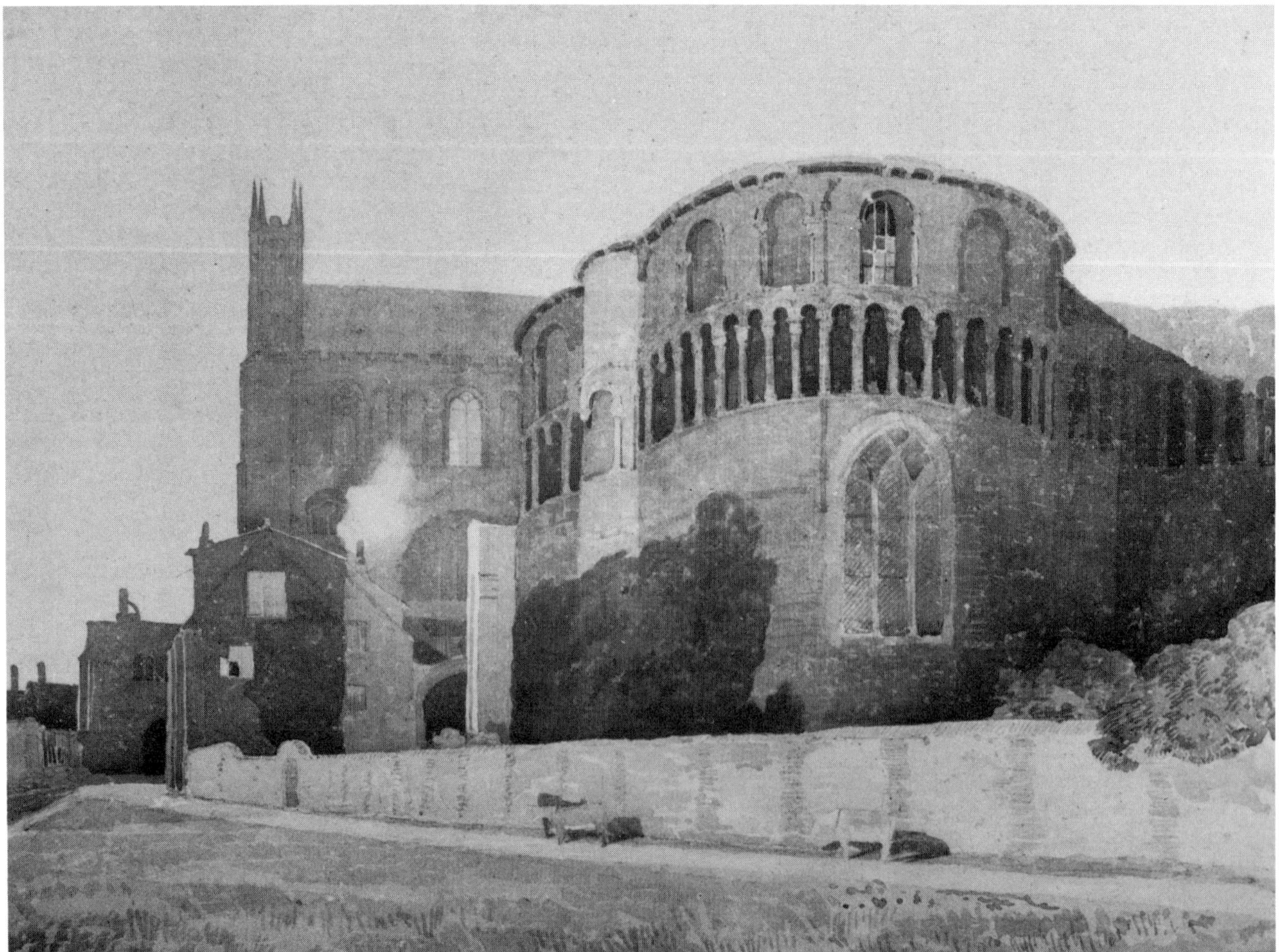

37 St. Luke's Chapel, Norwich Cathedral, East, 1808

5
At Norwich
1807-1810

Within a matter of days of writing to Dawson Turner to inform him of his intention to open a School of Drawing and Design in Wymer Street, Cotman had placed a lengthy advertisement with the *Norwich Mercury*. This appeared on 20 December 1806:

SCHOOL For Painting in Water Colours and for Designs. J. S. COTMAN RESPECTFULLY informs his Friends and the inhabitants of Norwich in general, that he has taken a HOUSE, in WYMER—STREET, near the Public Library, for the accomodation of those Ladies and Gentlemen who may favour him by becoming his pupils. That the Public may be enabled to form an accurate estime of his merit and of his claim to their patronage, he has been advised to open an EXHIBITION of his works, a Scheme almost too daring for an individual, did [he] not flatter himself that the labours of seven years might justify him in the attempt. The Exhibition, which opens on Monday, the 29th December, will consist of his coloured sketches, sketches in Light and Shade, and in Pencil, and a few Finished Drawings, which are to be on sale. Admittance by catalogue, one shilling.

The advertisement was repeated seven days later, with the additional information that the number of works would be 'upwards of Four Hundred Drawings'. The response was such that Cotman was emboldened, on 10 January, to append to his advertisement the information that he would 'commence his Instructions on Monday January the 19th, 1807. TERMS OF TEACHING. In the Academy by the quarter——£2.2s.0d. Four Private Lessons——£1.1s.0d.'

This was the beginning of an extremely busy and prolific period for Cotman. The method by which he chose to make his impression upon his home town was effectively as a drawing master and major exhibitor with the recently formed local artists' association, known as the Norwich Society. He worked hard and 'seems in better spirits about his undertaking' by the end of January.[1] However, his financial success whilst at Wymer Street was not considerable, a fact which Dawson Turner appears to have appreciated at an early stage. Cotman was to write to his patron of this period in his life in a manner which reveals the optimism of his time at Wymer Street: 'to speak further of myself; I am still the hard-working person you first found me in Wymer Street—and years after told me that you had appreciated me for it, and that it was the cause of your attention being directed to my advancement. But it was not hard work to me: it was my play.'[2] The sheer volume of work exhibited at the Norwich Society annual exhibition, 1807-1810 (149 works in total) and the sustained originality of those works ascribable to this period which survive today, attest to the prodigious creativity of Cotman during these years.

On 27 June 1807 a further advertisement appeared in the *Norwich Mercury* which demonstrates his continuing belief in the value of 'Drawings from Nature'. 'In addition to his other teaching, he has commenced giving Lessons from Nature, which comprehend the Pencil sketch, the Chiaro Oscura, and colouring,—specimens may be seen at his house in St. Andrew's, Broad Street'. During his first year back in Norwich he also executed a number of interior views of the Cathedral, including the Jesus Chapel and views of the ambulatory (see No. 37). Kitson has suggested that Dawson Turner could have influenced such a choice of subject matter, but this is purely hypothetical. Cotman's original treatment of his subjects at this time was far removed from the antiquarian interests of Dawson Turner. A series of views of Walsingham Abbey which may also be ascribed to the years 1807-8[3] similarly reveals Cotman's sustained interest in architectural subjects.

The Norwich Society of Artists had held the first of their annual exhibitions in the rooms of Sir Benjamin Wrenche's Court in 1805 during the August Assizes week. Cotman's first showing with the group in 1807 was of twenty works, a substantial presence which was relatively modest compared to his contributions for the next two years. The majority of subjects were architectural or portraiture (see Nos. 35, 36 and Section 11), with only one pure landscape scene, a *Distant View of Cader Idris.*[4] One of the exhibits, *A Coloured Sketch of the Market-place, Norwich, taken from Mr. Coopers',*[5] demonstrates Cotman's willingness to submit 'drawings from Nature' which do not show the degree of finish that might be expected of an exhibition piece. A more finished version, taken from a slightly more northerly viewpoint, was exhibited by Cotman two years later,[6] a composition subsequently lithographed by Henry Ninham.

Cotman continued to keep in touch with the Cholmeleys, but gradually it became apparent that he would not be able to respond again to invitations to return to Brandsby. On 22 April 1808 Cotman wrote to Francis Cholmeley: 'Your kind invitation I dare not think of. I shall only have the pleasure of seeing you in town, where I shall go about the end of the first week in May . . .'

The catalogue for the Norwich Society exhibition of 1808 describes Cotman for the first time as a portrait painter. It appears that he was attempting a further claim to the attention of the Norwich public by emphasizing this area of his talents. A significant number of his exhibits were also in oil (see Section 11), the result of serious experimentation with this more popular medium. This was the year in which Joseph Farington recorded that the passion for watercolours in London was subsiding: 'Haydon said, that a gentleman had laid a wager of 20 guineas that in *three years* there will be no Water colour Exhibition'.[7] Sound economic sense led Cotman to explore the medium of oil, as well as to advertise his talent as a portraitist. Nevertheless, although his talent was recognised, it did not bring financial security. It was at this period that Cotman applied to his friend and patron Sir Henry Englefield as security for the sum of £200 to assist his father. Although the money was forthcoming, Sir Henry wrote to Francis Cholmeley of his fears 'that [Cotman] must essentially want prudence as well as application or with his talent he could not have failed so totally. I am sure that he might have stood far above Varley if he had chosen to do so.'[8] Although such a comment was evidently only half-informed as to Cotman's standing in Norwich, it does reveal something of Cotman's metropolitan reputation.

Cotman also exhibited a number of Cromer-based subjects in 1808[9] (see No. 34), while a series of pencil sketches of small rowing boats survive of the period 1808-9 which also probably originate from visits to Cromer beach at this time.[10] The reason for such visits to this area was the young artist's court-

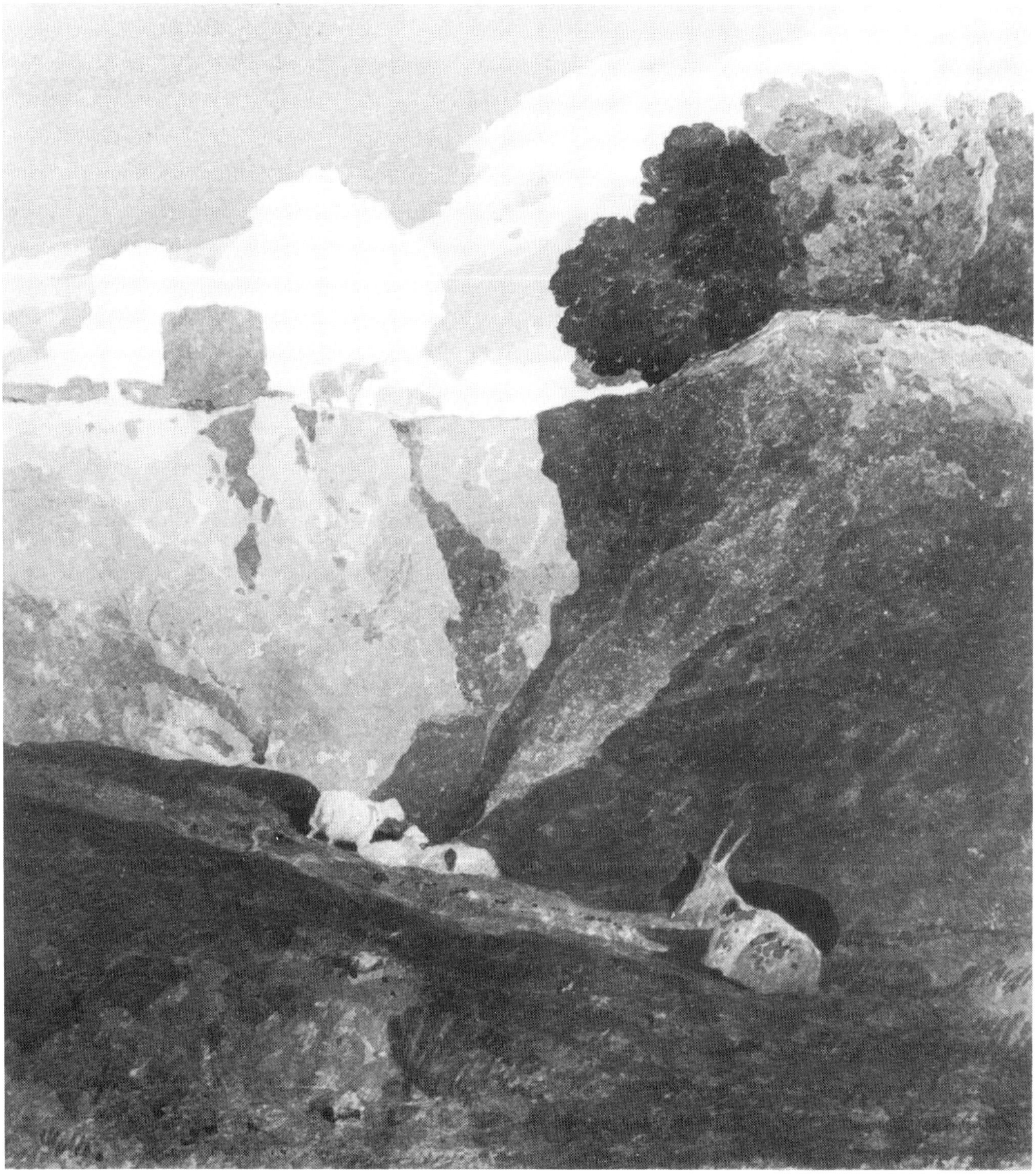

59 The Marl Pit, *c.*1809-10

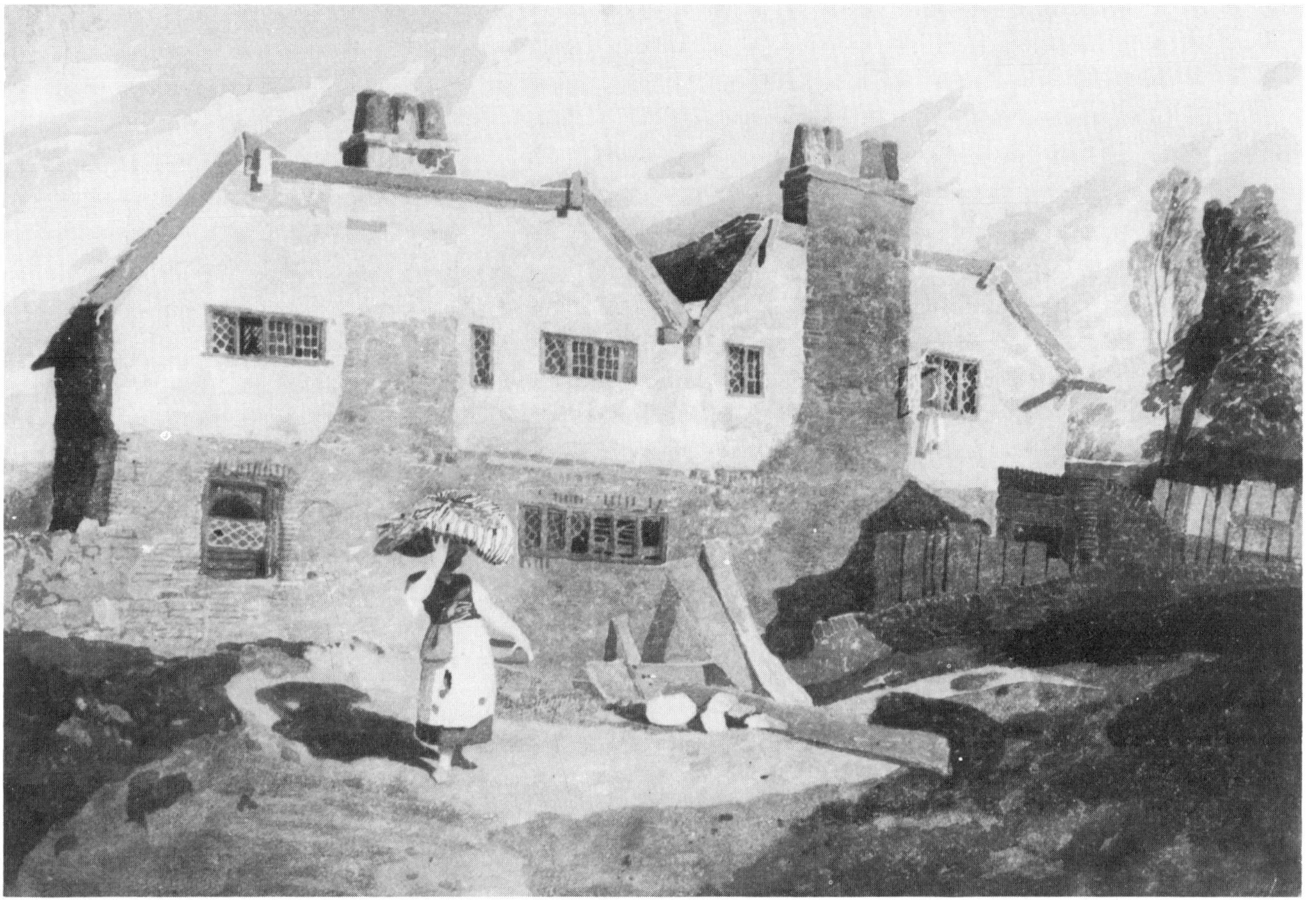

40 Cottages with Washerwoman *c.*1808-9

ship of Ann Miles, one of four daughters to a farmer of Felbrigg. He spent happy times with the Miles family and it was not long before he and Ann were married, on 6 January 1809 in Felbrigg Church, by the Curate John Lukin. When Anne Cholmeley met his new wife for the first time some three and a half years later, her one comment was that she thought him 'a very happy and very lucky man, tho' his wife is not a *beauty'.*[11] For his part, Cotman was devoted to his 'dear Nance'—'My Love, My Wife, My everything',[12] and remained so throughout his life (see No. 150). Their mutual affection, later shared with their sons and daughter, rings clear from the surviving family letters and evidently meant much to Cotman throughout his subsequent years, as indeed did the family's involvement in his professional career.

His new family obligations evidently persuaded him to extend his teaching commitments still further. On 15 July 1809 Cotman launched a new idea upon the Norwich public, again through the pages of the *Norwich Mercury:*

> A Circulating Collection of Drawings. J. S. COTMAN has opened to the Public, on the plan of a Circulating Library a collection of Six Hundred DRAWINGS, consisting of Landscapes, Compositions on Design & Figure, coloured sketches from Nature, sketches in Claro Obscuro, and his Original Pencil Sketches from the Saxon, Norman and Gothic Architecture, chiefly from the counties of Yorkshire, Lincolnshire, Essex, and Norfolk. The Drawings may be viewed on Monday the 17th and Tuesday the 18th inst. at J. S. COTMAN'S, St. Andrews Broad-street, and delivered to the subscribers on Monday, July 24. Quarterly subscriptions ticket One Guinea. J. S. Cotman will attend the delivery of the Drawings to the subscribers, that he may facilitate their copying of them by his instructions. Days of delivering, Mondays and Thursdays, between the hours of Twelve and Two.

The advertisement remained in the paper for the following three weeks, to coincide with the current exhibition by the Norwich Society. The majority of Cotman's exhibits in the catalogue for this year were marked with an asterisk, to indicate those selected from his 'Circulating Portfolios'.

Cotman's bid for recognition resulted in his first notice in a review of the exhibition in the local press, when his 'pencil sketches' in particular were singled out for praise. Unfortunately due to an error of punctuation, the piece read as though Cotman's works were simply 'copies after Old Masters' and the *Norwich Mercury* printed an apology the following week, on 5 August: 'we are assured he has not a single copy exhibited'. This is a confirmation of Cotman's practice at this most vital and productive period of his career, a time when he was entirely without assistants. His circulating collection was 'established for the use of students' the following year, with each of the six hundred drawings numbered consecutively. However, all Cotman drawing copies numbered below '600' surviving today do not necessarily date from this first series, due to substitutions of ruined drawings by later works. Similarly, earlier drawings could be introduced at any stage to serve as a later drawing copy.

His prestige within the Norwich Society of Artists was such that by the opening of the next exhibition in 1810 Cotman was elected Vice-President. That same year he made one more endeavour for his work to be acclaimed in London. He sent four oils to the British Institution and ten drawings to the Associated Painters in Water Colours in Old Bond Street, which he had joined as a member. There is, however, no evidence to suggest that he met with any success. Indeed the

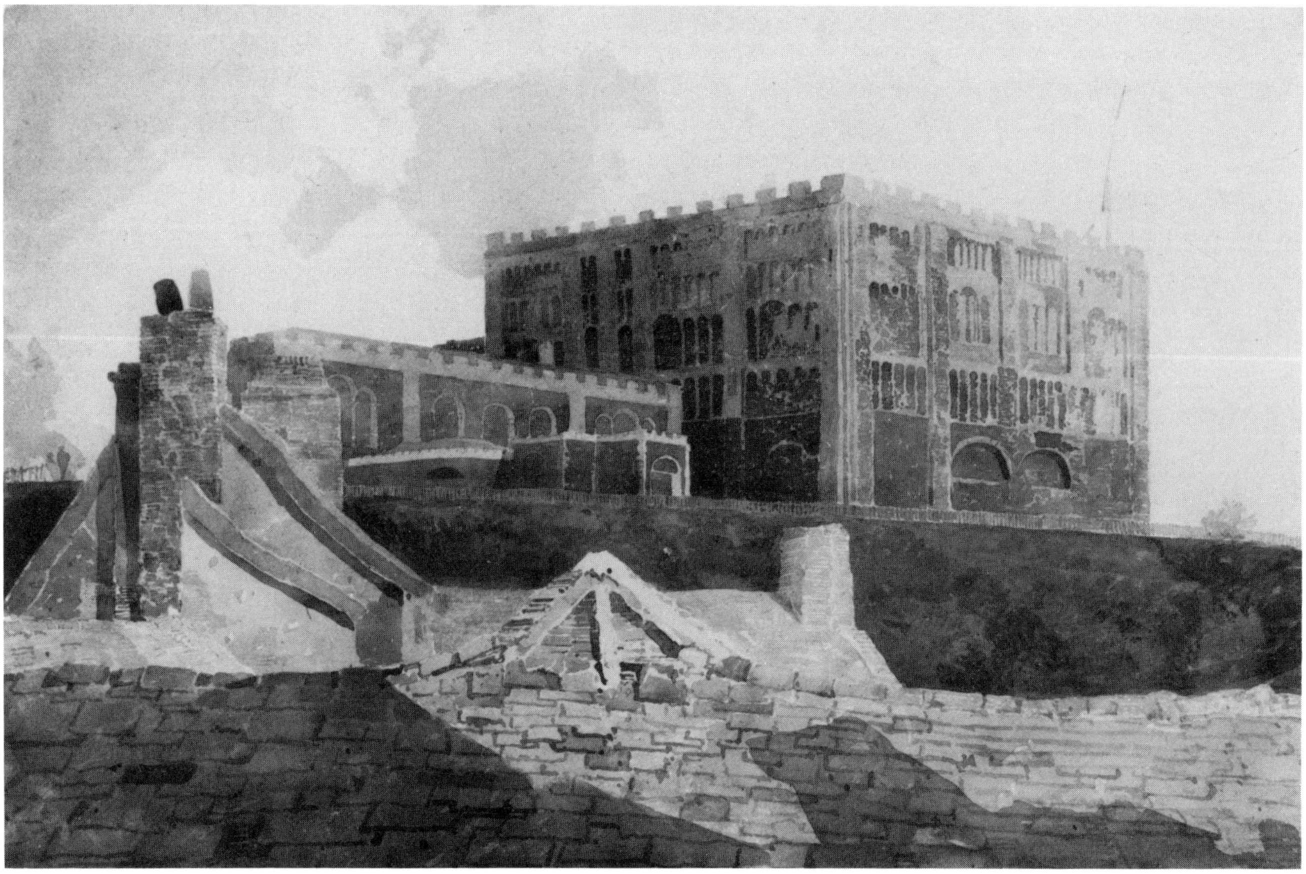

41 Norwich Castle, *c.*1808-9

Society was itself hard pressed to survive the competition of the Watercolour Society and disbanded in 1812. The following year he exhibited two drawings at Old Bond Street, but was not to show work in London again for fourteen years.

All twenty-three of Cotman's exhibited works in Norwich in 1810 were described in the catalogue as part of his 'circulating collection'. That summer he applied himself to a new project, the preparation of plates for the publication of a series of etchings, a decision which was to have considerable repercussions for his career. Stylistically, his watercolours had moved towards the use of a more heavily charged brush, laying solid blocks of colour on thick, fibrous paper, in a manner which encouraged Kitson to feel that he was emulating the oil painters. His creative impulse by the summer of 1810 was to express his visionary sense of design through the austere medium of the etching needle — a medium which would also enable him to reach a wider public. On 20 December 1810 he confided to Francis Cholmeley: 'This work save a few drawings to order has been my chief care; I am very fond of it, and being of a sanguine disposition, it gives me spirits, for I fancy a long line of patrons, and this being my first essay.'

Notes

[1]Mrs. Cholmeley to Francis, 31 Jan. 1807. [2]JSC to Dawson Turner, 12 Aug. 1841 (Barker Collection). [3]Kitson 1937 pp. 108-9. [4]1807 (67) [5]Norwich Society 1807 (130), now at Abbot Hall, Kendal. [6]Norwich Society 1809 (208); Tate 5636. [7]*The Farington Diary* (ed. J. Creig) 1 June 1808. [8]Sir Henry Englefield to Francis Cholmeley, 31 Oct. 1808. [9]1808 (162); (193); (226). [10]Rajnai & Allthorpe 1979 Nos. 77-79. [11]Anne Cholmeley to Francis, 16 July 1812. [12]JSC to his wife 11 August 1817. *Walpole Society* Vol. XIV p. 109.

33 Bishopsgate Bridge, Norwich, *c.*1806-7

illustrated on p. 40

Pencil, watercolour and gum on buff, laid paper; 25.4 × 45 (10 × $17\frac{11}{16}$). PROV: ?John Wodderspoon by Jan. 1863; ?his sale, G. H. Murrell, Norwich 15-16 Jan. 1863, 2nd day, lot 328 *Bishop Bridge, fine example,* bt. 120s William Dixon by 1867; Frederick Wedmore by 1876; by descent to his daughter Millicent Wedmore; her bequest 1965 (542.965). EXH: Norwich 1867 (765) lent by Wm. Dixon; Norwich, Art Circle 1888 (6) and BFAC 1888 (26) lent by F. Wedmore; Rouen 1967; Kenwood 1969; Colnaghi 1970 (38); Bordeaux 1977 (98) repro. REF: Kitson 1937 p. 112; Rajnai & Allthorpe No. 60.

This is a later watercolour version of the scene depicted in No. 3, showing the bridge from further downstream. It has unfortunately faded, but remains a remarkable work.

Kitson places this watercolour *c.*1807-8, the first two years of Cotman's return to Norwich. Rajnai and Allthorpe convincingly argue on stylistic grounds for a slightly earlier date of 1807 or possibly as early as autumn, 1806.

34 The Mars, riding at Anchor off Cromer, c.1807

illustrated in colour on p. 62

Pencil and watercolour, with birds scraped out, on buff, laid paper; 30.8 × 22 ($12\frac{1}{8}$ × $8\frac{5}{8}$). INSCR: *Recto,* signed in brown ink l.r. *J S Cotman.* PROV: The Palser Gallery; bt. from them by Percy Moore Turner, March 1926; bt. from him by R. J. Colman, March 1926; R. J. Colman Bequest 1946. (139.217.947). EXH: ?Norwich Society 1808 (193); Tokyo 1929; Norwich 1945; Norwich, Arts Council 1947 (8). REF: Kitson 1937 pp. 111, 112, 127, 179, pl. 48; Cordingly 1974 p. 127, pl. 74 in colour; Rajnai & Allthorpe No. 61.

'This is one of the most original compositions in the collection. The towering cumulus cloud, executed in a cool graduation of grey tones, gives the drawing a solemn majesty which is comparable to that of another watercolour of this date, [No. 30] *Devil's Elbow; Rokeby Park.'* (Rajnai & Allthorpe).

The 'Mars' was a seventy-four gun warship described by Ketton-Cremer in his *Felbrigg.*[1] It was commanded by William Lukin of Felbrigg, Cotman's contemporary and brother of the Rev. John Lukin who married Cotman and Ann Miles in 1809. On 31 July 1807, in squally weather, the 'Mars' anchored within sight of Cromer. Ketton-Cremer observed of Cotman's watercolour 'It cannot have been an exact reproduction of the scene: no ship of the line could conceivably have anchored so close inshore, and it is evident from the log that her position that night was some way east of Cromer. But the Mars and her captain, no doubt well known to the girl whom Cotman hoped to marry, must have appealed to his imagination, and inspired this superlative drawing'.

[1]R. W. Ketton-Cremer, *Felbrigg,* 1962 pp. 221-223.

35 Portrait of Tom Cotman (1783-1851), *c.*1807-9

Pencil and watercolour on cream, wove paper; 32.9 × 22.5 ($12\frac{15}{16}$ × $8\frac{7}{8}$). INSCR: *Recto,* signed in pencil l.r. *J S Cotman.* PROV: Anne Walne Cotman (1808-1881) daughter of the sitter; by descent to her grandson C. Noel Heath by 1922; bt. from him with the portrait of Mrs. Tom Cotman (No. 36), 1961. (1.305.961). EXH: Tate 1922 (66) lent by C. Noel Heath; Bedford & Cambridge 1966 (13). REF: Kitson 1937 p. 106; Rajnai & Allthorpe No. 63.

No. 35 dates from the period when Cotman was trying to establish himself as a portrait painter in Norwich. The sitter is traditionally said to be Thomas Cotman (1783-1851), Cotman's younger brother, who married Anne Walne of Starston, Norfolk, the subject of the next entry.

Stylistically No. 35 relates to the pure lines of Cotman's oil portraits (see No. 146) rather than his earlier pencil portraits[1] or his later ones.[2] It is close to another portrait[3] at Norwich and to a similar drawing,[4] *Study of a Head, after Vandyke* in the British Museum.

[1]Rajnai & Allthorpe No. 14. [2]Eg. V & A E1129 1927. [3]Rajnai & Allthorpe No. 62. [4]BM 1902-5-14-15; possibly Norwich Society 1807 (105).

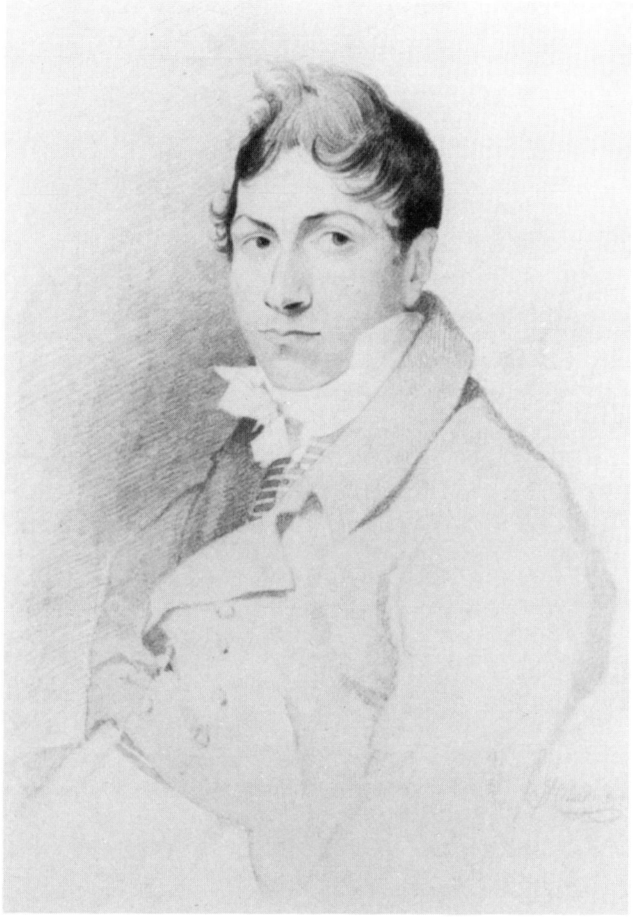

35 Portrait of Tom Cotman (1783-1851), *c.*1807-9

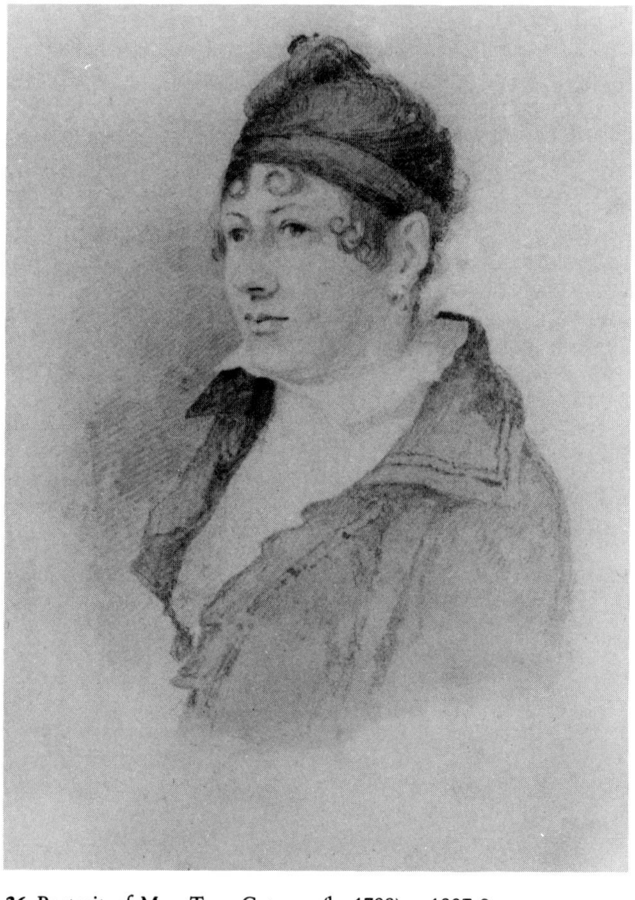

36 Portrait of Mrs. Tom Cotman (b. 1788), *c.*1807-9

36 Portrait of Mrs. Tom Cotman (b. 1788), *c.*1807-9
illustrated on p. 45

Pencil and watercolour on cream, wove paper; 30.4 × 21.8 ($11\frac{15}{16}$ × $8\frac{9}{16}$). PROV: See No. 35. (2.305.961). EXH: Tate 1922 (75). REF: Rajnai & Allthorpe No. 64.

This and the previous portrait have descended through the Cotman family and have always been regarded as a pair. Although the sitter is traditionally said to be Anne Walne, Mrs. Tom Cotman, Rajnai and Allthorpe point out that the age of the sitter appears to be more than 18 to 21 years. They also remark that its softer handling places it closer to the smaller pencil portraits of Cotman's wife Ann (see No. 150) and that of Mary Palgrave (No. 35 n. 4). They suggest that this similarity may derive from Cotman's endeavour to convey the softness of the female countenance rather than a difference in date from No. 35.

37 St. Luke's Chapel, Norwich Cathedral, East, 1808
illustrated on p. 40

Pencil and watercolour on buff, laid paper; 35.2 × 46.1 ($13\frac{13}{16}$ × $18\frac{1}{8}$). INSCR: *Verso,* of old backing paper (destroyed 1936) inscribed, dated and signed in pencil c.r. *St. Lukes Chapel Norwich Cathedral, East 1808/J S Cotman:* and further in pencil l.l., some of the inscription trimmed, *Mr J. S. Cotman / [ta]kes the liberty of presenting / . . . to Sir H Englefield / . . . is sorry he has not the pleasure [of] seeing him as he has much to [thank] him for — / . . . goes to town on Saturday / . . . Mail / no 4 M. . .field Rd / Soho.* PROV: John Wodderspoon; his sale, Murrell, Norwich, 15-16 Jan. 1863, lot 342, bt. ?William Dixon 3 gns.; certainly with William Dixon by 1867; his sale, Spelman, Norwich, 17 May 1882, lot 267, bt. J. J. Colman 12 gns.; J. J. Colman Bequest 1898. (19.4.99). EXH: Norwich 1867 (766) lent by Wm. Dixon; Norwich Art Circle 1888 (43); BFAC 1888 (20); RA Winter Exhibition 1892 (321); London, Guildhall 1896 (91); Tate 1922 (29); RA 1934 (739, Commemorative Catalogue 814, pl. CLXXVIII); Bucharest, British Council, 1935-36; NCM Picture of the Month, August 1943; British Council 1949-50 (22) pl. XV; Geneva & Zurich 1955-56 (23); King's Lynn 1956; Derby & Nottingham 1959 (1); Bedford 1960 (27); Manchester 1961 (31); RA 1961-62 (396); Japan 1970 (64) repro.; The Hague 1977 (12); Koblenz 1980 (12) repro. in colour; China 1982 (33) repro.; REF: Kitson 1937 p. 108; Rajnai & Allthorpe No. 65; *RSA Journal* Aug. 1979 repro. p. 598; Jacobs & Warner 1980 repro. p. EA23.

This is one of a number of views of the Cathedral which Cotman painted shortly after his return to Norwich and stands out in his oeuvre as a drawing of refined austerity and monumentality. While creating an impression of meticulous accuracy, it in fact presents a vastly aggrandized version of St. Luke's Chapel which here takes the place of the entire East End. Also omitted is the ambulatory, the tall clerestory and the tower with its spire.

Cotman did not exhibit any of his views of the Cathedral of this period. The 1807-8 series includes: the *Screen in Norwich Cathedral (South Transept);*[1] *In the Jesus Chapel* and an *Interior of the Nave,* both at Bedford;[2] *Interior of the Eastern Ambulatory of the Apse*[3] and *Norman Arcade in the Apse,* both in the Ashmolean; *The Jesus Chapel* now in Australia,[4] a *View of the Ambulatory,* now at Yale[5] and the *Tomb of Prior William de Walsham and Bishop Wakering* in a private collection.[6] There are in addition three Norwich Cathedral subjects, which may be early watercolours, now untraced,[7] and four later drawings.[8]

Three Norwich Cathedral subjects were exhibited with the Norwich Society in 1811 all apparently pencil drawings for unpublished etchings.[9]

[1] BM 1902-5-14-18; a version is in the Bacon collection. [2] Norwich Art Circle 1888 (3); also Kitson 1937 pl. 43. Both at Cecil Higgins Art Gallery. [3] Kitson 1937 p. 107 exh. Norwich, Art Circle 1888 (47). [4] Art Gallery of New South Wales, Australia. [5] Yale Center for British Art, New Haven, USA, B1975.2.571. [6] Norwich Art Circle 1888 (9). [7] See Rajnai & Allthorpe No. 65. n.16. [8] *Ibid,* n.17. [9] Norwich Society 1811 (124, 129 and 151). See also Popham Nos. 184, 185.

38 East Barsham Hall, Norfolk, *c.*1808
illustrated in colour on p. 98

Pencil and watercolour on buff, laid paper; 42.7 × 28.9 ($16\frac{13}{16}$ × $11\frac{3}{8}$). INSCR: *Recto,* signed in brown watercolour l.l. *J. S. Colman* (sic). PROV: Rev. James Bulwer; by descent to his son James Radford Bulwer; by descent to his younger brother Walter Bulwer; by descent to his son Henry A. Bulwer; sold by him to Walker's Galleries; bt. from them by R. J. Colman, 1926; R. J. Colman Bequest 1946. (155.235.951). EXH: London, Walker's Galleries 1926 (23); Norwich 1930-31; Norwich 1945. REF: Kitson 1937 p. 149; Rajnai & Allthorpe No. 66.

Barsham Hall (built *c.*1520-30) is situated to the north of Fakenham, about twenty five miles north-west of Norwich. Cotman saw the Hall early in 1808 as he wrote in a letter to Francis Cholmeley of 22 February 1808[1] of taking the road to Basham (sic) House en route to North Creake.

Rajnai and Allthorpe point out that No. 38[2] is stylistically close to *St. Luke's Chapel,* No. 37 and *Trentham Hall,* No. 39, being executed in light washes on a fibrous buff laid paper, while the sky in *East Barsham Hall* is an echo of that in *The Mars off Cromer,* No. 34.

No. 38 is a view of the East End of the South Front. It was etched and published in Cotman's *Architectural Antiquities of Norfolk* of 1818, when the plough was replaced by two figures and three dogs.[3] The plough itself was etched as plate 43 in the *Liber Studiorum.*[4]

Cotman returned to Barsham in 1811 for he wrote to Dawson Turner on 31 July: 'Basham [sic] House is really quite beautiful, this has afforded me fresh matter and as I think it has never been done justice to I have taken the more trouble about it'.[5] On this visit he appears to have sketched the west end of the South Front of the House[6] and the gatehouse,[7] both subjects which he subsequently etched.

[1] Letter dated 11 and 22 Feb. 1808. [2] A watercolour copy, not by Cotman, is at Corpus Christi College, Cambridge. [3] Popham No. 158. The etching is dated 1813. [4] Popham No. 336. [5] Barker Collection. [6] Popham No. 189, the etching is dated 1817. A drawing copy, numbered 2064, is NCM 468.235.951 and there are copies by F. A. Martineau, NCM 13.25.964, and Ellen Turner, dated 1826, NCM 6.26.31. [7] Not recorded by Popham. The etching is dated 1818. There are two copies: (a) inscribed *Gateway in Barsham House J. S. Cotman;* (b) Ellen Turner, dated 1825, NCM 5.26.31.

39 Interior of Trentham Church, Staffordshire, *c.*1808.
illustrated in colour on p. 63

Pencil and watercolour on buff, laid paper; 54.5 × 41 ($21\frac{7}{16}$ × $16\frac{1}{8}$). INSCR: *Recto,* signed in brown watercolour l.l. *J. S. Cotman.* PROV: The Palser Gallery; bt. from them by the Rev. G. W. Minns, Norwich; bt. from him by James Reeve, June 1890; bt. from him by H. S. Theobald, ?after 1903; bt. from him by R. J. Colman, Feb. 1910; R. J. Colman Bequest 1946. (133.217.947). EXH: RA Winter Exhibition 1892 (47); Norwich 1902 (220) and Norwich 1903 (16) lent by James Reeve; Manchester 1912 (326); Tate 1922 (60); Norwich 1945; Norwich, Arts Council 1947 (4). REF: Kitson 1937 pp. 97, 98; Rajnai & Allthorpe No. 67.

Cotman is known to have visited Trentham Hall, seat of the Marquess of Stafford, only once, in the summer of 1806. His invitation there probably followed his meeting with the 2nd Marquess's sister, Lady Carlisle, at Castle Howard the previous summer.

No. 39 is the only known work of Cotman to derive from this visit. It is dated by Rajnai and Allthorpe to *c.*1808. They observe that it is stylistically close to and executed on the same fibrous buff laid paper as Nos. 37 and 38.

The church interior depicted is that of St. Mary and All Saints, which was subsequently rebuilt by Barry in 1844. When the picture changed hands in 1890 the restoration is touched on by the vendor, the Rev. Minns, in a letter to the purchaser, James Reeve: 'The screen has unhappily been removed and the church restored. Observe the pulpit hangings, just such a bit of colour as Cotman would delight in. They have a history and are a tissue of gold and silver embroidery on rich velvet—anciently a gift of the 1st Marquis of Stafford to the Church, being a Moorish saddle cloth presented by the Emperor of Morocco to George III. They are not in use now and are kept in Trentham Hall. I have this from Mr. Pigott the present Vicar of Trentham'.[1]

[1] Typewritten extract from the letter dated 7 June 1890, Art Dept. archives, NCM.

40 Cottages with Washerwoman, *c.*1808-9

called *Cottages, Elm Hill*

illustrated on p. 43

Pencil and watercolour on cream, wove paper; 27.7 × 39.9 ($10\frac{7}{8}$ × $15\frac{11}{16}$). PROV: The Palser Gallery; bt. from them by Percy Moore Turner; bt. from him, with seven other Cotman watercolours, by R. J. Colman April 1926; R. J. Colman Bequest 1946. (142.235.951). EXH: Norwich 1945. REF: Rajnai & Allthorpe No. 68.

It is not possible to identify the houses here depicted with Elm Hill, Norwich. The former title, rejected by Rajnai and Allthorpe, derives from Cotman's exhibit with the Norwich Society 1809 (172*)[1] *Old Houses, Elm Hill.* The deep blue of the horizon suggests a coastal view.

Cotman's interest in this work lies in the rich patterning of colour and shape through variegated tone rather than in its topographical content. A washerwoman in a very similar pose can be seen in the left foreground of *Norwich Market Place,*[2] now in the Tate Gallery, London.

[1]The asterisk indicates that it was one of Cotman's drawings in his Circulating Portfolio. [2]Probably Norwich Society 1809 (208); Tate 5636.

41 Norwich Castle, *c.*1808-9

illustrated on p. 44

Pencil and watercolour on cream, wove paper; 32.4 × 47.2 ($12\frac{3}{4}$ × $18\frac{9}{16}$). INSCR: *Verso,* old backing board inscribed u.c.r. in pencil *Castle Norwich.* PROV: Mrs. M. Kemp; bt. from her, 1960. (98.960). EXH: USA 1981-82 (10) repro. p. 64. REF: Rajnai & Allthorpe No. 69.

This is a view of Norwich Castle from the north-west, taken from an elevated viewpoint over the housetops of Castle Ditches, now Castle Meadow. To the left is the Shirehouse built by Matthew Brettingham in 1749 and demolished in 1827-8.

No. 41 entered the collection at Norwich as an unattributed drawing but it is convincingly argued by Rajnai and Allthorpe to be Cotman's work of *c.*1808-9. They point out that a relationship can be observed between this view of Norwich Castle and *Cottages with Washerwoman,* No. 40; 'The paper, the torn sky, the palette, the underlying pencil work and the treatment of the brick chimneys compares well with *Cottages with Washerwoman'.*

Cotman's other works featuring Norwich Castle are all distant views from the east. Dating from the 1820s, these include an oil in the Bacon collection and thirteen pencil sketches.[1]

[1]See Rajnai & Allthorpe No. 69, n. 4.

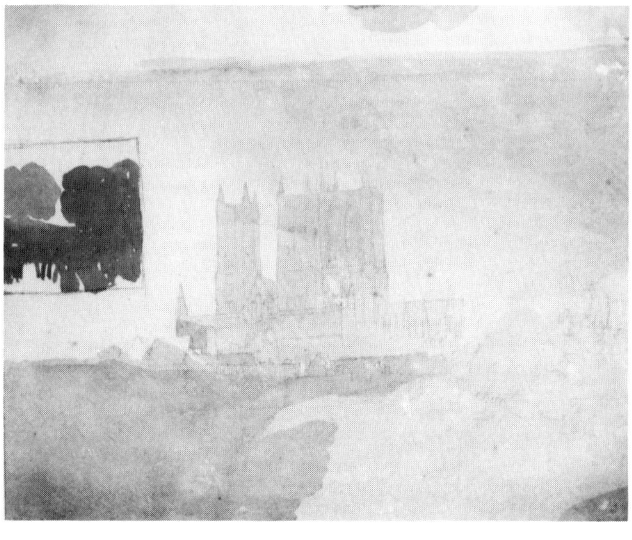

42 Lincoln Cathedral, *c.*1808-9

42 Lincoln Cathedral, *c.*1808-9

Pencil and watercolour on white, laid paper with watermark l.c.r. edge: a symbol like a capital *P,* the stem an inverted *4;* 32.9 × 39.9 ($12\frac{15}{16}$ × $15\frac{3}{4}$). INSCR: *Verso,* inscribed in pencil u.l. corner, not autograph, *Pictures at Kensington.* Prov: See No. 54. (236.235.951). REF: Kitson 1937 p. 74 n.1; Rajnai & Allthorpe No. 70.

This unfinished watercolour is presumably based on a sketch made while Cotman was passing through Lincoln on his way north to join the Cholmeleys in the summer of 1804. He wrote to Francis Cholmeley on 21 August, from Peterborough: 'I missed the Lincoln Mail this morg. it being quite full & I am told I may probably be detained here for a Week one coach only going thro the place.'[1] Cotman's method at this time, of underpainting in shades of light brown to provide a foundation for later washes, can here be clearly seen.

He was later to use this unfinished work as a stiffener for No. 54.

[1]JSC to Francis Cholmeley written 18-21 August 1804 (Barker Collection).

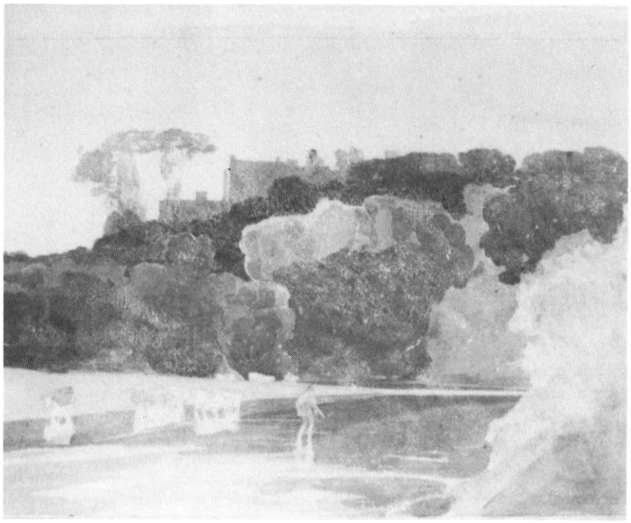

43 Gilling Castle, Yorkshire, *c.*1808-9

43 Gilling Castle, Yorkshire, *c.*1808-9

Pencil and watercolour on cream, wove paper; 32.9 × 40.2 ($12\frac{15}{16}$ × $15\frac{13}{16}$). PROV: Discovered in 1935 on the back of *Crosby Hall, 1830,* see No. 106. (235.235.951). REF: Rajnai & Allthorpe No. 71.

This unfinished watercolour is again a re-working of a subject first sketched[1] by Cotman on one of his Yorkshire trips. Kitson identified the subject as Gilling Castle in 1936, writing to the restorer S. Kennedy North on 8 October: 'I think the landscape you discovered on the back of "Crosby Hall" is undoubtedly Gilling Castle—3 miles from Brandsby Hall where Cotman stayed in the summer of 1803, 4 and 5. See photo of the pencil sketch which is evidently 1804 from the style. I suggest he did your watercolour in the winter of 1804-5, with this pencil sketch before him. There is no river in the foreground, but a small stream and evidence of a large pond, which has silted up and trees have grown in it. I went on Saturday last and examined the place anew.'[2]

Rajnai and Allthorpe dispute Kitson's suggestion that the watercolour dates from 1804-5 and convincingly assert that a date of *c.*1808 is more probable. Both the type of paper used and the broad uniform washes of colour ally No. 43 with both *St. Luke's Chapel, Norwich Cathedral* of 1808, No. 37, and *Cattle Watering* of *c.*1809-10, No. 48.

[1]Rajnai & Allthorpe No. 37. [2]Kennedy North, Report 1936, B. p. 28, Art Dept. archives, NCM.

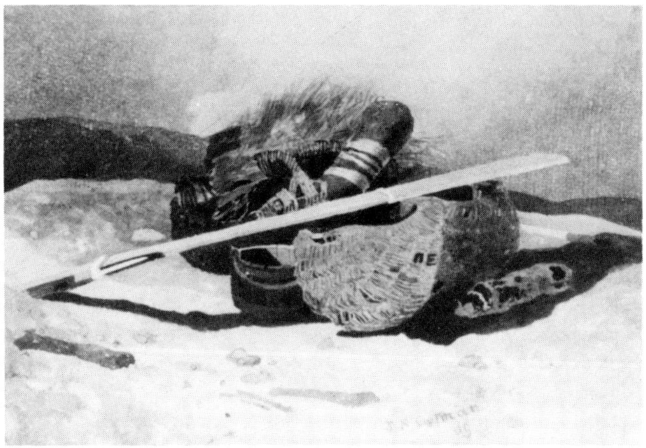

44 Fish Swills, Rudder, etc., 1809

44 Fish Swills, Rudder, etc., 1809
called *Gear of Fishing Boat*

Pencil and watercolour on cream, wove paper; 18.3 × 26.5 ($7\frac{3}{16}$ × $10\frac{7}{16}$). INSCR: *Recto,* signed and dated in brown watercolour l.c.r. *J. S. Cotman / 09.* PROV: See No. 40. (151.235.951). EXH: ?Norwich Society 1809 (169); Norwich 1945. REF: Kitson 1937 p. 196; Rajnai & Allthorpe No. 82.

This is one of the few dated drawings of 1809-10 and is a fine example of Cotman's technique at this period: 'the colours are applied over a warm buff ground with a "dry" brush and sometimes "dragged" across the canvas-like texture of an absorbent paper, adopted by the artist for its quality of adding lustrous depth to the thin medium'. (Rajnai & Allthorpe).

A pencil sketch[1] for this composition is also in the collection at Norwich. This bears colour notes which in No. 44 Cotman has followed, except in painting the rudder pink instead of the original grey.

[1]Rajnai & Allthorpe No. 81.

45 Moorland Landscape, 1809

Pencil and watercolour with some gum on cream, wove paper; 21.5 × 16.5 ($8\frac{7}{16}$ × $6\frac{1}{2}$). INSCR: *Recto,* signed and dated in brown watercolour l.c.l. *J S Cotman / 1809.* PROV: See No. 40. (153.217.947). EXH: Norwich 1945; Norwich, Arts Council 1947 (14). REF: Rajnai & Allthorpe No. 83.

This is another of the rare dated 1809-10 drawings, executed (as No. 44) on a textured paper.

It is possible that this watercolour or a related drawing may be *The Sheep Walk, near Alnwick Castle, Northumberland* which Cotman exhibited with the Norwich Society in 1809 (159*).

46 View of Jungfrau-Horn, a glacier in the canton of Bern, Switzerland, 1809
illustrated on opposite page

Pencil and watercolour with some gum on cream, wove paper; 65.5 × 46.3 ($25\frac{13}{16}$ × $18\frac{3}{16}$). INSCR: *Recto,* signed and dated in brown watercolour l.r. *J S Cotman, 1809.* PROV: J. Palser & Son; bt. from them by Col. H. Littlewood; his bequest 1921. (83.961). EXH: ?Norwich Society 1810 (55); Tate 1922 (138) and Aldeburgh, Third Festival 1950 (15) lent by Miss Littlewood; Bedford & Cambridge 1966 (7); King's Lynn 1970 (21); Paris 1972 (71) repro.; Bordeaux 1977 (99) repro.; Koblenz 1980 (10); Nottingham 1981 (45). REF: Kitson 1937 pp. 123, 131, 132; Rajnai & Allthorpe No. 84.

It was common practice amongst Cotman's contemporaries to copy works by other artists and this impressive watercolour is possibly the earliest example of Cotman's use of another artist's work. It is closely derived from a coloured aquatint after the Swiss artist Johann Ludwig Aberli, some of whose plates had been reprinted in London five years earlier.[1]

Cotman exhibited No. 46 with the Norwich Society in 1810 (55),

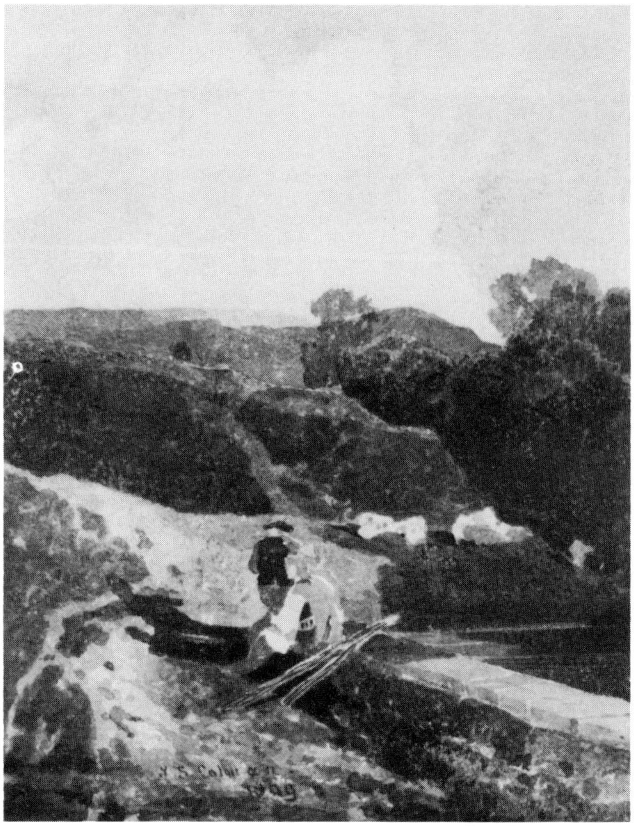

45 Moorland Landscape, 1809

where it was 'generally admired' and regarded as 'particularly well conceived and executed'.[2] It has been suggested by several writers that Cotman was influenced in his introduction of large scale figure groups in this and other compositions, by the work of Joshua Cristall whom he had met through the Sketching Society.[3]

[1]Pidgley p. 57 note 193 gives 'Aquatint by Chretien de Mechel after J. L. Aberli (1723-1786)'. [2]*?Norwich Mercury* Aug. 1810, undated transcript Reeve Coll. BM Print Room. Cotman showed a similar subject in 1824 (92). [3]The Cotman sale 1861 included lot 179 *Cristall, Girl Paring Turnips, upright drawing, outside measure 27 inches by 21.*

47 Byland Abbey, Yorkshire, *c.*1809
illustrated on p. 50

Pencil and watercolour with some gum, bird u.l. scraped out, on cream, wove paper; 52.1 × 43.5 ($20\frac{1}{2}$ × $17\frac{1}{8}$). PROV: ?Francis Cholmeley; by descent to Eleanor Cholmeley; Hugh C. Fairfax Cholmeley by 1922; Thomas Agnew & Sons by 1938; bt. from Agnew by S. Kennedy North on behalf of R. J. Colman, Feb. 1938, £725; R. J. Colman Bequest 1946. (233.217.947). EXH: London, Paterson Gallery 1913 (13); Tate 1922 (210) lent by Hugh C. Fairfax Cholmeley; London, Agnew 1938 (117); Norwich 1945; Norwich Arts Council 1947 (37). REF: Kitson 1937 pp. 122, 123, 144; Oppé *Burlington* Aug. 1945 p. 196; Rajnai & Allthorpe No. 85.

Rajnai and Allthorpe point out how well the extent of Cotman's development from his early work can be illustrated by comparison of this representation of *Byland Abbey* with the version dated 1804 (No. 19). 'The refined delicacy of the earlier version pales beside the robust monumentality of the later work. The solid mass of the West Front has become the undisputed focus of the composition. Its organic presence is juxtaposed to the menacing shape of a blasted tree on the right and to a theatrically posed pair of figures in the left foreground'.

Kitson is qualified in his praise of the work and observes: '. . . the drawing is fine in colour and so admirable in arrangement as almost to defeat its object as a picture, since there is no divine accident here to veil the completeness of its pattern'. Paul Oppé, meanwhile, concludes that it is 'the most sensational and overpowering of all Cotman's known work', and adds: 'In this drawing another and very different

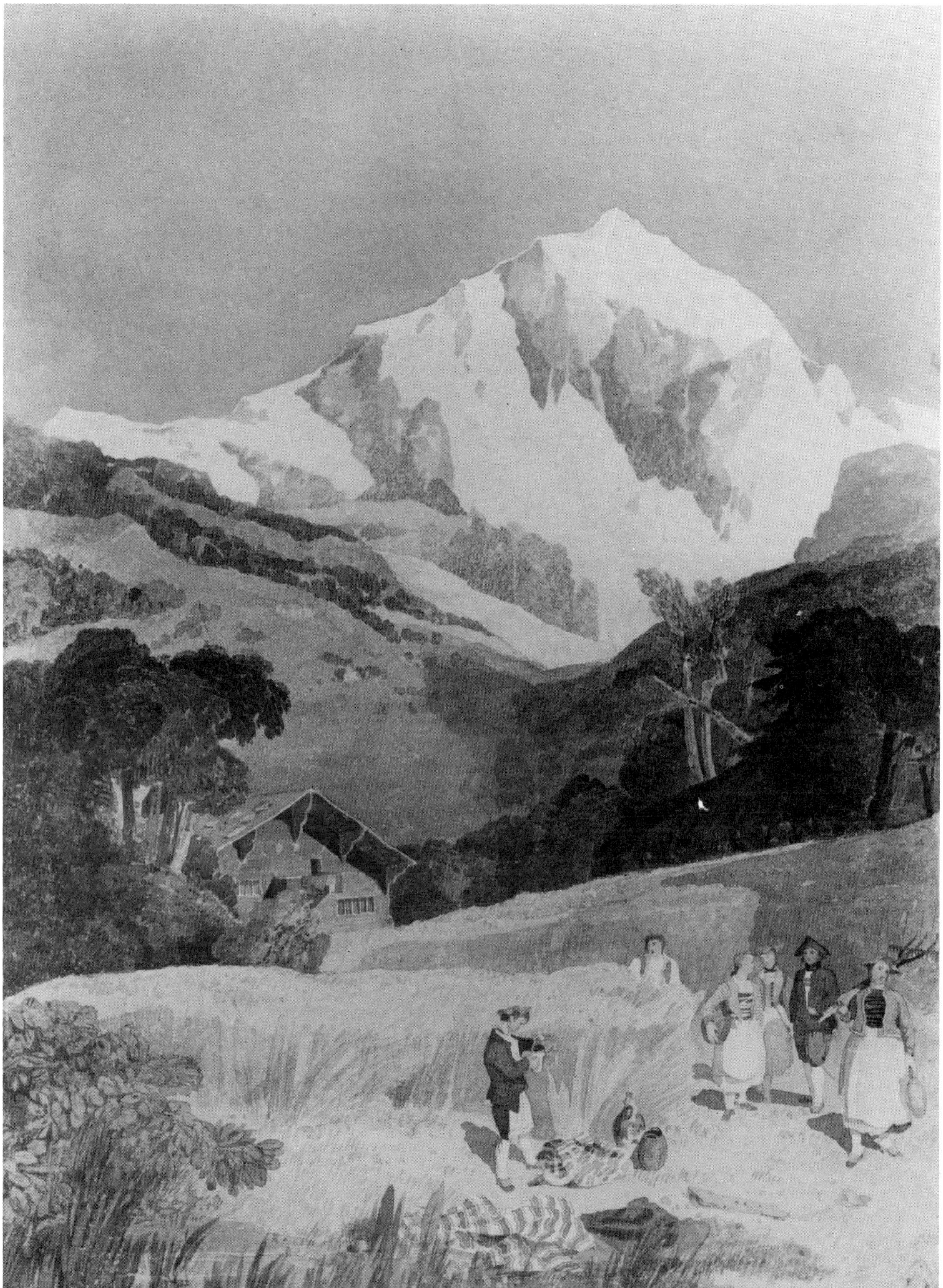

46 View of Jungfrau-Horn, a glacier in the canton of Bern, Switzerland, 1809

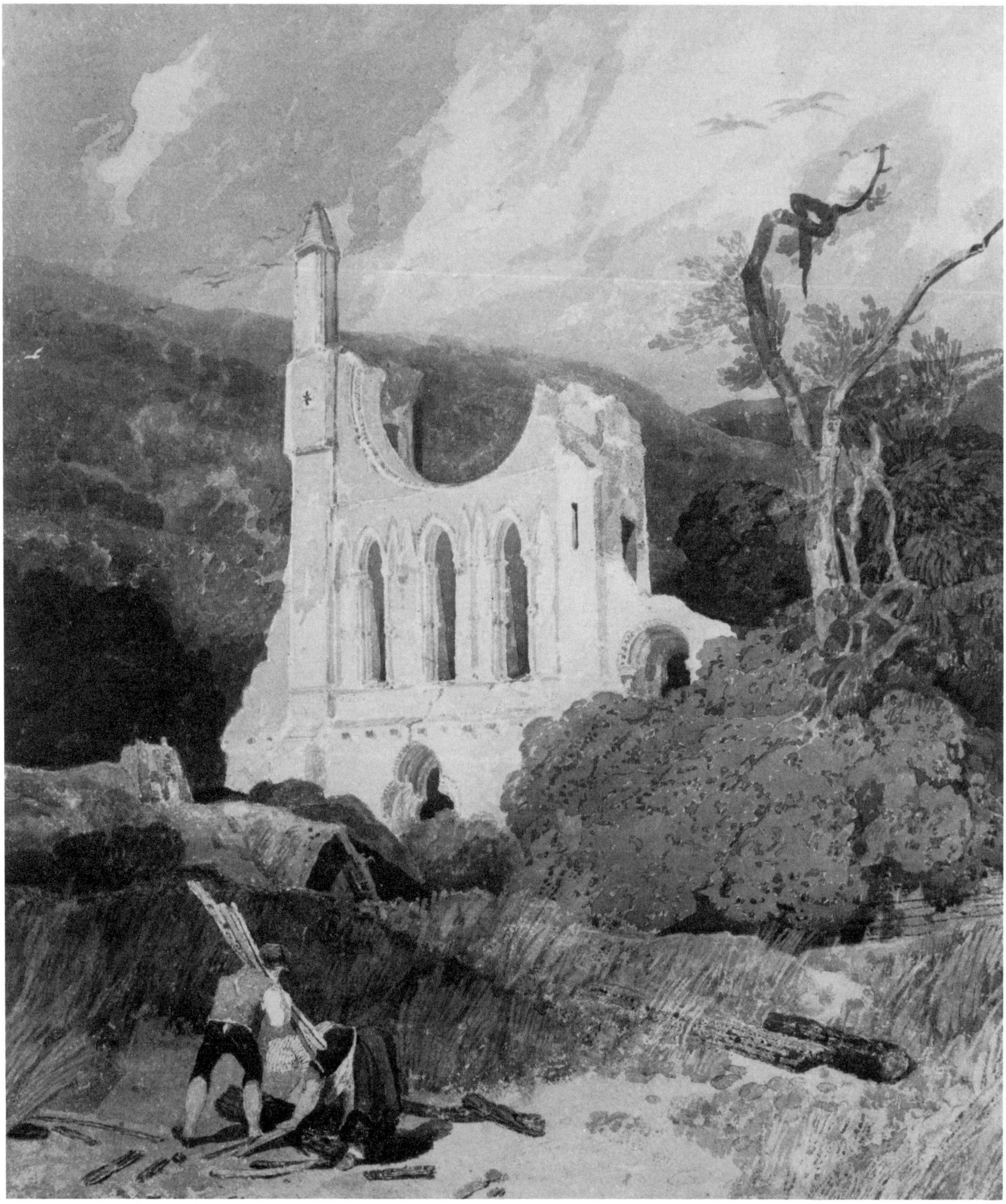

47 Byland Abbey, Yorkshire, *c.*1809

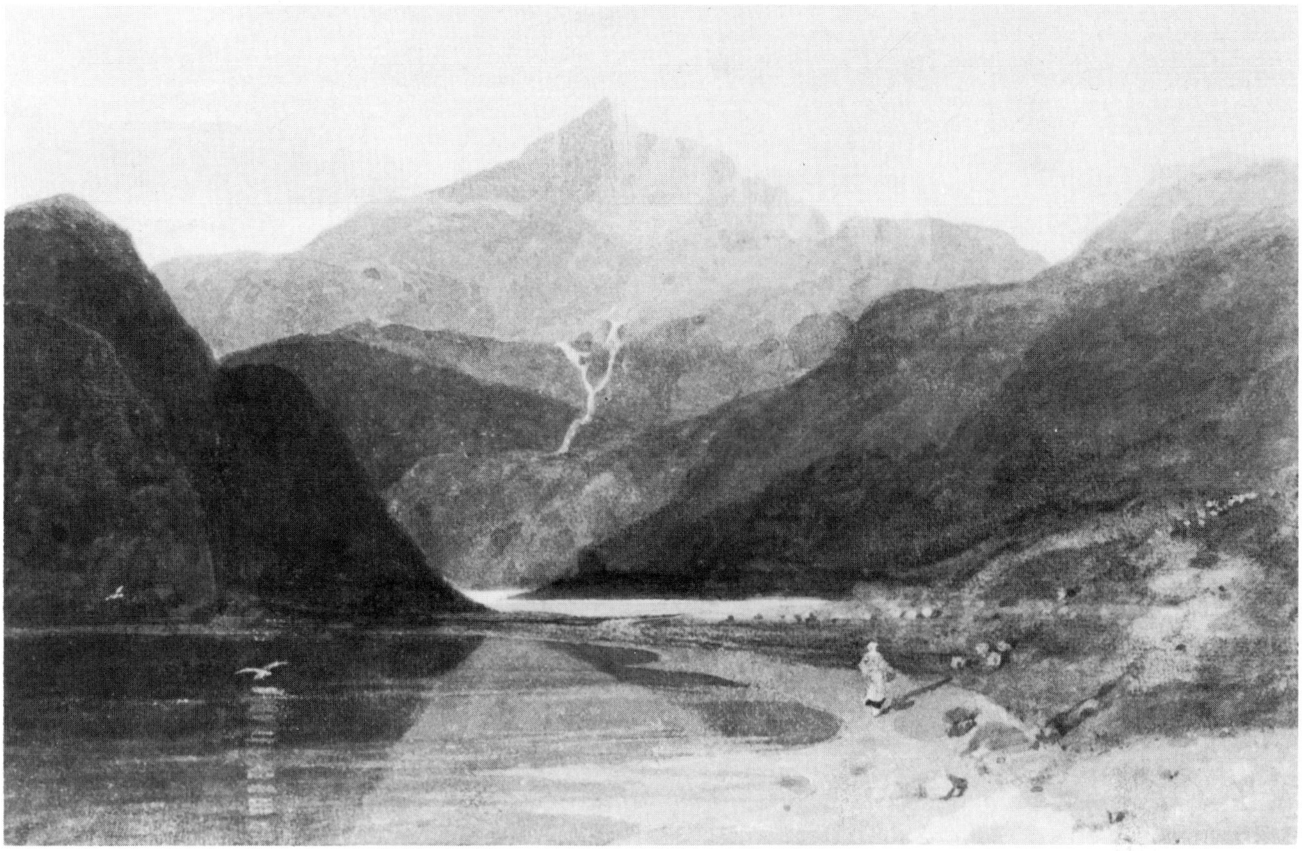

50 Snowdon, North Wales, *c.*1809-10

feature is apparent. The two cranes flying in the sky above a dead tree with a knotted bough cannot be anything but copies from some Chinese or Japanese ornament, and they must remove all doubts whether he had met with Oriental influences'. It is known that Cotman owned a collection of Chinese drawings (of figures and landscapes).

The other versions of Byland Abbey and an account of Cotman's visits there are given in the entry for No. 19.

48 Cattle Watering, *c.*1809-10

illustrated in colour on p. 28

Pencil and watercolour with some gum on buff, laid paper; 28.3 × 44.7 ($11\frac{1}{8}$ × $17\frac{7}{8}$). PROV: See No. 40. (148.235.951). EXH: ?Norwich Society 1809 (160*) as *Landscape with Cows;* Norwich 1945. REF: Rajnai & Allthorpe No. 87.

Such a large scale representation of cattle is unusual in Cotman's work, although the 'Cotman cow' features increasingly in his work either as staffage or the means by which to add touches of light or colour to his compositions.

Cattle Watering is a richly colourful and virtually unfaded watercolour in which a careful interplay of quasi-abstract forms is executed with absolute control.

A collection of Cotman's animal drawings is at Leeds. In these, Rajnai and Allthorpe discern the influence of George Morland and, to a lesser extent, that of La Cave, a collection of whose drawings was in the possession of Dawson Turner.[1]

[1]See Rajnai & Allthorpe Nos. 86 & 87.

49 'Trowse Hythe, Norwich', *c.*1809-10

illustrated in colour on p. 28

Watercolour, with scraping out, on cream, wove paper; 31.6 × 44.2 ($12\frac{7}{16}$ × $17\frac{7}{16}$). INSCR: *Verso,* inscribed in pencil u.r., not in the artist's hand, *Trowse Eye / J Sell Cotman.* PROV: F. T. Keith by 1878; his sale, Keith & Smith, Norwich 19 Feb. 1903, lot 296 *Trowse Hythe. (A very fine picture) J S Cotman,* bt. by R. J. Colman £19.10.0; R. J. Colman Bequest 1946. (156.235.951). EXH: Norwich 1878 (508) and Norwich 1885 (324) lent by F. T. Keith; Norwich 1903 (8) lent by R. J. Colman; Tate 1922 (19); Norwich 1930-31; Norwich 1945. REF: Rajnai & Allthorpe No. 88.

It is difficult to identify with absolute certainty this view as Trowse Hythe, the meeting point of the Rivers Yare and Wensum at Trowse, just south-east of Norwich.[1]

Another scene on the Yare, traditionally called *The Mumbles*[2] and held by the British Museum, is painted on a similar coarse-grained paper to that of No. 49 and is pointed out by Rajnai and Allthorpe as being very close in style.

[1]A late Cotman drawing called *Trowse Hythe* appears to be a view of the Wensum just before its confluence with the Yare, with Thorpe to the left, NCM 603.235.951. [2]BM 1859-5-28-116.

50 Snowdon, North Wales, *c.*1809-10

Watercolour, with some gum and with birds and waterfall scraped out, on white, wove paper; 23.7 × 36.4 ($9\frac{5}{16}$ × $14\frac{5}{16}$). INSCR: *Verso,* old backing paper (destroyed during removal, 1934) inscribed in pencil, ?in the artist's hand, *Peny / Sike / £.* PROV: George Holmes by 1874; his sale, Christie's, 25 April 1903, lot 2 as *Schellian* (sic), *Perthshire,* bt. Boswell on behalf of R. J. Colman 32 gns.; R. J. Colman Bequest 1946. (136.217.947). EXH: Norwich 1874 (160) as *Mountain Scenery, Perthshire* and Norwich, Art Circle 1888 (7) as *Schehallion in Perthshire* lent by George Holmes; Norwich 1945 and Norwich, Arts Council 1947 (6) as *Snowdon.* REF: Rajnai & Allthorpe No. 90; Jacobs & Warner 1980 repro. pp. WA2-3.

The poor condition of this watercolour makes it difficult to be certain in placing it with similar works of the same conjectural date, such as No. 51. Rajnai and Allthorpe have also remarked that the smooth paper is not characteristic of this period. The present title is based upon the similarity of the scene to that in an inscribed pencil sketch[1] which almost certainly shows a view of Snowdon.

Cotman exhibited views of Snowdon three times with the Norwich Society: in 1808 (186) *Snowdon, North Wales,* in 1810 (140) *View of*

Snowdon, from the lake of Llanberris, North Wales and in 1824 (74) *Snowdon with the Lake of Llanberris, from Dolbadden Castle, North Wales.*[2] The choice of viewpoint, while close to some of John Varley's views of Snowdon, was probably influenced by the oils of the subject by Richard Wilson.

[1]Rajnai & Allthorpe No. 89. [2]This is presumed to be the watercolour in the Mackintosh collection, repro. Rienaecker pl. 11 fig. 17.

51 Mountain Scene in Wales, 1810

illustrated in colour on p. 64

Watercolour and some gum, with birds scraped out, on cream, wove paper; 23.9 × 33.7 ($9\frac{3}{8}$ × $13\frac{1}{4}$). INSCR: *Recto,* signed in blue watercolour l.r. *J. S. Cotman; verso,* inscribed and dated in pencil, ?in the artist's hand, *From / P.S.M. / 1810.* PROV: See No. 40 (143.217.947). EXH: Norwich 1945; Norwich, Arts Council, 1947 (9). REF: Rajnai & Allthorpe No. 91.

It is suggested by Rajnai and Allthorpe that if the inscription on the *verso* of this watercolour is indeed autograph, it can be established not only that the date is 1810, but also that it may derive from a sketch by Munn. This assumes that the initials PSM stand for Paul Sandby Munn, in the company of whom Cotman probably made his second tour to Wales in 1802 (see section 2).

Apart from the Snowdon subjects (see No. 50) Cotman exhibited two additional Welsh scenes with the Norwich Society, in 1808 (199) *Llynn Ogwen, North Wales,* and in 1809 (206*) *Near Llanwryst, N. Wales.*

52 Durham Castle and Cathedral, *c.*1809-10

illustrated in colour on p. 61

Pencil and watercolour with some gum on cream, wove paper; 31.9 × 53.4 ($12\frac{9}{16}$ × 21). *Verso,* sketch in pencil of a landscape with figure and foliage, the left half framed with pencil lines. INSCR: *Verso,* illegible faint florid inscription in pencil. PROV: ?Cotman's sale, Christie's, 17-18 May 1843, 2nd day, lot 188 *Durham Cathedral* and a river scene, bt. Lukyn 4/-; William Bircham sale, Reepham, Norfolk, 4-5 Oct. 1883, lot 41 *Durham Cathedral,* bt. for J. J. Colman 9 gns.; his bequest to R. J. Colman 1898; R. J. Colman Bequest 1946. (127.217.947). EXH: ?Norwich Society 1810 (121) as *Durham Castle and cathedral;* ?APW 1810 (201) as *Durham Cathedral;* Norwich 1885 (326); Norwich, Arts Circle 1888 (13); BFAC 1888 (4); Norwich 1902 (217); Norwich 1903 (10); Manchester 1912 (322); Tate 1922 (42); Norwich 1945; Norwich, Arts Council 1947 (2). REF: Kitson 1937 pp. 51, 52; Rajnai & Allthorpe No. 92.

No. 52 is a view of the Castle and Cathedral from the north-west, which includes Framwellgate bridge as a key element of a powerful composition. The darkened tone of the picture is due partly to restoration[1] and also to the fading of the original blues.

Cotman made at least five drawings of the Cathedral and exhibited the subject four times. These must all derive from his visit to Durham in the summer of 1805. He was at first reluctant to go there, writing to Francis Cholmeley on 29 August: '. . . She [Mrs. Cholmeley] insists on my storming Durham . . . But seriously what have I to do with Durham? Am I to place it on my Studies of trees like a rookery. No and besides I have no time for Durham I want to get to Ray Wood—Durham I may take next Year as I most probably shall be at the Lakes and at Rokeby too . . .' Nevertheless he appears to have spent at least a week in the city and wrote to Francis Cholmeley from there on 6 September: 'It is a delightfully situated City — I have made but one outline since I've been here to my shame but I hope to be more industrious . . .'

Rajnai and Allthorpe suggest that No. 52 was Cotman's exhibit with the Norwich Society in 1810 (121) and with the Associated Painters in Watercolour, also in 1810 (201).

Four other views of this subject by Cotman are known: one is recorded by Dickes;[2] a monochrome study[3] of the bridge and cathedral is in the Tate Gallery, London; a more distant view[4] of No. 52 is held by the British Museum; and a magnificent view[5] from the south-east is in the same collection. Rajnai and Allthorpe suggest that the latter was Cotman's exhibit at the Royal Academy in 1806 (461) and with the Norwich Society in 1807 (18).

There is also a pencil study[6] and a watercolour[7] of the single-arched bridge at Durham. The watercolour may have been Cotman's exhibit with the Norwich Society in 1807 (47) entitled *Durham.*[8]

[1]Kennedy North, *Report* No. 6 states 'this drawing had been very heavily chalked'. [2]Dickes p. 263. [3]Tate 3634. [4]BM 1950-2-11-1. [5]BM 1859-5-28-119. [6]Fitzwilliam Museum, Cambridge, repro. Rienaecker pl. 22 fig. 39. [7]Bacon Collection, repro. Rienaecker pl. 22 fig. 38. [8]A watercolour called *A Church near Durham,* subject of Popham No. 329, was exhibited at the Tate 1922 (62).

53 Harlech Castle, North Wales, *c.*1809-10

called *Landscape, Wales*

illustrated on opposite page

Pencil and watercolour with some gum on cream, wove paper; 33.1 × 52.7 (13 × $20\frac{11}{16}$). INSCR: *Verso,* inscribed in pencil, not in the artist's hand, l.r. *Wales.* PROV: ?The Palser Gallery; ?bt. from them by Percy Moore Turner, March 1926; bt. from him by R. J. Colman March 1926; R. J. Colman Bequest 1946. (163.235.951). EXH: ?Norwich Society 1810 (59) or (161); Norwich 1945. REF: Rajnai & Allthorpe No. 93.

In this well preserved watercolour Cotman shows an awareness of the classical landscape tradition, but subserves it to his own idiosyncratic vision.

A splendid exhibition piece, comparable in scale to *Classical Landscape,* No. 55, *Harlech Castle, North Wales* was probably one of Cotman's two exhibits with the Norwich Society in 1810.[1] The composition almost certainly derives from drawings made on his first Welsh tour, when he sketched the southern aspect of Harlech in July 1800. (See Nos. 11 and 12; 186 and 187).

[1]See EXH.

54 Kirby Bedon Tower, Norfolk, *c.*1809-10

illustrated in colour on p. 97

Pencil and watercolour with some gum and with birds scraped out on cream, wove paper; 39.6 × 32.2 ($15\frac{5}{8}$ × $12\frac{5}{8}$). *Verso,* sketch in pencil of the composition in reverse of *Gilling Castle* (No. 43), bearing some watercolour. PROV: See No. 5. (147.217.947). EXH: ?Norwich Society 1810 (43); ?London, Paterson Gallery 1913 (63) as *Kirby Beedon, Norfolk;* Norwich 1945; Norwich, Arts Council 1947 (13). REF: Kitson 1937 p. 74 n.1 (title misprinted); Rajnai 1978 repro. in colour; Rajnai & Allthorpe No. 54.

This watercolour, which is in excellent condition, represents the tower of St. Andrew's Church in the village of Kirby Bedon, three miles to the south-east of Norwich. Rajnai and Allthorpe observe that: 'The figure group reappears in one of the 1811 etchings[1] and the stance of the seated man is imitated in one of the boys in the foreground of *Classical Landscape* [No. 55]. In the palette used, in the intensity of colours and more especially in the treatment of the sky, it is very close to [No. 62] of the same date'. Cotman shows a view of the tower from the south-west, but omits the body of the church.

No. 54 could well be Cotman's exhibit with the Norwich Society in 1810 (43) *Kirby Bedon tower.* There is also a smaller watercolour version[1] at Sheffield. Cotman exhibited the subject again at the Norwich Society in 1824 (89*) *Frame containing Tower of Kirby Bedon Church and Ruins at Llantissilio, North Wales.*[2]

[1]Popham No. 9. [2]Drawing Copy No. 1678, Graves Art Gallery, Sheffield. [3]There are two copies by pupils: (a) by Mrs. Dawson Turner, in the Ashmolean; (b) by an unknown hand, NCM 20.749.966.

55 Classical Landscape, *c.*1809-10

illustrated on opposite page

Pencil and watercolour on cream, wove paper; 44 × 59 ($17\frac{5}{16}$ × $23\frac{3}{16}$). INSCR: *Recto,* indistinctly ?signed in pencil l.r. *Cotman.* PROV: ?Forster sale 1922; Tooths; the Palser Gallery by 1923; bt. from them by Frank W. Keen; his sale, Christie's, 10 Nov. 1933, lot 81, bt. for R. J. Colman by Percy Moore Turner £273; R. J. Colman Bequest 1946. (160.217.947). EXH: Norwich 1945; Norwich, Arts Council 1947

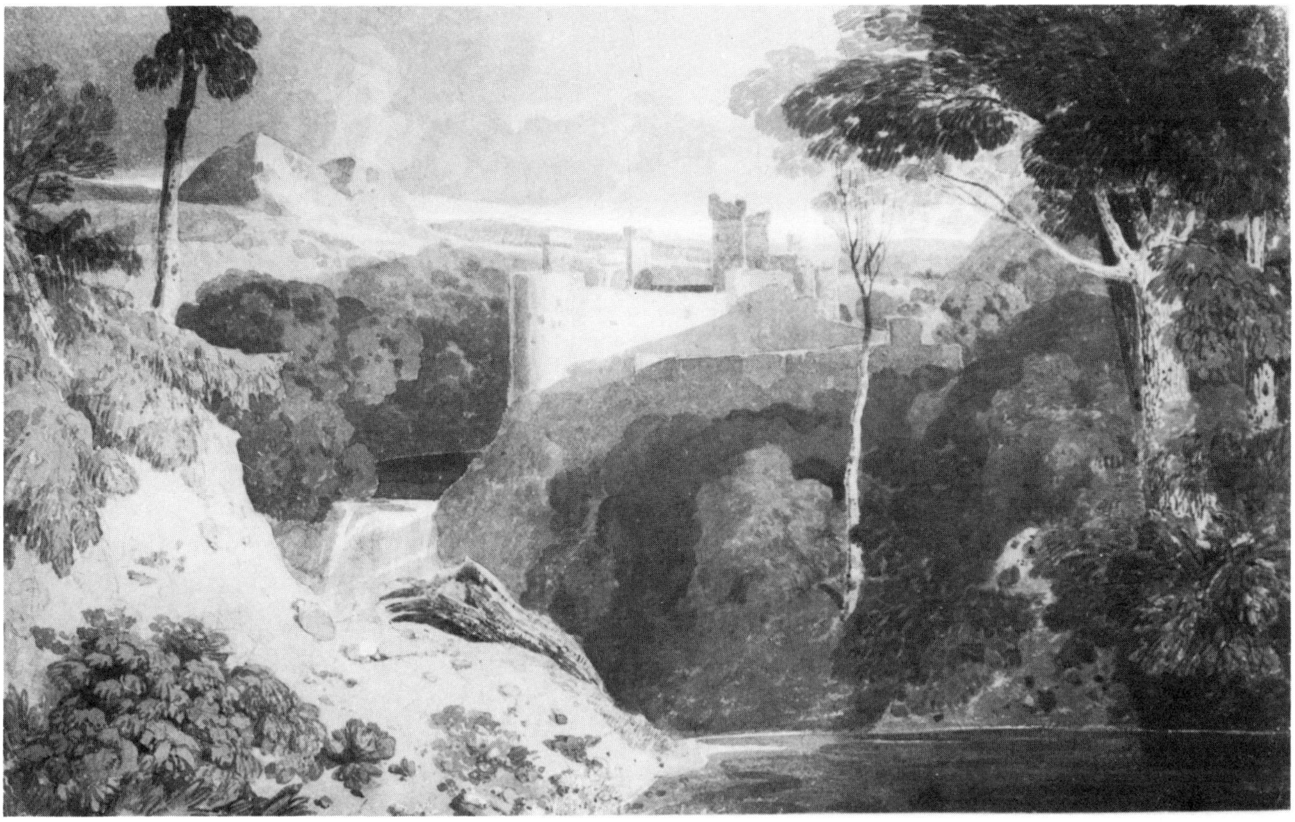

53 Harlech Castle, North Wales, *c.*1809-10

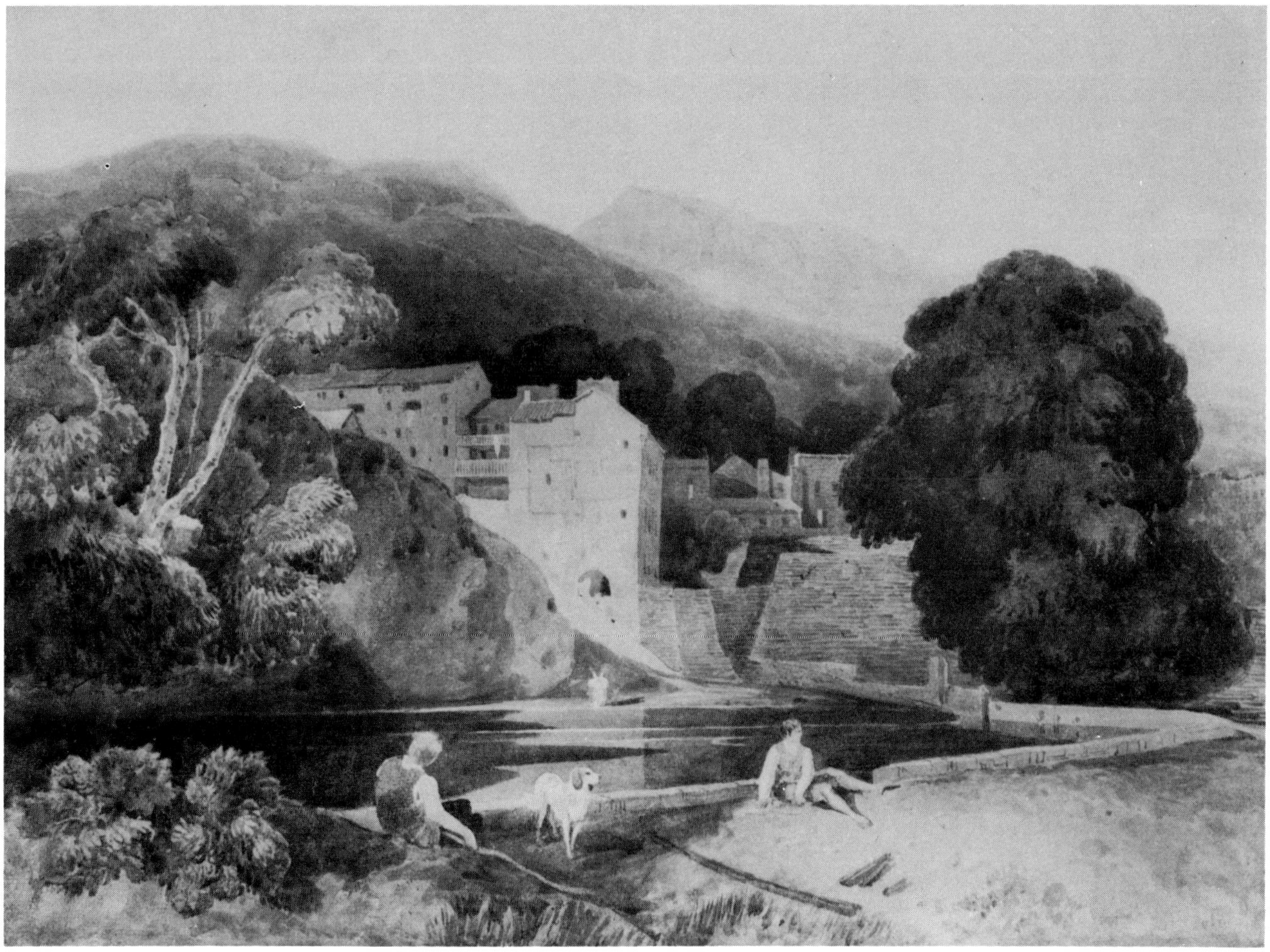

55 Classical Landscape, *c.*1809-10

(18). REF: Kitson 1937 pp. 74, 124; Rajnai & Allthorpe No. 95.

Like *Harlech Castle, North Wales,* No. 53, this richly-coloured composition again reveals Cotman's adaptation of his highly personal style to a traditional mode of landscape representation. Rajnai and Allthorpe point out that No. 55 is also partly derived from two drawings of a Welsh farmhouse scene.[1] They also suggest that it was exhibited in 1810, either as *Composition* with the Norwich Society (67) or as one of two works called *Landscape Composition* exhibited in London with the Associated Painters in Watercolour (83 and 140).

No. 55 relates to two early oils, *Classical Landscape Composition* in the Bacon collection and *The Judgement of Midas* (No. 149), both of which demonstrate the influence of Gaspar Poussin. Cotman was to develop similar classically-inspired compositions in his series of soft-ground etchings for the *Liber Studiorum.* In 1824 he exhibited with the Norwich Society (171) *A Landscape, with the Fable of the Judgement of Midas* (based on the oil), and a *View of Whitby, Yorkshire, part of a Series of Designs intended to illustrate a Work now publishing on Landscape Composition.* The latter plate, *Whitby,*[2] is closely related to the composition of *Classical Landscape.*

[1]Rajnai & Allthorpe No. 4 [2]*Liber Studiorum* pl. 22, Popham No. 316. A pencil drawing for the etching, in reverse of the plate, is NCM 612.235.951.

56 Cheyne Walk, London, *c.*1809-10

Pencil and watercolour with some gum on cream, wove paper; 23.5 × 29.8 ($9\frac{1}{4} \times 11\frac{3}{4}$). INSCR: *Recto,* numbered and signed in brown watercolour 1.1. *1053* and l.l.c. *J. S. Cotman; verso,* numbered in brown ink centre 453, the inner mount was formerly inscribed *Twickenham.* PROV: J. J. Cotman; purchased from him by Mr. Kent; bt. from him by James Reeve by 1888; bt. from him by H. S. Theobald, ?after 1903; bt. from him by R. J. Colman, Feb. 1910; R. J. Colman Bequest 1946. (164.217.947). EXH: As *Twickenham:* Norwich, Art Circle 1888 (53); BFAC 1888 (10); RA 1891 (69); Norwich 1903 (6) lent by James Reeve; Manchester 1912 (341); Tate 1922 (37); RA 1934 (726, Commemorative Catalogue 815). As *Cheyne Walk, London:* Norwich 1945; Norwich, Arts Council 1947 (19). REF: Kitson 1937 pp. 110, 111, 168, 370, pl. 51; Rajnai & Allthorpe No. 97.

This attractive watercolour is closely based on a pencil study inscribed *Chany Walk,*[1] also in the collection at Norwich. Although Kitson suggested a date of *c.*1807-8, Rajnai and Allthorpe observe that *Cheyne Walk*[2] 'accords well with watercolours of the period, *c.*1809-10, even though the palette is lighter and the handling looser than most. The foreground with its 'scumbled' texture, the brightly coloured figures in the middle distance, the rendering of the architecture and its foliate surrounds, compare surprisingly well with similar elements of the large *Classical Landscape* [No. 55], so different at first sight.'

Another London subject of this period is *Old Battersea Bridge*[3] which may well have been Cotman's exhibit with the Norwich Society in 1810 (138), *North End of Battersea Bridge.*

[1]Rajnai & Allthorpe No. 96. [2]A watercolour copy is in the V&A, P.178.1929, and a crude copy in oil was with Leggatt in 1925. [3]Bacon collection No. 672; a copy of this drawing is in the Spooner Collection, Courtauld Institute Galleries.

57 Castle by Water, *c.*1809-10

called *Ranza Castle*

illustrated in colour on p. 99

Pencil and watercolour, with some scraping out, on cream, wove paper; 26.4 × 20.8 ($10\frac{3}{8} \times 8\frac{3}{16}$). PROV: Percy Moore Turner; presented by him to R. J. Colman 1937; R. J. Colman Bequest 1946. (232.235.951). EXH: Norwich 1945. REF: Kitson 1937 p. 126; Rajnai & Allthorpe No. 98.

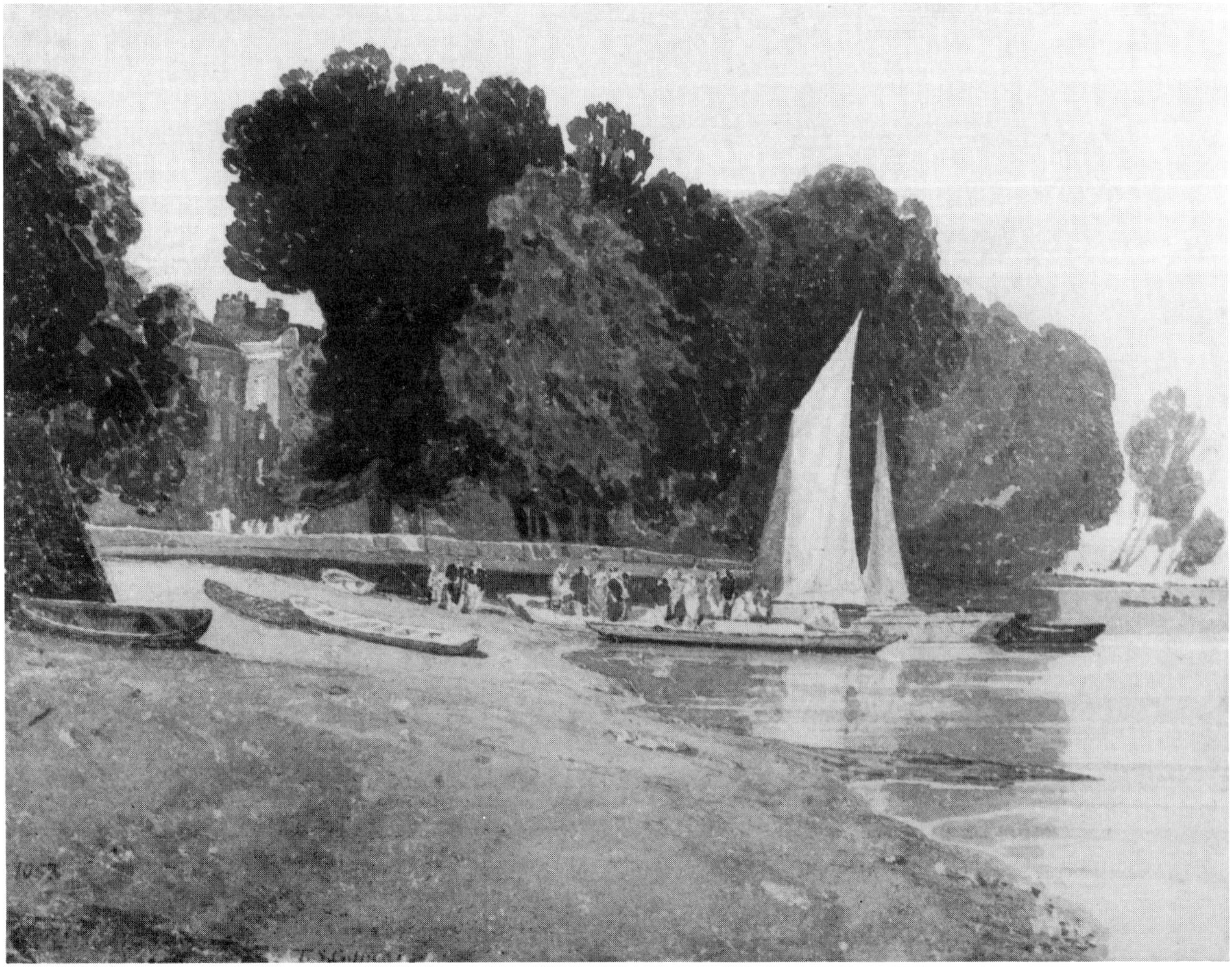

56 Cheyne Walk, London, *c.*1809-10

While Rajnai and Allthorpe point out that the colouring and the treatment of the sky of *Castle by Water* place it close to such works as *Ketts Castle, Norwich,* No. 58, they observe that it probably derives from an imaginative treatment of 'a print of Lochranza Castle which has two square towers and is set dramatically on a rock jutting into the northern bay of the Isle of Arran'. Cotman did not travel to Scotland[1] and as Kitson commented,[2] Cotman was not averse to 'invent[ing] Castles'. An imaginative treatment would certainly be consistent with the air of conjured subtlety evoked by the vibrant washes.

[1]For other Scottish subjects in Cotman's work, see Rajnai & Allthorpe No. 98, n.4. [2]Kitson 1937 p. 127.

58 Kett's Castle, Norwich, *c.*1809-10

illustrated below and in colour on front cover

Pencil and watercolour on cream, wove paper; 22.1 × 32.5 ($8\frac{11}{16}$ × $12\frac{13}{16}$). *Verso,* sketch in pencil of sailing boat on a choppy sea. PROV: See No. 5. (144.217.947). EXH: ?Norwich Society 1810 (175); Norwich 1945; Norwich, Arts Council 1947 (10). REF: Kitson 1937 p. 113, pl. 45; Rajnai & Allthorpe No. 100.

The schematic, abstract forms of this exquisite watercolour recall those of No. 57 but are closely based on a small pencil sketch[1] also at Norwich. No. 58 was almost certainly exhibited with the Norwich Society in 1810 (175) *Kett's Castle.*

Kett's Castle was the local name for the ruins of St. Michael's Chapel on Mousehold Heath. Blomefield describes the chapel as situated 'on the Brow of the Hill, on the North Side of the Road just out of *Bishop's* Gate: the Ruins of it are still [1745] visible and 'tis called KETT'S *Castle,* because it was the Place of Rendezvous of that Arch-Rebel.'[2]

[1]Rajnai & Allthorpe No. 99. [2]Blomefield's *Norfolk,* second edition, Vol. IV 1806 p. 426, first edition p. 797.

59 The Marl Pit, *c.*1809-10

illustrated on p. 42

Pencil and watercolour with some gum on cream, wove paper; 29.5 × 25.8 ($11\frac{5}{8}$ × $10\frac{1}{8}$). PROV: See No. 5 (154.217.947). EXH: Brussels 1929 (40); Norwich 1945; Norwich, Arts Council 1947 (15). REF: Kitson 1937 p. 122; Rajnai & Allthorpe No. 101.

This is one of the most successful and fascinating of all Cotman's works, in which a superbly patterned composition is achieved through a sensitive balance of light and shade, colour and shape.

Although the precise location of the scene is unknown, there were several marl pits in the Norwich area, one of which, *Whitlingham,* is the subject of a late Cotman watercolour at Norwich.[1] Rajnai and Allthorpe point out that a similar cloud to that in No. 59 can be seen in an earlier version of *Greta Bridge* in the British Museum,[2] while the two goats are based on a pencil sketch at Leeds[3] and also appear in a drawing of Moreton Hall of *c.*1808.[4]

It is typical of Cotman that the subtle patterning of quasi-abstract forms that constitute this image of harmony in fact derive from his close observation of and recordings of reality.

[1]NCM 214.235.951. [2]See No. 60. [3]Leeds 9.342/49. [4]Etched by John Smith and published 1 Oct. 1888 for Britton's *Architectural Antiquities* Vol. 2 opp. p. 82. See No. 147.

60 Greta Bridge, Yorkshire, 1810

illustrated in colour on p. 61

Pencil and watercolour with some gum, birds scraped out, on cream, wove paper; 30 × 50.1 ($11\frac{13}{16}$ × $19\frac{3}{4}$). INSCR: *Recto,* signed and dated in brown watercolour l.l. *J S Cotman / 1810.* PROV: ?Francis Stone, his sale, Spelman, Norwich, 19-23 Oct. 1835, 5th day, lot 124 *Greta Bridge, Yorkshire (no frame),* or ?David Wilkie, RA his sale, Christie's, 11-12 May 1836, 1st day, lot 29 *Greta bridge,* 8/-; Mr. Davis, London; bt. from him by James Reeve by 1903; bt. from him by H. S. Theobald; bt. from him by R. J. Colman, Feb. 1910; R. J. Colman Bequest 1946. (159.217.947). EXH: Norwich 1903 (15) as *On the Greta, Yorkshire* lent by James Reeve; Manchester 1912 (325); Tate 1922 (24); Norwich 1945; Norwich, Arts Council 1947 (17). REF: Kitson 1937 pp. 124, 370; Rajnai 1978 repro. in colour; Rajnai & Allthorpe No. 107; *RSA Journal* Aug. 1979 pp. 597, 598, repro. p. 597; Jacob & Warner 1980, repro. p. NH13 in colour.

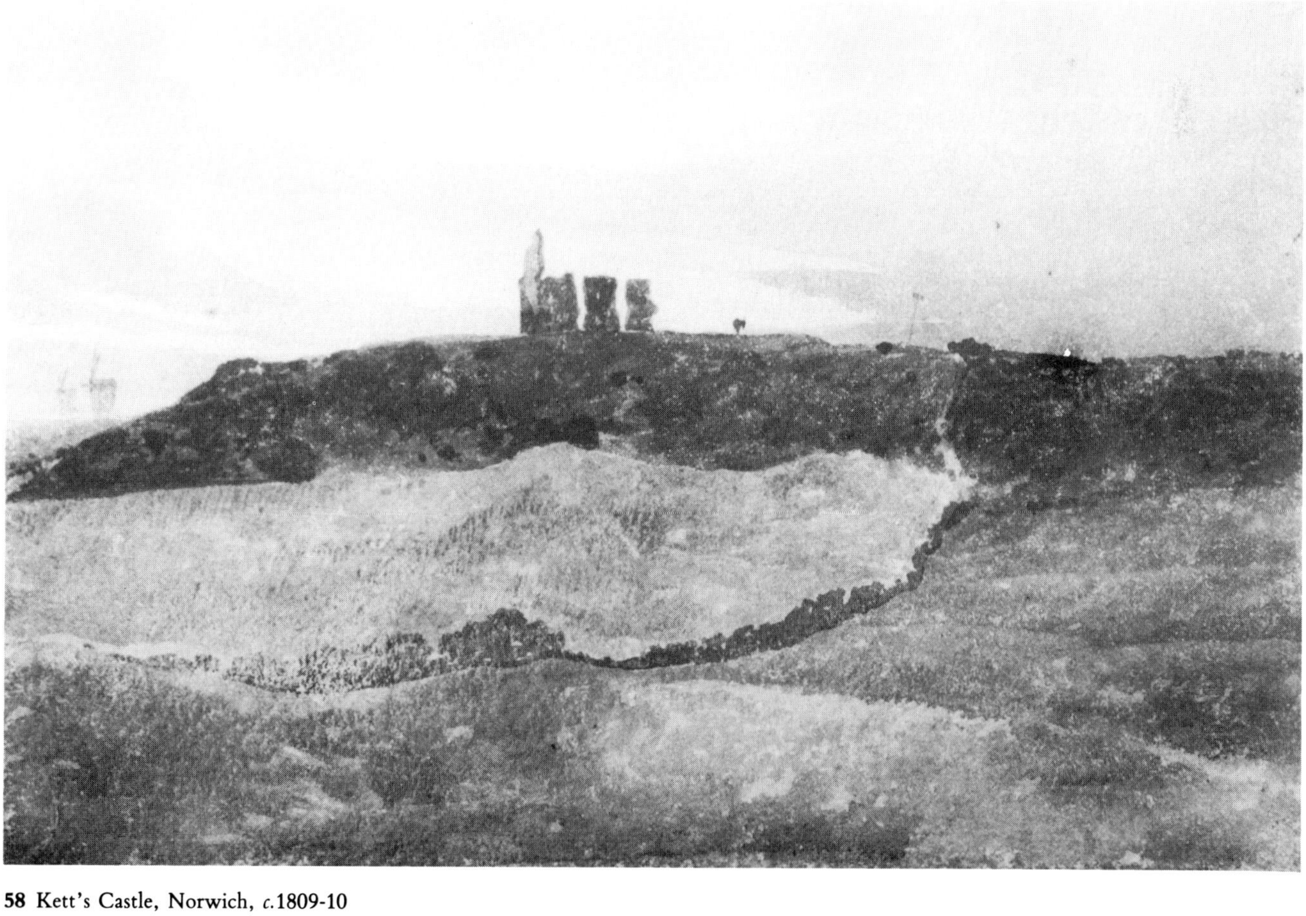

58 Kett's Castle, Norwich, *c.*1809-10

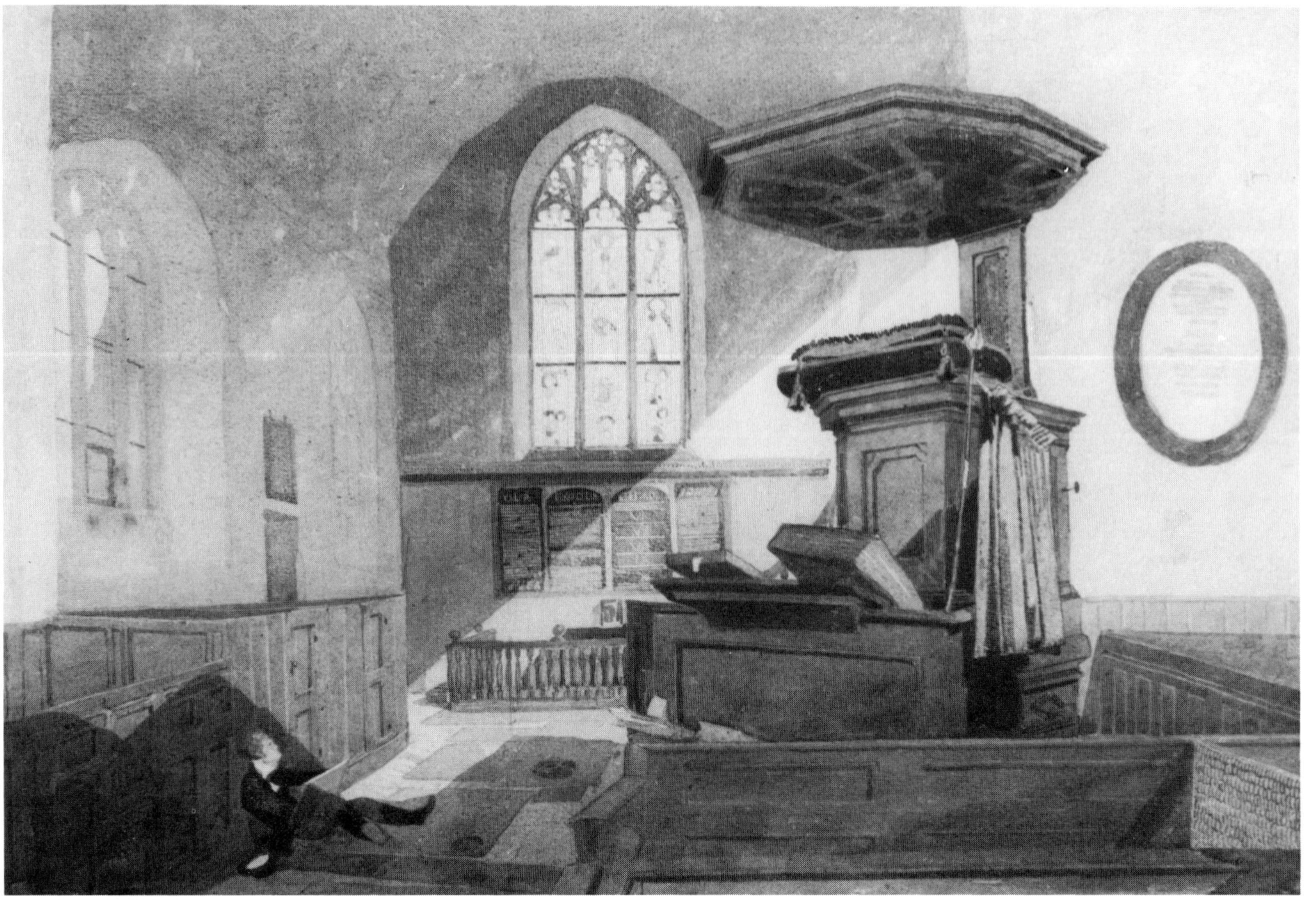

61 Interior of St. Peter Hungate Church, Norwich, 1810

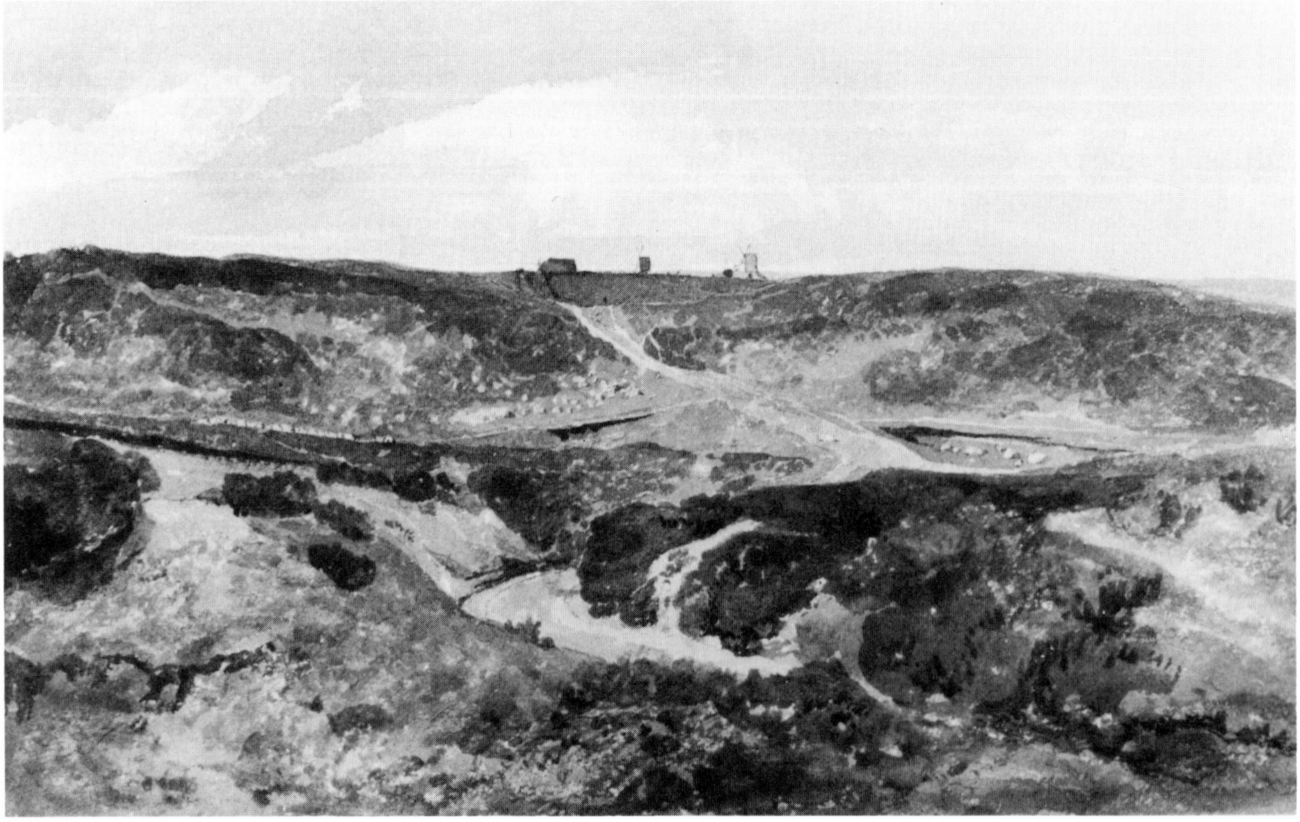

63 Mousehold Heath, Norwich, *c.*1810

This watercolour derives from the period of Cotman's visit to Rokeby in the summer of 1805. Greta Bridge spans the river at the south gates of Rokeby Park and it was at the inn by the bridge that Cotman stayed after leaving the house towards the end of August (see Section 4).

This superbly balanced composition, recalling scenes that are associated with one of the most fruitful periods of Cotman's artistic life, has provoked divergent reactions in Cotman scholars. Kitson criticised the work for being derived from Old Masters and devoid of an immediate emotional response to Nature. One writer regarded the work as a 'rank failure'[1] while Rienaecker, on the other hand, considered that Cotman 'never exceeded his achievement in Russell Colman's version of Greta Bridge which is the very bones and structure of his whole life work'.[2] Rajnai and Allthorpe conclude that the work is both 'masterly' in design and authoritative in its exploitation of watercolour as a medium. Despite this conflict of opinion it should not be regarded as inferior to the smaller watercolour version[3] of the same scene, *c.*1806-7, in the British Museum.

Neither of these two versions of the bridge appears to have been exhibited. A small pencil study[4] of the scene is in the British Museum and a watercolour,[5] probably *Distant View of Greta Bridge, Yorkshire* exhibited at the Royal Academy 1806 (494), is in the collection of the Tate Gallery, London.

[1]D. S. MacColl, *The Saturday Review* 15 April 1922. [2]Rienaecker p. 35. [3]BM 1902-5-14-17. [4]BM 1902-5-14-76. [5]Tate 3633.

61 Interior of St. Peter Hungate Church, Norwich, 1810

illustrated on opposite page

Pencil and watercolour with some gum on cream, wove paper; 33.7 × 48.1 ($13\frac{1}{4}$ × $18\frac{15}{16}$). INSCR: *Verso,* signed and dated in pencil c. from lower to upper edge *JSC / 1810.* PROV: Thomas Wells by 1888; by descent to Helen A. Wells by 1902; her sale, Spelman, Norwich, 2-3 March 1916, lot 176, bt. Boswell for R. J. Colman 20 gns.; R. J. Colman Bequest 1946. (137.217.947). EXH: Norwich, Art Circle 1888 (61) and BFAC 1888 (24) lent by Thomas Wells; Norwich 1902 (221) and Norwich 1903 (35) lent by Miss Wells; Norwich 1945; Norwich, Arts Council 1947 (7). REF: Rajnai & Allthorpe No. 108.

St. Peter Hungate church is situated at the west end of Prince's Street, at the top of Elm Hill, Norwich, only a short distance from Cotman's residence at the time. This watercolour is a view of the chancel, looking towards the east window and is one of Cotman's most successful church interiors, comparable with that of No. 39, *Interior of Trentham Church, Staffordshire.* The imposing pulpit achieves a monumental stature within the composition, acting as a focal point for the stunning correlation of washes, unified by the diagonal of the streaming sunlight.

Since 1933 the church has acted as a museum of church art.

62 Mousehold Heath, Norwich, *c.*1810

called *Heath Scene*

illustrated in colour on p. 64.

Pencil and watercolour on cream, wove paper in two pieces joined centre; 30.3 × 46.4 ($11\frac{15}{16}$ × $18\frac{1}{4}$). PROV: See No. 30,[1] (145.217.947). EXH: RA 1934 (724, Commemorative Catalogue 818) lent by R. J. Colman; Norwich 1945. REF: Rajnai & Allthorpe No. 109; Jacobs & Warner 1980 repro. pp. EA 20-21 in colour.

Mousehold Heath, which at the end of the eighteenth century was six miles long and three miles wide, was a popular subject with the Norwich artists and a favourite with Cotman himself. He exhibited the subject four times: with the Norwich Society in 1809 (181) *View on Mousehold Heath* and in 1810 (54, 60) both called *Mousehold Heath* and also with the Associated Painters in Watercolours in the same year (5) *A Mill on Mousehold Heath, near Norwich.*

Rajnai and Allthorpe relate No. 62, in terms of its depth of colour and use of foreground figures to emphasize scale, to *Old Tower, Kirby Bedon,* No. 54.

A contemporary version[2] of the same scene is in the British Museum, as is a preparatory pencil study[3] dated 20 April 1810. A third watercolour of the Heath is No. 63. Cotman was to return with great enthusiasm to the subject of Mousehold Heath towards the end of his life (see No. 130) especially during his last trip to Norfolk in 1841 (see section 10).

[1]Either this drawing or No. 63 was included with Colman's purchase of No. 30 from Percy Moore Turner, 22 April 1926. Colman made a further purchase from Turner on 27 April 1926 of eight Cotman watercolours including a *Mousehold Heath* (see No. 40). [2]BM 1902-5-14-20. [3]BM 1902-5-14-221.

63 Mousehold Heath, Norwich, *c.*1810

illustrated on opposite page

Pencil and watercolour on cream, wove paper; 28.5 × 44.5 ($11\frac{1}{4}$ × $17\frac{1}{2}$). INSCR: *Verso,* inscribed in pencil c., ?in the artist's hand, *Mousehold Heath / Norwich* (almost erased). PROV: See No. 62. (146.217.947). EXH: Norwich 1945; Norwich, Arts Council 1947 (12). REF: Rajnai & Allthorpe No. 110.

Rajnai and Allthorpe remark of this representation of Mousehold Heath: 'Executed on the rough textured paper used by Cotman at this time, [No. 63] is lighter in handling and colour than the other two versions of Mousehold Heath . . . [see previous entry]. The treatment of the sky is especially summary with its broad washes from a loaded brush. However the rough "scumbled" textures of the heath are more densely worked, the colours applied over a warm buff ground.'

They observe that the mottled effect in the foreground is similar to the foregrounds in Nos. 44 and 45, while the freshness of the green palette also recalls Nos. 48 and 49. It is therefore quite possible that this version could be earlier in date, making it eligible to be that work exhibited with the Norwich Society in 1809 (181), *View on Mousehold Heath.*

64 Cromer Church, Norfolk, *c.*1810-11

Pencil and grey wash on cream, wove paper; 29.9 × 21.9 ($11\frac{3}{4}$ × $8\frac{5}{8}$). PROV: See No. 38. (167.235.951). EXH: London, Walker's Galleries 1926 (48); Norwich 1930-31. REF: Kitson 1937 p. 174, pl. 64; Rajnai & Allthorpe No. 118.

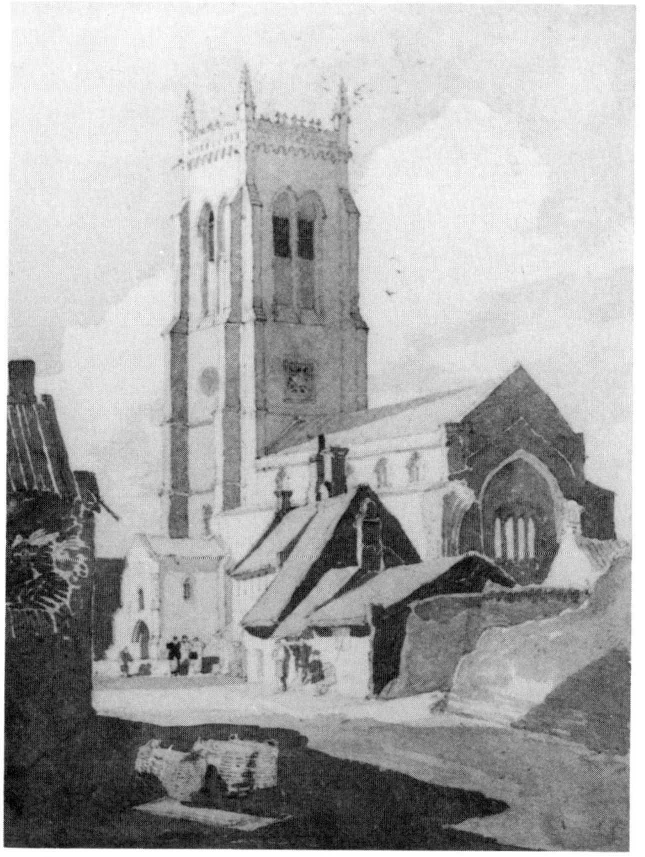

64 Cromer Church, Norfolk, *c.*1810-11

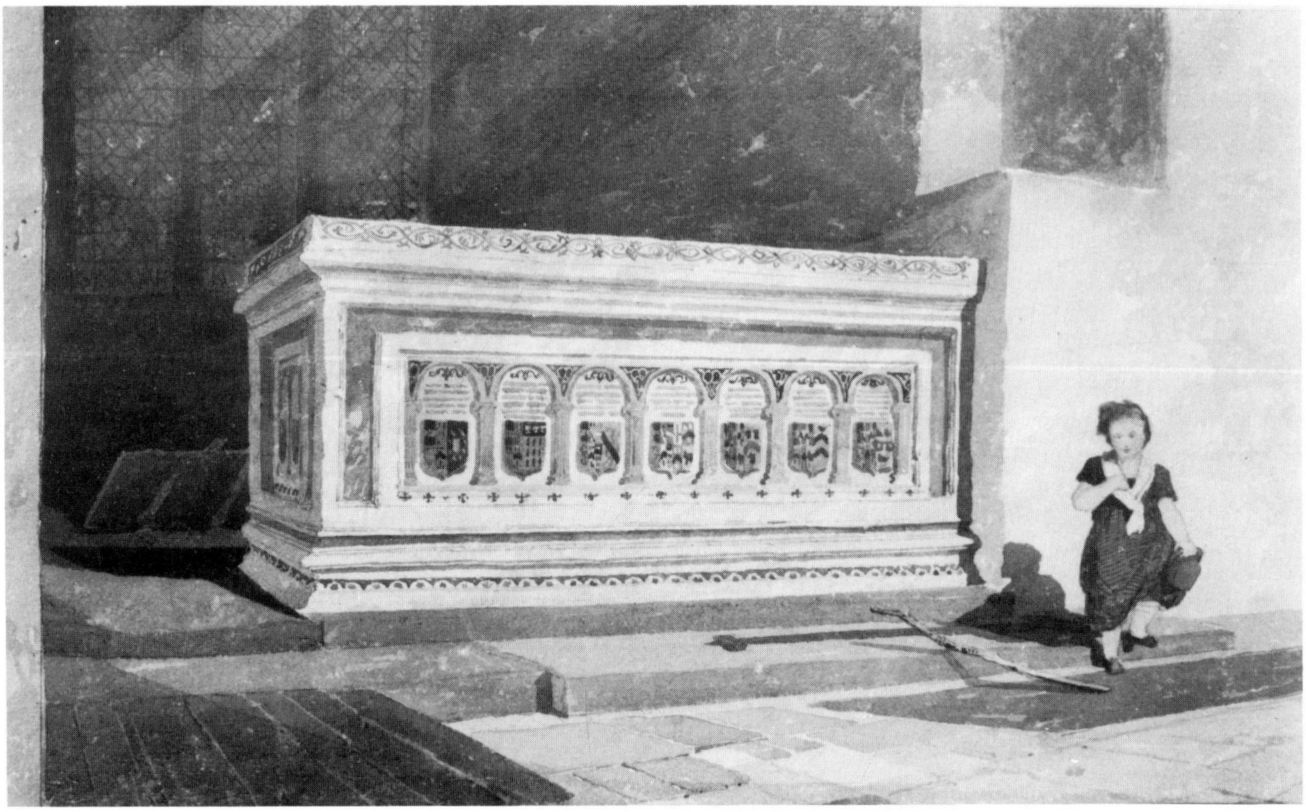

65 Tomb of Sir Edward Clere, Blickling Church, Norfolk, *c.*1810-11

By *c.*1810-11 Cotman had begun, at Dawson Turner's suggestion, to take drawings to illustrate Miller's edition of Blomefield's *Norfolk*. This monochrome of Cromer Church may have been made with this project in mind.[1]

The subject was familiar to Cotman as his wife's family lived at nearby Felbrigg. As Pevsner observes, the Church of St. Peter and Paul, Cromer is 'externally a very impressive church, the visual centre of what was once a prosperous little town. The tower is with its 160 ft. by far the tallest of any Norfolk parish church. It is moreover extremely lavishly detailed . . .'[2]

Cotman represented the subject twice more, taking a view from the west and the interior of the porch for *Excursions through Norfolk.*[3] See also No. 34[4] for an earlier Cromer subject.

[1] A copy by Mrs. Dawson Turner of No. 64 is in Dawson Turner's grangerised Blomefield in the BM. [2] Pevsner, *North-East Norfolk and Norwich* p. 118. [3] (a) Engraved by W. Wallis and published 1 July 1818, vol. 1 opp. p. 150; (b) Museum of Fine Arts, Boston, Massachusetts, USA, 62.756. Engraved by W. Deeble and published 1 July 1818, vol. 1 opp. p. 154. [4] He also drew the lighthouse at Cromer, Leeds 9.412/49. See also No. 151.

65 Tomb of Sir Edward Clere, Blickling Church, Norfolk, *c.*1810-11

Pencil and watercolour on cream, wove paper; 27.9 × 44.7 (11 × 17$\frac{5}{8}$). PROV: ?Rev. James Bulwer; by ?descent to his son J. R. Bulwer by 1888; by descent to his younger brother Walter Bulwer; by descent to his son Henry A. Bulwer; sold by him to Walker's Galleries; ?bt. from them by R. J. Colman, 13 July 1926, with four others, including Nos. 38 and 64 £393.15.0. (245.235.951). EXH: Norwich, Art Circle 1888 (56) and BFAC 1888 (21) as *Clere Tomb, Blickling Church,* lent by J. R. Bulwer; London, Walker's Galleries 1926 (43) as *The Clere Monument, Blickling Church, Norfolk.* REF: Rajnai & Allthorpe No. 119.

The tomb of Sir Edward Clere stands in St. Andrew's Church at Blickling, Norfolk and is 'a late Elizabethan tomb chest, now without its effigy. Against the chest sixteeen shields, under arches. They represent a faithful pedigree reaching back to 1066.'[1]

A second version of this composition, of similar size, is in the collection of Mr. Christopher Barker.[2] This is possibly lot 811 in Dawson Turner's sale 1859.[3]

Rajnai and Allthorpe comment that of the two known versions, No. 65 is 'deeper in palette and superior in draughtsmanship' and is executed on a rough textured paper characteristic of the period 1809-11. The subject indicates Cotman's developing interest in antiquarian subjects which was to encourage him to undertake the projects advocated by Dawson Turner. Cotman also painted an exterior view of the church — a watercolour known from a copy by Mrs. Dawson Turner in the Ashmolean.[4]

[1] Pevsner, *North-East Norfolk and Norwich* p. 96. [2] Tate 1922 (136) as *Boleyn Tomb in Blickling Church 1808,* possibly a copy by one of the Turner girls. [3] Cotman sale, 1861, lot 129 may represent another version. [4] Other Blickling subjects include (a) *South View of Blickling Hall,* Fitzwilliam Museum Cambridge, engraved by J. Webb and published 1 March 1819, for *Excursions through Norfolk,* vol. 1 pp. 170-171; (b) *View of the west Front of Blickling Hall,* engraved by J. Greig and published 1 July 1818 for *Excursions through Norfolk* vol 1 opp. p. 170; (c) Tate 1922 (214) *Piscina in Blickling Church;* see also No. 143.

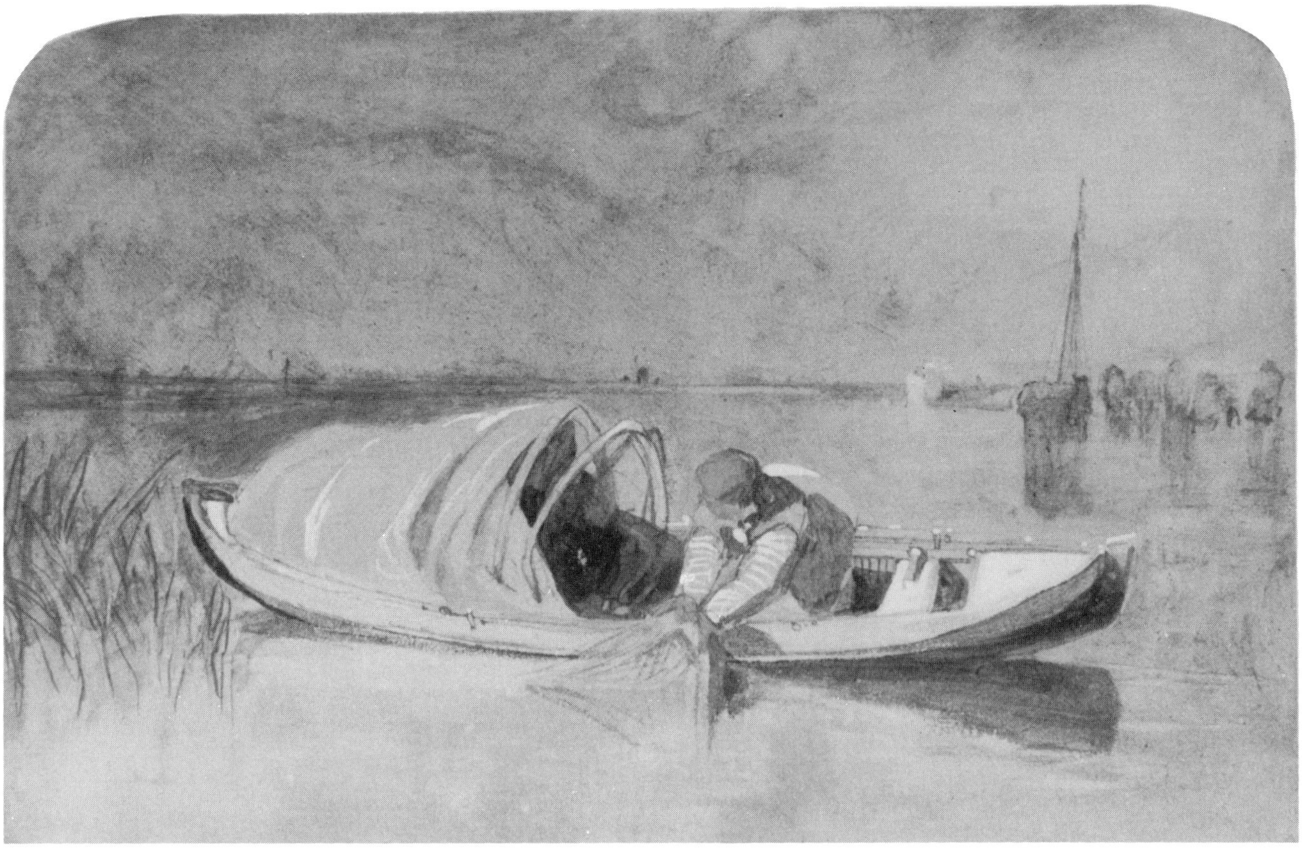

74 River Scene, *c.*1814

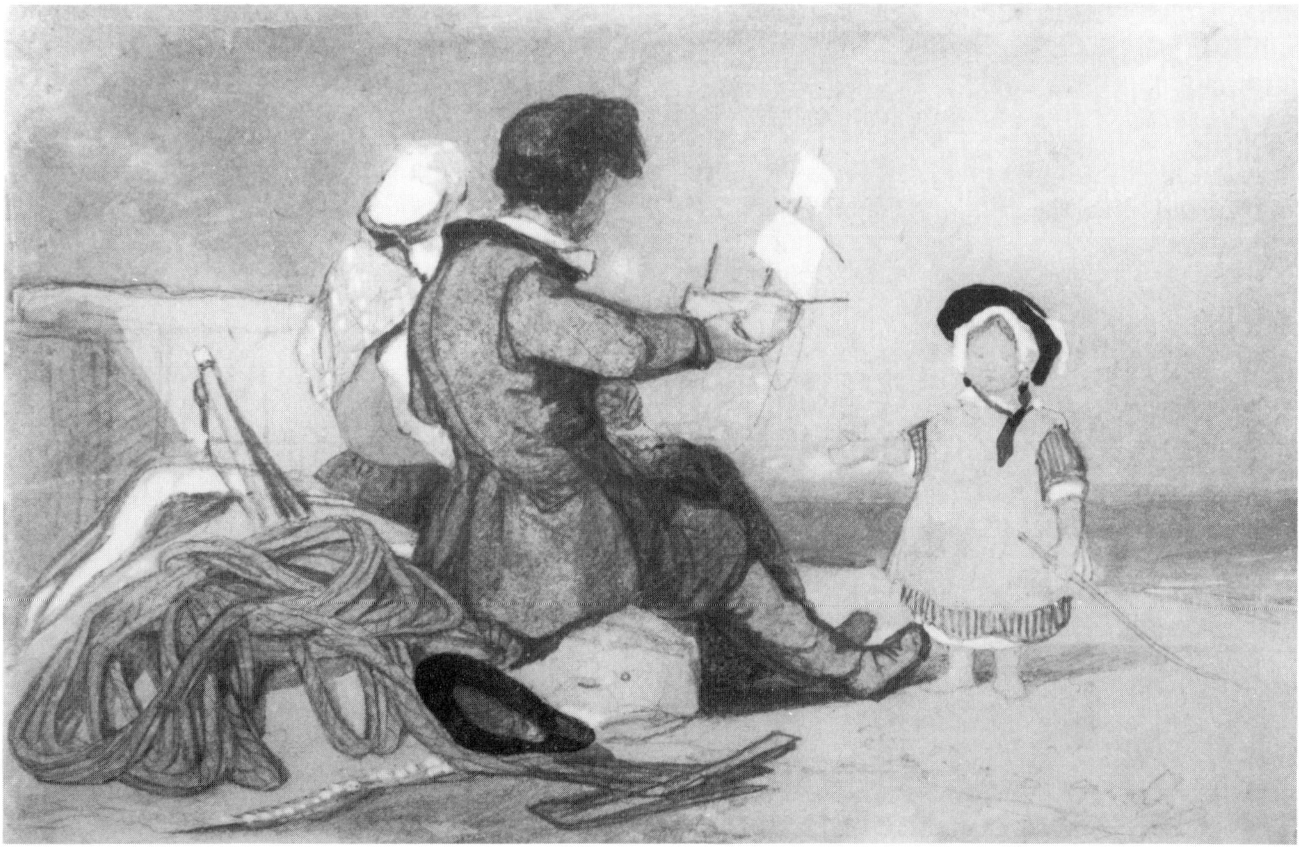

73 The Toy Ship, *c.*1814

6
The Change to Yarmouth and Archaeology 1811-1818

On 17 November 1810 the *Norwich Mercury* issued Cotman's first public announcement of his intention to publish, by subscription 'a collection of etchings in six numbers, consisting of picturesque specimens of Saxon, Norman and Gothic Architecture, Landscape, Shipping &c'. The etchings were recommended as 'a work of useful reference, both to the professional and to the amateur artist'. The wording of the advertisement was precisely that of a printed prospectus Cotman also sent to potential subscribers, including Francis Cholmeley.[1] In the event the last two categories proposed—landscape and shipping—were not included although there was one non-architectural subject, *Trees in Duncombe Park.*[2]

It is likely that this change in emphasis could have been influenced in part by the advice of Dawson Turner. Whilst still working on his first etching project, Cotman wrote to Dawson Turner on 10 February 1811 to inform him of a new idea and to seek his advice: 'This summer I am going to commence Etchings of all *Ornamented Antiquities* in Norfolk—and on this subject I shall be happy to receive any information that would lead me to proper subjects.'[3] Dawson Turner would undoubtedly have emphasised the potential value of architectural studies for the antiquary.

Cotman was well pleased with his new enterprise and was already working on other ideas by the end of February. He wrote to Francis Cholmeley on 28 February 1811: 'I have been doing several plates for other works, and shall do more as I am more known, so that my art is entirely changed'. On 5 June he was able to inform Cholmeley that the series of twenty-four etchings was complete. He added that he had been to London to see the exhibition of the Associated Painters in Water Colours, where the watercolours were 'not so good as former years, few sold, and the artists in despair'. For himself: 'I bless my stars at having now another [means] to support my family, save painting and drawing.'

The summer of 1811 was a busy time for Cotman. After a short tour in North Norfolk (Nos. 66, 67) and a visit to Yarmouth (Nos. 68, 69), he returned to Norwich to organise the distribution of his *Miscellaneous Etchings* and to attend the annual exhibition of the Norwich Society of Artists, of which he was now President. He himself exhibited thirty-four subjects, being drawings and etchings relating both to his *Miscellaneous Etchings* and his *Architectural Antiquities of Norfolk.* The day after the closing of the exhibition, Cotman again wrote to Dawson Turner,[4] seeking advice as to the best route to take for his next sketching tour in Norfolk (Nos. 70, 71).

While the influence of Dawson Turner upon Cotman at this time was both gradual and crucial, Cotman's own motivation should not be ignored. On 5 October 1811 Cotman issued an advertisement in the *Norwich Chronicle* of his intentions concerning the forthcoming *Specimens of Architectural Antiquities of Norfolk.* Of the list of 'conditions' set out, the third reveals the dichotomy inherent in Cotman's aims: 'Although it will be the principal object of the Author to exhibit faithfully the Styles of the various Structures, yet he will not be inattentive to the Selection of the most favourable points of view; being persuaded it will be the wish of his subscribers to see architectural fidelity combined with picturesque effect.' This summary of Cotman's intentions is supported by the works themselves.

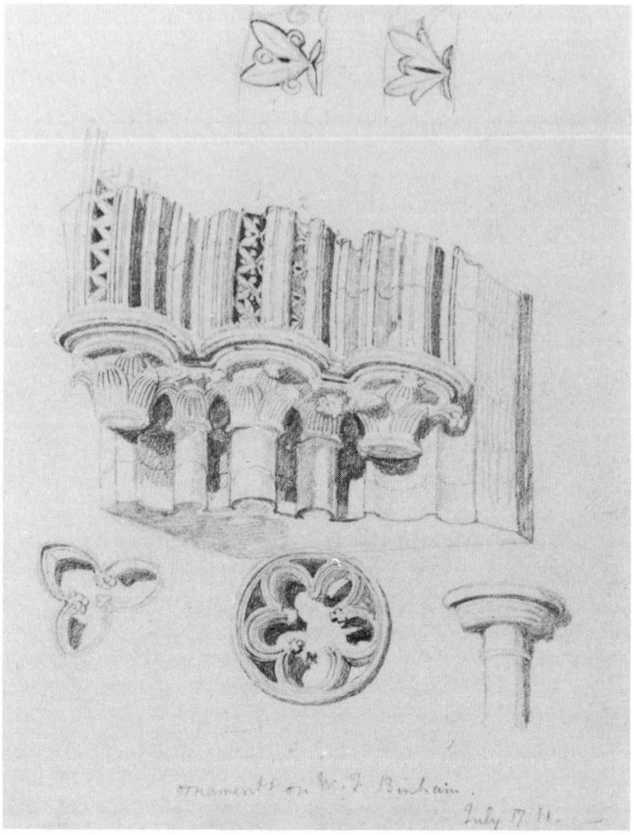

66 Ornaments on the West Front of Binham Priory, Norfolk, 1811

Cotman was not prostituting his talents by simply attempting to corner an antiquarian market, but rather responding to his own desire to combine an accurate representation of his subjects with his own sense of design, in a manner inspired by Piranesi (see section 12).

Dawson Turner, meanwhile, had determined to invite Cotman and his family to Yarmouth. Cotman's proven talents as a draughtsman, portraitist and drawing master, his recent demonstration of abilities as etcher of archaeological subject-matter and his obvious industry made his move to Yarmouth an attractive proposition to Turner. Cotman did not, however, leap at the opportunity, only gradually allowing himself to be persuaded. On 6 December 1811[5] he prevaricated by explaining that 'should my Norfolk work answer it would do away the cause of my residing at Yarmouth, particularly as I should not have time to dedicate to teaching. Then I should be sorry to remove to a house smaller than the one I am in now'. He was also concerned that his rent would be high, while he was determined to improve his own talents as an etcher 'having seen my first attempts approved of'. Nevertheless, he was later to admit that 'I had rather come than stay away'.[6] On 17 December[7] he confirmed that he would come providing a suitably 'pleasant and respectable' house could be found: 'In the meantime can you inform me the nature of teaching at Yarmouth, as I am a perfect stranger to teaching school-fashion? Saving for the best Scholars it's but a sorry drudgery and only calculated for

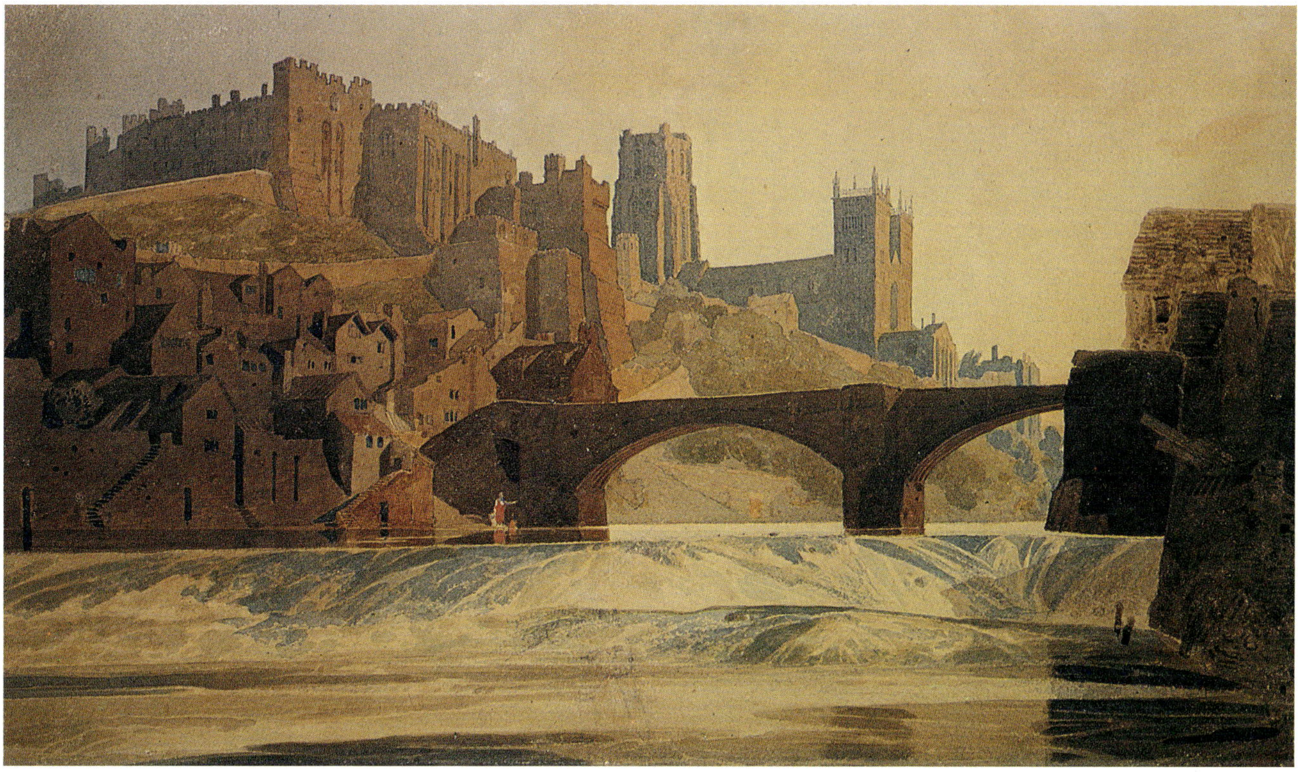

52 Durham Castle and Cathedral, *c.*1809-10

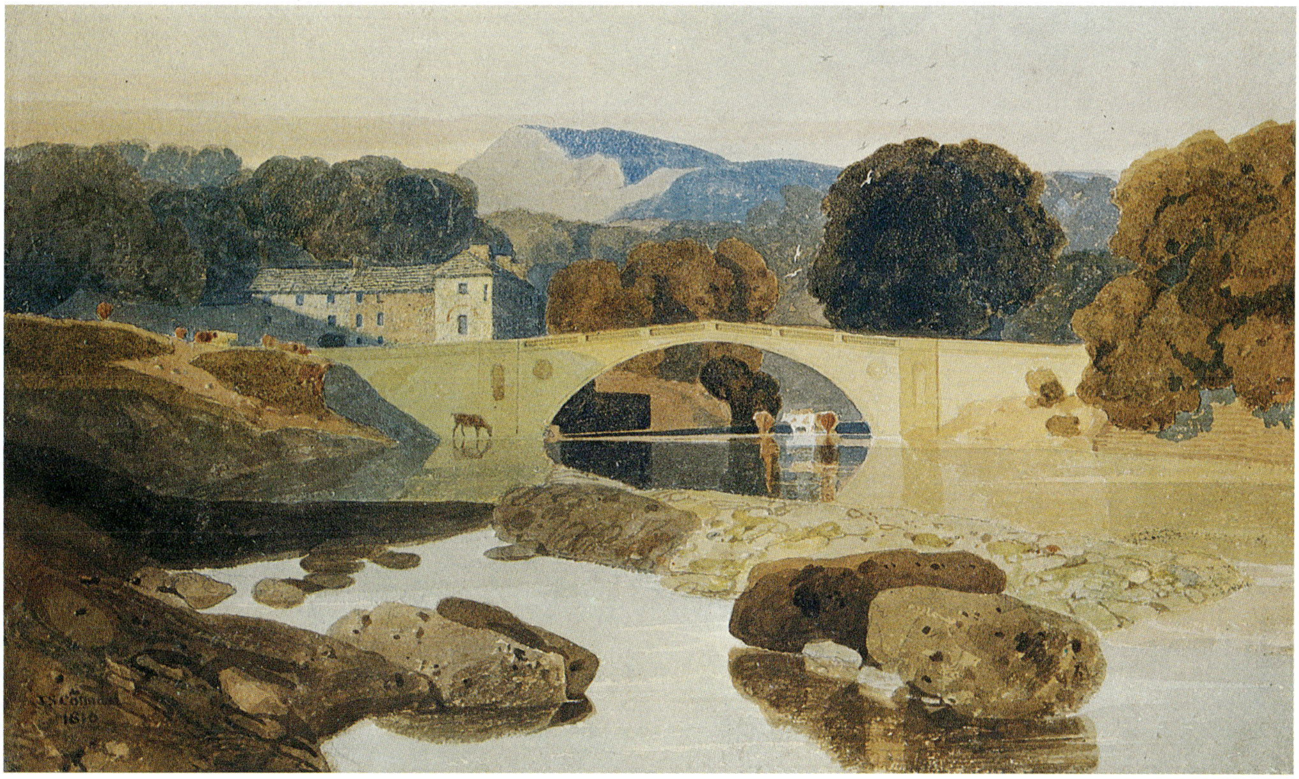

60 Greta Bridge, Yorkshire, 1810

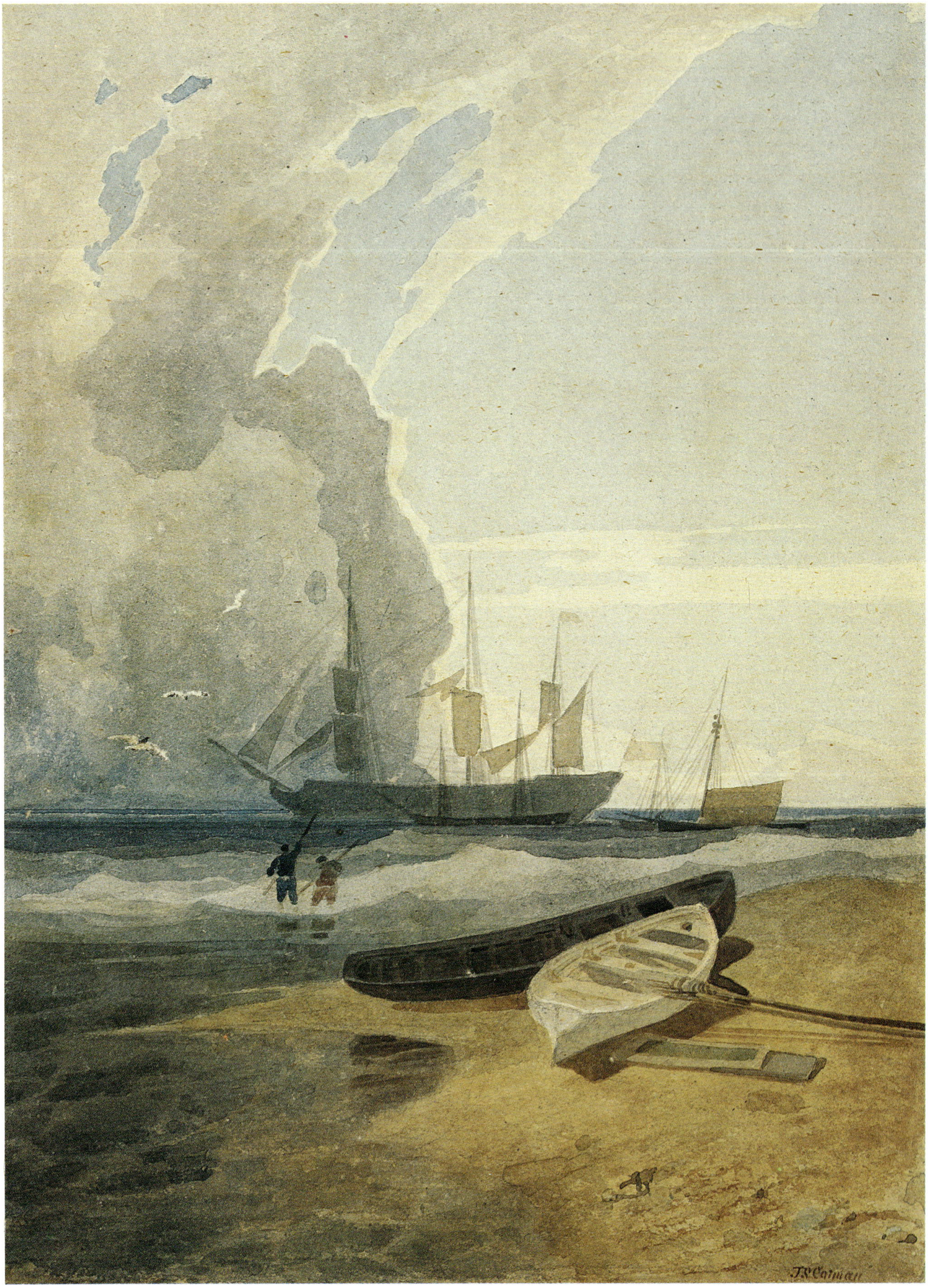

34 The Mars, riding at Anchor off Cromer, *c.*1807

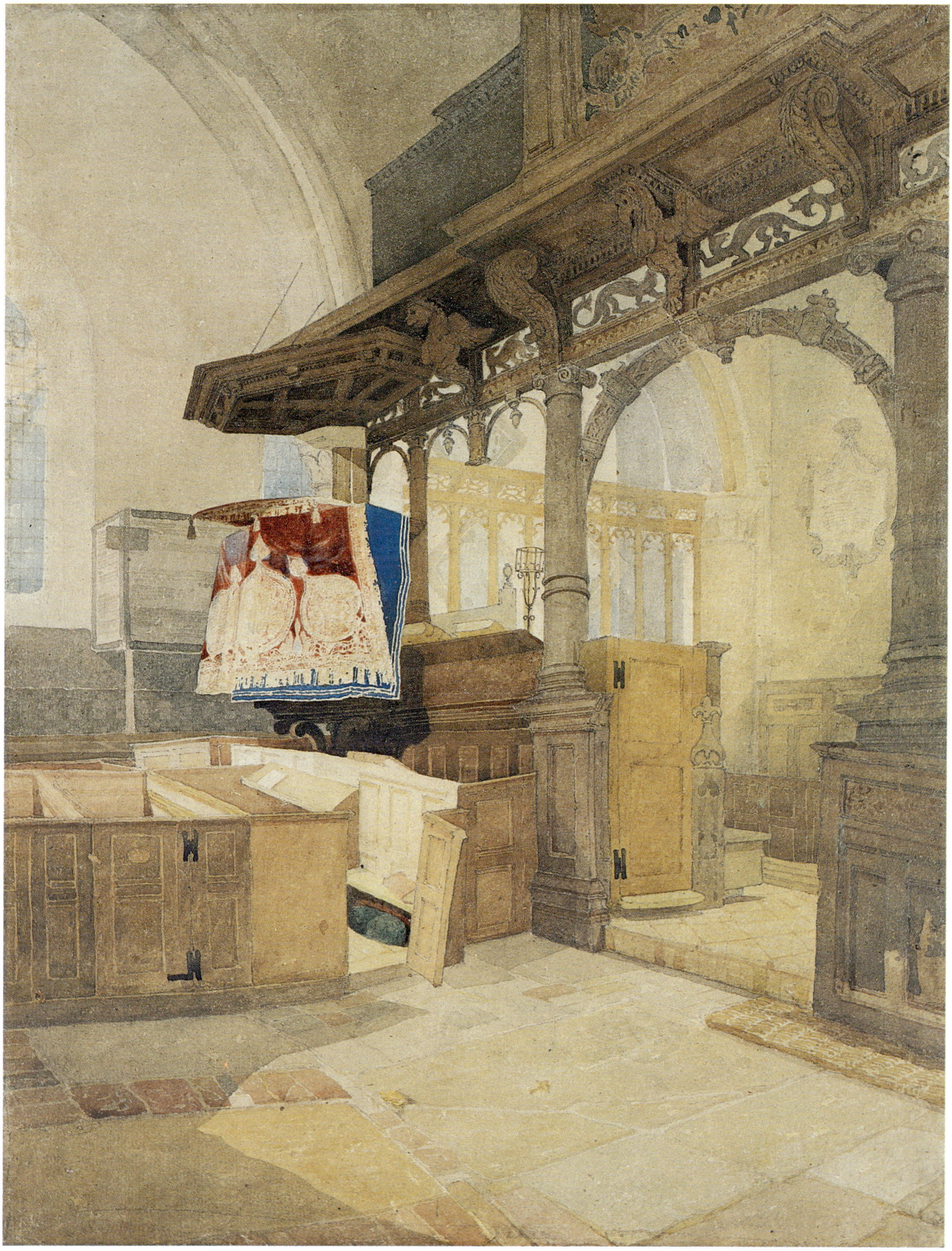

39 Interior of Trentham Church, Staffordshire, *c.*1808

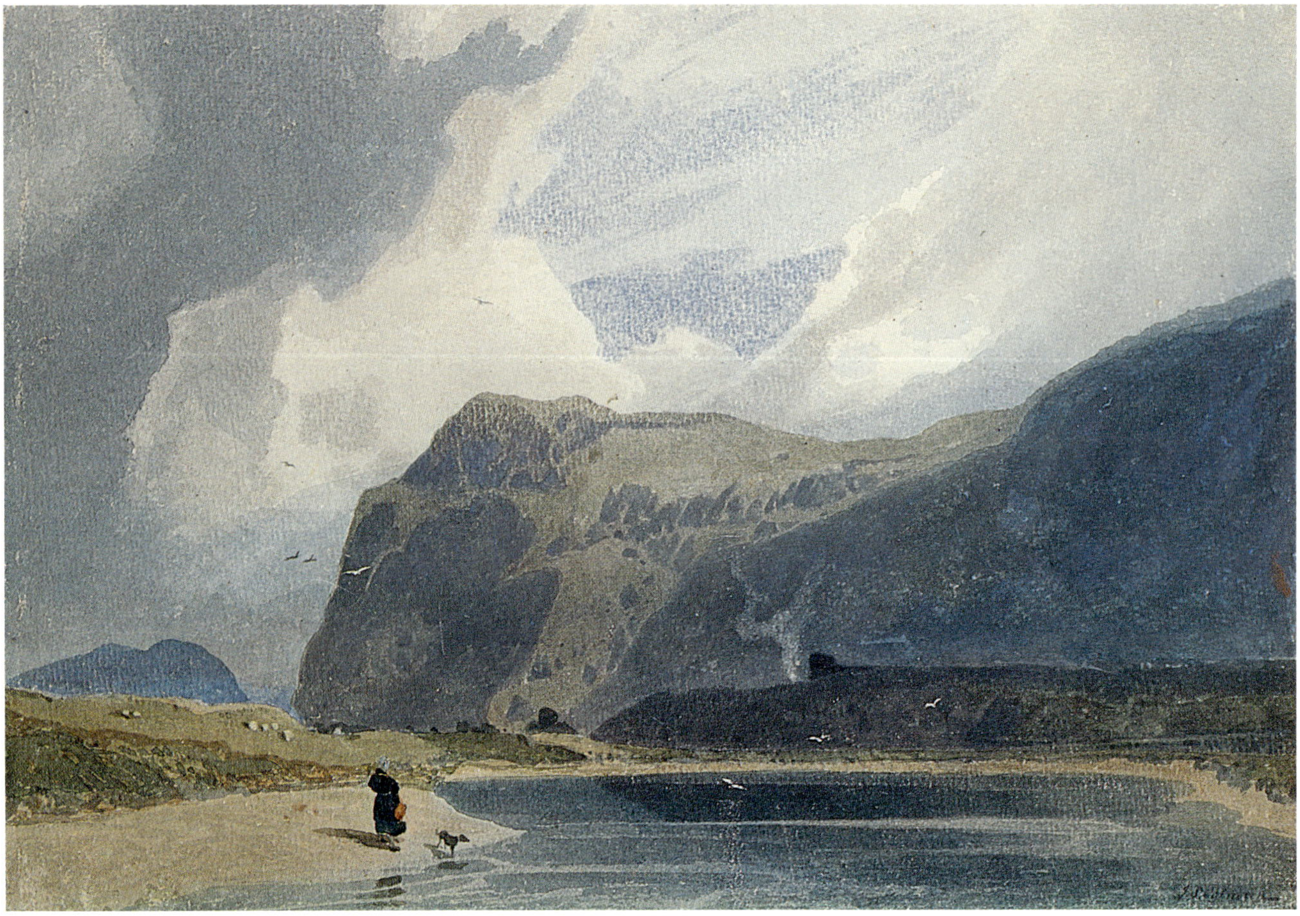

51 Mountain Scene in Wales, 1810

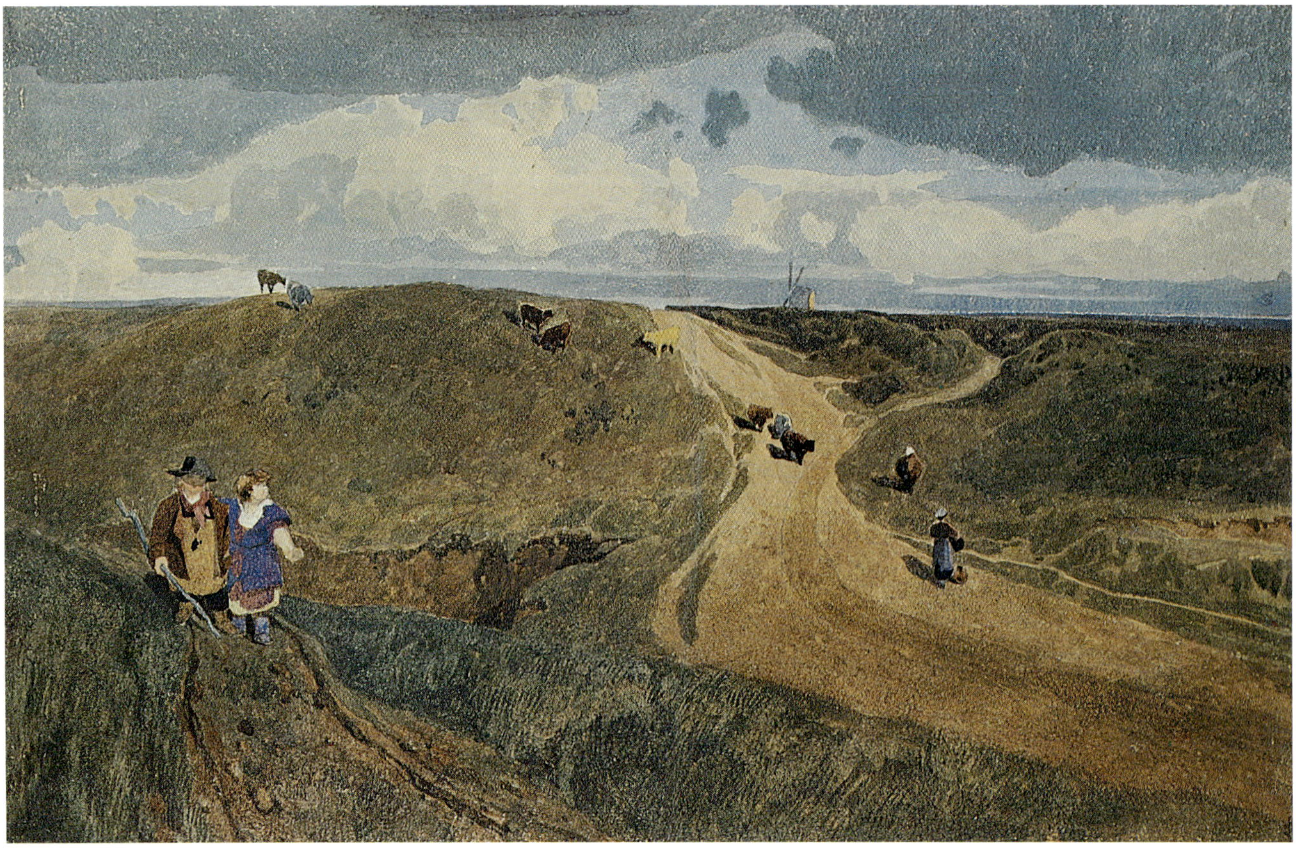

62 Mousehold Heath, Norwich, *c.*1810

money-making when a man fags from door to door merely for the pound sterling.'

It appears that Cotman made it clear that he did not intend to spend all his time teaching: a letter to Francis Cholmeley reveals that Cotman succeeded in reaching quite favourable terms with respect to teaching Mrs. Turner and her daughters, for he was required only two days a week and for them he received 'a clear £140'[8] per annum. Once persuaded, he admitted in a postscript to a letter of February 21: 'I shall feel most truly glad when I find myself a resident in Yarmouth.'[9] Cotman's move to Yarmouth was delayed as he was 'seized by a very fatiguing illness attended with fever',[10] which he attributed to overwork through 'severe attention to etching'. When he finally moved to his new house, at the beginning of April 1812, he soon wrote to Francis Cholmeley: 'it is really heavenly, and much as I have *travelled* I do not know where I could have choosen a spot more to my satisfaction.'[10] He appears to have lost little time in establishing himself and was 'much in request as a master'[11] by the middle of July.

Sydney Kitson, in his account of Cotman's Yarmouth period, tends to over-emphasize the drudgery of his existence, apparently inflicted upon him by Dawson Turner: 'it will be seen that Cotman was turning out during his first seven years at Yarmouth an etched plate in illustration of some Norfolk architectural subject at the rate of one every fortnight'.[12] Kitson did not, however, have the benefit of the Cholmeley correspondence covering this period, which is rich in enthusiastic references to his current projects and family circumstances. His output was prolific and he combined a high degree of accuracy with his idiosyncratic response to pattern and composition. Much of the routine work connected with his etching projects, meanwhile, was placed in the hands of assistants who must have proved increasingly capable (see section 12). Despite such help, the publication of *Specimens of Architectural Antiquities of Norfolk* was delayed. Originally advertised prior to the appearance of the first of ten quarterly numbers on 1 January 1812, the work was completed only in 1817. During these years he also suffered from poor health, including eye trouble for which he had a minor operation in the spring of 1814.[13]

The delay was the result not simply of unforeseen problems of illness, printing and production. Once at Yarmouth, Cotman undertook a number of other projects. On 22 May 1813, the forthcoming publication by subscription of *Engravings of the most remarkable of the Sepulchral Brasses in Norfolk and Suffolk* was announced in the *Norwich Mercury*. This was finally published in two volumes, in 1819. In the preface to the Norfolk volume, Cotman admits that he was 'not aware at its commencement of the magnitude of his task'. While much of the work was undoubtedly carried out by assistants (Cotman 'having employed apprentices and only finished the works'[13]), he also received the help of a number of 'gentlemen who . . . furnished him with impressions of brasses or otherwise directed his research'. He singled out for particular mention Rev. James Layton and Rev. Thomas Talbot, both of whom also received dedications in his *Specimens of the Architectural Antiquities of Norfolk*.[14] Nevertheless, he also collected impressions of brasses for himself, as evinced by a letter to Turner dated 14 July 1813.[15] From these he would compose his preliminary drawings for subsequent etching and tinting (Nos. 75, 76).

A measure of Cotman's recognition at this time may be seen in his selection by the London publisher, Longman, as one of the main artists employed to illustrate the guidebook *Excursions through Norfolk,* published in two volumes in 1818 and 1819 (No. 80). However his splendid series of seventy-six monochrome wash drawings were engraved by others, as was a subsequent series of eleven drawings for a companion volume. *Excursions through Suffolk.* These series of engravings are not an adequate translation of the subtlety of Cotman's drawings.

Dawson Turner's view of Cotman appears to have been essentially paternalistic. In 1830 Turner published privately a limited edition of a series of etchings by Mrs. Turner, called *One Hundred Etchings.* He inscribed a copy for Cotman with the dedication: 'Of the very few copies of this the present is, with the greatest pleasure, given to J. S. Cotman Esq., not only as a

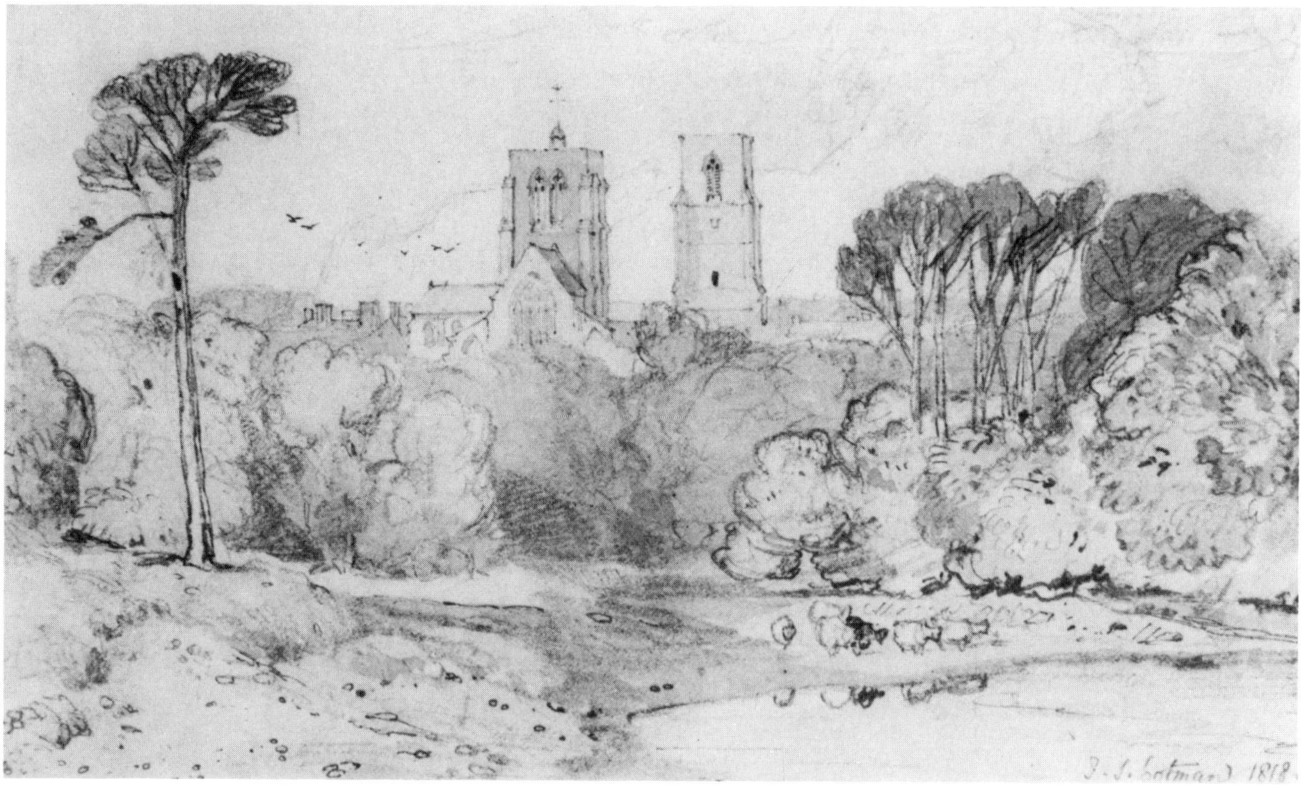

79 East Dereham, Norfolk, 1818

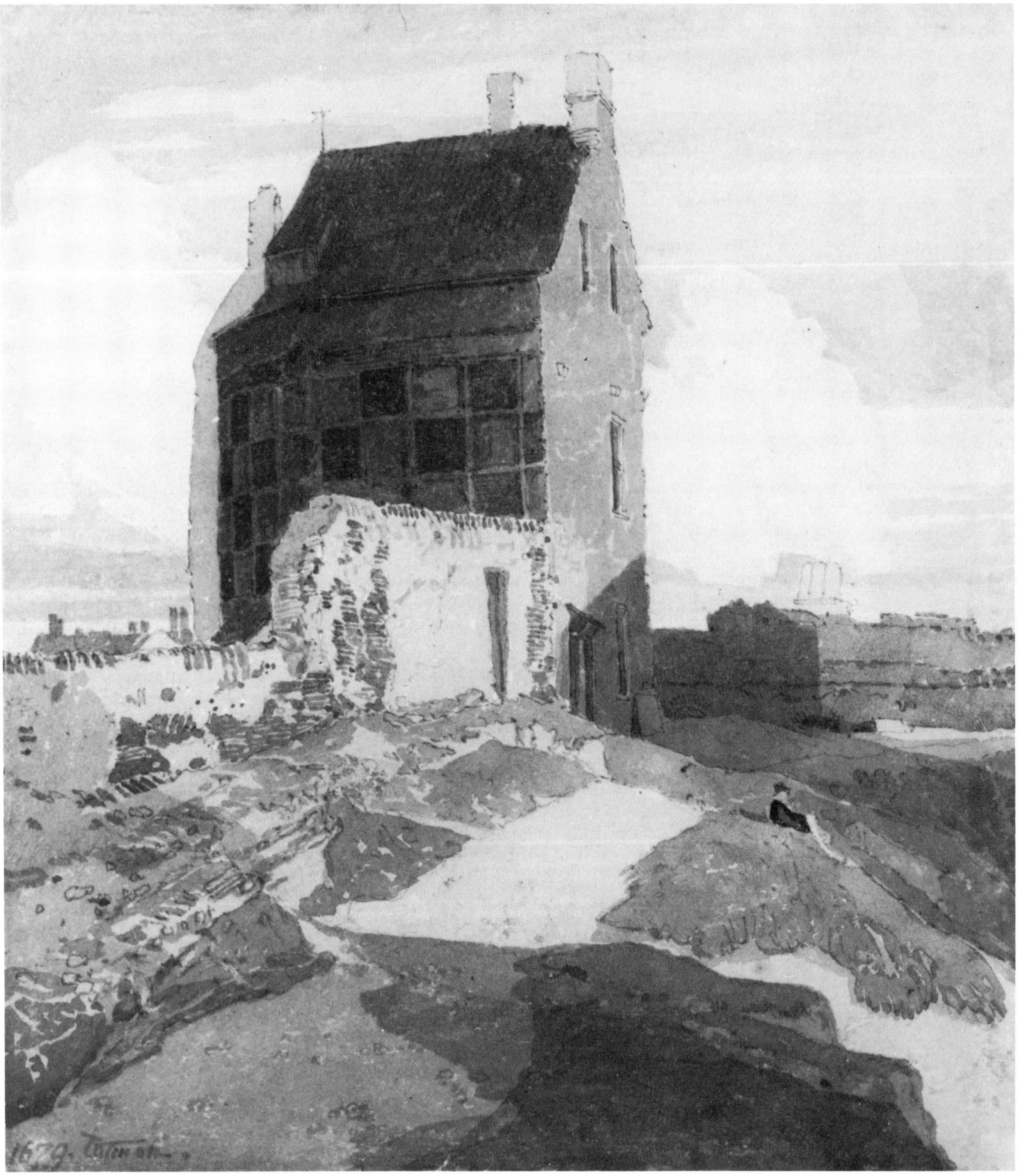

72 On the Walls, Yarmouth, *c.*1812

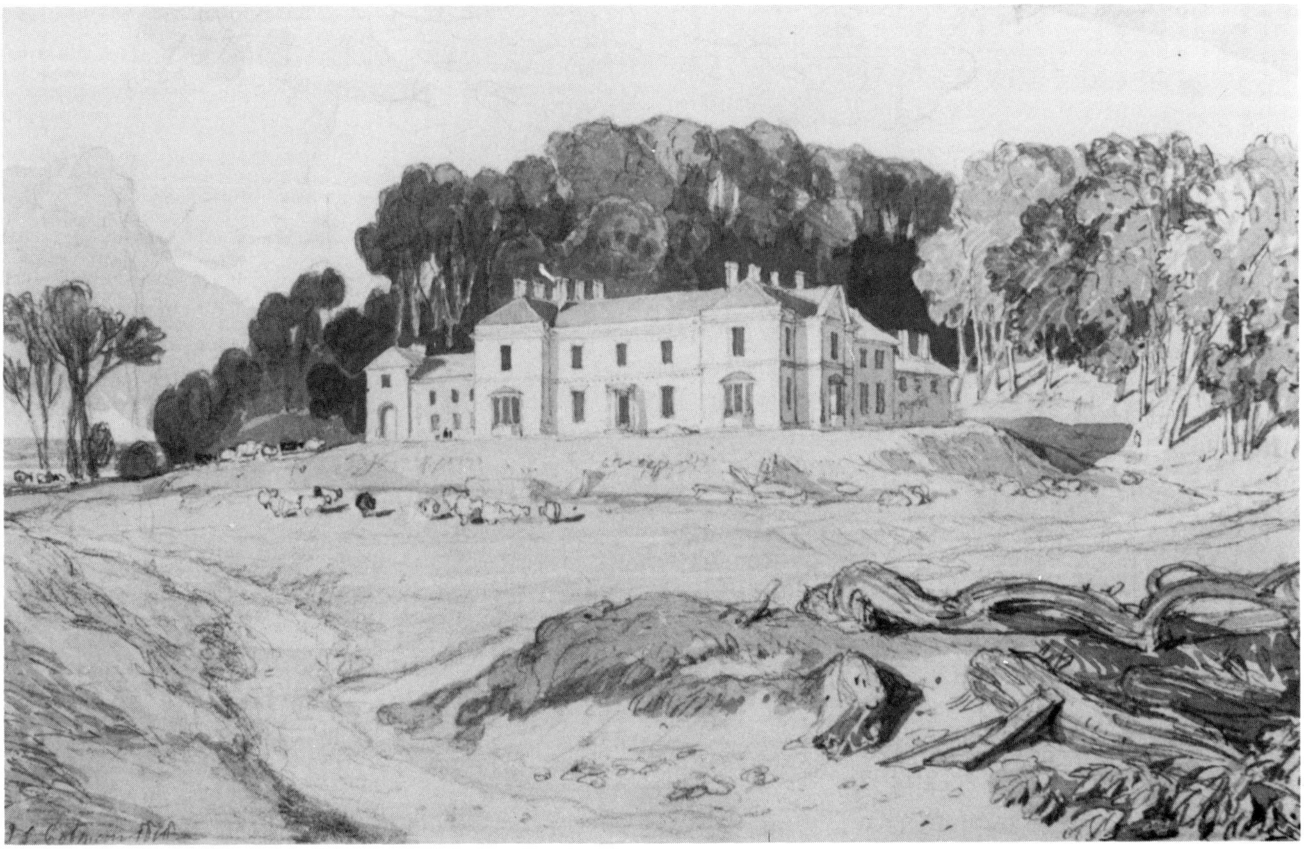

80 Sherringham Hall, Norfolk, 1818

memento of the regard entertained for him by all my family and of our high respect for his talents, but also as a proof of my thankfulness for the very great advantages which my daughters have derived from his very valuable instruction D.T.'[16] Turner was a canny businessman and would set his daughters to copy much of Cotman's original drawings which Turner had himself encouraged Cotman to produce in illustration of Blomefield's *History of Norfolk*. It was left to the Rev. James Bulwer to purchase the original drawings, while Turner was content with his daughters' copies.[17] In 1841 Dawson Turner acknowledged in the preface to a catalogue of these drawings: 'Whatever merit may be found in this collection of drawings is mainly attributable to Mr. Cotman. To him too, is ascribable that it was ever formed. My daughters . . . while they copied his sketches and listened to the tale of his discoveries, they could not but imbibe a portion of his enthusiasm'. Such an appraisal of Cotman's worth supports Benjamin Robert Haydon's view of Turner as a man 'with a searching quickness and excessive restlessness that kept his mind ever on the lookout, but never on the *look in*.'[18]

Cotman, for his part, responded to Turner's patronage in typically fulsome manner. In acknowledging Turner's catalogue he wrote: 'it refreshens the very, oh very many recollections of happy hours passed in your valuable society', while he also referred to his 'sincere and long-standing respect for your sound judgement.'[19] A few weeks later he remarked with characteristic exaggeration: 'I loved my employer—his family,—& all their doing.'[20] Whilst allowing for the evident extravagance of these words, there is no reason to doubt their sincerity. Throughout his years at Yarmouth, Cotman was assured of financial and domestic security under the paternalistic eye of Dawson Turner, enabling him to become totally absorbed in the creativity of archaeological draughtsmanship. While many of his etchings and drawings of this period are undoubtedly purely descriptive, it is rare for his archaeological work not to be executed in a line of the utmost sensitivity.

Notes

[1]A copy of the prospectus accompanied Cotman's letter to Francis Cholmeley of 24 Nov. 1810. [2]Popham No. 5. [3]BM. [4]JSC to DT, 25 Aug. 1811 (Barker Collection). [5]Barker Collection. [6]JSC to DT undated, but *c*.20 December 1811 (Barker Collection). [7]JSC to DT (Barker Collection). [8]JSC to Francis Cholmeley, 10 Jan. 1812. [9]JSC to DT (Barker Collection). [10]JSC to Francis Cholmeley, 13 April 1812. [11]Anne Cholmeley to Francis Cholmeley, 16 July 1812. [12]Kitson 1937 p. 170. [13]JSC to Francis Cholmeley, 1 June 1817. [14]Popham Nos. 179 and 152. [15]JSC to DT (R.C. Fiske Collection). [16]Norwich Local Studies Library. [17]Now in the BM. [18]*The Diary of Benjamin Robert Haydon* ed. W. B. Pope, Harvard, 1963 vol II p. 127. [19]JSC to DT, 11-12 Aug. 1841. [20]JSC to DT, 3 Sept. 1841.

66 Ornaments on the West Front of Binham Priory, Norfolk, 1811

illustrated on p. 60

Pencil on buff, wove paper; 28.1 × 21 ($11\frac{1}{16} \times 8\frac{1}{4}$). INSCR: *Recto,* inscribed and dated in pencil in the artist's hand, l.c.r. *ornaments on W. F. Binham / July 17.11.-.* PROV: Rev. James Bulwer; by descent to his son James Radford Bulwer; by descent to his younger brother Walter Bulwer; by descent to his son Henry A. Bulwer; acquired ?from him by Percy Moore Turner; bt. from him by R. J. Colman 9 June 1936; R. J. Colman Bequest 1946. (422.235.951). REF: Kitson 1937 p. 149; Rajnai & Allthorpe No. 120.

On the 31 July 1811 Cotman wrote to Dawson Turner[1] that after recovering from blindness caused by a severe cold he went for a short tour 'to fill up the vacant time between the printing of the Letter press & the actual sending the remaining setts out to my Subscribers . . . I have been at Binham, Walsingham[2] near which place is a very pretty West End of a Chapel, called Houghton with Dale [see No. 67] . . .'

The date of this drawing, when he also sketched the Priory's octagonal Perpendicular font,[3] is the earliest recorded in this tour. The drawing was etched as the lower part of a composite plate, No. XIV[4] in the 1818 Series, the top of which shows the South Front of Binham Priory. It was published shortly after Cotman left Norwich as it is dated 1812 Yarmouth.

Binham is just north-east of Walsingham, thirty miles north-west of Norwich. Cotman also etched the West Front of the Priory Church[5] which is still in use and a north-west view of the Priory,[6] while a south-west view[7] was engraved for the *Excursions through Norfolk.* The latter two compositions were from later drawings presumably deriving from this visit.

[1]Barker collection. [2]Rajnai & Allthorpe No. 122. [3]Yale Center for British

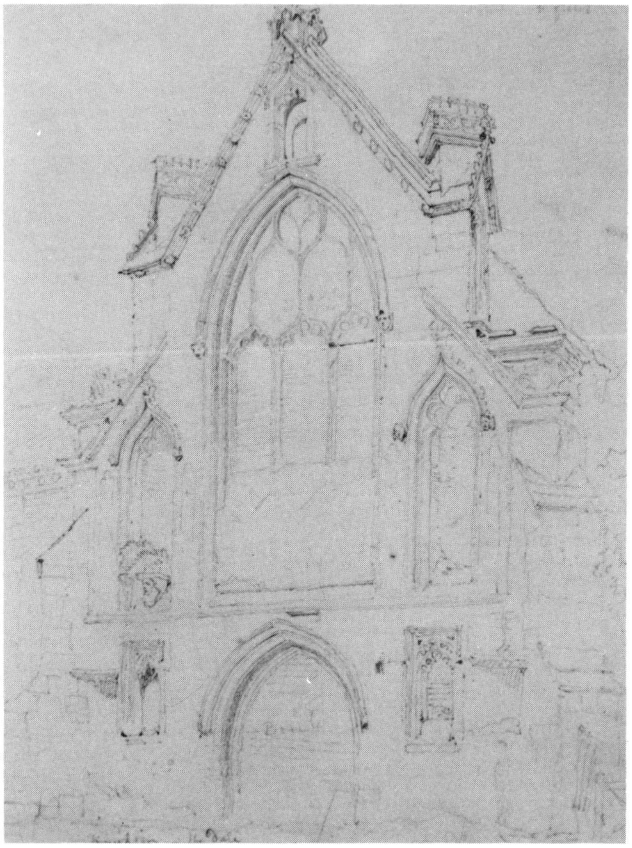

67 West Front of the Chapel, Houghton in the Dale, Norfolk, 1811

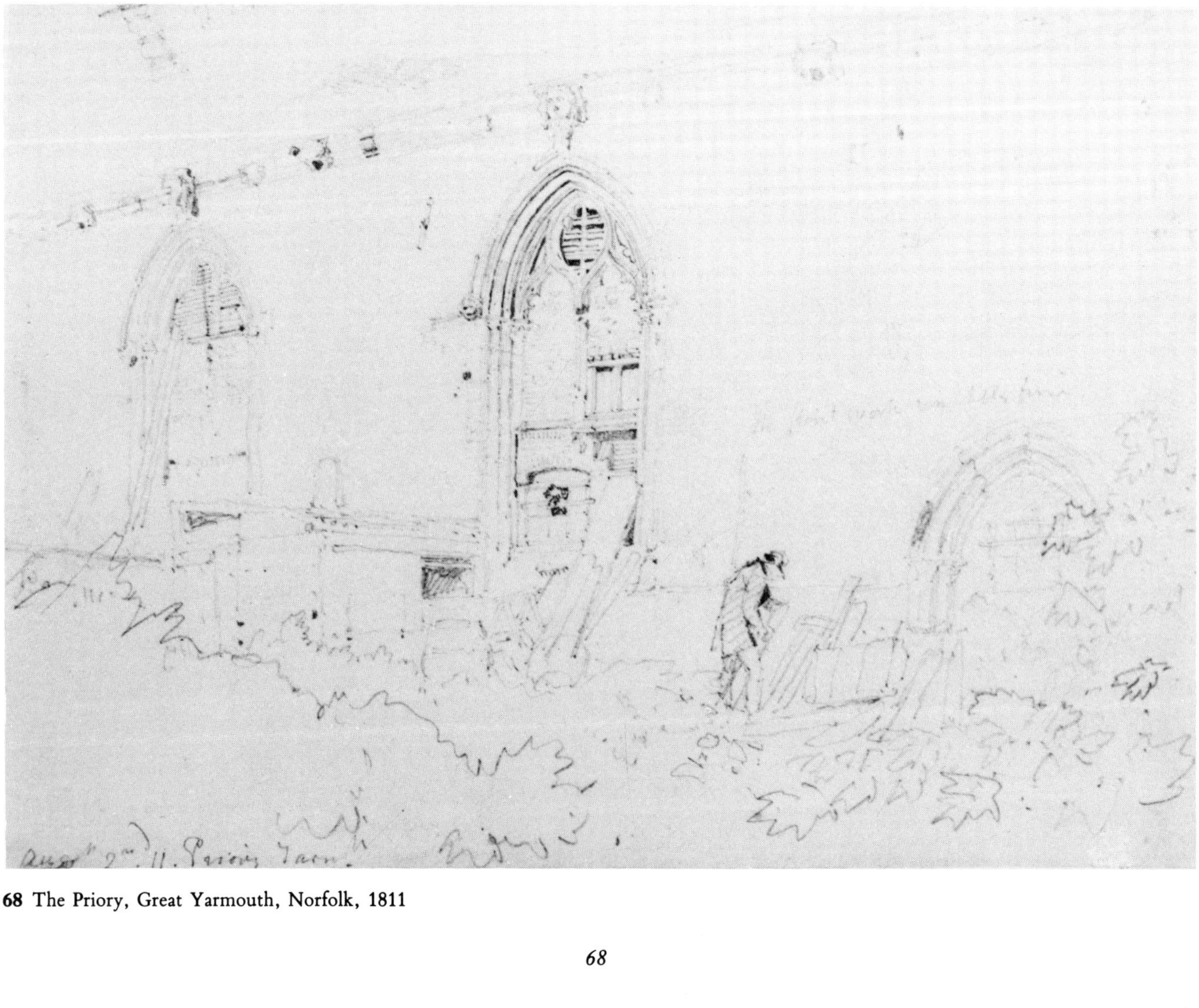

68 The Priory, Great Yarmouth, Norfolk, 1811

Art, New Haven, USA, B 1975.2.522. There are two copies: (a) by Mrs. Dawson Turner in the Ashmolean: (b) by Ellen Turner, NCM 9.26.31. [4]Popham No. 143. [5]Popham No. 142, the pencil drawing for the etching and the etching were probably his exhibits with the Norwich Society in 1811 (51) and in 1812 (88). [6]Popham No. 86; the drawing was in the Bulwer Collection, exh. Walker's Galleries 1926 (28) repro. in catalogue pl. VIII. [7]Bulwer collection, exh. Walker's Galleries 1926 (157), engraved by J. Greig and published 1 May 1819, vol. 1.

67 West Front of the Chapel, Houghton in the Dale, Norfolk, 1811

illustrated on opposite page

Pencil on buff, wove paper; 28.7 × 22.2 ($11\frac{5}{16} \times 8\frac{3}{4}$). INSCR: *Recto,* inscribed in pencil l.c.l. *Houghton in the dale / July 20 11* (the lower half of the date is trimmed off) lower.c.*Brick,* u.r. + *flint.* PROV: J. Smith; bt. from him with a collection of Norfolk prints by Walter Rye 1896; presented by Rye to the Norwich Central Public Library 1906; on indefinite loan from them since 1966 (6.749.966). REF: Kitson 1937 p. 149; Rajnai & Allthorpe No. 123.

After Walsingham (see No. 66) Cotman went to Houghton in the Dale, now Houghton St. Giles, just over a mile to the south-west. He wrote to Dawson Turner on 31 July 1811[1] 'I have been at Binham [see No. 66], near which place is a very pretty West End of a Chapel, called Houghton in the Dale, which stands rather out of the way, and have [sic] never been visited by the Pencil. Its chief beauty consists in its being so very small & the symmetry of the whole together.'

In fact, in 1809, an engraving by Hay after a drawing by the Rev. E. Edwards had been published in Britton's *Beauties of England and Wales.* Cotman's own etching,[2] after No. 67, was published within nine months, in the first quarter of 1812, just before he moved to Yarmouth. The etching was probably Cotman's exhibit with the Norwich Society in 1812 (69).

The mid-fourteenth century chapel is described by Dawson Turner in the text to the 1818 series: 'this interesting piece of antiquity is left unnoticed, even by Blomefield; but, as a specimen of architecture, it is at once beautiful and curious. The front, here given, alone remains; the rest is now turned into a cottage . . .' Now restored, it has recently become known as the Slipper Chapel which 'implies that from here the pilgrims to Little Walsingham walked barefoot'.[3]

[1]Barker Collection. [2]Popham No. 136. [3]Pevsner, *North-East Norfolk and Norwich* p. 174.

68 The Priory, Great Yarmouth, Norfolk, 1811

illustrated on opposite page

Pencil on buff, wove paper; 20.5 × 28 ($8\frac{1}{16} \times 11\frac{1}{16}$). INSCR: *Recto,* inscribed in pencil u.l. *The Corner,* l.c.r. *The flint work remarkably fine,* dated and inscribed in pencil l.l. *Augst 2nd 11. Priory Yarmth.* PROV: Rev. James Bulwer; by descent to his son James Radford Bulwer; by descent to his younger brother Walter Bulwer; by descent to his son Henry A. Bulwer; acquired ?from him by S. D. Kitson; presented by him to R. J. Colman; R. J. Colman Bequest 1946. (567.235.951). EXH: London, Walker's Galleries 1926 (30). REF: Kitson 1937 p. 150; Rajnai & Allthorpe No. 124.

Within two days of writing to Dawson Turner of his short tour of North Norfolk (see No. 66) Cotman was himself at Yarmouth where he sketched this sensitive study of the Priory. He also drew the interior,[1] which he etched[2] and published in the first quarter of 1812 before his removal to Yarmouth.

The Priory was founded in 1107 and stood opposite the south side of St. Nicholas' Church. By Cotman's time: 'the great hall had been filled with rubbish, and converted into stables, the windows being used for doors; the whole of the old buildings being then in a most dilapidated state, whilst a warehouse and stables had been erected in the courtyard.'[3]

[1]Yale Center for British Art, New Haven, USA. [2]Popham No. 133. Probably Cotman's exhibit with the Norwich Society in 1812 (68). [3]Palmer, *The Perlustration of Great Yarmouth* vol. 1 1872 pp. 63, 64.

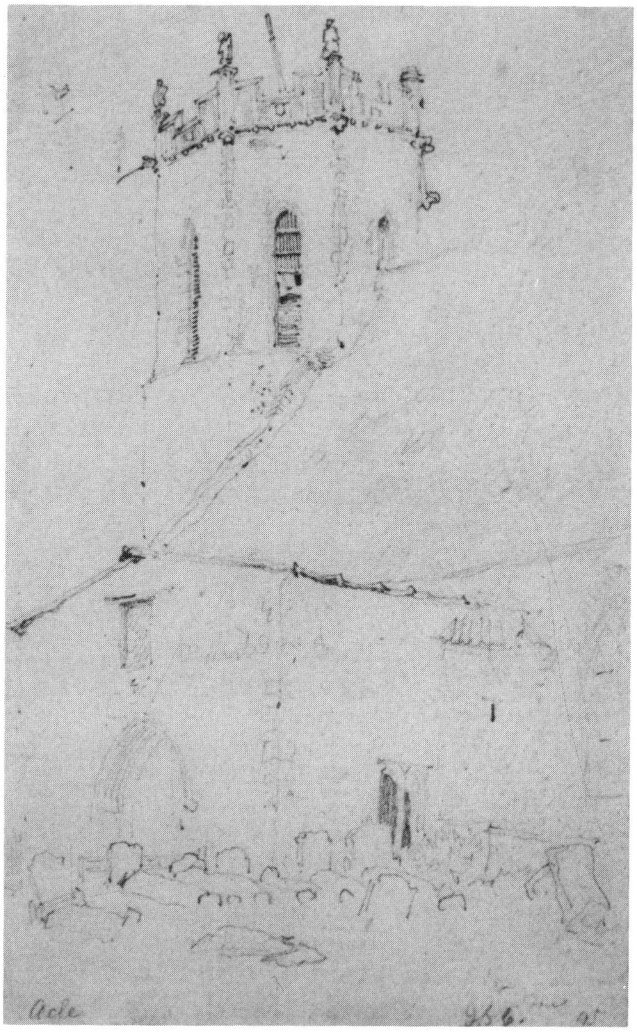

69 The Tower of St. Edmund's Church, Acle, *c.*1811

69 The Tower of St. Edmund's Church, Acle, *c.*1811

Pencil on buff, wove paper; 23.6 × 14.2 ($9\frac{5}{16} \times 5\frac{5}{8}$), u. edge roughly cut. INSCR: *Recto,* inscribed in pencil l.l. *Acle,* ?signed and numbered in pencil l.r. *J.S.C. / 95,* inscribed in pencil with colour notes u.c.l. *Plaster* and l.r. an illegible word. PROV: See No. 66. (412.235.951). REF: Rajnai & Allthorpe No. 125.

It was probably on his trip to Yarmouth (see No. 68) that Cotman made this drawing of the church tower at Acle, a village on the main road to the north-west of Yarmouth. Like No. 68 it must have been intended for the *Architectural Antiquities of Norfolk,* but like that drawing it was never etched.[1]

The view shows the west end of the church with the south porch and concentrates upon the octagonal top storey of the round tower, with its lancet windows and 'battlements with flushwork panelling and figures as pinnacles'.[2]

[1]He did etch *A Screen in Acle Church, Norfolk,* n.d. Popham No. 69, and *Cleristory in Acle Church, Norfolk,* 1818, Popham No. 62. The drawing for the former is NCM 413.235.951. [2]Pevsner, *North-East Norfolk and Norwich* p. 73.

70 Terracotta Screen in Oxborough Church, Norfolk, 1811

illustrated on p. 70

Pencil on buff, wove paper; 28.2 × 22 ($11\frac{1}{8} \times 8\frac{5}{8}$). INSCR: *Recto,* inscribed and dated in pencil u.r. *Oxburgh Church / Sepr. 9th 11.* PROV: See No. 67. (10.749.966). REF: Kitson 1937 p. 150; Rajnai & Allthorpe No. 126.

After his short tour of North Norfolk (see Nos. 66, 67) and his trip to Yarmouth (see Nos. 68, 69) Cotman returned to Norwich. But he wanted to gather more material for his new project, the *Architectural*

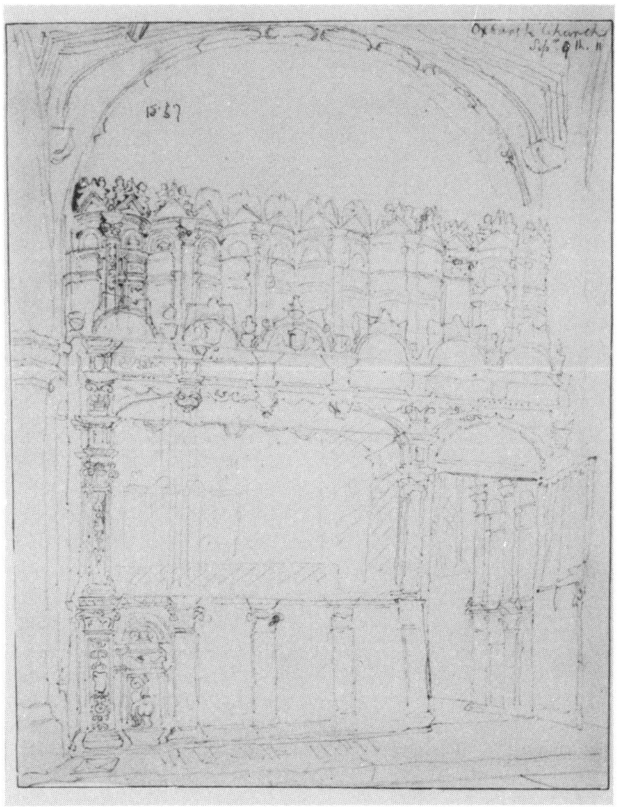

70 Terracotta Screen in Oxborough Church, Norfolk, 1811

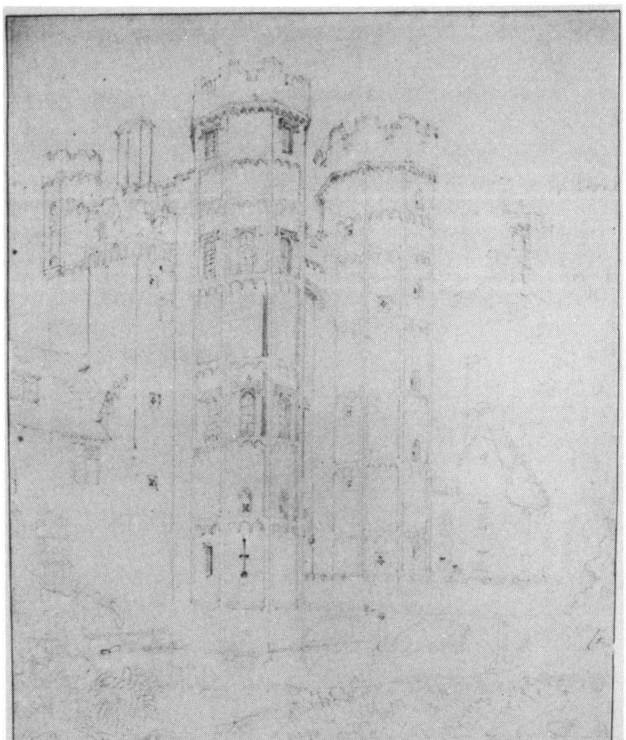

71 The Gateway of Oxborough Hall, Norfolk, 1811

Antiquities of Norfolk and he seems to have started his second, more extensive tour — concentrating on West Norfolk — towards the end of August.

On 20th September, Cotman wrote to Dawson Turner:[1] 'I have sketched a fine Screen to a dormitory at Oxburgh. — The Gateway id [see No. 71] — also an end of an old Parsonage at Methwold not totally unlike Basham [sic]'. He started in the south and progressed northwards, being at Methwold on the 6 September,[2] at Oxborough on the 9 and at Runcton Holme on the 12.[3] Although done with his projected publication in mind, No. 70 was never actually etched.

Rajnai and Allthorpe point out that Cotman's remark 'a fine Screen to a dormitory' is curious as he in fact sketched the terracotta screen which divides the South Aisle from Margaret Bedingfeld's chapel in the church of St. John Evangelist, Oxborough. An early manifestation of the Renaissance in England, the monument has 'ornamented pilasters and ornamented arched panels and a superstructure or canopy with short pendants and little semi-circular and triangular cresting motifs . . . It is all far from correct . . . but insouciant and lively.'[4]

[1]Barker Collection. [2]*Methwold Rectory,* pencil, inscribed and dated 6 Sept, 1811, Ashmolean, Popham No. 137. [3]See Rajnai & Allthorpe No. 128. [4]Pevsner, *North-West and South Norfolk* p. 281. A view of the church, dated 8 July 1819, is NCM 15.749.966.

71 The Gateway of Oxborough Hall, Norfolk, 1811

Pencil on buff, wove paper; 32.6 × 25.5 ($12\frac{13}{16}$ × 10). Inscr: *Recto,* inscribed in pencil with numbers denoting colour notes u.r. *x Stone* and l.r. *Oxborough, Oxburgh S/11* (paper trimmed along r. edge). *Prov:* See No. 67. (5.749.966). Ref: Kitson 1937 p. 150; Rajnai & Allthorpe No. 127.

This is the 'Gateway' mentioned by Cotman in his letter of 20 September 1811 to Dawson Turner (see No. 70). Seen from the north-east it served as a basis for an impressive etching[1] in his *Architectural Antiquities of Norfolk.* It was published in 1813.

Oxborough Hall, in the village of the same name, some thirty miles west of Norwich, was to be considerably rebuilt in 1835. Cotman sketched 'the chief survival of the late C15 house . . . the tremendous gatehouse, the most prominent of the English brick gatehouses of the C15.'[2] The etching is dedicated to the owner at the time of Cotman's visit, Sir Richard Bedingfeld, a descendant of its builder.

[1]Popham No. 165. [2]Pevsner, *North-West and South Norfolk* p. 282.

72 On the Walls, Yarmouth, *c.*1812

illustrated on p. 66

Pencil and watercolour on cream, wove paper; 24 × 20.6 ($9\frac{1}{2}$ × $8\frac{1}{8}$). Inscr: *Recto,* numbered and signed in brown watercolour l.l. *1679. Cotman.; verso,* inscribed in pencil, ?in the artist's hand, *On the Walls Yarm.* Prov: Mrs. Edwin Edwards, presented by her to the East Anglian Art Society 1883; presented by them with the rest of their collection 1894. (57.75.94). Exh: ?Norwich Society 1812 (73); Tate 1922 (220); Kettering 1952 (50); Stoke-on-Trent 1953; Art Exhibitions Bureau 1953-54 (19); Kidderminster 1954 (18); Derby & Nottingham 1959 (17); Bedford 1960 (32); China & Berlin 1963-64 (66); Bedford & Cambridge 1966 (10); Rouen 1967; Kenwood 1969; King's Lynn 1970 (18); Hamburg 1976 (249) repro.; The Hague 1977 (9) repro. in colour on cover; Ipswich 1978 (2); Koblenz 1980 (9) repro. in colour on back cover; Nottingham 1981 (48); China 1982 (31). Ref: NCM ?1897 (121); NCM ?1899 (135); Kaines Smith 1926 p. 166; NCM 1937 (43); Farmer, *East Anglian Magazine* Feb. 1970, repro. p. 131.

The gabled tower, with its distinctive dark, square patterned brickwork was one of sixteen similar towers on the defensive walls at Great Yarmouth. Similar decorative brickwork may be seen in Cotman's splendid etching of *South Gate, Yarmouth,* first published in January 1812.[1] The County Surveyor's Plan of the town, published 20 February 1803, suggests the tower to be on Dene side, where the wall angles around towards the South Gate. A later etching of the South West Tower by the Yarmouth artist Jane Worship (1809-1898), taken from a similar though lower viewpoint makes this tower a likely candidate, although the later view differs in some architectural details, as does a Cotman drawing, *c.*1812, of the same facade from further to the right, inscribed 'Old South Tower, Yarmouth'.[2]

The dainty pencilwork and delicately variegated washes establish this drawing as one of the finest of Cotman's watercolours of the Yarmouth period. There is a formal abstraction to the design which recalls the works of the end of the first Norwich period, while the use of rough, cream paper is also reminiscent of *c.*1809-10. The ascetic washes work with calculated simplicity. This use of wash is particularly successful in the delineation of the cumulus cloud, recalling the cloud effect of *The Mars, riding at Anchor off Cromer,* No. 34.

The number '1679' inscribed lower left, reveals that this watercolour was one of Cotman's circulating library of drawing copies. Two other drawing copies of similar date also bear close drawing copy numbers and are of Yarmouth subjects: 1676, *A Yarmouth Fisherwoman*[3] and 1677, *South Gate, Yarmouth.*[4] A further autograph drawing copy is number 1273, inscribed *A Tower on the Walls at Yarmouth.*[5] This shows the aspect of the tower from behind the wall to the left of the composition of No. 72. Two small and ramshackle outbuildings hug the wall, while the rounded end of the tower is clearly visible. The composition of this view was used directly by Cotman for his etching *A Tower on the Ramparts, Yarmouth Norfolk,*[6] first published in 1816, with the addition of two children in the foreground.

An on the spot thumbnail sketch on the reverse of drawing copy number 2520, *Man driving sheep through a ford,*[7] outlines briefly but precisely the main compositional elements of No. 72. Finally, the quality and style of No. 72 suggests that it may have been Cotman's exhibit with the Norwich Society for 1812 (73), *Tower on the Walls, Yarmouth.*

[1]Popham No. 130. [2]Bacon Collection, No. 698. [3]BM 1902-5-14-22. [3]NCM 158.217.947. [5]NCM 24.105.932. [6]Popham No. 128. [7]Manning Galleries April 1971.

73 The Toy Ship, *c.*1814

illustrated on p. 59

Pencil, watercolour and bodycolour on buff, wove paper; 17.4 × 26.3 ($6\frac{7}{8} \times 10\frac{3}{8}$). *Verso,* pencil sketches including boat tackle, an anchor and small girl. PROV: J. J. Colman by 1888; his bequest to R. J. Colman 1898; R. J. Colman Bequest 1946. (166.217.947). EXH: Norwich, Art Circle 1888 (45); Tate 1922 (223); Norwich 1945; Norwich, Arts Council 1947 (20). REF: Dickes p. 331; Kitson 1937 p. 165 pl. 70.

While a number of beach scene sketches exist which have been traditionally ascribed to Cotman's period at Yarmouth,[1] *The Toy Ship* is one of the rare watercolours to survive from these years. It suggests that Cotman continued to compose watercolour drawings for his own enjoyment, despite being swamped with work for Dawson Turner and his etching projects.

The intimacy of the family group, with the young man in a brown frock coat holding up a model ship to the young child, has led to a traditional belief that the figures are Cotman with his wife and their daughter Ann. There is no evidence to discount this theory, while the man's profile recalls that of Mrs. Turner's etching of the young Cotman after a drawing by J. P. Davis (see frontispiece). Stylistically, the drawing may be regarded as a transitional work. The little girl, with her pinafore over a striped dress, although unfinished, recalls the little girl of entry No. 65, of *c.*1810-11. The freedom in the use of pencil in those areas supporting the family group, together with the strong modelling of the male figure, foreshadows the increasing spontaneity of Cotman's later work.

If the tradition is accepted, then the little girl, some two years old in the drawing, suggests a date of *c.*1814, two years after the birth of Ann, Cotman's second child, in 1812. Two other Cotman compositions, subsequently published as part of his *Liber Studiorum* (1838) both contain as staffage similarly dressed children.[2] These figures are more obviously compositional elements, however, rather than integral subject-matter as in *The Toy Ship.*

[1]A number of such sketches are in the BM, V&A and at Leeds. [2]Popham No. 331, *Deptford* and Popham No. 333, *Lakenham near Norwich.*

74 River Scene, *c.*1814

called *The Eel Boat*

illustrated on p. 59

Pencil, watercolour and bodycolour on buff, wove paper, arched top; 17.2 × 26.3 ($6\frac{13}{16} \times 10\frac{7}{8}$). PROV: Christie's, ?Nov. 1889, bt. J. J. Colman; his bequest to R. J. Colman 1898; R. J. Colman Bequest 1946. (195.217.947). EXH: Norwich 1903 (36) as *River Scene;* Norwich 1945; Norwich, Arts Council 1947 (24). REF: Dickes p. 331 as *Babbing for Eels.*

This watercolour is extremely close to *The Toy Ship* in both technique and the identical type of paper used in each case. Similarly, they both bear the same experimental air. In *River Scene* perhaps the most experimental element is the free dragging of the brush in the blues of the sky, foreshadowing a technique Cotman was to develop much later in the second Norwich period.

The similarity between the two is heightened by the use of both lead white and the paper itself for the highlights, while the prominent placing of the red echoes that of *The Toy Ship.* The slight staining of the foreground with the lightest application of colour also complements a similar technique in the sky of the previous entry, while the treatment of the fisherman strongly recalls that of the woman in their identical colour scheme and lumpy delineation.

This picture has also been called *Babbing for Eels.*[1] The fisherman is not, however, baiting the eels, but drawing a net. It is tempting to identify the low flat landscape as Breydon Water, but the scene is undoubtedly an imaginary studio composition. A sheet of yellow paper, in the collection of the Victoria and Albert Museum, London bears two studies by Cotman of the same man in a fishing boat with a covered stern, hauling in a fishing net.[2] One of these is a preliminary sketch for *River Scene,* which includes all the features of the composition, including the rushes to the left and the curving shadow of the boat upon the water.

[1]Dickes p. 331. [2]V&A E726-1925.

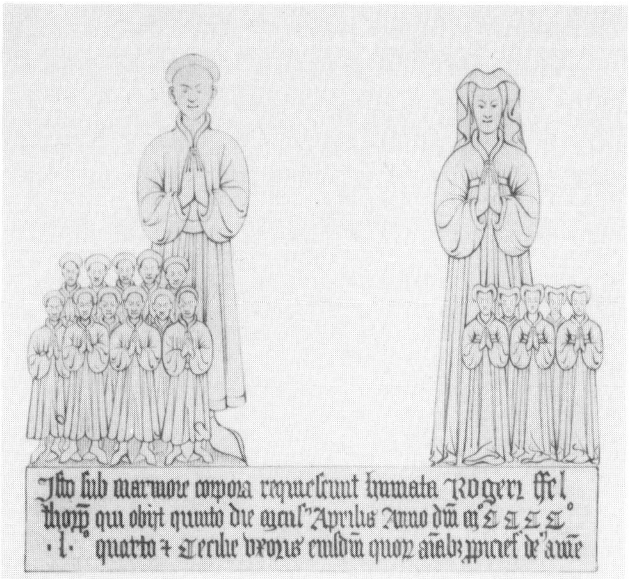

75 Monumental Brass, Blickling, Norfolk; Roger Felthorpe and Family (1454), *c.*1813-15

75 Monumental Brass, Blickling, Norfolk: Roger Felthorpe and Family (1454), *c.*1813-15

Pencil and watercolour on cream, wove paper; 22.2 × 23 ($8\frac{3}{4} \times 9\frac{1}{16}$). PROV: Probably from Bulwer Collection, see No. 77. (242.235.951).

The twelve-inch figures of this attractive memorial brass are located in the North aisle of Blickling Church, Norfolk.

This is the final study from which the corresponding plate in *Engravings of the Most Remarkable of The Sepulchral Brasses in Norfolk* (1819)

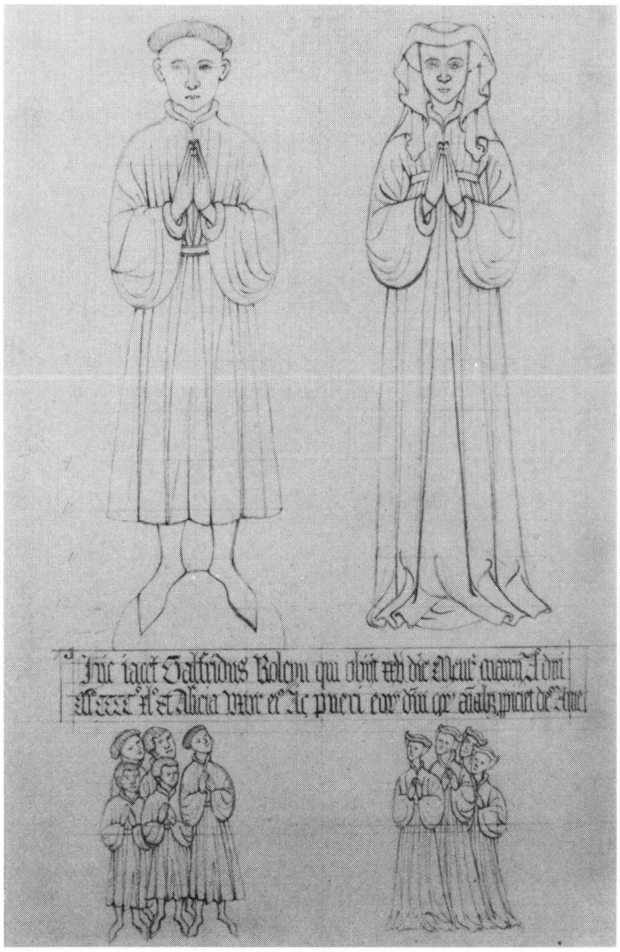

76 Monumental Brass, Salle, Norfolk: Geoffrey Boleyn and Family, (1440) *c.*1813-15

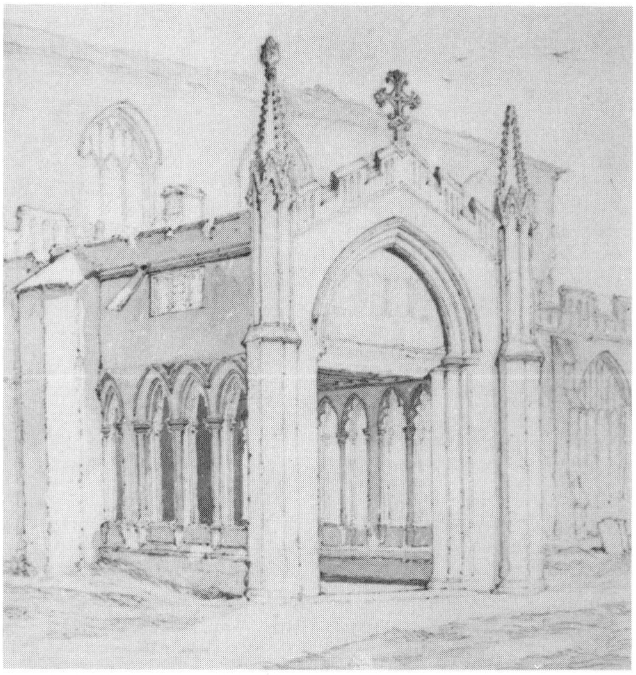

77 South Porch, Great Massingham Church, Norfolk, *c.*1816

was etched. The plate, according to its inscription, was first published by Cotman at Yarmouth in 1815. A comparison between the original monument,[1] No. 75 and the published plate reveals startling inaccuracies in the final etching, typical of a number which have subsequently given Cotman's publication of 1819 a poor reputation for accuracy. The etching shows only nine male children, instead of the correct number, eleven, together with changes of style which combine to falsify the quality and accuracy of Cotman's original drawing. The result is an unfaithful reproduction of the original brass which could be the result of a misinterpretation of Cotman's drawing by an assistant. This is an early indication of Cotman's reliance upon assistants, whose help he specifically acknowledges in a letter to Francis Cholmeley, 1 June 1817.

[1]Reproduced in R. Greenwood & M. Norris, *The Brasses of Norfolk Churches,* 1976 fig. 9.

76 Monumental Brass, Salle, Norfolk: Geoffrey Boleyn and Family (1440), *c.*1813-15.

Pencil on cream, wove paper; 29.3 × 19.1 ($11\frac{1}{2} \times 7\frac{1}{2}$). PROV: See No. 77 (423.235.951).

The memorial brass to Geoffrey Boleyn, his wife Alice and their children, lies in the nave of the church of St. Peter and St. Paul at Salle, Norfolk. The figures stand two feet, four inches high, while the sons and daughters are now missing from the bottom of the brass, one of seven brasses to this family in Norfolk.[1]

This subject is omitted from Cotman's *Engravings of The Most Remarkable of The Sepulchral Brasses in Norfolk,* (1819). This is surprising in view of the meticulous accuracy of this preliminary squared-up drawing. Cotman generally worked from impressions of brasses taken either by himself or on his behalf. His drawing is remarkably faithful to the style of the original monument. A copy of this drawing, by Elizabeth Turner, was used as an illustration to Dawson Turner's copy of Blomefield's *History of Norfolk.*[2] The one brass at Salle which Cotman did publish was that of John Brigge. Another Salle drawing by Cotman at Norwich is *Salle, Gothic Doorway.*[3]

[1]R. Greenwood & M. Norris, *The Brasses of Norfolk Churches,* 1976, p. 50. [2]Signed and dated *E.T. 1815* (BM 23,043 folio 94). [3]NCM 486.235.951.

77 South Porch, Great Massingham Church, Norfolk, *c.*1816

Pencil and brown wash on off white, wove paper with watermark r. edge *WHATMAN;* 22.9 × 21.7 ($9\frac{1}{16} \times 8\frac{9}{16}$). PROV: Rev. James Bulwer, by descent to his son James Radford Bulwer; by descent to his younger brother Walter Bulwer; by descent to his son Henry A. Bulwer; sold by him to Walker's Galleries; acquired by Percy Moore Turner; bt. from him with the rest of the Bulwer Collection of drawings by R. J. Colman, 9 June 1936; R. J. Colman Bequest 1946. (297.235.951). EXH: London, Walker's Galleries 1926 (53).

This fine drawing is a preliminary study of St. Mary's Church, Great Massingham, for the etching[1] of the same subject, which is inscribed on the plate to the effect that it was drawn, etched and published by Cotman at Yarmouth in 1817. The etching departs from the study in a number of minor instances, most notably in the removal of the four leaded windows of the tympanum, which are lightly sketched in the wash drawing. These features are more prosaically outlined in a pen, ink and sepia wash drawing attributed to William Taylor of Lynn,[2] which is taken from an almost identical viewpoint. Pevsner has observed that the porch was rebuilt in 1863.[3]

The sensitive and decorative pencil work of this sketch is similar to that of a Cotman drawing of the entrance porch of Cromer Church,[4] engraved by W. Deeble for Webb's *Excursions through Norfolk,* vol. I, and must date from the same period, *c.*1817. The south porch of St. Mary's, with its polygonal angle buttresses and decorative spirelets finds sensitive expression in Cotman's drawing style at this time. The drawing was copied by Mary Ann Turner in 1816 as an illustration to Dawson Turner's copy of Blomefield's *History of Norfolk.*[5]

Another Cotman drawing deriving from the same visit to the Church of St. Mary is *Great Massingham Church Carving,*[6] which represents a monk at a pulpit.

[1]Popham No. 107. [2]NCM Todd Collection, vol. IV Box 18 p. 172. [3]*North-West and South Norfolk* p. 439. [4]Fogg Art Museum, Cambridge, USA, No. 62.756. [5]BM Add. Ms. 23,035, folio 54. Ascribed to *MAT* in the MS index (BM Add. MS. 29738, folio 88). [6]NCM 489.235.951; Bulwer Collection, *Walker's Quarterly,* 1926, Nos. 19-20 p. 40 No. 82.

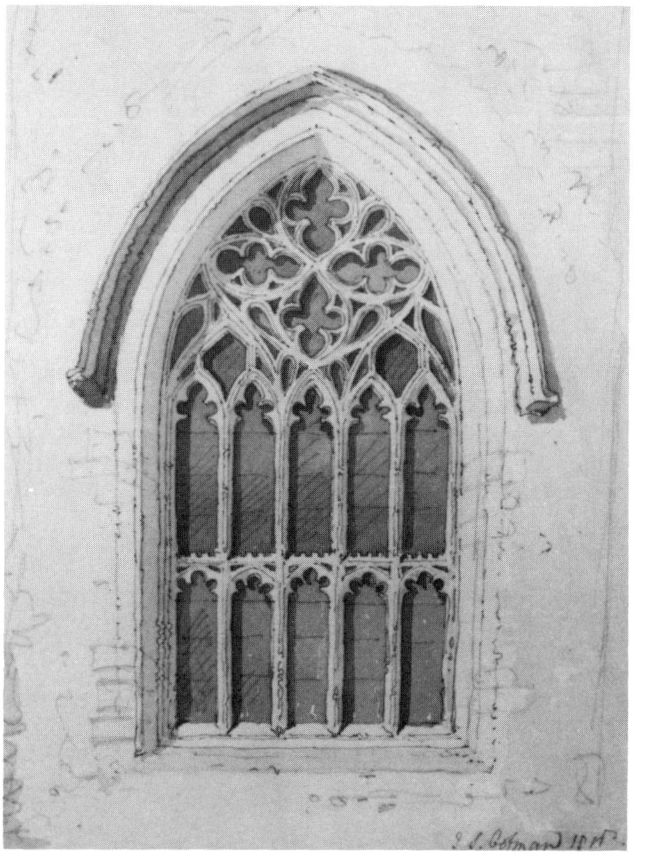

78 A Norfolk Church Window, *c.*1815-18

78 A Norfolk Church Window, *c.*1815-18

Pencil and brown wash on off white, wove paper; 22.2 × 16.5 ($8\frac{3}{4}$ × $6\frac{1}{2}$). INSCR: signed and dated in pencil l.r. *J. S. Cotman 1818.* PROV: R. J. Colman Bequest 1946. (298.235.951).

This delightful sketch is one of Cotman's most picturesque sepia wash drawings of any architectural feature dating from his Yarmouth period. The 'four-petalled flower' motif[1] of the tracery is a distinctive Norfolk type. Traditionally defined as the east window of Great Massingham Church, the tracery in fact bears no relationship to that window. It is, however very similar to that of the west window of Heacham Church, although the proportions of the elements are not exact and the window is set tightly beneath the gable of the roof and not within a larger wall as might be inferred from the drawing. Nevertheless, the Church of St. Mary at Heacham remains a possible candidate.[2]

This drawing does not appear to have been etched or engraved. The quality of the pencil work and wash suggests that, although originating from studies of an earlier visit to the Heacham area,[3] it was worked up in 1818, possibly with the intention of including it in Longman's *Excursions through Norfolk* (1818) or Cotman's own publication of the same year, *The Architectural Antiquities of Norfolk.*

[1]Pevsner, *North-West and South Norfolk,* p. 35. [2]Thanks are extended to Dr. Frank Woodman for his guidance. [3]JSC published a view of the nearby *West End of The Church at Snettisham,* inscribed *Drawn Etched & Published by J. S. Cotman 1815* (Popham No. 174), suggesting a visit to the area that year.

79 East Dereham, Norfolk 1818

illustrated on p.65

Pencil and brown wash on off white, wove paper; 14 × 22.9 ($5\frac{1}{2}$ × 9). INSCR: Signed and dated in pencil l.r. *J. S. Cotman 1818-* PROV: Colonel Bulwer; his sale, Quebec Hall, East Dereham, George Cubitt, 19-22 Aug. 1912, lot 1268, bt. Mase 9 gns; bt. from him by R. J. Colman ?1912; R. J. Colman Bequest 1946. (290.235.951). EXH: Norwich 1930-31.

This is one of a series of sensitive drawings in pencil and monochrome washes of distant Norfolk views. Of similar size they are all dated 1818, an example being *Walsingham Priory*[1] —which was engraved for reproduction in Longman's *Excursions through Norfolk,* published in two volumes in 1818 and 1819. *East Dereham* was not, however, included amongst those finally selected for reproduction, although it was copied by one of the Turner girls as an illustration to Dawson Turner's copy of Blomefield's *History of Norfolk.*[2]

The focal point of the view is the church of St. Nicholas, at the west end of the town of East Dereham. The church has a noble outline, thanks to the 'mighty detached bell tower and the grouping of the church itself round its crossing tower. Both towers lack parapets, battlements, and pinnacles, which makes them appear somewhat forbidding'.[3] No. 79 shows the south-east view of the church. The second tower was traditionally referred to as the 'new clocker'.[4]

Cotman had previously published as one of his *Specimens of Norman and Gothic Architecture in the County of Norfolk,* in 1817, a view of the *South Porch East Dereham Church, Nork*[5] for which two related drawings are a preliminary drawing[6] and a separate study of the *Piscina in the South Porch, East Dereham.*[7]

[1]Fitzwilliam, No. 747. [2]BM Add. Ms. 23028, folio 170. Ascribed to *MAT* in the Ms. index (BM Add. Ms. 29738, folio 44, verso). [3]Pevsner, *North-West and South Norfolk* p. 141. [4]Blomefield p. 1187. [5]Popham No. 48. [6]Fogg Art Museum, Cambridge, USA, No. 48. 1103. [7]NCM 458.235.951.

80 Sherringham Hall, Norfolk, 1818

illustrated on p. 67

Pencil and brown wash on off white, wove paper; 17.3 × 26.2 ($6\frac{13}{16}$ × $10\frac{5}{16}$). INSCR: Signed and dated in pencil l.l. *J S Cotman 1818.* PROV: Rev. James Bulwer; by descent to his son James Radford Bulwer; by descent to his younger brother Walter Bulwer; by descent to his son Henry A. Bulwer; bt. from him by Walker's Galleries; bt. from them by R. J. Colman, 13 July 1926 with three others £393.15.0.; R. J. Colman Bequest 1946. (305.235.951). EXH: London, Walker's Galleries 1926 (149) as *Sherringham Hall, Norfolk, the Seat of Abbot Upcher, Esq.*

In 1818 and 1819 the London publisher Longman issued the guidebook *Excursions through Norfolk,* in two volumes. The total number of one hundred engravings illustrating the text were produced after drawings by artists such as Thomas Higham and John Thirtle. The bulk of the designs, however, were after a series of 76 drawings by Cotman, including frontispieces to both volumes.

The drawing of Sheringham Hall is one of a series of monochrome wash drawings produced by Cotman for the engravers employed on the project. Engraved by William Wallis, *Sherringham Hall* was published 1 June 1818. Although placed opposite page 149 of the first volume, there is no textual reference to the Hall, presumably because, built to the design of Humphrey Repton's son John Adey Repton between 1812 and 1817, it had only recently been completed. Indeed, as Cotman's drawing clearly shows, the grounds were still in the process of being landscaped to the design of Humphrey Repton.

Repton later called Sheringham Hall his favourite work.[1] Built for Abbot Upcher, it has remained in the family, surrounded by beautiful grounds not yet apparent in Cotman's view. This shows the west facade with its porch supported by two pairs of Tuscan columns. The drawing is unusual in its forceful response to the unfinished site; the majority of Cotman's studies of the Country seats of Norfolk for this project reveal a more restrained and harmonious vision. This is the case with two other drawings from the series, both in the Colman Collection, *Langley Hall*[2] and *Melton Constable Park.*[3] In this picture, however, the delicate pencilwork of the hall itself is set in opposition to the spiky, strident drawing of the foreground and the resonant application of washes in the distant trees. The effect of the composition as a whole is one of purposeful vigour. The composition was copied by Elizabeth Turner as an illustration for Dawson Turner's copy of Blomefield's *History of Norfolk.*[4]

[1]Pevsner, *North-East Norfolk and Norwich* p. 314. [2]NCM 299.235.951, engraved by J. Hawksworth for *Excursions,* vol. I, opp. p. 91. [3]NCM 301.235.951, engraved by J. Webb for *Excursions,* vol I, opp. p. 173. [4]BM Add. MS. 23043, folio 187. Ascribed to *ET* in the Ms index (BM Add. Ms. 29738, folio 163).

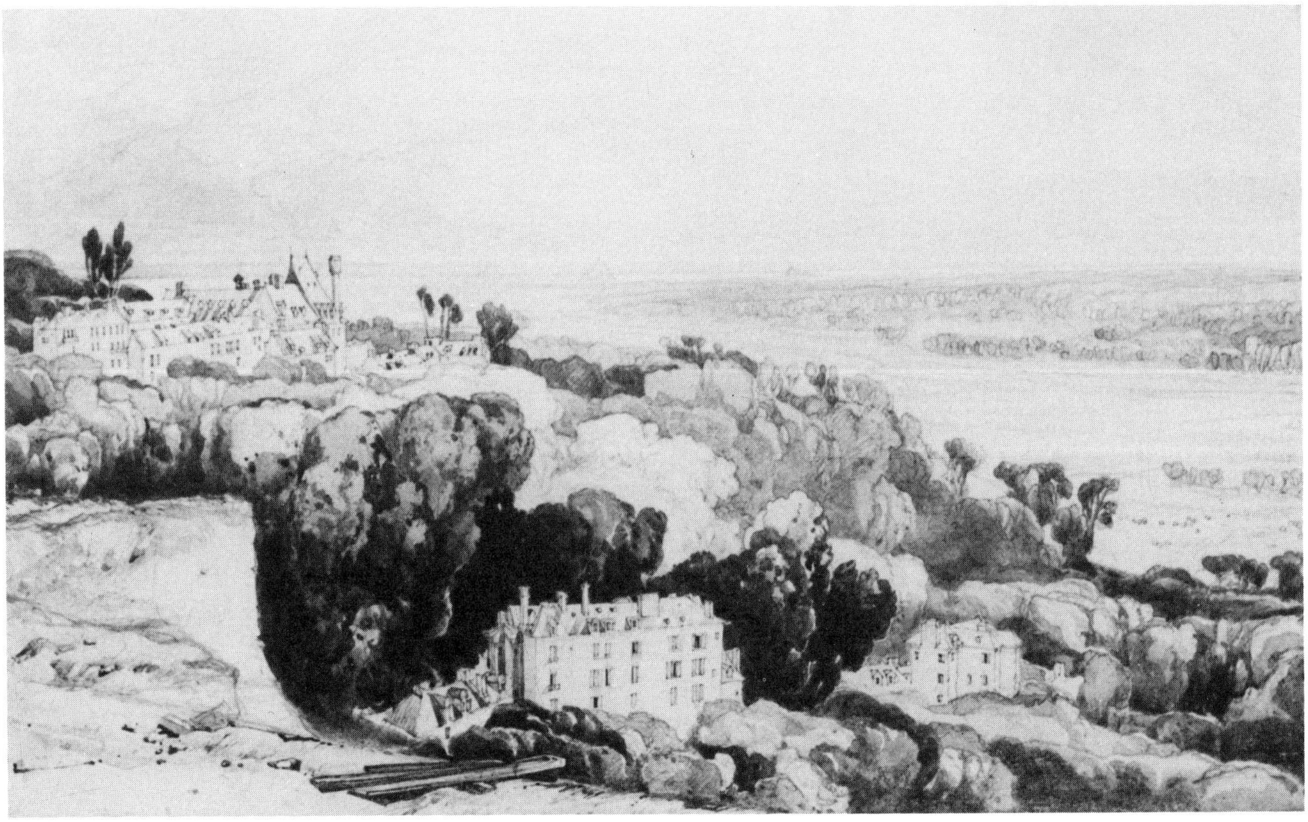

82 Distant View of Mont St. Michel and Tombelaine from the Terrace of the Cathedral of Avranches, *c.*1817-24

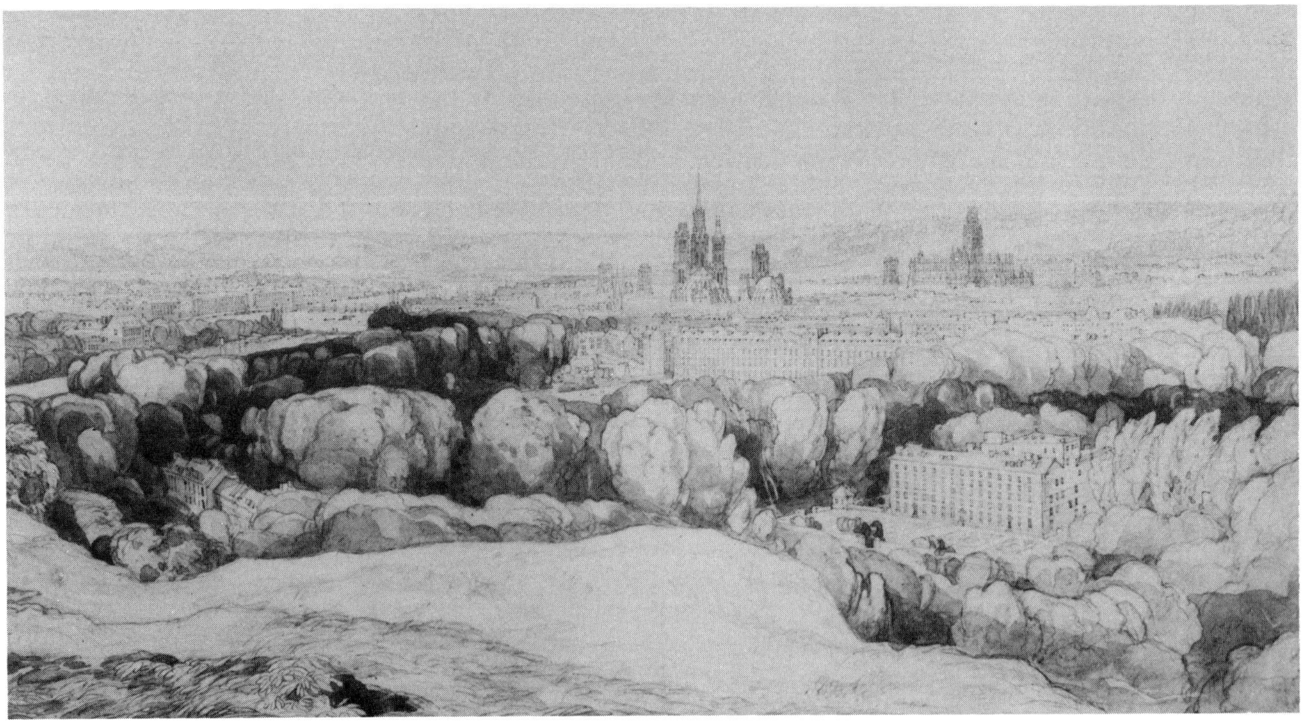

83 Rouen from Mont Ste. Catherine, *c.*1817-24

7
The Three Normandy Tours and their Outcome 1817-1823

During his period at Yarmouth, Cotman made three major visits to Normandy, in the summers of 1817, 1818 and 1820. Although there is no indication of Dawson Turner's specific involvement in Cotman's announcement to Francis Cholmeley on 1 June 1817: 'On Saturday I quit home for Normandy to collect fresh materials for my pencil and my etching needle',[1] it appears that the first tour was Turner's brainchild. Turner had himself visited Normandy with Thomas Phillips RA in September 1815, primarily to see the works of art brought back to Paris by Napoleon. The following year Turner had informed M. Lamouroux, Professor of Botany at Caen, of his desire to collect volumes about Normandy, a move which resulted in the addition to his library of a number of important works on French and Norman antiquities.[2] It was but a short step to conceive the notion of publishing his own volume on the antiquities of Normandy, illustrated by the well-proven talents of John Sell Cotman.

Cotman's three Normandy tours are extremely well documented.[3] By prior agreement, Cotman wrote full accounts of his travels both to his wife and to Dawson Turner, who subsequently made full use of them in the text of his own *A Tour of Normandy* (1820). Cotman's first letter to Dawson Turner at the outset of his initial trip was from London.[4] He recounts the events of a busy few days, including the receipt of a camera lucida from Sir Henry Englefield who had also given him 'an unlimited order' for drawings of Amiens, Abbeville and Beauvais. He had, in addition, visited the Royal Academy, the Old Water-Colour Society and the Elgin Marbles, newly installed at the British Museum. He subsequently sailed from Brighton on 18 June, arriving at Dieppe after a forty-two hour voyage. The following day he made his first excursion into the countryside where despite being 'exhausted from Heat', he later exclaimed 'good heavens what a lovely country! Everything is picturesque.'[5]

Cotman's method during the five and a half weeks of this first tour and indeed the subsequent tours of 1818 and 1820, was to rely almost entirely upon his sketchbook and pencil to record the buildings and scenery he visited. As Kitson commented: 'No sepia or water-colour drawings, made on the spot, survive among his Normandy sketches, and it seems that Cotman did not take painting materials with him . . . He relied upon his pencil and upon his memory.'[6] In addition he made considerable use of the camera lucida, primarily for the more mechanical recording of the detail and proportions of church and cathedral facades.

Cotman left Dieppe on 25 June, having visited the Castle of Arques on two separate occasions (Nos. 97, 98). He proceeded via Fécamp (No. 95) and Montivilliers to Le Havre, from where he visited Graville and Harfleur, before proceeding to Bolbec and Tancarville 'a place more romantic I have never seen, a perfect picture'.[7] The next day he sketched at Lillebonne, arriving at Rouen on 3 July, at three o'clock in the morning: 'a fine old city, the front of the cathedral here most gorgeous. I was a week drawi[n]g the front with a camera lucida which Sir Henry gave me, but not knowing how to use it, I so misused it that I am afraid my labour is entirely lost, from getting different focuses'.[7] He made two excursions from Rouen—to Lery and St. Martin de Boscherville—before moving on to Caen, 'full of interesting specimens of the *circular* style of arch, my object'.[7] He made Caen (Nos. 81, 84) his base for some ten days, visiting Allenagne and Langrune sur Mer whilst there. He then moved on to Avranches, via Bayeux and St. Lô. He disliked this stay at St. Lô—'people here all barbarians'[7]—whilst his inn he found nauseous: 'my ascent to my chamber was through every stench in nature'.[8] His experience of the next town, Coutances (No. 87) was little better, as he was 'followed by a troop of greasy night Caps of every color, & with no very inviting grimaces.'[8]

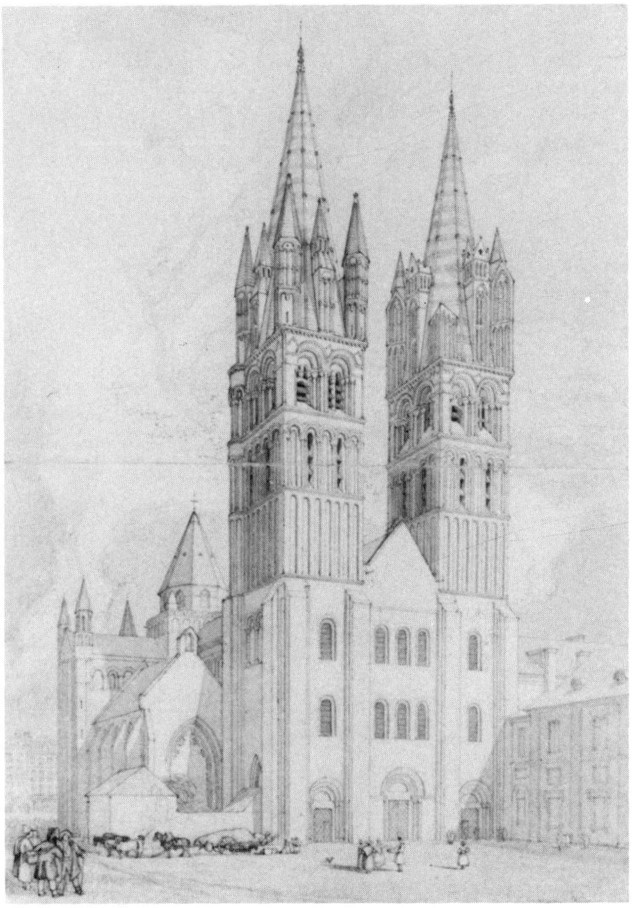

81 Abbey Church of St. Etienne Caen, West Front, *c.*1817-19

He travelled on to Granville and Avranches (No. 82), 'both beautifully situated, from the latter visited that most curious and awful Mont St. Michel.'[7] This was the first of three visits to this mountain fastness, which affected him with 'astonishment mixed with terror'[8] at its looming magnitude. After this experience he retraced his steps by the most direct route back to Le Havre, passing through Vielledieu-les-Poeles, Vires, Caen and Harfleur. He sailed from Le Havre for Southampton on 10 August and wrote to his wife from London the next day: 'business may take me there [Normandy] again, but never, oh never shall I be led there by Pleasure.'[9]

Cotman was in fact persuaded to return to Normandy the following summer. On this occasion he visited the region east of Rouen as well as the environs of Valognes and Cherbourg, in addition to revisiting a number of the towns with which he was already familiar. In 1818 his trip was twice as long as the previous year and spent in the company of Dawson Turner's family for over seven weeks. An additional manuscript source to Mrs. Turner's letters describing their tour is Mary Ann Turner's Diary,[10] which records their journey from London to Rouen and subsequently through parts of Northern Normandy during June and July. The group was joined by Dawson Turner for a short period at the end of July, when he personally visited Caen and Falaise.

Mrs. Turner and her daughters arrived at Rouen on 10 June, escorted by her son-in-law, William Hooker. However, he soon departed for a tour of Italy and Mrs. Turner confided in her husband: 'I long for Mr. Cotman's arrival . . . He will be very useful both as a man and an artist'.[11] The ladies were at this time having considerable difficulty both with the camera lucida and their own talents. Elizabeth Turner had looked upon Rouen Cathedral 'with fear and amazement as a subject for her pencil'.[11] Cotman set sail from Dieppe on 19 June and, travelling down to the north east of Rouen, arrived at Gournay on 22 June, where he met the Turner ladies the next day. They set off immediately by carriage to Les Andelys and visited Château Gaillard (No. 181) on 24 June.

On 25 June, the party returned to Rouen, where they met M. Le Prevost, the Bernay archaeologist and historian who was Dawson Turner's main contact in France. They remained there —apart from one excursion into the surrounding countryside —until 6 July. On 26 June Elizabeth Turner wrote to her father a revealing account of Cotman's practice: 'I hope that his plans will be accurately chalked out for him, for on looking over the map with him yesterday I find that he has left something unfinished in almost every large town so that he must retrace almost all he did last year . . . This has been owing to a sad defect of management, not of industry; for no one works harder at all times when he is before a subject he likes.'[12] While the charge that 'he left something unfinished in almost every large town' is undoubtedly true, he nevertheless covered much new ground on his second visit, whilst a certain retracing of his steps was perhaps inevitable. He remained a good companion to the ladies and Mrs. Turner was grateful for his presence, adding to her daughter's letter: 'he is so encouraging in the spirit he imparts and the help that he gives'. Cotman was certainly pleased with the results, sending Dawson Turner a list of 'seventy one subjects, out of which twenty five or thirty may be fairly selected for publication. For so short a time nothing more cd. have been expected.'[13]

Cotman left Rouen in the company of the Turner family, travelling with them as far as Honfleur, before making his own way on to Caen, which he reached on 24 July. He was joined once again by the Turner ladies and Dawson Turner himself finally arrived at Caen on 28 July. During the first two weeks of August Cotman was in the constant company of the Turners and the English community at Caen. He made sketching forays only after the Turner family had departed for England, visiting Thaon, Fontaine-Henry (No. 84) and Creully (No. 85) over the weekend of 14-17 August. On 20 August he left Caen for Valognes, where he took a letter of introduction to M. de Gerville, who became a warm friend and accompanied him on a second visit to Mont St. Michel. His return journey included Avranches, Valognes and Falaise. He was at Honfleur by 7 September, having been in Normandy for almost twelve weeks.

Under Dawson Turner's guidance the essential aim of Cotman's first two visits to Normandy had been to gather material for the publication of his *Architectural Antiquities of Normandy*, with a letterpress by Turner. His two tours had provided him with ample material, but he nevertheless conceived the idea of a third tour. In a long retrospective letter to Francis Cholmeley, Cotman reveals the two reasons for his embarking yet again for Normandy. Writing from Coutances towards the end of this

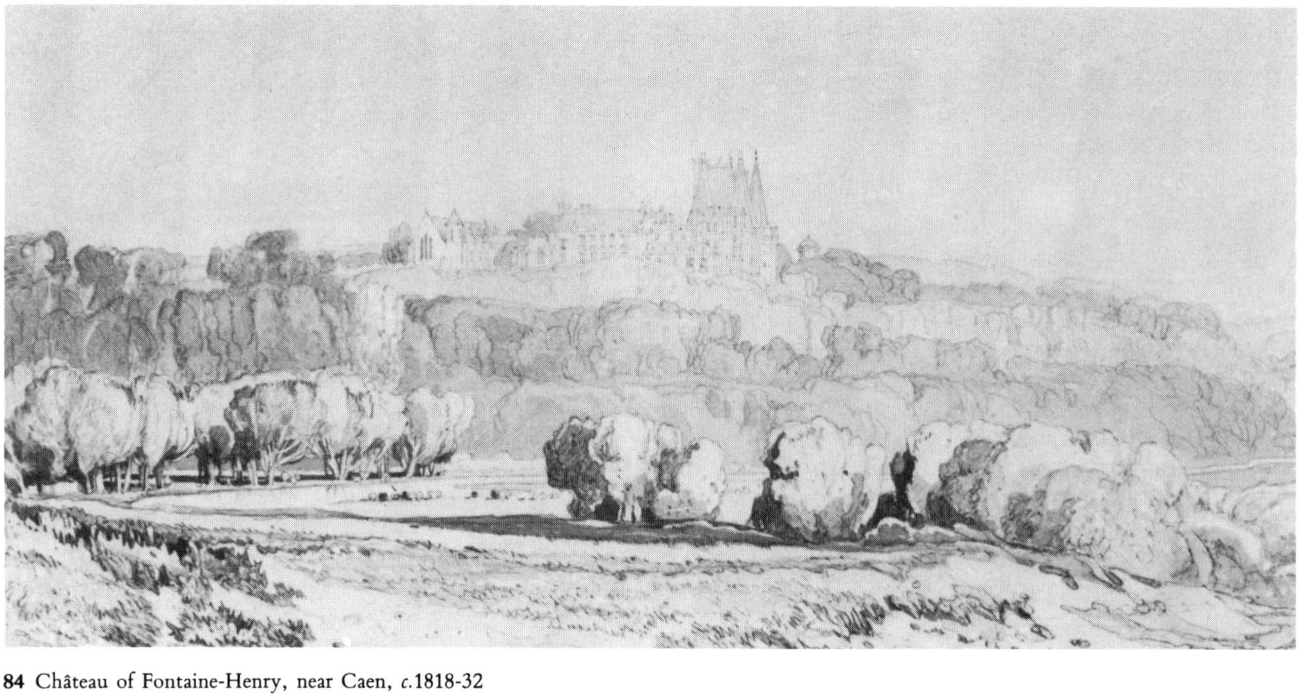

84 Château of Fontaine-Henry, near Caen, *c.*1818-32

final tour he explains:[14] 'I entered France for my health and to unite if possible business with it, though of a doubtful kind for I had settled no plan, except[in]g probably of [a] collection [of] views of the cathedrals and by so doing, adding another part, making them in all 5 p[ar]ts. But I had also an *idea* that the country afford[s] features sufficie[n]tly striking, of giving a picturesque tour distinct from the first work. This I have found to a most surprising degree and I beli[e]ve I shall be able to shew that Normandy is not a *flat country* at least.' He remarked that it reminded him of 'the most beautiful parts of Yorkshire.' In like vein he had written a month earlier to his wife of the country between Domfront and Mortain at the southernmost region of Normandy, that it was 'everything a Painter could wish for . . . the Wales of France'.[15] He was enraptured by the region and determined whilst there to 'announce to the public in some way not yet decided upon my firm intention of showing them the picturesque tour of Normandy.'[15] Although these plans never materialised into published form, the majority of the views selected here reveal the sublimity of his picturesque vision of Normandy which he grew to love: 'the more I see of it and of the people, the more I like both'[14] — an overall view which compensated for some of the more uncomfortable exploits and direct hostility that he had encountered at times. His vision was kindled by 'the picturesque scenery of this most delightful country'[16] and his letters of this visit are filled with a sense of enchantment.

Cotman's last tour of Normandy was cut short through illness. Having journeyed north to Valognes he was troubled by a swollen leg, no doubt exacerbated by his mode of transport. This was now usually by the main public form of transport, the Diligence 'which, however much I may have condemned them — are *easy chairs* to Coaches & cabriolets and their packhorses . . . everything is good or bad but by comparison'.[17] He paid repeat visits to Cherbourg and again to Mont St. Michel, before returning home across familiar territory via Avranches, Granville and St. Lô to Caen. Here he was confined to bed, before leaving 'in a condition that was worrying for his friends.'[18]

Cotman's last three years at Yarmouth were characterised by the 'Herculean labor'[19] of completing the plates for his *Architectural Antiquities of Normandy,* finally published in two volumes in 1822. As he confided to Francis Cholmeley, his habit was to work solidly from 8.30 a.m. until dusk, with only an hour's break for dinner, 'whether it was winter or summer'.[19] He left his house to go into Yarmouth only once a week, a habit 'fatal as poison'. Thus it comes as no surprise that on a visit to London he suffered a collapse, brought on by a liver complaint and the belief that he had swallowed a pin. He gradually recovered during the autumn, when his thoughts turned once again towards Norwich.

Notes

[1]JSC to Francis Cholmeley, 1 June 1817. [2]Rajnai 1975 p. 1. [3]See Isherwood Kay, *The Walpole Society* and in particular Rajnai 1975. [4]JSC to DT, 12 June 1817, *Walpole Society* vol. XIV pp. 93-94. [5]JSC to DT, 12 June 1817, *Ibid.* pp. 96-98. [6]Kitson 1937 p. 194. [7]JSC to Francis Cholmeley, 5 Jan. 1818. [8]JSC to DT, 3 Aug. 1817, *Walpole Society* vol. XIV pp. 106-108. [9]JSC to Mrs. Cotman, 11 Aug. 1817, *Ibid.* p. 108-109. [10]NCM 3.483.970. [11]Kitson 1937 pp. 203-4. [12]Barker Collection. [13]JSC to DT, 12 July 1818, *Walpole Society* vol. XIV pp. 112-115. [14]JSC to Francis Cholmeley, 25 Sept. 1820. [15]JSC to his wife, 26 Aug. 1820, *Walpole Society* vol. XV p. 116. [16]JSC to his wife, 17 Sept. 1820, *Ibid.* p. 121. [17]JSC to his wife, 2 Sept. 1820, *Ibid.* p. 118. [18]De Gerville to DT, 5 Nov. 1820 (Trinity College, Cambridge, quoted Rajnai 1975 p. 4). [19]JSC to Francis Cholmeley, 23 July 1822.

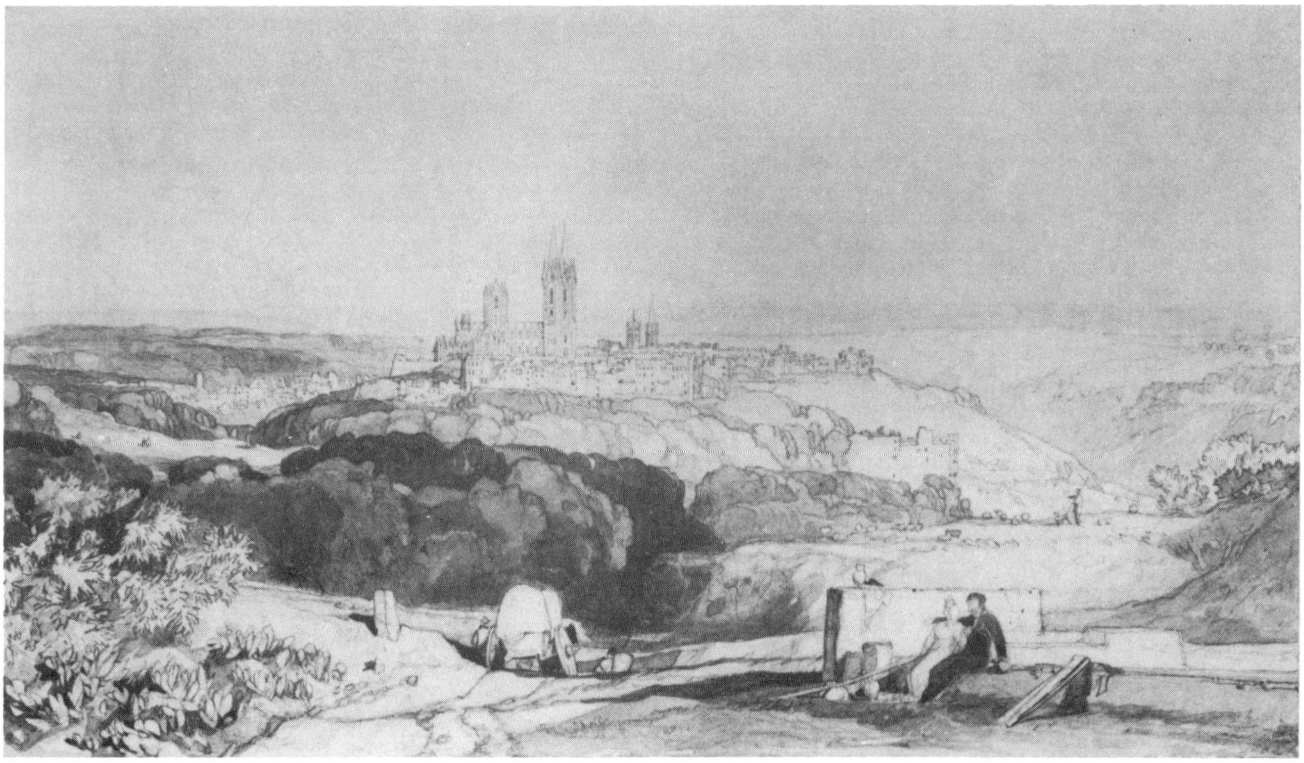

87 Coutances, *c.* 1818-24

81 Abbey Church of St. Etienne, Caen, West Front *c.*1817-19
illustrated on p. 75

Pencil and grey wash on cream, wove paper in two pieces; 47.1 × 32.7 ($18\frac{9}{16}$ × $12\frac{7}{8}$). INSCR: *Recto,* signed and dated in pencil l.r. *J. S. Cotman 1817.;* inscribed by the artist in margin in pencil l.l. *Abbey Church of St. Stephen at Caen.* PROV: ?The artist's sale, Christie's, 1 May 1824, lot 53, bt. Taylor £1.0.0.; James Reeve by 1902; bt. from him after 1903 by H. S. Theobald; bt. from him by R. J. Colman, Feb. 1910; R. J. Colman Bequest 1946. (285.235.951). EXH: Norwich 1903 (18) lent by James Reeve: Norwich 1930-31; Norwich 1969 and V & A 1970 (13). REF: Kitson 1937 pp. 197-198; Rajnai 1975 No. 11.

Rajnai observes that: 'Cotman spent more time in Caen than any other place in Normandy, consequently the Caen subjects are the most numerous in his Normandy output. His stay amounted to nearly two months spread over five visits: two visits in 1817 (11 and 2 days), one in 1818 (26 days) and two in 1820 (8 and 13 days).'

Cotman visited the Abbey of St. Stephen (i.e. St. Etienne or Abbaye-aux-Hommes) on each of his tours of Normandy. By the sixth day of his stay in Caen in 1817, he had already finished a sketch of it, presumed by Rajnai to be that of the west front: 'I am sketching St. Stephens Abbey from an awkward position from an oblique window from which I am obliged to lean out.'[1]

In 1818 he seems to have gone directly to St. Stephen's on arrival, but wrote to Mrs. Turner: 'I have been visiting the Abbey St. Etienne & fell asleep in y Nave—so much for enthusiasm over exhausted nature'.[2] He also reports sketching inside the church on his last full day in Caen during this visit.

In August 1820 he returned to Caen and recorded: 'Wednesday 9th. Cut all Friends today & filled my bag with good game. Met Mr. Lewis as he was drawing the towers, St. Etienne at Caen—'.[3]

No. 81 is a full scale design for an etched version[4] published on 7 October 1819. The date, 1817, signifies the year in which he sketched the subject and is not necessarily the date of execution. The same view appears in a watercolour version[5] and there is also a copy, but without the figures, by Elizabeth Turner.[6]

Cotman exhibited the etched version with the Norwich Society in 1820 (213), when it was praised as one of two etchings 'of very commanding excellence' by the *Norfolk Chronicle* 29 July 1820. The subject was shown again with the same Society in 1828 (154) and possibly with the OWCS two years earlier in 1826 (215), *Abbey church of St. Stephen, at Caen.*

St. Stephen's provided three more subjects for Cotman: *Military School and Abbey Church,*[7] etched by Mary Anne Turner;[8] *The Great West Doorway,* one of the three items in lot 54 in Cotman's 1824 sale;[9] *Elevation of part of the nave,*[7] also in lot 54 and etched in *Normandy* 1822, pl. 23.[10]

[1]JSC to DT, Caen 22 July 1817 (BM). [2]JSC to Mrs. DT, Caen 24 July 1818 (BM). [3]JSC to his wife, Caen 6 Aug. 1820 (BM). [4]Popham No. 221. [5]Discussed Rajnai 1975 pp. 55, 56. [6]Book of Drawings, No. 25. [7]Probably now in the Mellon Collection (Rajnai). [8]*A Tour in Normandy* 1820 vo. 2 pl. 41. [9]A copy by Elizabeth Turner is in the Book of Drawings, No. 26. [10]Popham No. 222. Other known Caen subjects by Cotman are listed in Rajnai 1975 pp. 56, 57.

82 Distant View of Mont St. Michel and Tombelaine from the Terrace of the Cathedral of Avranches, *c.*1817-24
illustrated on p. 74

Pencil and brown wash with some scraping out on white, wove paper; 29.5 × 46.8 ($11\frac{9}{16}$ × $18\frac{3}{8}$). INSCR: *Verso,* numbered ?in watercolour l.c. *No. 8.* Prov: ?Cotman sale, Spelman, Norwich, 16 May 1861, included in lot 81, bt. James King £25.4.0.; John Thomas Mott; ?his sale Christie's, 28 Feb. 1885, included in lot 125 bt. Martin Colnaghi £215.5.0 for R. H. Benson;[1] his sale Christie's, 13 March 1893, bt. Watson £21, presumably for J. J. Colman; his bequest to R. J. Colman 1898; sold by him Christie's, Red Cross sale, 12th day, 20 April 1918, lot 1807, bt. Carfax 36 gns.; bt. Sir Michael Sadler—returned to R. J. Colman 8 Dec. 1929 in exchange for an oil by Signac; R. J. Colman Bequest 1946. (176.235.951). EXH: ?Norwich Society 1824 (198*); Norwich 1903 (65); Manchester 1912 (347); Tate 1922 (159) lent by Sir Michael Sadler; Norwich 1945. REF: Rajnai 1975 No. 10.

Cotman visited Avranches on each trip to Normandy. In 1817 he arrived at 8 o'clock in the evening, 1 August. Rajnai suggests that he may well have sketched the view for No. 82 on Monday, 3 August when he had an unexpected extra day at Avranches and planned to 'employ [his] pencil in something to fill up [his] time'.[1]

Cotman passed through Avranches again in 1818, staying overnight on the 28 August, this time in the company of M. de Gerville, the Valognes antiquarian. His third and last visit was from 21-24 September 1820 when he used Avranches as a base for an excursion to what he calls 'my fav[o]urite Mont'.[2]

Cotman's viewpoint in No. 82 is near La Plat-forme, the site of the former Cathedral which had collapsed in 1794 and was subsequently demolished. Rajnai quotes a verbal description of the view from this site, given by Mrs. Charles Stothard, the wife of the antiquarian draughtsman, who was travelling with her husband in Normandy in 1818 at practically the same time as Cotman: 'the valley below, covered with woods and fine verdure, appears far distant, extending for many miles. The town winds round the hill in gentle descent—In the bottom the river [Sée] serpentines through many Branches, till it falls into a large arm of the sea. The thick woods grow to the extreme verge of the shore, and form a beautiful contrast to the wide expanse of waters, in which they seem to have their branches. Beyond, in the midst of the sea, arises 400 feet above the surface of the water, the majestic rock of Mount St. Michael, and near it another, but smaller rock called the Tombalaine'.[3]

The building on the left is a Benedictine Priory.

[1]JSC to DT, Avranches 3 Aug. 1817 (BM). [2]JSC to his wife, addressed to DT, Avranches 23 Sept. 1820 (BM). [3]Mrs. Charles Stothard 1820 p. 178.

83 Rouen from Mont Ste. Catherine, *c.*1817-24
illustrated on p. 74

Pencil and brown wash on white, wove paper with watermark r. edge *J WHATMAN;* 25.1 ×45.5 ($9\frac{7}{8}$ × $17\frac{15}{16}$). INSCR: *Recto,* paper squared. PROV: Cotman sale, Spelman, Norwich, 16 May 1861 ?included in lot 81, bt. James King 24 gns.; bt. from him by J. J. Colman; his bequest to R. J. Colman 1898; R. J. Colman Bequest 1946. (177.235.951). EXH: ?Norwich Society 1824 (191*); Norwich 1903 (63); Manchester 1912 (358); Tate 1922 (182); Norwich 1945. REF: Kitson 1937 pp. 206-7; Rajnai 1975 No. 33.

Cotman visited Rouen both in 1817 and 1818. On his first visit he spent ten full days there, excluding excursions. His second visit from 25 June to 15 July 1818 was made in the company of Mrs. Turner and her two daughters, Elizabeth and Mary Anne.

Elizabeth Turner records in her diary their descent into Rouen: 'we proceeded straight to Rouen which we entered by a road near Mont Ste. Catherine. The whole view of the town & river opened suddenly on us in the finest manner possible & Mr. Cotman immediately determined on making a drawing of it from that spot.'[1]

The next day Elizabeth gives this account of the drawing to her father: 'Mr. Cotman has been making a charming drawing of Rouen from a spot near Mount Ste. Catherine, looking down on the river & the beautiful green islands, & taking in the Cathedral, the bridge of boats & all the faubourg St. Sever.'[2]

This was, however, the second view sketched by Cotman from the heights to the south-east of the town. The first had been from the Côte Ste. Catherine 'very early' on Sunday, 13 July 1817.[3]

As No. 83 is a view from the Côte Ste. Catherine it must be based on the earlier sketch of 1817. Rajnai observes that Cotman 'was standing at the edge of a sheer drop to get the view he wanted, a low enough position to allow the towers of the Cathedral and St. Ouen's tower to break the skyline but not so low as to lose from sight the river, the Ile de Lacroix, the Bridge of Boats and the faubourg of St. Sever on the other side of the Seine. The three major landmarks of the townscape are the cathedral in the centre of the drawing, with its central tower . . . St. Maclou slightly to the right and further right St. Ouen, still without its two western towers.'

Elizabeth Turner concluded that this view: 'is indeed when seen from this distance accompanied by the rich country, the fine river, & the distant blue mountains, all receiving a glow from the setting sun, a truly romantic town.'[4] Cotman has responded to the view by producing one of his most sensitively-observed panoramas which combines delicate attention to the detail of the buildings with the broad treatment of the foreground and foliage.[5]

[1]Elizabeth Turner's Diary p. 45. [2]ET to DT, Rouen 26 June 1818 (Barker Collection). [3]JSC to wife in letter to DT, Rouen 6 July 1817 (BM). [4]Elizabeth Turner's Diary p. 30. Elizabeth is looking at the city from higher up, not from Cotman's more precarious viewpoint. [5]Other known Rouen subjects by Cotman are discussed in Rajnai 1975 No. 33 n. 23.

84 Château of Fontaine-Henry, near Caen, *c.*1818-23

illustrated on p. 76

Pencil and brown wash on cream, wove paper; 19.7 × 39.5 (7$\frac{3}{4}$ × 15$\frac{1}{2}$). Inscr: *Recto,* signed and dated in pencil l.r. *J S Cotman 1818* (lower part of signature and date missing, paper cut); *verso,* l.l. *No. 11 / No. 4* (indistinct). Prov: Same as No. 82; R. H. Benson sale, Christie's, 13 March 1893, bt. Watson 19 gns, presumably for J. J. Colman; his bequest to R. J. Colman 1898; R. J. Colman Bequest 1946. (180.235.951). Exh: ?Norwich Society 1823 (146). Ref: Kitson 1937 pp. 214, 215; Rajnai 1975 No. 26.

Until 1975 the subject of No. 84 was unidentified and known simply as *Château in Normandy.* Rajnai has, however, identified the view as of the eastern side of the Château of Fontaine-Henry which Cotman visited on 15-16 August 1818: '. . . & to Fontaine Henry, the Château of Monsieur le Vicomte Henry de Canissy, —*one of the most beautiful* & elegant residences you can well conceive—fitted up with taste & *comfort* perfectly English—The old walls, once surrounding it, entirely thrown down, & a good carriage way made in their stead— flower beds directly up to the windows—grass plots & shrubberies at a little distance with fruit trees intermixed—extensive garden, 4 carriages, &, in one stable, 12 fine carriage & riding horses of the finest breed—such is the state of Fontaine Henry.

15th. To this place I rode, & on the carriage way made a dead halt; such a one as Sancho-Panza might have made when most surprized; & not unlike my equipage—a vile brute, with my *pack & stool & table fixed behind.* Well, I rang at the bell, & demanded permission to draw the Château which was granted immediately, & I saw no more of my poor beast till the 16th when I left Fontaine for Creully—.'[1]

The date on the drawing probably records the year in which the subject was sketched. The pencil sketch from which the Norwich drawing was developed is in Leeds City Art Gallery[2] and a pencil drawing in outline is in a private collection.[3] Cotman drew two other aspects of the Château, known by plates 62 and 63 in *Architectural Antiquities of Normandy* 1822, showing the west front and its middle section.[4] These must have been based on the two drawings in lot 60 of Cotman's sale in 1824: *Château of Fontaine le Henri, near Caen; Central Compartment of Ditto.* He also drew a *Sculpture in the Castle,* which was one of three drawings in lot 61 of that sale (a copy by Elizabeth Turner is in the book of Drawings, No. 48).

[1]JSC to DT, Caen 18 Aug. 1818 (BM). [2]Leeds 9.124/49. [3]Dr. J. F. Young 1975. [4]Popham Nos. 260 & 261. [5]Cotman also drew two details of the romanesque chancel of the village church (see lot 61 in Cotman's 1824 sale), presumably the drawings etched in *Architectural Antiquities of Normandy* 1822, pls. 60 & 61. (Popham Nos. 258 & 259).

85 Castle of Creully, *c.*1818-24

Pencil and brown wash on cream, wove paper; 18.7 × 38.7 (7$\frac{3}{8}$ × 15$\frac{1}{4}$). Inscr: *Recto,* signed and dated in pencil l.r. *J. S. Cotman 1818* (last digit indistinct, paper cut); *verso,* numbered in pencil l.c.l. . . . *14* (indistinct). Prov: Same as No. 82; R. H. Benson sale Christie's, 13 March 1893, lot 73, bt. Watson £15.4.6., presumably for J. J. Colman; his bequest to R. J. Colman 1898; R. J. Colman Bequest 1946. (168.235.951). Exh: ?Norwich Society 1824 (204*); Norwich 1945. Ref: Kitson 1937 p. 217 as *Brest;* Rajnai 1975 No. 20.

Cotman paid a short visit to Creully during his second tour, 1818, when on a four days' excursion from Caen: '[August] 16, Sunday, left Fontaine for Creully—well received by Genl. Hodgson—sketched the Château—17th, Monday, sketched the church, returned to Caen, . . .'[1]

Dawson Turner's account of the castle is only brief both in his *Tour* and in the second volume of Cotman's *Architectural Antiquities of Normandy* 1822: '. . . the baronial castle is still standing, and displays, in two of its towers and in a chimney of unusual form, a portion of its ancient character: the rest of the building is modernized into a spruce, comfortable residence, and is at this time occupied by a countryman of our own, General Hodgson.'[2]

Rajnai has established that the traditional belief that No. 85 represents Brest is entirely mistaken. It is a view of Creully Castle from the north-west with the River Seulles at its foot.[3] The polygonal spire to the right of the square tower is that of the church behind, which Cotman says he sketched on Monday 17 August. The subject of the sketch must have been the interior view etched in *Architectural Antiquities of Normandy* 1822, pl. 91.

[1]JSC to DT, Caen 18 Aug. 1818 (copy in BM). [2]*A Tour in Normandy* 1820 vol. 2, p. 264. [3]The identification was made by Judy Hines, 1974.

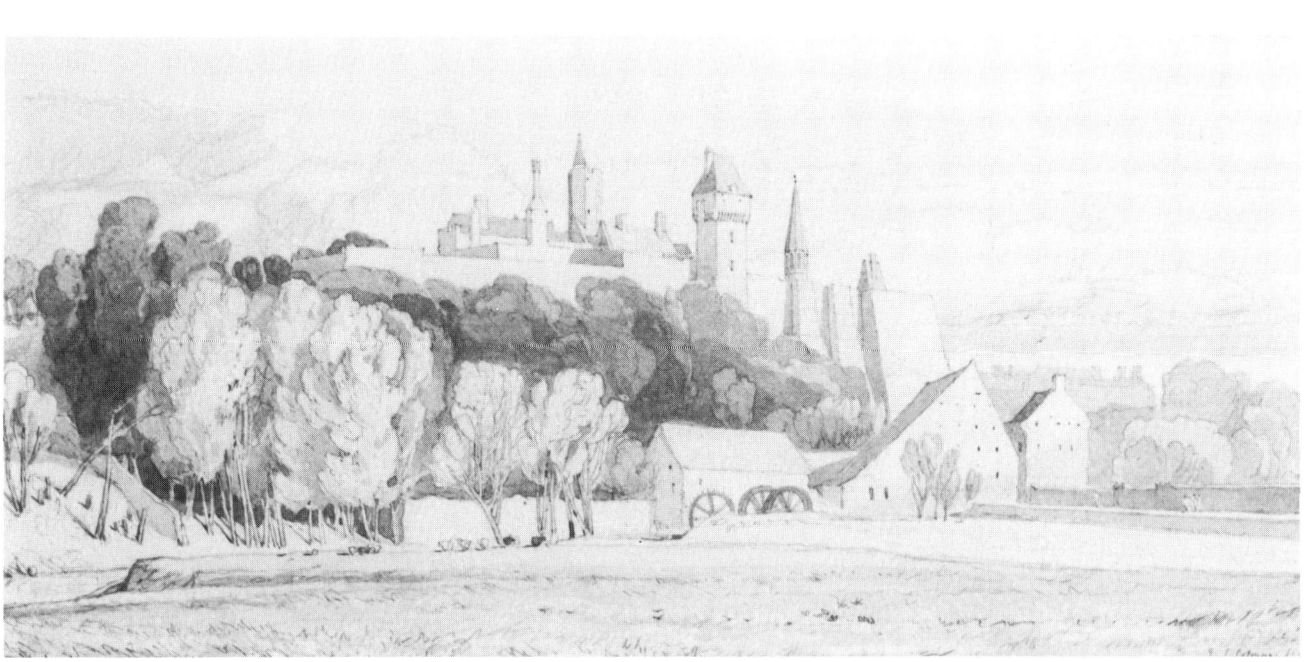

85 Castle of Creully, *c.*1818-24

86 St. Sauveur-le-Vicomte, *c.*1818-24

Pencil, pen and brown ink, on white, wove paper; 23.5 × 39.1 ($9\frac{1}{4}$ × $15\frac{3}{8}$). INSCR: *Verso,* in pencil lower c. *No. 3.* PROV: Same as No. 82; R. H. Benson sale Christie's, 13 March 1893, bt. Watson 19 gns. presumably for J. J. Colman; his bequest to R. J. Colman 1898; R. J. Colman Bequest 1946. (170.235.951). REF: Kitson 1937 pp. 238-239 (reference to the etching of the castle); Rajnai 1975 No. 41.

Cotman makes no mention of a visit to St. Sauveur-le-Vicomte.[1] Rajnai conjectures that it 'could have been one of the places visited on the "circuitous route to Mont St. Michel" he made in the company of de Gerville between 23 and 30 August 1818, or at least during his stay with de Gerville between 22nd August and 5th September.'

This drawing is a view of the banks of the River Douve beneath the village of St. Sauveur le Vicomte.[1] It is one of the most vigorous drawings of the Normandy series. A series of fractured planes and levels in the foreground is contrasted with the amorphous shapes of the central pair of trees.

An outline version of No. 86 is in a private collection.[2]

[1]In his sale Christie's 1 May 1824, Cotman included lot 71 *Ruins of the Castle of St. Sauveur le Viscomte,* etched in *Architectural Antiquities of Normandy* 1822, pl. 13, and in the same lot, *View of the Abbey Church of Ditto,* etched in *Architectural Antiquities of Normandy* 1822 pl. 14 (Popham Nos. 213 & 214). [2]E. D. Levine, 1975.

87 Coutances, *c.*1818-24

illustrated on p. 77

Pencil and brown wash on cream, wove paper with watermark r. edge *J WHATMAN;* 26.6 × 45.4 ($10\frac{7}{16}$ × $17\frac{7}{8}$). INSCR: *Verso,* numbered in pencil l.l. *No. 15.* PROV: Cotman sale Spelman, Norwich, 16 May 1861, ?included in lot 81, bt. King 24 gns.; John Thomas Mott; ?his sale Christie's, 28 Feb. 1885, included in lot 125, bt. Martin Colnaghi £21.5.0. for R. H. Benson; his sale Christie's, 13 March 1893, lot 79, bt. Watson 24 gns. for J. J. Colman; his bequest to R. J. Colman 1898; R. J. Colman Bequest 1946. (178.235.951). EXH: Norwich 1903 (64); Manchester 1912 (349); Tate 1922 (175); Norwich 1945. REF: Rajnai 1975 No. 17.

Cotman visited Coutances during each of his three Normandy tours, perhaps more than once in 1818 and apparently twice in 1820.

Although in 1817 Cotman remarks on the beauty of the countryside surrounding Coutances, Rajnai points out that it is unlikely that he had the opportunity then to take this panoramic view of the city as: 'it rained the whole time I was in the town.'[1] Cotman is more likely to have sketched this view, taken from the Valognes road a few kilometres from Coutances, at the start of his homeward journey from there on 30 August 1818. Another possible time is 4 or 5 September 1820, when Cotman might have travelled again on the same route after diverting from St. Lô to Coutances.

'The view is one of the most successful in Cotman's series of monochrome landscapes. Although the composition is almost naively simple—the town sits in the very centre of the picture area, perched on a hill which is itself in the middle of a bowl-like hollow—it presents a most satisfying balance between nature and artefact'. (Rajnai).

A larger version in watercolour of this composition, but called *Coutances Cathedral* is recorded,[2] while a preparatory study is at Norwich Castle Museum.[3]

[1]JSC to DT, Avranches 3 Aug. 1817 (BM). [2]Dickes pp. 338-9. [3]Rajnai 1975 No. 18; for other known Coutances subjects by Cotman see *Ibid* No. 19.

88 Rouen, looking up the Seine, Mont Ste. Catherine in the distance, *c.*1818-24

illustrated on opposite page

Pencil and brown wash on white, wove paper; 24.3 × 48.1 ($9\frac{9}{16}$ × $18\frac{15}{16}$). INSCR: *Verso,* in pencil lower c. *No. 1* (indistinct). PROV: Same as No. 87: R. H. Benson sale, Christie's, 13 March 1893, lot 83, bt. Watson 26 gns. for J. J. Colman; his bequest to R. J. Colman 1898; R. J. Colman Bequest 1946. (181.235.951). EXH: Norwich 1903 (69); Norwich 1945. REF: Kitson 1937 p. 256; Rajnai 1975 No. 35.

The sketch for No. 88 must have been done between 25 June 1818, when Cotman arrived in Rouen and 12 July, when in his letter[1] to Dawson Turner of that date he included 'St. Catherine & Boulevards' among his list of the subjects already sketched.

Rajnai observes that: 'It is probably the most elegant composition among Cotman's series of Normandy monochromes and it is of a more complicated design than he usually adopts. The focus of interest, the fine group of trees with the Porte and row of houses behind the animated scenes, is off centre. All the lines of the left foreground converge on the trees standing apart and donning a silhouette borrowed from the strange figurations of his Rokeby trees almost twenty years

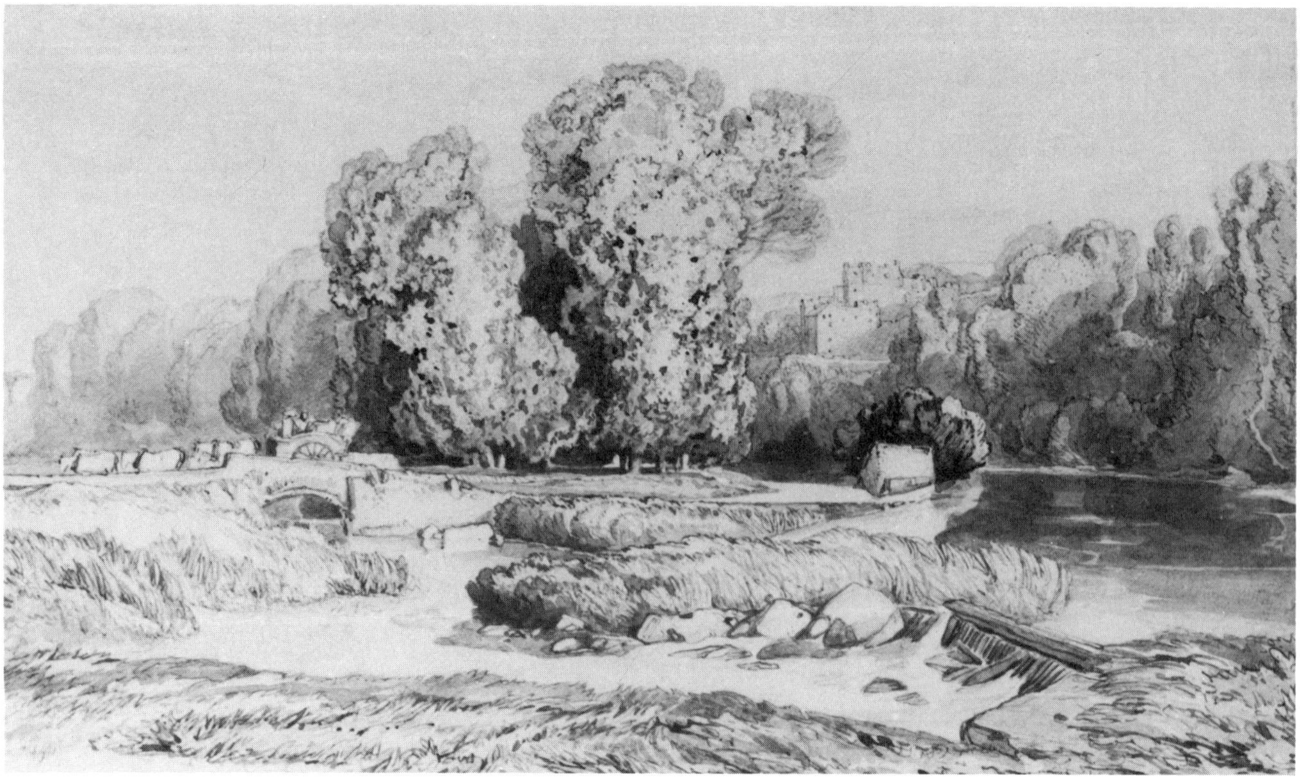

86 St. Sauveur-le-Vicomte, *c.*1818-24

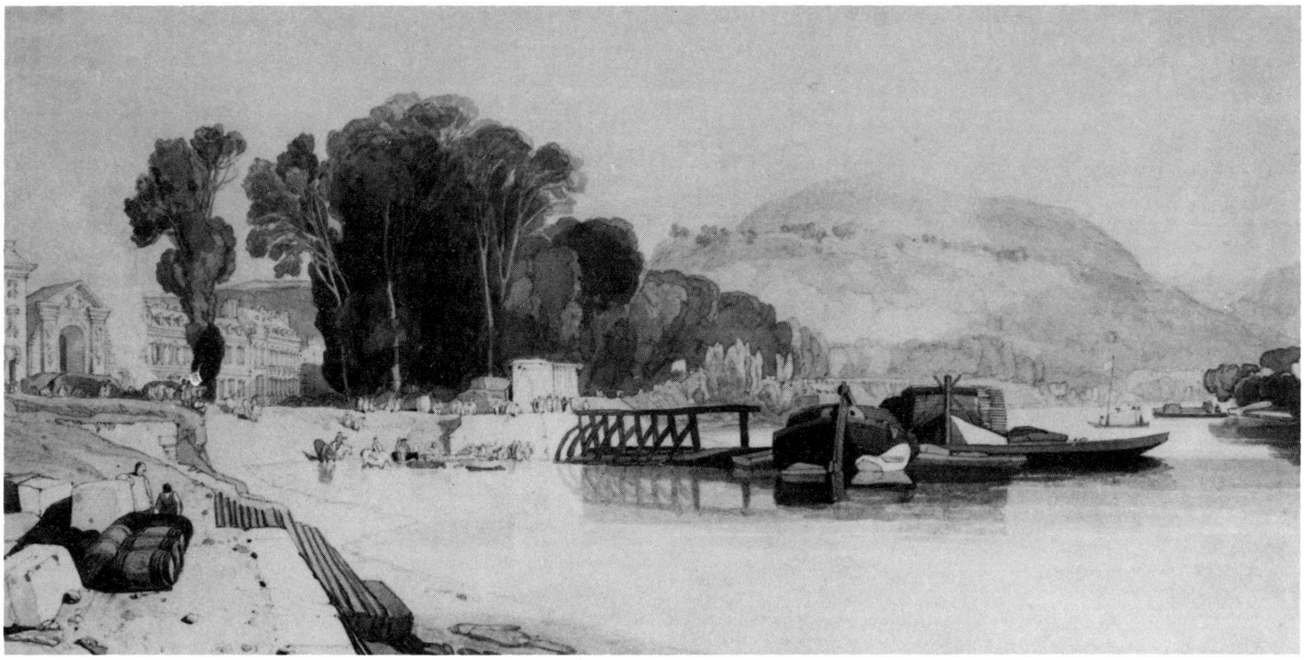

88 Rouen, looking up the Seine, Mont Ste. Catherine in the distance, *c.*1818-24

before. From this solitary tree the attention slides down and inwards in the direction of St. Catherine, much less prominent in tone but equal in mass to balance the clump of trees. The vista on the river is closed by a screen of boats giving the space in front a more intimate, more domestic character.'

Cotman first showed what was probably a watercolour version of the same view in the 1823 Norwich Society exhibition (155). A drawing of the same title was also included in Cotman's sale of 1824 (96). Two watercolours of this view survive: one of which may be the 1823 exhibit or a replica of it, autograph or otherwise; the second is a monochrome, probably by M. E. Cotman, now in a private collection, London.

[1]JSC to DT, Rouen 12 July 1818 (BM). [2]a) P. Danger sale, Christie's 15 June 1971, lot 49, bt. Leger; b) ex Inglis Palgrave and Viscount Mackintosh of Halifax, now Private Collection, Norfolk. [3]The corners are cut so as to turn it into an elongated hexagonal.

89 Domfront, *c.*1820-23

Pencil and brown wash on white, wove paper; 24.8 × 45.8 ($9\frac{3}{4}$ × 17 $\frac{7}{8}$). Prov: Same as No. 87; R. H. Benson sale Christie's, 13 March 1893, lot 82, bt. Watson 29 gns. for J. J. Colman; his bequest to R. J. Colman 1898; R. J. Colman Bequest 1946. (184.235.951). Exh: ?Norwich Society 1823 (162); Norwich 1903 (68); Manchester 1912 (348); Tate 1922 (148). Ref: Kitson 1937 p. 224 (reference to Cotman's visit to Domfront); Rajnai 1975 No. 22.

From *c.*1893 until 1975 this drawing was always incorrectly titled *Château Gaillard,* despite the evident differences between the two castles (see No. 181). Rajnai has corrected this error and observes that No. 89 is a view of Domfront Castle and town from the north-west, taken from the top of the Tertre Grisiere and looking over the deep Val des Rochers.

Cotman's only visit to Domfront was in 1820. He arrived on 20

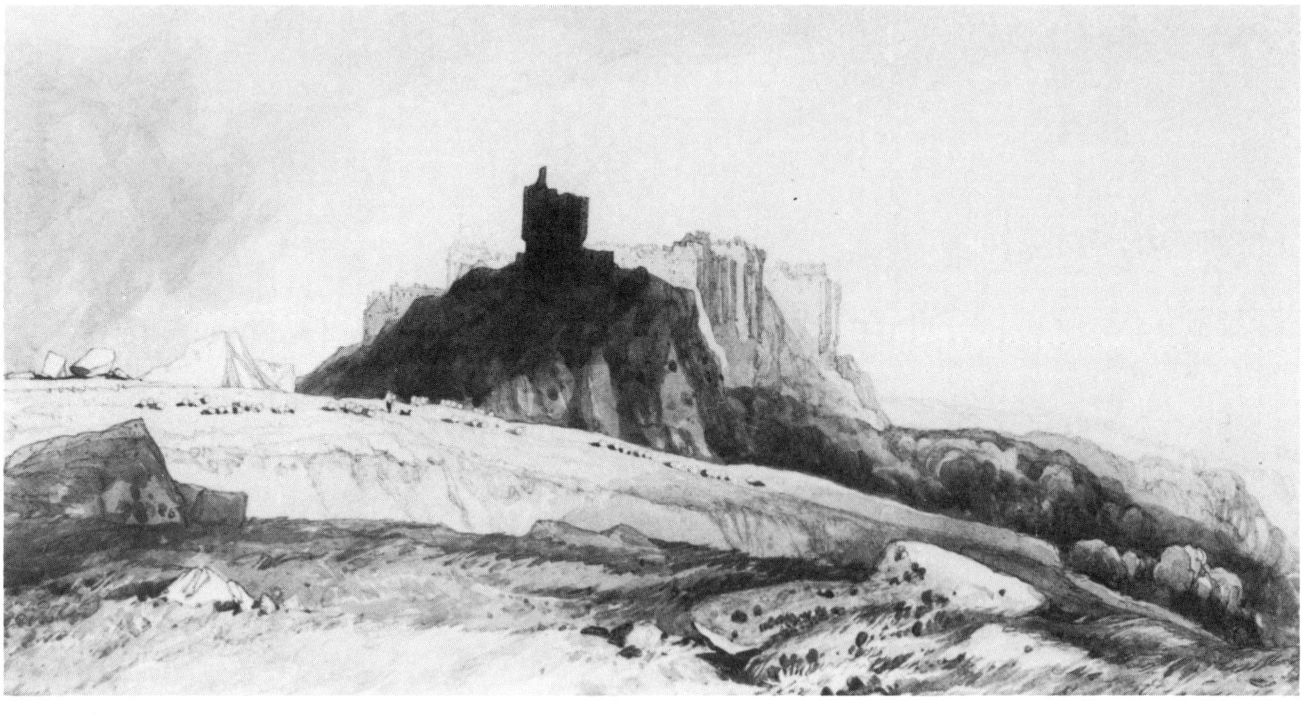

89 Domfront, *c.*1820-23

August and stayed there for several days:

> Next day [after arrival] 21st looked about me, & soon found plenty to do. — a good old Church of N. Dame, and Views of Town, & Rocks extremely grand, so as to outdo what I so much praisd at St Quentin de le Roche near Falaise — This day commenced with Rain, & Thunder the whole of the day at distance. In the Evening it was a grand storm, such a one as to add to the magnificence of the place & the flashes were so vivid & appearing so near that thinking my umbrella no protection but rather likely to be a conductor, I hastened to my Inn where I enjoyd it from my loop hole of a window that commanded a grand view for 30 miles over the most woody country possible one mass of forest. — Tuesday, 22nd, heavy Rain whole day so as to prevent my drawing though I made repeated attempts & began several — Wednesday. The Ducks in high glory at 4 o'clock, tremendous rain more heavy than ever, though the Night had been fine with much wind — Nay a hurrican, so as to blow down Chimnies, logs & heavy masses continually falling & glass, rattling to atoms everywhere, with the music of the Sign of a hotel de Bretagne grating like the setting of a saw — it cleared up & I managd to do something between showers. — The clearing up of the mist, & passing clouds over the forest gave inexpressible beauty to the already most superb & fine situation — .[1]

In 1823 Cotman exhibited with the Norwich Society of Artists two drawings of Domfront, one from the town (147) and the other of the town (162) and his sale in 1824 included lot 109 *A Pair of Highly interesting Views of the Town of Domfront and of the Rocks in the Neighbourhood of the same, in Water Colours, not published.* Cotman seems to have done three landscape compositions of the environs of Domfront: from the rocks on the side of Tertre Grisiere looking south-east towards the hilltop town; from the town towards the rocks (see No. 90) and the view seen in No. 89. Whilst the first two views are known by several versions[2] the third seems to exist only in No. 89.

[1]JSC to DT, Mortain 26 Aug. 1820 (BM). [2]For a discussion of these and other known Domfront subjects by Cotman see Rajnai 1975 No. 22 n. 8.

90 Domfront, View from the Town, *c.*1820-23

Pencil and brown wash on white, wove paper; 26.2 × 40.4 ($10\frac{5}{16}$ × $15\frac{7}{8}$). PROV: C. J. Winter; acquired from him by James Reeve by 1903; bt. from him by H. S. Theobald; bt. from him by R. J. Colman, Feb. 1910; R. J. Colman Bequest 1946. (289.235.951). EXH: ?Norwich Society 1823 (147); Norwich 1903 (71) lent by James Reeve; Tate 1922 (160). REF: Kitson 1937 p. 224 (reference to the subject, the Leeds version is repro. pl. 98); Rajnai 1975 No. 23.

This is the view of 'Rocks extremely grand' mentioned by Cotman is his letter of 26 August 1820 which is quoted in No. 89. The view is taken from the hillside below the castle, looking into the Val des Rochers, the gorge of the river Varenne, and at the Tertre Grisiere, from the top of which Cotman drew the scene shown in No. 89. Rajnai comments that No. 90 is 'one of his most successful Normandy drawings with such crisp and sensitive rendering of the rocky scenery that it could hardly be bettered.'

There is a replica of this drawing in the collection at Norwich which also came with the Colman Bequest but was unregistered. Faithful in all detail, Rajnai suggests that it may be attributed to Miles Edmund Cotman.

An autograph version, also in pencil and brown wash, is in Leeds City Art Gallery.[1] It was copied by Elizabeth Turner in the Book of Drawings, No. 43. A watercolour of the same subject was formerly in the Arthur Colegate Collection.[2]

[1]Leeds 29.30/38 (1352). [2]Repro. Rienaecker pl 39, fig. 77.

91 Campeaux between Vire and St. Lô, *c.*1820-24

illustrated on opposite page

Pencil, reed pen and brown ink, brown wash on cream, wove paper; 25.3 × 41.7 ($9\frac{15}{16}$ × $16\frac{7}{16}$). INSCR: *Recto,* previously inscribed with title in the artist's hand, but removed in cleaning, 1936. PROV: Cotman sale, Spelman, Norwich, 16 May 1861, ?included in lot 81, bt. James King 24 gns.; bt. from him by J. J. Colman by 1874; his bequest to R. J. Colman 1898; R. J. Colman Bequest 1946. (185.235.951). EXH:

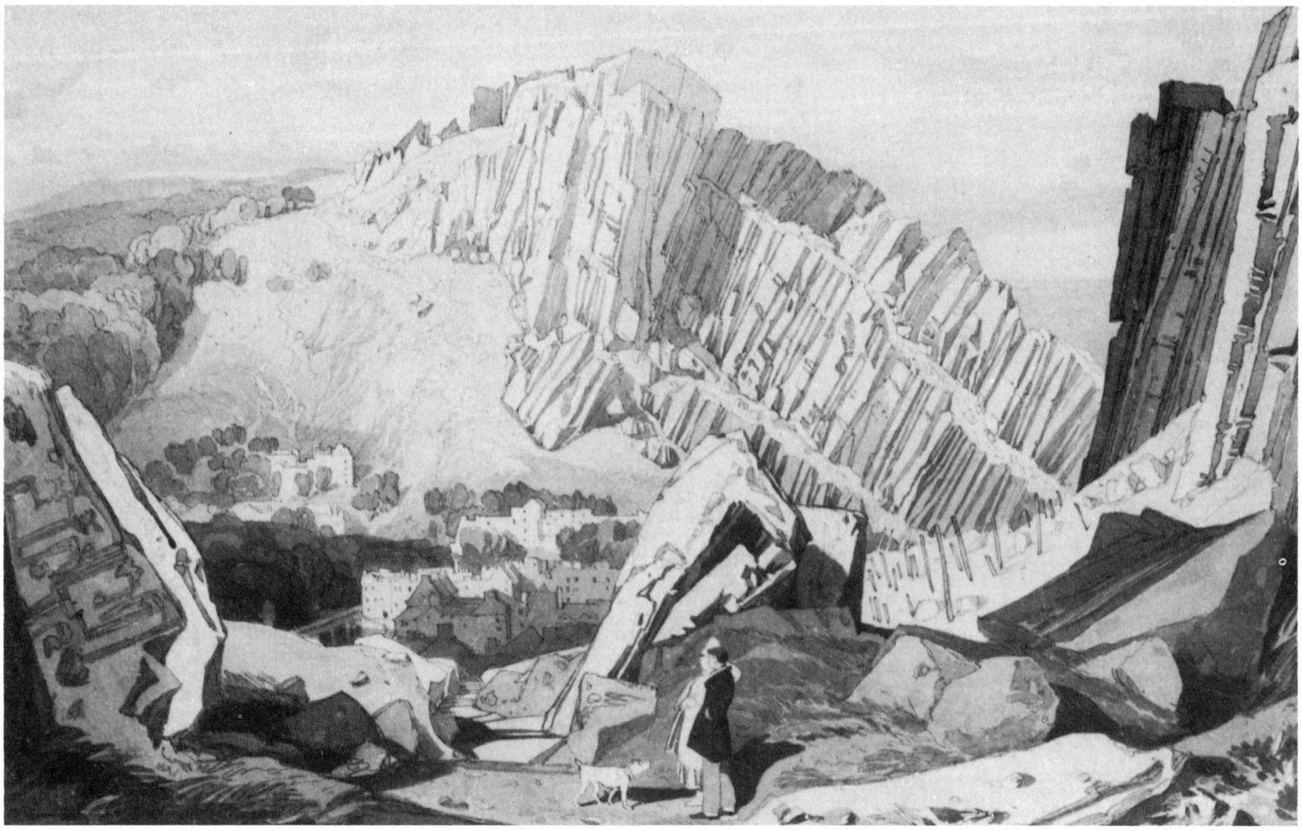

90 Domfront, View from the Town, *c.*1820-23

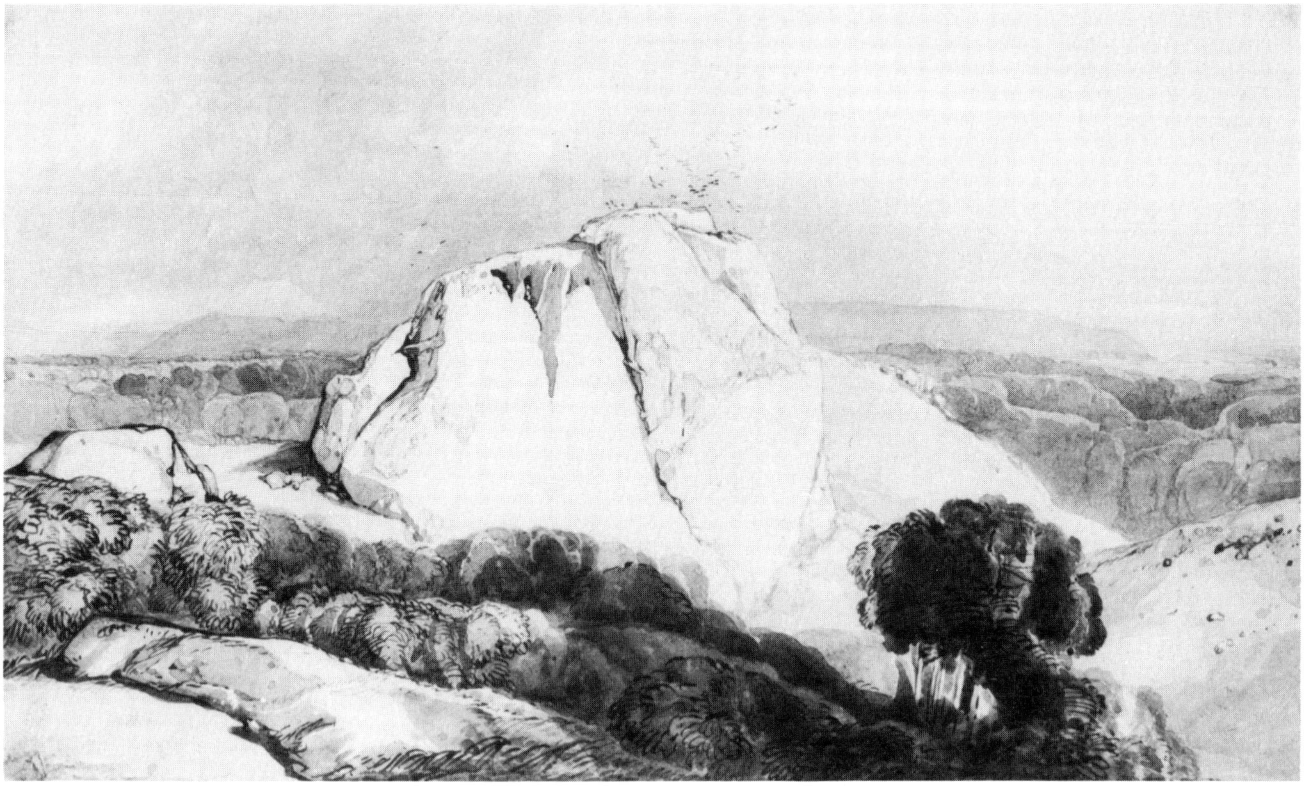

91 Campeaux between Vire and St. Lô, *c.*1820-24

London, International Exhibition 1874 (26) lent by J. J. Colman; ?Norwich 1878 (83); Norwich, Art Circle 1888 (141); Manchester 1912 (357); Tate 1922 (154); Norwich 1945. REF: Rajnai 1975, No. 14.

Cotman passed through Campeaux on his way from Vire to St. Lô on 1 September 1820. The journey of 30 miles took nine hours with apparently only one stop at Torigni. 'Friday 1st Sept left Vire at 4 o'clock *in a Coach* with 2 *wheels,* alias a Cart with one horse for which I paid 18 francs, — and of all the Carriages I ever was in this was the very worst, and accorded well with the road. The very worst I have ever seen, a road torn up by the Roots. . . . My coat pockets shook off, — My watch stopped, and I was going to say my money was in a fair way of being made smooth by the violent friction.'[1]

It was on this journey that Cotman must have made a sketch of this solitary and rocky hilltop which dominates the wooded landscape.[2]

[1]JSC to his wife, St. Lô 2 Sept. 1820 (BM). [2]A second version was once with the Walker's Galleries (Witt photo.).

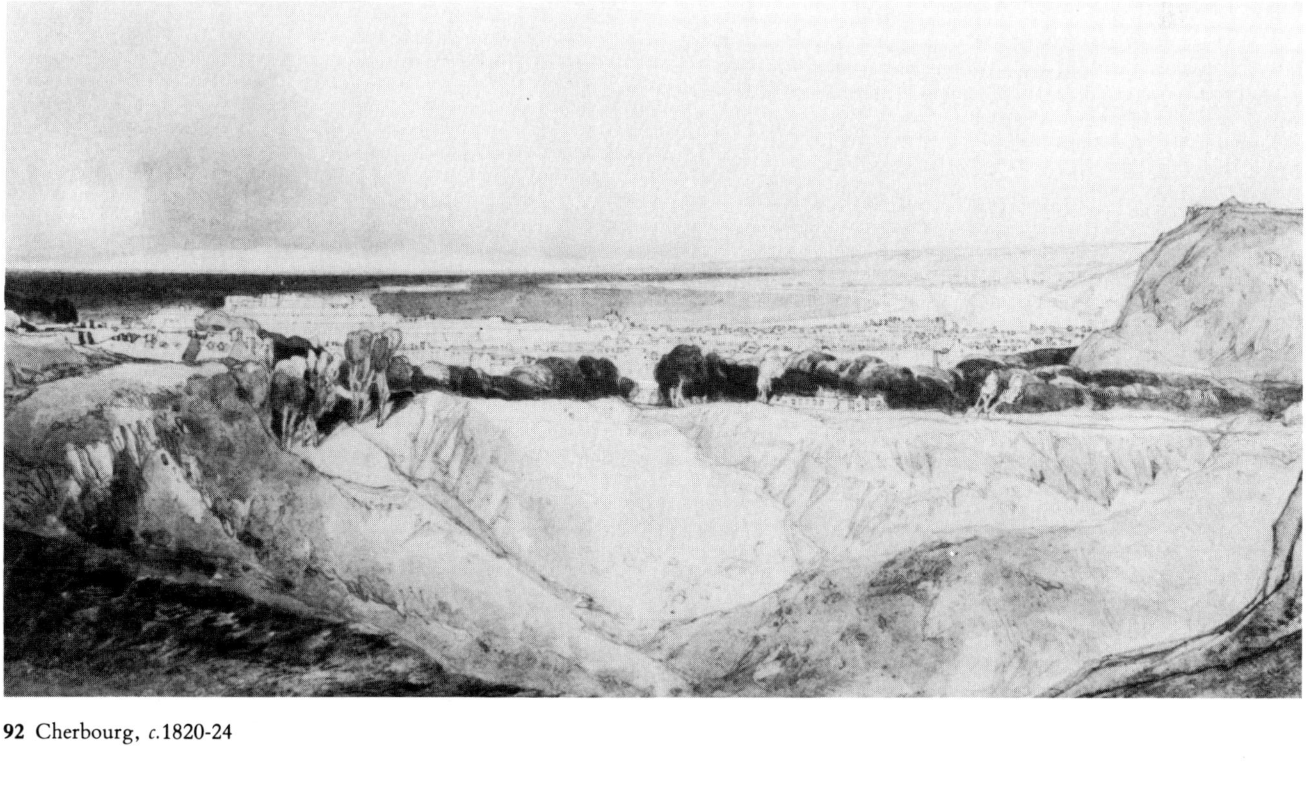

92 Cherbourg, *c.*1820-24

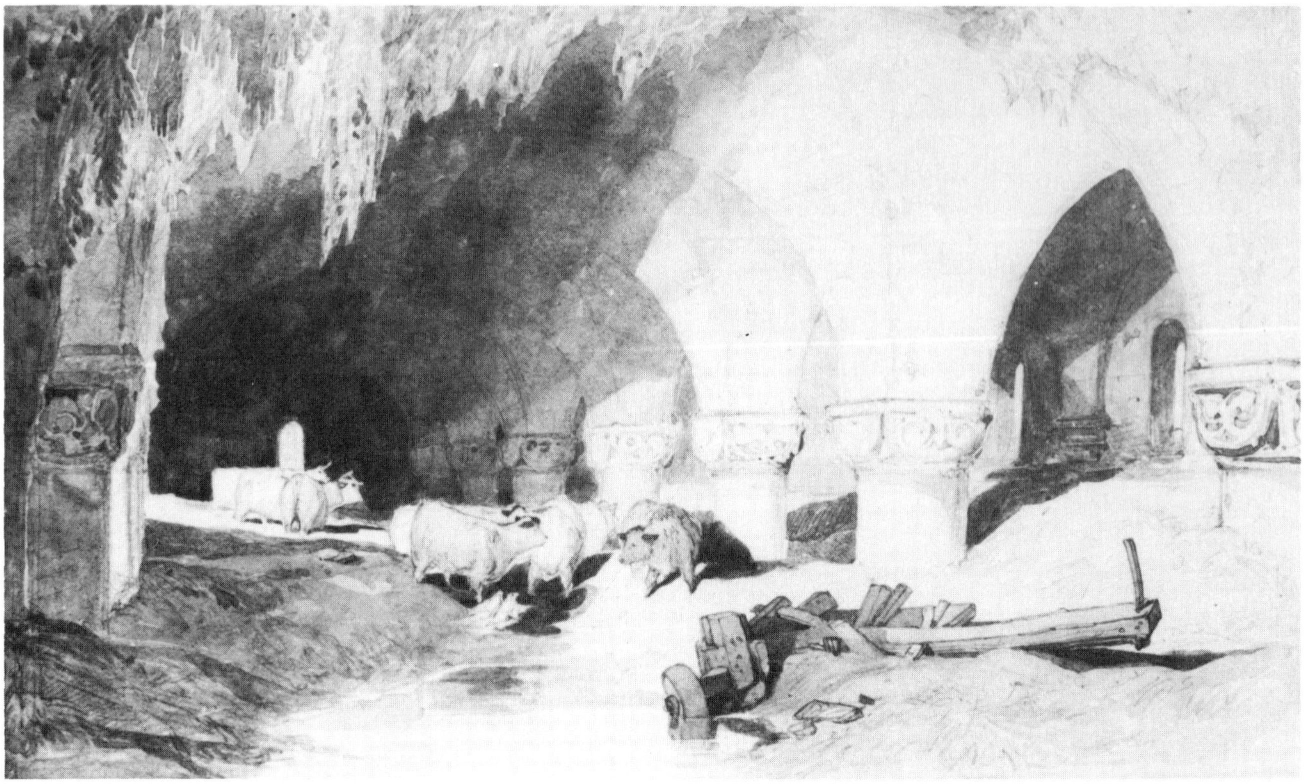

93 Cattle in a Norman Crypt, *c.*1820-24

92 Cherbourg, *c.*1820-24

illustrated on p. 83

Pencil and brown wash on cream, wove paper; 25.2 × 45.8 ($9\frac{15}{16}$ × $18\frac{1}{16}$). INSCR: *Verso,* in pencil l.r. *No. 10.* PROV: Same as No. 82; R. H. Benson sale Christie's, 13 March 1893, lot 80, bt. Watson £20.9.6., presumably for J. J. Colman; his bequest to R. J. Colman 1898; R. J. Colman Bequest 1946. (175.235.951). EXH: Manchester 1912 (355); Tate 1922 (153); Norwich 1945. REF: Kitson 1937 pp. 228-9, pl. 93; Rajnai 1975 No. 16.

Cotman visited Cherbourg twice, both times in the company of M. de Gerville, the Valognes antiquarian. On 31 August 1818 he writes: 'Sept. 1st we shall be at Cherbourg to copy a section of the Mount & church of St. Michel which will prove of the utmost importance, as the whole was done by an Engineer.'[1] They returned in 1820 on 13 and 14 September Cotman drew the Church of Octeville near Cherbourg on the first day and the rest of the day, according to de Gerville 'was devoted to the view, which is lovely in the neighbourhood of Cherbourg. Mr. Cotman seemed very pleased with it, and returned there yesterday morning before we left for Valognes. On the road from Cherbourg to Valognes, he got off his horse again to draw the view, the beauty of which had struck him two years ago.'[2]

Rajnai observes that this view is undoubtedly the one in No. 92. The scene is described in splendid detail by Cotman himself: 'The two Days we were at Cherbourg were *perfectly Cloudless not one speck to be seen.* — The ascent to the top of Hill from which you descend into the Town is granite for 3 miles & by being a perfect straight road bordered by high trees, gives it a grandeur not to be conceived for you might imagine it going even to the Heavens. & the effect and cause are the same that give the sublime to Waterloo Bridge. — When sufficiently near to the Town you look down upon it as upon a fine quarry of *dead silver* with here & there a tinge of gold & the light & shadowed sides both coming off from *the deep azure of the bay,* as one mass of [?] rich glowing *pearl color.* The wood, & meadows & mountains & the fine look of the Roul the most conspicuous of all with its fortress closing the scene to the right. The left is occupied with the fort d'artois — and the center by the breakwater formed by art — & fort royal. The foreground is a fine Stone quarry into which you cast a fearful glance. Such is *My* account of Cherbourg.'[3]

The Montagne du Roule, on the right, is to be seen in another view presumably sketched during the same visit, taken from the direction of the town.[4] A drawing of a tower and fortification by the harbour, inscribed *Cotman* and *Cherbourg,* suggests a third subject derived from one of the two visits.[5]

[1]JSC to DT, Valognes 31 Aug. 1818 (copy in BM). [2]M. de Gerville to DT, Valognes 15 Sept. 1820 — translation (Trinity College, Cambridge). [3]JSC to his wife, St. Lô 17 Sept. 1820 (BM). [4]Leeds 29.29/38, a preliminary pencil study is in the Fry collection. [5]Bradford City Art Gallery (145 Gill 1925).

93 Cattle in a Norman Crypt, *c.*1820-24

Pencil and brown wash on cream, wove paper; 25.6 × 42.5 ($10\frac{1}{16}$ × $16\frac{3}{4}$). INSCR: *Verso,* in pencil l.r. *6.* PROV: Cotman sale, Spelman, Norwich 16 May 1861, ?included in lot 81, bt. James King 24 gns.; bt. from him by J. J. Colman by 1888; R. J. Colman Bequest 1946. (182.235.951). EXH: Norwich, Art Circle 1888 (133) lent by J. J. Colman; BFAC 1888 (94); Norwich 1903 (67); Tate 1922 (147). REF: Rajnai 1975 No. 42,

Although the subject of this drawing has not been identified, it forms part of a group of eleven brown wash drawings of similar size and proportion, all of which possibly form a series.[1] The combination of free pencilwork, ruled perspective lines and broad application of wash in this drawing renders it close to No. 91 *Campeaux* and No. 94 *Ruined tower Normandy.*

This composition may have been the subject of a watercolour, *Cattle in a Norman Crypt* which was brought by Palser for 7s in the Cotman sale of 1843.[2]

[1]Nos. 82 *Avranches;* 83 *Rouen from Mont Ste. Catherine;* 87 *Coutances;* 88 *Rouen, looking up the Seine, and Mont Ste. Catherine in the distance;* 89 *Domfront;* 90 *Domfront, View from the Town;* 91 *Campeaux;* 92 *Cherbourg;* 94 *Ruined Tower, Normandy;* 96 *Pont-de-l'Arche* and this drawing. [2]Christie's, 1st day, 17 May 1843, under *Drawings, in Water-Colours,* lot 136.

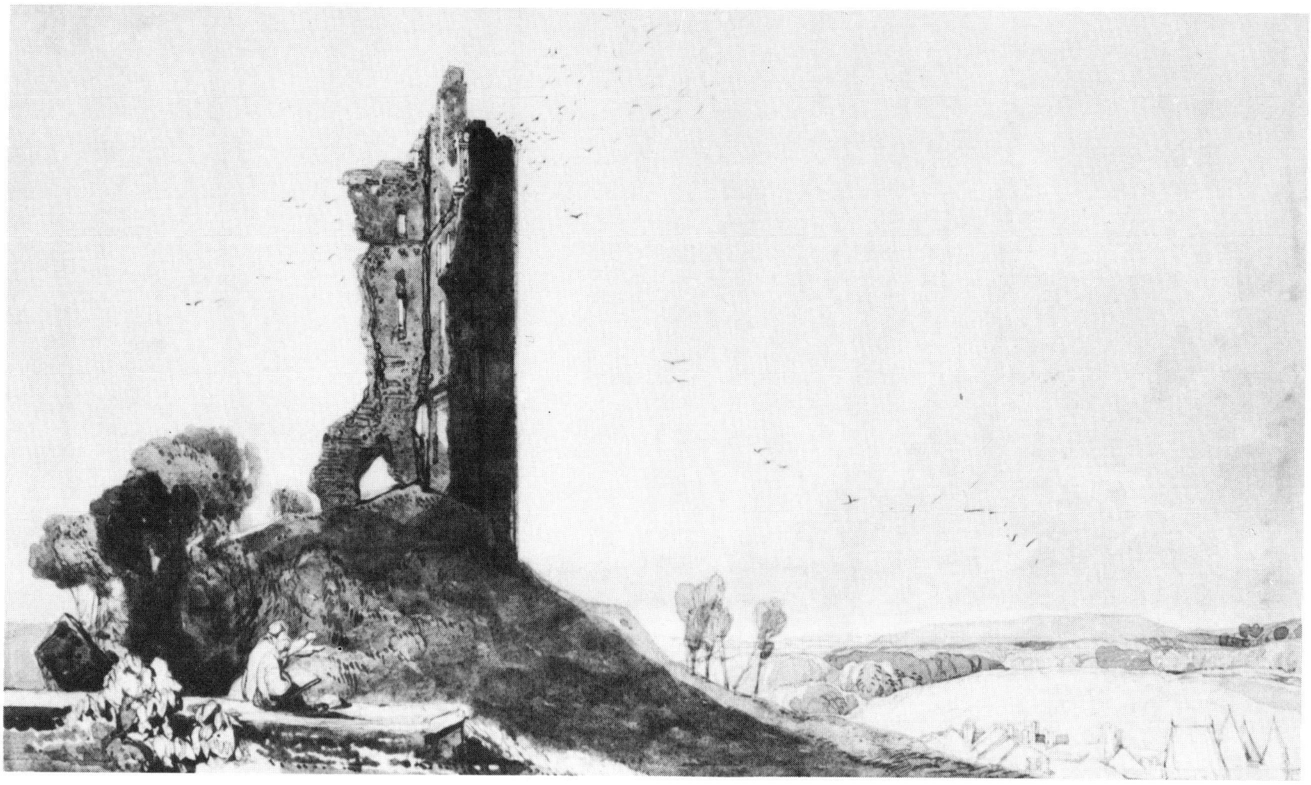

94 Ruined tower Normandy, *c.*1820-24

94 Ruined tower Normandy, *c.*1820-24

Pencil, pen and brown ink, brown wash on white, wove paper; 25.9 × 43.4 ($10\frac{3}{16}$ × $17\frac{1}{16}$). PROV: See No. 93. (183.235.951). EXH: Norwich, Art Circle 1888 (147) lent by J. J. Colman. REF: Rajnai 1975 No. 43.

The buildings, lower right, clearly indicate a French location for this subject, but while there are a number of similar castle ruins in Normandy, such as Vire, the subject remains unidentified.

The rich brown washes of this drawing ally it with No. 93.

95 View of the Inner Harbour and Cliffs at Fécamp, 1821

Pencil and grey wash on white, wove paper with watermark left edge *WHATMAN:* 20.3 × 43.2 (8 × 17). INSCR: *Recto,* signed and dated in pencil l.r. *J. S. Cotman 1820.1821; verso,* lower c. *No. 4.* PROV: ?The artist's sale, Christie's, 1 May 1824, lot 21, bt. Trant £1.7.0.; John Thomas Mott; ?his sale Christie's, 28 Feb. 1885, included in lot 125, bt. Martin Colnaghi 205 gns. for R. H. Benson; his sale Christie's, 13 March 1893, bt. Watson 21 gns. presumably for J. J. Colman; his bequest to R. J. Colman 1898; R. J. Colman Bequest 1946. (172.235.951). EXH: Norwich 1903 (66). REF: Rajnai 1975 No. 25.

This elegant composition is a view of the harbour of Fécamp looking

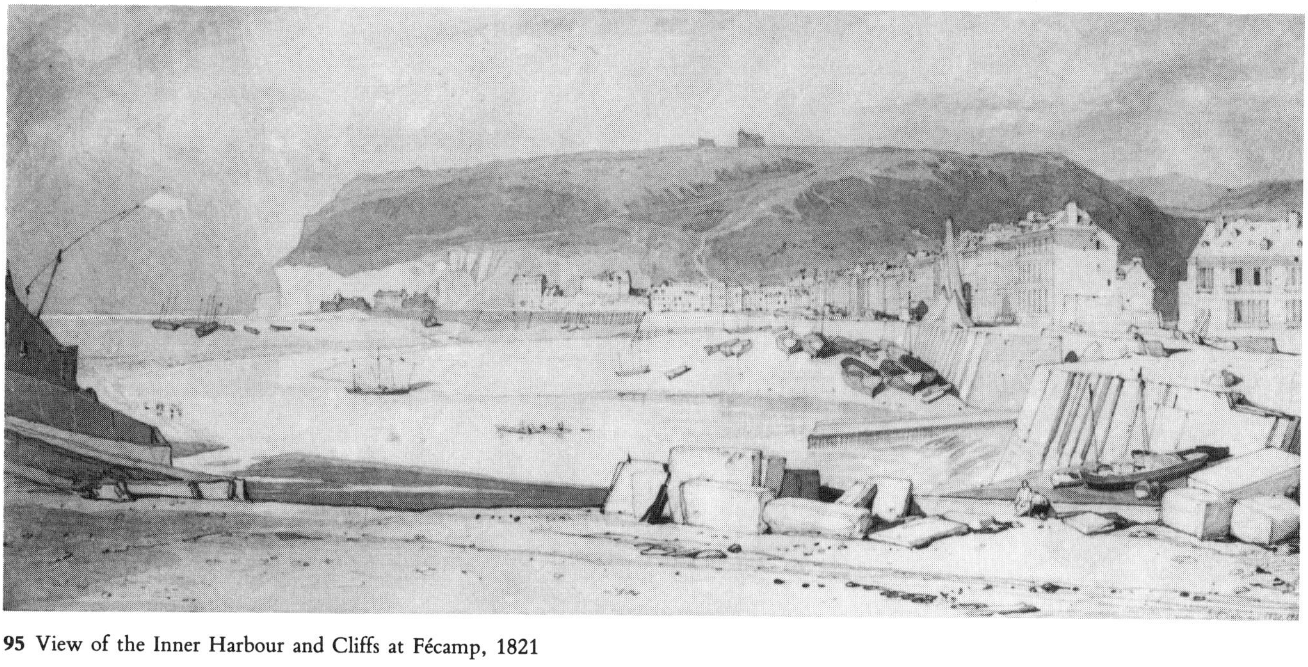

95 View of the Inner Harbour and Cliffs at Fécamp, 1821

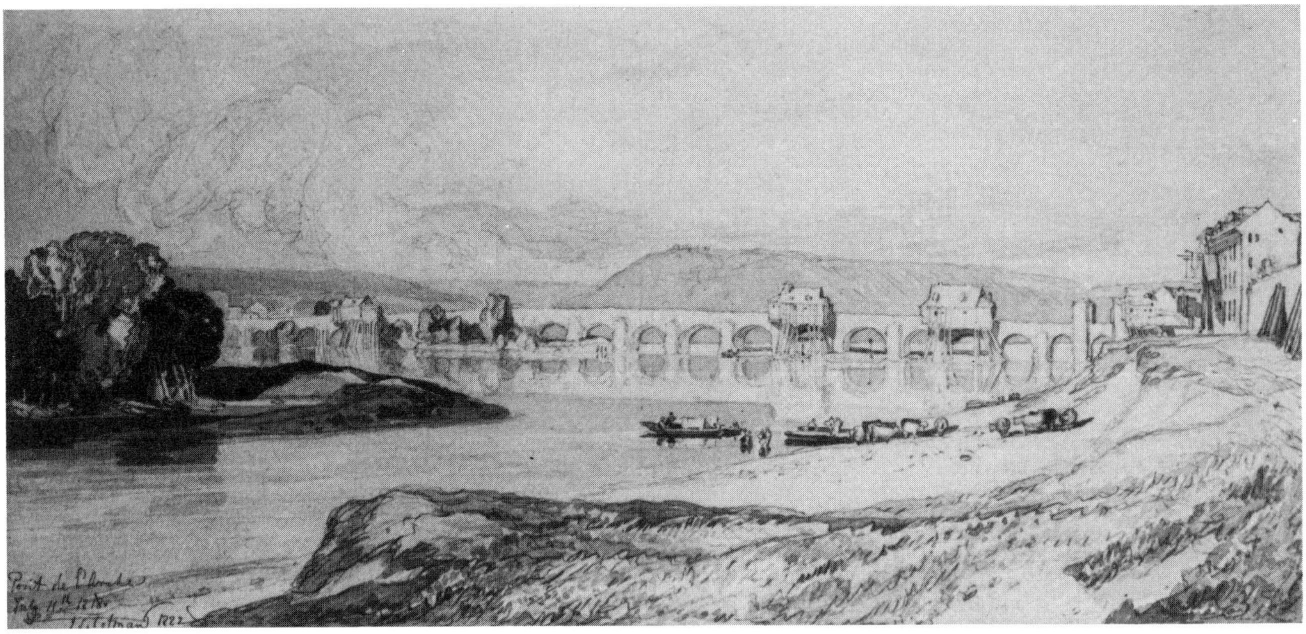

96 Pont-de-l'Arche, 1822

north towards the Côte de la Vierge with the church of Notre-Dame-de-Salut on the top. Until it was correctly identified by Rajnai the view was thought to be of Dieppe.

Cotman visited Fécamp twice. In 1817 he arrived there within a few days of landing at Dieppe on 20 June: '25. left Dieppe for Fecamp & was much disappointed in the Cathedral there, — & sketched only the south front of y Church of St Etienne — I had a letter to Monsr. Dupin, & by him was first introduced to a french Lady, Madame Dupin, very young & handsome & at her toilette, Monsieur was engaged & he left us to manage as well as we could, she not speaking a word of french & I not a word of English. She was very polite, — & I tried to be so — They did not understand my motions & led up walk after walk up Cliffs & Vales &c. — .'[1] He moved on two days later.

Cotman returned to Fécamp during his last tour in 1820 when he made a special excursion there from Le Havre — where he landed on 26 July: '27th. Visited Fecamp — & sketched a few things there, & returned on the 29th — .'[2] Among 'a few things' must have been the sketch for this drawing for the first of the double date is a reference to the date of the sketching of the subject.

A view[3] of the harbour looking to the north-west, from behind the buildings to the right of this composition, was with Spinks in 1982.[4] Signed and dated 1818, this composition must derive from materials gathered on his first visit.[5]

[1]JSC to DT, Rouen 6 July 1817 (BM). [2]JSC to DT, Havre de Grace 31 July 1820 (BM). [3]Spink & Son Ltd., *English Watercolour Drawings*, Annual Exhibition 1982, No. 53. [4]Other known Fécamp subjects by Cotman are listed in Rajnai 1975 No. 25 n.5. [5]An outline drawing of No. 95 was with Sotheby's, New York, 3 June 1981 (199). This was on paper bearing a watermark date, *1823*.

96 Pont-de-l'Arche, 1822

Pencil and brown wash on cream, wove paper; 20 × 41.4 ($7\frac{7}{8}$ × $16\frac{5}{16}$). INSCR: *Recto*, in pencil l.l. *Pont de l'Arche / July 11th 1818. / J. S. Cotman 1822.* PROV: J. J. Colman by 1874; his bequest to R. J. Colman 1898; R. J. Colman Bequest 1946. (173.235.951). EXH: ?Norwich Society 1823 (161); London, International Exhibition 1874, lent by J. J. Colman; Norwich 1945. REF: Kitson 1937 p. 211, pl. 91; Rajnai 1975 No. 32.

Cotman visited Pont-de-l'Arche on 11 and 15 July 1818. As the inscribed date makes clear, the subject was sketched on the first visit. He was accompanied on the second occasion by Mrs. Turner and her two daughters. Elizabeth Turner described their passage over the bridge in the following terms: 'Pont de l'Arche lies in a valley — we walked over the bridge by permission of the Conducteur — it is of a frightful height above the water which is here locked in consequence of two water mills built on the bridge itself . . . from the bridge we saw the côte des Deux Amants with the convent on the top of it.'[1]

The Museum's drawing shows the bridge from the south bank looking east towards the promontory of the Côte des Deux Amants, with the remains of the 'abbey' just visible on the top. The bridge was damaged beyond repair in the 1856 floods and has since been replaced. The drawing is one of considerable economy, with the shapes and masses in fine balance around the bridge and its reflected image.[2]

[1]Elizabeth Turner's Diary, p. 57. [2]A drawing copy of this title is recorded in Art Dept. archives, NCM. An outline drawing of No. 96 was with Sotheby's, New York, 3 June 1981 (199).

97 Castle of Arques, *c.*1822-4

illustrated on opposite page

Pencil and brown wash on cream, wove paper; 18.9 × 39 ($7\frac{7}{16}$ × $15\frac{3}{8}$). INSCR: *Recto*, signed and dated in pencil l.r. *J. S. Cotman 1819.* PROV: ?Cotman sale, Spelman, Norwich, 16 May 1861, included in lot 81, *Original Normandy Sketches, including 34 in sepia and colours, in portfolio*, bt. James King 24 gns.; bt. from him by J. J. Colman; his bequest to R. J. Colman 1898; R. J. Colman Bequest 1946. (169.235.951). EXH: ?Norwich Society 1824 (200*) as *Castle of Arques, France, a Sketch;* ?Norwich, Art Circle 1888 (155); BFAC 1888 (101); Norwich 1945. REF: Rajnai 1975 No. 6.

Arques was the second place visited by Cotman in Normandy; and its castle provided him with the subject of his first drawings on French soil.

He visited Arques on Saturday, 21 June 1817. He had arrived at Dieppe at 3 o'clock on the previous afternoon after 'a very long passage of 42 Hours'[1] which had started at 9 o'clock on Wednesday morning at Brighton. At Dieppe he contacted M. Gaillon 'an obliging, sensible, and well-informed young man, as well as an ardent botanist.'[2] Gaillon had been informed of Cotman's arrival by Auguste le Prevost, [3]the Rouen antiquarian, who assisted Dawson Turner in preparing Cotman's tour.

The next day Cotman walked with Gaillon to the château which he found: 'a very fine ruin of an immense size, & not totally unlike Conway or Harlech, but four times their size & thickness. Many of the Towers going to a great depth below y outward base of the vaults — which are of a frightful depth and are seen in various places open on the hill, — I have several sketches of it.'[1] On the evidence of lot 24 of his sale in 1824 we know that he drew these details: (1) *Entry to Castle,* (2) *Angular Tower,* (3) *Part of Keep,* (4) *Inner Gateway.*[4]

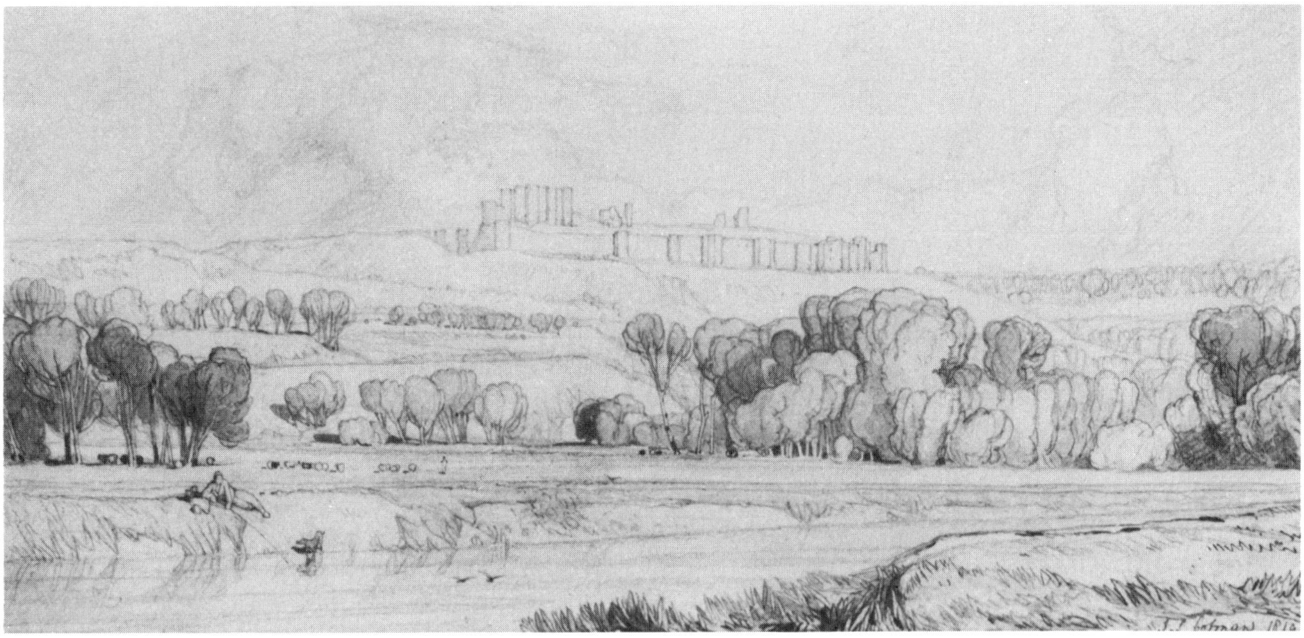

97 Castle of Arques, *c.*1822-4

98 Castle of Arques, *c.*1822-4

It seems to have been on the homeward walk that Cotman encountered the view presented in No. 97. The castle is seen from the east; the river in the foreground is the Béthune.

This fine monochrome drawing has, in common with the others of this series, an air of serene tranquillity, conveying pictorially Dawson Turner's verbal description: 'I do not think that any of ours [i.e. castles] are of an equal extent; nor can you well conceive a more noble object than this, when seen at a distance: and it is only then that the eye can comprehend the vast expanse and strength of the external wall, with the noble keep towering high above it.'[5]

For an outline version of this composition see No. 98. A copy by Elizabeth Turner is in the Book of Drawings, No. 6, and an etching by her is in *A Tour of Normandy,* 1820.[6]

[1]JSC to DT, Dieppe 21 June 1817 (BM). [2]*A Tour in Normandy,* 1820, vol. 1, p. 28. [3]Auguste le Provost to DT, Bernay 5 June 1817 (Trinity College, Cambridge). [4]See Rajnai 1975 No. 6 nn. 7-10 for related drawings. [5]*A Tour in Normandy,* 1820, vol. 1, pp. 39-40. [6]*Ibid,* pl. 12.

98 Castle of Arques, *c.*1822-4

Pencil on white, wove paper; 19.5 × 39.1 ($7\frac{11}{16}$ × $15\frac{3}{8}$). INSCR: *Recto,* numbered in pencil l.r. *78.* PROV: Dr. John Sell Cotman; his widow Mrs. Dorothy Cotman; sold by her Sotheby's, 12 July 1967, Part II, lot 186 with another, bt. Folio Fine Art £25; bt. from them 1967. (624.967). REF: Rajnai 1975 No. 7.

For the circumstances of Cotman's visit to Arques on 21 and 22 June 1817, see the previous entry.

Rajnai suggests that this outline drawing of No. 97 might well be a preparation for an etching—presumably for his projected publication of a picturesque tour of Normandy (see p. 76, f). No. 98 is one of a set of outline drawings, most of which relate to the group of monochromes of which No. 97 is an example.[1] 'All of these compositions in outline, although copies, are of high quality and display such verve and assuredness that their attribution to Cotman can hardly be doubted.' (Rajnai).

[1]See also No. 95 n. 5 and No. 96 n. 2

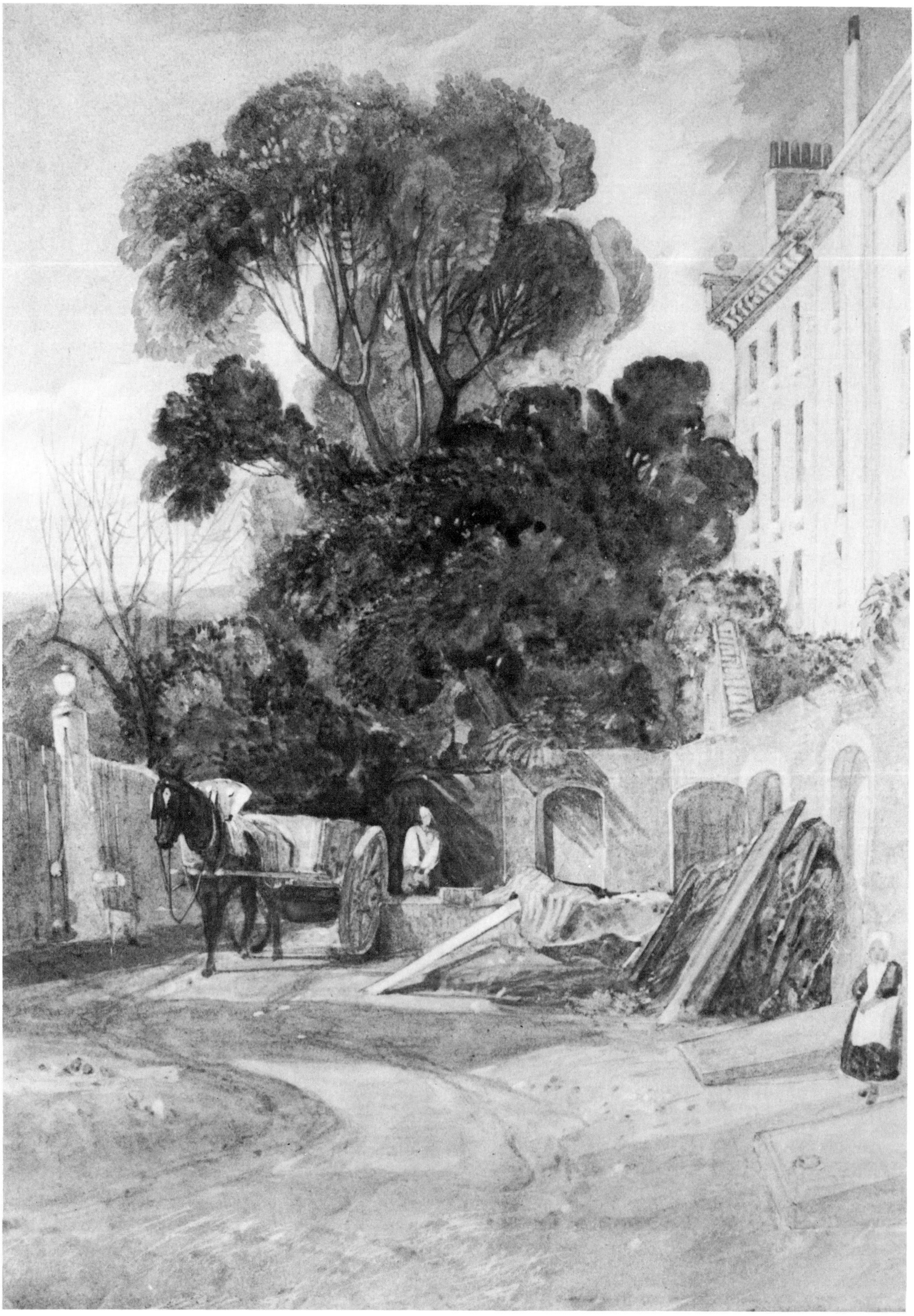

104 Houses, Surrey Street, Norwich, *c.*1829-30

8
The Return to Norwich
1823-1833

In the summer of 1823 Cotman exhibited nineteen works with the Norwich Society. This was the first occasion on which his works had been seen on a significant scale in Norwich since he had left the City eleven years previously. He was well received by the reviewers of both the local papers. The *Norwich Mercury* of 2 August observed: 'It is a sincere gratification to us to see MR. COTMAN'S works once more gracing the room. He is a man of uncommon powers, both intellectual and practical, and while he strikes out a style of his own the very licence he uses is an indication of talent which sets him above the level of common faculties. His design is always magnificent, and the practised eye of the artist discovers this, the capital property of his mind, at a glance . . . there is whether in his pencil or water-colour drawings, an elegance and taste pervading the whole, which is as delightful as it is rare . . . the period drawings might safely challenge exhibition with those of any artist in Britain.' Also singled out for praise were a number of the Normandy monochrome drawings. Cotman could hardly resist the lure of returning to Norwich in the role of established artist.

On 3 January 1824 the *Norwich Mercury* carried the simple announcement that Cotman 'intends immediately, after the Christmas vacation, to open in Norwich a SCHOOL for Drawing, professedly to embrace every construction necessary to form the professional student and Amateur Artist'. In order to help finance his new residence, a three storey red-brick Georgian house on St. Martin-at-Palace-Plain, he sold over two hundred of his Normandy drawings and other works relating to his recent etching projects, by auction through Christie's, in London on 1 May 1824. Despite his expectations, the financial outcome was a mere £165.6s.4d.,[1] which must have seemed a crushing blow after the positive acclaim that had greeted his work the previous year. The buyers were in the main dealers, such as Colnaghi and Palser.

Nevertheless, Cotman was again critically well received on his showing of a formidable fifty-two items at the 1824 summer exhibition of the Norwich Society. These included a number of oils and commissioned pictures from local patrons such as the collectors John Bridgman (No. 156) and J. Eager Esq.,[2] the former archdeacon of St. Albans the Rev. Charles Parr Burney[3] (see No. 100) and Dawson Turner's son-in-law, John Brightwen,[4] as well as examples from his portfolio for the use of his students. In the words of the *Norwich Mercury* critic: 'MR COTMAN (drawing-master of Norwich) is a man of unquestionably superior genius . . .'[5] The writer did, however, express his confusion when faced with *Trees at Kimberley—Clearing up after a storm at Mid-day* as a composition 'adopting a manner so removed from the common course' as to leave 'virtuosi' and public 'wholly unable to catch the effect'. Cotman was to be dogged throughout the remainder of this period at Norwich by this ambivalent reception of his work, both locally and in London.

During the mid 1820s Cotman gradually re-established himself as a Drawing Master in Norwich. On 2 November 1827 Hudson Gurney wrote to Dawson Turner:[6] 'as for Cotman, I am told he is getting on very well as a Drawing Master, and that if he goes on regularly in that employ he will have all

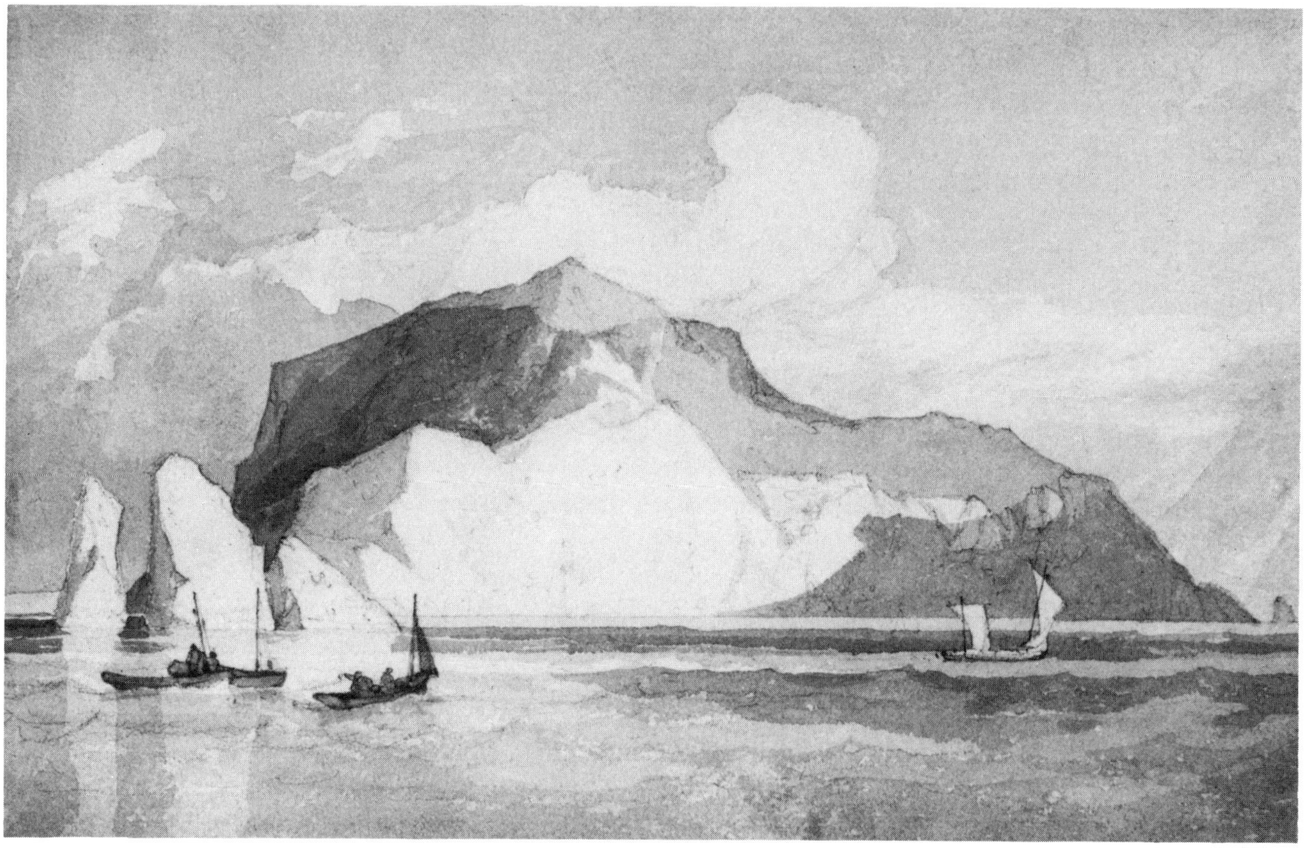

99 The Needles, *c.*1823

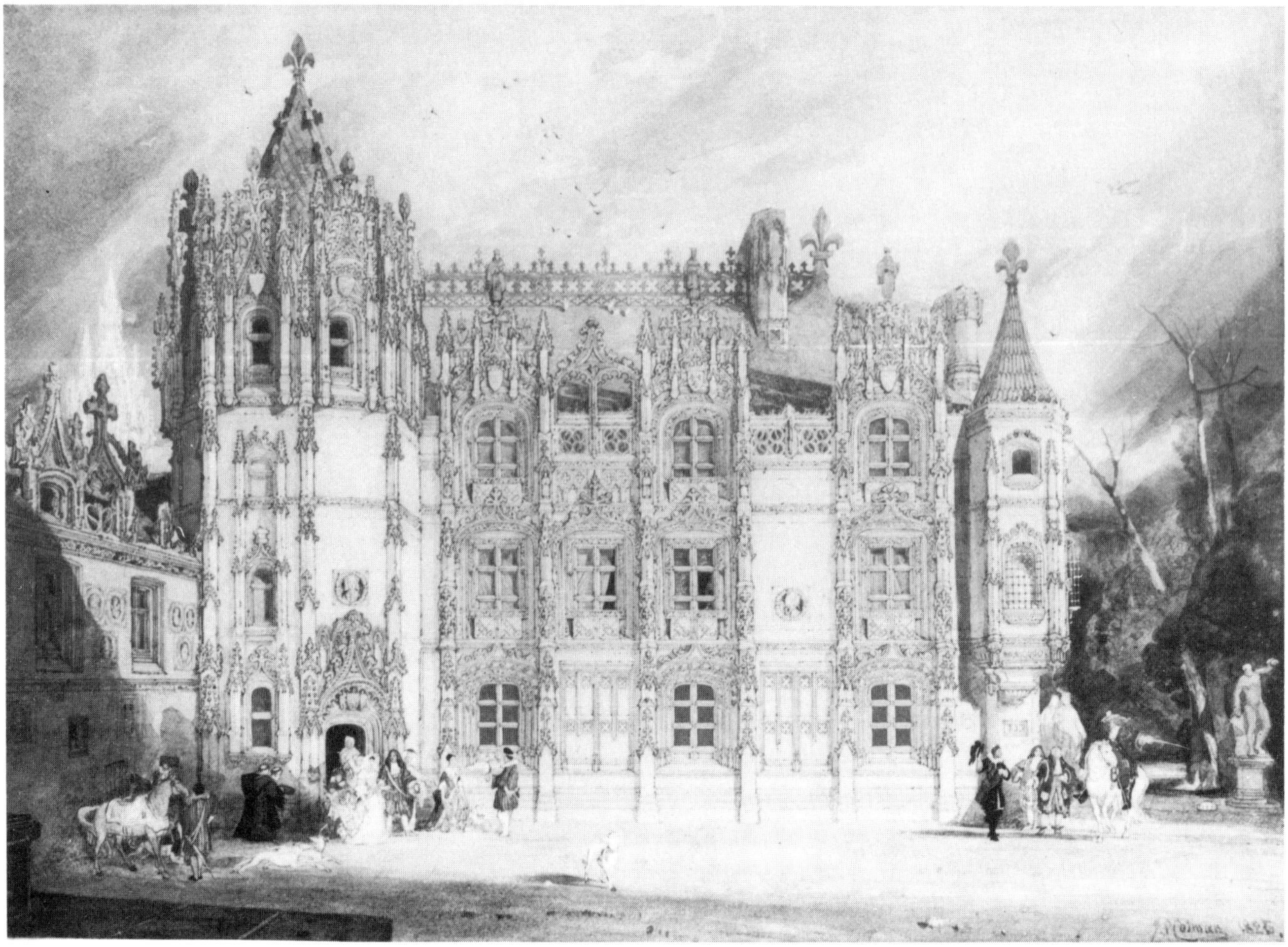

100 Abbatial House of the Abbey of St. Ouen at Rouen, ?1825

that it affords in this place—so that possibly his skirting off for things much more to his taste would add nothing to his means of living. Old John Crome had everything here, and while he lived there was but a Bad Chance in Norwich for another Drawing Master.' Gurney also comments that at that time John Berney Crome was 'losing his pupils rapidly', in all likelihood to Cotman. Cotman's 'skirting off' was presumably a reference not only to his work in oils and watercolour, but to that 'manner so removed from the common course' that was baffling to some.

The precise nature of the problem posed to the public by some of Cotman's work during the late 1820s and early 1830s is not easy to ascertain. His standing was high in Norwich at the beginning of 1825 and Dawson Turner's daughter, Mrs. Palgrave interceded on Cotman's behalf with Charles Wild, the treasurer of the Old Water-Colour Society, in order to obtain an exhibition venue for him in London. Mrs. Palgrave reported to her father that if Cotman were to apply for admission at once, he would be able to exhibit that spring. 'Mr. Wild was earnestly desirous that Mr. Cotman's drawings should have this advantage, which he considers a great one. The usual way for a person desirous of admission is to send drawings for approval; but Mr. Wild said Mr. Cotman's known talents rendered that unnecessary.'[7] Cotman duly exhibited three drawings that April as an associate of the Society that had 'blackball'd' him nearly twenty years previously. According to a correspondent in the *Norwich Mercury* at the end of the month the drawings were 'three most exquisite views', all of which were sold at the private view 'and we have heard them applied for more than once this morning'.[8] One of these exhibits was in his new, highly coloured style, one of a number of versions of his *Abbatial House of the Abbey of St. Ouen at Rouen* (No. 100). Cotman himself was pleased with the reception of his pictures: 'it was higher than I calculated upon' as he informed Dawson Turner in a letter of 2 July 1825.[9] That summer he exhibited only five subjects with the Norwich Society and they received the same mixture of high praise tinged with some bafflement: 'Mr. Cotman (we believe we speak the language of everybody who looks at his pictures—and who is not attracted to them?) always surprizes, delights and confounds us . . . But when and where did we ever see his colouring in Nature? . . .'[10] It seems that Cotman was to the forefront of the public attention, in both London and Norwich, while public taste was not necessarily abreast of contemporary developments, in the field of watercolour painting. His works at the Old Water Colour Society in 1825 were strongly criticized by Robert Hunt of *The Examiner* for his 'sudden opposition of reds, blues and yellows.'[11]

It was against this frustrating background of qualified success that Cotman applied unsuccessfully in the spring of 1825, for the post of drawing master in the School of Military Engineering at Chatham. His thoughts at this time were all for London. He eventually succumbed to a period of emotional crisis exacerbated by financial worries. A series of letters between Cotman and Dawson Turner during the summer of 1826 provided a focal point for Kitson's account of a period of 'penury and despair'.[12] Dawson Turner recommended the practical step of returning to Southtown, Yarmouth where he could re-occupy his former home—a regression which would have been anathema to Cotman. Dawson Turner's advice was always

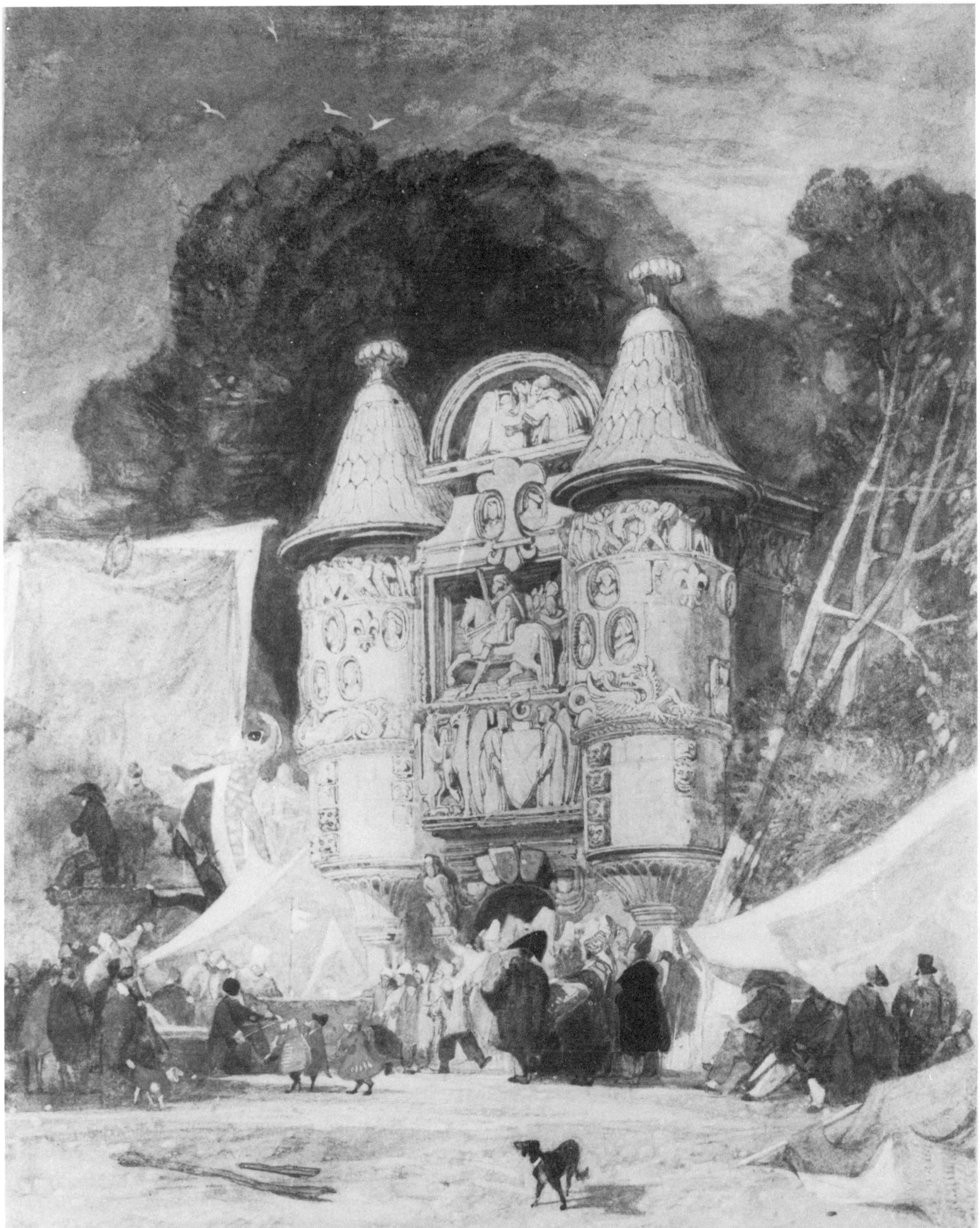

109 Gateway, Abbey Aumale, 1832

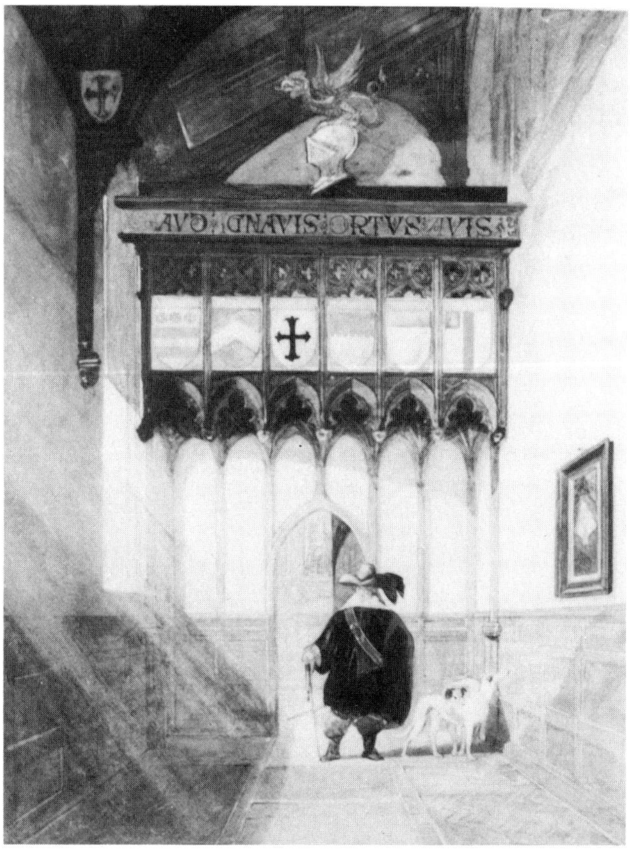

118 The Interior of Spruggins' Hall, Manor of Dolfuddle, Bedfordshire, leading to the Picture Gallery; Arms of Spruggins, Gull, Whittington, Bagnigge, KingWaddle and Sucklethumkin over the doorway — *vide* Lady Morley's *Spruggins Gallery*, 1833

practical, but in this case totally uncomprehending of Cotman's complex emotional state of mind. He advised him that 'your present style will not succeed, and you have talent enough to adopt any other. The public is a body that cannot be forced. Some extraordinary geniuses may have succeeded in guiding it; but they are few.'[13] Such advice was unlikely to ease Cotman's mind and their correspondence continued with Turner at one point becoming alarmed 'lest by brooding over his misfortunes, his mind sh[oul]d become totally unhinged'.[14] Yet it seems that the very process of letter-writing was one of catharsis for Cotman. Even as he wrote 'the sun has set for ever on my career and all is darkness before me . . . My pupils diminish to such a degree that it is impossible for me to live in any, save a *Workhouse* or a *Prison*'[15] he was on the brink of another period of vital and creative energy.

No surviving work by Cotman may be safely attributed to 1826, although in a letter on 1 November to Dawson Turner he comments that he has once again returned to oil painting (see section 11). There were no exhibitions locally in 1826 or 1827 as the Norwich Society Exhibition rooms were closed during the building of a new Corn Exchange on the same site. By November 1827 Cotman felt that the tide was once again in his favour as the numbers of his pupils increased and he determined to begin a series of drawings 'for Reputation—and I hope, for Profit.'[16] A year later, he was even more in command of his circumstances and determined to delight the public in the contemporary taste for 'city and town scenery and splendid architecture', such as that evinced by Prout (see Nos. 103, 104, 107). Nevertheless, while his subject-matter continued to please the local press reviewers, his heightened colouring remained controversial, being described in 1829 as 'too gaudy, and we regret in them the absence of that sweet grey tone which is so charming in nature'.[17]

Cotman continued to succumb to periods of elation and depression whilst developing a new technique to match his heightened awareness of colour (see Nos. 104, 113). One notable period of elation came at the start of 1830 when Cotman was a leading instigator of a series of 'artist conversaziones', no doubt encouraged by similar functions in London: 'It was the most brilliant thing ever witnessed for Norwich Art. Not one thing went amiss. We, the Artists, have reason to be perfectly satisfied. It was as far beyond my expectations as possible.'[18] In recognition of the leading role he had adopted, in 1831 and 1832 he was re-elected Vice President of the local society, now the Norfolk and Suffolk Institution for the Promotion of Fine Arts, becoming President for the second time in its final year, 1833. His contribution of eleven pictures in 1833 was praised once more in the press[19] for being the product of 'a man of genius', while it was noted that his works 'were all sold to London this spring'— possibly a reference to his works shown at the Old Water-Colour Society (No. 118). That October, the same review was reprinted in *Arnold's Magazine of the Fine Arts,*[20] the foremost art periodical of the day. Cotman's reputation was once again in the ascendant, just as negotiations began within the Turner family to promote his cause once again, this time for his appointment as Professor of Drawing at King's College School, London.

Notes

[1]J. Christie to JSC, 21 May 1824, Kitson 1937 pp. 249, 250. [2]Nos. 63 & 64. [3]No. 94. [4]Nos. 75 & 95. [5]*Norwich Mercury* 14 Aug. 1824. [6]Barker Collection. [7]Mrs. Palgrave to DT, Jan. 1825, Kitson 1937 pp. 261-2. [8]30 April 1825, Pidgley p. 61. [9]*Ibid.* p. 62 (Barker Collection). [10]*Norwich Mercury* 6 Aug. 1825. [11]Pidgley p. 122. [12]Kitson 1937 pp. 263-8. [13]DT to JSC, 22 June 1826, Kitson 1937 p. 264-5. [14]DT to Edmund Cotman, 22 July 1826, Kitson 1937 p. 267-8. [15]JSC to DT, 3 Aug. 1826 (Barker Collection). [16]JSC to DT, 10 Nov. 1827 (Barker Collection). [17]*Norfolk Chronicle* 1 Aug. 1829. [18]JSC to DT 22 Jan. 1830, Kitson 1937 p. 288. [19]*Norwich Mercury* 10 Aug. 1833. [20]Oct. 1833 p. 573 (Pidgley).

99 The Needles, *c.*1823

illustrated on p. 89

Pencil and watercolour on white, wove paper; 21.1 × 32.6 ($8\frac{5}{16}$ × $12\frac{7}{8}$). PROV: James Reeve; bt. from him by H. S. Theobald 1903; bt. from him by R. J. Colman, Feb. 1910; R. J. Colman Bequest 1946. (188.235.951). EXH: RA 1934 (728, Commemorative Catalogue 819); Norwich 1945. REF: Kitson *OWCS* 1930 pl. X in colour; Binyon 1933 p. 148; Kitson, *Country Life* 7 Nov. 1936 repro fig 1; Kitson 1937 p. 199, pl. 88; Binyon, *Burlington* July 1942 p. 163; *Colman Collection Guide* 1951 p. 6, pl. 7A; Rienaecker pl. 4 in colour; Clifford pp. 53, 70; Hardie vol. 2 p. 86, pl. 76; Day 1969 vol. III repro. p. 27 in colour; Cordingly 1974 pp. 126, 128, pl. 75; Pidgley p. 148; Conrad 1977 pl. 2.

This watercolour is one of the most successful results of Cotman's Normandy tours. The considered balance of forms combined with absolute tonal harmony reveals the essence of Cotman's inherent sense of structure. The masses are simplified to a degree which recalls the works of his first Norwich period, such as *The Marl Pit* (No. 59) and *The Mars off Cromer* (No. 34). The white chalk cliffs, the small outlying rocks and their reflections broken by three fishing boats to the left, the two white sails of the boat to the right catching the sunlight, the white clouds in the limpid blue sky above blend into a composition which still retains the spontaneity of dexterously applied washes.

Cotman had the opportunity to sketch the south-west aspect of the Isle of Wight on two occasions: his homeward bound journey on 10 August 1817 and on his outward voyage to Le Havre on 25 July 1820. He wrote to his wife of the first journey that 'the passage was a most boisterous one'. They had reached the harbour when 'opposite to Cowes Castle, Isle of Wight, it fell a perfect calm, which delayed our positive arrival at Southampton some four or five hours.'[1] It appears that the weather was still 'boisterous' when Cotman was first able to sketch the Needles from the south-west. It is probably on this day that he produced the small sketch[2] of a low horizontal viewpoint, from which the watercolour[2] *Boats off the Needles in Stormy Weather*[3] was worked up. The voyage of 25 July 1820 was however 'a most delightful passage'[4] and it seems likely that No. 99 derives from a sketch made at this time.

The underlying drawing of soft pencil, in combination with the translucent washes of watercolour, recall the technique and vision of the later monochrome views of Normandy deriving from his last visit. The central rocky outcrop of *Campeaux between Vire and St. Lô* (No. 91) is an example of a similar motif, but the treatment of the cliffs in *View of the Inner Harbour and Cliffs at Fécamp* (No. 95) is the closest parallel among the Normandy drawings. Another view of the Needles by Cotman is heavily worked in pencil with white bodycolour[5] and, although presumably derived from a sketch, is a less successful composition.

[1]JSC to his wife, 11 Aug. 1817 (*The Walpole Society*, vol. XIV, pp. 108-109) [2]BM 1902-5-14-53. [3]Chalk and watercolour on grey paper, $5\frac{3}{4}$ × $12\frac{1}{4}$, Private Collection. [4]JSC to DT, 31 July 1820 (*The Walpole Society*, vol. XV, p. 106). [5]NCM 532.235.951.

100 Abbatial House of the Abbey of St. Ouen at Rouen, ?1825

illustrated on p. 90

Pencil, pen and brown ink, watercolour and bodycolour with scraping out on white, wove paper with watermark u.l. *JWHATM[AN]*; 42.3 × 57.3 ($16\frac{5}{8}$ × $22\frac{9}{16}$). INSCR: *Recto*, signed and dated in brown watercolour l.r. *J S Cotman 1825* (?) PROV: ?J. Webster 1825; T. Humphrey Ward; bt. from him by J. J. Colman by 1888; his bequest to R. J. Colman 1898; R. J. Colman Bequest 1946. (191.217.947). EXH: ?OWCS 1825 (105); Norwich, Art Circle 1888 (164) lent by J. J. Colman; BFAC 1888 (61); RA Winter Exhibition 1892 (102); Norwich 1903 (53); Manchester 1912 (330); Tate 1922 (144); Norwich, Arts Council 1947 (21). REF: Kitson 1937 p. 257, pl. 131; Rajnai 1975 No. 36.

Cotman's visits to Rouen are discussed in the entry for No. 83.

As in the case of the *Gateway Abbey Aumale* (Nos. 108, 109), Cotman did not see the subject of this watercolour, as it was demolished by 1817. Rajnai suggests that Cotman must have used the engravings in J. F. Pommeraye's *Histoire de l'Abbaye de St. Ouen* 1662,[1] although details such as the courtly scene in the foreground and the statues on the right seem to be Cotman's own invention.

During his lifetime Cotman exhibited the subject four times: twice with the Norwich Society of Artists in 1824 (94) and 1829 (132) and twice with the Old Water-Colour Society in 1825 (105) and 1831 (105). According to its catalogue entry the 1824 exhibit was painted for the Rev. C. P. Burney. However, as it did not have his 'idea of finish', Cotman took it back with the promise to paint a more finished one for him.[2] The original Burney drawing of 1824 Cotman then sold probably to Charles Turner of Norwich[3] and it remains in private hands.[4] The 1829 version was possibly the replacement which was still not accomplished by November 1827,[2] but subsequently entered the collection of the Victoria & Albert Museum.[5] Another watercolour version, with a pond introduced in the foreground, now in a Norfolk private collection, was probably the 1831 exhibit.[6] A chalk drawing on grey paper, probably by M. E. Cotman, is in another private collection.[7] Of all these versions No. 100 is the only one that shows the building the right way round; as shown in the 1662 engraving. Rajnai has convincingly argued that the strongest likelihood is that No. 100 was the version exhibited with the Old Water-Colour Society in 1825 and purchased by J. Webster Esq.

Cotman himself commented on the anxiety that he faced concerning the repetition of this subject in 1827: 'Unaccustomed to repeat my drawings, it was a task more so that I cd. possibly calculate upon & I sickened in my work and independant of this I had said I would leave off drawing architecture but wd, leave off with the best subject I ever touched upon, to shew I did it from choice & not because I cd. not go on with duel subjects!!! What a retribution.'[2]

[1]This was probably available to him in the library of Dawson Turner (included in his book sale Sotheby's, 7-12 and 17-24 March 1853, 10th day, lot 2541). [2]JSC to Rev. C. P. Burney, Norwich 12 Nov. 1827 (Norfolk and Norwich Record Office). [3]Chambers *Norfolk Tour* 1829 p. 115 reveals that he owned a version by this date. [4]The Charles Turner drawing became the property of A. E. Alston and remains with the family. [5]V&A P30-1934. [6]Repro. Rienaecker pl. 41, fig. 80. [7]Possibly Cotman sale, Murrell, Norwich, 27 Nov. 1862, lot 206.

101 South Porch of the Church of Louviers, *c.*1825-6

illustrated on p. 94

Pencil, pen and brown ink, watercolour and white bodycolour on white, wove paper; 46.8 × 32.7 ($18\frac{3}{8}$ × $12\frac{7}{8}$). INSCR: *Recto*, signed in brown watercolour l.r. *J S Cotman*. PROV: Rev. Canon Bulmer sale, Spelman, Norwich, 2nd day, 28 Feb. 1900, lot 421, bt. R. Levine for R. J. Colman 50 gns; R. J. Colman Bequest 1946. (197.235.951). EXH: ?OWCS 1826 (192); Norwich 1903 (25); Tate 1922 (101); Norwich 1930-31. REF: Kitson 1937 p. 258; Rajnai 1975 No. 31.

Cotman visited Louviers during his second Normandy tour, probably on 11 or 12 July 1818. In his letter[1] to Dawson Turner, dated 12 July 1818, Cotman includes 'Louviers, South Porch of y Ch' in his 'list of subjects' already drawn.

No. 101 is developed from a preliminary drawing[2] also in the collection at Norwich. The finished composition is more elaborate and Kitson observes that: 'Among the other water-colours derived from his Normandy portfolios, *The Church Porch at Louviers* shows the same preoccupation with elaborate detail as *The Abbot's House.* In such drawings as these Cotman was parading his virtuosity as a draughtsman to the prejudice of his other qualities.'

The watercolour is almost certainly one of Cotman's seven exhibits with the Old Water-Colour Society in 1826. A drawing of the same subject is in the Barker Collection. This is inscribed, apparently in Cotman's hand, with the apology that was printed in the text of the etched version, plate 79 in *Architectural Antiquities of Normandy* 1822: 'Mr. Cotman very much regrets that it was not in his power to do this porch the justice it deserved, in consequence of the continual interruptions to which he was exposed from the lower class of the inhabitants.'

[1]BM. [2]Rajnai 1975 No. 30; a full scale design for the etching (Popham No. 276).

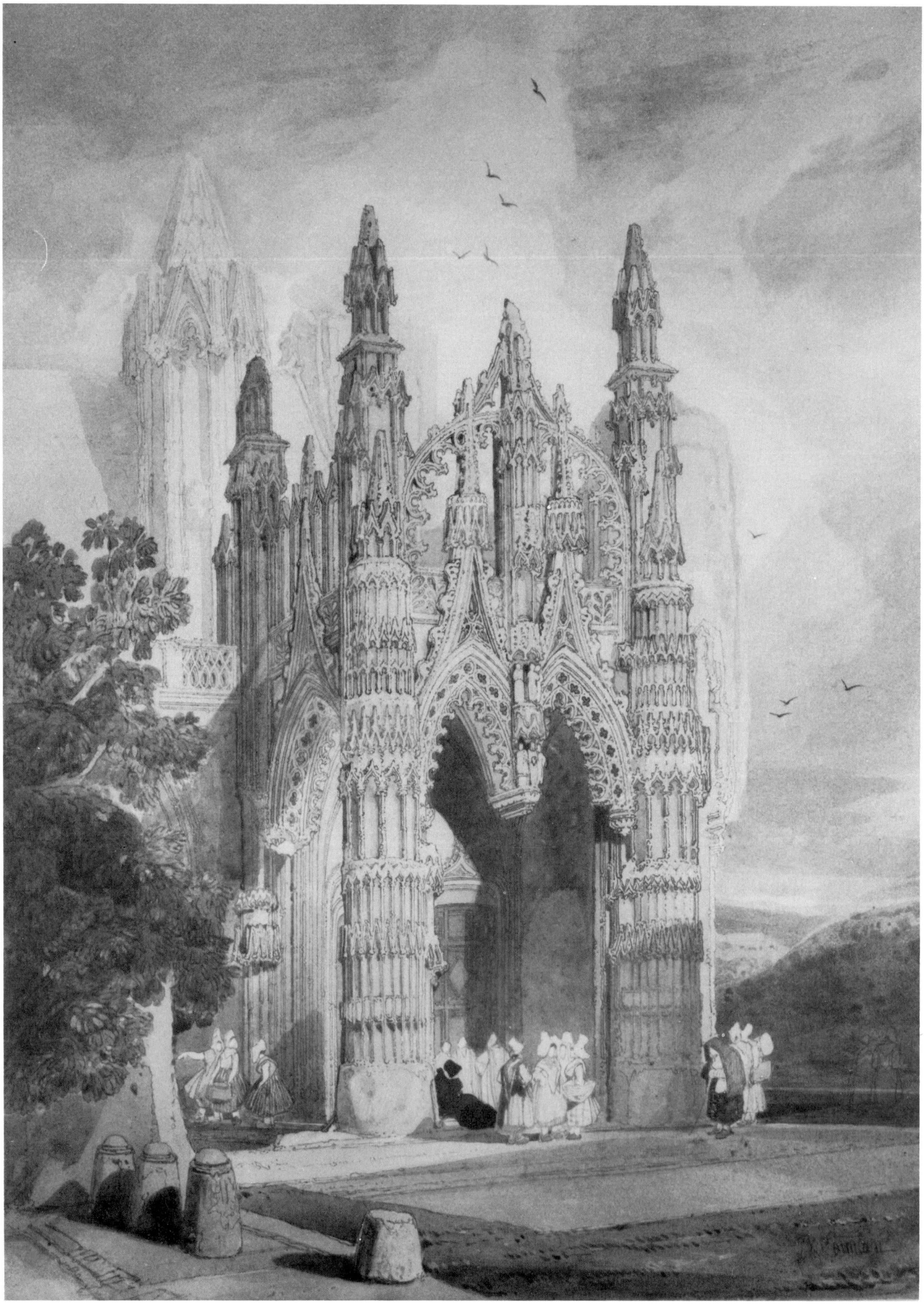

101 South Porch of the Church of Louviers, *c.*1825-6

102 Tower of Lillebonne, *c.*1826-31

Pencil, watercolour and bodycolour on white, wove paper; 33.8 × 24.1 ($13\frac{1}{4} \times 9\frac{1}{2}$). INSCR: *Verso,* in pencil c. *Cotman* (indistinct). PROV: ?Cotman sale, Spelman, Norwich, 16 May 1861, lot 169, bt. Titlow £1.12.6; ?Rev. Samuel Titlow sale, Spelman, Norwich, 13 June 1871, lot 214, 65s.; Palser Gallery; bt. from them by Percy Moore Turner, March 1926; bt. from him by R. J. Colman, March 1926; R. J. Colman Bequest 1946. (200.235.951). REF: Rajnai 1975 No. 27.

Cotman's only visit to Lillebonne was made on 2 and 3 July 1817, during his first Normandy tour.

It is not clear, however, that the tower in No. 102 actually relates to the environs of Lillebonne. No tower of this type seems to be recorded in the town or its vicinity and Rajnai suggests that the composition is probably a *capriccio.* It is a work created at least ten years after his original visit to Lillebonne and displays the heightened colour range of the late 1820s when Cotman was reworking and exhibiting a number of Normandy subjects in watercolour (see also Nos. 100, 101, 109). The lively groups of figures in the foreground recall those of other works of this period such as Nos. 101, 107 and 108.

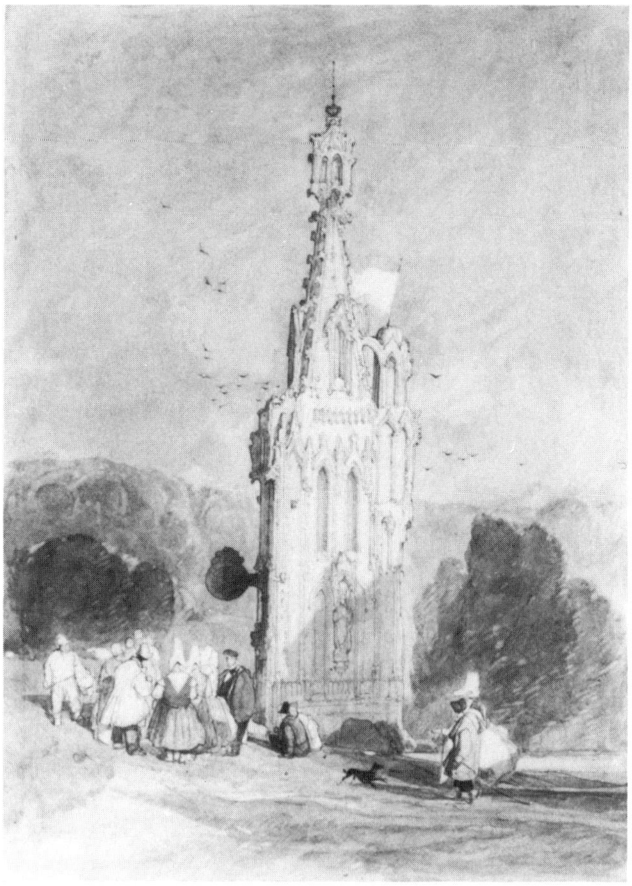

102 Tower of Lillebonne, *c.*1826-31

103 Houses, Surrey Street, Norwich, 1829

Pencil heightened with white and orange chalk on white, wove paper; 30.6 × 22.3 ($12 \times 8\frac{3}{4}$). INSCR: Signed with initials and dated in pencil l.r. *JSC. Nov. 13.29.* PROV: See No. 99. (510.235.951). REF: Kitson 1937 p. 278.

This drawing is important in Cotman's oeuvre as one of the few securely dated examples of his drawing style which by this period had developed a more flamboyant flourish. His vigorous pencilwork combines the use of the sharp point of the pencil to outline the essential structure, whilst foliate or shadowed areas are achieved with rapid hatched work employing the softer side of the pencil. No. 103 is the preliminary sketch for the watercolour (No. 104).

Almost a year previously Cotman had written to Dawson Turner of his intentions to follow contemporary fashion and select city and town subjects which combined architecture and scenery 'to which I can give a local interest and a name'.[1] Surrey Street was an excellent choice, being 'a Georgian Street of distinction'.[2] Cotman has selected the range of tall, three and a half storey terraced houses designed by Thomas Ivory. Built between 1761-1771, the terrace on the south side of Surrey Street is still largely intact. It was in this terrace that the celebrated botanist, Sir James Edward Smith had lived until his death in 1828, while the house which appears to be undergoing alterations is traditionally regarded as that of the Solicitor Thomas Brightwell, the father of Cotman's pupil, Lucy Brightwell.

Another sketch of a street scene, comparable in both style and subject matter, is in the collection of the Victoria and Albert Museum.[3] Although not readily identifiable it is a further example of Cotman's efforts to sketch urban scenes at this time.

[1]JSC to DT, 25 Nov. 1828 (Barker Collection). Kitson 1937 p. 274. [2]Pevsner *North East Norfolk and Norwich* p. 278. [3]V&A E711-1925.

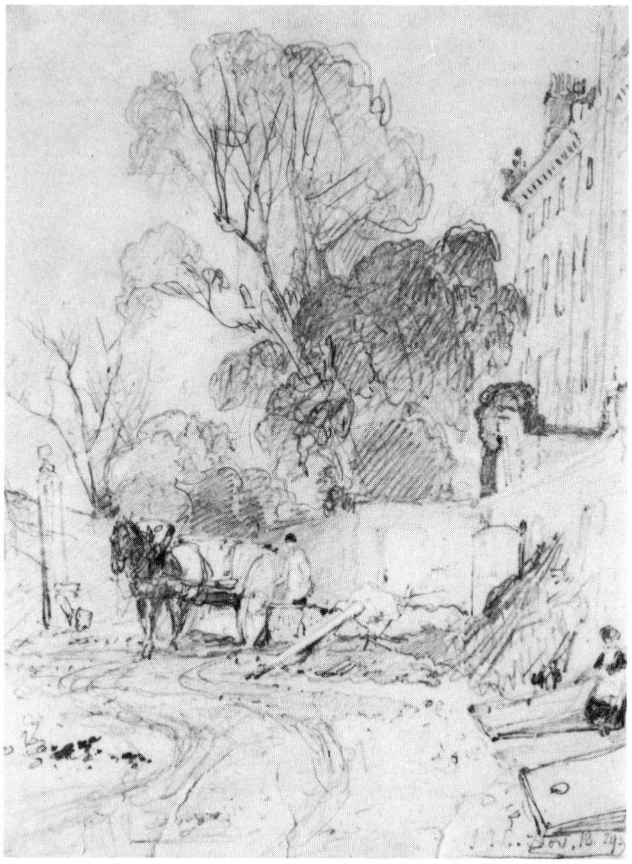

103 Houses, Surrey Street, Norwich, 1829

104 Houses, Surrey Street, Norwich, *c.*1829-30
illustrated on p. 88

Pencil and watercolour with some scraping out on white, wove paper; 32.6 × 22.4 ($12\frac{13}{16} \times 8\frac{13}{16}$). PROV: John King by 1874; ?by descent to Dr. H. D. King; bt. from him by James Reeve; bt. from him by H. S. Theobald 1903; bt. from him by R. J. Colman, Feb. 1910; R. J. Colman Bequest 1946. (198.235.951). EXH: Norwich 1874 (110) lent by John King; Norwich 1903 (24) lent by James Reeve; Manchester 1912 (332); Tate 1922 (100); Norwich 1930-31; Norwich 1945. REF: Kitson 1937 pp. 278-9.

This watercolour is developed from Cotman's pencil and chalk sketch of 13 November 1829 (No. 103). For a discussion of the subject see the previous entry.

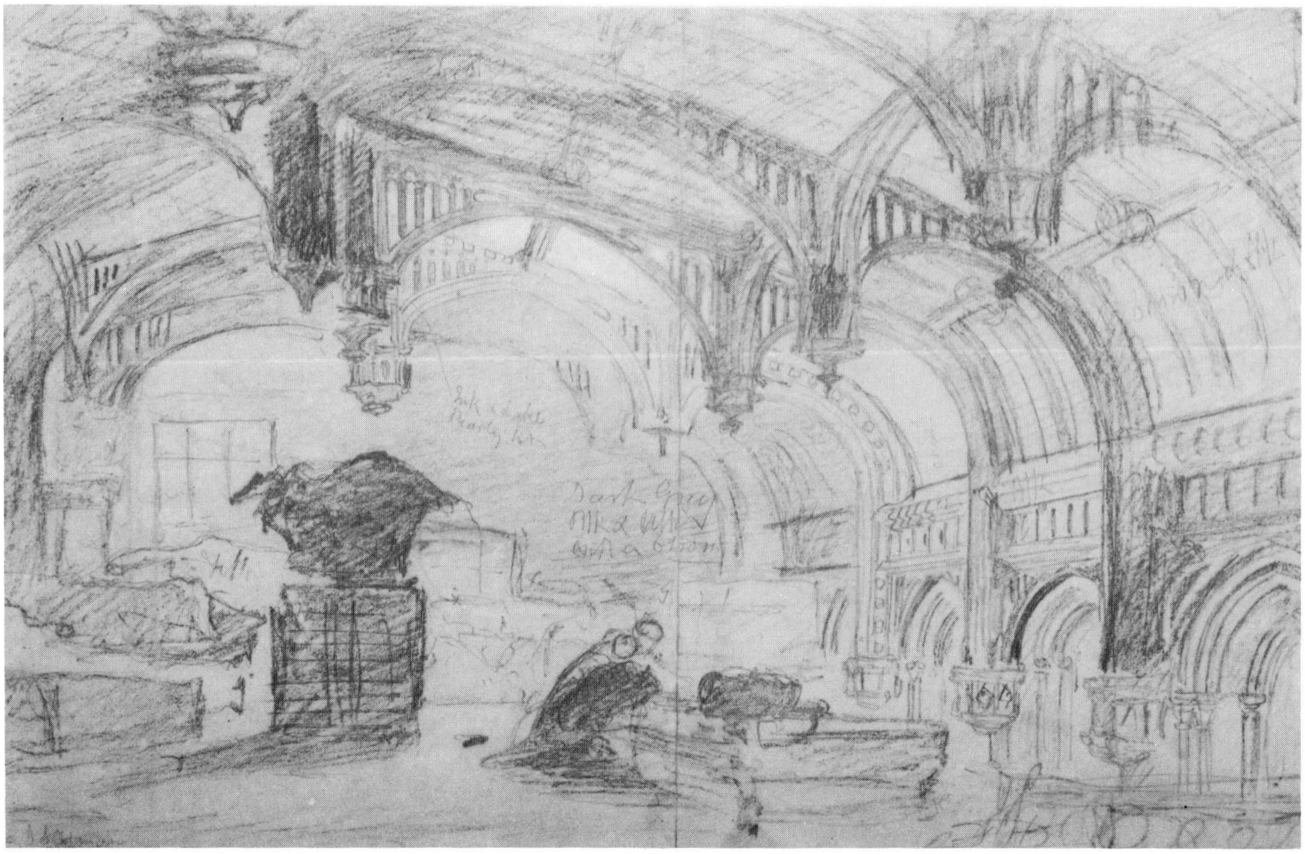

105 Crosby Hall, 1829

The virtuosity of pencilwork in the preliminary study has become a bravura performance in colour values. While his palette remains similar to that of his first Norwich period, as does his eye for decorative detail, his use of the medium has changed dramatically. Washes are no longer abstract hues staining the paper with two-dimensional blocks of colour. Instead the colour is now teased and worked into more representational forms.

While the scale and proportions of the sketch remain, the effect of the watercolour is one of brazen colour, tempered in tone through the gradation from the raw sienna of the foreground through to the variegation of the cooler blues and the blotting of the foliage to achieve a softened hue. The strident foreground colour is textured by scratching with a pointed tool, a technique Cotman used intermittently.

105 Crosby Hall, 1829

Pencil and black chalk heightened with white on two sheets of brown, wove paper, joined centre right; 28.6 × 43.5 ($11\frac{1}{4}$ × $17\frac{1}{8}$). INSCR: signed in pencil l.l. *J S Cotman* and inscribed with colour notes. PROV: R. J. Colman Bequest 1946. (457.235.951).

Cotman spent Christmas 1828 and the start of the new year with the artist George Cooke and his brother William. George's son Edward kept a diary and a number of his entries reveal some of Cotman's movements in London during this visit. He made a number of sketches with a view to providing subjects for George Cooke's *London and its Vicinity* and sketched Crosby Hall on 10 January 1829.[1] No. 105 is undoubtedly the preliminary drawing of this visit.

Crosby Hall, then 'situated on the eastern side of Bishopsgate-Street, London, at a short distance from the parish church of St. Helens'[2] was a subject steeped in historical association calculated to appeal to Cotman's romantic sense of the past. However, the hall 'though one of the most elegant specimens of ancient domestic architecture in England; the residence of princes, and the theatre of great and interesting transactions [was] now converted into a common warehouse.'[2] The lease of Messrs. Holmes and Hall, Packers, expired in 1832, when a committee was formed to restore the building.

In Cotman's day, therefore, the hall was 'greatly mutilated, and obscured by bales of goods',[2] leaving the highly ornamented timber-work of the roof as the single dominant feature visible. The hard edge of the pencil is worked over in black chalk to achieve an exploration of light and shade on the grandest scale. A discussion of the two water-colour versions derived from this drawing is in the following entry.

During the period 1908-10, as a result of the continuing effort to restore the building, Crosby Hall was dismantled and transported to Chelsea where it now stands.

[1]Pidgley p. 247. [2]John Britton, 'Some account of Crosby Hall, London', *Architectural Antiquities of Great Britain*, vol. 4, 1814, pp. 185-188.

106 Crosby Hall, *c.*1829-30

illustrated in colour on p. 136

Pencil, watercolour, bodycolour and pen and ink on cream, wove paper; 34.8 × 51.9 ($13\frac{11}{16}$ × $20\frac{7}{16}$). INSCR. Signed and dated in brown ink l.l. *J S Cotman—1830.* PROV: Cross sale, Foster, Norwich 19 Dec. 1860, lot 27, bt. Andrews £2.15.0; Christie's sale, 16 May 1862, lot 156; E. W. Cooke RA; his sale, Christie's, 24-26 May 1880, lot 156, bt. William Cox 9 gns.; bt. from him by J. J. Colman by 1888; his bequest to R. J. Colman 1898; R. J. Colman Bequest 1946. (204.217.947). EXH: Norwich Society 1830 (40*); Norwich, Art Circle 1888 (163) illus. with litho. by S. F. Howitt, lent by J. J. Colman; BFAC 1888 (78); Norwich 1894 (56); Earls Court 1897 (20); Norwich 1903 (43); Manchester 1912 (343); Tate 1922 (103); Norwich 1945; Norwich, Arts Council 1947 (27). REF: Binyon 1903 pl. C31; Dickes p. 369 repro. p. 370; Batchelor, *EDP* 13 April 1922; Kaines Smith 1926 pp. 66, 106, 137; Kitson, *OWCS* 1930 p. 16; Rutter, *ILN* Sept. 1936 p. 492 repro; Kitson 1937 p. 294, pl. 129; Rienaecker pl. 48 fig. 94; Mallalieu 1974 pl. IV in colour; Pidgley pp. 197 n.100, 198; Rajnai & Allthorpe No. 71.

Edward Cooke's diary records that Cotman called in April, 1830 to deliver a watercolour of Crosby Hall which he intended as a contribu-

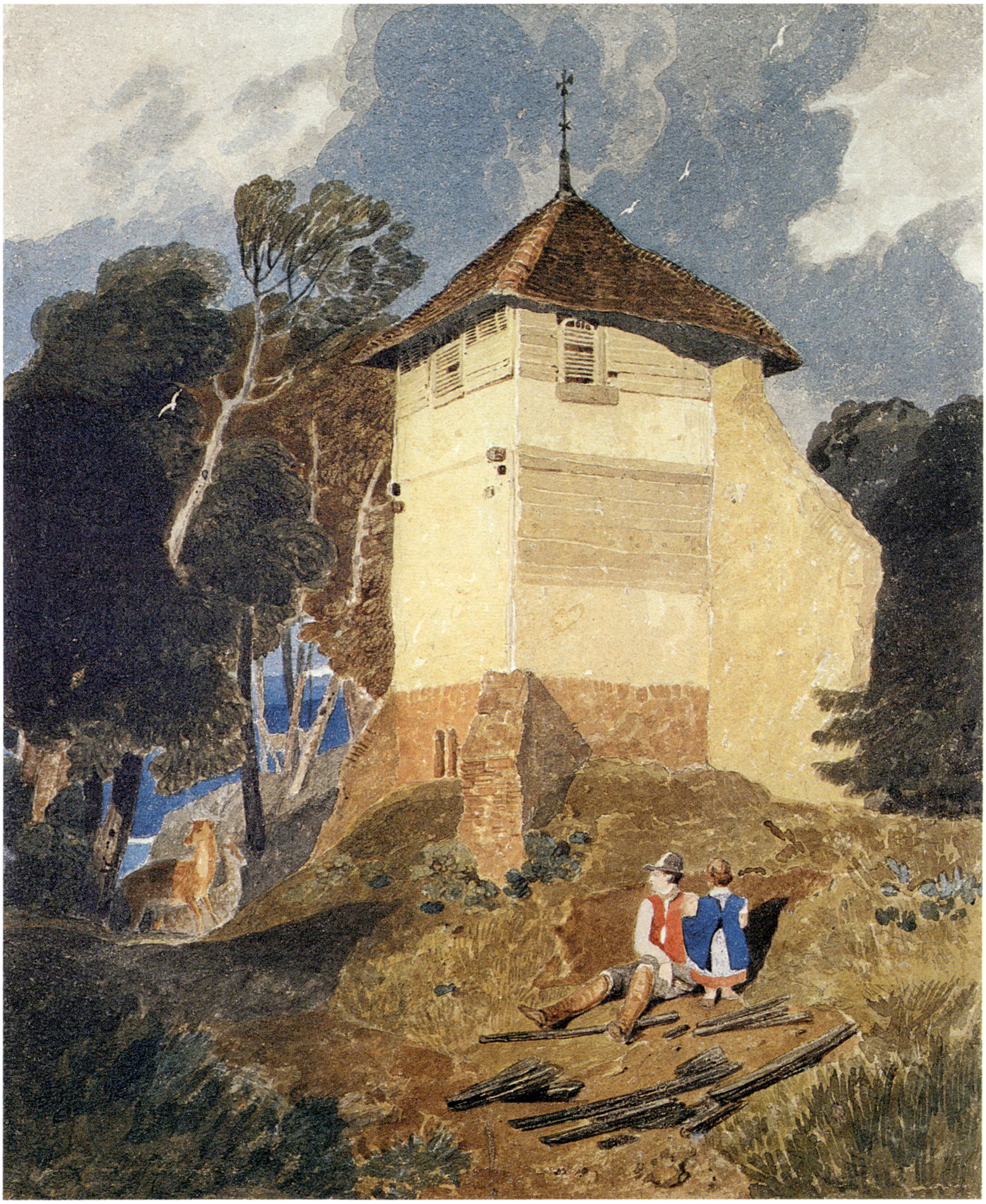

54 Kirby Bedon Tower, Norfolk, *c.*1809-10

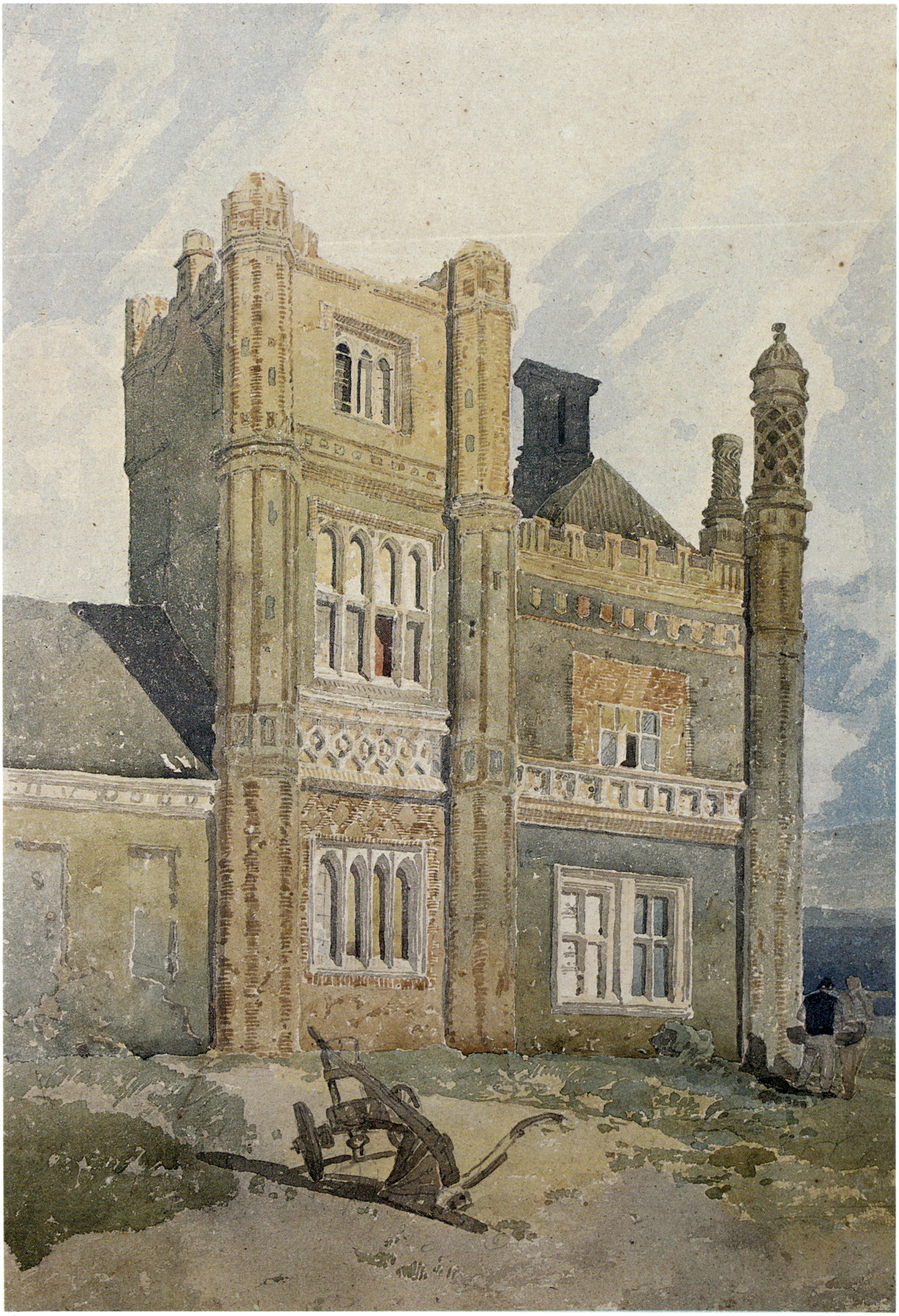

38 East Barsham Hall, Norfolk, *c.*1808

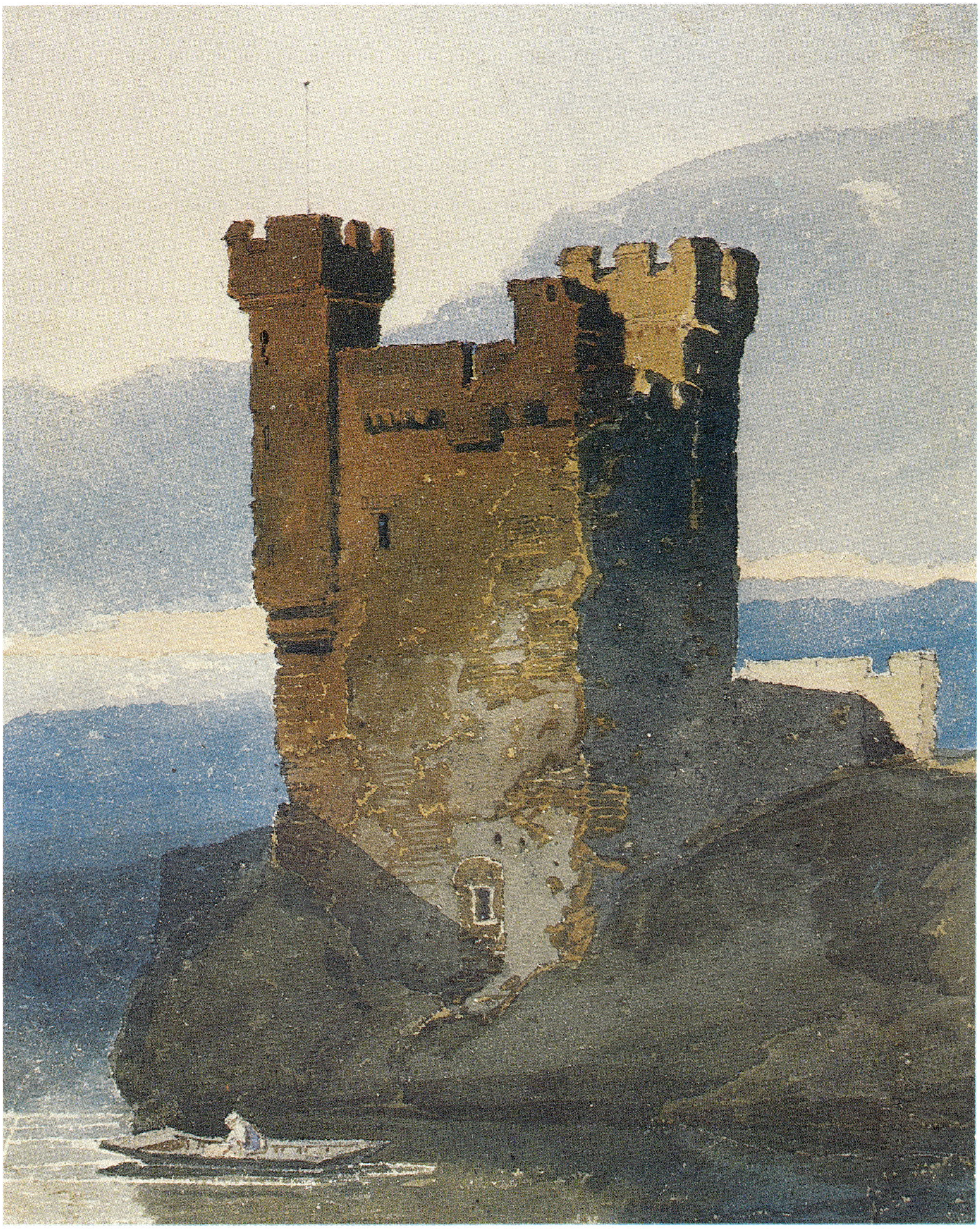

57 Castle by Water, *c.*1809-10

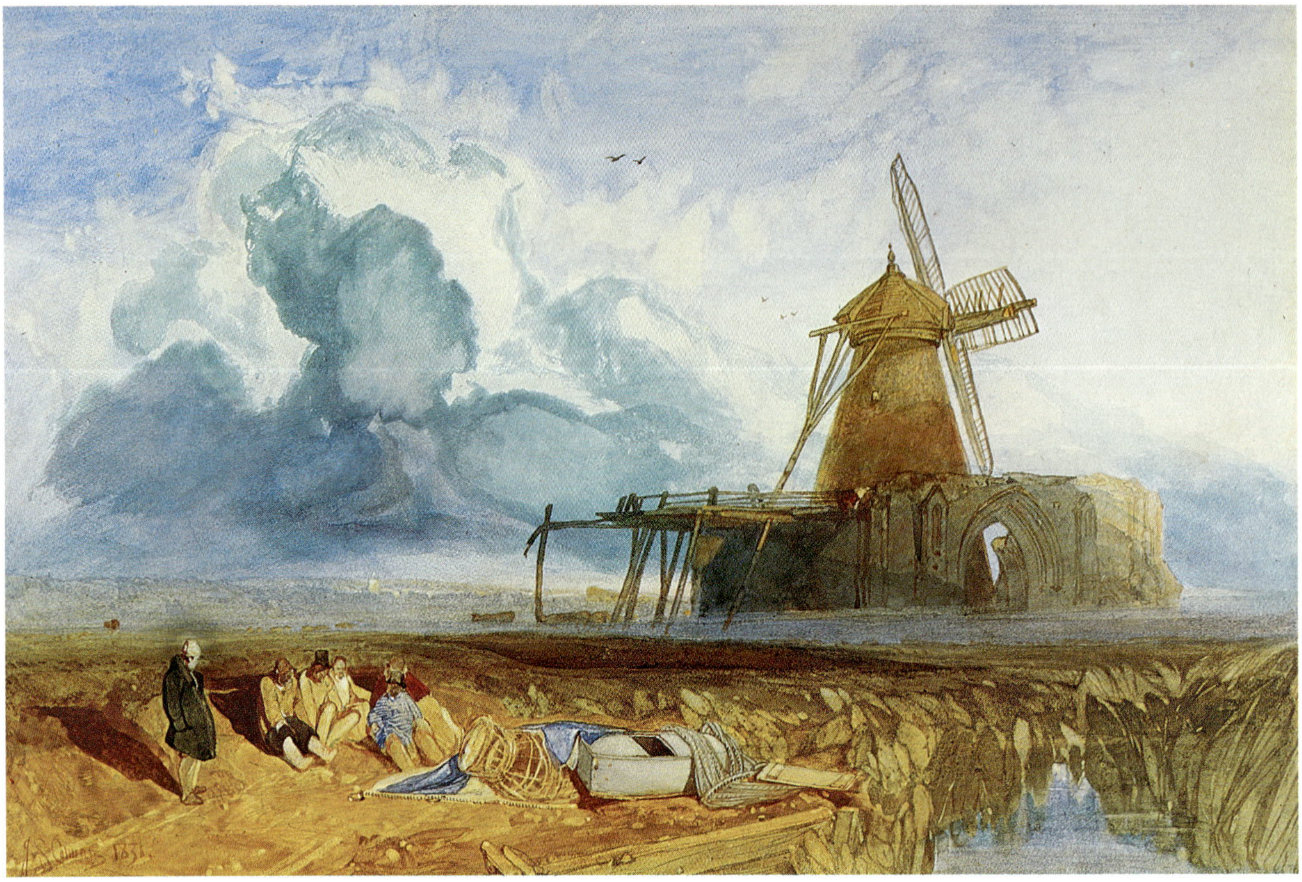

112 St. Benet's Abbey, Norfolk, 1831

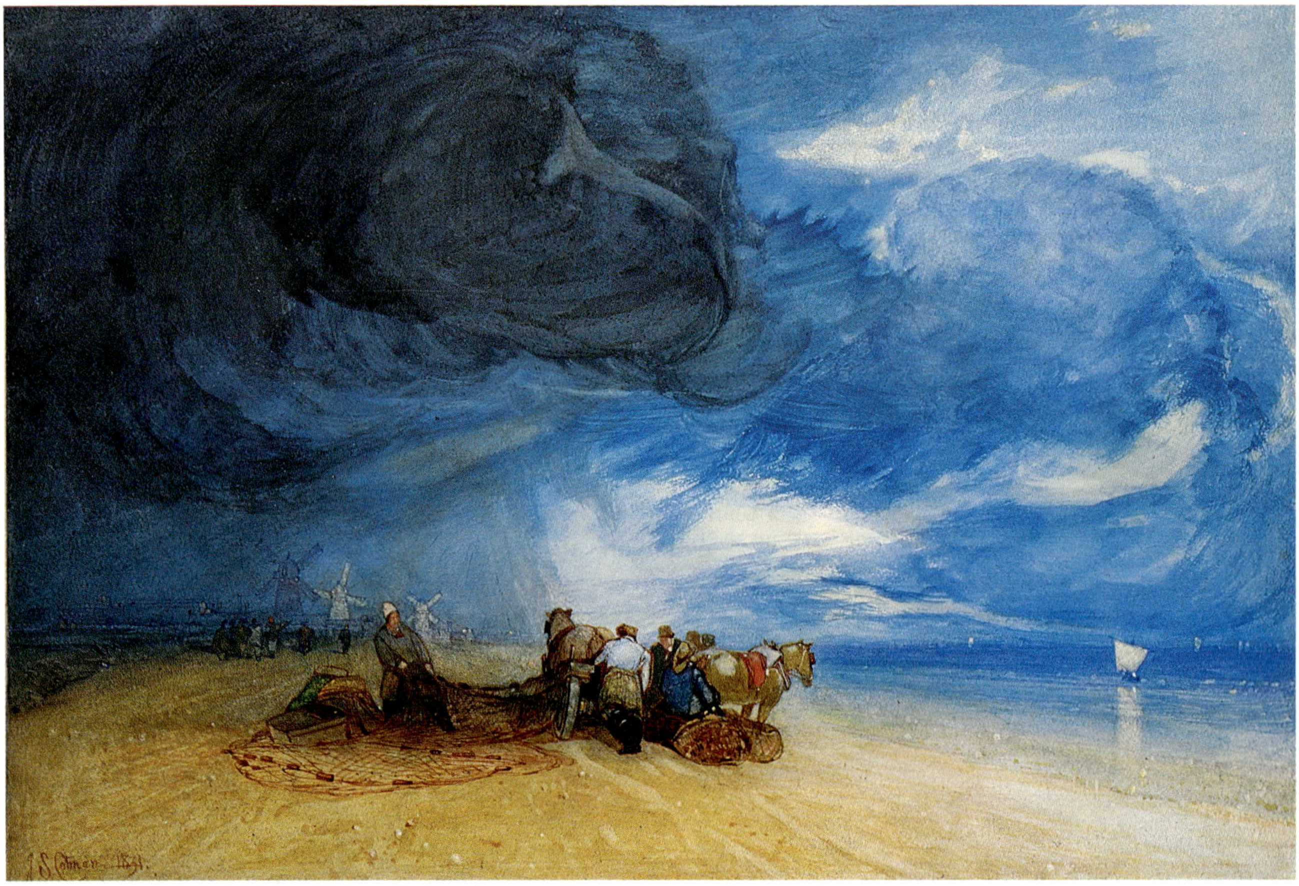

113 Storm on Yarmouth Beach, 1831

tion to George Cooke's *London and its Vicinity.*[1] In the event it was not engraved, but probably returned to Norwich in time to be shown at the Norfolk and Suffolk Institution exhibition that summer. No. 106 is derived from the study of the previous entry, while the identification of this watercolour with the Cooke family is evidenced not only in its provenance, but in the inscriptions 'Cooke' and 'G. Cooke' to be seen on the bales of merchandise at the back of the hall.

The colour notes of the initial study have been closely followed: 'pearly white' effects are achieved through scraping out, while 'dark grey blk' is retained for the background, 'oker' is echoed in the roof, and 'brown & blk' is followed in the painting of the architectural elements. A heavy use of gum enhances the depths of the shadows, while dazzling areas of light are achieved through reserved and scraped areas. A powerful sense of romantic reaction to the historic setting of a building which features in Shakespeare's *Richard III* is strongly evoked. In Kitson's words: 'a like wizardry is seen in Turner's contemporary visions of interiors at Petworth'.[2]

A second watercolour version,[3] exhibited the following year with the Old Water-Colour Society, is now in the collection of the Victoria and Albert Museum. This is more prosaically worked up by comparison and departs further from the original drawing. A pair of scales is added to the tabletop, together with an extra archway to the right. One feature loosely indicated in the drawing but worked up only in the second watercolour version is a roll of ornately decorated material in the right foreground. The architecture and incident are more specifically details in the second, larger watercolour version.

[1]Pidgley p. 247. [2]Kitson 1937 p. 294. [3]V&A P19 - 1927.

107 Statue of King Charles I, Charing Cross, *c.*1829-30

illustrated on p. 102

Pencil, watercolour, bodycolour and brown ink on cream, wove paper, ?watermark lower edge; 46.2 × 31.6 ($18\frac{3}{16}$ × $12\frac{7}{16}$). PROV: bt. from the artist by John Gurney of Earlham for £5; Rev. W. N. Ripley by 1874; Christie's sale, 26 April 1912, lot 30, bt. Paterson ?on behalf of R. J. Colman, 170 gns. (90 gns. in annotated catalogue, Art Dept. archives, NCM); R. J. Colman Bequest 1946. (203.217.947). EXH: Norwich 1874 (145) lent by Rev. W. N. Ripley; Norwich 1878 (478); Norwich 1885 (292); Norwich, Art Circle 1888 (180) illus. with litho. by C. J. Watson; RA Winter Exhibition 1892 (104); Norwich 1894 (76); Norwich 1902 (224) as *Trafalgar Square, Statue of Charles I;* Norwich 1903 (41); Tate 1922 (121); Norwich 1945; Arts Council, Norwich 1947 (26). REF: *The Academy* 21 July 1888; *EDP* 1 Dec 1888; Dickes p. 370 repro. opp.; Cundall, *The Studio* 1920 pl. XLIV; *Pall Mall* 12 April 1922; MacColl, *Saturday Review* 15 April 1922 p. 388; Kaines Smith 1926 pp. 106, 137; Kitson, *OWCS* 1930 p. 16; Rutter, *Sunday Times* 20 Sept. 1936; Gordon, *Observer* 20 Sept; 1936 repro; *The Christian Science Monitor* Oct. 1936 repro; Kitson 1937 pp. 294-295; *Colman Collection Guide* 1951 p. 6, pl. 9.

It is likely that this composition derives from a sketch made during Cotman's visit to London between late December 1828 and 20 January 1829,[1] when he sketched monuments which included *Crosby Hall* (Nos. 105, 106) and the *Monument and St. Philip Magnus Church.*[2]

The scene shows Northumberland House on the right, the Golden Cross Inn on the left and the spire of St. Martin's Church beyond. The composition is dominated by the statue of Charles I on horseback, the work of the Huguenot sculpture Sueur, standing since 1675 on the site of the original Charing Cross.

This watercolour is a splendid example of that style by which Cotman proposed 'to appear once more before the public in borrowed plumes'.[3] He had announced to Dawson Turner his intention to concentrate upon City architecture and to follow the example of Canaletto. It is possible that Caneletto's rigorously composed townscapes lie behind the selection of this subject, which is as theatrical in its effect as a number of Cotman's interiors of this period.

It is perhaps this element which has evoked divergent responses in its critics. The critic of *The Academy* in 1888 found the watercolour 'a treatment of architecture at once learned and free. It has atmosphere— the atmosphere of the town'. D. S. MacColl of *The Saturday Review,* however, recoiled at the colour values demonstrated in the picture in which he upbraided Cotman for having 'deck[ed] out his yellow with

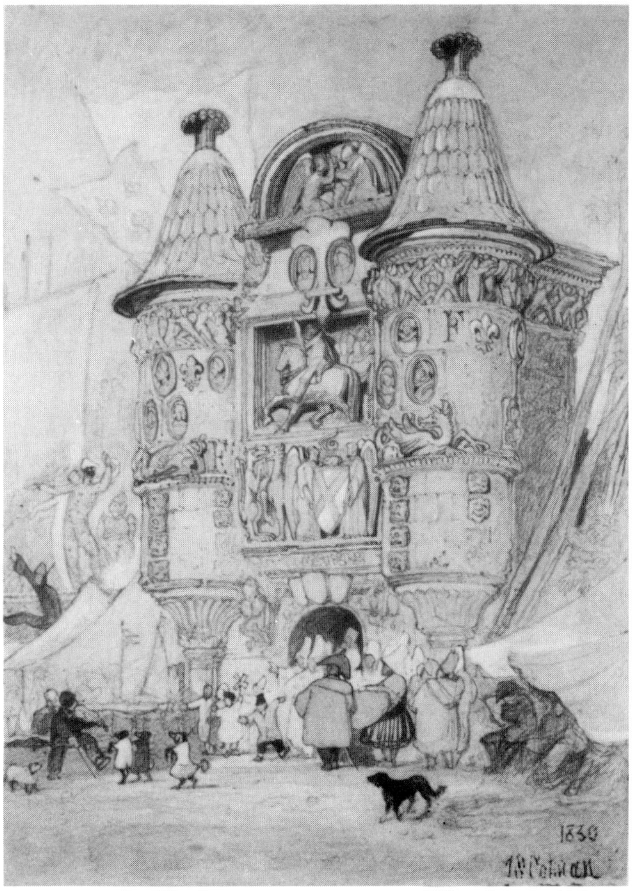

108 Gateway, Abbey Aumale, 1830

bright crimson and green figures as in that climax of falsity, the Charing Cross . . . He had given up harmony for brilliance'.

[1]Pidgley p. 246. [2]V&A E689-1925. [3]JSC to DT, 25 Nov. 1828 (Barker Collection). Kitson 1937 p. 274.

108 Gateway, Abbey Aumale, 1830

Pencil and white bodycolour on buff, wove paper; 33.8 × 23.9 ($13\frac{5}{16}$ × $9\frac{3}{8}$). INSCR: *Recto,* in pencil c.r. *Aumarl* (sic: indistinct) signed and dated in brown wash l.r. *1830 / J S Cotman.* PROV: R. J. Colman Bequest 1946. (411.235.951). REF: Rajnai 1975 No. 9.

There is no direct evidence to confirm that Cotman visited Aumale during his Normandy tours, although he is known to have been in the vicinity at the beginning of his second tour in 1818. However, there is no need for Cotman to have been to Aumale in order to draw this subject, as the Abbey Gate had been demolished in the early nineteenth century. The composition by Cotman related to this subject, like that of No. 100, must have been taken from a print.

No. 108 is a preliminary study for the watercolour version of 1832 (see No. 109). It corresponds to a second preliminary study[1] which is in the collection of the Whitworth Art Gallery, Manchester. A tracing[2] of No. 108 is also at Norwich but, as Rajnai has pointed out, this is 'such a crude and clumsy affair' that it cannot possibly be by Cotman.

[1]Whitworth, Manchester D.1.1917. [2]621.B22.235.951, exhibited at Tate 1922 included in (197) *Book of tracings by J. S. Cotman of Sketches by Harriott and others.*

109 Gateway, Abbey Aumale, 1832

illustrated on p. 91

Pencil, pen and brown ink, watercolour and bodycolour on white, wove paper with watermark left edge *J WHATM[AN] / TURKEY M[ILL],* paper cut; 44.6 × 33.6 ($17\frac{9}{16}$ × $13\frac{3}{16}$). INSCR: *Recto,* signed and dated in brown ink l.l. *J. S. Cotman 1832.* PROV: ?Anon. sale (a

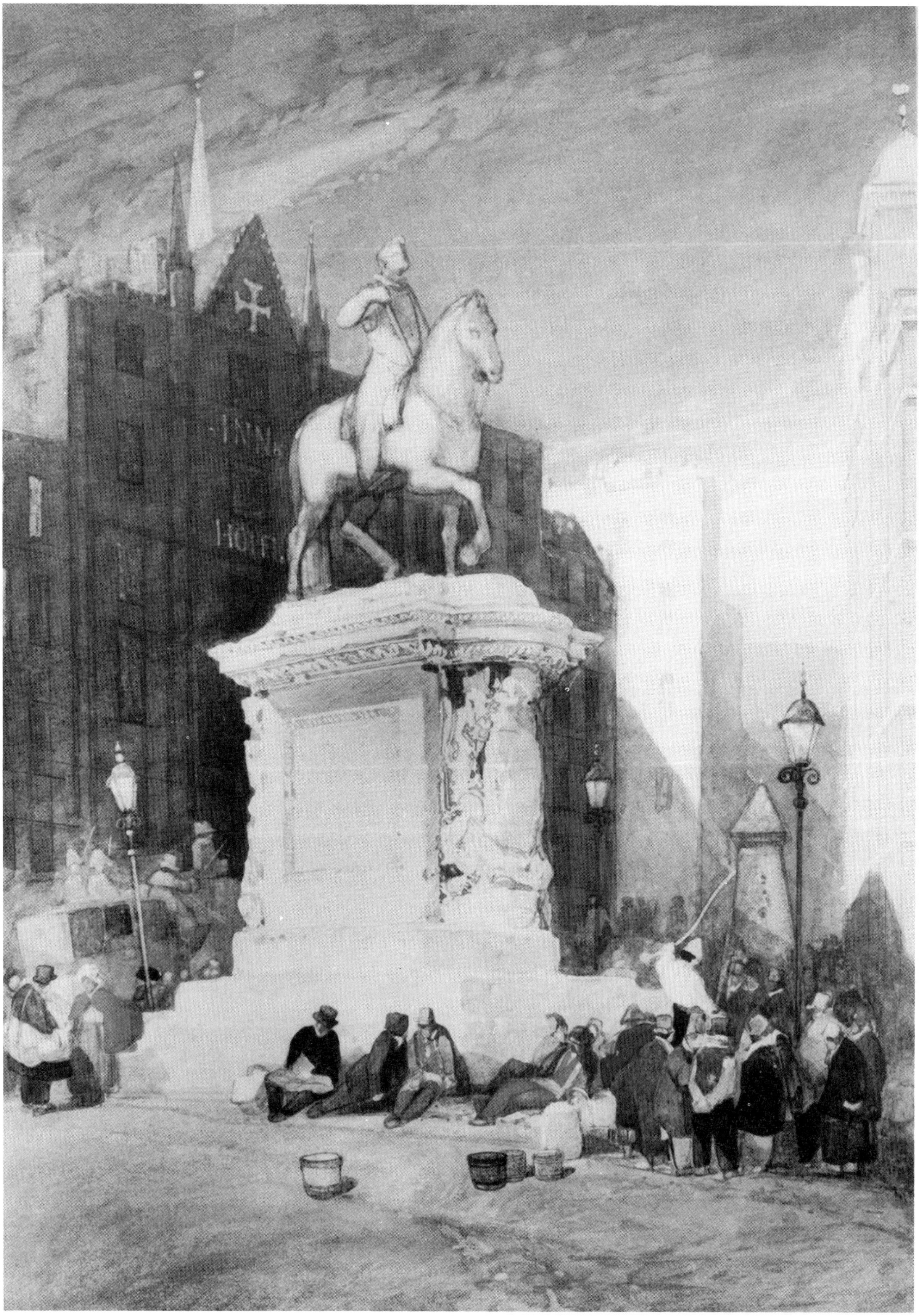

107 Statue of King Charles I, Charing Cross, *c.*1829-30

lady, possibly Saunders), Foster & Son, 1 May 1867, lot 116, bt. Hogarth £9.19.6; Sir William Richard Drake FSA by 1888; his sale Christie's, 27 & 29 June 1891, 2nd day, lot 200, bt. J. J. Colman 26 gns.; his bequest to R. J. Colman 1898; R. J. Colman Bequest 1946. (217.217.947). EXH: BFAC 1888 (80) lent by Sir William Drake; Norwich 1902 (215); Norwich 1903 (37), incorrectly dated 1836; Manchester 1912 (331); Tate 1922 (106); Norwich, Arts Council 1947 (33). REF: Rajnai 1975 No. 8.

No. 109 is a fully worked up watercolour version of No. 108, in which the gateway is set within a larger space. This includes a background of foliage, while additional figures populate the scene to the left and right, enhancing the lively atmosphere.

A smaller version of this composition is also in the Colman Collection.[1] Rajnai has convincingly argued that differences in quality and technique declare this to be a copy of No. 109. The subject was first exhibited by Cotman at the Old Water Colour Society in 1830 (237), *Abbey Gate of St. Martin at Aumale.*

[1] NCM 129.377.965.

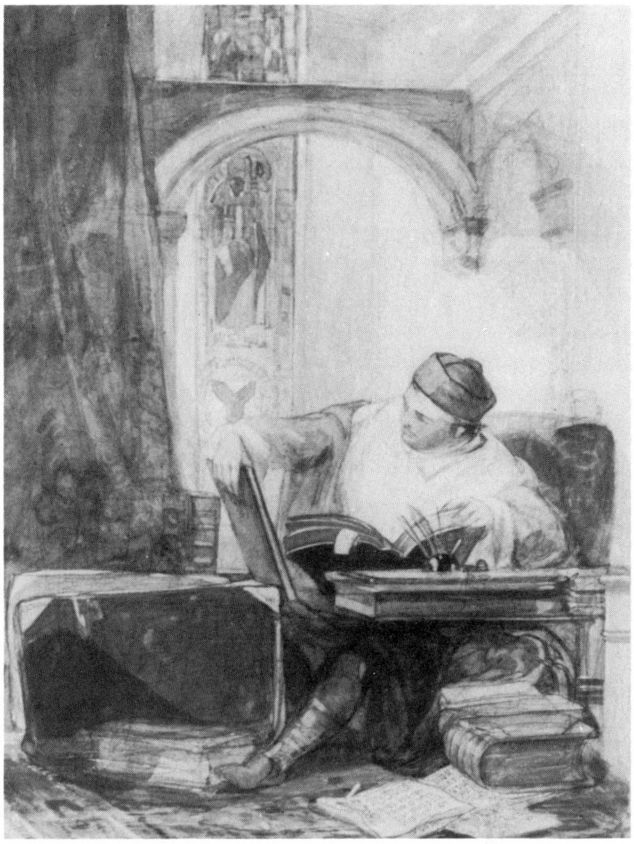

110 The Student, *c.*1830-33

110 The Student, *c.*1830-33

Pencil, watercolour and bodycolour with some gum on off-white, wove paper; 33.7 × 25.2 ($13\frac{1}{4} \times 9\frac{15}{16}$). PROV: James King; bt. from him by J. J. Colman by 1874; his bequest to R. J. Colman 1898; R. J. Colman Bequest 1946. (220.235.951). EXH: London, International Exhibition 1874 (324) lent by J. J. Colman; Norwich, Art Circle 1888 (192) illus. with litho. by C. J. Watson; Norwich 1894 (59); Norwich 1903 (55); Manchester 1912 (344); Norwich 1945. REF: Binyon 1903 pl. C28 as *The Antiquary;* Dickes pp. 384-6, repro. p. 385.

Almost every element of the composition finds an echo in other works by Cotman dating from this period. The antiquarian interests first fostered by Dawson Turner became, during the 1830s, a rich source of ideas. Cotman was responding both to his own intellectual background and to the current fashion amongst such artists as C. R. Leslie and Sir David Wilkie in pursuing antiquarian subjects. In terms of technique, the pencilwork of No. 110 compares with Cotman's soft, loose drawing style of *c.*1830-33, while the use of bodycolour recalls *The Belfry* (No. 111) dated 1831 and *A Study in Armour etc.* (No. 117) dated 1832.

The antiquary or student at his studies recurs in other Cotman compositions of this period. A pencil drawing, entitled *A Man in his Study*[1] shows a similar scene, while the posthumously published etching *The Student* (No. 182) was executed, according to Dawson Turner, in 1833. The figure in the latter is similarly at a table amongst manuscripts and portfolios, but the student in No. 110, seated beneath the image of a Saint, is more overtly ecclesiastical. The dramatic effect of the light falling in the midst of brown shadows recalls the work of Rembrandt, an influence more manifest in the etching.

[1] Private Collection, Oxford.

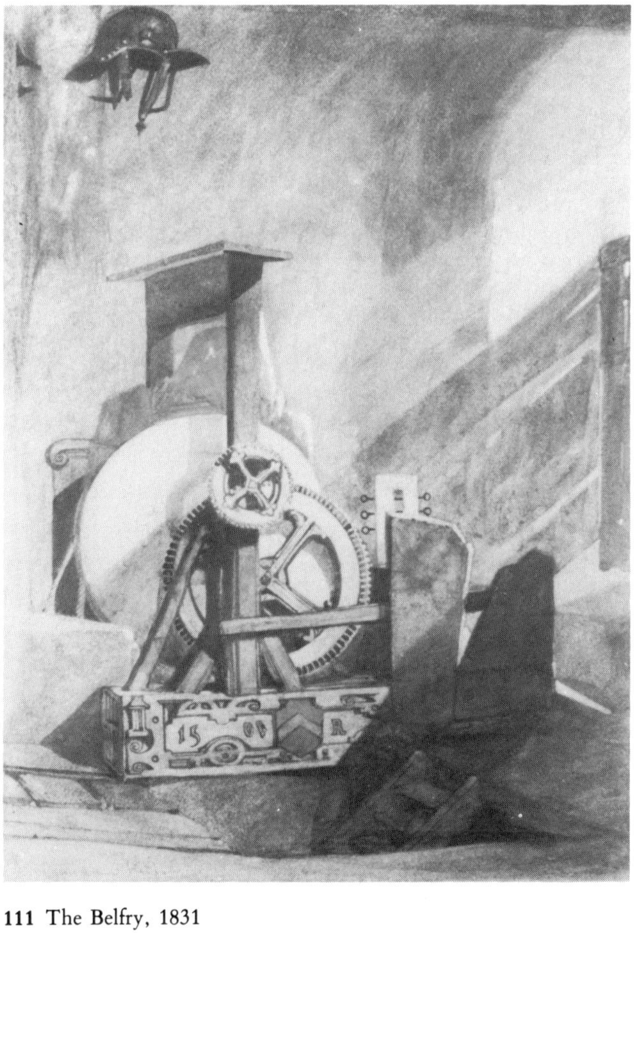

111 The Belfry, 1831

111 The Belfry, 1831

Pencil, watercolour, bodycolour and brown ink with some gum on off-white, wove paper; 33.3 × 23.9 ($13\frac{1}{16} \times 9\frac{7}{16}$). INSCR: Signed and dated in brown watercolour l.l. *J S Cotman 1831.* PROV: W. Boswell & Son, Norwich; bt. from them by H. S. Theobald; bt. from him by R. J. Colman, Feb. 1910; R. J. Colman Bequest 1946. (212.217.947). EXH: Manchester 1912 (360); Tate 1922 (211); Norwich 1945; Norwich, Arts Council 1947 (31). REF: Kitson 1937 p. 298, pl. 130; Rienaecker pl. 52, fig. 99.

Kitson considered this watercolour 'a beautiful still-life study, admirably drawn and perfect in its rich tonality'. The darker tonality and colour range is similar to that of other interior scenes of this period, particularly *Crosby Hall* (No. 106) and *A Study of Armour etc.* (No. 117). The use of gum adds resonance to the darker tones of these pictures. The shafts of light streaming through the shuttered window to the right both dramatise and romanticise the subject, similar in effect to *Crosby Hall* (No. 106).

Cotman's ability to imbue a scene with romantic historical associations is fully exemplified here. The medieval reference of the still life of steel helmet and banner (now sadly damaged) in the top left hand corner of the composition is echoed by the decorated supporting beam beneath the cogs of the machinery, carved with dated strapwork, and a shield of 'gules chevron argent'.

Another interior scene of this period is the undated *Interior of a small room in Norwich Cathedral,*[1] now in the Courtauld Institute, 'where discarded ecclesiastical trappings are stored in picturesque disorder'.[2]

[1]Witt 3294. [2]Kitson 1937 p. 278.

112 St. Benet's Abbey, Norfolk, 1831

illustrated in colour on p. 100

Pencil, watercolour, bodycolour and brown ink with some gum arabic and wiping out on cream, wove paper, with watermark r. edge *J WHATMAN / 1830;* 31.8 × 46.9 ($12\frac{1}{2}$ × $18\frac{7}{16}$). INSCR: Signed and dated in brown watercolour l.l. *J S Cotman 1831.* PROV: C. H. T. Hawkins, 10 Portland Place, London; his sale, Christie's, 26 March 1904, lot 13,[1] bt. Boswell £71.8.9.; bt. from him by R. J. Colman 1904, £100; R. J. Colman Bequest 1946. (211.217.947). EXH: Manchester 1912 (338); Tate 1922 (128); Norwich 1945; Norwich, Arts Council 1947 (30). REF: Batchelor, *EDP* 13 April 1922; Kaines Smith 1926 p. 98; *EDP* 18 Sept. 1936 repro.; *British Heritage* 1948 pl. XV in colour; *Colman Collection Guide* 1951 p. 6, fig. 11A; Rienaecker pl. 50, fig. 96; *EEN* 24 Feb. 1955 repro.; *RCH Magazine* Christmas 1964 p. 60 repro. in colour; Day 1969 vol III repro. p. 33; Farmer, *East Anglian Magazine* Feb. 1970 repro. p. 133.

The stone and flint ruin of St. Benet's Abbey is situated near the north bank of the River Bure, approximately three miles south of Horning, Norfolk. The eighteenth-century brick tower draining mill was built into the ruins of the original gateway, the only part to have survived. This highly picturesque subject dominates the surrounding landscape and has attracted almost every Norwich School artist. Cotman has selected a view from the north west, a viewpoint different from that of his etching of St. Benet's Abbey first published in 1813 and reprinted with a dedication to Mrs. Dawson Turner in 1818.[2]

No. 112 is removed in both concept and execution from the archaeological work of Cotman's Yarmouth years. The relative accuracy to be seen in the etching of 1813 and a contemporary watercolour[3] of the same subject is no longer a relevant consideration for Cotman in the 1830s and he exercises considerable licence in his representation of the abbey for compositional effect. A later oil version[4] by Cotman, also from the north west, is idiosyncratically placed within a heavily wooded landscape with a similar disregard for actual topography.

Despite the mature virtuosity of this piece, it does not appear to have been exhibited in Cotman's lifetime. The hot contrasts of blue and yellow, mellowed only in the green reeds of the right foreground herald the maturity of Cotman's new paste technique, with wiping out in both cloud and foliate forms. The outlining of the figures in brown ink with a reed pen is also a technique common to another work of this period (No. 113).

Other sketches of St. Benet's Abbey by Cotman exist, although none relates directly to this composition.[5] One sketching trip by Cotman is recorded in the diary of Mrs. Gunn, one of the Turner daughters. On 5 July 1832,[6] she visited the abbey by boat with Cotman and his daughter Ann. This was possibly the occasion on which he sketched a view of the abbey from the edge of the Bure, now in the collection of the Castle Museum at Norwich.[7] A 'late' watercolour of St. Benet's Abbey in the National Museum of Wales is likely to be the work of Miles Edmund Cotman.[8]

[1]R. J. Colman left a commission for 52 gns. with Christie's for this lot (CC Records). [2]Popham No. 154. [3]Lady Lever Art Gallery, Port Sunlight; another version, Private Collection. [4]NCM 109.235.951; a watercolour version was once with the Fine Art Society. [5]BM 1902-5-14-255; V&A E651-1925: traditionally a study for the oil, although earlier and not directly related; Leeds 9.391/49. [6]Kitson 1937 p. 290. [7]NCM 381.235.951. The Cotmanesque view, NCM 380.235.951, is possibly the work of Joseph Geldart. [8]No. 3030.

113 Storm on Yarmouth Beach, 1831

illustrated in colour on p. 100

Watercolour, pen and ink with some scraping out on cream, wove paper; 36.6 × 53.6 ($14\frac{7}{16}$ × $21\frac{1}{8}$). INSCR: Signed and dated in brown ink l.l. *J S Cotman 1831.* PROV: ?Christie's sale, 11 May 1836, lot 66 *Yarmouth Sands, with fishermen,* bt. 'Cob:' (?Cobbett), £2.10s.; George Holmes, Brooke Hall, Norwich by 1874; his sale, Christie's, 25 April 1903, lot 1, bt. Boswell & Sons on behalf of R. J. Colman, 245 gns.; bt. from Boswell by R. J. Colman; R. J. Colman Bequest 1946. (210.217.947). EXH: Norwich 1874 (152) as *Yarmouth Beach* lent by George Holmes; Norwich, Art Circle 1888 (167) as *Yarmouth Beach* illus. with litho. by Miss H. Wells; RA 1891 (?); Norwich 1894 (70); Manchester 1912 (334); Tate 1922 (132); Norwich 1945; Norwich, Arts Council 1947 (29). REF: *Norfolk Chronicle* 14 July 1888; *The Academy* 21 July 1888; Binyon 1903 pl. C30; Dickes p. 372 repro. opp.; Kaines Smith 1926 pp. 88, 136; Kitson 1937 p. 296, pl. 127; Barnard pl. 15; *Colman Collection Guide* 1951 p. 6; Iolo Williams p. 165; Clifford pp. 58, 63, 69, pl. 38a; Hawcroft, *RCH Magazine* p. 12; Hardie vol. 2 p. 92; Farmer, *East Anglian Magazine* Feb. 1970 p. 132 repro.

This watercolour displays the technical virtuosity of the period 1830-33 and 'is probably as fine a watercolour in Cotman's late style as exists.'[1] It is a relatively early use of the technique which Martin Hardie has described 'from experiment, just a simple method of using ordinary flour or rice paste, not necessarily sour or rotten, with perhaps an admixture of some Chinese white, as a medium to mix with pure colour.'[2] The semi-opaque quality of the medium results in an intensity of colour which remains moist upon the paper for longer. This enables Cotman to wipe, drag or otherwise manipulate the colour in a manner which reflects the imaginative intensity of his vision. The central group, outlined in brown watercolour, locks the composition into place and enables Cotman to conceive an effect of storm both elemental and emotional.

The composition barely suggests the town of Yarmouth in the distance to the left, while three windmills dominate the horizon. These are probably the same mills which occur as a group in an earlier drawing[3] by Cotman and also drawing copies[4] from his circulating portfolio. A series of cloud studies[5] by Cotman, now at Norwich, indicate his interest in the drama of natural cloud formation. Yarmouth beach remained a rich source of inspiration to Cotman in all the media in which he worked, throughout his career (see Nos 68, 72, 155, 156, 173, 174, 176).

[1]Iolo Williams p. 165. [2]Hardie, *Burlington* July 1942, p. 175. [3]NCM 620.235.951; cf. Leeds 9.456/49. [4]NCM 616.235.951 (copy no. 2122), identified by an inscribed copy by Ellen Turner (NCM 26.31); NCM 619.235.951 (copy no. 251). [5]NCM 6 & 8-13.L1967.9.

114 Stormy Weather, *c.*1831-3

illustrated on opposite page

Watercolour, bodycolour and brown ink on cream, wove paper, with watermark l.l. edge *[WHA]TMAN / . . .9;* 26.7 × 17.1 ($10\frac{1}{2}$ × $6\frac{3}{4}$). PROV: Mrs. Pelham, Liverpool; William Cox, picture dealer of London; J. J. Colman by 1888; his bequest to R. J. Colman 1898; R. J. Colman Bequest 1946. (193.217.947). EXH: Norwich, Art Circle 1888 (196) lent by J. J. Colman; BFAC 1888 (67); RA Winter Exhibition 1892 (49); Norwich 1903 (56); Manchester 1912 (337); Norwich 1945; Norwich, Arts Council 1947 (23). REF: Dickes p. 288.

Although undated, this watercolour compares well with *Storm on Yarmouth Beach* (No. 113). The subtle blending of blue through to yellow at the shoreline is similar in both technique and effect to the shoreline of No. 113. The dragging of the blue is also similar to that area of the sky in No. 113 which is not instantly darkened by storm clouds, while the figures are similarly outlined in brown watercolour.

The figures are reproduced in one of Cotman's etchings published subsequently by Charles Muskett in 1846 (No. 183). This shows the figures set in a wider context and, according to a note by Dawson Turner in his copy of the posthumous set of etchings,[1] dates from 1833. The etching acts as a natural conclusion to the compositional elements of both *Storm on Yarmouth Beach* and *Stormy Weather.*

A contemporary watercolour, *Yarmouth Beach,* which also features two fishermen, this time with a boat drawn up on the beach, is in a private collection and appears to be a joint work by both Cotman and his son, Miles Edmund.[2]

[1]Kitson 1937 pp. 300-301. [2]Two related pencil studies by Cotman are BM 1902-5-14-84 and a similar study formerly in the collection of P. M. Turner. An oil version of the former, attributed to M. E. Cotman, is NCM 628.235.951; of the latter see Sotheby's 27 May 1935, lot 18. (not JSC).

115 Landscape Composition — Classical Landscape I, *c.*1832-3

illustrated on p. 106

Pencil, watercolour and bodycolour with wiping out on cream, laid paper, with watermark u.l. ?*T. GREEN* and impressed stamp l.r. corner; 35.3 × 45.9 ($13\frac{7}{8}$ × $18\frac{1}{16}$). INSCR: Signed in brown watercolour l.r. *J S Cotman.* PROV: ?Cotman's sale, Christies, 17-18 May 1843, lot 41, *A pair of classical landscapes,* bt. Palser 6s.; Sir William Richard Drake by 1888; his sale, Christie's, 27 & 29 June 1891, lot 201, bt. J. J. Colman 20 gns.; J. J. Colman Bequest 1898. (17.4.99). EXH: ?OWCS 1833 (45) as *Landscape — Composition, with the Story of Bathsheba;* BFAC 1888 (86) lent by Sir William Drake; RA Winter Exhibition 1892 (?); ?Norwich 1894 (73 or 79); Earls Court 1897 (22); Tate 1922 (80); Cambridge, Arts Council 1948 (5); Lowestoft 1948 (14) and Leeuwarden 1948 (12) either this drawing or its pair (No. 116); Colnaghi 1970 (42); Sudbury 1978 (10); Koblenz 1980 (7). REF: NCM ?1897 (Q or S); NCM ?1899 (152 or 162); *Norwich Mercury* 13 Feb. 1899; NCM 1904 (249 or 254); Dickes p. 349; NCM 1909 (266 or 271); NCM 1937 (40 or 41); Kaines Smith 1926 p. 166; Kitson 1937 p. 299; Barnard, *The Studio* Aug. 1947 p. 30; Clifford p. 66, fig. 38b as *The Story of Bathsheba.*

Cotman's interest in the classical landscapes of Bourdon and Gaspar Poussin is discussed in Nos. 32 and 148. The selection of classical motif in this composition and its pair (No. 116) is however more likely to derive from the example of George Barrett who had established himself as a painter of atmospheric effects and classical scenes without reference to specific locality.

Nos. 115 and 116 were criticised by Kitson for being 'artifical in sentiment' whilst Clifford regards the figures as resembling 'half filled feather-bolsters'. Yet the work is not devoid of magic, in common with other 'composition' drawings[1] of this period by Cotman. In these works the control of the paste medium, allowing of both chance in application and careful wiping out of reserved areas, is a *tour de force.*

Two landscape compositions were exhibited in the spring of 1833 with the Old Water-Colour Society[2] and it is possible that these were Nos. 115 and 116. One was entitled *Landscape — Composition, with the story of Bathsheba*[3] and No. 115 has been thought to represent Bathsheba who is traditionally depicted at the waters edge, aided by attendants. Nevertheless the scene could similarly depict other classical scenes such as Diana and Callisto or Nausicaa with her maidens prior to the arrival of Ulysses.

Two classical landscape compositions[4] were also exhibited at the Norfolk and Suffolk Institution in the summer of 1833, the year of Cotman's Presidency. It is possible that these were identical to those shown in London during the spring, as was the case with two other drawings that year.[5]

The influence of J.M.W. Turner may also be seen in Cotman's choice of composition. The disposition of masses and elements such as the trees, classical pediment, discarded masonry and the use of foreground figures reflects Cotman's knowledge of Turner, most evident in his studies after Turner's *Liber Studiorum.*[6]

[1]cf. National Museum of Wales, 3026, dated 1830. [2]OWCS 1833 (36 and 45). [3]No. 45. [4]Norwich Society 1833 (36 & 47). [5]OWCS 1833 (304) and Norwich Society 1833 (77); OWCS 1833 (222) and Norwich Society 1833 (35). [6]cf. BM 1902-5-14-267 : *Isis.*

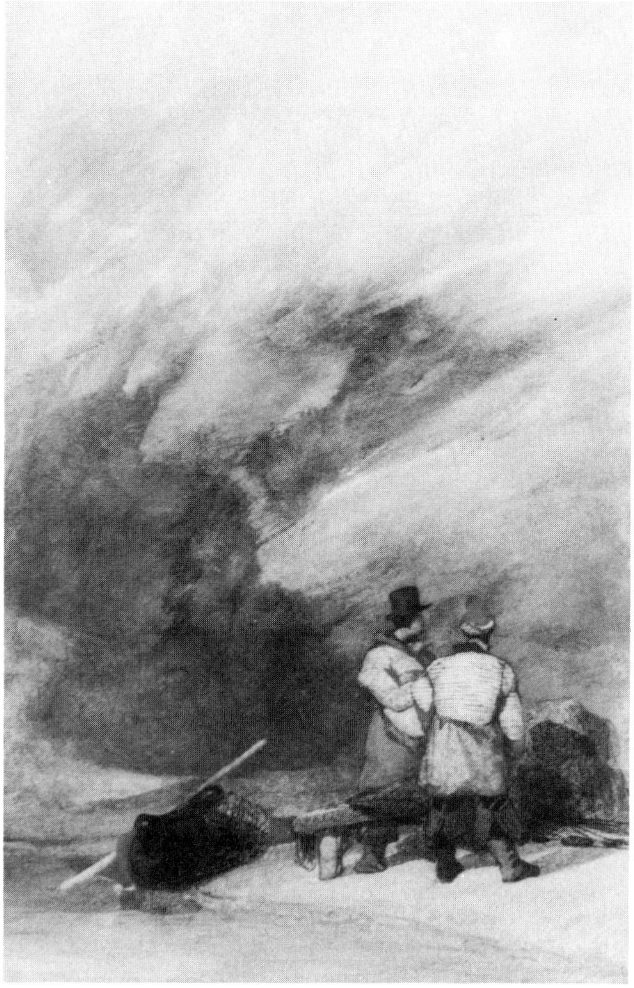

114 Stormy Weather, *c.*1831-3

116 Landscape Composition — Classical Landscape II, *c.*1832-3

illustrated on p. 106

Pencil, watercolour and bodycolour with some gum arabic and wiping out on cream, laid paper; 34.7 × 45.8 ($13\frac{11}{16}$ × $18\frac{1}{16}$). INSCR: Signed in red watercolour l.l. *J S Cotman.* PROV: See No. 115. (lot 199 in Sir William Drake's sale). (18.4.99). EXH: BFAC 1888 (88) lent by Sir William Drake; RA Winter Exhibition 1892 (?); ?Norwich 1894 (73 or 79); Earls Court 1897 (21); Tate 1922 (90); Cambridge, Arts Council 1948 (6); Lowestoft 1948 (14) and Leeuwarden 1948 (12) either this drawing or its pair (No. 115); British Council 1949-50 (24); Colnaghi 1970 (43) repro. pl. X; Sudbury 1978 (11). REF: NCM ?1897 (Q or S); Binyon 1897 repro. p. 101 as *Landscape Composition with Figures;* NCM ?1899 (152 or 162); *Norwich Mercury* 13 Feb. 1899; NCM 1904 (249 or 254); Dickes p. 349 repro.; NCM 1909 (266 or 271); NCM 1937 (40 or 41); Kaines Smith 1926 p. 166; Kitson 1937 p. 299; Barnard, *The Studio,* Aug. 1947 p. 30.

Unlike the Doric architecture depicted in No. 115, the building just visible to the left is Corinthian in derivation. Two drawing copies[1] are known which witness Cotman's concern for accuracy in the depiction of classical architecture as with the 'curious antiquities' of Norfolk and Normandy with which he was more familiar.

For a further discussion of this drawing see the previous entry.

[1]Drawing copy no. 3069, *The Temple of Vesta,* formerly Barker Collection; no. 3072, *Remains of the Temple of Jupiter,* Sotheby's, 10 April 1980 (117).

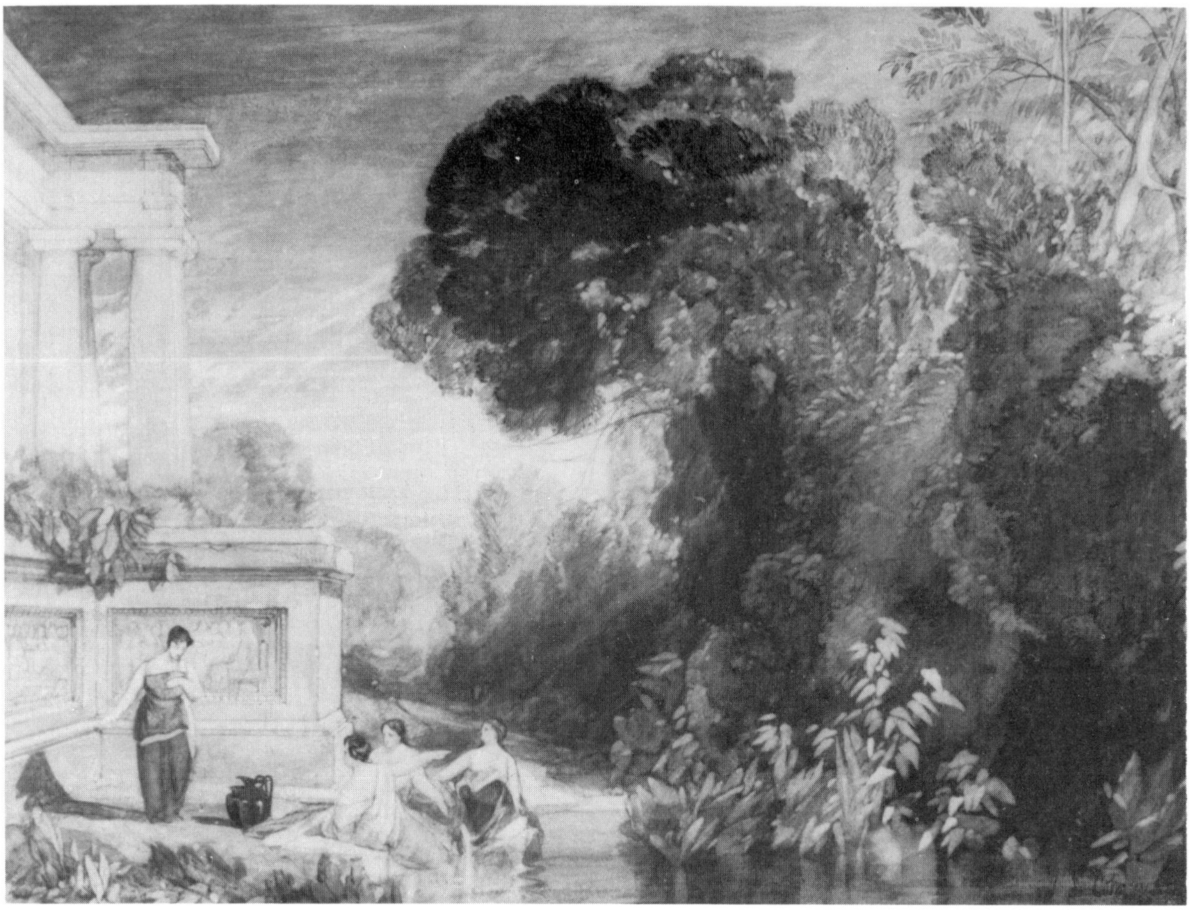

115 Landscape Composition — Classical Landscape I, *c.*1832-3

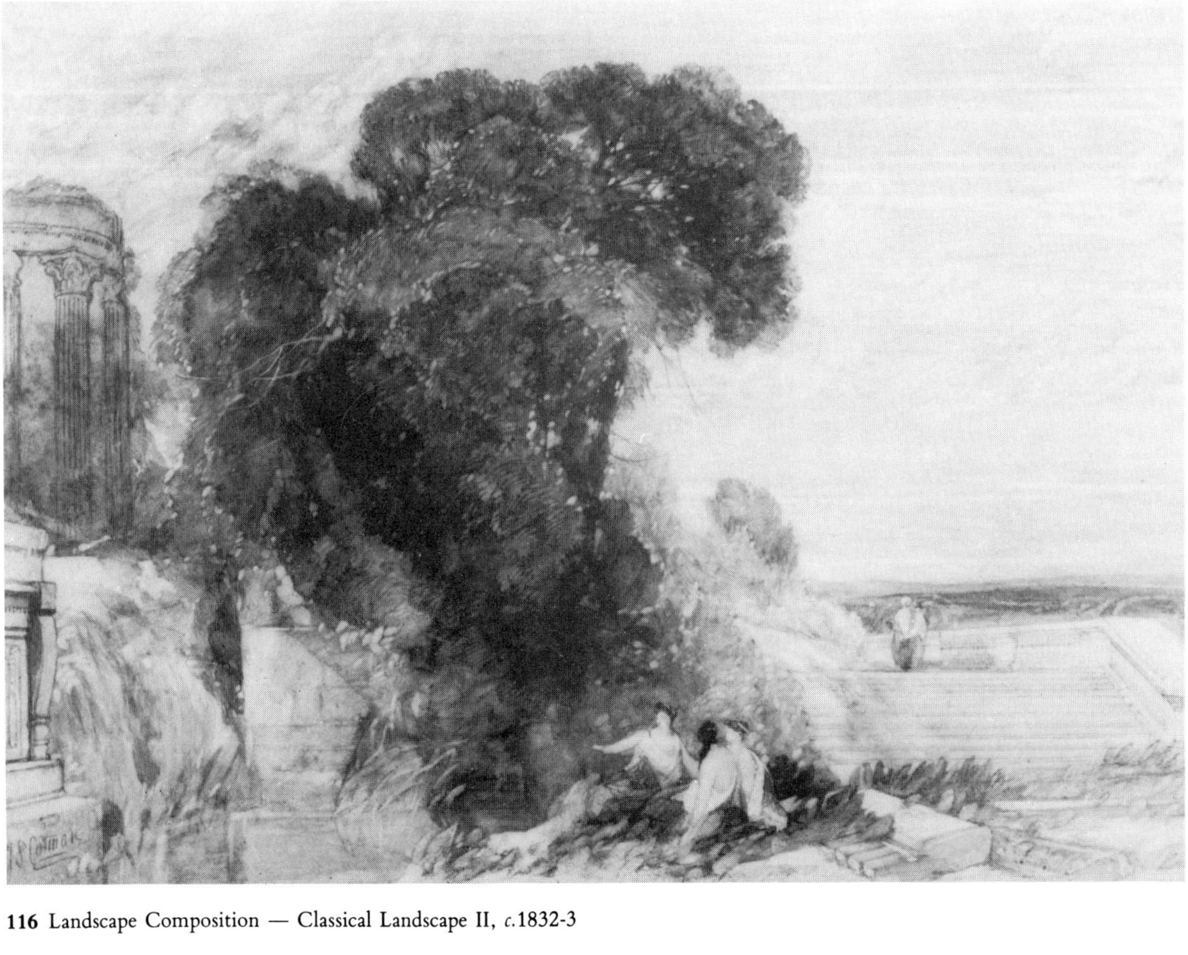

116 Landscape Composition — Classical Landscape II, *c.*1832-3

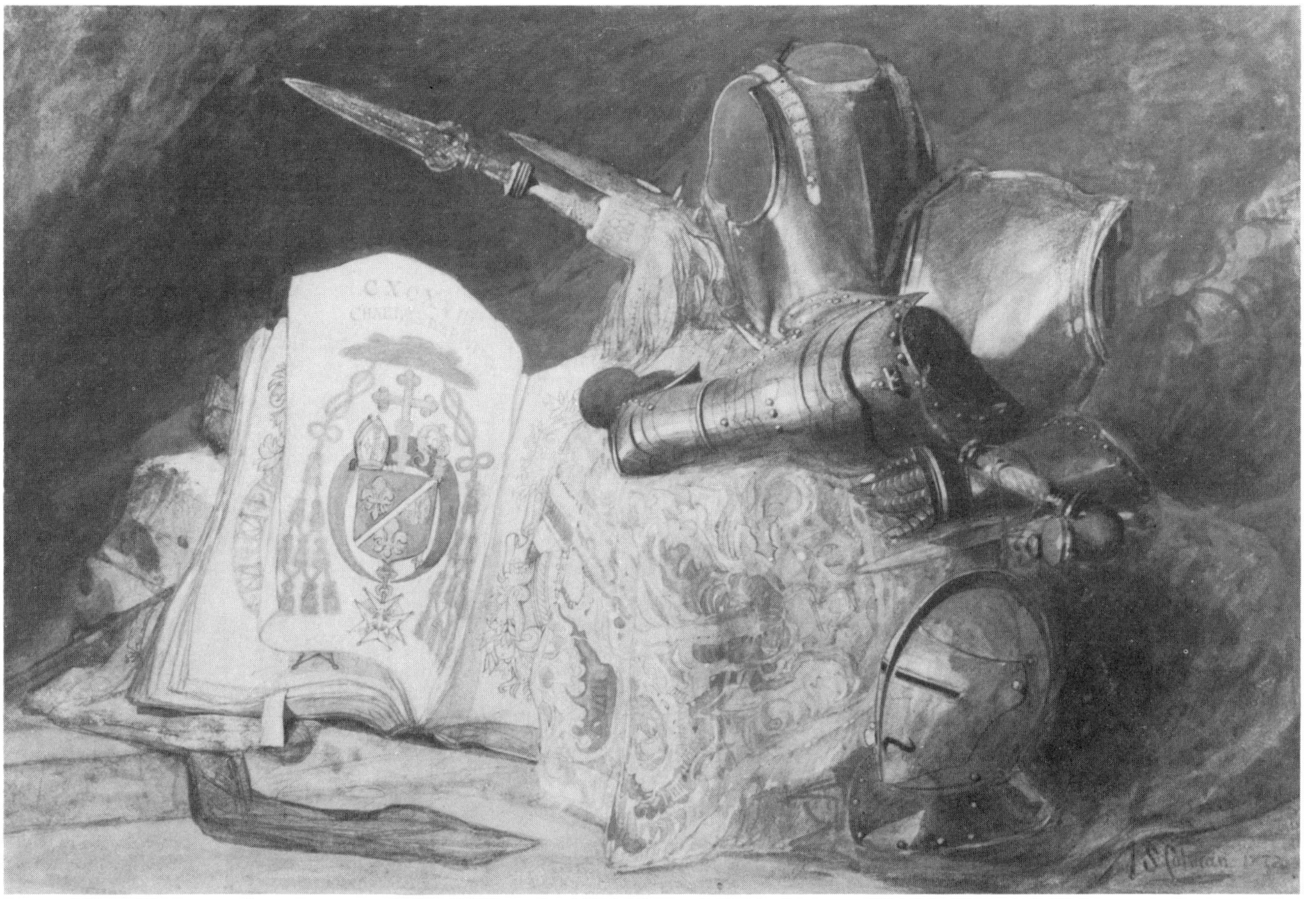

117 A Study of Armour etc., 1832

117 A Study of Armour etc., 1832

Pencil, watercolour, bodycolour and gum on cream, wove paper; 36.5 × 52.7 ($14\frac{3}{8}$ × $20\frac{3}{4}$). INSCR: Signed and dated in brown watercolour l.r. *J S Cotman 1832.* PROV: Cotman's sale, Christie's, 17-18 May 1843, lot 152, as *A study of armour and illuminated books brilliantly coloured,* unsold;[1] ?Cotman sale, Spelman, Norwich, 16 May 1861,[2] lot 177 as "*Armour*". *This lot is in his best style, very rich in colour, outside measure 30 inches by 24,* bt. Wells 7 gns.; John Norgate; H. S. Theobald; W. Boswell; bt. from him by R. J. Colman, 30 May 1904, £50; R. J. Colman Bequest 1946. (213.217.947). EXH: Norwich Society 1832 (39); OWCS 1834 (237);[3] Manchester 1912 (359) as *Still Life;* Tate 1922 (131); Norwich 1945; Norwich, Arts Council 1947 (32) as *Missal and Armour.* REF: *Norwich Mercury* 4 Aug. 1832; Kitson 1937 p. 298 (wrongly discussed as two separate pictures: *Illustrated Missal* and *Study of Armour*); Rienaecker pl. 52, fig. 100.

In 1832 Cotman was Vice-President of the Norfolk and Suffolk Institution, but exhibited only two works, while his son Miles Edmund exhibited eight works. The critic for the *Norwich Mercury* commented: 'Messrs. Cotman occupy the first rank. The *Study of Armour,* no. 39, possesses extraordinary force and accuracy with a lustrous brilliancy of colour'. Miles Edmund also exhibited a *Study of Armour and Tapestry*[4] that year, presumably influenced by his father's example.

The catalogue for the three day sale of Cotman's library and collections,[5] prior to his departure for London, reveals the considerable range of his collecting fervour. Despite the romantic conception of this still life, it is evident that the individual items were all culled from his own collections. On the third day of the sale, amongst nineteen lots of 'ancient armour' may be found 'a beautiful black steel helmet, with moveable visor, temp. James I' (lot 145), 'breast-plate and 1 epauliére, supposed to be of the same date' (lot 146), 'a pair of gauntlets' (lot 148) and lot 150 'two pikes (one engraved)'. Lot 147 was a complete suit of armour, which sold for £9.5s.0d.[6] instead of the fifteen guineas[7] hoped for. Cotman himself owned a 'sketch of armour' attributed to Paolo Veronese, from Sir Thomas Lawrence's collection.[8]

The illustrated book is open at the page showing the arms of Cardinal Charles de Bourbon (1523-90) uncle to Henry IV of France. The description of the plate on the opposite page is obscured, but the book may be identified from the 1834 sale catalogue (first day, lot 213): 'Les Noms, Armes et Blassons de l'Ordre et Milice de Benoist Sainct Esprit, handsomely bound in russia, gilt edges Paris, 1643'. The volume sold for nineteen shillings.[9]

This watercolour reveals Cotman as a fully fledged member of the 'School of Chivalry' along with Nash, Cattermole and Bonington. It was the one subject he chose to show at the Old Water-Colour Society in 1834, the year of his removal to London.

[1]Copy of annotated sale catalogue, Art Dept. archives, NCM, is inscribed with 'MEC' (Miles Edmund Cotman) as the purchaser and the price £1.8s. crossed out. [2]A *Study of Armour* by J. S. Cotman was also exhibited at Norwich 1860 (253) lent by C. Steward, Yarmouth. [3]Pidgley Ch. One n.202. [4]Norwich Society 1832 (32). [5]Spelman, at the residence of John Sell Cotman Esq., St. Martin's Palace Plain, 10-12 Sept. 1834. [6]Annotated sale catalogue, NCM 87.943. [7]Dickes pp. 379-380. [8]Christie's, 6 June 1843, lot 309. [9]NCM 87.943 *ibid.*

118 The Interior of Spruggins' Hall, Manor of Dolfuddle, Bedfordshire, leading to the Picture Gallery; Arms of Spruggins, Gull, Whittington, Bagnigge, KingWaddle and Sucklethumkin over the doorway—*vide* **Lady Morley's** *Spruggins Gallery,* 1833

illustrated on p. 92

Pencil, watercolour, bodycolour and brown ink with some gum arabic on cream, wove paper; 43.9 × 32.7 ($17\frac{5}{16}$ × $12\frac{7}{8}$). INSCR: Signed and dated in red bodycolour l.l. *J S Cotman 1833.* PROV: Rev. G. W. Minns, Norwich; bt. from him by J. J. Colman by 1888; his bequest to R. J. Colman 1898; R. J. Colman Bequest 1946. (205.235.951). EXH: OWCS 1833 (83); Norwich, Art Circle 1888 (157) illus. with litho. by Miss M. Bolingbroke, lent by J. J. Colman; BFAC 1888 (69); Norwich 1894 (65); Norwich 1902 (211); Norwich 1903 (45). REF:

Roget vol. ii 1891 (1972) p. 34; Binyon 1897 p. 95; Dickes p. 374 repro. p. 375; Kitson, *OWCS* 1930 p. 15; Kitson 1937 pp. 299-300; Clifford p. 65; Pidgley pp. 164-165 n.23; Hemingway 1979 p. 72, pl. 63.

This drawing is a reflection of Cotman's love of burlesque although it adds nothing to our knowledge of his technical brilliance as a watercolourist. The particular feature of this baronial setting is the splendid screen bearing arms which lampoon the fashion for family pedigree, beneath the solemn inscription 'Haud ignavis ortus avis' ('Descended from Famed Ancestors'). Cotman's source, referred to in the title, was a volume of forty-four lithographic caricatures after drawings by Walter Sneyd, published in 1829.[1]

Cotman had exhibited a similar subject at Norwich in 1831: *Sir Simon Spruggins. Knt. the tall fellow of the family of that ilk—vide Lady Morley's Spruggin's Family,*[2] which he also sent to London the next year.[3] This picture is now untraced. Another historical costume piece of this period is a chalk drawing[4] of a cavalier with his wife and child in a Gallery setting which is likely to be Sir Simon Spruggins with his wife Lydia, daughter and heiress of John Fulbotham, Esquire.

Pidgley first pointed to the resemblance of the screen shown in No. 118 to that at Attleborough Church, Norfolk. The panels, cusping and proportions are close to those of one of the chancel entrances at Attleborough. In a letter[5] of 25 February, 1833 to Rev. William Gunn, Cotman relates a recent visit with E. T. Daniell to Attleborough Church 'to see a very fine and curious screen there . . . Its principle feature is the Arms of all the Bishops running horizontally at the top . . . though these things are rather out of my line now. I have thought of nothing else but it since I saw it'. He resolved to return on 27 February to 'make a sketch', which presumably formed the basis of the design for the entrance to Spruggins' picture gallery.

[1]Pidgley p. 46 n.25. [2]Norwich Society 1831 (43). [3]OWCS 1832 (58). [4]NCM 347.235.951; cf. NCM 345.235.951. [5]BM.

119 The Wind in the Trees, *c.*1832-4

illustrated on opposite page

Watercolour and bodycolour with some gum arabic and wiping out on cream, wove paper, with watermark r. edge *J WHATMAN / 1831;* 41 × 29.2 ($16\frac{1}{8}$ × $11\frac{1}{2}$). PROV: William B. Paterson by 1913; bt. from him by R. J. Colman June 1913; R. J. Colman Bequest 1946. (196.217.947). EXH: London, Paterson Gallery 1913 (35); RA 1934 (720, Commemorative Catalogue 823); Norwich 1945; Norwich, Arts Council 1947 (25). REF: Clifford fig. 39b.

This is a watercolour version of the earlier oil, *Silver Birches* (No. 161). The dated watermark confirms the stylistic evidence that the watercolour postdates 1831. The use of wash is far removed from that of abstract, flat planes of colour. The more representational use of brush strokes and the use of a bristle brush recalls the technique of oil painting. The branches bend with the sweep of the brush suggesting the agitation of the wind. A dating of 1832-4 is suggested by the watercolour's close stylistic affinities with Nos. 115, 116 and 120.

It was this element of Cotman's style which most influenced that of his second son, John Joseph, who was responsible for a watercolour of *Trees in Gunton Park*[1] now at Norwich and traditionally attributed to John Sell Cotman. Another example of this aspect of Cotman's development is *At Whitlingham*[2] in the British Museum.

A first thumbnail pencil sketch[3] related to this composition is also at the British Museum. The motif of broken branches and a rocky gorge are repeated in other Cotman family productions, such as *The Torrent*[4] and a related drawing, *Waterfall.*[5]

[1]NCM 201.125.951. [2]BM 1902-5-14-35. [3]BM 1902-5-14-244. [4]NCM 199.235.951. [5]NCM 398.235.951.

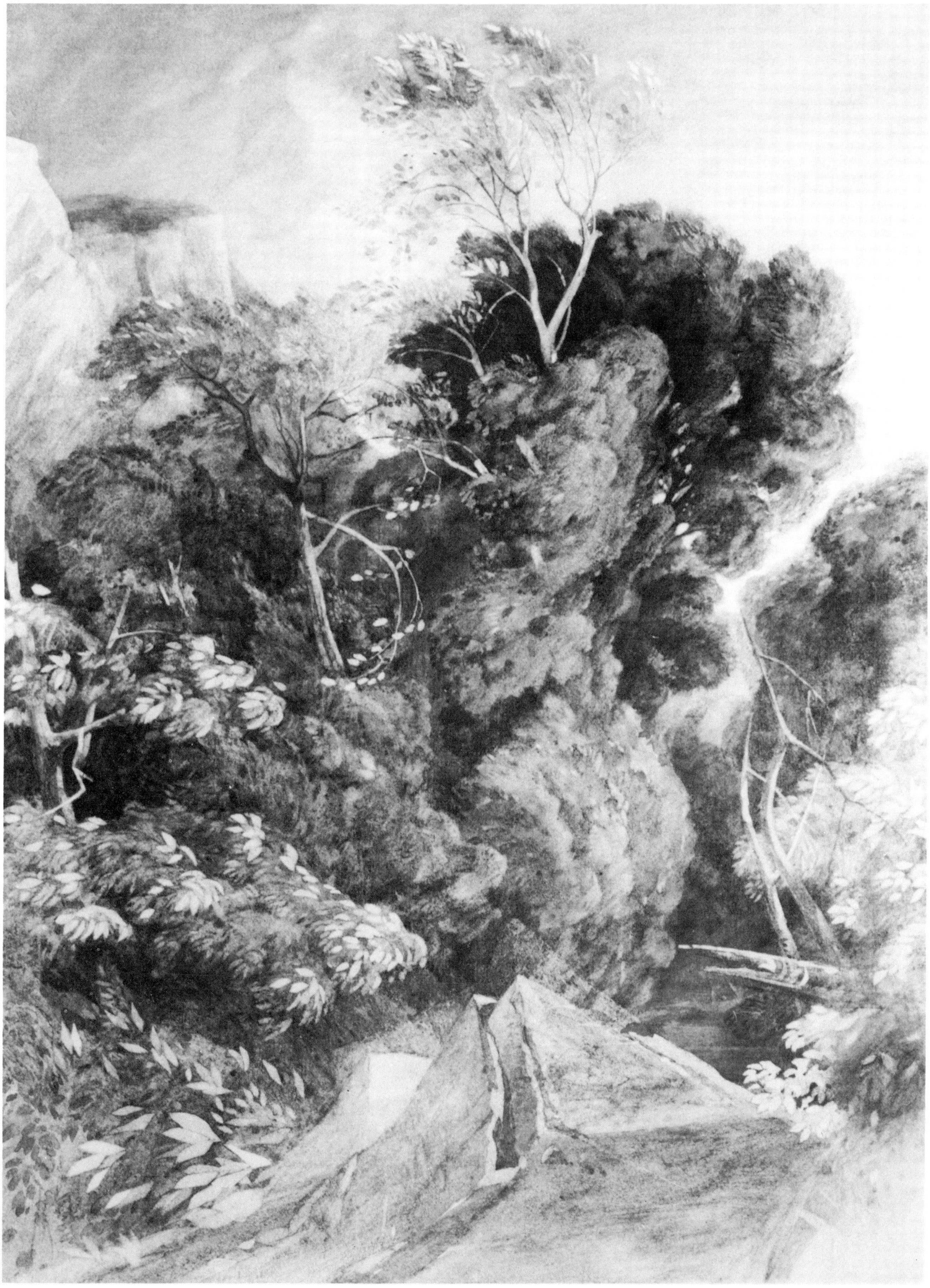

119 The Wind in the Trees, *c.*1832-4

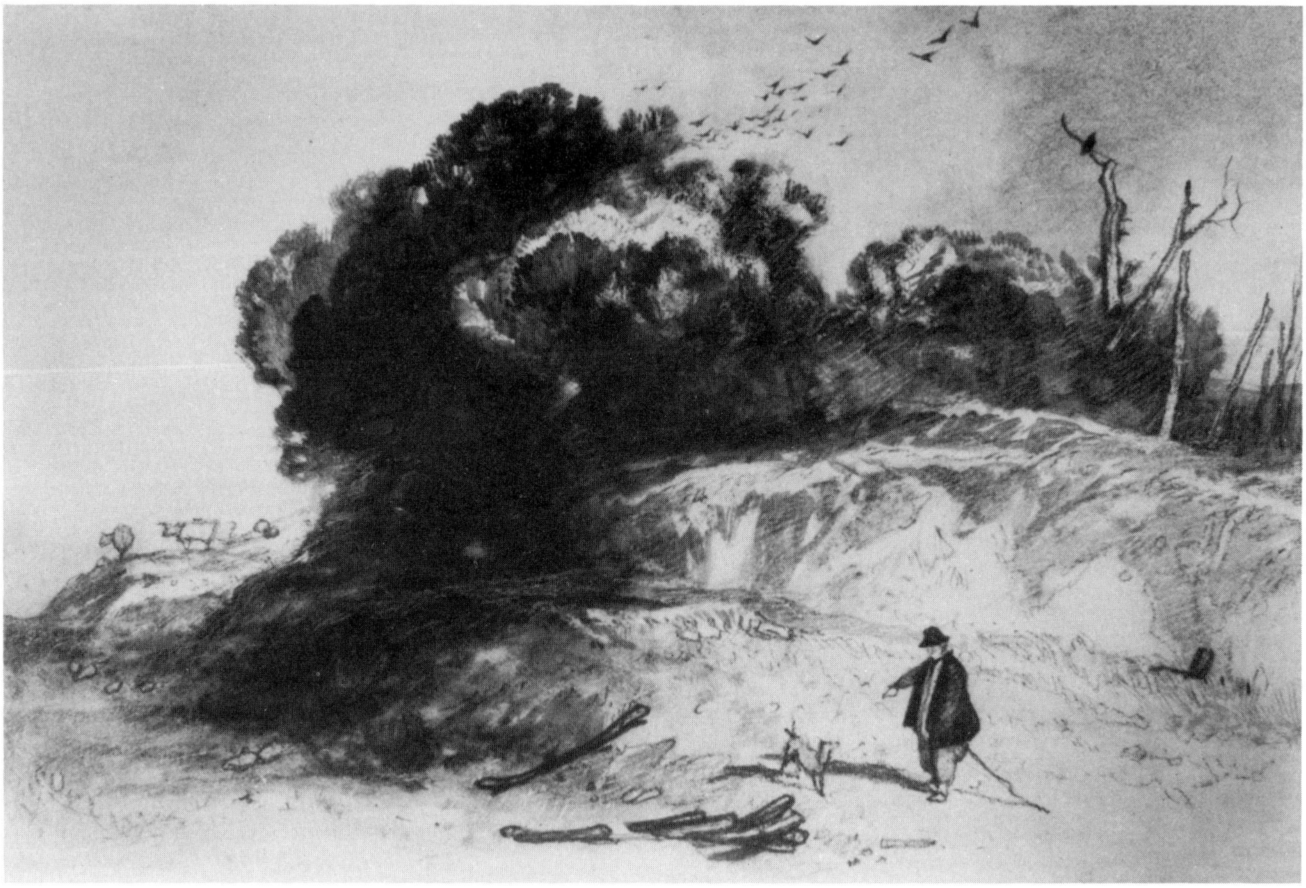

130 Mousehold Heath, *c.*1838-41

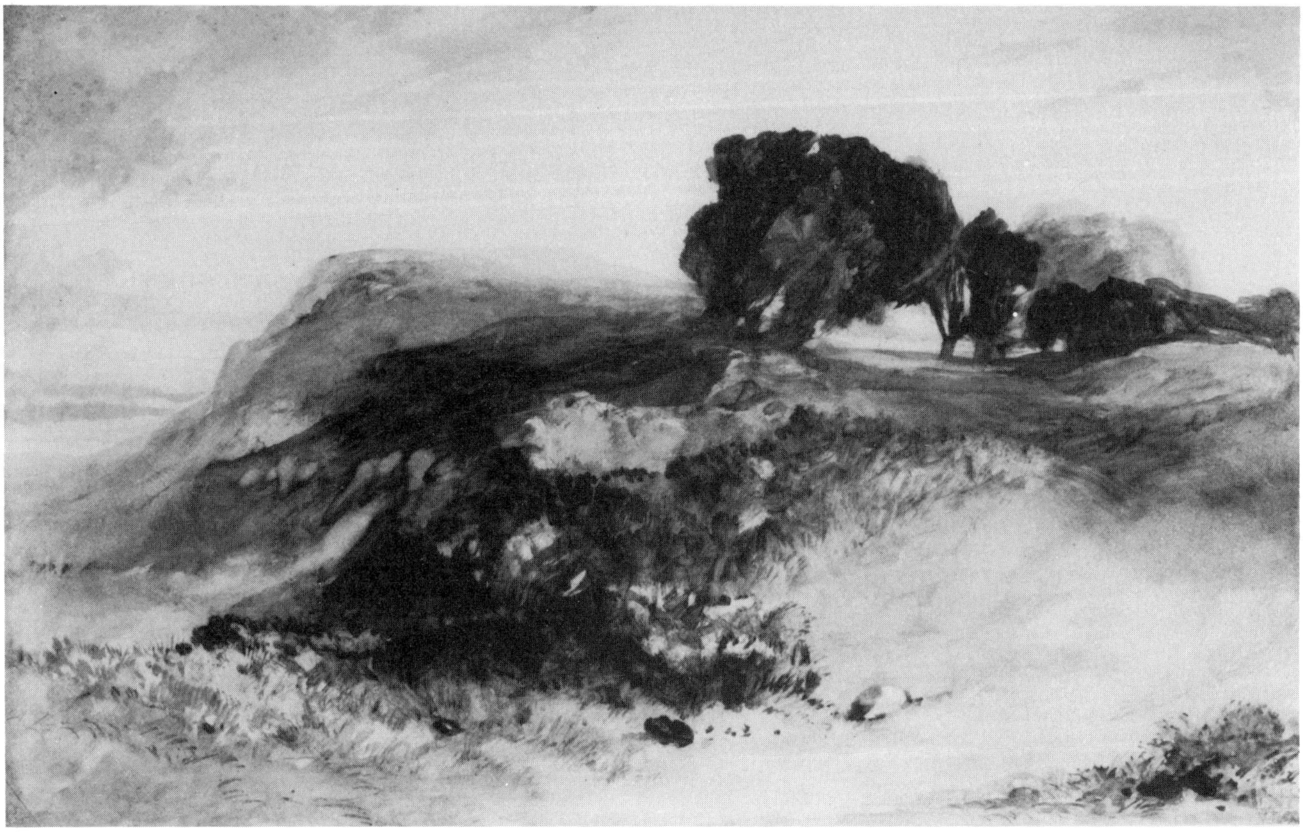

131 Trees on a Hill, *c.*1838-41

122 Cader Idris, *c.*1835-9

9
Professor of Drawing at King's College, London 1834-1841

In the course of seeking the advice of the Principal of the King's College School, London concerning a tutor for their children, the Palgraves learnt of the possibility of the appointment of a drawing master at the school. Whilst Sir Francis Palgrave recommended Cotman, his wife wrote[1] to her father, Dawson Turner, to seek his opinion as to Cotman's suitability for the post. Once Cotman knew of the opening, he pursued his cause relentlessly. He obtained a glowing testimonial from Samuel Bignold, the Mayor of Norwich, who testified not only to his ability to teach drawing, but also to his 'habits and character'.[2] In the week before Christmas, 1833, he went to London, hoping to 'get at Sir M. A. Shee, P.R.A.; Calcott, R.A.; and, perhaps, J. M. W. Turner, R.A., through Mr. Phillips.'[3] On New Year's Eve he wrote to his wife: 'I have obtained a Testimonial from Wilkins, R.A. . . . this excitement suits me, as you all know. I die in a calm.'[4] On 15 January, 1834 he was able to write to Dawson Turner: 'the Battle is fought and won. The Principal has congratulated me as Professor of Drawing to King's College.'[5]

The post came as the fulfilment of a lifelong ambition: 'This is what I have ever loved and tried to realize . . . Much as I have ever loved London I have never trod its gold paved streets feeling so much a man of business, and so much to belong to it, as now.'[6] London, for Cotman, meant not only 'the excitement and pleasure of seeing so many old friends'[3] such as George and Edward Cooke, James Stark and the Rev. James Bulwer, but the visual stimulus of the artistic confraternity. On one occasion he 'saw above three hundred most splendid drawings by Lewis. Words cannot convey . . . their splendour. My poor Reds, Blues and Yellows—for which I have, in Norwich, been so much abused and broken-hearted about are faded fades to what I saw there.'[7] On 25 February 1834 he wrote further to Dawson Turner of a party he had given the night before during which he had been impressed by the sketchbooks of David Roberts and J. F. Lewis: 'an entirely new light was burst upon me'.[8] It was little wonder that his only true regret on leaving Norwich was for the demise of the Norwich Society. He did not, however, approve of the behaviour of the local artists who set about canvassing 'the ground my son is about to take.'[9] On 26 January 'the full body of our decomposed Society of Artists met at my house for the last time.'[10] Only John Berney Crome, Cotman's traditional rival as a drawing master, had declined to scramble for custom, 'fairly hint[ing] it was a lost game to him.'[10]

Cotman's second son, John Joseph, accompanied him to London to help him with his work and remained there for a

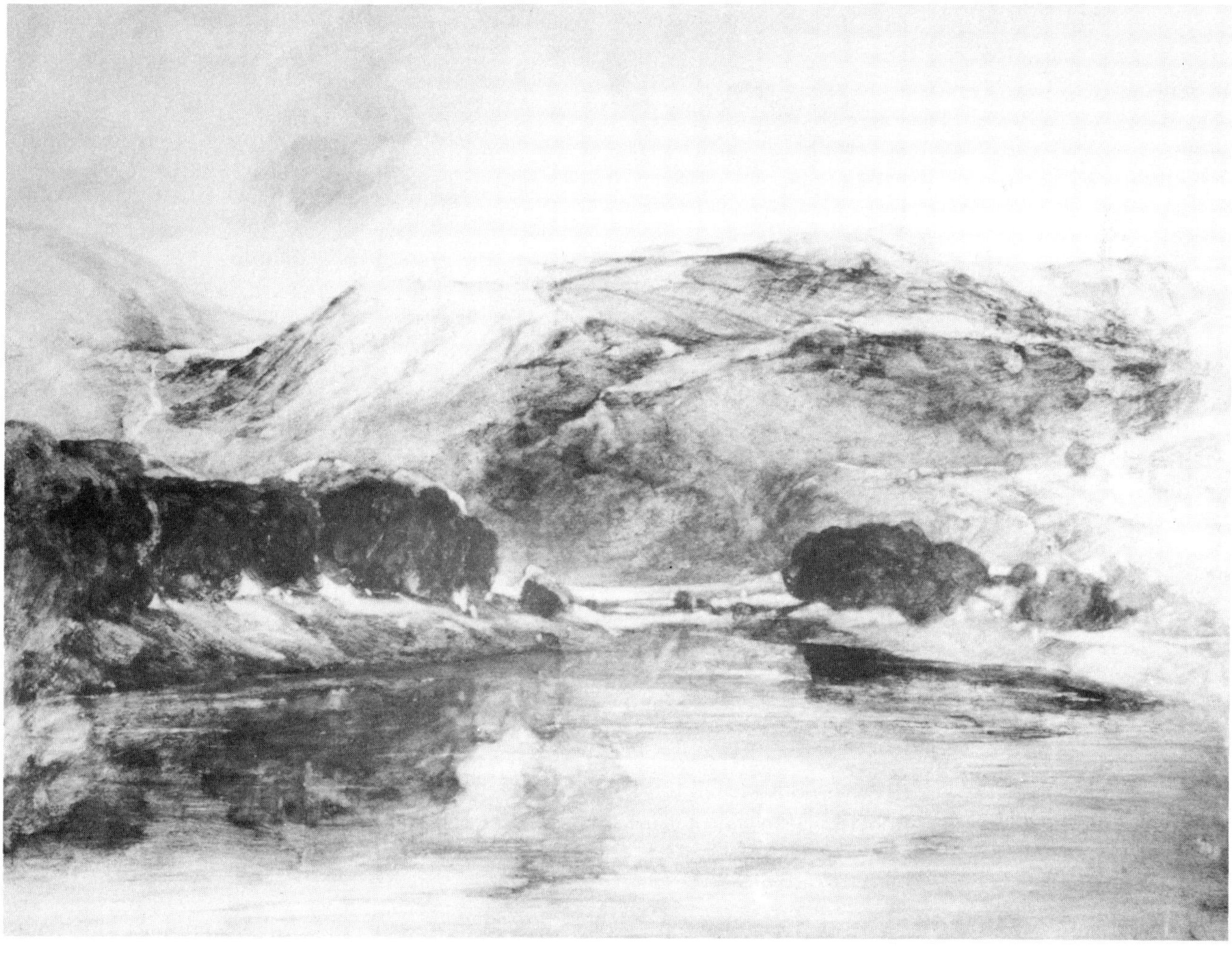

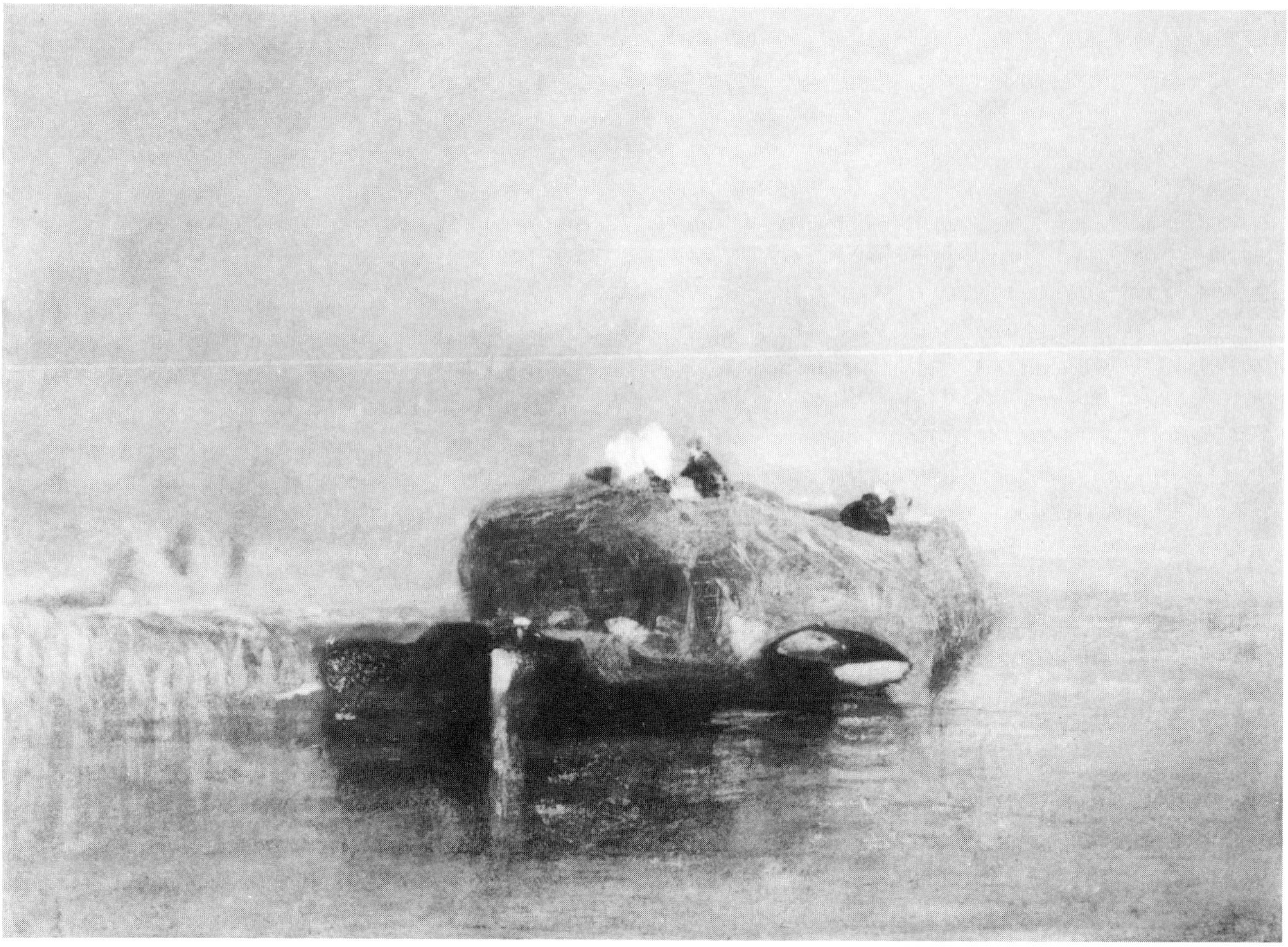

124 The Hay Boat, *c.*1835-9

short period when Cotman returned to Norwich for Easter, 1834. Cotman wrote a postcript to a letter from his daughter to John Joseph which precisely captures his sentiments about both cities: 'Tombland Fair never was so gay or so full. The afternoon sun is now shining most brilliantly on the folks and makes them all shine like gems. At night the lights on the stalls look as gay as Norwich can well look—but very, very far below the firefly appearance of a London Street with its regular and magnificent sweep of gas lamps and its accompaniment of fine architecture.'[11]

It was again through the intervention of Lady Palgrave and Dawson Turner that Cotman was finally able to settle in a house large enough to reunite him with his family in London at the end of the year. The Cotman family was to move to London at 42 Hunter Street, Brunswick Square, after Christmas. On 28 November he wrote to Dawson Turner: 'I feel now perfectly happy. I have commenced work in earnest. I have some of my books, a beautiful lamp and a most delicious colour-box and a good workshop. My room begins to look like my room in Yarmouth or Norwich—full of books, sketches and colour boxes'. In the same letter he acknowledged: 'To your family I am indebted for all this—to my kind pupil, Lady Palgrave!'[12]

It had taken the full year for Cotman to settle in London and the period had not been without its difficulties. His financial affairs were once again in disarray until he was able to gather his family under one roof in London. Early in the year he visited Dawson Turner to ask him for a loan. Dawson Turner refused him, but pointed out that Cotman's voracious habits as a collector meant that he held considerable assets. Cotman acted upon his advice and arranged for his collections of books, prints, paintings, drawings, casts, furniture and miscellaneous items such as a collection of armour to be sold by auction in September.[13] Cotman spent much of the summer prior to the auction in low spirits, but the sale raised the sum of about £500[14] which did indeed help Cotman out of his predicament. In November he wrote[15] to Dawson Turner to atone for his 'ungrateful' behaviour to 'my loved and valued friend of many a long year'. Couched in characteristically hyperbolic terms, his words reveal the dichotomy of the relationship between the level-headed banker and Cotman's more histrionic temperament: 'A money-lending friend, I now see, is not the best friend a man can have. I have acted on your advice, and—as you then said I should be if I did so—I am the happier for it; though allow me to say at that time it went to my very soul. For who can part with his Hobby—be it ever so small a one—without deep, deep regret? Mine, for me, was a great Horse, almost my idol, my business, my existence, my pack-horse, and I its slave. And I knew if I lost it that I should be what I have been, a mere idler, wretched and sad. I have now been all these for more than a year—aye, even in London—most wretched, and without doing anything but for the college.'

The 1834 sale catalogue reveals Cotman to have been a prodigious collector, while his library sale held at Christie's on 6 June 1843 makes it clear that he continued to amass an 'interesting library of German, French and English books, curious antiquarian works and books of prints' whilst in London. On 23 February 1836 he wrote to John Joseph[16] 'I have added most wonderfully to my library; very, very fine and most rare volumes, and most useful to me—and also very cheap'. The

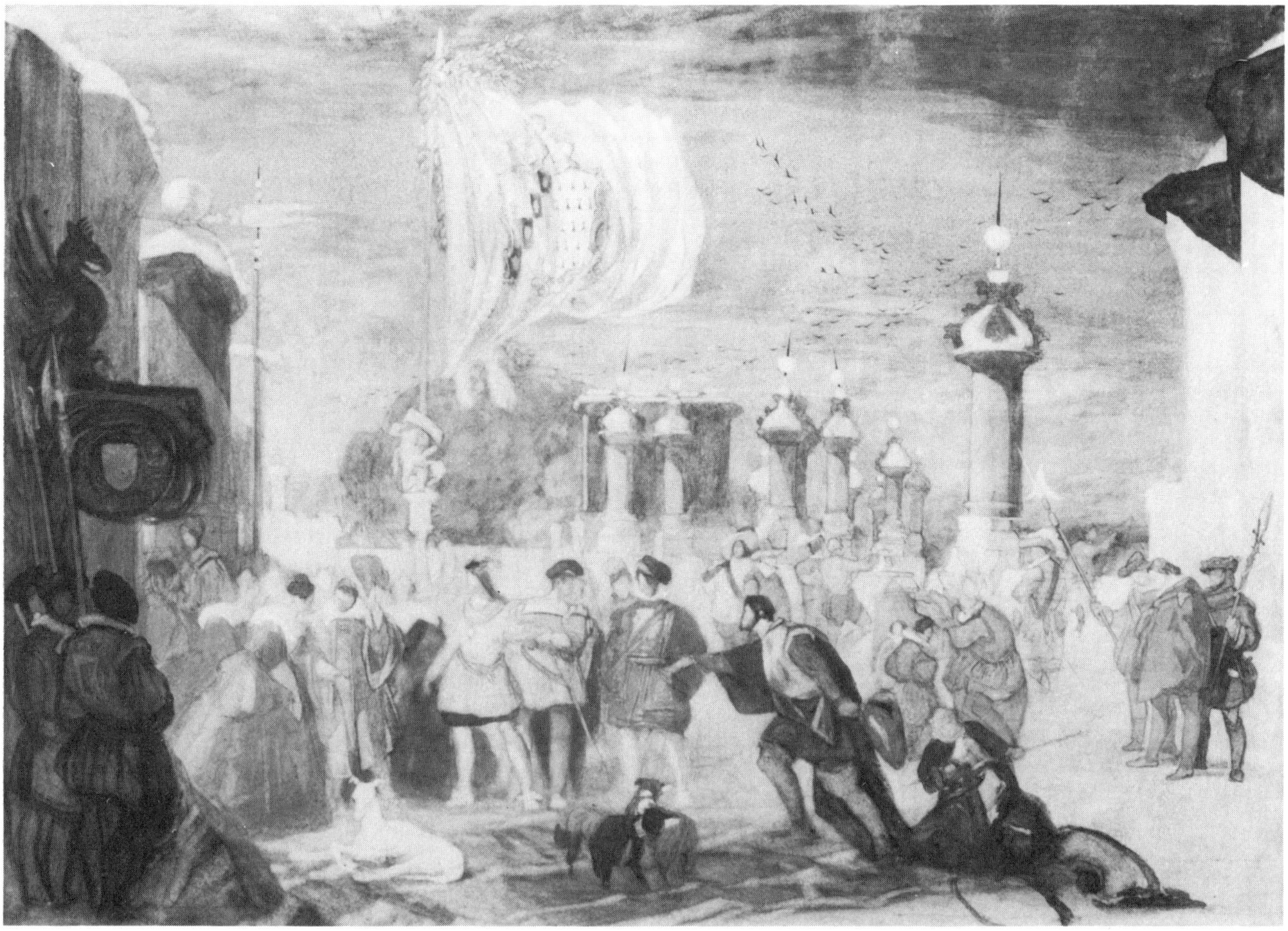

126 The Presentation of a Rose and Sword to the Lady of the Manor of Flixton, 1838

same letter recounts his delight in buying a print after Murillo: 'I should have been miserable if I had lost it.' He also attended the sale of John Constable's collection of books and engravings at Foster's in Pall Mall over 11 and 12 May 1838: 'I have added *all* I believe you liked *& more* of the Sebastian Bourdon landscapes. These I will give you, as the severest landscapes I know of . . . At the same sale I bought a Vol. of *244* prints drawn by Teniers.'[17] Throughout his working career Cotman combined his passion for collecting with the practical need to amass sources of reference material for both himself and his students. He endeavoured to equip his classroom at King's College as 'an exhibition one for the visitors—Casts, Models, Drawings and Prints on all subjects to raise the character of my department, even should I be obliged to be at the sole expense.'[18] His collecting even extended towards buying 'an old German carved frame' for three pounds.[17]

Cotman's duties as professor of drawing at King's College School were relatively light. He was required to attend only on Wednesdays and Saturdays.[19] His teaching method was to provide drawing copies which demanded increased proficiency from his pupils. The provision of these copies was not the tedious task that it might have been, as he was helped by his family in an atmosphere 'all full of life and fun.'[20] Cotman described the process in a letter to John Joseph who had remained in Norwich to continue to teach those pupils who wished to learn the Cotman style: 'Edmund, Ann, & Alfred and I are all drawing-mad; Ann and Alfred working for the college pupils with great effect [in] every way. They have done crack subjects, and they take wonderfully. Little do they ken by Whom they are done, when given under my name.'[21] The method was evidently successful, for his pupils grew in number from 185 in February 1834[22] to 323 in the autumn of 1841.[23] The number of pupils per class was in the region of fifty and from the beginning Cotman appears to have made a success of handling a large class, astonished at the 'electrical' effect of his commands for silence. He wished at all times 'to gain the love and respect'[22] of his pupils and appears to have succeeded. He was particularly pleased by the account of him contained in a book entitled *The Poetry of Life* by a former pupil, Sarah Stickney: 'It is much read and has been reviewed in different journals of the day, and the part relative to me quoted. This sort of puff, you know, I don't disrelish.'[20] The puff included a description of Cotman as 'one of the most poetical artists of the present day.'[24]

Two pupils who joined Cotman's class in 1837 were Dante Gabriel Rossetti and his younger brother, William. The latter, writing with the benefit of hindsight in 1895,[25] described Cotman as 'the most interesting pedagogue of all . . . an alert, forceful-looking man, of modest stature, with a fine well-moulded face, which testified to an impulsive nature, somewhat worn and worried.' He refers to the common conception that 'the seeds of madness lurked in this distinguished artist, although apart from a rather excitable or abrupt manner in ruling his bear-garden, I never saw any symptoms of it.' Cotman's physical and mental health during these years appears, in fact, to have been relatively stable. The 'worn and worried' mould of his demeanour during the last five years of his life appears to have been the result of considerable domestic problems. The mental health of both John Joseph and Cotman's youngest son, Alfred, collapsed. John Joseph's first breakdown in 1837 was relatively short, but he remained

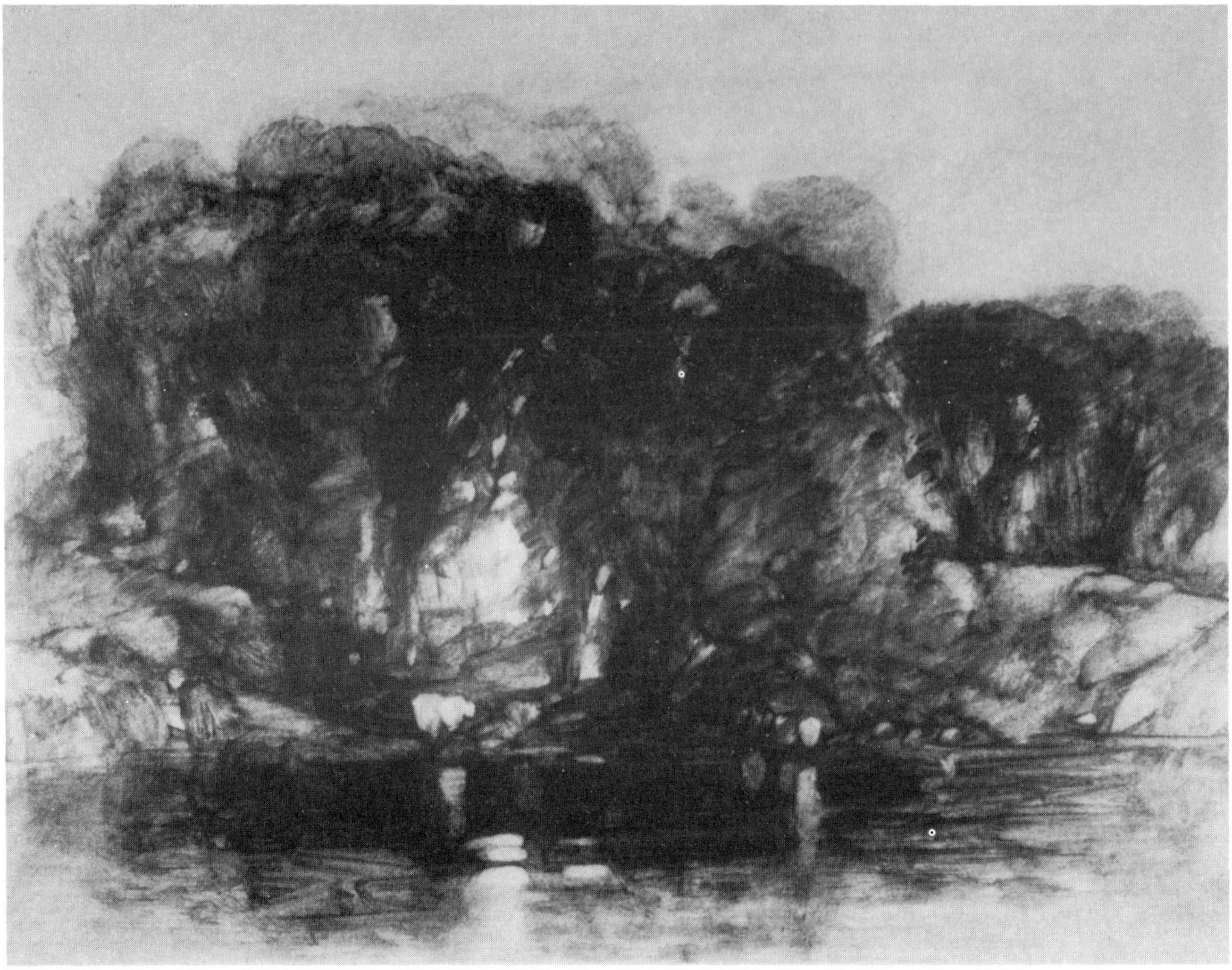

132 Watering Pool, *c.*1838-41

thereafter a source of anxiety to his father. Cotman wrote of Alfred, however, that he would have to be committed although 'he has not been so violent as formerly though more *varied* in his attacks upon us than ever which draws from us all our resources to meet or repel.'[26]

By his own account, Cotman remained busy but in good health, 'thanks to the Thames, Medway, fresh air and walking.'[27] On 12 September 1839 he wrote to his son Walter:[28] 'It seems that all my letters relate to my voyages up and down the Thames, breathing health and spirits. Today I took Alfred with me to Woolwich. It was such a glorious day, such clouds, such forms and colouring. I was quite beside myself and everything appeared animated.' It was during this autumn that he showed his work once again at Norwich, with the first exhibition of the Norfolk and Norwich Art Union (No. 166). His output during this period bespeaks an imaginative response to technique that recalls the creativity of his first Norwich period. Whilst indulging in baroque fantasy (Nos. 126, 127), he also teased his paste medium to achieve effects of lyrical virtuosity in both colour (Nos. 122, 123) and monochrome (Nos. 129-133).

Notes

[1]Lady P to DT, 17 Oct. 1833. [2]Kitson 1937 p. 304. [3]JSC to his wife, 26 Dec. 1833 (BM). [4]*Ibid.* 31 Dec. 1833. [5]JSC to DT, 15 Jan. 1834 (Barker Collection). [6]JSC to his wife, 15 Jan. 1834 (BM). [7]JSC to DT, 6 Jan. 1834 (Barker Collection). [8]*Ibid.* 25 Feb. 1834. [9]*Ibid.* 30 Jan. 1834 (Barker Collection). [10]*Ibid.* 27 Jan. 1834. [11]Ann Cotman to JJC, 28 March 1834 (Barker Collection.). [12]Barker Collection. [13]Spelman, Norwich, 10-12 Sept. 1834. [14]Kitson 1937 p. 317. [15]JSC to DT, 28 Nov. 1834 (Barker Collection). [16]BM. [17]JSC to JJC, 19 May 1838 (BM). [18]JSC to DT, 16 Dec. 1836 (Barker Collection). [19]JJC to A. Dixon, undated but March 1834, and JSC to JJC, 24 April 1838. [20]JSC to JJC, 27 Oct. 1835 (BM). [21]JSC to JJC, 13 Nov. 1835 (BM). [22]JSC to DT, 25 Feb. 1834 (Barker Collection). [23]Oppé, *Burlington* July 1942 p. 171. [24]Quoted, Kitson 1937 p. 322. [25] *Memoir of D. G. Rossetti,* by W. M. Rossetti (1895), quoted by Dickes, p. 391. [26] JSC to JJC, 9 Sept. 1841 (BM). [27]JSC to FWC, 30 Aug. 1839 (Kitson 1937 p. 338). [28]*Ibid.* 12 Sept. 1839.

120 An Oriental Figure holding a Flintlock, *c.*1833-4

called *The Mountaineer*

Pencil, watercolour and bodycolour with some gum arabic and wiping out on cream card; 26.2 × 21.3 ($10\frac{5}{16} \times 8\frac{3}{8}$). Prov: Bequeathed by Miss Norah Morley Shipstone, 1966. (356.966). Exh: Rouen 1967; Kenwood 1969; King's Lynn 1970 (8); Bordeaux 1977 (101) repro.; Sudbury 1978 (9). Ref: *EDP* 7 July 1966; Pidgley p. 192 n. 89; Rajnai & Allthorpe No. 48.

The extensive wiping out of colour on the leaves recalls that of No. 115, *Classical Landscape I,* and No. 119, *The Wind in the Trees.* Arabic gum has preserved the reds, although some of the greens have faded, revealing the free pencilwork beneath. A more finished version, formerly in the Bulwer collection, remains in a private collection.

Both watercolour versions relate to Cotman's etching,[1] *An Oriental Figure holding a Flintlock,* published by Charles Muskett in 1846, but originally conceived in 1833. The Bulwer version, known as *The Wolfhunter,* is directly related to the etching in both size and composition, but the Norwich version is a larger, more freely handled variation, which introduces a cool, blue, mountain landscape in the background. This latter feature has led to the traditional title of *The Mountaineer.*

Pidgley has suggested that the figure was probably inspired by Bonington's exotic armed figures such as *An Albanian,* published by J. D. Harding as a lithograph in 1830. Cotman's first essay at a similar figure was etched at the house of his friend W. H. Harriott. Although the plate[2] is dated 19 May 1832, it remained unpublished. This figure holds a furled banner, as opposed to the flintlock gun, which may correspond with lot 158 of Cotman's 1834 sale: 'A Moorish rifle the barrel beautifully embossed in silver'.

[1] Popham No. 343. [2] *Ibid.* No. 356.

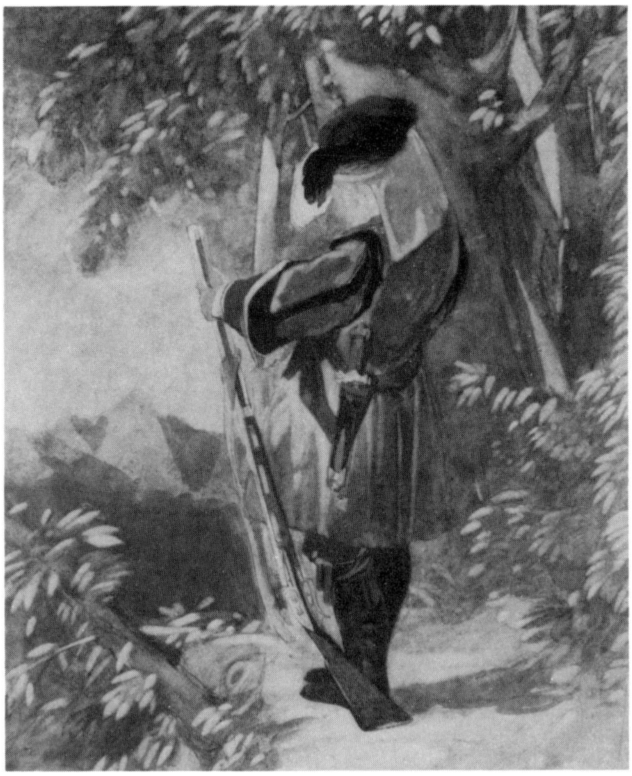

120 An Oriental Figure holding a Flintlock, *c.*1833-4

121 The Old Abbey, *c.*1835-9

Pencil, watercolour and bodycolour with some wiping out and scraping out on off-white, wove paper; 19.4 × 26.7 ($7\frac{5}{8} \times 10\frac{1}{2}$). Prov: Charles Muskett; his sale 1857, bt. M. J. Stark; ?by descent to Mrs. M. J. Stark; bt. from her by J. J. Colman, 1877; his bequest to R. J. Colman 1898; R. J. Colman Bequest 1946. (226.217.947). Exh: Norwich, Art Circle 1888 (9) illus. with litho. by S. H. Baldrey; BFAC 1888 (59); Norwich 1894 (75); Norwich 1903 (40); Norwich 1945; Norwich, Arts Council 1947 (36). Ref: Dickes p. 329.

The substantial use of black in Cotman's depiction of foliage is first apparent after 1835. Here the use of black is juxtaposed with the naked pencilwork of the abbey, thus highlighting the subject. The foreground is enlivened by touches of green while spots of yellow and red enrich the dark foliage. The dark areas are further textured through scraping with both a pointed tool and the end of the brush.

This treatment is similar to that of No. 129, *Mousehold Heath,* while the jaw of the ridge biting out from the right is a common element. The continued use of washes of colour argues, however, for a slightly earlier date than that for No. 129.

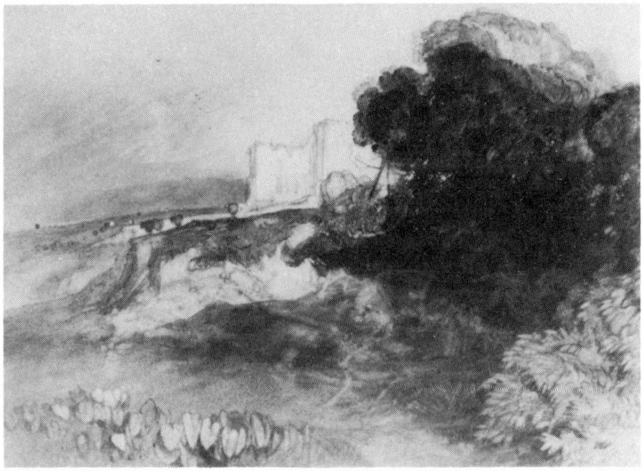

121 The Old Abbey, *c.*1835-9

122 Cader Idris, *c.*1835-9

illustrated on p. 111

Watercolour, bodycolour and gum arabic, with some scraping out on cream, wove paper; 35.2 × 44.7 ($13\frac{7}{8} \times 17\frac{5}{8}$). Prov: H. G. Barwell by 1883; by descent to his daughter Miss Barwell; bt. from her by R. J. Colman, Dec. 1911; R. J. Colman Bequest 1946. (209.217.947). Exh: Norwich 1883 (2, Room E); Norwich, Art Circle 1888 (176) illus. with litho. by Bagge Scott; BFAC 1888 (64); Norwich 1903 (22) lent by Miss Barwell; Manchester 1912 (323); Tate 1922 (120); Norwich 1945; Norwich, Arts Council 1947 (28); Norwich 1956 (23). Ref: Dickes p. 330; Cundall, *The Studio* 1920 pl. XLV; Kitson 1937 p. 349, pl. 142.

Cotman had seen the formidable Cader Idris during both his Welsh tours (section 2). The image of the blue mountain ridge remained with him and No. 122 is one of the last of the many compositions inspired by its haunting silhouette (see also the oil version, No. 163).

Cotman's use of the paste medium at this period reached a creative and imaginative peak to match that of his earlier drawings. A number of these works feature the mountains of Wales, most of which derive from the remembered image of Cader Idris. Examples are *Cader Idris*[1] and *Mountain Tarn*[2] in the British Museum, London and *Cader Idris*[3] in the National Museum of Wales, Cardiff. Each work in this series combines blues and browns thickened with paste and dragged in a manner similar to No. 113, *Storm on Yarmouth Beach,* and prefigures the final flourish of the technique in monochrome (see Nos. 129-133).

Accurate representation of the landscape was far removed from Cotman's imaginative purpose at this time. *Rocky Landscape: Sunset*[4] in the Victoria and Albert Museum, London, is an example of a similar use of the paste technique in which colour has been laid on and worked whilst viscid, with some scraping out, on a sheet of thick, cream wove paper. No. 122 is, by contrast, on a thinner sheet, necessitating a smoother treatment to achieve an effect of translucent colour.

[1] BM 1902-5-14-26. [2] BM 1902-5-14-28. [3] No. 3029. [4] P.21-1926; cf. also P.20-1926, *The Lake* and BM 1902-5-14-27, *Cattle on a Mountain, North Wales.*

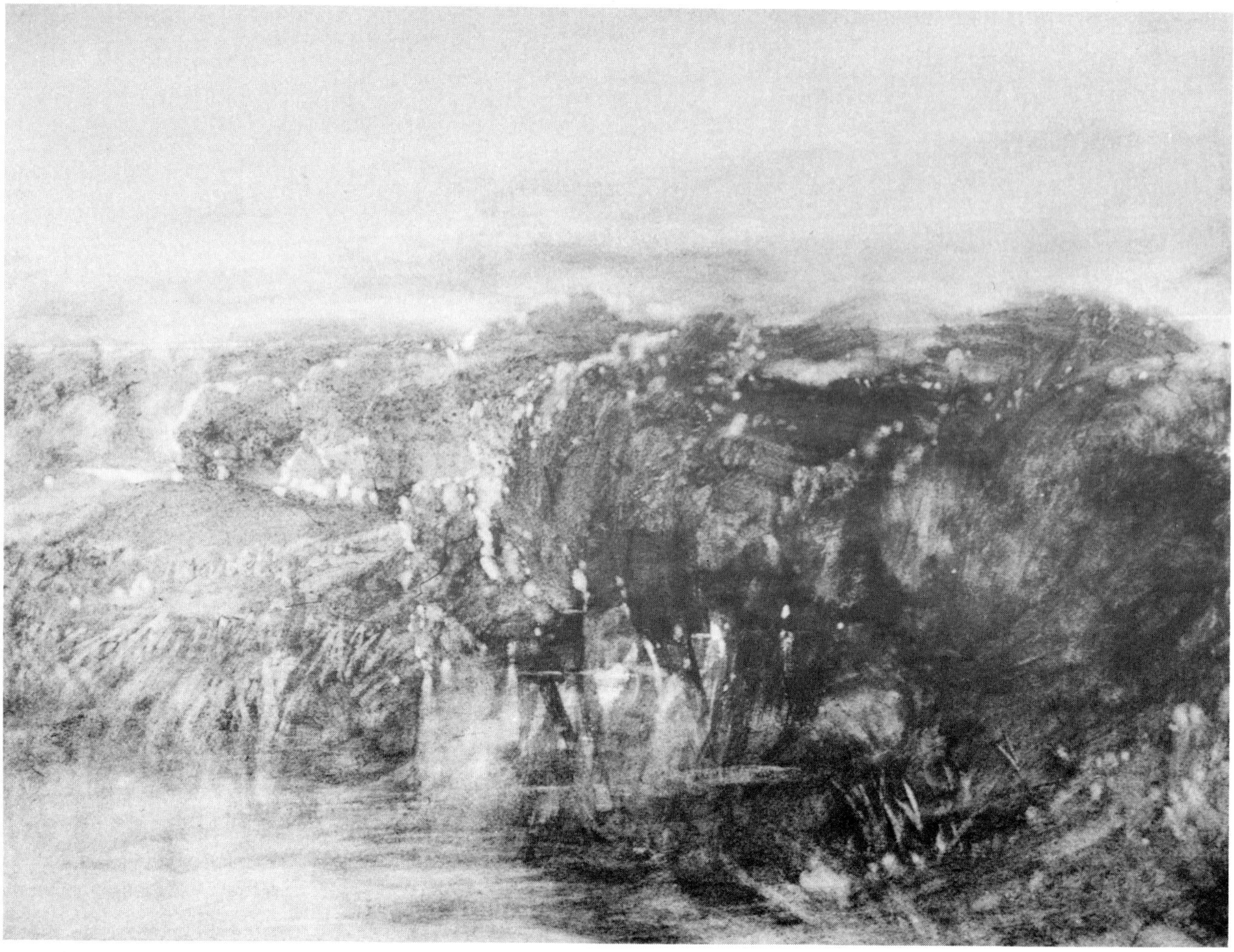

123 Woodland Stream, *c.*1835-9

123 Woodland Stream, *c.*1835-9

Watercolour and bodycolour with wiping out on cream, wove paper; 24.6 × 31.9 ($9\frac{11}{16}$ × $12\frac{9}{16}$). PROV: J. J. Colman by 1888; his bequest to R. J. Colman 1898; R. J. Colman Bequest 1946. (221.217.947). EXH: Norwich, Art Circle 1888 (185) lent by J. J. Colman; BFAC 1888 (45); Norwich 1903 (32); Norwich 1945; Norwich, Arts Council 1947 (34). REF: Dickes p. 331.

It is typical of Cotman's visual eloquence that his technical mastery should match his imagination. *Woodland Stream* marks the final flowering of Cotman's experiments with the paste medium to convey the abstract qualities of landscape.

The apparent abstraction of greens and blues, however, belies a remarkable verisimilitude. A distant landscape of meadowland to the left is bounded by the silhouettes of foliate trees traced out with the stump of the brush, leaving a distinct edge to the lights. The stream in the foreground is vigorously brushed in with vertical strokes, hatched with horizontal wiped marks which leave a single highlight of paper at the heart of the composition. The swirl and sweep of the scene, reminiscent of No. 119, *The Wind in the Trees,* is subtle and restrained. While a number of water-colours of this period use similar techniques (see No. 122, *Cader Idris*), few achieve the lyricism of *Woodland Stream.*[1]

[1]cf. Agnews, *108th Annual Exhibition of Watercolours and Drawings* 1981 (150).

124 The Hay Boat, *c.*1835-9

illustrated on p. 112

Bodycolour with some gum arabic and scraping out on cream, wove paper with watermark lower edge *J WHATMAN / 1833;* 25.7 × 34.9 ($10\frac{1}{8}$ × $13\frac{3}{4}$). PROV: ?John Joseph Cotman;[1] Murrell's sale, Norwich 26-27 Nov. 1862, lot 255 as *The Hay Boat,* unsold;[2] bt. by James Reeve;[2] ?Dr. Hamilton;[1] J. J. Colman by 1870;[2] his bequest to R. J. Colman 1898; R. J. Colman Bequest 1946. (192.217.947). EXH: London International Exhibition 1874 (315a); Norwich 1894 (81); Norwich 1902 (216); Manchester 1912 (365); Tate 1922 (116); Norwich 1945; Norwich, Arts Council 1947 (22); Norwich 1956 (22). REF: Dickes p. 331; *EDP* 13 April 1922; *The Architect* 21 April 1922; Kaines Smith 1926 p. 136 repro. p. 138; Kitson, *Country Life* 7 Nov. 1936 repro. figs. 3 & 4; Kitson 1937 p. 293; Allthorpe-Guyton 1979.

The heavy use of bodycolour in *The Hay Boat* is a further example of Cotman's assertive and creative experimental approach to his work during the 1830s. This picture gives some credence to the traditional statement that Cotman would attempt to vie with oils in his water-colour painting. When Kitson knew the picture it was covered in varnish which was only removed during restoration in 1935-6. Until that date the scene was believed to be in oil. It remains one of the most Turneresque of Cotman's works in oil or watercolour, with an effective use of blue applied with a dry brush to suggest shadow. A unique tone of blended blue-green atmosphere is evoked, against which the shadows are as richly worked and scraped as the subjects portrayed.

A compositional pencil study[3] for *The Hayboat* reveals that the wedge of land stretching across to the right was a key element from its conception, as were the shadows, acting here almost as highlights. A related pencil sketch,[4] dated 19 September 1828, depicts the original incident from which the composition developed: a hayboat being loaded from the bank of the River Medway. The colour notes along the bottom edge of the sketch accord well with the scheme finally chosen by Cotman:[5] 'Boat warm raw sienna, black and ash. Rudder a spot of light. Men white and ultramarine . . . Distance greyish purple: do. color to ye right and in middle distance. Bank to ye left golden green.'[6] Miles Edmund both etched and painted[7] a similar subject, prosaic by comparison.

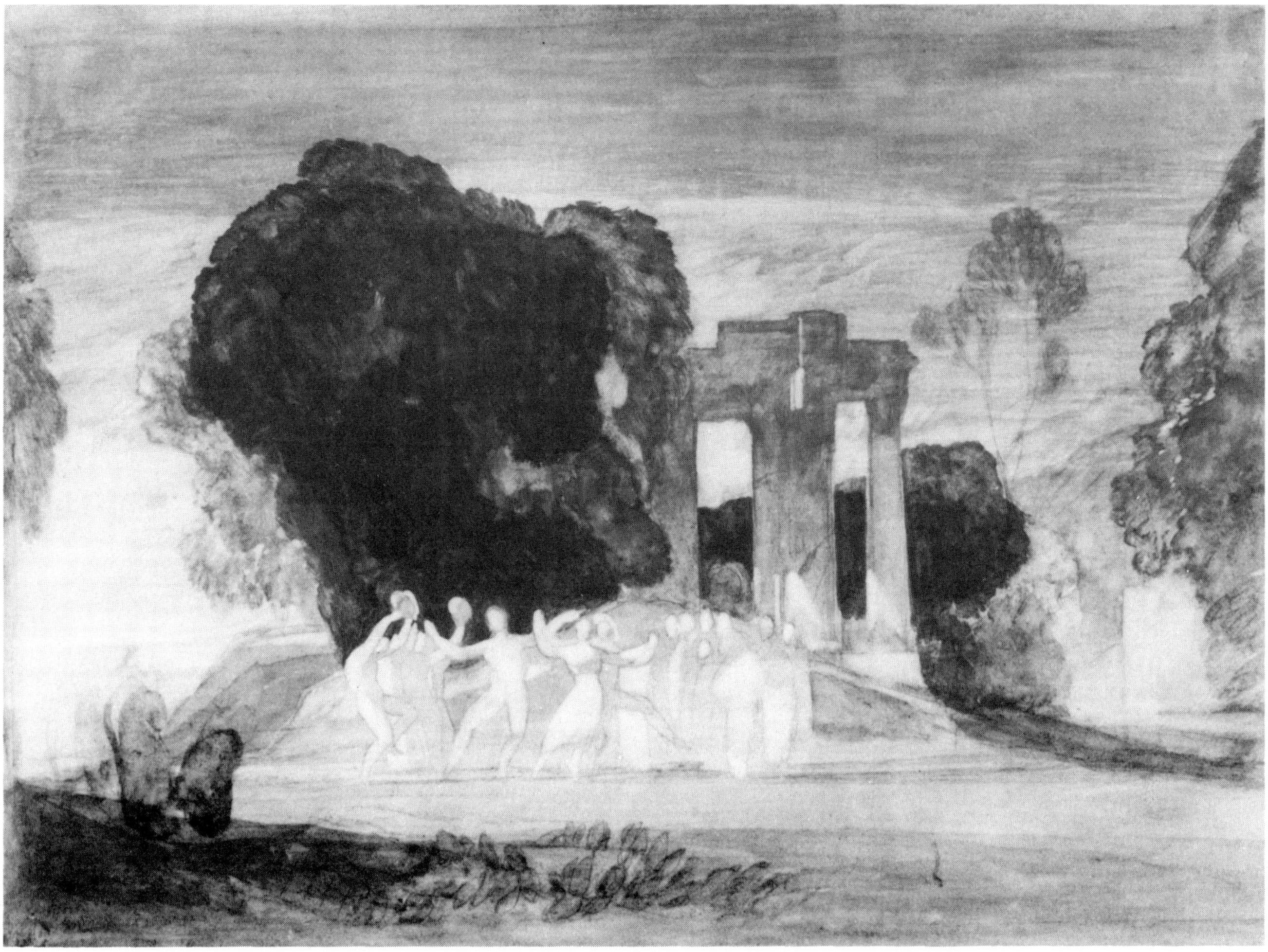

125 Figures Dancing in a Classical Landscape, *c.*1835-9

[1]CC records. [2]Annotated catalogue, Art Dept. archives, NCM, indicates that it was bt. by Bulwer, £11.0s.6d., but a later note states that it was 'Bought in. Sold afterwards to J. Reeve. Now in possession of J. J. Colman Esqr. 1870'. [3]BM 1902-5-14-201. [4]BM 1902-5-14-227. [5]From the corrected wording of Kitson 1937 p. 278. [6]A drawing copy (King's College) is BM 1902-5-14-136; a reverse copy of which is NCM 2.105.932. [7]Oil, Private Collection; formerly H. N. Holmes Collection.

125 Figures Dancing in a Classical Landscape, *c.*1835-9

Pencil, watercolour, bodycolour and gum arabic on cream, wove paper; 34.3 × 45.5 ($13\frac{9}{16}$ × $17\frac{15}{16}$). PROV: Cotman's sale, Christie's, 17-18 May 1843, lot 135, bt. Taylor 5s.; A. W. Preston; bt. from him by R. J. Colman, Jan. 1927; R. J. Colman Bequest 1946. (223.235.951). EXH: Norwich 1945. REF: Kitson 1937 repro. fig. 144 as *Classic Dance.*

This composition has been associated with Cotman's interest in Poussin.[1] Although No. 125 is classical in both subject and composition, the effect is reminiscent more of Fuseli's extravagant and stylized romanticism than of the works of Poussin. The figures also recall Cotman's early work with the Sketching Society, such as those in *Weird Scene,*[2] now in the British Museum. The composition differs little from the preliminary sketch[3] in brush and sepia on grey paper, heightened with white, also in the British Museum.

In common with other works of Cotman's second London period, the colour black is used extensively in the representation of foliage (see Nos. 129-133). The black pigment is thickly flooded in on a sheet of paper which is smooth and thin in texture, similar to those of Nos. 130 and 132. The colour range, despite the rich blue, is relatively monochromatic, suggesting a date towards the end of the period when Cotman turned away from the 'very gay and gawdy' work exemplified by No. 126.

[1]For which see No. 148. [2]BM 1902-5-14-39. [3]BM 1902-5-14-50.

126 The Presentation of a Rose and Sword to the Lady of the Manor of Flixton, 1838

illustrated on p. 113

Pencil, chalk, watercolour and bodycolour on buff, wove paper; 57.1 × 78.3 ($22\frac{1}{2}$ × $30\frac{13}{16}$). PROV: William Cooper, London Street, Norwich; by descent to his son; bt. from him by W. Boswell; bt. from him by Mr. Sandford, Cromer; bt. from him by James Reeve 1889; bt. from him by R. J. Colman, 9 Dec. 1903, £105; R. J. Colman Bequest 1946. (224.235.951). EXH: Norwich 1903 (39); Tate 1922 (86); Norwich 1945. REF: Binyon 1897 pp. 95-96; Dickes p. 395 repro; *EDP* 13 April 1922; Kitson 1937 pp. 344-345; Oppé *Burlington* Aug. 1945 pp. 199-200, pl. II, fig. B; *Colman Collection Guide* 1951 p. 6; Clifford pp. 66, 67, 70; Pidgley pp. 193-194.

A letter from Cotman, written on 7 April 1838 to his son Francis Walter[1] refers at some length to this subject: 'One entirely my own in every sense of the word, being very gay and gawdy and full of frippery, is a view on the top of Flixton Hall, Suffolk, sketched[2] when Anne was with me some six years ago and somewhat better, with about twenty large figures, very principal, and about the same number of supernumeries or figurantes, as we say at the opera. The Story—The Presentation of a Rose and Sword to the Lady of the Manor of Flixton —a story altogether fictitious. A huge banner of Henry VIII waving over the battlements . . . A fine subject and promises to be a very fine drawing, if so it will be 60 guineas.'

Cotman had written three weeks earlier to his friend J. H. Maw, commenting that the story was set in 'the noble time of Elizabeth with soldiers &c. as on guard'.[3] These surviving comments accord well with the composition of No. 126, although not with regard to the number of 'supernumeries'. It appears that the original conception was never completed and that it was indeed No. 126 to which Cotman referred the following May: 'Flixton is all but sold for *60 guineas* . . .

my first trophy in this my determined campaign For reputation—of course profit For the one *never* comes without the other.'[4]

Although founded upon sketches of the roof of Flixton Hall, first built in 1615 by John Tasburgh Esq., the drawing is a work of pure fantasy. The costumes of the figures are not uniformly of the Elizabethan era, while Binyon remarked that although 'a splendid failure . . . The glow, the pomp, the gorgeous unreality of romantic art are here'. The gorgeous treatment of the left foreground prefigures that of *The Drawing Master* (No. 127) while the introduction of bright orange to the more customary combination of vermilion and emerald adds to the fanciful 'riot of colour'.[5]

[1]BM. [2]See Tate, 1922, no. 26 for another watercolour derived from this visit. [3]15 March 1838 (BM), Pidgley. [4]JSC to JJC 19 May 1838 (BM). [5]Kitson.

127 The Drawing Master, 1839
called *The Green Lamp*
illustrated in colour on p. 136.

Pencil, chalk, watercolour and bodycolour with some gum arabic on cream, wove paper, lamp cut out and pasted on; 33.1 × 47.6 (13 × $18\frac{3}{4}$). INSCR: Signed, dated and inscribed in black chalk lower edge *J S Cotman—1839* -. . . (illegible). PROV: given by the artist to Dr. Charles Firth; by descent to his daughter Miss Firth; bt. ?from her by Leggatt Bros; bt. from them by Percy Moore Turner 1928; bt. from him by R. J. Colman, 30 June 1928, £180; R. J. Colman Bequest 1946. (225.217.947). EXH: ?Norwich 1839 (267) as *The Drawing Master;* Norwich, Art Circle 1888 (165) as *Interior (unfinished)* lent by Charles Firth; Norwich 1945; Norwich, Arts Council 1947 (35). REF: *Norfolk Chronicle* 12 Oct. 1839; *Art Union* Oct. 1839 p. 151;[1] Kitson 1937 pp. 346-347; Rienaecker pl. 55 fig. 105; Hardie vol. 2 p. 91, pl. 78; Pidgley pp. 165, 241; Rajnai 1978 repro. in colour; Allthorpe-Guyton 1979; Allthorpe-Guyton & Stevens 1982 repro. p. 19.

This drawing was one of six Cotman submitted for the first exhibition of the Norfolk and Norwich Art Union, only two[2] of which did not relate directly to his capacity as Drawing Master at King's College, London. The *Norfolk Chronicle* commented that 'the subject, being probably a secondary consideration with our respected fellow-citizen, may be designated by the above as well as by any other title'. The critic found the picture 'remarkable for freedom of manner and richness of tone; for massiveness and depth of shadow in contrast with equal breadth and vivid effect of light'. The inscription, now illegible, has been read as 'unfinished' which is, however, unlikely.

The subject is, like No. 126, one entirely his own. The setting traditionally shows Cotman with his wife and daughter Ann in their drawing room at Bloomsbury. Pidgley has pointed out that the lamp 'was the one Cotman worked by in the evenings. He sketched it in a letter to Turner (Nov. 28 1834), and called it his "Lamp of Aladdin" because it worked wonders for him'. The table is equipped with materials for the drawing lesson, in an arrangement similar to that of the Sketching Society's table, as it is depicted in a contemporary lithotint vignette.[3] Nevertheless, the scene is rendered fantastic by the palatial baroque decorative scheme more reminiscent of an opera house than a drawing room. The pictures on the wall, although influenced by Cotman's knowledge of the primitives, such as those in the collection of Dawson Turner and the National Gallery, are purely imaginary. There is no evidence that Cotman owned a crucifixion triptych, while the mannerist Virgin and Child in its ornate gold frame was originally sketched in a horizontal format.

No. 127 was, for 'an esteemed correspondent' of the *Art Union* 'A brilliant and beautiful piece of colouring, in that rich and gorgeous style for which Mr. C. has lately rendered himself famous'. The writer did, however, deprecate the use of a coloured piece of paper pasted on as the lamp shade, finding it 'somewhat derogatory to Art for a painter such as Mr. Cotman to continue these practices'. While *The Drawing Master* represents the height of Cotman's romantic virtuosity and the latest of his securely datable works in this style, the picture is close in almost every aspect of colouring technique and composition to his watercolour of Crosby Hall, composed nine years earlier (No. 106).

[1]Pidgley. [2]Nos. 125 & 218. The identification of *The Drawing Master* was first made by Pidgley. [3]Title page of *Evening sketches by A. E. Chalon etc.*, London, 1840.

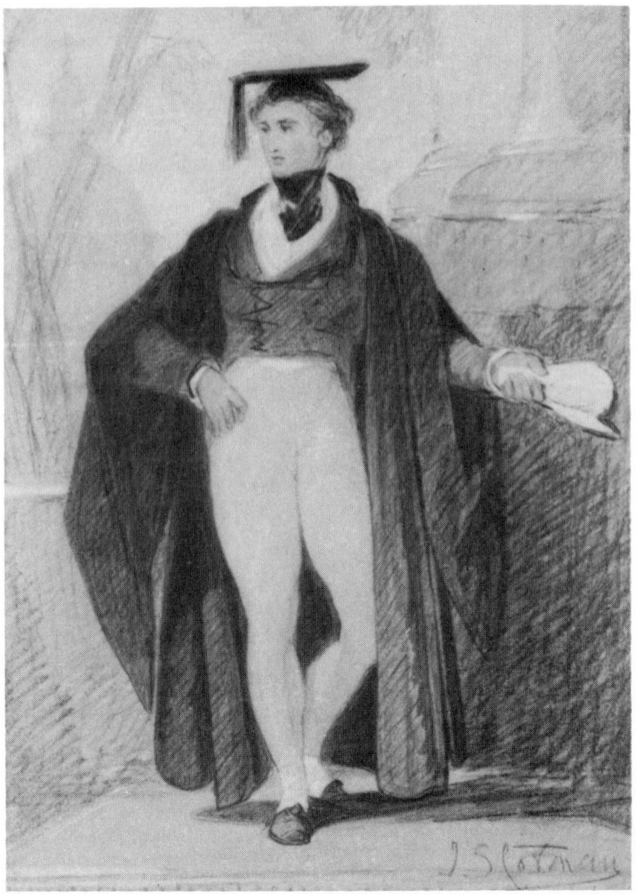

128 Cap and Gown, *c.*1835-9

128 Cap and Gown, *c.*1835-9

Black and white chalk touched with red chalk on brownish, wove paper; 42.9 × 30.4 ($16\frac{7}{8}$ × $11\frac{15}{16}$). INSCR: Signed in black chalk l.r. *J S Cotman.* PROV: R. J. Colman Bequest 1946. (326.235.951). EXH: ?Norwich 1839 (320) as *Portrait of a Collegian.*

In a spirit akin to that of *The Drawing Master,* Cotman gives his subject a romantic treatment flattering to both student and scholarship. The figure stands in a portico, with trees beyond, framing a view of the dome of St. Paul's.

From the beginning of his employment at King's College, London, Cotman had hoped 'to gain the love and respect of my pupils. They are and shall be my best friends.'[1] A number of sketches indicate that he was pleased to portray his pupils. A pencil sketch of a standing figure, now in Chicago,[2] may well be of a similar student, as is a pencil sketch[3] heightened with white, known simply as *Scholar.* A sketch of a similar portrait head, with mortarboard and black cravat, is on the verso of *The Fisherman,* No. 133.

No. 128 could well be an exhibition piece. The white highlights and touches of red to the flesh tones reveal Cotman's full colour sense with absolute economy. In 1839, together with five other works including *The Drawing Master* (No. 127), Cotman exhibited at the first exhibition of the Norfolk and Norwich Art Union, a similar subject: *Portrait of a Collegian,*[4] which may well have been No. 128.

[1]JSC to DT, 25 Feb. 1834 (Barker Collection). [2]Art Institute of Chicago, 22.1171. [3]Christie's, ?March 1978: a family production, probably MEC. [4]No. 320.

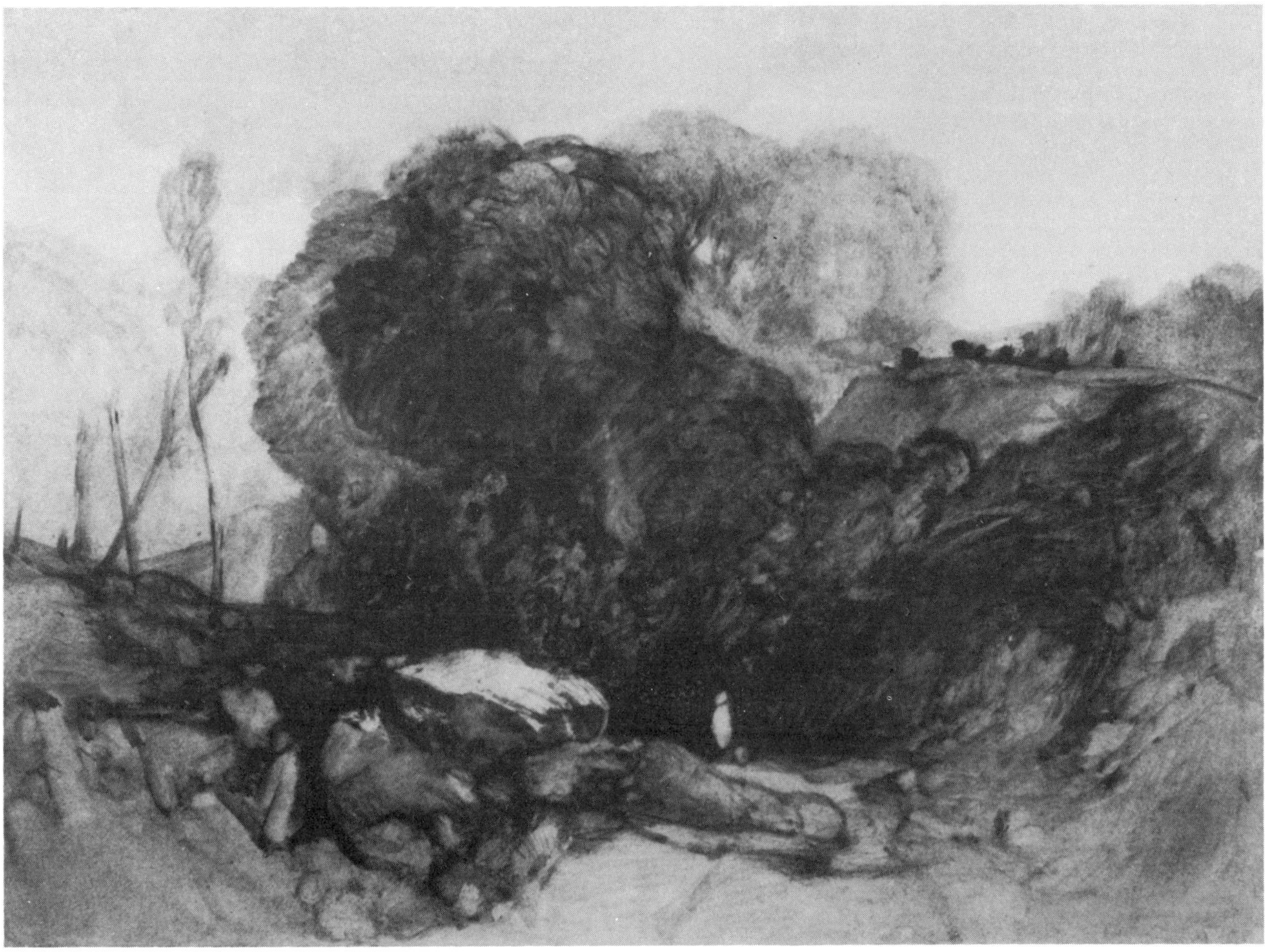

129 The Sunken Road, *c.*1838-41

129 The Sunken Road, *c.*1838-41

Brownish-grey watercolour and bodycolour with some gum arabic on off-white, wove paper, with watermark lower edge *RUSE & TURNER / 1834;* 17.2 × 22.8 ($6\frac{3}{4}$ × $8\frac{15}{16}$). PROV: The artist, Thomas Price Downes; bt. from him by J. J. Colman by 1888; his bequest to R. J. Colman 1898; R. J. Colman Bequest 1946. (227.235.951). EXH: Norwich, Art Circle 1888 (126) as *A Composition* lent by J. J. Colman; Norwich 1903 (77) as before; Norwich 1945.

The Sunken Road, together with Nos. 130-133, represent as a group the final phase in Cotman's development as a colourist. Whilst eliminating the heightened colour contrasts apparent in his work since the mid 1820s, he returned towards the end of the 1830s to the monochromatic scale of his Normandy drawings. He introduced touches of colour into the drawings only on rare occasions (No. 130). The resulting drawings, although very different, are as effective in their suggestion of the moods of landscape as are the Normandy monochrome drawings or the tonal modulations of the Greta period work.

His compositions within this mode of expression remain fundamentally similar. The use of the paste technique, in which the deepest blacks are reinforced with bodycolour, necessitates reservoirs of 'colour' on the paper from which to work the representational textures of an imaginative landscape. Thus *The Sunken Road* develops as the central mass is dragged and wiped into a composition remarkable for a velvety softness last seen in Cotman's oeuvre in some of the more heavily-worked Normandy monochromes (Nos. 93, 94). The motif of stark and blasted trees silhouetted against the horizon recalls earlier works, and is a recurring theme at this time, (see No. 130).

130 Mousehold Heath, *c.*1838-41

illustrated on p. 110

Pencil and black watercolour and bodycolour touched with brown ink and brown watercolour with some scraping out on cream, wove paper; 17.9 × 26.3 (7 × $10\frac{5}{16}$). PROV: The artist, Thomas Price Downes; bt. from him by J. J. Colman; his bequest to R. J. Colman 1898; R. J. Colman Bequest 1946. (231.235.951). EXH: Norwich 1945.

The thick sheet of paper of *Mousehold Heath* allows a greater degree of scraping out than in *The Sunken Road* (No. 129), but it is not taken to the extent of the scoring and scouring of the surface to be seen in *The Fisherman,* (No. 133). The use of soft pencil is also prominent in No. 130, particularly in outlining the figures, the stark trees to the right of the composition and the contours of the bank. The black watercolour is scraped and worked in both trees and shadows. The touches of brown relate to another monochrome watercolour of this period, *The Edge of The Broad,*[1] where spots of red and yellow heighten the effect. The motif of a single bird perched on a branch to the right recalls that in *Cattle Watering,* (No. 48) and the oil, *The Mishap* (No. 159).

Although an imaginative creation, this scene relates to the view to the left of Colonel Harvey's house on Mousehold Heath, which Cotman sketched[2] on 18 November 1841 (see p. 123). The scene may well be based upon a reminiscence of that view, with which he later familiarised himself once again.

[1]NCM 228.235.951. [2]BM 1902-5-14-168.

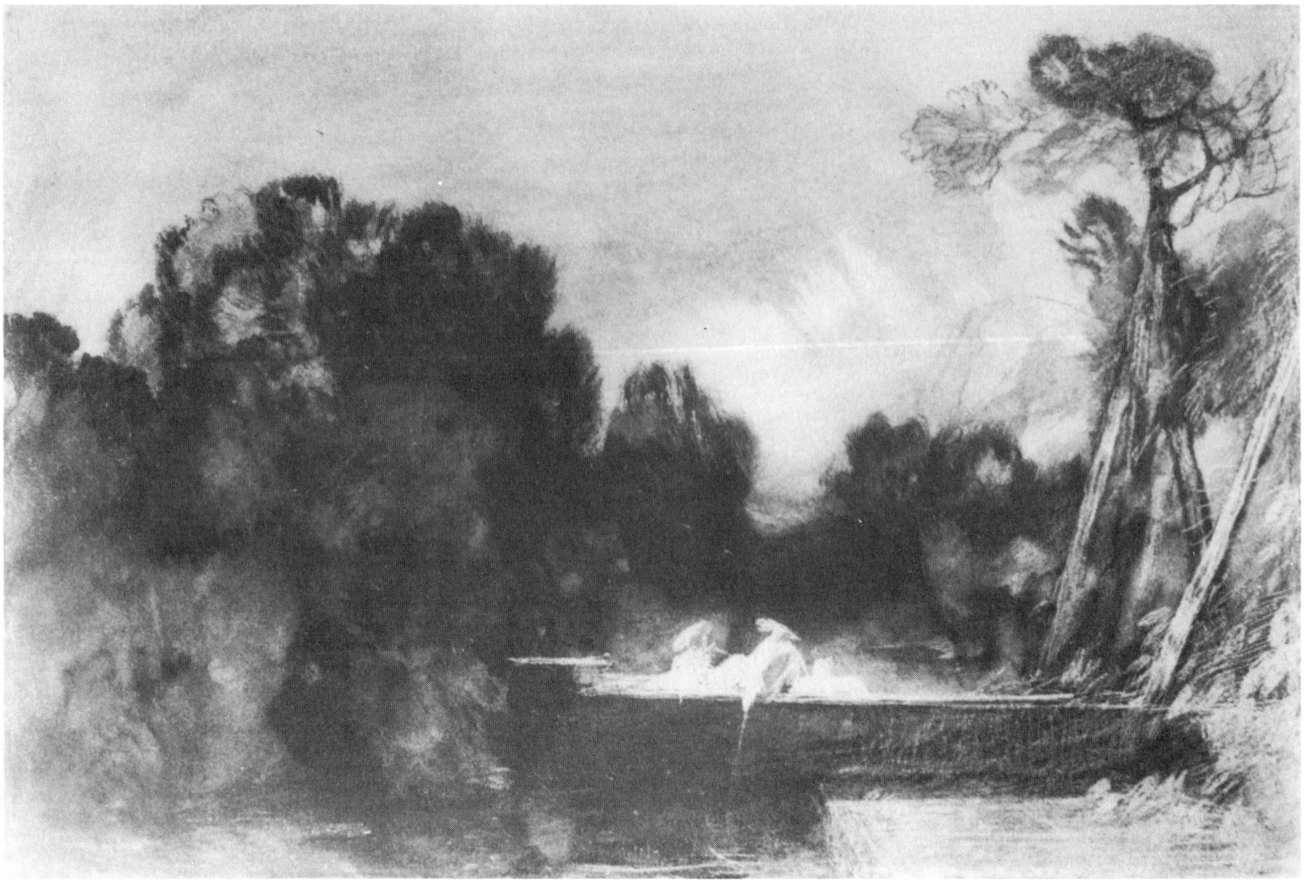

133 A Composition, *c.*1838-41

131 Trees on a Hill, *c.*1838-41
illustrated on p. 110

Brown and black watercolour and bodycolour on cream, wove paper with impressed stamp l.r. *London Superfine Board;* 22.4 × 34.8 ($8\frac{13}{16}$ × $13\frac{11}{16}$). PROV: See No. 130. (229.235.951). EXH: Norwich 1945. REF: Cundall, *The Studio* 1920 pl. XLVII as *Water Colour Study;* Clifford fig. 40b; Maas 1969 repro. p. 57.

This drawing represents another remembered heathscene, achieving subtle modulations of brown and black, grey and cream. The short strokes of a coarse-haired brush emphasize the scrub and stubble of heathland in the foreground, which is in contrast to the gentle undulating sweep of the path leading up between the trees. Cotman continues to modulate the tones of the composition even within the silhouettes of the trees. See also No. 129 for a further discussion of this technique.

132 Watering Pool, *c.*1838-41
illustrated on p. 114

Brown and black watercolour and bodycolour on cream, wove paper; 17.2 × 21.7 ($6\frac{3}{4}$ × $8\frac{1}{2}$). PROV: John Joseph Cotman; Mrs. King; her sale 1880, bt. ?J. J. Colman; ?his bequest to R. J. Colman 1898; R. J. Colman Bequest 1946. (309.235.951).

No. 132 achieves in monochrome the modulated tones and shadows, reflections, lights and darks of a scene that is presumably imaginary, but tightly controlled in the manner of an earlier composition of similar effect, *Woodland Stream,* (No. 123). The use of the paste medium, worked with the wooden stub of the brush, is particularly effective. A twilight scene of cattle watering at a pool, with light beckoning from beyond the trees, is conjured into existence, evoking and surpassing the eighteenth century blot technique of Alexander Cozens. See also No. 129 for a further discussion of this technique.

133 A Composition, *c.*1838-41
called *The Fisherman*

Pencil, black wash and bodycolour with some gum arabic and scraping out on cream, wove paper; 17.7 × 26 ($6\frac{15}{16}$ × $10\frac{1}{4}$). *Verso,* in pencil sketch of head of a man[1]. PROV: See No. 129. (230.235.951). EXH: Norwich, Art Circle 1888 (103) lent by J. J. Colman; BFAC 1888 (111); Norwich 1894 (72); Norwich 1903 (73); Tate 1922 (150); Tokyo 1929; Norwich 1945. REF: Rutter, *Sunday Times* 20 Sept. 1936 repro.; Gordon, *Observer* 20 Sept. 1936; *Burlington* Nov. 1936 repro.; Kitson 1937 pl. 145; Hardie vol. 2 p. 92.

This composition reveals Cotman at his most experimental in this medium. The deep black forms and shadows are heavily scored, or, as the restorer Kennedy North observed, 'etched', in a technique of 'brilliant audacity'. As one might expect, the sheet of paper is heavy and thick in order to withstand the extensive scouring and parallel strokes of scraping out. This consistent use of parallel scraped lines is to be found in another splendid monochrome of this period, *A Shadowed Stream.*[2] See also No. 129 for a further discussion of this technique.

[1]See No. 128. [2]BM 1902-5-14-57.

10
The Last Year
1841-1842

Nothing survives of Cotman's correspondence from November 1839 until July 1841. Kitson surmised that Cotman suffered a serious breakdown during this period, but there is little evidence to support this. Indeed, Cotman's earliest surviving letter from 1841[1] is to Dawson Turner, telling him about a copy of Rubens' *The Judgement of Paris* by Jordaens which he might like to add to his collection. In the event Dawson Turner was not interested, and Cotman bought it for himself: 'I could not resist it and I have bought it. By lamplight it is a golden sun.'[2] It appears that Cotman was living in much the same fashion as before the break in correspondence.

In the summer of 1841 Cotman was as close to his long-standing patron as he had ever been. In thanking Turner for a copy of the catalogue of his illustrations to Blomefield, Cotman remarked: 'I have profited by your advice in all things, save one —that of buying books . . . With all my faults I have ever glassed myself at your glass, however far I may be from your fashion. It is the truest and surest proof I can render you of my sincere and longstanding respect for your sound judgement.'[3] Three weeks later Cotman reminds Turner how he had written to say that he would visit his old protegé in London 'and shake me by the hand once again before we died . . . I know of no man, save Hudson Gurney, whose esteem I more truly value and always did, than yourself.'[4]

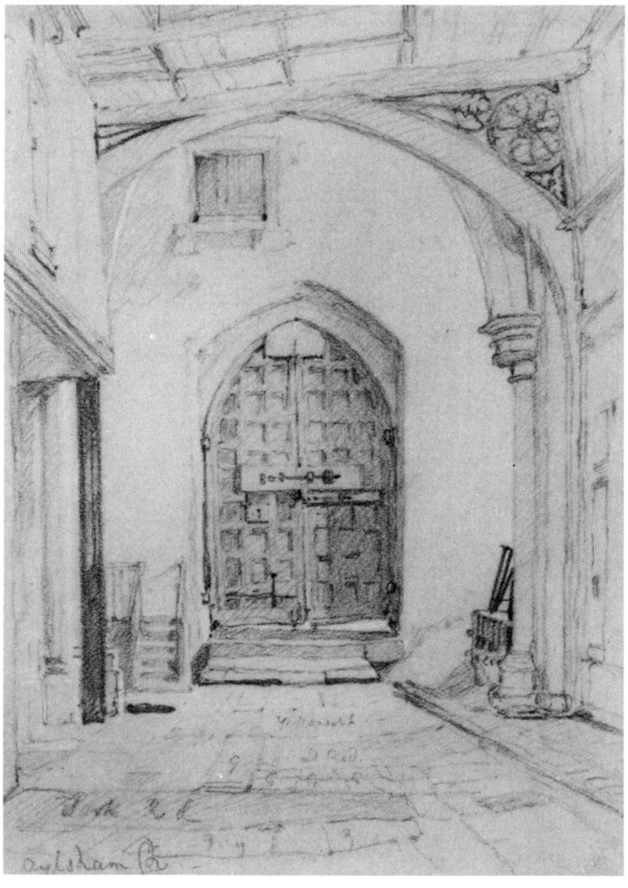

135 Aylsham Church, Norfolk, Interior, ?8 October 1841

In September 1841 Cotman determined to take a holiday, to return to Norfolk to revisit old haunts and friends, including the Rev. James Bulwer, the Rev. John Gunn and his wife Harriet and the Turner Family at Yarmouth. His monochrome paste drawings of remembered Norfolk scenes indicate that his thoughts had often returned to his native county (Nos. 129-133). His friend James Bulwer had himself only recently moved back from London to Norfolk, shortly after the death of his father the previous year, to live in the Manor House, Aylsham. In August 1841 Bulwer was licensed to the Curacy of Blickling, with Erpingham, within the Diocese of Norwich. Bulwer was also an amateur artist who shared Cotman's passion for sketching the churches of Norfolk. On 24 September 1841 Cotman wrote to Bulwer: 'Get your sketching maps in good order, my dear Bulwer, for I meditate a descent on you; and 'tis hard if, between us, we don't demolish a church or two. The Principal of King's College has given me a holiday of a fortnight, but I shall stretch it to three weeks or nearly so, for Edmund can do my duty, (though he is really ill), till I return to meet my extra duties in the upper department.'[5]

Cotman was away in Norfolk for almost two months, such was his enthusiasm, despite intermittent torrential rains which caused flooding in the area. Kitson refers to Cotman as an 'elderly truant'[6] at this time, sketching with the carefree abandon of his youth in Wales and Yorkshire. The evidence of his many surviving drawings in black and white chalks, often dated and inscribed, reveal the joy with which Cotman sketched the scenes of his native county. In addition to facilitating the reconstruction of Cotman's itinerary for much of his holiday, the drawings represent the consummation of Cotman's late career, being 'among the most purposeful studies done direct from Nature which have ever been produced by a landscape painter'.[6] Although many are annotated with colour notes, indicating that Cotman envisaged taking them further in the mediums of watercolour and perhaps oil, the drawings were the focus of admiration at a 'conversazione' held at the end of the holiday.[7] Miles Edmund subsequently selected twelve which he published as lithographs after his father's death.

It seems likely that Cotman's first subject was Devil's Tower, Norwich (No. 134). Three sketches survive, all bearing the date of 2 October, which find Cotman sketching near the Geldarts' house at Whitlingham,[8] on the banks of the Yare[9] and at Colonel Harvey's meadow at Thorpe.[10] It is possible that over the next few days he visited west of Norwich, an undated sketch of *Kimberley (a Falgate)* being subsequently lithographed by his son. On 7 October he was again on the banks of the Yare, sketching the Red House near Norwich.[11] The following day appears to be the first occasion on which he is likely to have visited Bulwer, giving him an opportunity to sketch Bulwer's Church at Aylsham (see Nos. 135, 136) and Wickmere Church on 9 October (No. 137). The next day he travelled to stay the night at Irmingland Hall (Nos. 139-141) sketching Hanworth Hall briefly on the journey (No. 138). He continued to Cromer, sketching the lighthouse on 13 October.[12] Cotman then returned to Norwich where he was staying with his son John Joseph at his lodgings at Heigham Terrace. It was from here that he wrote to Dawson Turner on 17 October to announce his forthcoming visit to Yarmouth: 'I

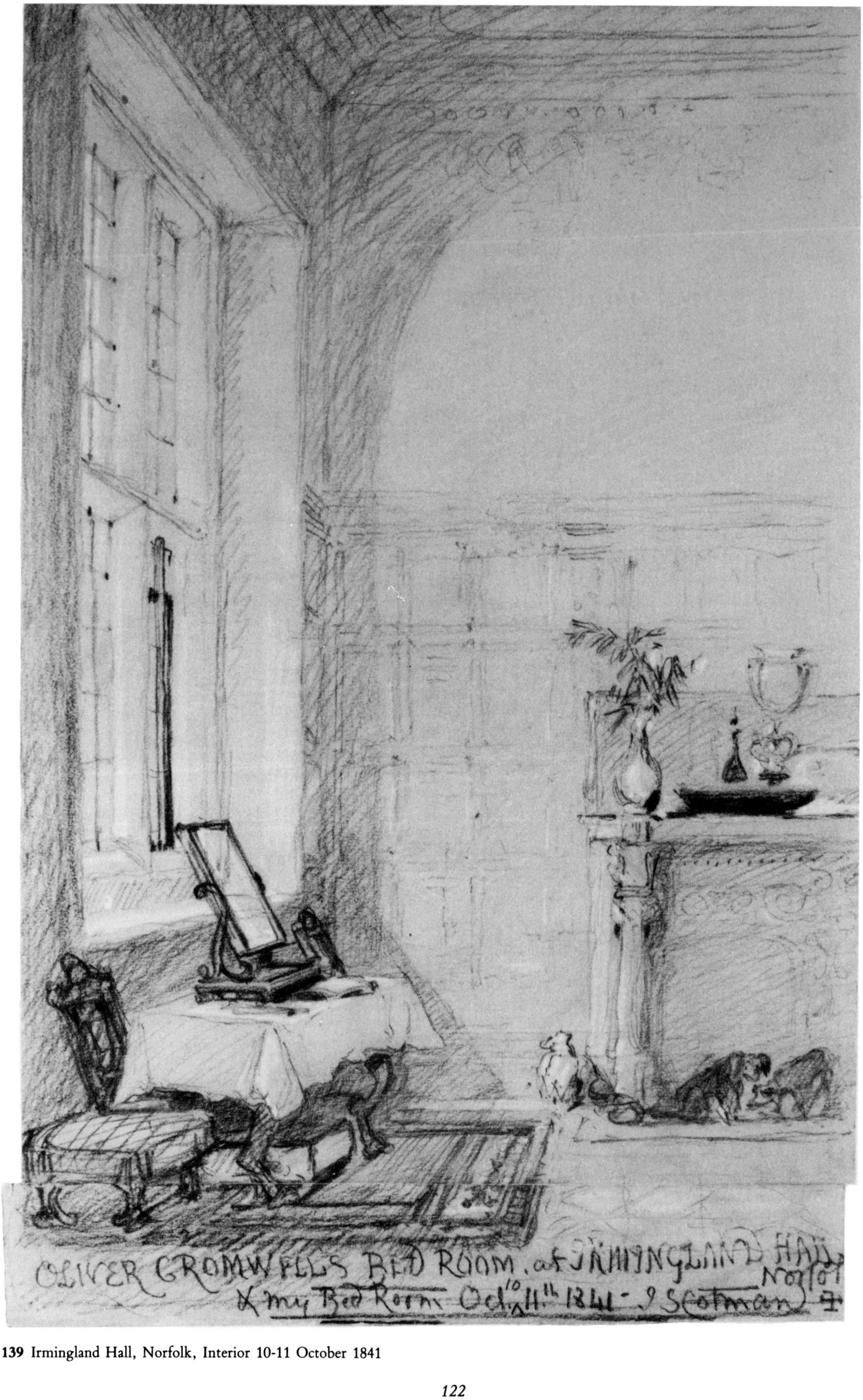

139 Irmingland Hall, Norfolk, Interior 10-11 October 1841

have been sketching on our River, and at Hanworth, Cromer and Sheringham, the wilderness of Norfolk . . . I came here really for my health. Judge for yourself my happiness on finding your Norfolk flints capable of once more creating a blaze in my heart, and I have been hard at work at my delightful profession, as when you first saw me at work in my room at Wymer Street.'[13]

Cotman set off for Yarmouth by steamer, accompanied by John Joseph, on 19 October. Three sketches survive from this trip, which reveal considerable flooding of the countryside, while the trees bend to the fury of the wind. One view, of windmills *Below Langley,*[14] was later lithographed by Miles Edmund while another, *Below Hardley Cross,*[15] is inscribed with the comment 'The Wold Afloat'. Cotman and his son stayed for some ten days at Bank House with the Turners. One drawing of the North Sands at Yarmouth dates from this visit, known by Miles Edmund's subsequent tracing for an unpublished lithograph.[16] They travelled back to Norwich by steamer, on 29 October, a journey recorded by three drawings, including a view of Postwick Grove[17] under heavy floodwater and a view of Reedham.[18]

The following day Cotman wrote to Dawson Turner to thank him for his hospitality: 'On the return journey the deck of the steamer opened up to me scenes that I must never hope to witness again. All was desolation and dreariness. It was sublime. It was a day to be remembered, entirely and especially by an artist, for it gave a power to wildness that I never before ever imagined.'[19] That same day he sketched[20] the view from his son's lodgings, while Robert Geldart's diary records that 'the Cotmans etc. spent the evening at my house, and Old Cotman put a new foreground in chalk to one of my brother Joseph's sketches.'[21] The next morning Robert Geldart visited Heigham Terrace 'and saw some of Old Cotman's sketches which he has recently made. The valleys round here are all flooded on account of the incessant rains.'[21] That day Cotman sketched 'Thorpe Meadows during a great flood.'[22]

Both Miles Edmund and Dawson Turner wrote to express concern that Cotman should not over-exert himself in search of subjects to sketch, but he explained that ''tis as impossible to pass a fine subject and not to book it as it is for a miser to pass a guinea and not pick it up.'[23] This letter also states his intention to dine with his father that day, when he probably sketched the view *From my Father's House at Thorpe* (see No. 168) and possibly a drawing inscribed 'Quite at home. November 3 1841 JSC.'[24] The next day Cotman and his son went to Irstead to stay with the Gunns, arriving on the 4 November and leaving two days later. At least three drawings[25] survive of the area around Irstead and Barton Broad sketched during this visit.

The following week Cotman again visited Bulwer in order 'to demolish a church or two'. He visited Marsham Church (No. 142) on the way, and was probably accompanied by Bulwer on his visits to Blickling (No. 143) and Tuttington (No. 144). They visited Itteringham[26] on 12 November, on their way to Wolterton Hall where they wished particularly to see Rubens' *The Rainbow Landscape,* now in the Wallace Collection, London. When they arrived Cotman paused in the portico to sketch 'A remarkable & beautiful coincidence a fine rainbow appearing at the very moment we alighted under the portico of Wolterton to see the glorious one painted by Rubens.'[27] A sketch[28] also survives in the British Museum executed on the drive back to Aylsham that day. It was probably during this visit that Cotman sketched the Hollyhock Walk in Bulwer's garden at Aylsham.[29] On 14 November Cotman braved the stormy weather to make a last excursion to Cromer.[30] The next day he sketched a final half-length portrait of his host, which he set in an elaborately depicted frame which he inscribed 'To the Revd Jas. Bulwer $\frac{1}{2}$ past 12 o'clock pm Nov. 15th 1841—sketched during a heavy Gale of Hail, Sleet & Wind.'[31] An inscribed and dated drawing, *Norwich from the Cromer Road*[32] reveals that the storm abated enough for Cotman to return to Norwich that afternoon.

Cotman's thirst for subjects to sketch remained insatiable to the very end of his truancy. On 17 November he sketched Mousehold Heath[33] and returned again the following day, as he recounts with characteristic enthusiasm in his letter to Dawson Turner, after his return to London on 20 November: 'I galloped over Mousehold Heath on that day, for my time was short, through a heavy hail-storm, to dine with my Father—but was obliged to stop and sketch a magnificent scene on the top of the hill leading down to Col. Harvey's house, of trees and gravel pit. But Norfolk is full of such scenes. Oh! rare and beautiful Norfolk.'[34] The resulting sketch[35] is a vast composition, executed on three sheets of conjoined paper, subsequently lithographed by Miles Edmund.

Back in Bloomsbury Cotman was faced once again with family problems, particularly over the 'distressing and dangerous scenes'[34] caused by Alfred. While some sketches reveal that he proceeded to work up some of his compositions,[36] there are no letters or dated drawings for the last six months of his life. The entry in Robert Geldart's diary for 20 June 1842 finds him visiting the Cotmans in London: 'Old Cotman, who was seriously ill, showed us Normandy

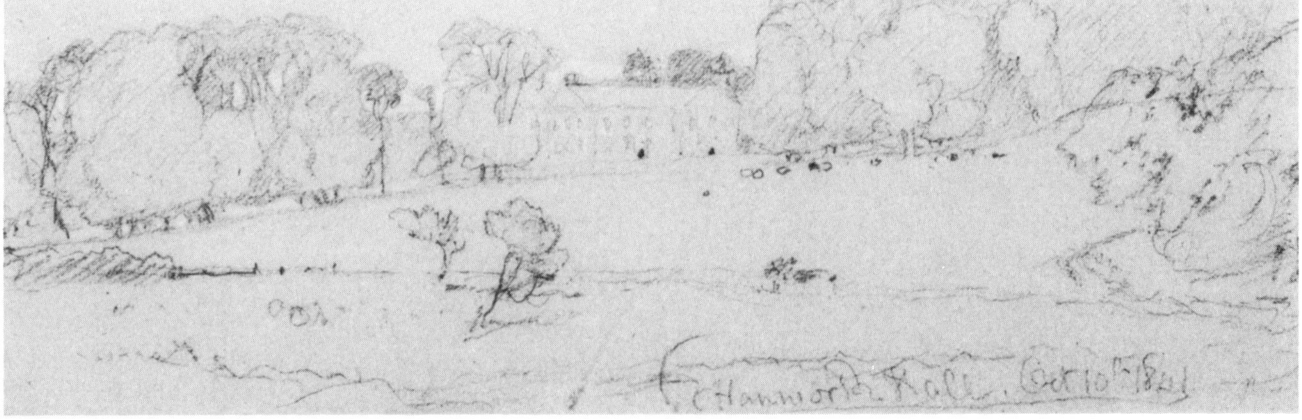

138 Hanworth Hall, Norfolk, 10 October 1841

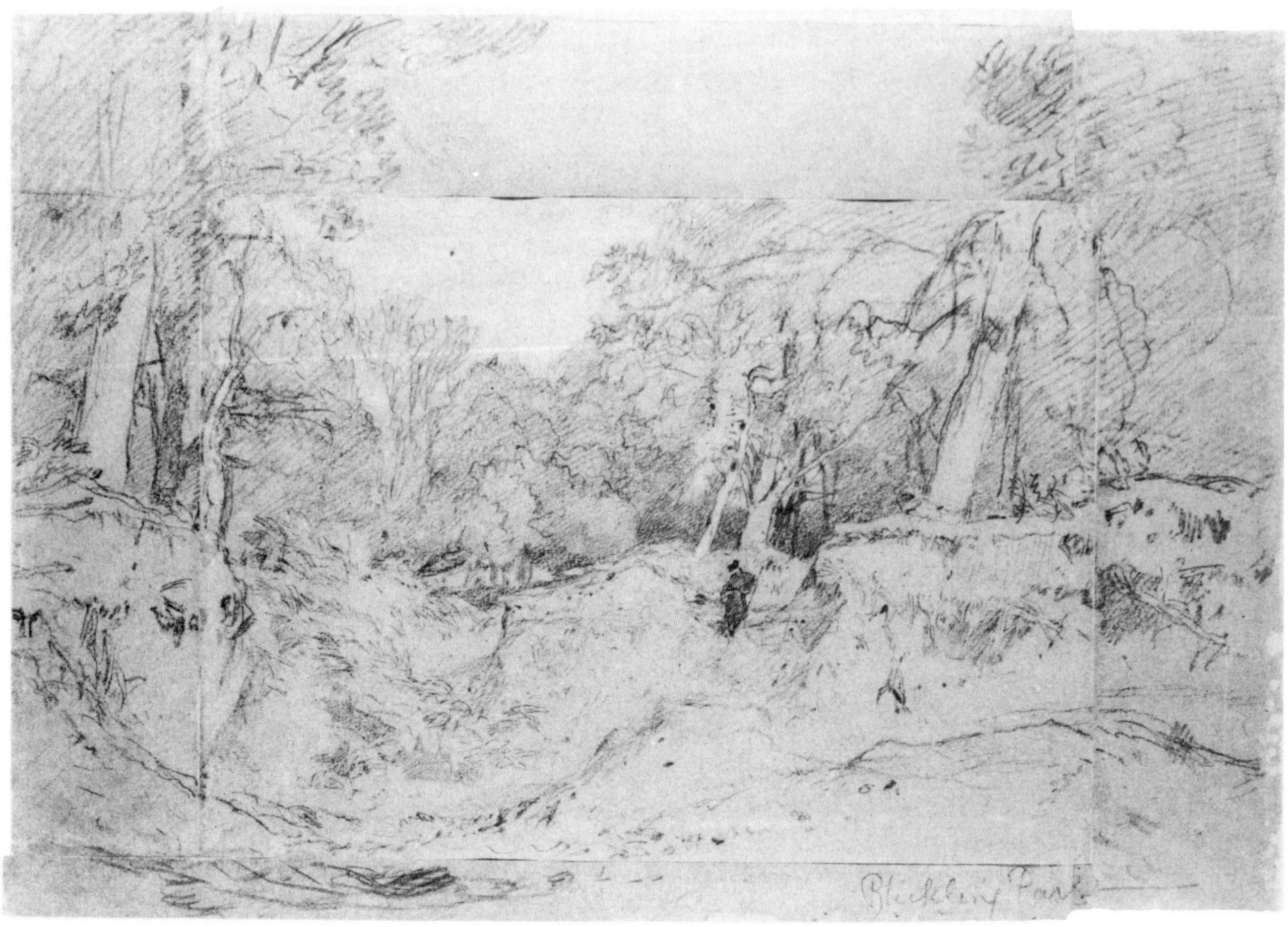

143 Blickling Park, Norfolk, ?10 November 1841

drawings in sepia.'[37] On 22 July Ann wrote to John Joseph a touching account of their father's last days. Neither family nor doctors could encourage him to eat or sleep: 'I am quite sure he does not wish to get well, or he would have made some effort to do so.'[38] On 24 July Cotman died. He was buried six days later in St. John's Wood Chapel Churchyard, Marylebone.

Notes

[1]JSC to DT, 21 July 1841 (Barker Collection). [2]JSC to JJC, undated but August 1841 (BM). [3]JSC to DT, 12 Aug. 1841 (Barker Collection). [4]*Ibid.* 3 Sept. 1841. [5]JSC to JB, 24 Sept. 1841 (Kitson, 1937, p. 354). [6]Kitson 1937 p. 355. [7]*Ibid.* p. 361. [8]BM 1902-5-14-142. [9]BM 1902-5-14-143. [10]BM 1902-5-14-173 is the tracing by MEC for the lithograph. [11]Bacon No. 822, lithographed by MEC. [12]Kitson 1937 p. 356, whereabouts unknown. [13]Barker Collection. [14]BM 1902-5-14-145 (the preparatory tracing by MEC is NCM 319.235.951). [15]BM 1902-5-14-146. The third drawing of this date is BM 1902-5-14-147. [16]NCM 364.235.951. [17]BM 1902-5-14-149. [18]Manning Galleries, June 1968 (26). See also BM 1902-5-14-148. [19]Barker Collection. [20]BM 1902-5-14-150. [21]Kitson 1937 p. 358. [22]BM 1902-5-14-151. [23]JSC to DT, 3 Nov. 1841 (Barker Collection). [24]Kitson 1937 p. 359, whereabouts unknown. Kitson suggests a visit to Heydon Hall, but this is unlikely. [25]BM 1902-5-14-153 and 154; NCM 317.235.951. [26]Bacon Collection, No. 824; the tracing by MEC for the lithograph is NCM 353.235.951. [27]BM 1902-5-14-158. [28]BM 1902-5-14-157. [29]BM 1902-5-14-159. [30]BM 1902-5-14-160. [31]BM 1902-5-14-163. [32]BM 1902-5-14-161. [33]BM 1902-5-14-164. [34]JSC to DT 20 Nov. 1841 (Barker Collection). [35]BM 1902-5-14-168. [36]cf. BM 1902-5-14-170 and 172. See also No. 168. [37]Kitson 1937 p. 363. [38]AC to JJC, 22 July 1842 (BM).

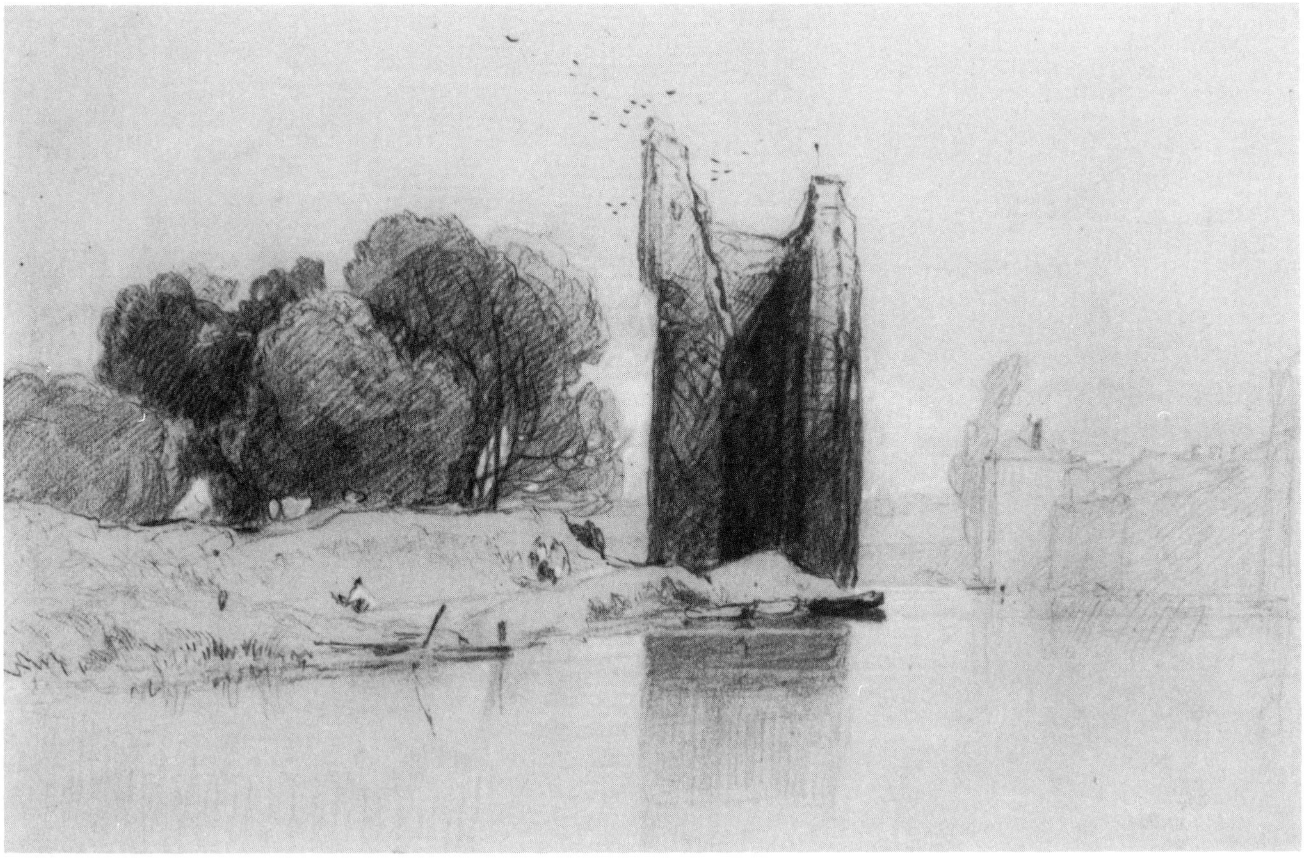

134 The Devil's Tower, Norwich, October 1841

134 The Devil's Tower, Norwich, October 1841

Black chalk heightened with white chalk on brown, wove paper; 24.1 × 36.9 ($9\frac{1}{2} \times 14\frac{1}{2}$). PROV: John Joseph Cotman; bt. from him by James Reeve 1864; bt. from him by R. J. Colman; R. J. Colman Bequest 1946 (338.235.951). REF: Kitson 1937 p. 356; Rajnai & Allthorpe No. 1 n.6.

This is possibly the earliest of the series of drawings executed by Cotman during his last visit to Norwich and Norfolk in the autumn of 1841. The drawing was one of twelve sketches from his last holiday which were lithographed by Miles Edmund Cotman and published as a set after Cotman's death. The lithograph version reveals the inscribed title and the date 'Oct 1841', at some stage cut from the bottom edge of the drawing.

The maturity of Cotman's powerful vision is apparent in a comparition of No. 134 with the depictions of the same subject executed at the outset of his career (see Nos. 1 and 2). The assured handling of the dominant silhouette of the tower is emphasised by the subtlety with which the backs of the King Street buildings to the right are lightly sketched in profile. The scene is a view from up river and shows the further deterioration of the fabric of the tower since the beginning of the century (see No. 1).

135 Aylsham Church, Norfolk, Interior, ?8 October 1841
illustrated on p. 121

Black chalk heightened with white chalk on brown, wove paper; 36 × 26 ($14\frac{3}{16} \times 10\frac{1}{4}$). INSCR: inscribed in black chalk l.r. *Aylsham Ch.* and with colour notes. PROV: See No. 134. (314.235.951).

Cotman appears to have visited James Bulwer at his home in Aylsham on two occasions during his autumn holiday in Norfolk. Cotman had written to Bulwer from London to suggest sketching in harness to 'demolish a church or two'[1] and he visited him on 8-9 October and again on 9-15 November.[2]

It is perhaps most likely that Cotman would choose to 'demolish' Bulwer's local church at the first available opportunity. No. 135 shows the west door as the central feature of a design which, as evidenced by the extensive colour notes, Cotman intended to transform subsequently into a watercolour version. Miles Edmund lithographed this drawing[3] together with eleven others after Cotman's death. The preparatory drawing made from No. 135 for the lithograph is in a private collection.[4] See No. 136 for a further drawing presumably executed during the same visit.

[1]JSC to Rev. J. Bulwer, 24 Sept. 1841 (Barker Collection). [2]See section 10, pp. 121, 123 [3]MEC omitted all but one of JSC's colour notes. [4]Oxford (1973).

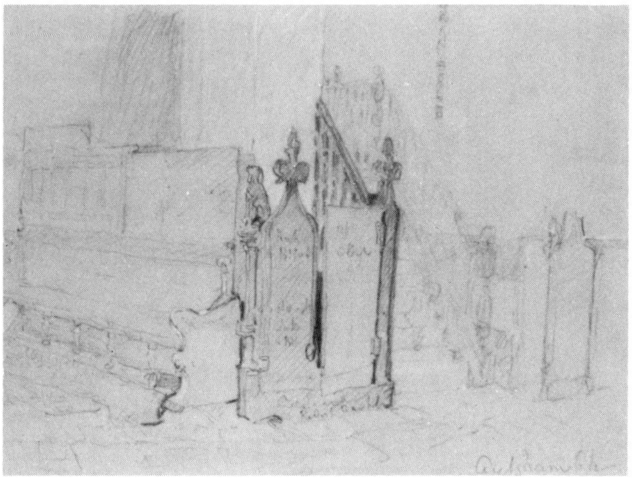

136 Aylsham Church, Norfolk, Pew Ends, ?8 October 1841

136 Aylsham Church, Norfolk, Pew Ends, ?8 October 1841

Black chalk heightened with white chalk on grey-brown, wove paper; 26.1 × 34.4 ($10\frac{1}{4} \times 13\frac{1}{2}$). INSCR: inscribed in black chalk l.r. *Aylsham Ch-* [cut] and with colour notes. PROV: See No. 134. (315.235.951).

One of the features of St. Michael's Church, Aylsham is the West

Gallery, to which the staircase featured in this drawing, leads. As in No. 135, there are extensive colour notes. The same staircase and viewpoint is featured in a watercolour[1] by Bulwer which appears to date from a later period, possibly after the restoration of the church which took place in 1852.[2]

[1]NCM 27.B29.235.951. [2]Pevsner, *North-East Norfolk and Norwich* p. 77.

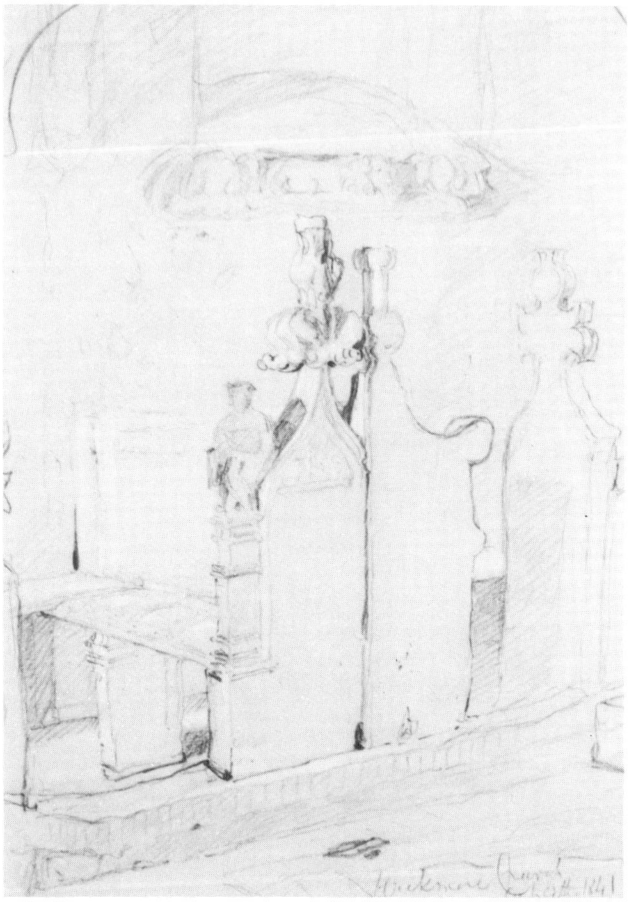

137 Wickmere Church, Norfolk, Poppy Heads, 9 October, 1841

137 Wickmere Church, Norfolk, Poppy Heads, 9 October 1841

Black chalk heightened with white chalk on light brown, wove paper; 37.5 × 26.1 ($14\frac{3}{4}$ × $10\frac{1}{4}$). INSCR: inscribed and dated in black chalk l.r. *Wickmere Church / Oct. 9th. 1841* [cut]. PROV: See No. 134 (403.235.951).

The church of St. Andrew at Wickmere is some four miles north of Aylsham. This rapid but noble sketch shows the carved poppy heads of the pews in the north aisle together with the large corbel which is a feature of that aisle. James Bulwer accompanied Cotman on this visit and also sketched the same corbel.[1] Bulwer's version, dated 1841, shows the carving of the corbel to consist of a crouching lion, bordered by the head of an angel to each side. A later drawing[2] of the same view by Bulwer, but dated 1847 and prosaic by comparison, shows the carved figure on one of the poppy heads playing a lute.

There are a number of drawings of Wickmere Church by James Bulwer in the collections at Norwich of which three[3] show the compositional influence of Cotman and may date from this visit. Cotman himself made a second sketch[4] of the interior at Wickmere on 9 October, which was subsequently lithographed by Miles Edmund Cotman.[5]

[1]NCM, Todd Box 13, Part II p. 136. [2]NCM 27.B252.235.951. [3]NCM 27.B72.235.951; 27.B183.235.951; 27.B239.235.951. [4]BM 1902-5-14-144. [5]Preparatory tracing by MEC: NCM 404.235.951.

138 Hanworth Hall, Norfolk, 10 October 1841

illustrated on p. 123

Black chalk heightened with white on blue-grey wove paper; 12.7 × 37.6 (5 × $14\frac{3}{4}$). INSCR: inscribed and dated in black chalk l.r. *Hanworth Hall. Oct. 10th. 1841.* PROV: See No. 134.[1] (346.235.951). REF: Kitson 1937 p. 356.

Kitson postulates that James Bulwer accompanied Cotman throughout his excursion through north east Norfolk, but there is no evidence to support this. Cotman was on his way to spend the night at Irmingland Hall, but was able to make this rapid sketch en route.

Cotman was already familiar with the Hall, and had sketched it when still under the ownership of Robert Lee Doughty (died June 1819). His original drawing was engraved by J. Acon for *Excursions through Norfolk*, published in 1818. On the occasion of his visit in 1841 Cotman was not concerned to delineate the architectural details of this fine, early eighteenth-century, red-brick house, although his sense of composition recalls his earlier sketches of Halls for the *Excursions through Norfolk* (see No. 80).

[1]Robert Leman's sale, Spelman, Norwich, 23 April 1863, lot 118, *A Series of 34 Drawings . . .* included a chalk drawing by J. S. Cotman of Hanworth Hall.

139 Irmingland Hall, Norfolk, Interior, 10-11 October 1841

illustrated on p. 122

Black chalk heightened with white chalk on two pieces of grey-green, wove paper joined along lower edge; 41.5 × 26.1 ($16\frac{5}{16}$ × $10\frac{1}{4}$). INSCR: *Recto*, inscribed, dated and signed in black chalk lower edge *OLIVER CROMWELL'S BED ROOM, at IRMINGLAND HALL / NORFOLK / & my Bed Room Oct. 10 11th.—J S COTMAN; verso,* sketch in black chalk of a portrait of a small girl, inscribed lower edge *MARTHA. Daughter of / George & Katherine Cross. / of ARMINGLAND* [sic] *Hall / Norfolk / Born Sep 10th. 1840.* PROV: See No. 134. (352.235.951). REF: Kitson 1937 p. 356.

This drawing documents Cotman's overnight stay at Irmingland Hall, Norfolk on 10 October 1841. Kitson supposes that Bulwer was with him, but there is no evidence to support this assumption. The inscription on the reverse of the drawing suggests that Cotman was a guest of the owners, George and Katherine Cross. The sketch of their baby daughter on the reverse of the sheet is a delightful portrait of Martha at the age of thirteen months. Kitson's assertion that 'Cotman, still unwearied, made a drawing of his bedroom by candlelight after everyone else had retired to rest' seems to have little foundation. The sun streams through the window, while the inscription adds the date of the 10 October as an afterthought, suggesting that Cotman made the drawing on the morning of 11 October.

It is typical of Cotman that he should respond to the tradition that Cromwell, whose son-in-law General Fleetwood once lived at Irmingland Hall, had stayed at Irmingland. Built in 1609, only the east wing of the Hall now remains.[1]

[1]Pevsner, *North-East Norfolk and Norwich* p. 178.

140 Irmingland Hall, Norfolk, Interior, 10-11 October 1841

illustrated on opposite page

Black chalk heightened with white chalk on four pieces of grey-blue, wove paper, joined; 41.9 × 56.3 ($16\frac{1}{2}$ × $22\frac{1}{8}$). INSCR: inscribed in black chalk lower edge *(This room 20 feet in height) / Now used as a Kitchen. Armingland* [sic] *Hall. a residence of Oliver Cromwell. vide Blomfields / Norfolk,* and with colour notes. PROV: ?Cubitt sale, Norwich, 10 Sept. 1917, lot 20, *Two pencil sketches—Kitchens at Armingland Hall,* 24s.; R. J. Colman Bequest 1946 (351.235.951).

This drawing presumably arises from the same circumstances as those outlined in the previous entry and is executed on the same coloured paper as No. 139.

Another view of Irmingland Hall Kitchen[1] is in the collections at Norwich and must date from the same visit, albeit drawn on a buff coloured sheet, in contrast to the paper used for Nos. 139 and 140. See also No. 141 for another drawing made on this visit.

[1]NCM 350.235.951.

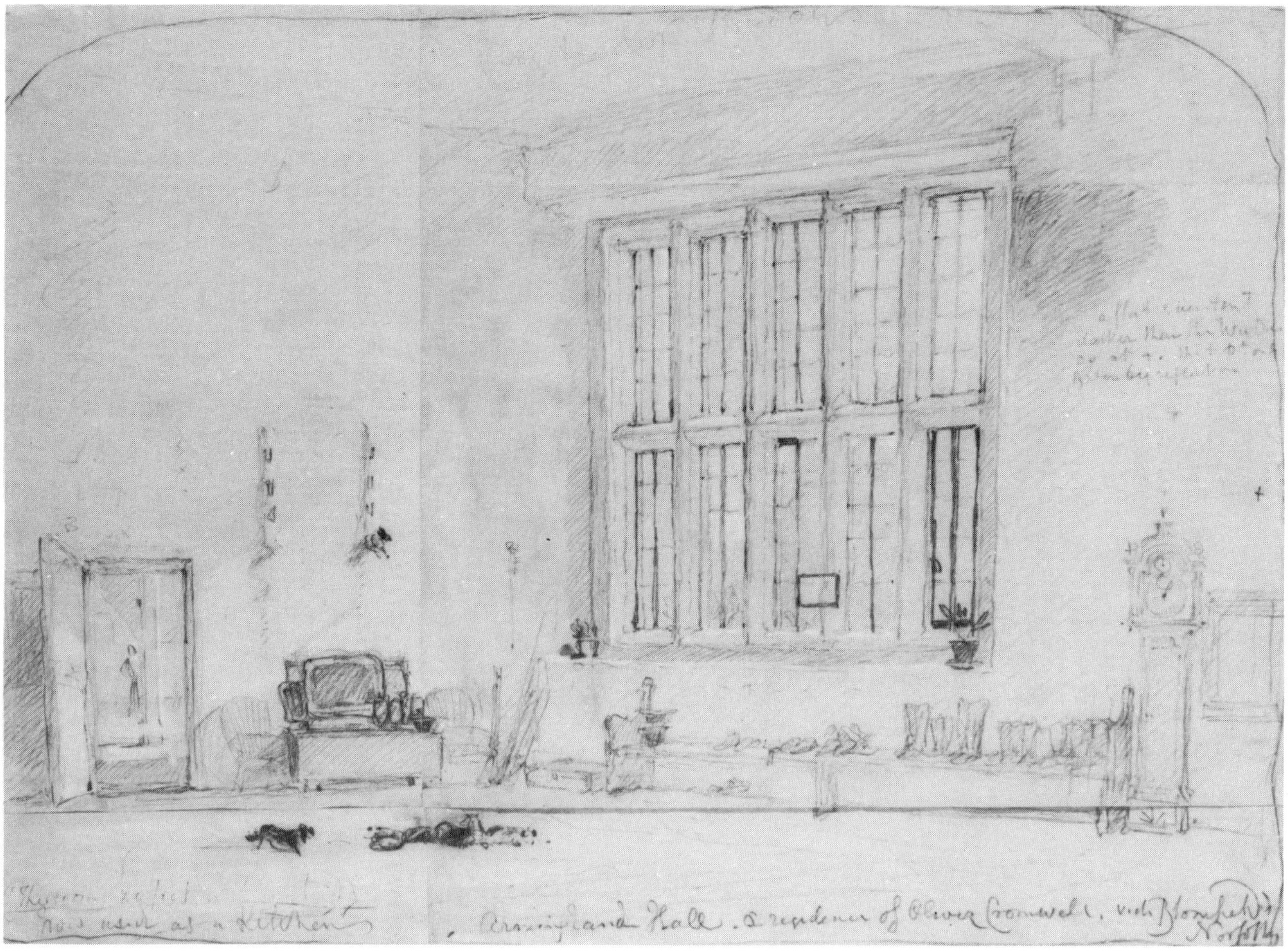

140 Irmingland Hall, Norfolk, Interior, 10-11 October 1841

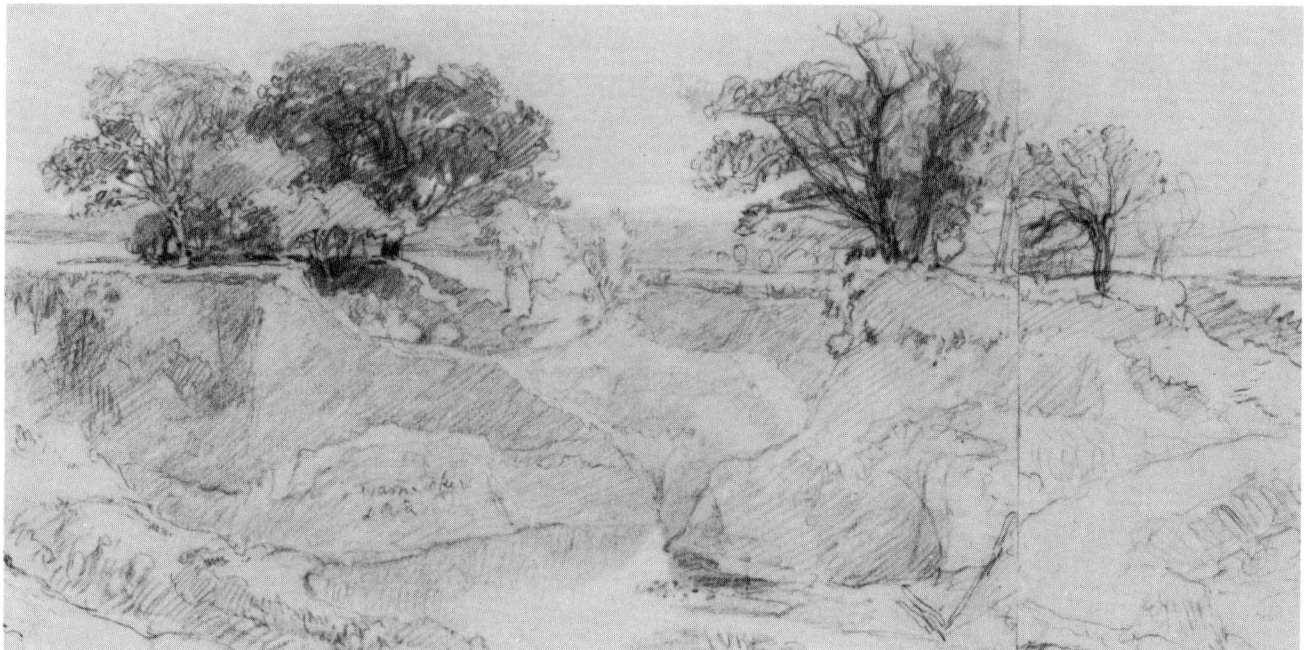

141 Irmingland, Norfolk (Trees and Vale), 10-11 October 1841

141 Irmingland, Norfolk (Trees and Vale), 10-11 October 1841
illustrated on p. 127

Black chalk heightened with white chalk on dark brownish-grey, paper joined at right; 26 × 48.1 ($10\frac{1}{4}$ × $18\frac{15}{16}$). INSCR: inscribed in black chalk l.l. *Irmingland* and with colour notes. PROV: See No. 134 (349.235.951).

Irmingland is a small parish and village, just over five miles to the north-west of Aylsham, with a recorded population of thirteen inhabitants in 1841.

This rapid sketch, with hasty, hatched shading, illustrates the continued breadth and grandeur of Cotman's inherent sense of design. The scene appears to represent a flooded quarry. The hieroglyphs of the design create a composition of absolute poise and equilibrium.

For further details concerning Cotman's visit to Irmingland Hall see Nos. 139 and 140.

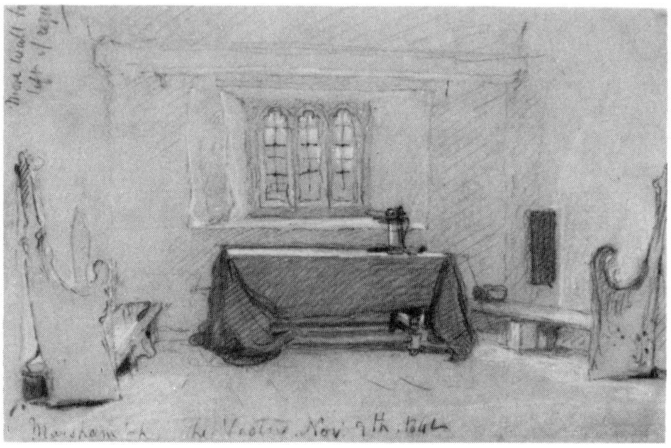

142 The Vestry, Marsham Church, Norfolk, 9 November 1841

142 The Vestry, Marsham Church, Norfolk, 9 November 1841

Black chalk heightened with white on brown, wove paper; 24.5 × 37.7 ($9\frac{5}{8}$ × $14\frac{13}{16}$). INSCR: inscribed and dated in black chalk l.l. *Marsham Ch. The Vestry. Nov. 9th. 1841.* and note u.l. (cut). PROV: ?Anon. sale, Mealing Mills, Norwich, 9 July 1918, lot 238 *Marsham Vestry 1842* [sic], 12s.6d.; R. J. Colman Bequest 1946. (360.235.951).

Cotman visited the Rev. James Bulwer for a second time in the autumn of 1841, shortly after spending three days with his son John Joseph at the home of the Rev. John Gunn at Irstead.[1] Despite a number of drawings by Bulwer of the stained glass and interior of the church of All Saints, Marsham there is no evidence that Bulwer accompanied Cotman on 9 November.

Cotman executed at least three drawings of the interior of Marsham Church. No. 142 shows the interior of the vestry in a simple sketch, on which the inscribed aide-memoire, 'More wall to [the] left if requ[ired]' indicates his intention to produce a more finished design at a later date. A second view of the vestry, sketched at the same visit but this time in a vertical format, is now in the Fitzwilliam Museum.[2] A third interior view,[3] subsequently lithographed by Miles Edmund Cotman, shows the steps and rails leading to the altar. Cotman's company on this occasion was a black cat, depicted asleep at the foot of the carpet-covered steps.

James Bulwer subsequently painted a watercolour copy[4] of No. 142 and also executed a similar version[5] of the scene lithographed by Miles Edmund.

[1]See section 10, p. 123. [2]Fitzwilliam Museum, 3273. [3]BM 1902-5-14-155. [4]NCM 27.B266.235.951. [5]NCM 27.B194.235.951.

143 Blickling Park, Norfolk, ?10 November 1841
illustrated on p. 124

Black chalk on five sheets of blue-grey wove paper, joined; 34.7 × 48.2 ($13\frac{11}{16}$ × 19). INSCR: inscribed in black chalk l.r. *Blickling Park* PROV: H. S. Theobald; bt. from him by R. J. Colman, Feb. 1910; R. J. Colman Bequest 1946. (322.235.951). EXH: Tate 1922 (180).

A vigorous drawing[1] by Cotman inscribed 'The Pound at Blickling Nov. 10 1841' reveals the date on which No. 143 was almost certainly sketched.[2] It seems that Cotman was again accompanied by James Bulwer, who may be the figure depicted in this drawing. The grounds of Blickling Park were a favourite sketching spot for Bulwer. A number of watercolours by him of this area are in the collections at Norwich, of which two similar views[3] may be derived from sketches made on this visit. He had been licensed to the curacy of Blickling with Erpingham on 14 August that year.

[1]BM 1902-5-14-156. [2]For another sketch from this visit, see *An Old Chest* inscribed *Blickling* and dated 10 Nov. 1841, Leeds 9.682.49. [3]27.B33.235.951 and 27.B34.235.951.

144 Tuttington Church Interior, 11 November 1841
illustrated on opposite page

Black chalk heightened with white chalk on brown, wove paper; 36.9 × 26.7 ($14\frac{1}{2}$ × $10\frac{1}{2}$). INSCR: *Recto,* inscribed and dated in black chalk u.l. *Tuttington Ch / Nov. 11th. 1841* and with colour notes u.r.; *verso,* inscribed in black chalk:

Blake. Swanton Abbots
William Spinks 80. } *died this day*
John Wright—36. or 37. }
Flora. died this day. Nov. 11th 1841

PROV: See No. 134. (395.235.951). REF: Kitson 1937 p. 360.

Kitson comments on the 'picturesque confusion' of the benches with their carved poppy-heads. Cotman has arranged the components of his composition to include certain features of the church of St. Peter and St. Paul at Tuttington. The south door has swung open to reveal its exterior ironwork, while one of the pews to the right is foreshortened to reveal two carvings: a woman making butter and a woman with a basket and pig.

James Bulwer accompanied Cotman on his visit to Tuttington. A drawing[1] of the church font and cover by Bulwer is dated 'Nov. 11 1841'. Bulwer's viewpoint, similar to that of Cotman, reveals the extent to which Cotman selected his elements, in this case ignoring the font and repositioning the pew to the right. Bulwer was to return to Tuttington five years later in order to sketch this same poppy-head.[2]

No. 144 is the most attractive of Cotman's church interiors from this last autumn of his life in Norfolk, and was lithographed by Miles Edmund Cotman. It is interesting to note from the inscriptions on the reverse of the drawing that Cotman chose to record the news, probably via Bulwer, of recent deaths in the parish. In addition to two deaths on that day, he notes the untimely death of Frances Mary Jex Blake, aged twenty-five years, in the nearby parish of Swanton Abbot, on 29 October 1841.[3]

[1]NCM 27.B260.235.951. [2]NCM 27.B209.235.951, one of a series of which another is dated 1846. [3]NCM Todd Box 13, pt. I, p. 123 records the memorials to the Blake family placed in the church of St. Michael, Swanton Abbott.

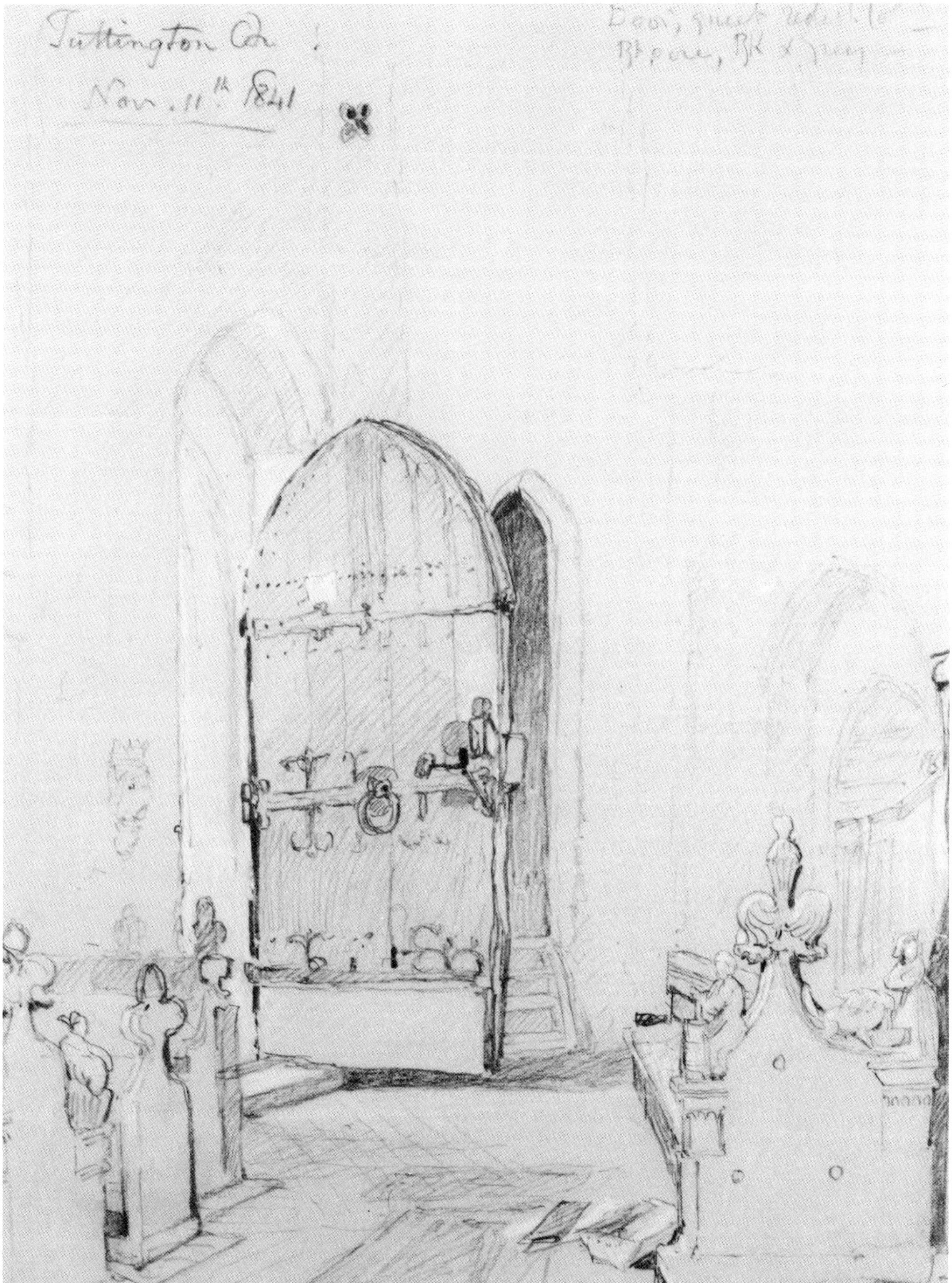

144 Tuttington Church, Interior, 11 November 1841

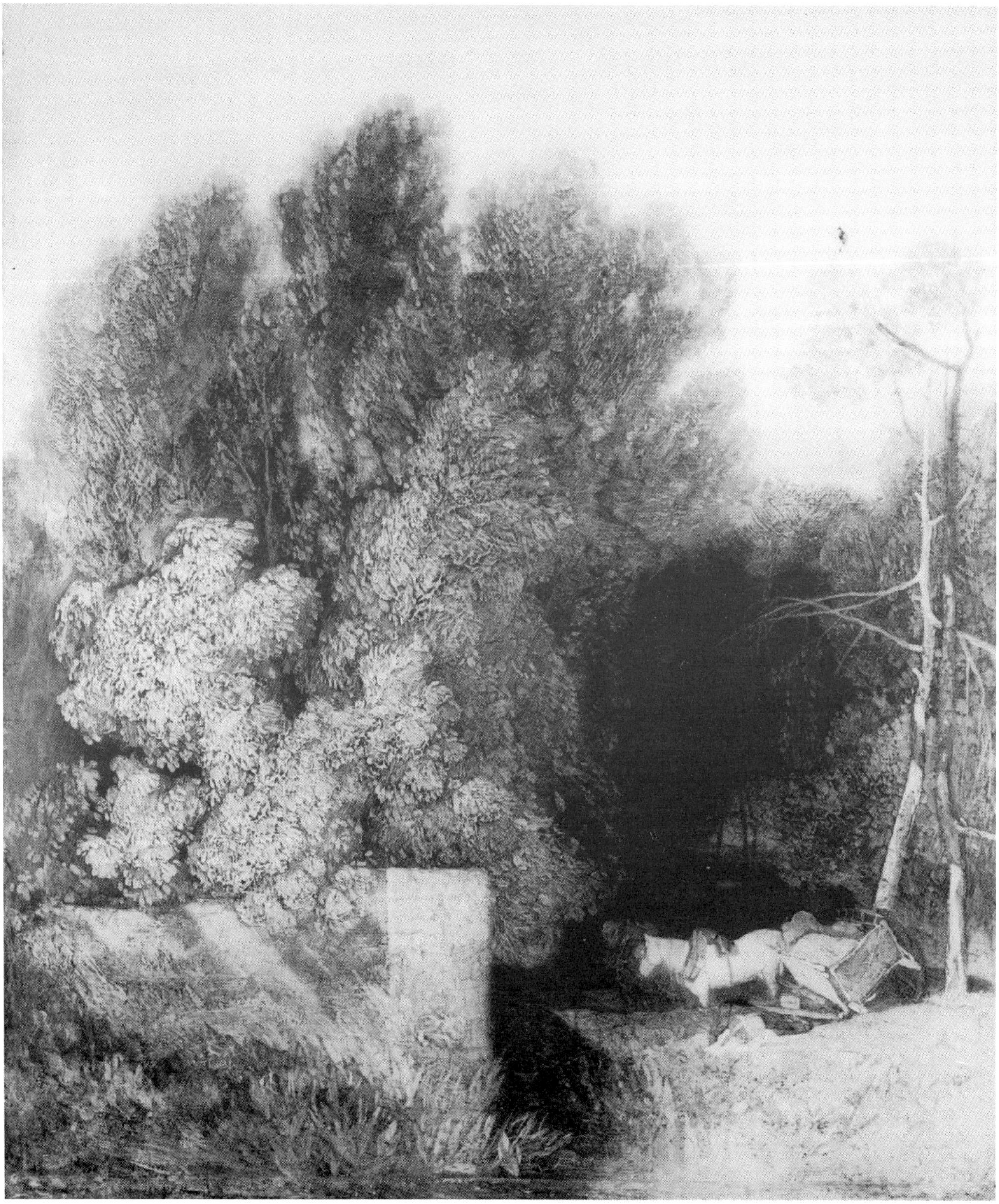

159 The Mishap, *c.*1824-8

11
The Oil Paintings

While Cotman is an undisputed master of watercolour, his achievement as an oil painter has invariably been underrated. Cotman's reputation in this field has suffered from judgements based upon works often either insecurely dated or wrongly attributed. Although it remains difficult to date firmly Cotman's oil paintings through a lack of documentary evidence, it is possible to follow his concerted progress in oils, which reaches a summit at the end of his life, when, on 31 May 1839, he writes to his friend James Bulwer: 'I have been, and am, painting hard, and I am so fond of it that I think I shall never execute another drawing.'[1] Bulwer had recently returned from London to Aylsham and Cotman adds: 'How you are to be envied in your occupation of planning and building, to say nothing of looking after your garden, and watching the ripening of your first strawberries. I know nothing to equal this—but painting.'

Cotman was actively painting in oil at least by the summer of 1806. On 15 October that year he wrote to Dawson Turner of his desire to improve: 'I have much to learn in this great field of study to become tolerably good; for more must be done in this branch of Art than in Water Colours—or nothing is done.'[2] He specifically mentions having almost finished a first effort at oils, a composition of 'Shipping, sea-shore and figures.' On 1 July 1806 he was confident enough to place an advertisement, whilst still residing in London, in the *Norwich Mercury*. The advertisement appeared four days later: 'Mr. J. S. COTMAN Begs leave to inform his Friends, that he intends being in Norwich the beginning of next week, and during his short stay there will give Lessons in Painting and in Water Colours.' This suggests some proficiency in oil painting before his return to Norwich. His London contacts and the annual shows at the Royal Academy, at which he had exhibited drawings regularly from 1800-6, would have provided him with ample contemporary models in this field.

The collection of Cotman's oils at Norwich Castle Museum provides a unique opportunity to survey the breadth of his achievement as an oil painter. It is evident from the early oils of this collection, dating from the period *c.*1807-10 that Cotman was as much dependent upon the work of the Old Masters as upon that of his contemporaries. The catalogues to both his sales in 1834 and 1843 reveal his lifelong habit of collecting prints and the work of both ancient and modern masters. The influence of such masters, however, is rarely as direct as in the field of watercolour where the transition from print to drawing is perhaps more easily accomplished. A debt to Murillo in No. 145 is one of subject, while that to Gaspar Poussin in No. 149 is no more than a painterly reference, as is that to Sebastian Bourdon in *The Waterfall* (No. 148).

Cotman was more attracted to a personal representation of Nature, as can be seen from at least four such subjects exhibited with the Norwich Society in 1808. In addition to *Old Merton* [Moreton] *Hall* (see No. 147), these include the titles *Sketch from Nature, in Oil*[3] and *Study in Oil: Still Life.*[4] From 1807-9 he also exhibited a number of portraits with the Society, some of which were almost certainly in oils, such as *The Beggar Boy* (No. 145) and *Boy at Marbles,*[5] both exhibited in 1808. Both the 1808 and 1809 exhibition catalogues style Cotman as 'Portrait-Painter'. The consummation of this first phase of Cotman's career as an oil painter may be seen in his exhibition of four oils at the British Institution, London, in 1810. Two of these pictures were entitled *Dutch Fishing Boats.*[6] At least one of the exhibits had previously been shown at Norwich in 1808, *Old Merton Hall, Cheshire* (see No. 147) while another subject, *Dutch Boats laying in the river, Yarmouth*[7] could also have been shown at Norwich in 1808 as *Dutch Hoys, Yarmouth River.*[8]

Perhaps the most significant influence upon Cotman's work in oils was the example of J. M. W. Turner. Apart from the evidence of the oils themselves, an illuminating comment upon Turner's work survives in a letter from Cotman to his friend, Francis Cholmeley, written on 5 June 1811. In discussing the current exhibition at the Old Water-Colour Society, he remarks: 'Turner as usual—as usual fine in his pictures, his drawings the compleat opposite of his oils, the lat[te]r pure and silvery, the former yellow and brown, false colour[e]d as if 'twas done as a foil to painting, which is now getting much in fashion, thanks to good taste.' Elsewhere in the same letter he writes of the despair of the watercolourists, the standard of the works being 'not so good as former years, few sold', with Varley being 'blacker than ever, consequently cannot reflect much brilliancy.' It is this 'brilliancy' that Cotman looks for in watercolour, but equally a 'pure and silvery' tone in oil—an effect he achieves most remarkably in No. 153, *Sea View (Fishing Boats),* a composition strongly reminiscent of Turner's early seascapes.

Cotman appears to have painted in oil only intermittently during his Yarmouth years, increasing his work in this medium only after the demands of his Normandy tours were over. He exhibited two oils with the British Institution in 1823 (see No. 155). J. M. W. Turner continued to be a signal influence upon him, a fact recognised by his patron John Bridgman: 'By the way, I think you are very partial to Turner. This may be well to a certain extent, as it may be with Cuyp and Claude; from each of whom whatever they may possess—take it. But do not copy them. You have sufficient excellence to be as original as either of them. Knowing what you do, and possessing an eye so correct in the discernment of colour, you have only to look at Nature in her finest hours, and—taking the most favoured scenes—produce Pictures equal to any of them.'[9] Bridgman's references to Cuyp and Claude are less apposite in the context of Cotman's more original and contemporary vision at this time, but reflect the current conservative notion of the most correct examples to follow.

Having returned from Yarmouth to Norwich in December 1823, Cotman advertised in the *Norwich Mercury* on 17 July 1824 'that his course of instruction in the departments of DRAWING, PAINTING IN OIL and in WATER COLOURS, will Recommence on Monday, the 28th inst.' The next month he exhibited a number of oils with the Norwich Society, and gained a welcome puff from the *Norfolk Chronicle* reviewer: 'The varied products of his fertile pencil ever welcome to our eyes, have served strongly to impress us with the conviction that there is hardly a province of the Arts, whether practised in water colours or in oil, in which by the native force of Genius, if seconded by the impulse of inclination, he would not have arrived at success and distinction.'[10] This approbation came at a time when Cotman was embarking

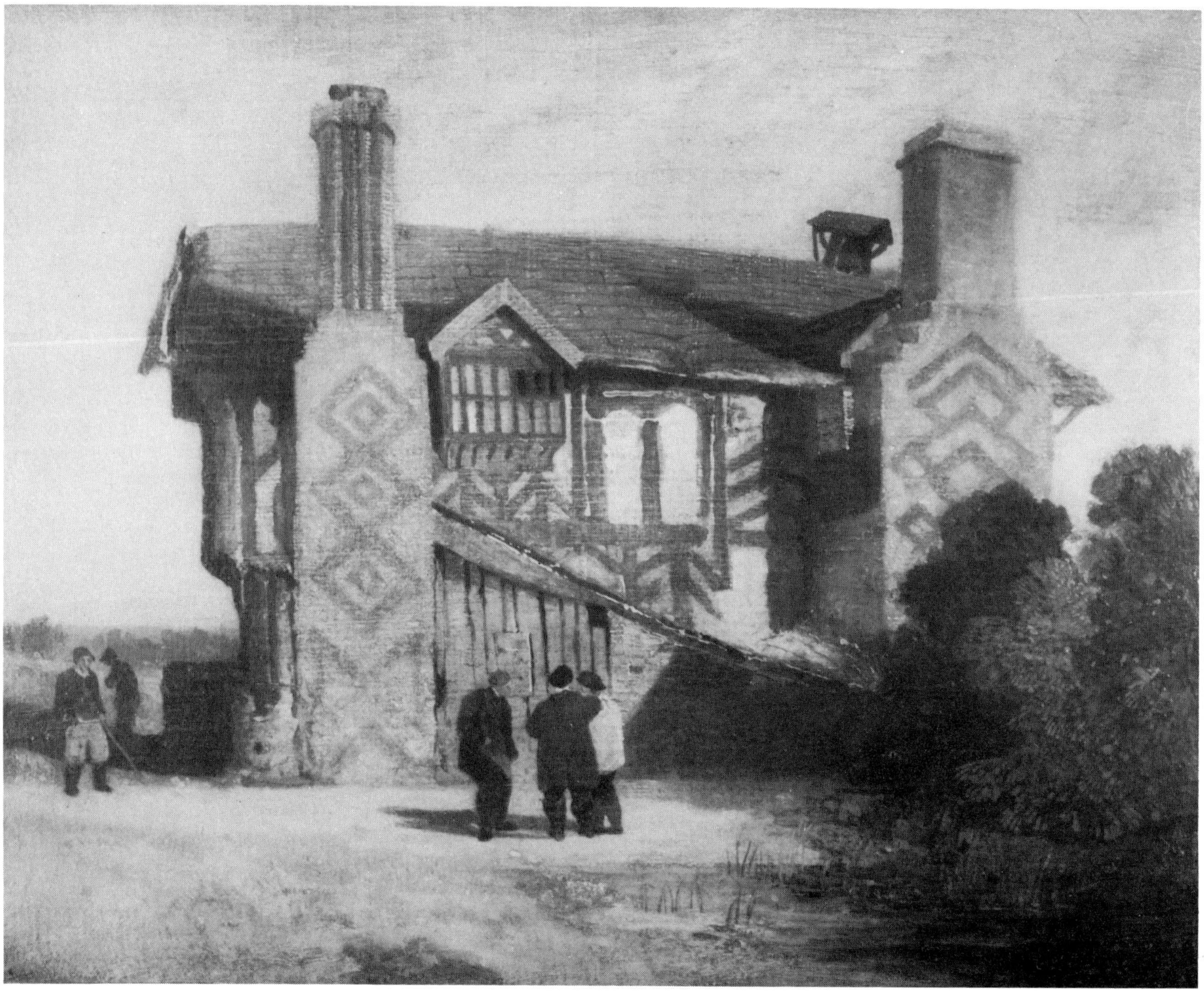

147 Old Merton [Moreton] Hall, Cheshire, *c.*1807-8

upon painting in oil once again in earnest. His work surviving from the mid 1820s reveals him at his most innovative and accomplished as an oil painter (see Nos. 157-161).

As with his drawings of this period, Cotman's oils had a mixed reception. Dawson Turner for one, seems to have encouraged Cotman to continue with his drawing in preference to painting. On 2 July 1825 Cotman responded: 'It will give you pleasure to assure you that I shall go on with Drawings— but I have received additional orders for two Pictures 18 guineas each, which must be attended too [sic].'[11] Thus he was evidently still being commissioned to paint in oil and it was at this time that he appears to have undertaken a series of closely-related landscape compositions which all feature luxuriantly leafy trees painted with a full and 'fatty' brush. A comment by Cotman in a letter[12] to Dawson Turner of 1 November 1826 seems to relate to this new phase in his production: 'I can no longer bear the stigma that Trees I can neither draw nor paint.' It is an enigmatic reference as it is not clear whether Cotman's oils featuring trees are the object of, or a response to this criticism. He exhibited a number of tree subjects with the Norwich Society over the period 1824-8. On 14 August 1824 the *Norwich Mercury* critic had expressed his bewilderment at the picture *Trees at Kimberley*[13] then showing at the Norwich Society. Whilst being 'satisfied that he has some particular aim in adopting a manner so removed from the common course', the reviewer continues: 'we regret to find that it is in this instance as unintelligible to virtuosi as to the public. We were wholly unable to catch the effect.' It is not, however, certain whether this picture was an oil or a watercolour.

Cotman submitted three oil landscapes to the British Institution, London in 1827,[14] while the evidence of works such as *Palace of Prince Beauharnais* (No. 162) and *Cader Idris* (No. 163) confirms that he continued to paint in oil whilst residing in Norwich. A number of his oils 'In Richly Carved and Gilt Frames' were included in the sale of his collections held by Spelmans in September 1834[15] after his removal to London. A letter from Cotman to his son John Joseph confirms that he had taken up oil painting again by October, 1836 (see No. 164). This was the beginning of a final phase in his work in this medium. He also encouraged John Joseph to try his hand, writing to him in May, 1837: 'I am painting a little in oils, so when you come you must try too. The Royal Academy Rooms are well lighted but look small. Wilkie, Landseer, and Etty are the principal painters. Turner's pictures are very extraordinary and require to be looked at a good deal to give an opinion of them.'[16] Cotman had evidently retained his interest in Turner but did not attempt to emulate that artist's increasingly idiosyncratic approach.

It was two years later that Cotman confessed to Bulwer that he was so fond of painting that he could consider never executing another drawing (see p. 131). In a postscript to that letter Cotman adds: 'I am just from Etty's "Pluto & Proser-

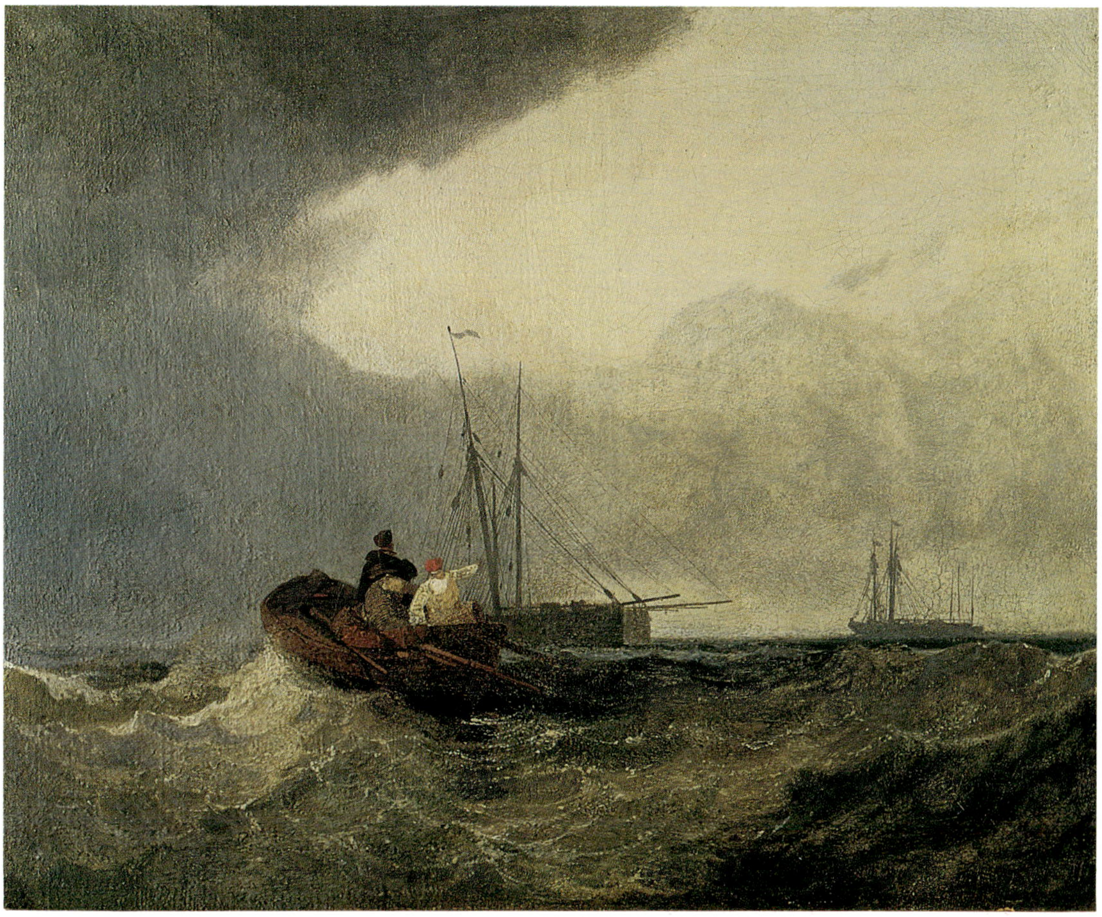

153 Sea View (Fishing Boats), ?1820s

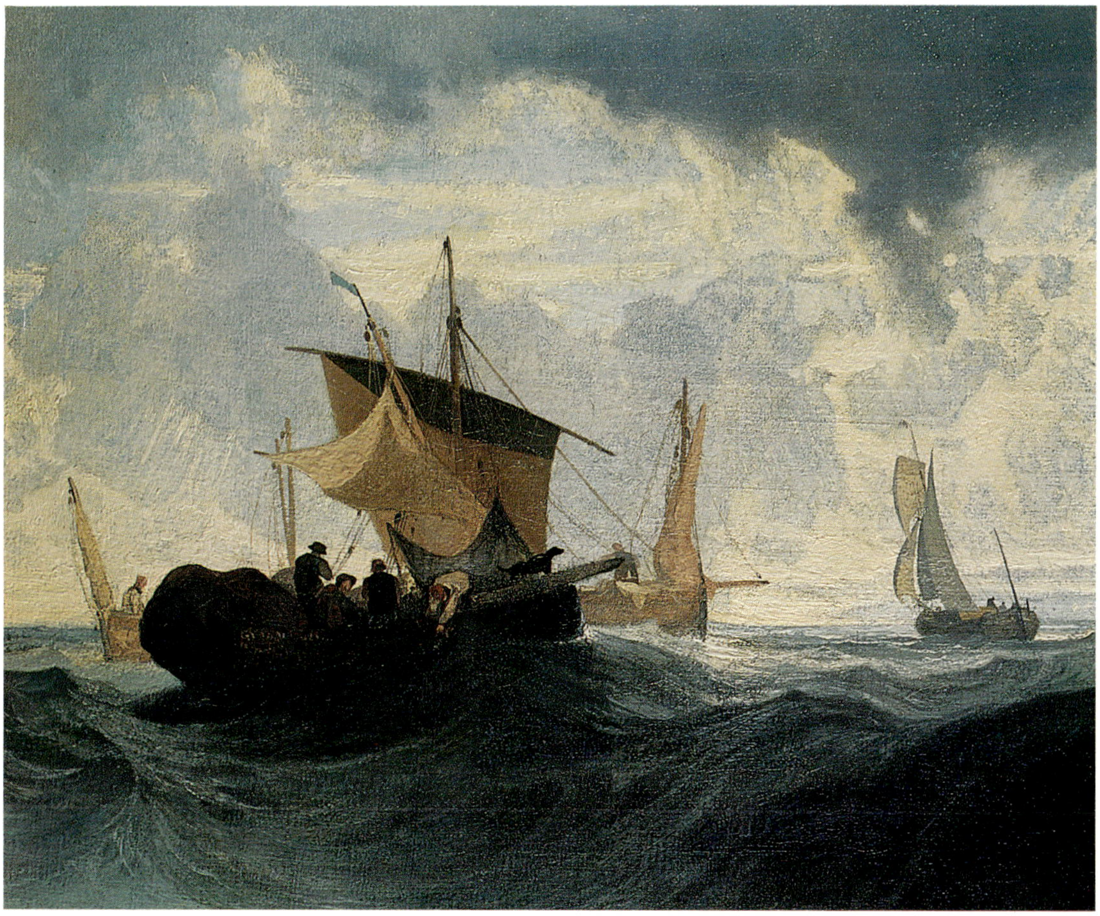

154 After the Storm, ?1820s

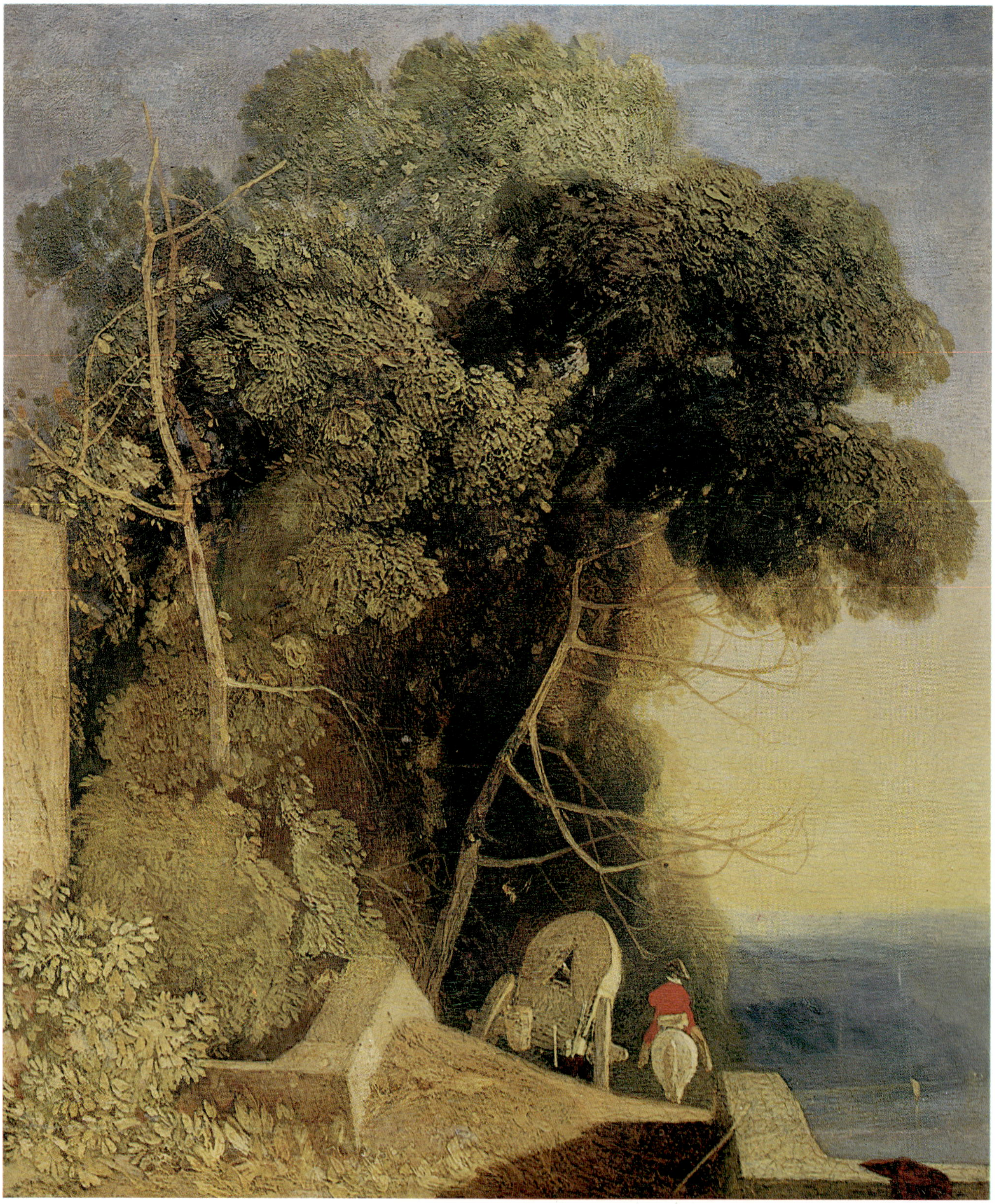

158 The Baggage Wagon, *c.*1824-8

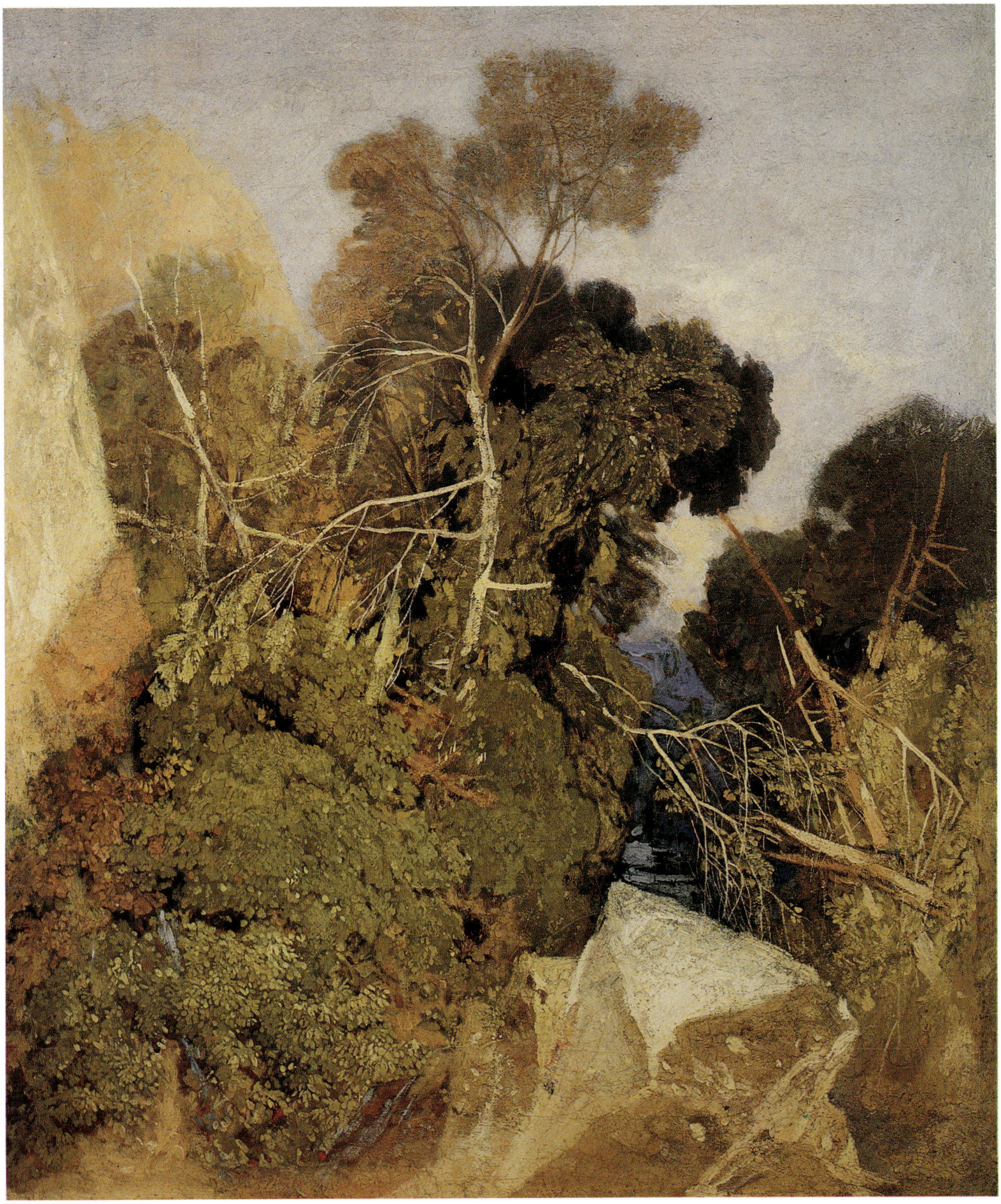

161 Silver Birches, *c.*1824-8

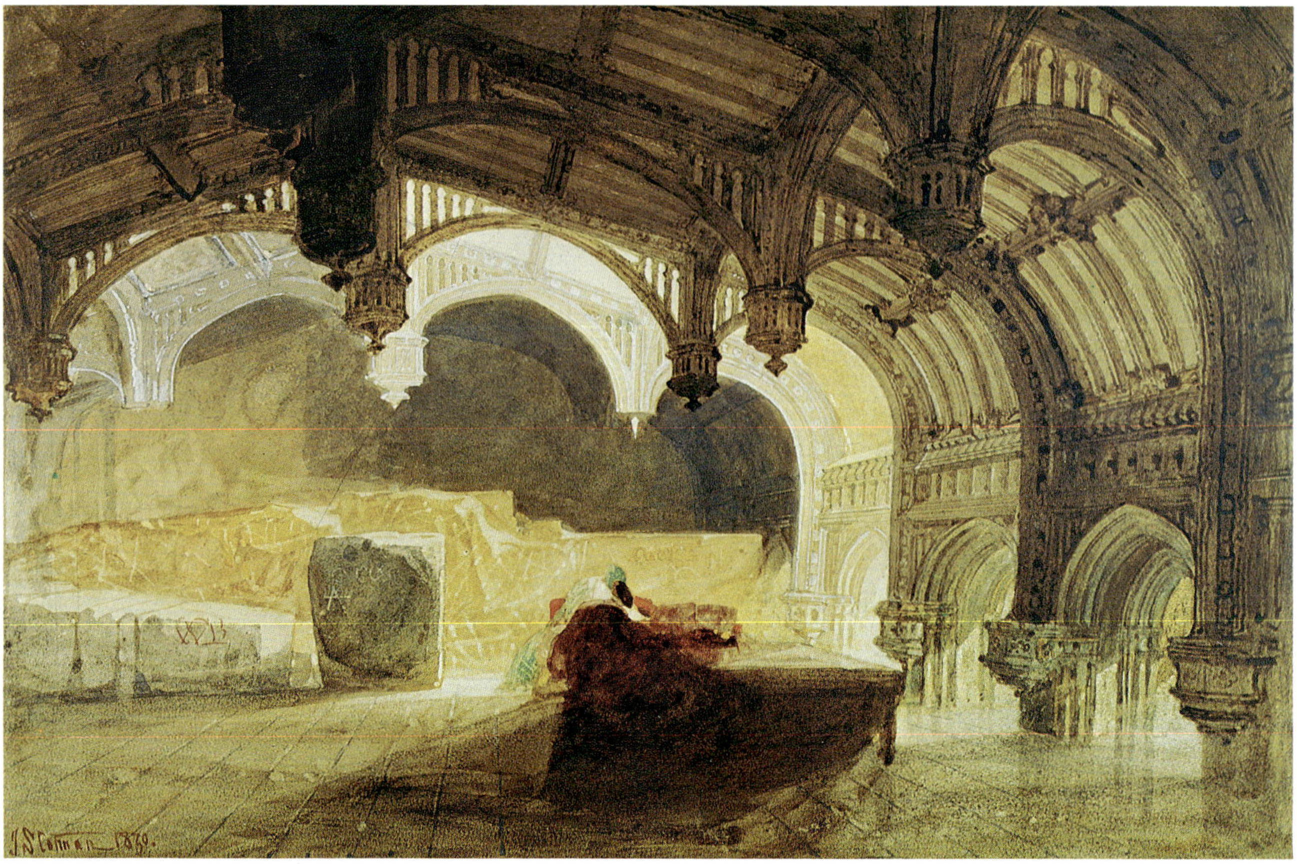

106 Crosby Hall, *c.*1829-30

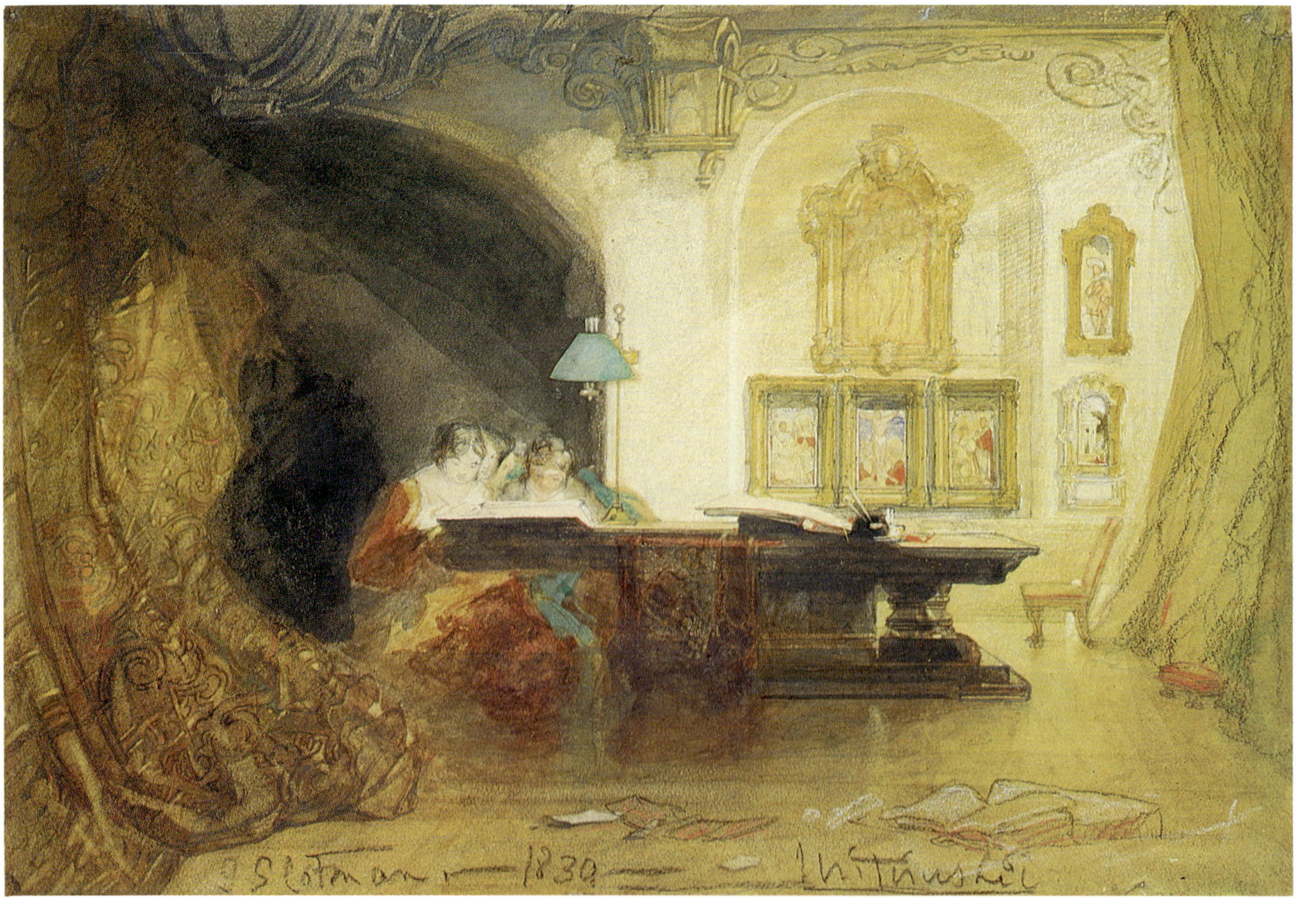

127 The Drawing Master, 1839

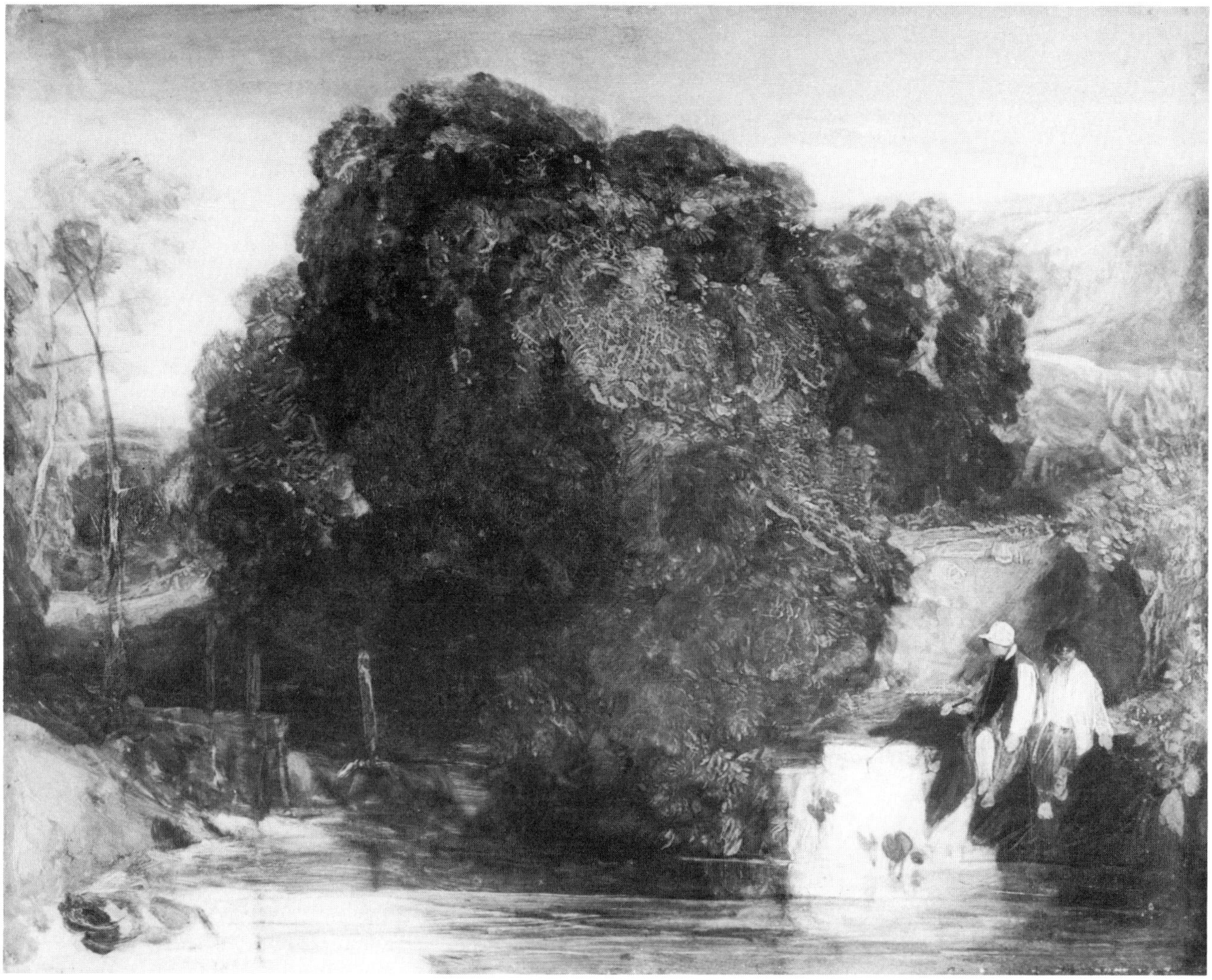

166 Henley on Thames — Boys Fishing, *c.*1837-9

pine''. I hold it by far the best coloured pictures in the Academy', revealing that his heightened sense of colour at this period found echoes in his appreciation of oil as well as water-colour painting. *Henley on Thames — Boys Fishing* (No. 166) confirms the brilliance of his colour sense at this time.

In terms of technique, the oils in the collection at Norwich reveal three distinct stages in Cotman's use of oil. His early works are executed with a fluid yet comparatively dry use of the medium. In the early 1820s the distinctively 'fatty', almost clotted, spots of colour herald a series of oils that may be regarded as the height of his achievement in the medium. Nevertheless, he appears to have recognised the dangers inherent in an overloaded use of oil, and certainly by 1836, had gradually developed a more liquid technique (No. 164). Drying cracks in a number of the works suggest an over-hasty approach to his oils, confirmed by his own account to James Bulwer of a painting intended for an exhibition at Manchester in the summer of 1839: 'That evening the sketch was made and the sky was laid in the following day. On Thursday[1] it will be finished and off on Saturday. The subject is *The Phantom Ship* by Captain Marryat . . . The size of the jay is three feet six inches by two feet six. I have had no difficulty with it. It went as a plaything and I have enjoyed my labours hugely.'[17] The 'sketch' was often on an ochre ground as can be seen most clearly in Nos. 167 and 168, but was also the case in earlier examples such as Nos. 155, 162 and 166.

Cotman's oeuvre as an oil painter remains comparatively small. It is, indeed, smaller than might be imagined, as the number of ugly paintings sometimes attributed to him bear no relation to his individual contribution to the medium. Thus while imitators may copy his compositions (notably his etched work) and others may have 'finished' or 'improved' the oil sketches auctioned together with his remaining works at Christie's in 1843,[18] the finest examples of his work at Norwich stand as one of the most distinctive and original achievements in British painting of the first half of the nineteenth century.

Notes

[1]Barker Collection, Rienaecker pp. 151-152. [2]Barker Collection. [3]Norwich Society 1808 (27). [4]Norwich Society 1808 (157). [5]Norwich Society 1808 (7); see also No. 145, *The Beggar Boy.* [6]BI 1810 (82) and (289). [7]BI 1810 (293). [8]Norwich Society 1808 (165). [9]JB to JSC, 1 July 1825 (BM). [10]14 August 1824. [11]Barker Collection. For Kitson's misdating of this letter see Oppé *Burlington* Aug. 1945, p. 199. [12]Barker Collection. [13]Norwich Society 1824 (15), *Trees at Kimberley — clearing up after a Storm at Mid-day.* [14]BI 1827 (129); (381); (383). [15]Spelman, Norwich 12 Sept. 1834 (3rd day) lots 109-116, 118, 120-128. [16]BM. [17]JSC to JB, 23 July 1839, see also Kitson 1937 p. 342. [18]Christie's 18 May 1843 lots 260-278, 280-301.

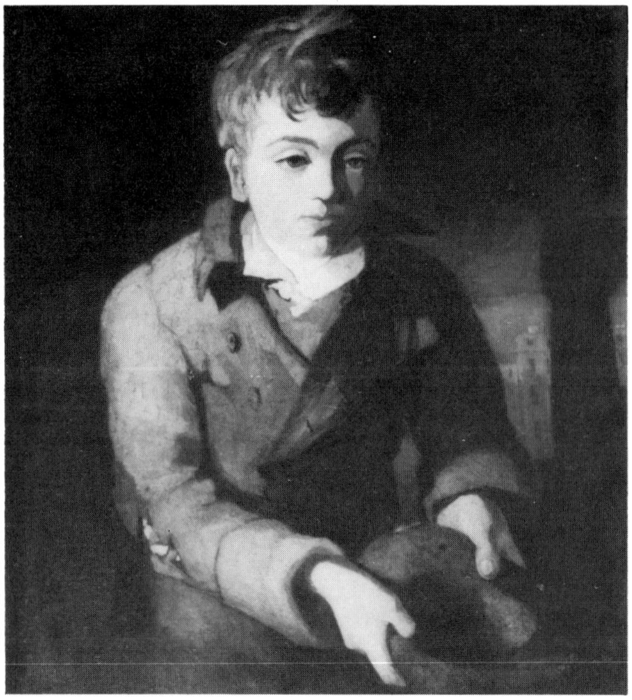

145 The Beggar Boy, 1808

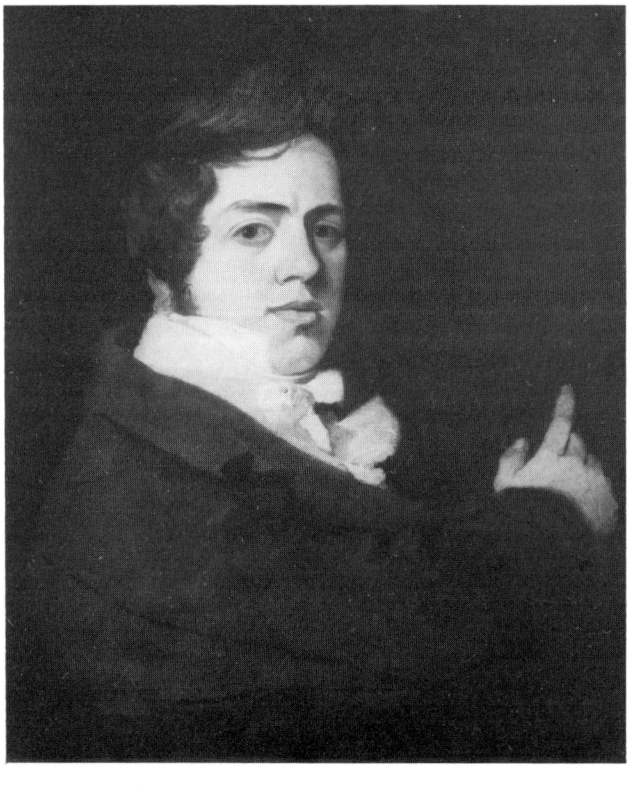

146 Portrait of a Young Man, *c.*1807-9

145 The Beggar Boy, 1808

Oil on millboard; 72.7 × 61.5 ($28\frac{5}{8}$ × $24\frac{3}{16}$). PROV: Cotman sale, Spelman, Norwich, 16 May 1861, lot 192, bt. Hunt £12.1s.6d; Christopher Steward; his sale, Spelman, Norwich 15 & 16 August 1864, 1st day, lot 177; William Dixon; his sales Spelman, Norwich 30 Nov. 1871 lot 220, ?unsold (£17.17s. in annotated catalogue, Art Dept. archives, NCM) and Spelman, Norwich 17 May 1882, lot 229, bt. Francis Taylor 30 gns.; R. J. Colman by 1922; R. J. Colman Bequest 1946. (92.235.951). EXH: Norwich Society 1808 (6); Tate 1922 (76) lent by R. J. Colman; Norwich 1930-31. REF: Kitson 1937 pp. 105-106; *Colman Collection Guide* 1951 p. 5.

The Beggar Boy was one of thirteen portaits Cotman exhibited with the Norwich Society in 1808, the year in which he is first credited as 'Portrait-Painter' in the exhibition catalogues. It is likely that a number of these portraits were in oil, as were at least nine other subjects exhibited by Cotman that year (see Nos. 147, 148).

The sitter is traditionally Cotman's younger brother Henry, born twenty years later than Cotman and represented in another oil also exhibited in 1808, *Boy at Marbles.*[1] It is also probable that Henry was the sitter for another canvas, *Portrait of a Boy,* now in a private collection.[2]

Cotman's oil portrait style combines a free handling of the medium with a crisp delineation of features reminiscent of his contemporary pencil and wash portraits (Nos. 35, 36).

[1] Norwich Society 1808 (7); Kenneth Cotman Family Collection. [2] Yorkshire.

146 Portrait of a Young Man, *c.*1807-9

Oil on canvas; 61.2 × 50.8 ($24\frac{1}{8}$ × 20). PROV: bt. from a London picture dealer by R. J. Colman; R. J. Colman Bequest 1946. (91.235.951). EXH: Tate 1922 (67) as *Portrait of Francis Walter Cotman.*

The former identification of the sitter as the artist's son, Francis Walter (born 1816) has long been recognised as mistaken. The style of the picture suggests a date at the beginning rather than the end of Cotman's career. The portrait shows a young man in his early twenties, whose features recall those of Cotman's younger brother, Thomas (see No. 35). Although the eyes and nose of both sitters are extremely close, the full mouth of the young man in No. 146 finds a more direct parallel in that of another pencil and wash portrait of a similar date in the collection at Norwich, *Portrait of a Gentleman.*[1] Rajnai and Allthorpe have suggested[2] the latter may be Edmund Cotman junior, (1786-1851) the younger brother of Cotman. The close similarity between the hair style, browline and full face of both sitters suggest that they may be the same person. The family resemblance between Tom Cotman and John Sell (see frontispiece) may be extended to No. 146, making Edmund Cotman a most likely sitter for this portrait.[1]

This is the most finished portrait by Cotman in the collection at Norwich. The features are characteristically modelled with formal simplicity, while the crisp folds of the cravat are broadly handled.

[1] NCM 254.235.951. [2] Rajnai & Allthorpe No. 62.

147 Old Merton [Moreton] Hall, Cheshire, *c.*1807-8

illustrated on p. 132

Oil on coarse weave canvas; 62.3 × 75.5 ($24\frac{1}{2}$ × $29\frac{3}{4}$). PROV: the artist's sale, Spelman, Norwich 10-12 Sept. 1834, 3rd day, lot 116 as *Merton Hall, in Chester, and figures,* bt. J. Norgate £1.13s.; Christie's sale, 28 Feb. 1863, lot 27 as *Old Merton Hall, Cheshire with figures,* ?bt. in by Radcliffe £5;[1] J. Norgate sale, Christie's 26 March 1877, lot 127 as *Merton Hall,* bt. Cox £32.11s.; Foster's sale, 1 May 1879, lot 229, unsold;[2] bt. from Cox by Thomas Woolner, RA, 1882;[2] by descent to Miss Woolner by 1912;[2] bt. from her by W. B. Paterson by 1913;[2] bt. from him by W. A. Coates; bt. from sale of Coates Collection through W. B. Paterson by Percy Moore Turner 1927;[2] bt. from him by R. J. Colman, 5 March 1927; R. J. Colman Bequest 1946. (116.235.951). EXH: ?Norwich Society 1808 (220) as *Old Merton Hall, Cheshire;* ?BI 1810 (306) as before; London, Suffolk Street 1878 (185) as *Merton Hall, Near Norwich;* London, Conduit Street 1882 (32);[2] Grosvenor Gallery 1888 (78) as *Merton Hall, Norfolk* lent by T. Woolner; London, Paterson Gallery 1913 (24) as *Morton Hall, Cheshire;* London, Suffolk Street 1927 (51) as *Morton Hall;* Norwich 1945. REF: Roget vol. i. 1891 (1972) p. 501; Dickes p. 304; *EDP* 9 Jan. 1931 repro; Isherwood Kay, *Connoisseur* Feb. 1936 pp. 68-71, repro. p. 68; Kitson 1937 p. 117; Oppé, *Burlington* Aug. 1945, pp. 196, 199.

Cotman probably visited Old Moreton Hall, near Congleton, Cheshire in the summer of 1806. The hall is some fourteen miles north of Trentham (see No. 39). The Tudor mansion is richly decorated with timbers, plaster and brickwork and provided Cotman with a subject for which at least six drawings survive. Two of these were engraved for Britton's *Architectural Antiquities of Britain,* one of the *South side*[3] published 1 October 1808 and the other of the *Kitchen Gable and Great Hall Doorway*[4] published 2 June the following year. A third drawing[5] presents the same view of Old Moreton Hall as that in the oil and includes the two figures to the left of the composition.[6]

The oil represents a freer version than the meticulous drawing, which was probably produced initially with a view to being engraved for Britton. The coarse grained use of paint suggests an instinctive response to both the medium and the coarse wove canvas. The paint-surface has suffered and Isherwood Kay has pointed out that the picture at one stage was overpainted with additional groups of sheep. The entry in the Grosvenor Gallery exhibition catalogue for 1887-8 reads: 'It is formed of red brick and half timbered with dark roofs and high quaint chimnies, in front a farmer and his man seem to be discussing with a butcher the price of sheep seen near the house and further off.'[7] It appears that this overpainting has subsequently been removed; the only significant touches of modern paint today being in the rushes of the right foreground.

The treatment of the foliage to the right of the composition relates to that of another oil probably also exhibited in 1808, *Water-fall, composition* (No. 148). It is likely that this canvas was exhibited with the Norwich Society in 1808 and was one of Cotman's first submissions to the British Institution in 1810.

[1]Copy of annotated catalogue, Art Dept. archives, NCM. Isherwood Kay p. 69 records that it was bought in at Murrell's rooms, Norwich, 1863. [2]Isherwood Kay p. 69. [3]Etched by John Smith, Vol. 2 opp. p. 82. [4]*Ibid* opp. p. 83. [5]C. E. Russell Collection, 1936, repro. Isherwood Kay, see REF:. [6]Two Cotman pencil interiors are Whitworth D.14.1972 and Colnaghi, May/June 1972 no. 45; an early drawing copy (no. 246) inscribed *Old Merton Hall, Cheshire,* is in the Clifford Collection. A second drawing copy (no. 333) dated 1815 is NCM 75.105.932. [7]See Isherwood Kay (REF).

148 The Waterfall, *c.*1807-8

Oil on canvas; 57.3 × 43.2 ($22\frac{9}{16}$ × 17). PROV: given by the artist to William Kinnebrook; by descent to his wife, Mrs. Kinnebrook; bt. from her by John Berney Ladbrooke, 25s.; bt. from him by James Reeve and Charles Clowes, 25s.; bt. from them by John Wigger, £12; acquired from him in exchange by William Dixon; his sale Spelman, Norwich, 17 May 1882, lot 228 as 'The Falls of Tivoli, *a rare example,*' bt. Clowes for J. J. Colman 54 gns.; his bequest to R. J. Colman 1898; R. J. Colman Bequest 1946. (118.235.951). EXH: ?Norwich Society 1808 (221); Norwich 1885 (59); Norwich 1894 (31); RA Winter Exhibition 1894 (15) as *Landscape;* Carfax Gallery 1911 (16); Manchester 1912 (318); Tate 1922 (31); Wembley 1924 (V.13); Norwich 1925 (24); Ipswich 1927 (91); Brussels 1929 (33); Norwich 1930-31; RA 1934 (621, Commemorative Catalogue 397); Norwich 1945. REF: Binyon 1897 pp. 68, 88, repro. p. 87; Binyon 1903 pp. JSC viii, x; Holmes, *Burlington* 1904 p. 79; Dickes p. 306, repro. opp.; Cundall, *The Studio* 1920 p. 20; *Daily Chronicle* 6 April 1922; *Times* 8 April 1922; *EDP* 13 April 1922, 30 Aug. 1922; Kaines Smith 1926 pp. 89, 91, 138; Kitson, *OWCS* 1930 p. 10; *EDP* 8 Jan. 1931 repro., 30 Dec. 1933 repro.; Wilenski 1933 p. 210; *EDP* 6 Jan. 1934; Rutter, *Sunday Times* 20 Sept. 1936; Kitson 1937 pp. 118, 119, pl. 55; Binyon, *Burlington* 1942 pp. 159, 160; Oppé, *Burlington* Aug. 1945 p. 199; Barnard pl. 6; *Colman Collection Guide* 1951 p. 5; Rienaecker pp. 32, 43, pl. 30 fig. 58; Day 1969 vol. III p. 17; Rajnai & Allthorpe No. 59; Allthorpe-Guyton 1979.

For a discussion of the pencil and wash versions of this composition see the entry for No. 32. Both Binyon and Dickes suggest a date of *c.*1815-16 for this canvas. However, later critics such as Kitson and Rienaecker have recognised the strong affinity between Cotman's work in oils and watercolour during his early Norwich period. No. 148 represents a natural extension of Cotman's work at this time. As Rienaecker remarks: 'in its austere pattern, and flat distribution of panels of soberly coloured tone, it is remarkably similar to the Greta and Rokeby group of drawings.'

It may also be that Cotman is indebted to the classical examples of Sebastian Bourdon and Gaspar Poussin. While Cotman's interest in Bourdon is discussed in the entry for No. 32, his interest in the Poussin brothers is confirmed by lot 49 in the Cotman sale of 1861, 'Solitude and the Cascade after *Poussin.*' A sketch by Cotman entitled *A Roman Road, after Poussin,*[1] ascribed to the period *c.*1809-10 by Rajnai and Allthorpe, is in the collection at Norwich. Cotman's library sale in 1843 included prints by Moucheron after Poussin,[2] as well as 'A volume of Landscapes after G. Poussin and Claude, half bound.'[3] The debt to Gaspar Poussin lies not simply in Cotman's sense of compostion, but equally in his use of flat, solid, and almost dry layers of paint of a low key, an affinity perhaps more pronounced in No. 149.

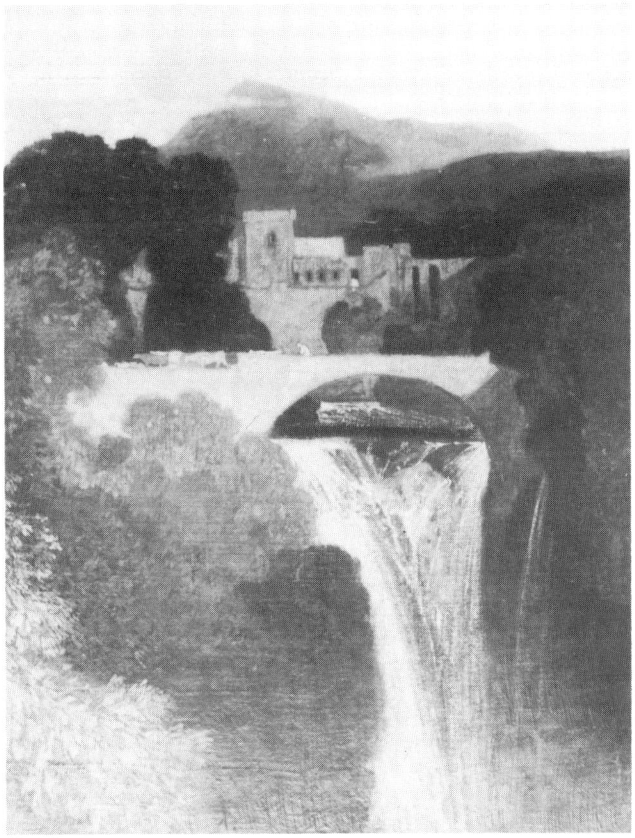

148 The Waterfall, *c.*1807-8

[1]NCM 51.L1967.9, Rajnai & Allthorpe No. 104. [2]Lot 395. [3]Lot 423.

149 The Judgement of Midas, *c.*1808-9

illustrated on p. 140

Oil on canvas; 60.8 × 73.7 ($23\frac{15}{16}$ × 29). PROV: Turner, picture dealer; Robinson & Fisher's sale, Oct. 1935, bt. by Percy Moore Turner; bt. from him by R. J. Colman, 27 Nov. 1935, £1,200; R. J. Colman Bequest 1946. (117.235.951). EXH: Norwich 1945. REF: Kitson 1937 p. 119; Oppé, *Burlington* Aug. 1945 pp. 196, 199; *Colman Collection Guide* 1951 p. 5; Holcomb 1978 p. 12, pl. 38; Rajnai & Allthorpe No. 95.

The subject of this oil is confirmed by the title of a softground etching,[1] *The Judgement of Midas* published as plate 6 in Cotman's *Liber Studiorum* of 1838. The drawing[2] for the design of the etching is dated 1814 and is a faithful replica of the oil which differs in only minor details. The tale is derived from Ovid's *Metamorphoses*[3] and Cotman's scene shows Midas present among those listening to the musical contest of Pan and Apollo. Pan may be seen playing a rustic melody on his pipes, while Apollo awaits his opportunity to render a more harmonious and lyrical tune. The mountain god Timolus is present to give his verdict. King Midas was subsequently to be endowed with ass's ears for questioning the judgement in favour of Apollo.

This is the most consciously allegorical composition of Cotman's oeuvre. The tale is one of Arcadian nature versus art and Cotman selects that moment when a verdict has yet to be given. The air of natural harmony which invests Cotman's Classical landscapes is also present in another oil of this period *Classical Landscape — Composition* in the Bacon Collection, which also echoes No. 148, *The Waterfall.* A comparable composition of this period is No. 55, *Classical Landscape.*

During the summer of 1937 the full size preliminary drawing for No. 149 was discovered[4] on the back of another oil, *The Beggar Boy* (No. 145), whilst that picture was undergoing restoration. This draw-

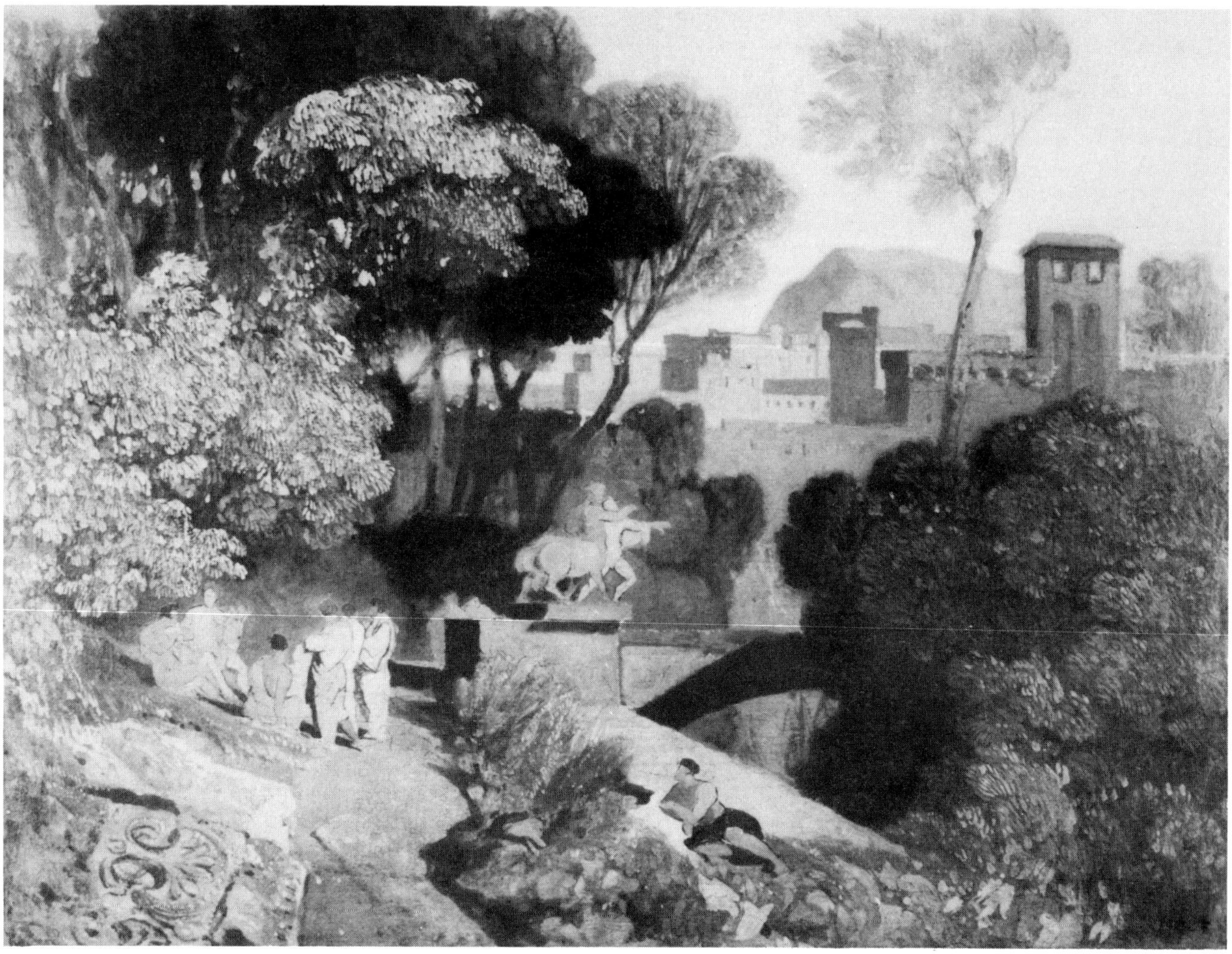

149 The Judgement of Midas, *c.*1808-9

ing was unfortunately destroyed during removal. The initial drawing on the canvas itself is also visible, particularly that of the figures. For a discussion of the influence of Poussin upon Cotman's work see the entries for Nos. 32 and 148.

[1]Popham No. 301. Either this or the corresponding study was exhibited with Norwich Society 1824 (171). [2]BM 1902-5-14-111. [3]Ovid Met. 11, fab. 5 (see Cotman's 1843 Library Sale, 1st day, lots 116, 117). [4]CC 1942.

150 Mrs. John Sell Cotman, *c.*1808-9

illustrated on opposite page

Oil on millboard; 54.6 × 40 ($21\frac{1}{2}$ × $15\frac{3}{4}$). PROV: bequeathed by Dr. John Sell Cotman, great-grandson of the artist 1952 (195.952). EXH: Arts Council 1947 (45); Stoke-on-Trent 1953; Hampstead 1953 (21); Art Exhibitions Bureau 1953-54 (3); Agnew 1958 (3); Derby & Nottingham 1959 (10); Sudbury 1978 (2). REF: Kitson 1937 pp. 120, 128, pl. 60.

Kitson suggests that this profile portrait of Ann Cotman — 'a masterly portrait sketch' — is probably one of the last of Cotman's early phase in painting in oil. The dashes and spatters of paint along the bottom edge of the panel reveal the vitality of the painting session. Although a raw sketch, the composition is a harmonious one. The burnt sienna and ochre collar provide a rich contrast to the green coat and background, while the flesh tones are balanced by the cool blue of the eye.

Ann and her two sisters Harriet and Elizabeth were the daughters of Edmund Miles, a tenant farmer of Swifts Grove Farm, Felbrigg.[1] She married Cotman on 6 January, 1809. Cotman's letters declare his devotion both to her and the six children she bore him. Writing from Normandy on 23 September 1820, Cotman recalls their courtship, prompted by his meeting 'three very pretty country farmers daughters, well dressed and arm in arm . . . and I thought on Felbrigg & old times.'[2] In 1812 her sister Elizabeth was to marry the Norwich artist John Thirtle.

Two apparently later pencil drawings by Cotman of his wife survive, one in Leeds[3] and the other in a private collection. The latter is closely related to the oil in most details apart from the substitution of the angular collar with a frilled bodice. Her portrait was also painted by D. B. Murphy as a pair to one of Cotman, traditionally commissioned by the artists of Norwich and presented to the couple as a wedding present.[4] D. B. Murphy also exhibited her portrait with the Norwich Society in 1824 (126), *Portrait of Mrs. J. S. Cotman.*

[1]M. Allthorpe-Guyton, *John Thirtle,* 1977 p. 14. [2]*Walpole Society,* vol. XV p. 126. [3]No. 9.694/49. [4]Now in the Kenneth Cotman Family Collection.

151 Boats on Cromer Beach, *c.*1808-10

illustrated on opposite page

Oil on mahogany panel; 37 × 46.7 ($14\frac{5}{8}$ × $18\frac{3}{8}$). PROV: Percy Moore Turner; bt. from him by R. J. Colman with three other pictures, 5 March 1927; R. J. Colman Bequest 1946. (96.235.951). EXH: ?Norwich Society 1808 (162); REF: Rajnai & Allthorpe No. 77.

Traditionally called *Boats on Yarmouth Beach,* the true location of the scene may be identified from the inscription on a later drawing copy[1] which shows the same central motif of the covered boat. No. 151 is a similar version in oil of a fine watercolour[2] now in the Victoria and Albert Museum, signed and dated 1809. Slight differences in composition between the watercolour and the oil include the addition of an extra mooring post and the dog[3] in the latter, while the watercolour includes a cart with two horses and figures on the horizon to the right. The vessels on the horizon of the watercolour have their sails furled.

A pencil study[4] in the collection at Norwich of the same boat as in No. 151 is inscribed with colour notes which correspond to the colours of both the oil and watercolour versions. This is one of a number of pencil studies of boats and anchors which have been ascribed to this period by Rajnai and Allthorpe.[5]

Major restoration has confused some passages in the oil, particularly the awkward painting of the small vessel to the left. However, the dry texture of the paint is consistent with the work of Cotman during the period 1807-9, and this version could have been that exhibited with the Norwich Society in 1808 (162) *Cromer Beach.* Another Cotman oil of a similar subject and date is *Seashore with Boats.*[6] A third beach scene in oil of this period is also in the Colman Collection, known as *Yarmouth Beach.*[7] Rajnai and Allthorpe have suggested that the latter may be Cotman's exhibit with the Norwich Society in 1808 (15) *Dealers waiting the coming in of the Herring Boats, Yarmouth.*

[1]NCM 13.105.932. See also Norwich Society 1809 (22*) for a drawing copy of the same subject. [2]V&A 2-1875. [3]A similar dog first appears in Cotman's etched work in 1811, *Kirkham Priory, York* (Popham No. 11). [4]48.L1967.9. [5]Rajnai & Allthorpe Nos. 75-81. [6]Tate 4785. [7]NCM 94.235.951 (Mr. T. Colman).

152 Old Houses at Gorleston, *c.*1815-23

illustrated on p. 142

Oil on canvas; 45.5 × 35.3 ($17\frac{7}{8}$ × $13\frac{15}{16}$). PROV: the artist's sale, Spelman, Norwich, 10-12 Sept., 1834, 3rd day, lot 120 as *Old House at Yarmouth,* bt. John Norgate £1.10s.; bt. by the artist John Middleton, bequeathed[1] by him to Thomas Lound; his sale, Spelman, Norwich, 6 March 1861, lot 259 as *Cottages,* bt. James Mills at reserve price of 20gns.; his sale Spelman, Norwich, 12-14 June 1865, 3rd day, lot 191 as *Old Houses,* bt. James Reeve 12 gns.; bt. from him by Samuel Harvard, 18 gns.; bt. from him by J. J. Colman 1878, £100; J. J. Colman Bequest 1898. (8.4.99). EXH: Norwich 1860 (60) as *Ancient House* lent by Thomas Lound; RA 1878 (30); Norwich 1885 (60); Earls Court 1897 (51); Tate 1922 (18); Wembley 1925 (W.48) repro.; RA 1934 (607, Commemorative Catalogue 401, pl. CXV); Norwich 1942; Norwich 1945; Arts Council, *Norwich School of Painting* 1947 (3) repro.; Leeuwarden 1948 (9) repro.; British Council 1949 (8); British Council 1949-50 (20); Paris 1953 (25); Harrogate 1953; Agnew 1958 (63); Derby & Nottingham 1959 (11); Council of Europe 1959 (80); Manchester 1961 (16); British Council 1966-67 (11); Paris 1972 (65) repro.; Tate 1973 (265) repro. REF: NCM ?1897 (E); NCM ?1899 (20); NCM 1904 (10); Holmes, *Burlington* 1904 pp. 74-75; Dickes pp. 304, 309-311, repro. p. 310; NCM 1909 (10); *Times* 8 April 1922; Kaines Smith 1926 p. 165; NCM 1937 (35); Kitson 1937 p. 117; Barnard, *The Studio* Aug. 1947 p. 30, repro. p. 33 in colour; Goldberg 1978 p. 255; Hemingway 1979 p. 22; Jacobs & Warner 1980 p. EA10.

No. 152 is one of a number of compositions of cottages and gable ends painted by Cotman in oil. This subject recurs throughout Cotman's first Norwich and Yarmouth periods and the oils are difficult to date in consequence. No. 152 echoes *Old Moreton Hall, Cheshire* (No. 147) in its use of figures to lend scale and solemnity to the scene with their quiet, dissociated poses, but the oil technique is more advanced, arguing for a later date.

The subject, composition and treatment closely resemble those of an oil in a private collection known as *Ruined Cottage,*[2] which is also probably a Yarmouth subject. A watercolour version of this, in the collection of the Ashmolean Museum, Oxford, must also date from Cotman's Yarmouth years. A further oil of similar subject is *Gable End of Old Houses,*[3] also in the Colman collection. Whilst the treatment of areas such as the painting of the plasterwork is close to that of *Old Houses at Gorleston,* the crispness of finish is dissimilar in effect to the remainder of Cotman's oeuvre in oil. This may be explained by the fact that the composition is derived from an etching, *Hertfordshire, St. Albans,* published by Francis Stevens in 1815,[4] which Cotman also used as the basis for a drawing copy.[5] A fourth oil belonging to this group, known as *An Old House at St. Albans,*[6] is in the collection of Manchester City Art Gallery.

Two subjects exhibited with the Norwich Society in 1824, the year in which Cotman again exhibited oils, may be ascribed to this group.

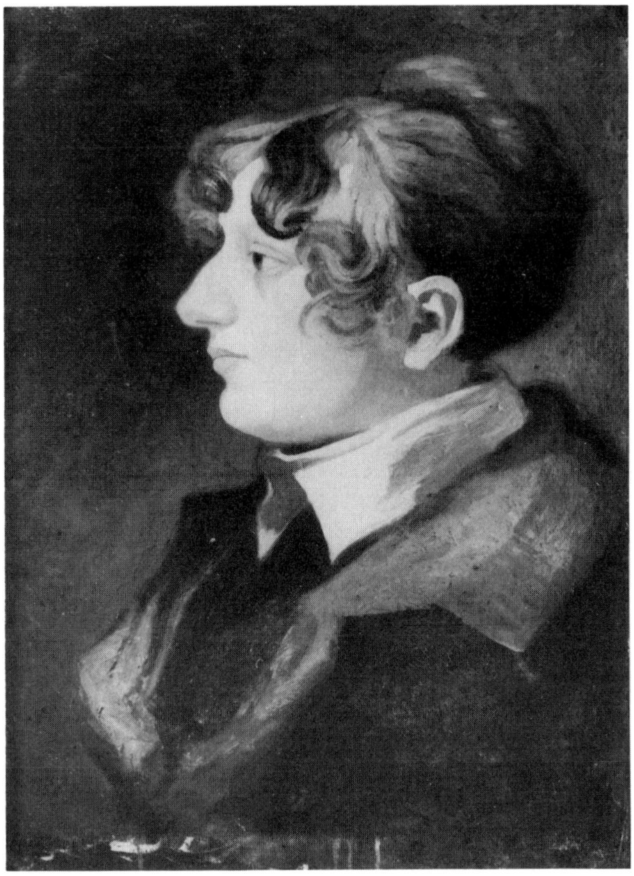

150 Mrs. John Sell Cotman, *c.*1808-9

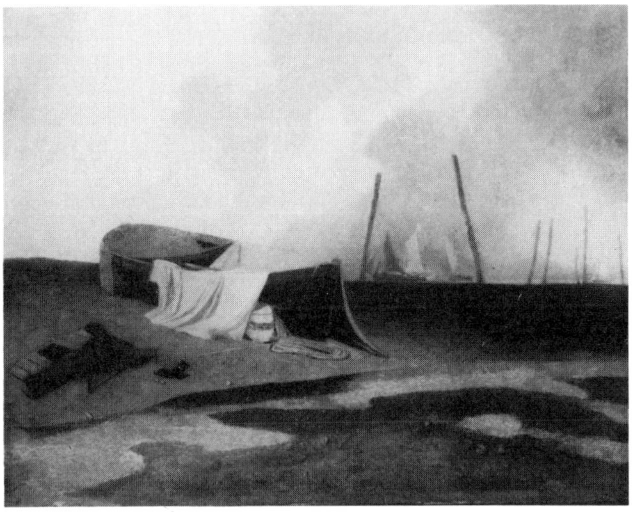

151 Boats on Cromer Beach, *c.*1808-10

Number 48, *An Old House at St. Albans* could relate to either the Manchester or Norwich pictures, while number 72, *Old Houses and Figures* could be either *Old Houses at Gorleston* or *Ruined Cottage.*

[1]It is not included in Middleton's will. The information for the Provenance comes from a MS catalogue by James Reeve, 1909, in Art Dept. archives, NCM. [2]With Colnaghi, London 1970. [3]NCM 100.235.951. An oil copy was with W. B. Paterson, London, 1927. [4]JSC Sale, 1834, 2nd day, lot 111: 'Stevens Cottages and Farmhouses of England and Wales, hf. bd. 1815' (sold for ten shillings). [5]NCM 69.105.932; a copy after JSC by S. C. Edwards is NCM 136.377.965. [6]A copy is in the Bacon collection. This subject was also painted by W. Mulready, V&A, Sheepshanks Gift, No. 157.

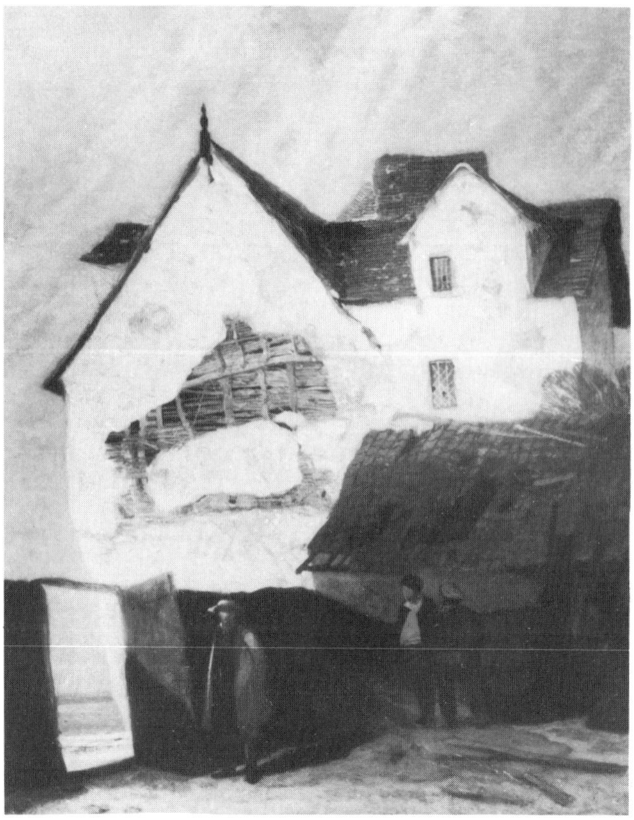

152 Old Houses at Gorleston, *c.*1815-23

153 Sea View (Fishing Boats), ?1820s

illustrated in colour on p. 133

Oil on canvas 63.2 × 76 ($24\frac{7}{8} \times 29\frac{15}{16}$). Prov:[1] the artist's sale, Spelman, Norwich, 10-12 Sept. 1834, 3rd day, lot 126, bt. John Thirtle 3 gns.; by descent to his wife; bt. from her by W. Boswell, £3; bt. from him by John Thomas Mott by 1856, £5; by descent to his son; bt. from him by J. J. Colman 1895, £600; J. J. Colman Bequest 1898. (7.4.99). Exh: Norwich 1856 (220) as *Sea View* lent by J. T. Mott; Norwich 1867 (908) as *Sea View;* Norwich 1874 (50) as *Gale at Sea;* RA 1878 (43) as *Sea Piece;* Earls Court 1897 (42 or 50) as *Sea Piece;* Tate 1922 (15); Norwich 1930-31; RA 1934 (601, Commemorative Catalogue 398); Norwich 1945; Leicester 1956 (38); Agnew 1958 (53); Derby & Nottingham 1959 (12); Manchester 1961 (15); Paris 1972 (66) repro.; Bordeaux 1977 (100) repro.; Brighton 1979 (59) repro. Ref: NCM ?1897 (D); Binyon 1897 pp. 68, 86, 88, 102, repro. p. 89; NCM ?1899 (15); Binyon 1903 p. JSC xi, pl. C1; NCM 1904 (8); Dickes p. 307 repro. opp.; NCM 1909 (8); Cundall, *The Studio* 1920 p. 21; *Morning Post* 7 April 1922; Batchelor, *EDP* 13 April 1922; Kaines Smith 1926 p. 165; NCM 1937 (36); Kitson 1937 pp. 254, 343.

A range of possible dates have been suggested for the painting of this canvas and the following oil, No. 154. Pidgley has suggested *c.*1810-1815,[2] Binyon *c.*1815, Reeve *c.*1820 and both Kitson and Rienaecker propose post 1823. Critics have, however, been united in praise for the picture. While Dickes considers it 'wonderful for its breadth, atmosphere and reality,' Binyon describes the picture as 'perhaps Cotman's masterpiece in oils.'[3]

It is almost impossible to reach a definitive conclusion concerning the date of execution of this oil. Although Kitson considers the picture to derive from pencil sketches made towards the end of Cotman's period at Yarmouth, the dry, gritty treatment of the oil is akin to the technique associated with works of the period *c.*1810, such as *The Waterfall,* No. 148. The ragged cloud shapes of both No. 153 and *After the Storm* also find a parallel in Cotman's watercolours of *c.*1810.

Both No. 153 and *After the Storm* (No. 154) reflect the influence of J. M. W. Turner. Cotman's interest in Turner's seascapes is borne out by his copy[4] of Turner's oil known as the *Bridgewater Sea Piece,*[5] exhibited in 1801, which also shows a similar boat[6] cresting the waves. The ship on the horizon in No. 153 echoes a number of Turner's early seascapes,[7] as does the low colour key in both sea and sky. In a letter to Francis Cholmeley of 5 June 1811 Cotman writes specifically of his admiration for the 'Pure & Silvery' effect that Turner achieved in his oils, an effect Cotman successfully emulates in this work.[8]

The existence of a close watercolour version[9] of this composition, signed and dated *J. S. Cotman 1832,* perhaps supports a date from the 1820s in that it is consistent with Cotman's execution of other watercolour versions of his oils of that period (e.g. *Silver Birches,* No. 161 and *Wind in the Trees,* No. 119).

[1]The information for the Provenance comes from a MS catalogue by James Reeve, 1909, in Art Dept. archives, NCM. [2]Catalogue: Paris 1972 (66). [3]Binyon 1897 p. 88. [4]BM 1902-5-14-284. [5]Butlin & Joll. No. 14. [6]A pencil sketch of the fishing boat and crew is in a private collection; see Whitworth Art Gallery, Manchester 1961 (15). [7]e.g. Butlin & Joll Nos. 85 and 91 (both exhibited, Turner's Gallery, 1809 and 1810). [8]An oil copy of No. 153 was in Capt. A. Hamond sale, Case and Dewing, Dereham, Norfolk. 30 Oct. 1975 (160). [9]Sotheby's, 8 July 1982 lot 158 (Miklós Rajnai).

154 After the Storm, ?1820s

illustrated in colour on p. 133

Oil on canvas; 63.2 × 75.6 ($24\frac{7}{8} \times 29\frac{3}{4}$). Prov: bt. by J. J. Colman from a London picture dealer by 1885; by descent to R. J. Colman 1898; R. J. Colman Bequest 1946. (103.235.951). Exh: Norwich 1885 (47) as *After a Breeze* lent by J. J. Colman; Newcastle 1887 (727); Gt. Yarmouth 1889 (50); Earls Court 1897 (43); Manchester 1912 (320); Tate 1922 (51); Norwich 1930-31; RA 1934 (616, Commemorative Catalogue 399, pl. CXIV); Paris 1938 (33); Norwich 1945. Ref: Dickes p. 309 repro.; *Connoisseur* May 1906 repro. p. 37; *Morning Post* 7 April 1922; Batchelor, *EDP* 13 April 1922; Kaines Smith 1926 pp. 89, 91, 98, 103, repro. p. 98; *EDP* 23 Dec. 1933 repro.; Kitson 1937 p. 254; Binyon, *Burlington* July 1942 pp. 159, 160; Oppé, *Burlington* Aug. 1945 p. 199; Rienaecker p. 33.

No. 154 is closely related to the preceeding oil *Sea View (Fishing Boats)* in both style and conception and has deservedly received full praise from past writers. Kitson finds it 'one of the most convincing and powerful renderings of such a scene that have ever been painted,' while Binyon considers 'it is as original in design as masterly in its rendering of the moment.' The disposition of the masses, particularly the contours of the waves and cloud formations, is parallelled in *The Dismasted Brig,*[1] a watercolour now in the British Museum.

A number of thumbnail sketches[2] of shipping at sea proclaim Cotman's continuing interest throughout his career for shipping scenes as subjects for fully-worked compositions in oil as well as watercolour. Other studies survive of shipping in stormy weather,[3] at least one[4] of which is derived from Turner and may have been a source of inspiration for *After the Storm.*[5] A pencil and wash study[6] for No. 154 was formerly in the collection of C. J. Watson. A similar composition in oil which may be attributed to Cotman is in a private collection.[7]

The difficulties in dating No. 154 are similar to those in *Sea View (Fishing Boats),* discussed in the previous entry.

[1]BM 1902-5-14-32. Kitson dated this *c.*1823, but it is more consistent with watercolours of *c.*1807-9. [2]e.g. BM 1902-5-14-180; 191-3; 251. [3]e.g. Leeds 9.70/49; 9.74/49; 9.71/49. [4]BM 1902-5-14-281 *Mouth of the Humber* after Turner, *Rivers of England.* [5]N.B. also Cotman's sale, 1834, lot 55: 'Eleven Prints of Shipping (including Turner's Storm).' [6]Norwich, Art Circle 1888 (70). [7]London, 1971.

155 Dutch Boats off Yarmouth, Prizes during the War *c.*1823-4

illustrated on opposite page

Oil on mahogany panel; 43.5 × 63.5 ($17\frac{1}{8} \times 25$). Prov: bt. by John Bridgman from ?the 1823 British Institution Exhibition; by descent to his grandson George Bridgman; bt. from him by Frederick John Nettlefold by 1933; bt. from him by R. J. Colman *c.*1945 (Oppé 1945); R. J. Colman Bequest 1946. (115.235.951). Exh: ?BI 1823 (8) as *Dutch Prizes off Yarmouth;* Norwich Society 1824 (41); Norwich 1945. Ref: *Norfolk Chronicle* 14 Aug. 1824; Binyon 1897 p. 92; Dickes p. 311; *Nettlefold Catalogue* p. 118 repro. opp. in colour; Kitson 1937

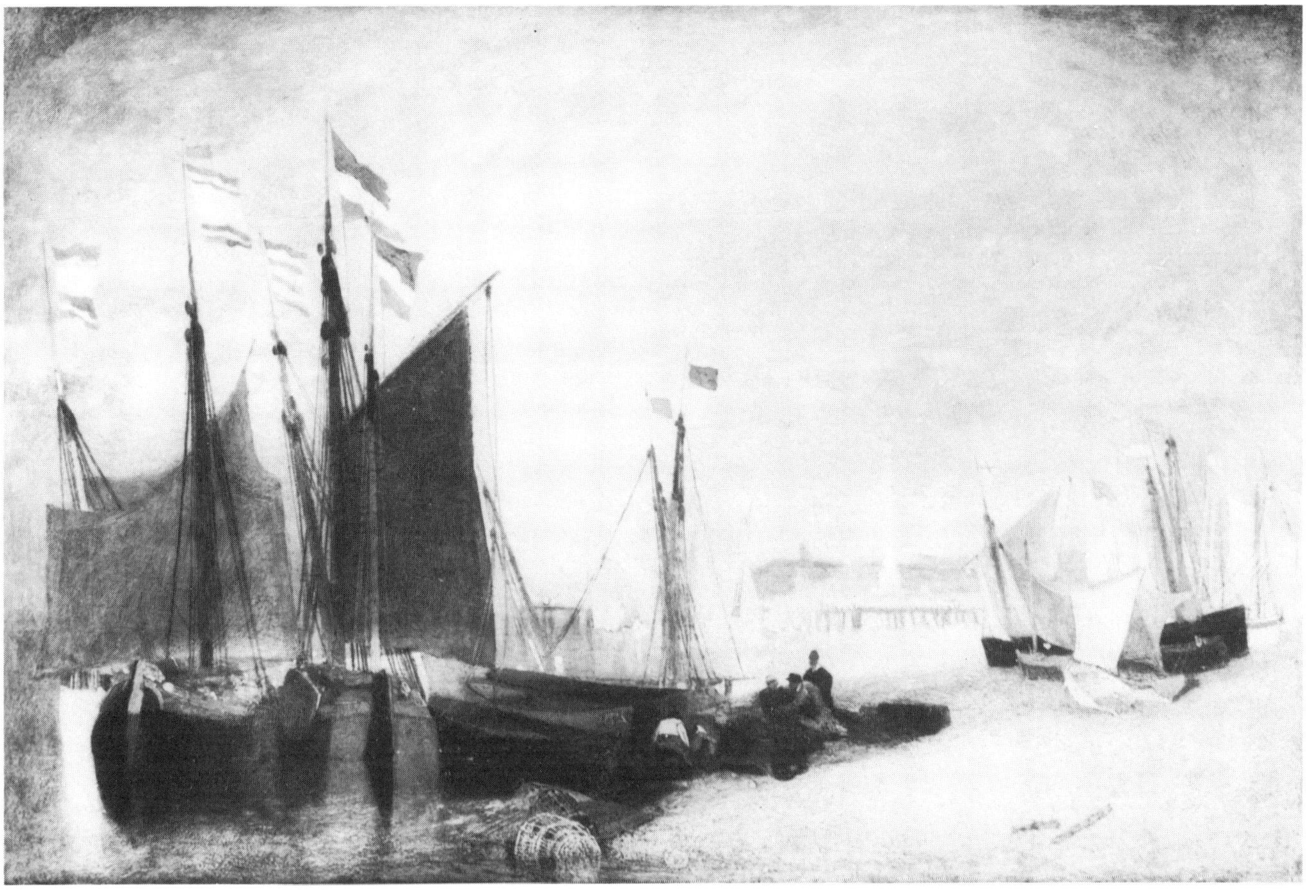

155 Dutch Boats off Yarmouth, Prizes during the War, *c.*1823-4

pp. 252-3, pl. 107; Oppé, *Burlington* Aug. 1945 p. 199; Rienaecker pl 2 in colour; Day 1969 vol. III repro. p. 33; Pidgley pp. 60, 155; Hemingway 1979 p. 73, pl. 61 in colour.

Having recently returned to Norwich from Yarmouth, Cotman exhibited in strength with the Norwich Society in August 1824. The critic of the *Norfolk Chronicle,* in reviewing the show, celebrated Cotman's work by first selecting this oil for especial praise : 'This is really a *multum in parvo* of cleverness for design, colouring, and management of light and shade, a most delectable "bit" of what all so wish but few have "the power" to produce, in marine painting. Not unworthy to stand beside "the studies" of a Vandervelt or a Backhuysen, the attention which though "small in size" it attracts and the admiration it excites, become mingled with our regret, that such subjects have not been early cherished ones with Mr. Cotman, composed as they might be on a larger scale, for the display of his most finished style.'[1]

Cotman had exhibited a similar subject,[2] possibly this oil, at the British Institution the previous year. It is likely that it was here that the collector Mr. John Bridgman of Wigmore Street first became aware of Cotman's oils, subsequently commissioning a picture from him (see the following entry). Both these oils were exhibited with the Norwich Society in 1824 and it may be assumed that Bridgman purchased No. 155 on the strength of its similar size and appeal to the oil he had already ordered.

The oil is a fully worked up composition derived from a small on-the-spot pencil sketch[3] of Yarmouth sands. The incident and general disposition of the masses in the sketch is retained, but Cotman enhances the oil with additional flags and mastheads among both the Dutch boats[4] to the left and the Yarmouth yawls to the right. The Nelson Monument confirms the view to be from the north side of the jetty looking along the sands across the Denes, with Gorleston in the distance. The Monument adds a final note of British naval jingoism to the scene. The panoply of sails and masts beneath a sky of billowing clouds makes this one of Cotman's gayest compositions.

[1]14 Aug. 1824. [2]See Exh. [3]NCM 10.139.949. Similar Dutch boats feature in a Cotman watercolour, NCM 149.235.951 and related drawing copies.

156 View from Yarmouth Bridge, looking towards Breydon, just after sun-set, *c.*1823-5

illustrated on p. 144

Oil on millboard; 44.4 × 63.3 ($17\frac{1}{2} \times 24\frac{15}{16}$). Prov: commissioned by John Bridgman, 1823-24, £14; by descent to his grandson George Bridgman; bt. from him by Frederick John Nettlefold by 1933; bt. from him by R. J. Colman *c.*1945 (Oppé 1945); R. J. Colman Bequest 1946. (114.235.951). Exh: Norwich Society 1824 (18); Norwich 1945. Ref: *Norfolk Chronicle* 14 Aug. 1824; Binyon 1897 pp. 77, 92, 102; Dickes p. 311; Kaines Smith 1926 p. 89; *Nettlefold Catalogue* p. 116 repro. opp. in colour; Kitson 1937 pp. 252-3, pl. 108; Oppé, *Burlington* Aug. 1945 p. 199; Rienaecker p. 32, pl. 1 in colour; Pidgley p. 60.

This picture was singled out for qualified praise by the *Norfolk Chronicle* critic reviewing the Norwich Society exhibition on 14 August 1824: 'Here we have judicious choice of situation; the waning glow of light immediately consequent on sun-set well represented; in short the composition and arranged materials of a truly good picture, yet quitted prematurely by the artist. We are no friends to "sketches" in oil painting.' While this criticism may be interpreted as an insensitive response to the picture's breadth and lack of definition, wherein lies its true subtlety of atmosphere, it is probable that Cotman exhibited the picture whilst still unfinished. It was to be almost a year before John Bridgman received the picture, despite having commissioned it. Cotman wrote to excuse the delay, while Bridgman's reply on 1 July 1825 records the patron's reactions:

> I have received the Picture safely and am much pleased with it. The composition is excellent, the distances are beautifully toned and well preserved, while the vessels in the foreground are in colour and handling masterly. I had expected a different sky. You proposed giving—about the centre of the Picture—rays of light from the sun which was just hid by passing clouds. These were to illumine the picture, and would have given a fine and natural effect, certainly a more brilliant one than the present. It would seem

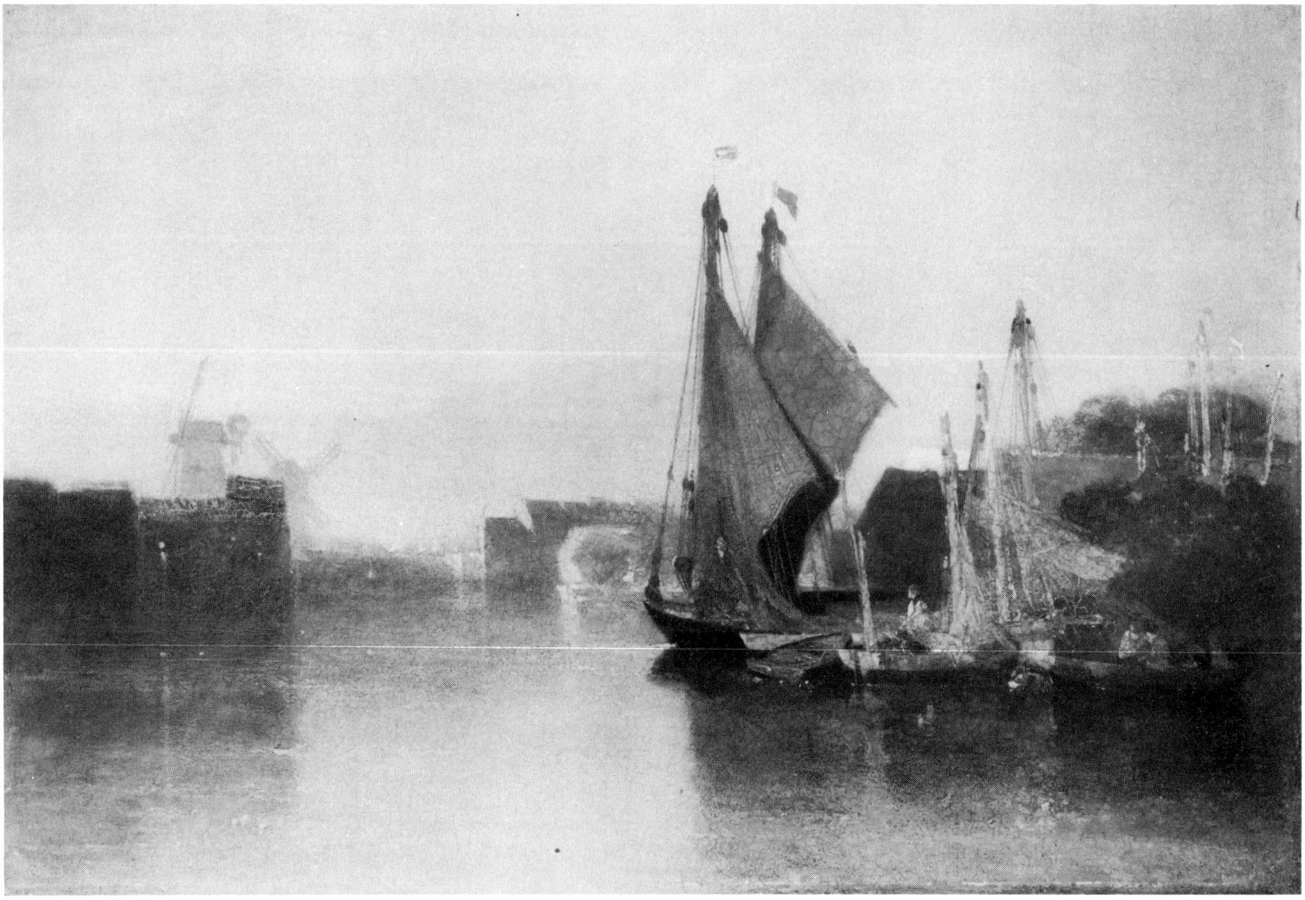

156 View from Yarmouth Bridge, looking towards Breydon, just after sun-set, *c.*1823-5

that, giving up your first intention, you have been undecided about the sky. This deviation has given you considerable trouble. Still the sky harmonizes with the foreground and is much better when seen nearer. The objects being small, we are drawn close to the Picture, and then the clouds appear broken, little, trifling—anything but broad and grand—very like some of the extravagances of Turner.[1]

Nos. 155 and 156 are among the most Turneresque of Cotman's oils dating from the early 1820s when Cotman's subjects appear to have featured shipping and seascapes akin to the example of Turner (see also Nos. 153, 154). Bridgman paid a reasonable price of ten guineas for the picture, with a further '£3.16.0 paid for Colours, Brushes, etc.'[1]

[1] Both Dickes and Rienaecker recognise that this letter must relate to this picture. However, Kitson ascribed it to No. 155. For further reference to this letter see p. 131.

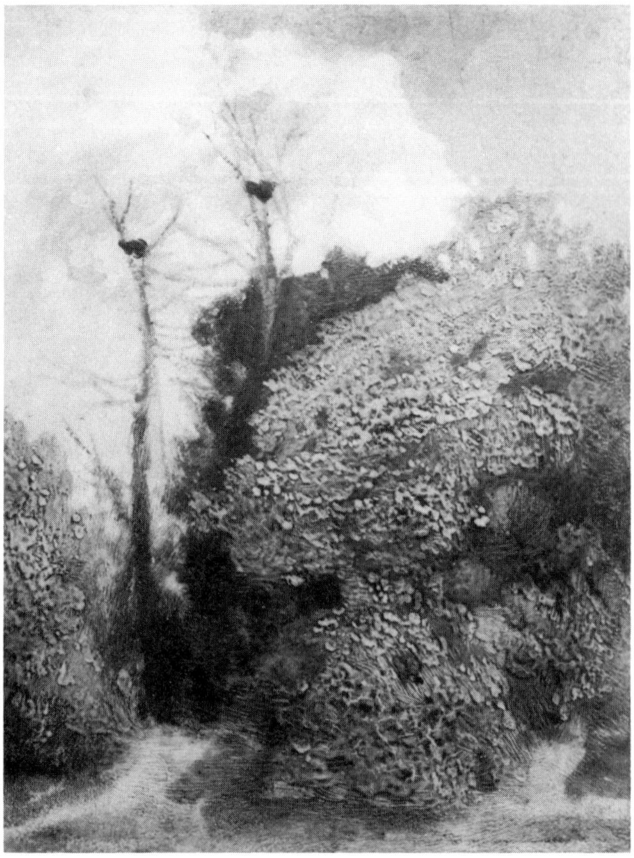

157 In the Bishop's Garden, Norwich, *c.*1824-5

157 In the Bishop's Garden, Norwich, *c.*1824-5

Oil on millboard; 25.6 × 18.9 ($10\frac{1}{16} \times 7\frac{7}{16}$). PROV: Ann Cotman;[1] by descent to John Joseph Cotman;[1] sale, Murrell, Norwich, 26-27 Nov. 1862 (ex catalogue),[2] bt. Charles Clowes 1 gn.; bt. from him by Mr. Mower of Trowse, Norwich; bt. from him by Mr. Hunt, bookseller, on behalf of Reuben Levine by 21 June 1899; bt. from him by William H. Booth; his sale, Robert Bond & Sons, Ipswich, 18-21, 23 April 1906, lot 832 (with pencil sketch), bt. H. S. Theobald £37; bt. from him by R. J. Colman, Feb. 1910; R. J. Colman Bequest 1946. (107.235.951). EXH: Norwich 1902 (204); Norwich 1930-31. REF: Dickes p. 321; *EDP* 9 Jan. 1931 repro.

This small sketch represents a signal point in Cotman's developing technique as an oil painter. Although there is little evidence to support the traditional location as the garden of the Bishop's Palace off St. Martin's at Palace Plain, it is a reasonable assertion: on his removal to Norwich Cotman took up residence on St. Martin's at Palace Plain and a number of drawings show the view from the house of the Palace and its surrounding trees.[3] A compositional pencil sketch[4] for No. 157 is in the collection at Norwich. Inscribed with colour notes, it is the briefest of preparatory sketches and bears the date 'May 20, 1824', soon after Cotman's arrival in Norwich.

No. 157 is the first of a series of tree subjects painted during the mid 1820s which represent the highest and most individual achievement of Cotman's career as an oil painter (see Nos. 158-161). At this time Cotman developed a 'fatty' or 'clotted' texture to his brushstrokes which became the counterpart of his idiosyncratic 'banana' shapes in his depiction of foliate forms in watercolour. No. 157 is perhaps the 'fattiest' of these oils in which both texture and foliage are achieved through brush strokes which are loaded with oil. Despite the supremely confident handling, however, the paint surface has crept and cracked on drying. This reveals a weakness in Cotman's technique not apparent in the following works of this series,[5] confirming that he was both experimenting and learning from these experiments at this time.

[1]According to MS note by James Reeve, Art Dept. archives, NCM. [2]Added in MS in James Reeve's copy of the sale catalogue, Art Dept. archives, NCM. [3]Kitson 1937 p. 259, pl. 117. [4]NCM 2.107.235.951. [5]Some wrinkling due to the drying process is apparent, however, in No. 159 *The Mishap.*

158 The Baggage Wagon, *c.*1824-8

illustrated in colour on p. 134.

Oil on mahogany panel; 43 × 35.2 ($16\frac{15}{16}$ × $13\frac{7}{8}$). PROV: the artist's sale, Spelman, Norwich, 10-12 Sept. 1834, lot 111 as *Landscape,* bt. Paul Squires £5; his sale ?1864, bt. J. J. Colman with No. 159, £75; J. J. Colman Bequest 1898. (5.4.99). EXH: London, International Exhibition 1874 (148); RA 1878 (45) as *Landscape;* Norwich 1883 (D19); Norwich 1885 (36); Newcastle 1887 (778); Earls Court 1897 (41); RA 1934 (598, Commemorative Catalogue 403, pl. CXV); London, Wildenstein's Galleries 1937 (12); Paris 1938 (34); Agnew 1958 (62); RA 1961-62 (181) repro.; British Council 1966-67 (12) repro. REF: NCM ?1897 (F); Binyon 1897 p. 91, repro. p. 93; NCM ?1899 (21); Binyon 1903 pl. C4; NCM 1904 (6); Holmes, *Burlington* 1904 p. 82; Dickes pp. 319-20, repro. p. 320; NCM 1909 (6); Cundall, *The Studio* 1920 p. 21; *EDP* 6 April 1922; Kaines Smith 1926 pp. 91-92, 99, 136, 138, 165; Wilenski 1933 pp. 95, 210, pl. 30; *EDP* 8 Feb. 1933, 17 Jan. 1934 repro.; 22 April 1937; NCM 1937 (33); Kitson 1937 pp. 271, 272; *EDP* 8 March 1938 repro.; Oppé, *Burlington* Aug. 1945 p. 199; Barnard, *The Studio* Aug. 1947 p. 30; Barnard repro. frontispiece; *Colman Collection Guide* 1951 p. 5. pl. 2; Rienaecker pp. 27, 33, 49, pl. 44 fig. 85; Davis, *ILN* 1965 p. 31 repro.; Hawcroft, *RCH Magazine* p. 12, repro. p. 14 in colour; Eurich 1966 p. 45 repro.; Herrmann 1967 pl. XXI in colour; Day 1969 vol. III p. 17; Hemingway 1979 p. 73.

Perhaps the most significant tendency in Cotman's oils of this period is the increased awareness of the three dimensional possiblities in representing the patterns of nature. Such possibilities could not be obtained either through flat planes of coloured washes, or a sole dependence upon the etched line.

The Baggage Wagon, a pair to No. 159, is closely related to No. 157, *In The Bishop's Garden.* The same 'fatty' application of paint is at its most subtle in foliage at the lower left of the composition, while the juxta position of stark and leafy trees is also developed. Critics have struggled to account for the simple splendour of Cotman's technique and composition in his oils of this series. Dickes remarks inexplicably: 'The composition reminds one of Cuyp. The solidity of the painting is thoroughly Dutch.' Kitson refers instead to the pointillism of Camille Pissarro. Writers have also perpetuated the fantasy that the picture is painted 'on paper to save the cost of canvas.'[1]

A number of related pencil sketches survive for this composition. A first variant[2] on the design is at the Castle Museum, Norwich which shows the same scene but with two figures other than the baggage wagon. A thumbnail sketch, *Trees by a road,*[2] is another view of these figures on the same road. A third study,[4] on light grey paper is the first in which the wagon appears, with its distinctive tilt and the posture of the rider clearly established.

[1]Rienaecker p. 33. [2]NCM 7.139.949. [3]NCM 77.L1967.9. [4]V&A E679-1925.

159 The Mishap, *c.*1824-8

illustrated on p. 130

Oil on mahogany panel; 43 × 35.4 ($16\frac{7}{8}$ × $13\frac{15}{16}$). PROV: the artist's sale, Spelman, Norwich, 10-12 Sept. 1834, lot 112, bt. Paul Squires 5 gns.; his sale ?1864, bt. J. J. Colman with No. 158, £75; J. J. Colman Bequest 1898. (6.4.99). EXH: Norwich 1860 (159) as *The Broken Wheel;* London, International Exhibition 1874 (168) as *The Breakdown;* Norwich 1878 (95); RA 1878 (41) as *Landscape;* Norwich 1883 (18) as *The Upset;* Norwich 1885 (35); Newcastle 1887 (779); Earls Court 1897 (45); Tate 1922 (49); RA 1934 (599, Commemorative Catalogue 404); Paris 1938 (35); Agnew 1958 (64); USA 1967 (28) repro. REF: NCM ?1897 (C); Binyon 1897 pp. 88, 91, repro. p. 91; NCM ?1899 (14); Binyon 1903 pl. C5; NCM 1904 (11); Holmes, *Burlington* 1904 p. 83; Dickes pp. 319-320, repro. opp. p. 319; NCM 1909 (11); Cundall, *The Studio* 1920 p. 21; *EDP* 6 April 1922; Kaines Smith 1926 pp. 91-92, 99, 136, 138, 165; *EDP* 17 Jan. 1934 repro.; NCM 1937 (34); Kitson 1937 pp. 271, 272; Oppé, *Burlington* Aug. 1945 p. 199; Barnard *The Studio* Aug. 1947 p. 30; *Colman Collection Guide* 1951 p. 5; Rienaecker pp. 27, 33; Hawcroft, *RCH Magazine* p. 12; Goldberg, *Connnoisseur* Feb. 1967 p. 96, fig. 6; Hemingway 1979 p. 73.

A pair to No. 158, *The Mishap* displays a decorative use of colour similar to that of No. 155, while the richly scumbled foliage is absolutely idiosyncratic. The two leafless saplings echo Cotman's vision in Nos. 158 and 161, while the treatment of the blue background recalls the traditionally earlier oil now in the Tate Gallery, London, known as *Duncombe Park.*[1]

A pencil study[2] by Cotman now in the Victoria and Albert Museum, London shows the original mishap of the cart with its broken wheel and spilled contents in isolation. Other pencil sketches in the same collection, including one dated 27 January 1824, may also relate to the incident. A thumbnail sketch[4] also survives which outlines the final composition almost exactly.

[1]Tate 3572. [2]V&A E.728-1925. [3]V&A E.681-1925. [4]NCM 598.235.951.

160 The Silent Stream, Normandy, *c.*1824-8

called *Normandy River*

illustrated on p. 146

Oil on canvas; 40.2 × 33.5 ($15\frac{7}{8}$ × $13\frac{3}{16}$). PROV: ?Dawson Turner 1827; ?given by him to his daughter Harriet on her marriage to Rev. John Gunn 1830; by descent to his second wife Eliza, 1890; her sale, Christie's, 26 April 1912, lot 14 as *The Silent Stream, Normandy,* bt. W. A. Coates, Edinburgh, 130 gns.; bt. from him by Percy Moore Turner 1927; bt. from him by R. J. Colman 4 Dec. 1936, £5,000; R. J. Colman Bequest 1946. (120.235.951). EXH: London, Paterson Gallery 1913 (8); London, Suffolk Street 1927 (82); Norwich 1945. REF: Binyon 1897 p. 91; ?Dickes p. 320 as *A Tree Piece;* Wilenski 1933 pp. 95, 210-211, 275, pl. CXVIII; Rutter, *Sunday Times* 20 Sept. 1936; Kitson 1937 pp. 271, 272, pl. 119; Oppé, *Burlington* Aug. 1945 p. 199; *Colman Collection Guide* 1951 p. 5; Pidgley p. 44.

There appears to be no obvious connection between this composition and a Normandy setting. In fact, the remainder of the works in this group seem to all have their origins in Norfolk.[1] Dawson Turner's daughter, Mrs. Harriet Gunn, owned this and another oil dating from the same period, *Silver Birches* (No. 161), traditionally given to her as a wedding present on her marriage to John Gunn.

No. 160 has suffered, with areas such as the boat and bottom corners repainted, while the surface has been severely flattened during relining. However it is still possible to appreciate the soft and delicate colour scale of greens and greys in a composition which recalls all the surviving oils[2] of this period. A pencil sketch of *c.*1827-8 now in the British Museum is of an upright landscape composition and appears to be a study for another oil destined to relate to this series.[3]

[1]Contemporary with this series is *The Drop Gate,* (Tate 3632) which may be identified as *Costessey Watering, Norfolk* from a watercolour version of that title (NCM 1.78.949). [2]cf. also *Salmon Spearing,* Agnews, July 1958 No. 69 (Private Collection). [3]BM 1902-5-14-243.

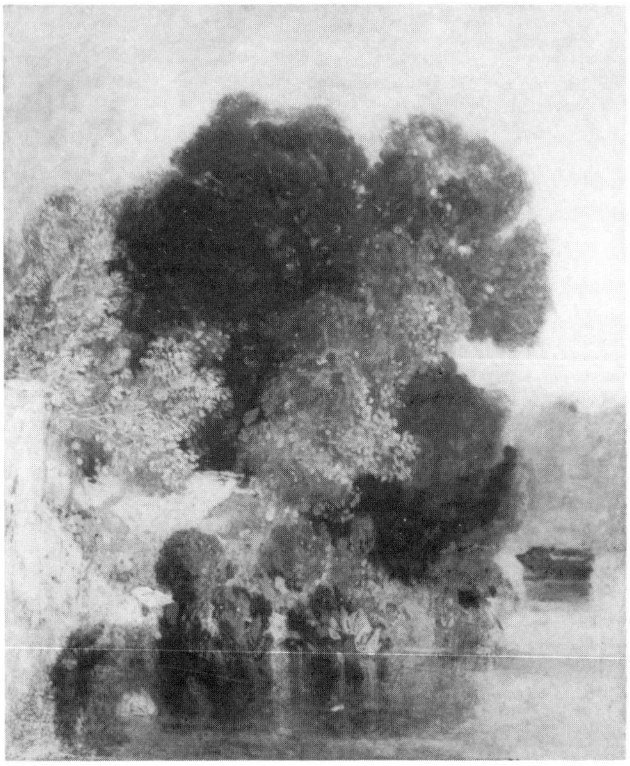

160 The Silent Stream, Normandy, *c.*1824-8

161 Silver Birches, *c.*1824-8

illustrated in colour on p. 135

Oil on canvas; 76.2 × 62.7 (30 × $24\frac{3}{4}$). PROV: ?Dawson Turner 1827; ?given by him to his daughter Harriet on her marriage to Rev. John Gunn 1830; by descent to his second wife Eliza, 1890; her sale, Christie's, 26 April 1912, lot 13 as *A Rocky Gorge, with trees,* bt. W. A. Coates, Edinburgh, 170 gns.; bt. from him by Percy Moore Turner 1927; on loan to NCM 1927-33; bt. from Percy Moore Turner by R. J. Colman, 15 April 1935, £8,000; R. J. Colman Bequest 1946. (119.235.951). EXH: London, Paterson Gallery 1913 (3); London, Suffolk Street 1927 (61); London, Olympia 1927 (X9) and 1928; Norwich 1945. REF: Binyon 1897 p. 91; ?Dickes p. 321 as *A Composition of Trees; EDP* 2 May 1927 repro., 5 May 1927; Collins Baker & James 1933 pl. 93; Rutter, *Sunday Times* 20 Sept. 1936; Kitson 1937 pp. 271, 272, 293, pl. 118; Binyon, *Burlington* July 1942 pp. 159, 163, pl. IIIB; Oppé, *Burlington* Aug. 1945 p. 199, pl. I; Barnard ref. & pl. 7; *Colman Collection Guide* 1951 pl. 3; Rienaecker pl 43 fig. 83; Mallalieu 1974 pl. III in colour; Pidgley p. 44; Parker, *In Britain* 1975 repro. p. 27 in colour; Allthorpe-Guyton 1979; Hemingway 1979 p. 73.

The lyrical quality of Nos. 158-160 reaches its climax in this composition. While Kitson finds *Silver Birches* 'one of the most distinguished of all Cotman's paintings', Binyon echoes his sentiments, describing it as 'one of Cotman's finest and most fortunate works.' Kitson suggests that *Silver Birches* was one of Cotman's exhibits with the British Institution in 1827, but there is no evidence to support this. Nevertheless Cotman did exhibit three landscapes with the British Institution that year[1] and it seems likely that they would belong to this series.

One more anomaly which exists concerning this picture is the traditional assertion that Dawson Turner purchased both this and *The Silent Stream, Normandy* as a wedding present for his daughter (see previous entry, No. 160). Oppé reveals that Kitson's account is based upon a misdating of one letter from Cotman to Turner, while Dickes states that Mrs. Gunn's two oils by Cotman were *The Silent Stream, Normandy* and 'A Composition of Trees' apparently founded on the view from the window of the house at St. Martin's Palace Plain. It seems that the latter must be *Silver Birches,*[2] while Dickes' assertion, based upon a comment by Binyon[3] may be a confusion with the oil sketch *In the Bishop's Garden* (No. 157).

[1]BI 1827, Nos. 129, 381, 383. [2]See PROV. [3]Binyon 1897 p. 91.

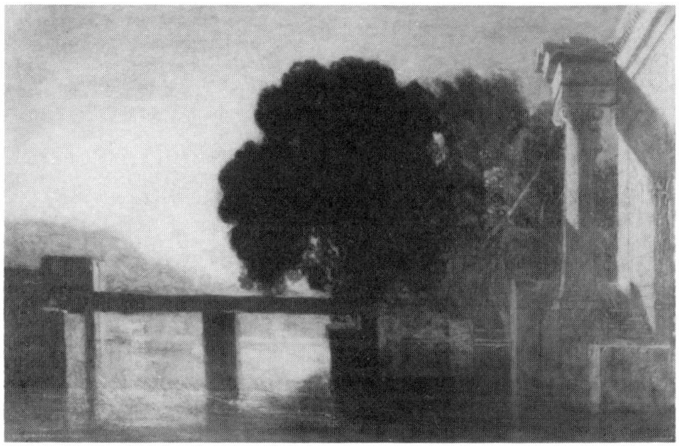

162 Palace of the Prince Beauharnais, *c.*1827-30

162 Palace of the Prince Beauharnais, *c.*1827-30

Oil on oak panel; 28 × 43 (11 × $16\frac{15}{16}$). PROV: the artist's sale, Spelman, Norwich, 10-12 Sept. 1834, lot 113 as *Landscape and Palace of the Prince Beauharnois,* bt. Edmund Cotman,[1] father of the artist, £3; by descent to Henry Cotman, brother of the artist; by descent to Henry's son, Frederick George Cotman by 1874; bt. from him by Thomas Brightwell *c.*1874, £40; bequeathed by him to Charles Foster by 1902; his sale, Spelman, Norwich, 12-14 March 1907, lot 274, bt. Boswell on behalf of R. J. Colman, 8 gns.; R. J. Colman Bequest 1946. (108.235.951). EXH: London, International Exhibition 1874 (96a) lent by F. G. Cotman; Norwich 1878 (86) lent by T. Brightwell; Norwich 1902 (166) lent by Charles Foster; Manchester 1912 (314); Tate 1922 (53); Norwich 1930-31. REF: *EDP* 8 Jan. 1931 repro.; Kitson 1937 p. 254.

Cotman visited the Château Navarre, seat of the Beauharnais family at Evreux only once, with the Dawson Turner family during a hot day on 16 July 1818.[2] No. 162 is a shimmering landscape memory of that visit, painted some ten years later, but founded upon sketches probably made at the time, but now lost.

Two compositional sketches survive which relate to this oil. One[3] in pencil is a less classical version which may be dated *c.*1828. The building to the right is almost hidden by foliage, while the bridge has span arches to the pillar supports. A more developed sketch[4] in black chalk is much closer to the finished oil and also includes forms under the left span of the bridge. These were later worked up as cattle in a watercolour version[5] traditionally painted for Dawson Turner.[6] Either the watercolour or the oil version could have been that exhibited with the Norwich Society in 1828 (167*) *Château Navarre, the late Property of Beauhamais.*

[1]According to letter on reverse of picture from F. G. Cotman, 11 Nov. 1874, quoting extract from Edmund Cotman's diary, 8 Sept. 1834. [2]Rajnai 1975 p. 17. [3]BM 1902-5-14-212. [4]BM 1902-5-14-107. [5]Norwich, Art Circle 1888 (189), lent by Mr. R. H. Inglis Palgrave; also BFAC 1888 (70). [6]A. H. Wild sale, Christie's, 16 June 1922, lot 29.

163 Cader Idris, *c.*1828-33

illustrated on opposite page

Oil on oak panel; 24.4 × 31.6 ($9\frac{5}{8}$ × $12\frac{7}{16}$). PROV: Rothschild & Co.; bt. from them by Percy Moore Turner, 3 July 1941, £150; bt. from him out of Beecheno Bequest Fund, 2 Aug. 1941, £350. (103.941). EXH: Norwich 1942; Kettering 1952 (47); Paris 1953 (30) pl. 18; Harrogate 1953; Art Exhibitions Bureau 1953-54 (2); Rotterdam 1955 (26); Worthing 1957 (14); Agnew 1958 (59); Derby & Nottingham 1959 (13); Manchester 1961 (21); Swansea 1964; Paris 1972 (67); Milan 1975 (135) repro.; Sudbury 1978 (1). REF: *Apollo* Nov. 1941 p. 122; *Times* 22 Nov. 1941 repro.; *Apollo* Jan. 1942 p. 19 repro.; Barnard, *The Studio* Aug. 1947 p. 30; Barnard pl. 8.

The mountain ridge of Cader Idris remained a haunting image in Cotman's mind throughout his lifetime. A number of versions in different media survive (see No. 122) but perhaps No. 163 is the most lyrical in atmospheric effect, and may be compared to the vision

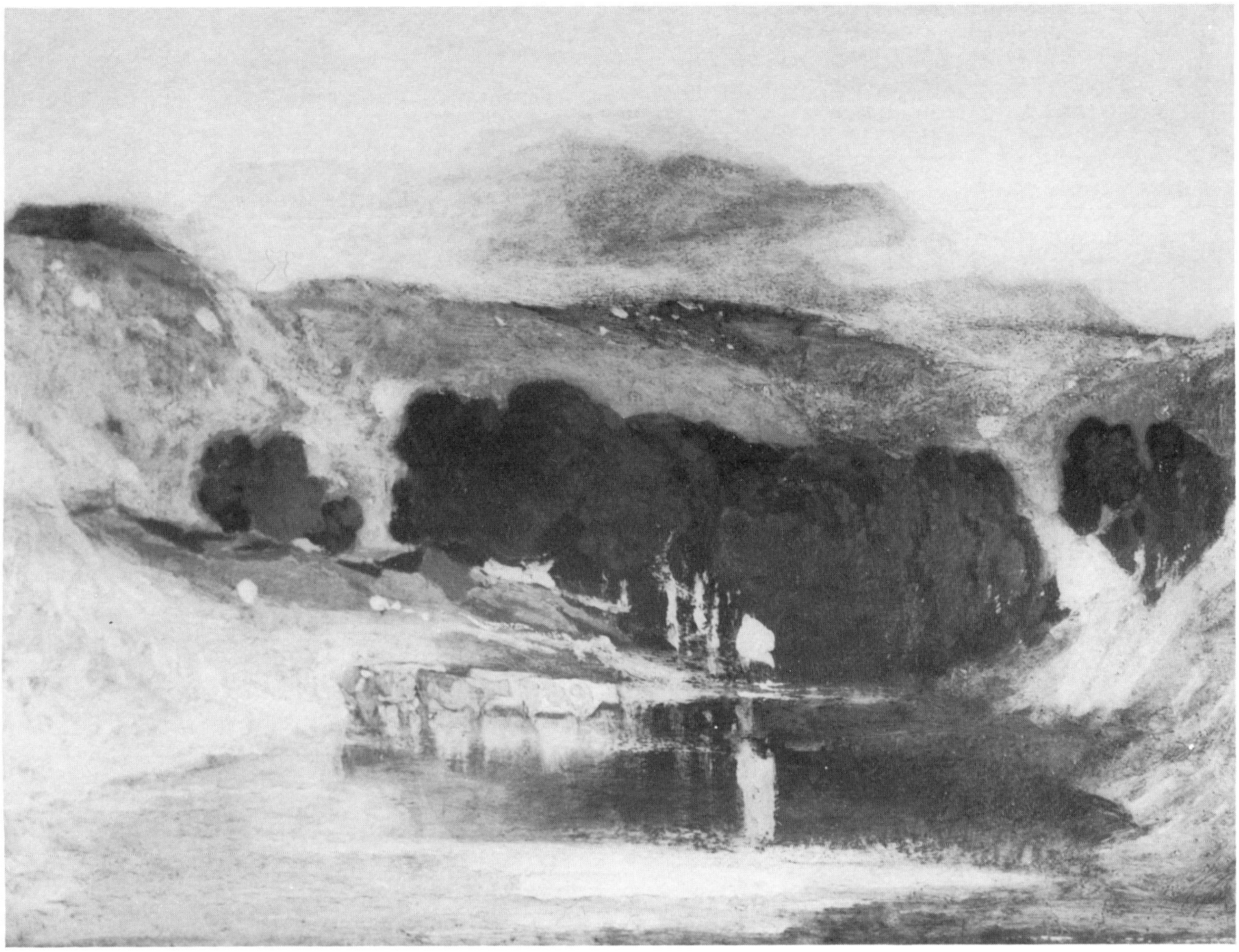

163 Cader Idris, *c.*1828-33

developed in his paste drawings of this period. The painterly technique of Nos. 158-161 is here developed with total freedom. The blobs of colour retain some of their 'fattiness' but achieve a more atmospheric and less decorative effect, while the palette is more subdued.

The composition is taken directly from a drawing[1] dated 1808, which was also reproduced in reverse as a soft ground etching,[2] plate 15 of Cotman's *Liber Studiorum* published in 1838. Slight variations between the original design and the oil version reveal that the latter is no slavish copy. Another oil version[3] of this subject is also in the collection at Norwich.

[1] Paterson Collection, London 1923. [2] Popham No. 309. [3] NCM 101.235.951.

164 An Ecclesiastic, 1836

Oil over pencil on mahogany panel, *verso* impressed *BROWN / HOLBORN;* 44.7 × 33.9 ($17\frac{9}{16}$ × $13\frac{5}{16}$). Prov: Cotman's sale, Christie's, London, 17 May 1843, lot 291 as *A priest in his robes before the altar in a church, capitally painted,* bt. by 'Mr Cotmans friend' (?Sandford) £2.6s.; J. R. Nutman; Percy Moore Turner; bt. from him by R. J. Colman with seven other pictures, 12 Dec. 1930; R. J. Colman Bequest 1946. (110.235.951). Ref: Kitson 1937 p. 340.

The date of this unfinished oil is established in a letter from Cotman to his son, John Joseph, written on 31 October 1836: 'I have nearly completed a picture of a Monk, & hope to finish another, its companion, in about a fortnight, both these to be sent to the Bath exhibition. The large one [of two figures praying] has been at a stand still in consequence of getting these done as pot-boilers.'[1] No record exists of either having been exhibited at Bath, while it is apparent that Cotman never did finish this work. Its companion, known as *The Monk*[2] is in the Colman Collection and both are in their original arched frames.

164 An Ecclesiastic, 1836

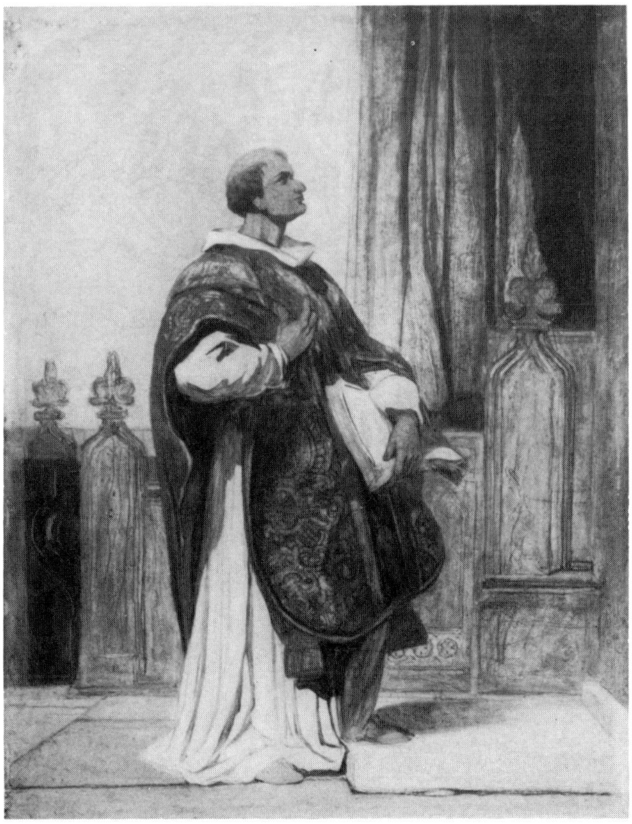

Although Cotman rightly regarded these works as 'pot-boilers', they remain of interest as being the only securely datable works in oil surviving from Cotman's time as Professor of Drawing at King's College prior to *c.*1839 (see No. 166). The choice of subject recalls his early oil of *St. James De Compostella,*[3] also in the Colman Collection, but also mirrors a concurrent preoccupation with figure subjects in his watercolours of the 1830s. It is interesting to note Cotman's use of a light coloured ground, suggesting that it was not his unvarying practice to work up a composition from an ochre ground, as might be inferred from his other unfinished oils (see Nos. 167, 168). His initial pencilwork is also clearly visible as is his method of colour composition. Colours are applied to echo each other across the depth of the composition. The background is securely blocked in, while movement is achieved through the gesture, glance and tread of the figure.

[1]BM. [2]NCM 111.235.951. [3]NCM 93.235.951 (Kitson 1937 pp. 119-120); two other oil sketches of Church Interiors, attributed to Cotman, are NCM 112.235.951 and NCM 47.949.

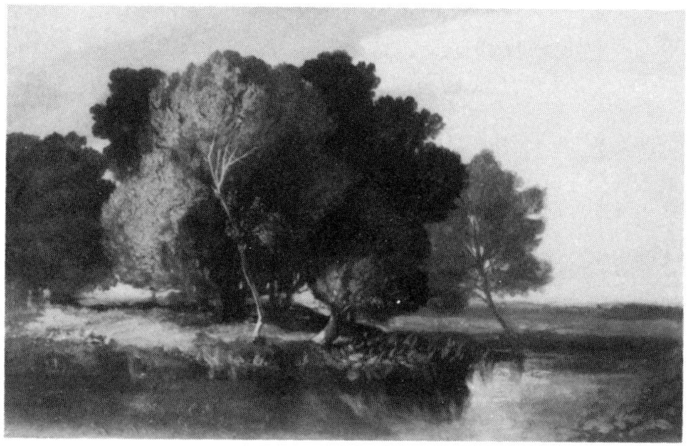

165 Alder Carr, *c.*1830s

165 Alder Carr, *c.*1830s

Oil on mahogany panel; 33.5 × 52.2 ($13\frac{1}{4}$ × $20\frac{1}{2}$). PROV: Edwin Edwards; bt. from him by Messrs. Leggatt; bt. from them by Dr. J. S. Cotman (d. 1902); by descent to his son Dr. Harold H. Cotman (d. 1930); by descent to his son Dr. J. S. Cotman; bt. from him by Percy Moore Turner 1935; bt. from him by R. J. Colman, 30 Sept. 1938, £500; R. J. Colman Bequest 1946. (106.235.951). EXH: Tate 1922 (12); Norwich 1945. REF: Binyon 1897 p. 88; Dickes p. 316; Kitson 1937 p. 293.

The traditional title, Alder Carr, is a generic term for any swampy wood in which alder trees predominate. This composition exists in a number of versions and with more than one title, making it difficult to be sure of the original location of the subject. A sketch in chalks entitled *Marshland Trees*[1] shows a similar view whilst a second, related but unfinished oil[2] possibly by Cotman, is variously known as *Postwick Grove* or *Scene on the Bure.* Finally, No. 165 is directly related to a watercolour version[3] by John Joseph Cotman, entitled *Gunton Park, Norfolk.* A third oil by Cotman of a similar group of trees, now in the Bacon Collection, is also entitled *Postwick Grove.*

A thumbnail sketch[4] by Cotman in the collection at Norwich, formerly ascribed to No. 165, is in fact more closely related to the oil *Postwick Grove* in the Bacon Collection. There is little to substantiate Kitson's claim that it was No. 165 which Cotman exhibited with the Norfolk and Suffolk Institution in 1830 (49*) *Alder Carr Reach* as it is not certain that this work was in oil. The low, sombre key of the sky and trees seems removed from the sparkle of works such as *Silver Birches* (No. 161) and *Cader Idris* (No. 163), suggesting a date of post 1830.

The watercolour version by John Joseph Cotman is a faithful replica of No. 165 but also conveys a conscious effort to improve the balance of the composition with the addition of buildings and smoke on the horizon to the right and changing the direction in which the righthand tree bends. Cotman himself made a similar but more successful change in another version of this composition (see No. 167).

[1]BM 1902-5-14-133. [2]Mackintosh Collection, Rienaecker pl. 54. A related drawing ascribed to M. E. Cotman is NCM 702.B5.235.951. [3]V&A 53-1896; a broader view is *Riverside Trees,* BM 1902-5-14-141. [4]NCM 6.139.949.

166 Henley on Thames — Boys Fishing, *c.*1837-9

illustrated on p. 137

Oil on mahogany panel; 35.1 × 43.3 ($13\frac{13}{16}$ × $17\frac{1}{16}$). PROV: bt. from the artist by Rev. James Bulwer 1839; bt. from him by William Boswell; bt. from him by Thomas Woolner RA by 1874; bt. from him by R. J. Colman, Jan. 1912; R. J. Colman Bequest 1946. (121.235.951). EXH: Norwich 1839 (125); London, International Exhibition 1874 (98) lent by T. Woolner; RA 1882 (8); Grosvenor Gallery 1888 (296); Manchester 1912 (311); Tate 1922 (48); Norwich 1930-31; Norwich 1945. REF: Dickes p. 305; Cundall, *The Studio* p. 21, pl. XLIX; *Artwork,* Autumn 1930 (Kitson); *EDP* 8 and 9 Jan. 1931 repro.; Kitson 1937 p. 341, pl. 133; Rienaecker p. 45 n. 2; Pidgley p. 133.

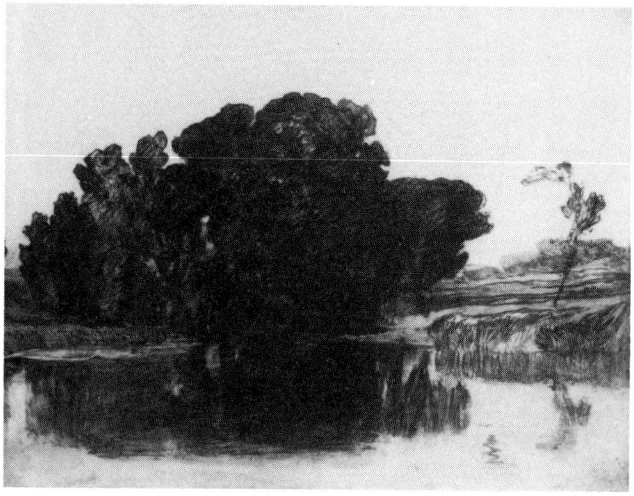

167 Alder Carr, *c.*1839-42

Pidgley has established that in 1839 James Bulwer, as the winner of the highest Art Union prize of fifteen pounds in the first Norfolk and Norwich Art Union draw, selected this picture as his prize. Bulwer was aware of Cotman's renewed delight in oil painting that year as two of Cotman's letters to him survive, written in May and July 1839, articulating that pleasure: 'I am so fond of it that I think I shall never execute another drawing' (see pp. 131, 137).

A more liquid application of the medium is evident in this fine and rare example of his finished style at this period. The design is tightly controlled, enlivened by single blotches of colour. Luxuriant foliage is offset by translucent green glazes. Painted upon an ochre ground, this picture gives some indication of the finished splendour that Nos. 167 and 168 might have achieved.

A study[1] of No. 166, *Landscape with Boys Fishing,* is now in the British Museum, London. This too is enlivened with touches of yellow and red, while the style and composition recall the late monochromes such as No. 129.

A watercolour[2] of a similar subject also survives, together with a related oil.[3]

[1]BM 1902-5-14-58, also known as *Dewy Eve* (Norwich, Art Circle 1888, No. 109). [2]Fine Art Society, 40th Exhibition, 1960 (10). [3]Broadbent sale, Sotheby's, London 14 Dec. 1938, lot 330, bt. Agnews. Probably not JSC.

167 Alder Carr, *c.*1839-42

Oil over chalk on mahogany panel; 35.1 × 45.7 ($13\frac{13}{16}$ × 18). PROV: John Joseph Cotman; bt. from him by John King; bt. from him by James Reeve; exchanged by him for etchings from Edwin Edwards; sold by Mrs. Edwards, Christie's, bt. by W. Boswell & Sons; bt. from them by W. H. Booth, Ipswich, 1898, £10; bt. from him by H. S. Theobald; bt. from him by R. J. Colman, Feb. 1910; R. J. Colman Bequest 1946. (113.235.951). EXH: Tate 1922 (152).

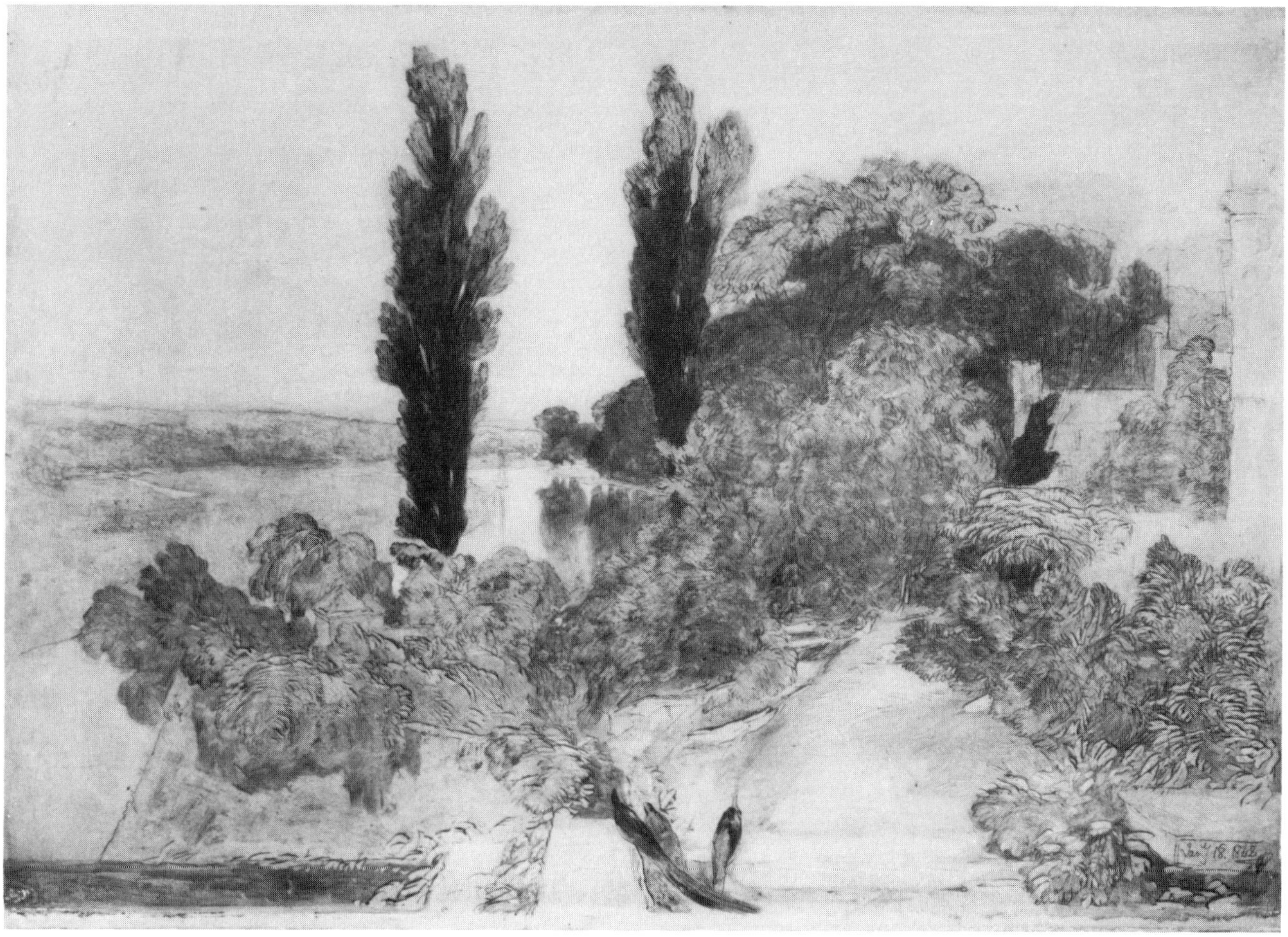

168 From My Father's House at Thorpe, *c.*1841-2

Of all the versions of this composition, No. 167, although unfinished, is the most dramatic. Freely drawn with both brush and chalk, the dual masses of grove are given scale by the lone tree and their reflections. The graceful silhouette of the sapling tree to the right, together with the dark central mass, recall the forms of Cotman's late monochrome watercolours (see Nos. 129, 132).

See No. 165 for a discussion of related compositions.

168 From My Father's House at Thorpe, *c.*1841-2

Oil over black chalk on canvas; 68.4 × 94 ($26\frac{15}{16}$ × 37). INSCR: dated in chalk l.r. *Jany 18. 1842.* PROV: W. Boswell; bt. from him by the Rev. George W. Minns, Enfield; presented by him to the East Anglian Art Society 1877; presented by them with the rest of their collection 1894. (1.75.94). EXH: Tate 1922 (151); Arts Council, *Norwich School of Painting* 1947 (5); Kettering 1952 (51); Stoke-on-Trent 1953; Harrogate 1953; Worthing 1957 (38); Agnew 1958 (4) repro.; Derby & Nottingham 1959 (14); Manchester 1961 (24); RA 1961-62 (182) repro.; USA 1967 (30) repro.; Sudbury 1978 (4). REF: *Norfolk Chronicle* 26 Jan. 1878; NCM ?1897 (21); Binyon 1897 p. 98; NCM ?1899 (16); Binyon 1903 pp. xii-xiii; NCM 1904 (7); Holmes, *Burlington* 1904 p. 83; Dickes pp. 323, 405, repro. p. 404; NCM 1909 (7); Cundall, *The Studio* 1920 p. 23; *Morning Post* 7 April 1922; *EDP* 25 Oct. 1925; Kaines Smith 1926 pp. 54-55, 88, 91, 95, 100, 138, 155; NCM 1937 (37); Kitson 1937 pp. 4, 359, 362-3, pl. 156; Rienaecker pp. 31-32, 35, pl. 56 fig. 107; Hawcroft, *MC News* 1959 p. 12 repro.; Hawcroft, *RCH Magazine* p. 13 repro.; Warren, *Norfolk Fair* 1968 p. 41 repro.; Maas 1969 repro. p. 55; Mallalieu 1974 pl. 23 and repro. back cover; Holcomb 1978 p. 17; Goldberg 1978 p. 147; Jacobs & Warner 1980 repro. p. EA23.

This remarkable canvas is developed from sketches made on Cotman's last holiday in Norfolk, possibly during his visit to his father on 3 November 1841. According to his plans recorded in a letter[1] to Dawson Turner that day, he intended to dine with his father.

A preliminary chalk sketch[2] now in the British Museum establishes those elements of the composition which may be closest to the actual view from his father's home at Thorpe. The sweep of the river Yare in the middle distance is framed by two tall poplars, as in the oil version. A few diminutive figures are dwarfed by trees and vegetation. A second chalk sketch[3] in the same collection establishes a more romantic view, which is closer to the final composition and introduces the three peacocks in the foreground. One change which was not adhered to in the final oil is the substitution of two fir trees for the poplars. The three studies together provide a last insight into the artist's creative and romantic imagination.

Both Cotman's sons paid tribute to this final work. While John Joseph executed a watercolour version[4] of the oil, Miles Edmund reproduced the composition as a lithograph in 1842. It is likely that it was Miles Edmund who inscribed the date on the canvas to record that day when his father last worked on the picture.

[1] Barker Collection. [2] BM 1902-5-14-165. [3] BM 1902-5-14-166. [4] Whitworth, Manchester, D.2.1933.

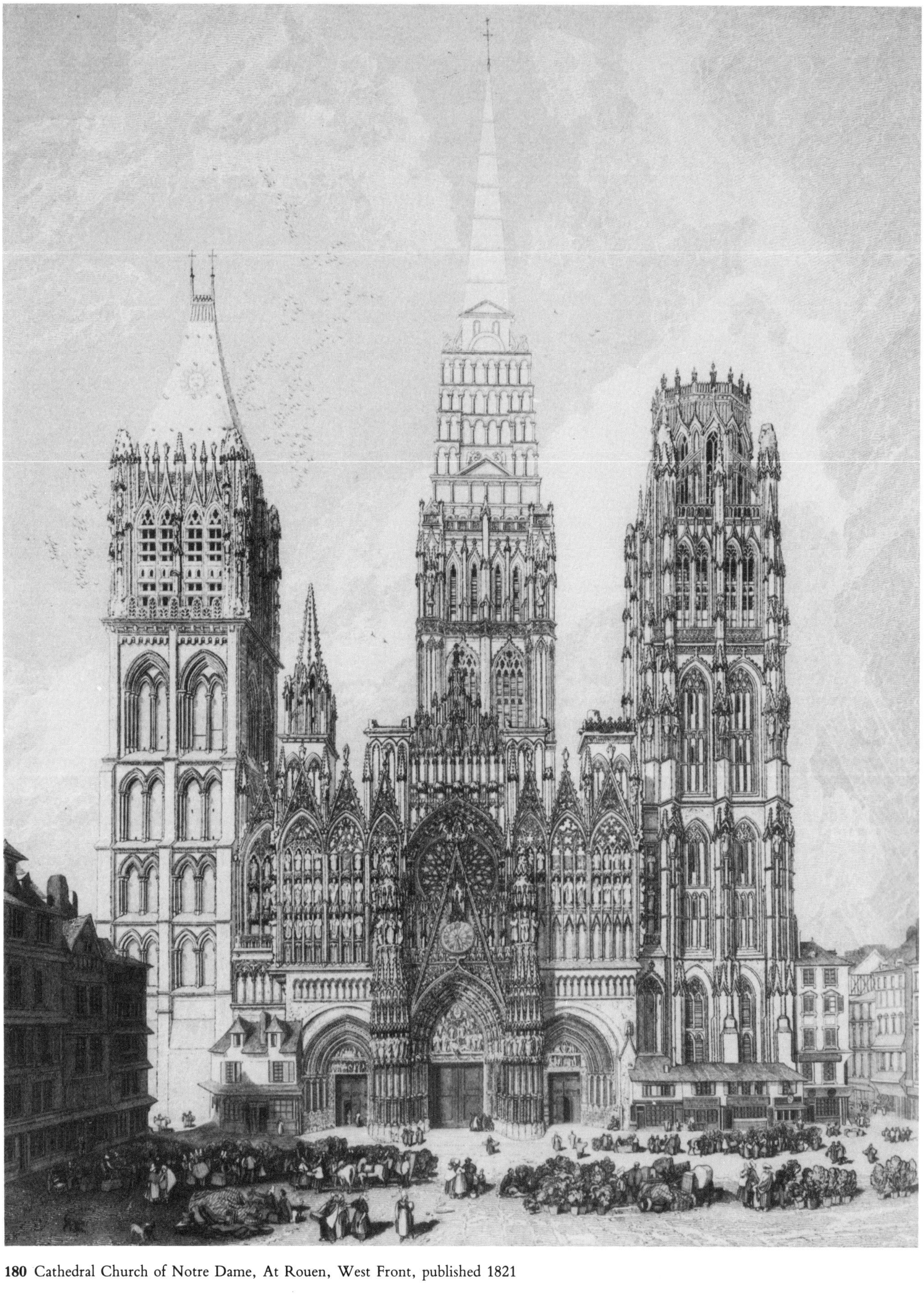

180 Cathedral Church of Notre Dame, At Rouen, West Front, published 1821

12
The Etchings

Almost all Cotman's etched work derives from the period 1810-22. This was a period of unremitting labour for him but it should not be assumed that the results were inevitably hack-work. While it is true that under the aegis of Dawson Turner Cotman undertook the prodigious task of executing over four hundred plates in the publication of six volumes of etchings, it is apparent that he was dedicated to the work. He spent most of his time in voracious pursuit of subjects and was helped by assistants in the production of plates. His passion for collecting and his career both before and after this period reveal his antiquarian and archaeological interests working hand in hand with his joy in the representation of Nature. Although the publication of etched work demanded *'A Herculean Labor',*[1] it also held out the 'distant view of reputation'[2] and the possiblity of a more secure livelihood. On 20 December 1810 Cotman wrote to Francis Cholmeley of his first publication *Miscellaneous Etchings:* 'This work save a few draw[in]gs to order has been my chief care; I am very fond of it, and being of a sanguine disposition, it gives me spirits, for I fancy a long line of patrons, and this being my first essay.'

Cotman's correspondence contains a good deal of discussion of his etched work, which reveals both the seriousness and the pleasure with which he tackled this essentially reproductive medium. In a letter to Dawson Turner of 25 January 1812 he gives short shrift to recently-published plates engraved by James Basire after John Ady Repton: 'I cannot help noticing that I think Mr. Repton's Plates of Barsham House are very vile things. I expected very much better, at least *correctness,* from an Architect — which they do not possess — so much for a bungling Engraver, giving finish where none was meant and altering that which he could not understand.'[3] This desire for accuracy is inherent throughout his etched work of archaeological subjects, but there is equally a visionary quality to his etchings which often finds a parallel in the grandeur of scale exemplified in the work of Piranesi.

Cotman's correspondence with the Cholmeley family in the year 1811 provides the touchstone to an appreciation of his technique and aspirations as an etcher, at a time when he was establishing both his method and his reputation in etching before his move to Yarmouth. On 14 January 1811 he wrote to Francis Cholmeley to seek criticism of some examples of his work: 'I shall be proud to be favoured with them, as a fresh eye (to my misfortune) may with ease detect the tottering state of my poor Howden, caused by too strict attention to parts, and rather too much care have been taken with the shadows for the good effect of the whole.' Cholmeley responded by approaching a good number of potential subscribers, including Todd, 'the first bookseller in York in the line of the Fine Arts, as well as in every other. He admired them and said he thought the work uncommonly cheap.'[4] Cholmeley also commented upon 'a want of delicacy and effect' in some of the earlier examples he had seen, whilst admiring others (see No. 169). *The Manor House, York* he found 'also very good and Rebrandtish, but some of the doors are rather coarse. Croyland is good, but Howden, alas! though excellent in other aspects, not only totters but tumbles, something must be done to it.' He considered that the etchings had 'the character of pencil sketches' rather than of finished drawings, but concluded that this was no bad thing: 'indeed you transfer *yourself* on to copper wonderfully'. Cholmeley's sister Katherine Charlton also appreciated this aspect of his technique, writing on 6th Arpil 1811: 'To say how nearly they resemble your pencil drawings is sufficient to prove how beautiful they are, but to me there is a strength and softness which excels even your original sketches. Those that particularly struck me are Croyland, Howden, the trees in Duncombe Park, and a gateway at Rivaulx.'[5] Anne Cholmeley added her own praise to the same letter: 'Perhaps *my* praise may not be *very* flattering to you, but I certainly have never seen any etchings I thought nearly so soft and forcible, except some of Rembrandt's Sir Harry shewed me. The trees at Duncombe Park I prefer to any, at least they strike me as most like Rembrandt's.'

Cotman found such references to Rembrandt 'a great compliment', but added that 'it would not do to follow that master in my subjects.'[6] His letter of 5 March to Francis Cholmeley is the most specific concerning his technique. Sir Henry Englefield's gift to Cotman of six etchings by Piranesi 'was the model I intended most religiously to bend my mind and judgment too. How far *I* and all modern etchers are behind him, both as to the execution . . . with the needle and conception of effect, no one can be a better judge than he who strives to copy him, where the broad black line *looks not coarse* but full and mellow.'[6] Later in the same letter, he concludes 'The style I have adopted is more difficult than that style of the Manor House, which is made up of scratches; the other style, *every line is studied* and is decided, consequently more calculated to show talent.'

Cholmeley took up Cotman's reference to Piranesi in a letter of 16 April.[7] Whilst commending the 'rapid and striking' improvement of Cotman's style he pointed to Cotman's habit of leaving the sky unworked in his early etchings. He recommended that Cotman 'put in skies in order to give the whole more the appearance of a finished piece. Piranesi's skies are many of them beautiful, I think, and add much to the richness of effect in his views.' He finished his letter by offering to lend Cotman 'several of Piranesi's etchings,' an offer which Cotman appears not to have pursued. This was despite having written the previous February to Dawson Turner expressing the hope that he might view a complete set of Piranesi etchings belonging to Hudson Gurney 'so that I can glean something from that vast mass of excellence.'[8] In the same letter he had admitted with some modesty: 'I decidedly follow Piranesi, however far I may be behind him in every requisite.'

At the end of 1811 a complete set of Piranesi etchings came on the market through the Norwich bookseller, William Stevenson, at a price of £120. Cotman informed[9] Dawson Turner of the set and he promptly purchased it, eliciting Cotman's response: 'As an Artist I cannot but most sincerely congratulate you on your purchase; for I do, without exception, think it the most superb book in your Collection — and by far, by very far, the cheapest.'[10] Such extravagant praise, whilst being totally in character, was given in the knowledge that by access to the set he 'should gain a most invaluable Study.'[9]

The twenty six plates of the *Miscellaneous Etchings* were completed with a *Dedication to Sir H. C. Englefield,*[11] issued on 1 July 1811. The earliest of the etchings contained in the final

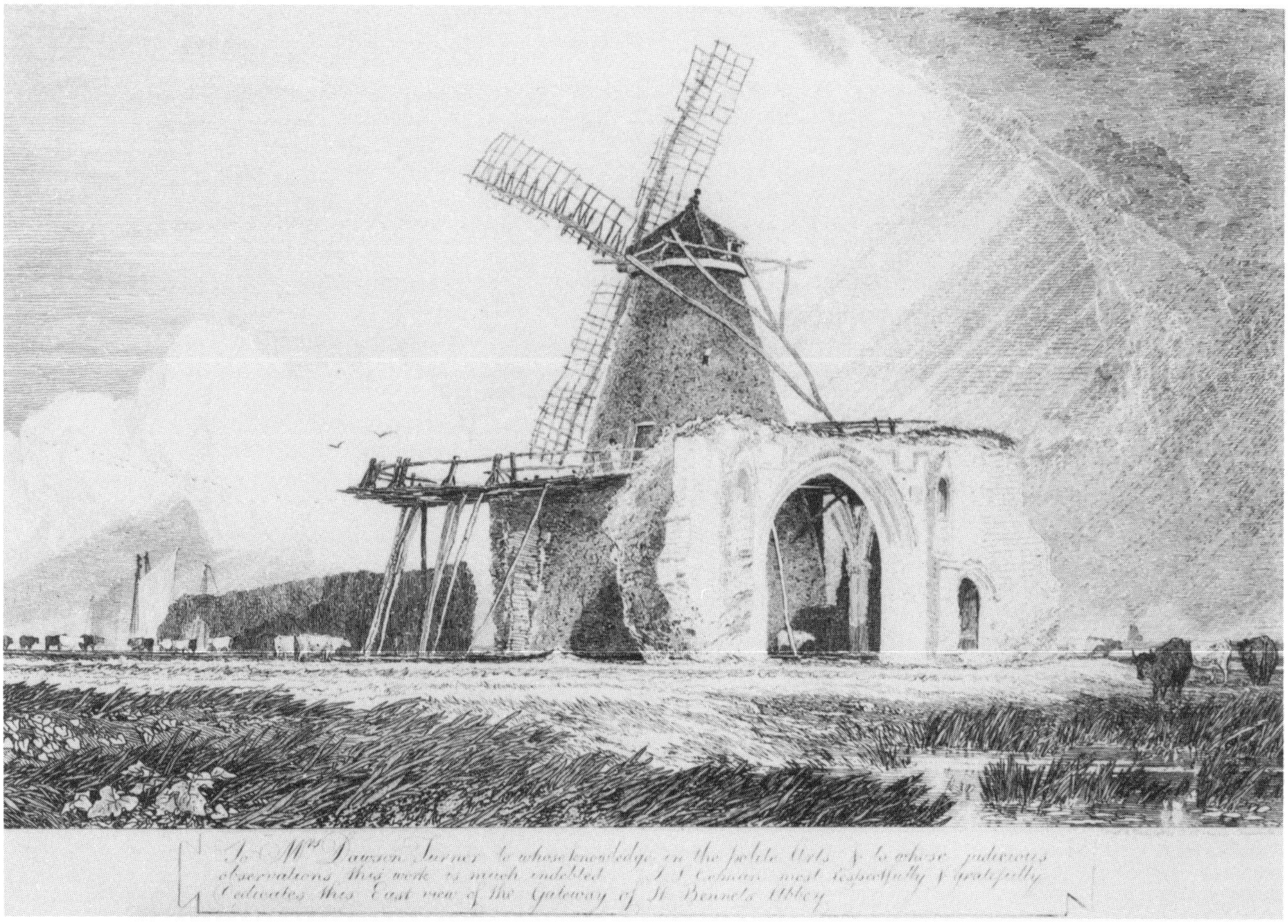

177 East View of the Gateway of St. Bennets Abbey, published 1813

volume was that of *South Birlingham Church,*[12] dated 29 August 1810. The compositions included mainly architectural subjects resulting from his tours in Yorkshire, Wales, Suffolk and Norfolk. This choice was presumably influenced by Cotman's interest in such subjects as much as by market forces. Although Francis Cholmeley had advised him that the York bookseller Todd 'said his subscribers did not like the view in Duncombe Park, because it might have been *anywhere.* Two-thirds of mankind, you know, mind more *what* is represented than *how* it is done' the advice had come too late to influence radically the compilation of the final selection.

Cotman embarked immediately upon the series of etchings of Norfolk antiquities which was to occupy him until their eventual publication in 1818 as *A series of Etchings illustrative of the Architectural Antiquities of Norfolk.* A presentation copy to Dawson Turner of this work is now in the British Museum.[13] In two volumes, it contains extra title pages and impressions of all the states of each plate, together with three additional plates. This was not, however, the only work of these years. He also produced a series of more than one hundred etchings of Norfolk architectural subjects, which he proposed to publish in 1823 as *Specimens of Norman and Gothic Architecture in the County of Norfolk.*[14] This was one of a number of projects which did not reach fruition,[15] although individual plates were published and often used as sources for drawing copies. The majority of this series are conceived purely as antiquarian records rather than for any larger aesthetic motive.

It is in these works, together with those of the *Engravings of the Most Remarkable of the Sepulchral Brasses in Norfolk* published in 1819,[16] that the work of assistants is most evident. In his letter to Francis Cholmeley of 1 June 1817, Cotman mentions 'having employed apprentices and only finished the works and sketched abroad . . . with these apprentices I have finished my Norfolk Antiquities.' It is likely that the etcher Henry Davey was one of these assistants. As Pidgley points out,[17] his style and sense of composition can be seen to be remarkably close to that of Cotman in a series of etchings of Suffolk antiquities published by Davey in 1818. Pidgley also hypothesises[18] that Frederick Crome is likely as a second apprentice: his signature appearing alongside that of Cotman in the plate of *Font, Chatgrave Church, Norfolk.*[19] For his last major etching project, the *Architectural Antiquities of Normandy,* Cotman relied heavily upon the assistance of Joseph Lambert. In a letter to his wife of 2 September 1820, Cotman wrote from St. Lô, Normandy, addressing himself at one stage to Lambert: 'I suppose by this time he has worked himself aground if so pray Lambert take up any of them to carry them on as far as you see is consistent with *my style*—I trust entirely to you & I don't fear but I shall be satisfied.'[20]

It was a blow to Cotman when the copper plates for his entire etched work were sold to the publisher Henry Bohn in December 1835 for a mere one hundred pounds,[21] having failed to reach their reserve price in his sale of September 1834. Bohn's subsequent complete edition of Cotman's etchings in 1838 included the previously unpublished series of soft ground etchings which Bohn called Cotman's *Liber Studiorum.* In the preface Bohn explains: 'The *Liber Studiorum* consists of studies in soft-ground, done more for practice and amusement than with any view to publication. This style of Etching which is not often resorted to, was preferred in the present instance from a feeling that it gave more of the freedom and effect of drawing. Mr. Cotman entertained some reluctance to

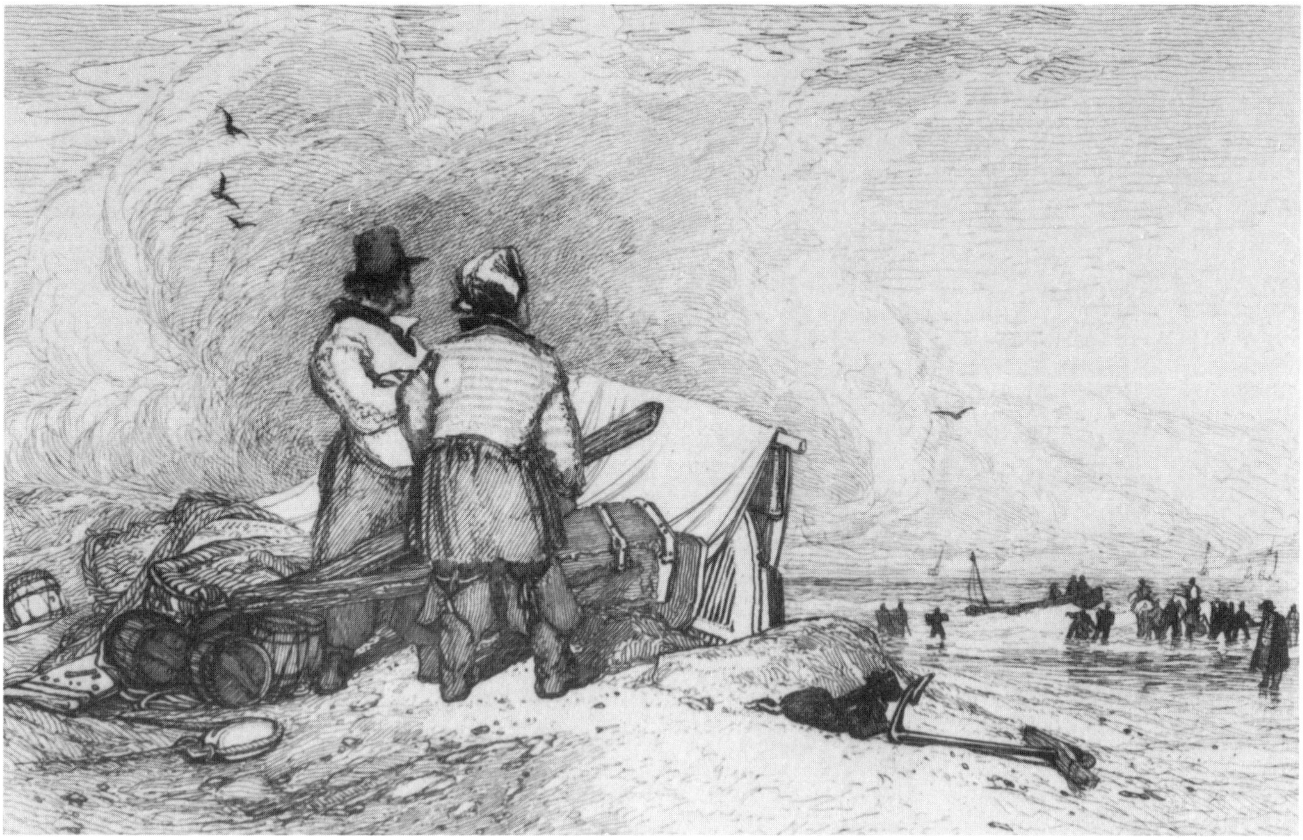

183 Scene on the Beach, published 1846

the publication of these early efforts, but the favourable opinions expressed of them by several distinguished artists overcame his objections.' A number of the original drawings for these etchings survive (see Nos. 186-188), most of which date from the period *c.*1808-17.[22] Cotman appears to have conceived the idea of publishing his soft ground etchings at least by 1824 when he exhibited four[23] with the Norwich Society as 'part of a Series of Designs intended to Illustrate a Work now publishing on Landscape Composition' (see Nos. 184, 185).

Only one was published at the time in a separate work (see No. 173). Thomas Phillips, RA in a letter to Dawson Turner of 11 April 1815 was pleased to receive an example: 'I don't know if we are indebted to the kindness of yourself or Mr. Cotman for the impression of his excellent softground.'[24] Certainly, some of the most personal and evocative examples of Cotman's etched work are to be found in the thirty-nine soft ground etchings contained within the *Liber Studiorum.* Nevertheless, Cotman's reputation increased steadily as his etchings were published, his *Architectural Antiquities of Normandy* receiving the most consistently high praise. In 1821 Cotman showed two etchings[25] with the Norwich Society (for one of which see No. 180). On 18 August the *Norwich Mercury* critic effused: 'Mr. J. S. Cotman has two magnificent etchings of buildings, from his work on Normandy. This gentleman's talent has been so highly appreciated by the world of art, that no commendation we can bestow would add a grain to his celebrity. This work is truly honorable to himself, his country, and his nation.'

Notes

[1]JSC to Francis Cholmeley, 23 July 1822. [2]JSC to Francis Cholmeley, 14 Feb. 1820. [3]Royal Academy, published by John Gage 'Documents of Crome and Cotman' *Burlington Magazine,* April 1969 p. 216. [4]Francis Cholmeley to JSC, 24 Feb. 1811 (BM). [5]BM. [6]JSC to Francis Cholmeley, 5 March 1811. [7]BM. [8]JSC to DT, 10 Feb. 1811 (BM). [9]JSC to DT, 11 Jan. 1812 (Barker Collection). [10]Barker Collection (Kitson 1937 p. 146). [11]Popham No. 2. [12]*Ibid.* No. 7. [13]DT received similar presentation copies of Cotman's *Antiquities of St. Mary's Chapel at Stourbridge, near Cambridge* (1819) and *Architectural Antiquities of Normandy* (1822). These are also in the BM. The number of states (exclusive of the final published state) in the presentation copies are listed in Popham, Nos. 130-296. [14]See JSC to Mrs. DT, 19 July 1823 (BM), Kitson 1937 p. 171 and *Norwich Mercury* 9 Aug. 1823. [15]Others include Cotman's plans for a *Picturesque Normandy* (see Section 7) and in 1837, *The Pageant* (see Kitson 1937 pp. 329-330). [16]111 unnumbered plates; reissued with the addition of numbers on each plate by Bohn in 1839 as *Engravings of Sepulchral Brasses in Norfolk and Suffolk,* 2 vols. with a supplement of 47 plates relating to Suffolk monuments. [17]Pidgley pp. 25-27 and nn. 80, 85. [18]*Ibid* p. 26 and n. 82. [19]Popham No. 96. [20]*Walpole Society* vol. XV p. 118. [21]H. G. Bohn to DT, 29 Dec. 1835 (Barker Collection), see Kitson 1937 pp. 323-4. [22]Kitson 1937 p. 136. [23]Norwich Society 1824 (171) and (172). [24]BM. [25]Norwich Society 1821 (129) and (131).

Cotman's Published Etchings

1811 *Etchings by John Sell Cotman*
London: Published for the Author by Messrs. Boydell & Co., Cheapside; Colnaghi & Co., Cockspur St.; Todd & Co., York; & Mr. Whyte Edinburgh, 1811 (26 etchings). Referred to in the text as *Miscellaneous Etchings* 1811.

1814 *A Narrative of the Grand Festival, at Great Yarmouth,* on Tuesday, the 19th of April, 1814 Yarmouth: Printed and Published by J. Keymer (3 etchings and 1 softground etching). Referred to in the text as *Yarmouth Festival* 1814.

1817 *Specimens of Norman and Gothic Architecture, in the County of Norfolk,* by J. S. Cotman. (50 etchings).

1817 *The Nelson Column at Yarmouth* (see No. 174).

1817(?) *Specimens of the Castellated and Ecclesiastical Remains in the County of Norfolk* (50 etchings).

1818 *A Series of Etchings* illustrative of the Architectural Antiquities of Norfolk; with References to the Authors who have Described or Figured them. By John Sell Cotman, author of a volume of miscellaneous etchings, and of Figures of the Sepulchral Brasses of Norfolk and Suffolk. London: Printed by C. Sloman, Yarmouth: Published by Longman and Co.; Lackinton and Co.; Colnaghi and Co.; and W. J. White, Brownlow-Street, Holborn: J. and W. Freeman, Norwich: C. Sloman, Yarmouth: and by the author at Southtown, Suffolk. 1818 (60 etchings). Referred to in the text as *Architectural Antiquities of Norfolk* 1818.

1819 *Engravings of the Most Remarkable of the Sepulchral Brasses in Norfolk* . . . by John Sell Cotman, . . . London: Published by John and Arthur Arch, Cornhill; also by J. and W. Freeman, Norwich; and by the Author, at Southtown, near Yarmouth. Printed by C. Sloman, Jun., Yarmouth. 1819 (111 plates).

1819 *Antiquities of Saint Mary's Chapel, at* Stourbridge, near Cambridge, etc., etc. by John Sell Cotman. Author of Architectural Antiquities of Norfolk, Architectural Antiquities of Normandy, &c., &c. Published by John S. Cotman, Yarmouth. Printed by C. Sloman, Yarmouth 1819 (10 etchings).

1822 *Architectural Antiquities of Normandy,* by John Sell Cotman; accompanied by Historical and Descriptive Notices by Dawson Turner, Esq., F. R. and A. S. London: Printed for John and Arthur Arch, Cornhill; and J. S. Cotman, Yarmouth. MDCCCXXII. 2 volumes (97 etchings). Referred to in the text as *Architectural Antiquities of Normandy* 1822.

1838 *Liber Studiorum* First published by H. G. Bohn as a separate work and in his collected edition of Cotman's etchings, 1838 (48 plates, 40 of which are softground etchings). Referred to in the text as *Liber Studiorum* 1838.

1846 *Eight Original Etchings* by the late John Sell Cotman. now first Published. Norwich: Charles Muskett. 1846. Referred to in the text as *Eight Original Etchings* 1846.

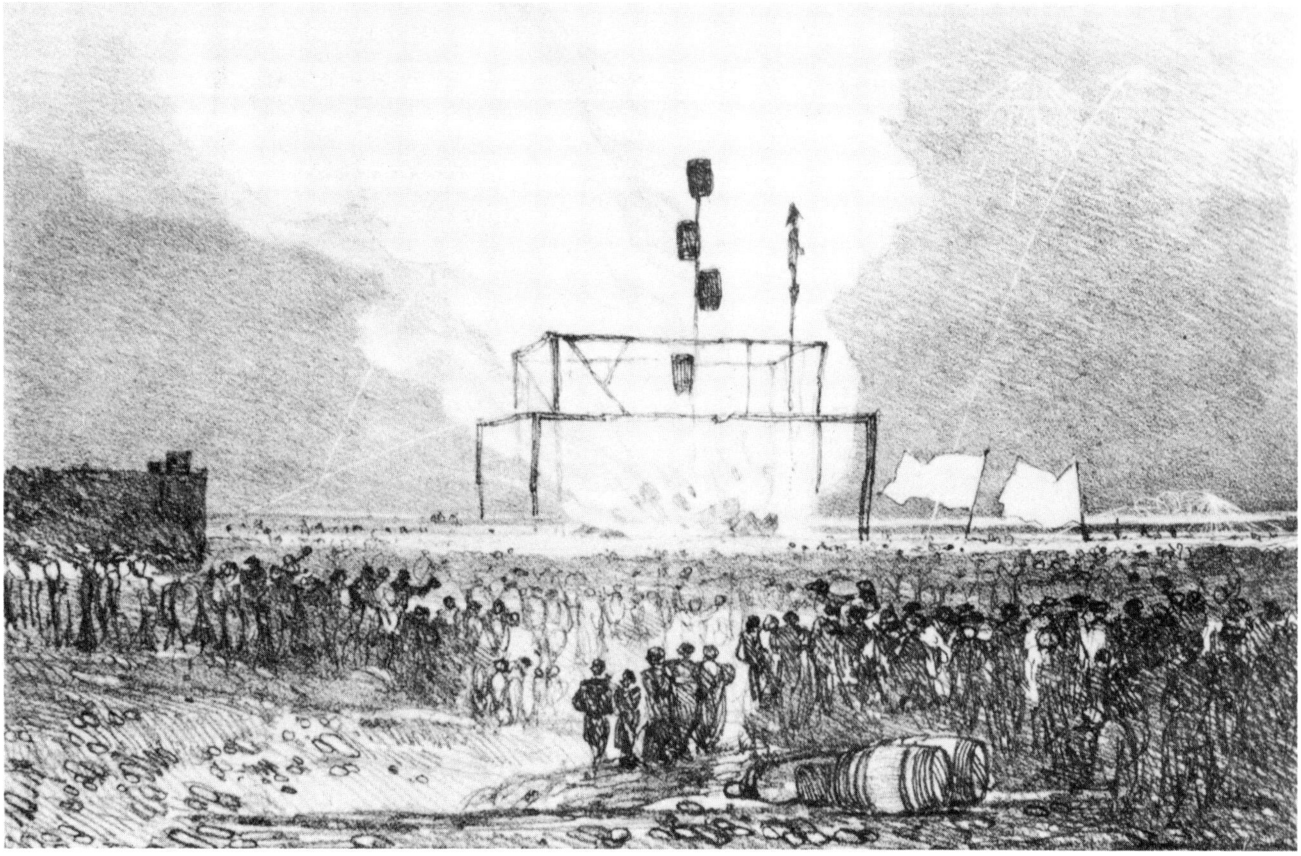

173 Grand Bonfire at the Yarmouth Festival, published 1814

169 A Doorway leading to the Refectory of Rivaulx Abbey, Yorkshire, published 1810

Etching on thick cream, wove paper; plate 30.2 × 22.6 ($11\frac{7}{8} \times 8\frac{15}{16}$) with full margin. INSCR: signed and dated in the plate l.r. *J. S. Cotman. Del. et. Sc. / Norwich. Published Novr 13th. 1810*—(before the scratch title). PUBL: *Miscellaneous Etchings* 1811 pl. 12. PROV: Mrs. Hodgson (one of a bound volume of *Miscellaneous Etchings,* 1811); her gift 1898. (41.98). REF: Popham No. 12; Kitson 1937 pp. 51, 141, 142.

This is one of three etchings[1] deriving from Cotman's visits to Rievaulx Abbey in 1803 (see section 3, p. 23). Mrs. Cholmeley reported to her son that Cotman and Paul Sandby Munn had thought 'it altogether the finest ruin they had ever seen.'

Cotman sent a proof of this etching to Francis Cholmeley at Brandsby, probably with those forwarded on 14 January 1811. Cholmeley replied on 24 February 1811: 'I think by the dates that you improve as you go on. There is a want of delicacy and effect I think, in some of the earlier ones, particularly some Gothic arches (I believe a Norfolk ruin), and some in Rievaulx, though not much. I particularly admire the Refectory door at Rievaulx, which is a work of art I prefer to any.'[2] Mrs. Cholmeley later wrote that she too was 'particularly struck'[3] by this composition.

Cotman exhibited this subject with the Norwich Society in 1811 (69) as *An Entrance to the Refectory of Rievaulx Abbey, Yorkshire.* This was presumably either the etching or the drawing for it.

[1]See also Popham Nos. 10 and 13. [2]BM; Kitson 1937 p. 141. [3]*Ibid,* p. 142.

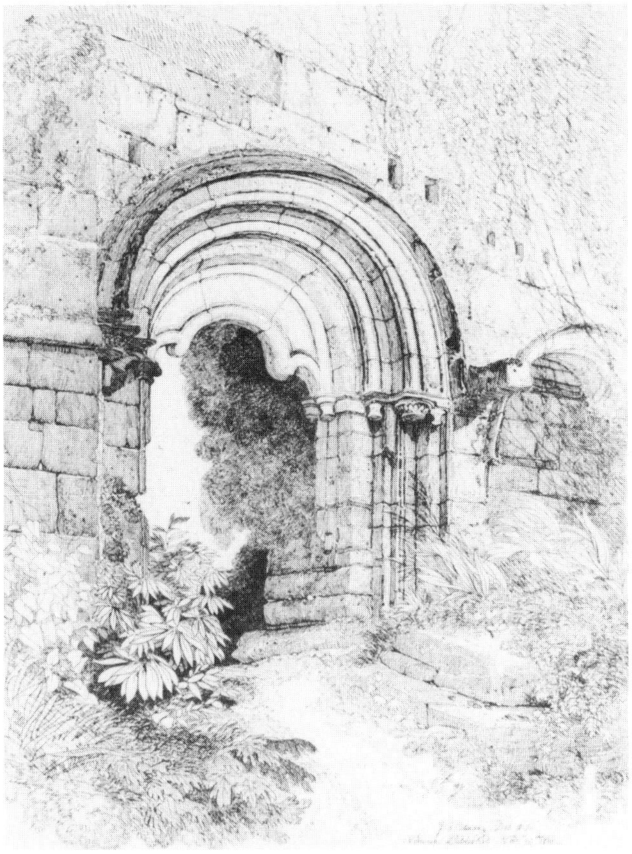

169 A Doorway leading to the Refectory of Rivaulx Abbey Yorkshire, published 1810

170 The Old College House, Conway, published 1811

Etching on thick cream, wove paper; plate, 30.5 × 21.5 ($12 \times 8\frac{7}{16}$) with full margin. INSCR: Signed, dated and titled in the plate, lower edge, *The Old College House Conway / Etched & Published May 30th 1811 by J. S. Cotman, Norwich.* PUBL: *Miscellaneous Etchings* 1811 pl. 18. PROV: Presented by Duncan Cotman, 1974. (52.474.975). REF: Popham No. 18.

Rajnai and Allthorpe have convincingly argued[1] that Cotman probably arrived in Conway in the middle of August 1800, when he must have sketched the Old College House. He exhibited the subject twice with the Norwich Society, in 1811 (57) and 1824 (154*). The former was presumably this plate or the drawing for it.

An early watercolour by Cotman and a later family drawing copy of this subject are known, as is a watercolour based on the etching.[2]

This picturesque subject was also sketched by Cornelius Varley and David Cox. Cotman makes the composition his own with a cloud formation which recalls that of No. 34, *The Mars off Cromer.*

[1]See Rajnai & Allthorpe No. 10. [2]*Ibid* n.7, for details of these versions.

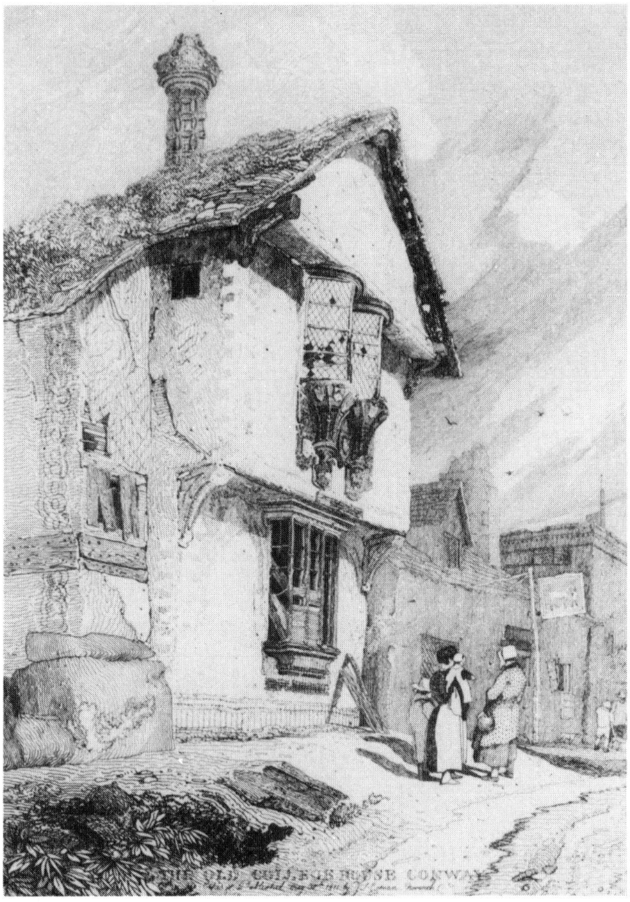

170 The Old College House, Conway, published 1811

171 West Front of Croyland Abbey, Lincolnshire, published 1811

illustrated on p. 156

Etching on thick cream, wove paper; plate 38 × 27.6 ($15 \times 10\frac{7}{8}$) with full margin. INSCR: signed and dated in the plate, l.l., *Published Jan^{ry} 6th. 1811 Norwich,* l.r. *J S Cotman Del et Sc;* in pencil in margin, l. *22,* l. margin r. *W. Front of Croyland Abbey:* PUBL: *Miscellaneous Etchings* 1811 pl. 24. PROV: Unknown. REF: Popham No. 24; Kitson 1937 pp. 73, 140-2, 144.

See the entry for No. 20 for a discussion of the circumstances of Cotman's visit to Croyland's twelfth century Benedictine Abbey and for other versions by Cotman of the subject.

Cotman last exhibited this subject with the Norwich Society in 1811 (64). This was presumably either the etching or the drawing for it. On 14 January 1811 Cotman sent his friend Francis Cholmeley some specimens of his etched work for his criticism. These included *Howden Church, Yorkshire*[1] and *Croyland Abbey, Lincolnshire:* 'Croyland proves a more perfect work, though not so perfect as I hope to render it some time hence, as well as Howden. Croyland bears the date of my wedding day and Howden that of the birth of my boy.'[2] In a reply of 24 February 1811 Francis Cholmeley informs Cotman of the admiration one of his colleagues held for this composition: '. . . Dr. Goldie an old Edinr. colleague of mine was here for a few days on his way thither.

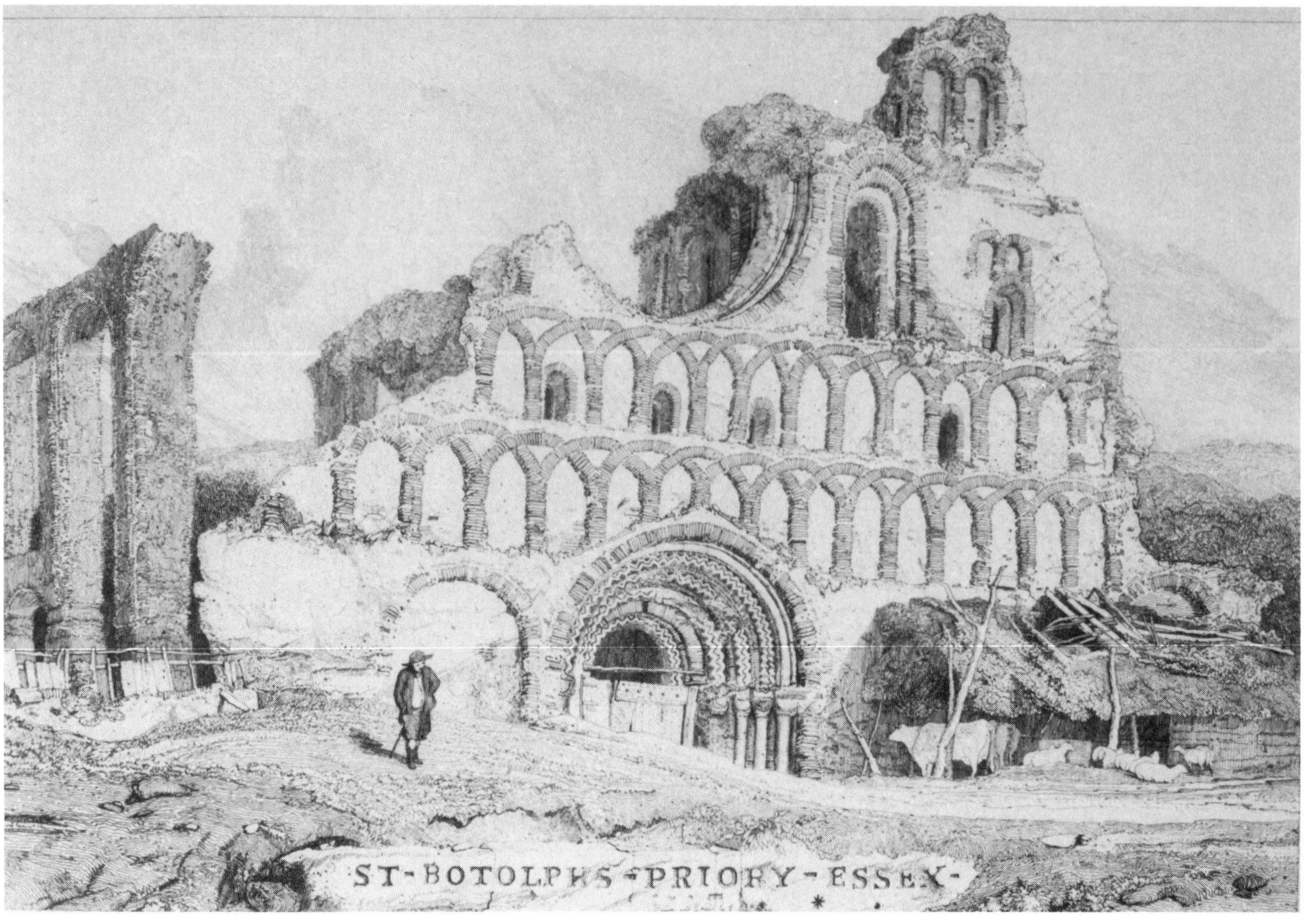

172 St. Botolph's Priory, Colchester, Essex, published 1811

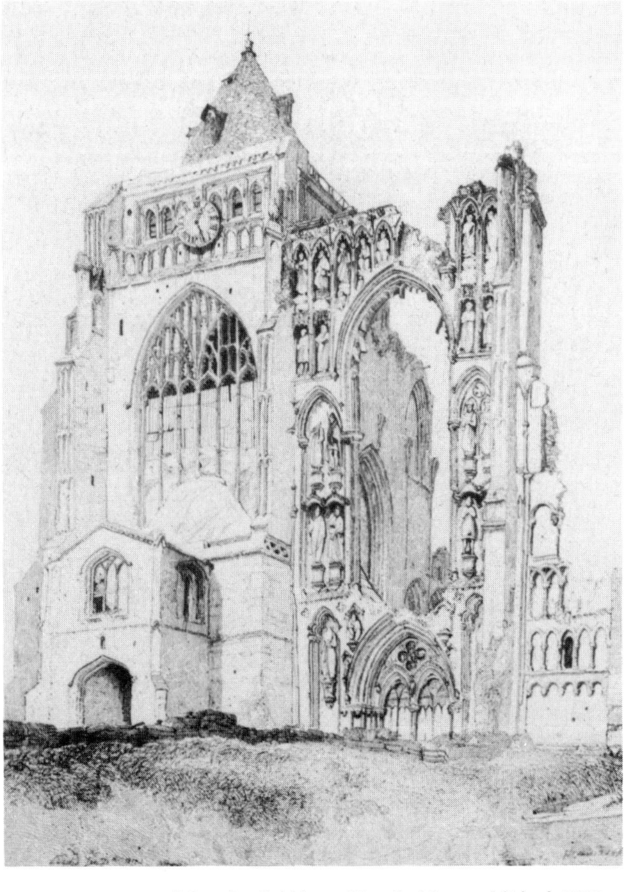

171 West Front of Croyland Abbey, Lincolnshire, published 1811

He admired Croyland that you sent me so much and thought his friends in the North would do so too, that I gave it him in hopes it might help to propagate subscriptions. I shall be most truly happy if your work answers and think it need only be known to make it do so . . . Croyland is good but Howden, alas!'

[1]Popham No. 25. [2]Both dates are anniversaries.

172 St. Botolph's Priory, Colchester, Essex, published 1811

Etching on thick cream, wove paper; plate 25.8 × 36.5 ($10\frac{3}{16} \times 14\frac{7}{16}$) with full margin. Inscr: signed and dated in the plate l.c. edge *St— Botolphs — Priory — Essex / Drawn and Etched by J. S. Cotman,* l.l. margin, *Norwich Published Febry—20th by J. S. Cotman St Andrews Street, 1811.* Publ: *Miscellaneous Etchings* 1811 pl. 26. Prov: Unknown. Ref: Popham No. 26; Kitson 1937 p. 145.

See the entry for No. 7 for a discussion of the probable circumstances of Cotman's visit to the ruins of St. Botolph's Priory and for other versions by him of the subject.

Cotman exhibited the subject, presumably the etching or the drawing for it, with the Norwich Society in 1811 (81), *The West Front of St. Botolph's Priory, Colchester Essex.* In his letter to Francis Cholmeley of 5 March 1811 Cotman describes the difficulty he experienced with this plate, a design in which he was emulating the work of Piranesi: 'An accident happened to the best plate I ever sketched; whilst biting, stopping out some p[ar]ts that ought to be feignt, the wax melted from too strong a heat and the whole bares the same proportion of tint. This plate took me nearly three weeks—it is St. Botolph's Priory, Colchester. You will have it in the work. This was etched decidedly for the Piranesi effect. As *coars[e]ness* does not proceed from thickness of line, but from want of variety of line, an etching may be coarse with every line as fine as a hair.'

A later pencil drawing by a copyist and a watercolour copy of the etching are also known.[1]

[1]See Rajnai & Allthorpe No. 36 n.6.

173 Grand Bonfire at the Yarmouth Festival, published 1814.
illustrated on p. 154

Soft ground etching on thick cream, wove paper laid down on archive paper; plate cut, 17.8 × 26.3 (7 × $10\frac{3}{8}$). INSCR: in ink on mount, l.c. *Yarmouth,* in pencil *209.* PROV: Part of the Todd Collection, a grangerised and illustrated *History of Norfolk* by Blomefield, presented by the Executors of Mrs. E. M. Colman, 1954. (138.954. Box 26 p. 209). PUBL: *Yarmouth Festival* 1814. REF: Popham No. 30; Kitson 1937 p. 183, pl. 79.

To celebrate the abdication of Napoleon in 1814, the town of Yarmouth elected to hold a splendid festival. The event was recorded by a Yarmouth antiquary, Cory, in a volume entitled 'A Narrative of The Grand Festival at Great Yarmouth, on Tuesday, the 19th of April, 1814 Yarmouth: Printed and Published by J. Keymer.' The title page[1] was etched by Cotman (with lettering as above), and he also included an etching of the table plan[2] and an elevation of the 'Funeral Pile of the Buonapartean Dynasty.'[3] No. 173 is the fourth and finest commemoration of the event and Cotman's first published soft ground etching. The silhouette of the burning effigy of Napoleon can still be seen amidst the swirling smoke and the flags and fireworks which relieve the night sky.

[1]Popham No. 27; see also vignette repro. on p. 168. [2]*Ibid* No. 28. [3]*Ibid* No. 29.

174 Column at Yarmouth to the Memory of Lord Nelson, published 1817

Etching on thick cream, wove paper, plate 47.6 × 29.9 ($18\frac{3}{4}$ × $11\frac{3}{4}$) with margin cut. INSCR: in plate l. edge: *Column at Yarmouth to the Memory of Lord Nelson. / To The Right Worshipful Isaac Preston Iuu^{r} Esqr Mayor of Yarmouth. / During whose Mayorality the First Stone of the Column was laid on the 15 Augst 1817. / and to whose exertions the town is greatly indebted for possessing it / this plate is most respectfully inscribed by his obedient servant / I. S. Cotman,* l.l. edge *Height of the column 140 feet,* l.c. edge *1817 Drawn, Etched and Published by J S Cotman Yarth* PROV: Unknown. REF: Popham No. 355; Kitson 1937 pp. 183-4, pl. 80.

The Nelson Column to the South of Yarmouth was designed by William Wilkins. The top of the pillar bears a drum on which Victories support a gilt statue of Britannia. Cotman's design, although a faithful representation of that projected by Wilkins,[1] differs in that his column supports a vessel with oars.

Cotman's version both captures the magnificent scale of the monument and expands upon the celebratory sentiment of his soft ground etching of 1814, No. 173. The visionary qualities of that earlier work are now surpassed in the depiction of the embattled ships off Trafalgar in the background to the design. An etching of this subject by Clark after Preston, published in Yarmouth two years later, pales by comparison.[2]

[1]NCM Todd Collection Box 26 p. 186. [2]*Ibid* p. 187.

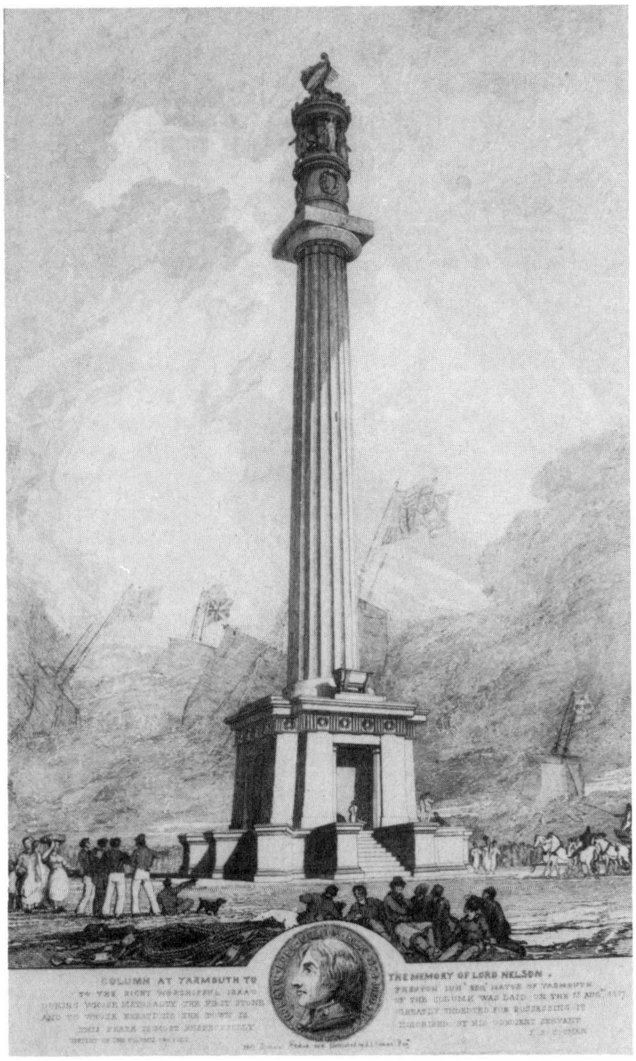

174 Column at Yarmouth to the Memory of Lord Nelson, published 1817

175 Saxon Arches in The Tower of Castle Rising Church, Norfolk, published 1812

Etching on thick cream, wove paper; plate 25.7 × 36.7 ($10\frac{1}{8}$ × $14\frac{7}{16}$) with full margin. INSCR: in plate, l.l. *Saxon—Arches—in— / The—Tower—of Castle—Rising—Church— / Norfolk,* l.l. edge *Norwich Etched & Published by J. S. Cotman—Jany 1812,* l.c. *To John Gurney Esqr / This Print is Respectfully Dedicated by his Obed^{t} Humble Servant / John S Cotman* with coat of arms, in pencil t.l. margin *2.* PUBL: *Architectural Antiquities of Norfolk* 1818 pl. 2. PROV: Unknown. REF: Popham No. 131.

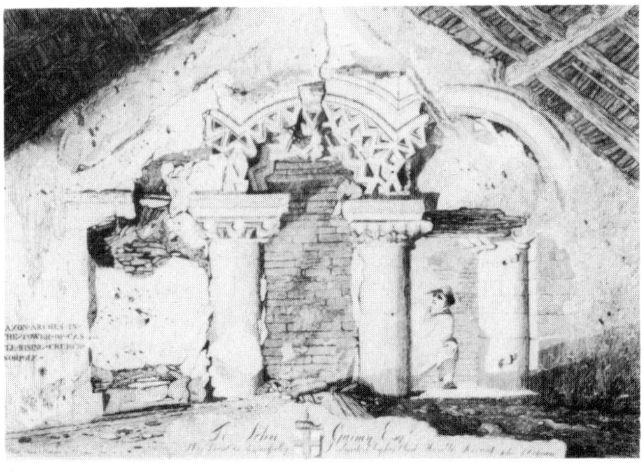

175 Saxon Arches in The Tower of Castle Rising Church, Norfolk, published 1812

On 25 August 1811 Cotman wrote[1] to Dawson Turner of his intention to begin another expedition through Norfolk in search of new subjects for his second series of etchings: 'I feel at a great loss where to find a good and profitable route, the want of which makes it seem more like a voyage of discovery. Lynn, however, will be my route: Castle Rising and Castle Acre my chief objects.' He had reached Castle Rising by 20 September, from where he wrote[2] to Dawson Turner of his plans. He decided to take a rest at Castle Rising, 'for I am really fatigued, both bodily and mentally. I have been at it, invariably by five o'clock a.m. till, sometimes five p.m., without dining, when dinner would have interfered.' Whilst at Castle Rising he gathered material for two etchings of the Castle[3] as well as a further four subjects developed from his sketches of the church, including the West Front,[4] the East window in the chancel,[5] elevations of the Font[6] and an exterior view.[7] A third view,[8] unrecorded by Popham but published in 1817, of the *Ruins of the Gate and Ramparts, Castle Rising Castle,* may derive from this visit.

Dawson Turner's uncredited letterpress to the 1818 volume of *Architectural Antiquities of Norfolk* corrects the etched title which erroneously suggests that the arches with their splendid zigzag decoration are Saxon rather than Norman. When in Rouen in 1817, Cotman was to find nothing 'so fine, so curious as our Castle Rising Church'.[9]

Cotman exhibited this subject with the Norwich Society in 1812 (64) as *Arches under the Tower of Castle Rising Church.* This was presumably either the drawing or the etching for this composition.

[1]Barker Collection, Kitson 1937 p. 150. [2]*Ibid* p. 152. [3]Popham Nos. 155 and 156. [4]*Ibid* No. 164. [5]*Ibid* No. 94, an initial drawing is NCM 437.235.951. [6]*Ibid* No. 53. [7]*Ibid* No. 93. [8]NCM 274.974. [9]JSC to DT, 6 July 1817, *Walpole Society,* vol. XIV p. 98.

176 The North West Tower, Yarmouth, published 1812

Etching on thick cream, wove paper; plate 36.9 × 25.9 ($14\frac{1}{2} \times 10\frac{3}{16}$) with full margin. INSCR: in plate, l. edge *The North West Tower, Yarmouth,* l.r. *Cotman f 1812* (2 in reverse). PROV: Unknown. PUBL: *Architectural Antiquities of Norfolk* 1818 pl. 3. REF: Popham No. 132.

This composition is one of a number of the towers of Yarmouth either drawn or etched by Cotman. For a discussion of some of these see the entry for No. 72. His etched views of similar subjects are *North Side South Gate Yarmouth,*[1] *A Tower on the Ramparts, Yarmouth,*[2] and *South Gate Yarmouth.*[3] He also exhibited a similar subject with the Norwich Society 1812 (73), as *Tower on the Walls, Yarmouth.* This could have been the etching or the drawing[4] for it, but see also No. 72.

A drawing based on this etching, formerly attributed to Cotman, is in the collection at Norwich.[5]

[1]Popham No. 80. [2]*Ibid* No. 128. [3]*Ibid* No. 130. [4]Yale Center for British Art. [5]NCM 16.749.966.

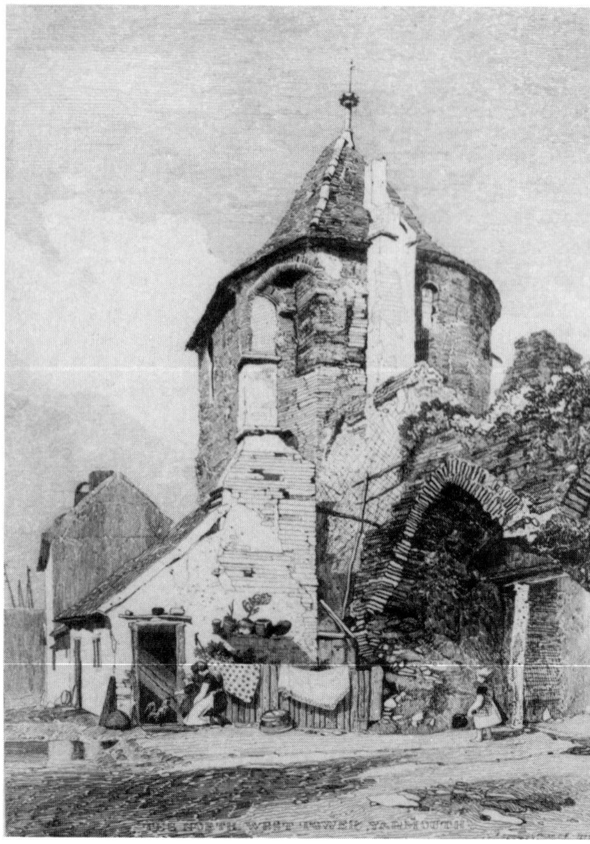

176 The North West Tower, Yarmouth, published 1812

177 East View of the Gateway of St. Bennets Abbey, published 1813

illustrated on p. 152

Etching on thick cream, wove paper; plate 27.7 × 38 ($10\frac{7}{8} \times 15$) with full margin. INSCR: in plate l. edge *To Mrs. Dawson Turner to whose knowledge in the polite Arts & to whose judicious / observations this work is much indebted J. S. Cotman most Respectfully & gratefully / Dedicates this East view of the Gateway of St. Bennets Abbey,* l.r. *Etched & Published by J. S. Cotman Yarmouth 1813.* PUBL: *Architectural Antiquities of Norfolk* 1818 pl. 25. PROV: Unknown. EXH: Tate 1973 (266). REF: Popham No. 154; Kitson 1937 pp. 153-4, 169, pl. 63; Jacobs & Warner, 1980 repro. p. EA27.

With the publication of his *Miscellaneous Etchings* almost complete, Cotman, anxious to continue with his Norfolk series, proposed to include St. Benet's Abbey.[1] The result, with its dedication to Mrs. Turner, is one of the most splendid of his etched designs. In 1815 Mrs. Turner was herself to etch this subject in a composition[2] which, although from a different viewpoint, is stylistically a tribute of her own to Cotman's work. Her husband, meanwhile, received equal tribute from Cotman in the magnificent plate of *South Gate Yarmouth,*[3] published in January, 1812.

For other versions by Cotman of this subject, see No. 112.

[1]JSC to DT, 9 July 1811 (Barker Collection). [2]NCM Todd Collection Box 24 p. 118. [3]Popham No. 130.

178 St. Ethelbert's Gate, Norwich, published 1817

Etching on thick cream, wove paper; cut to plate size 37.1 × 24.1 ($14\frac{5}{8} \times 9\frac{1}{2}$). INSCR: in the plate, l. edge *To The Rev Geo Anguish A.M. of Somerleyton Hall / This plate of St. Ethelberts Gate leading to the Cathedral / of which he is a Prebendary, is most respectfully dedicated / by his very obedient servant J. S. Cotman / 1817 Drawn, Etched and Published by J. S. Colman* (sic) with coat of arms. PUBL: *Architectural Antiquities of Norfolk* 1818 pl. 55. PROV: R. J. Colman Bequest. (621.B48.235.951). EXH: Norwich 1956 (90); Norwich 1980. REF: Popham No. 184.

St. Ethelbert's Gate dates from 1316[1] and is known as the Great Gate, to distinguish it from the slightly later Erpingham Gate[2] which acts as a second approach from the city to the Cathedral Close. Cotman renders his subject with a characteristic instinct for the decorative,

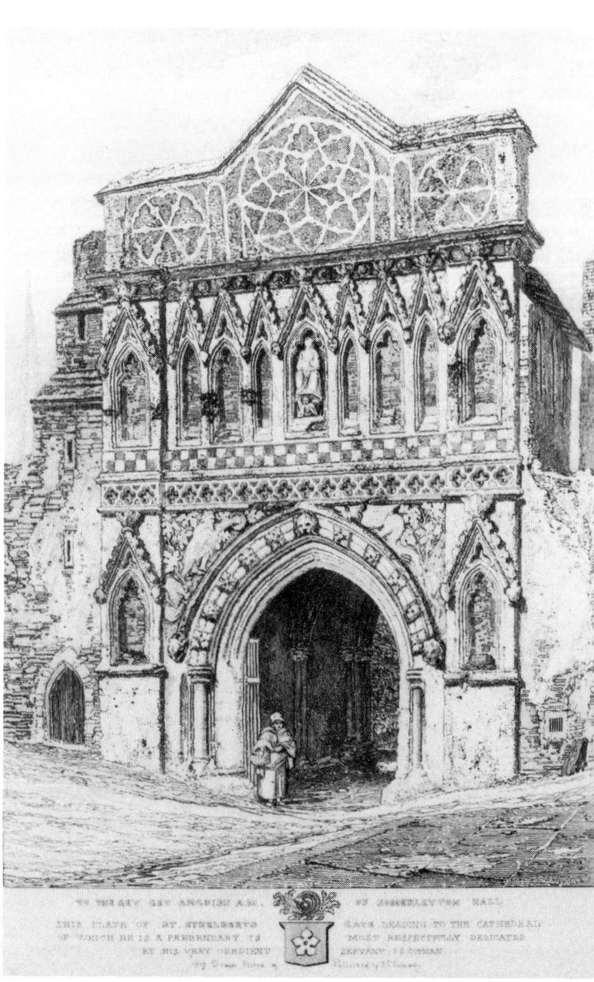

178 St. Ethelbert's Gate, Norwich, published 1817

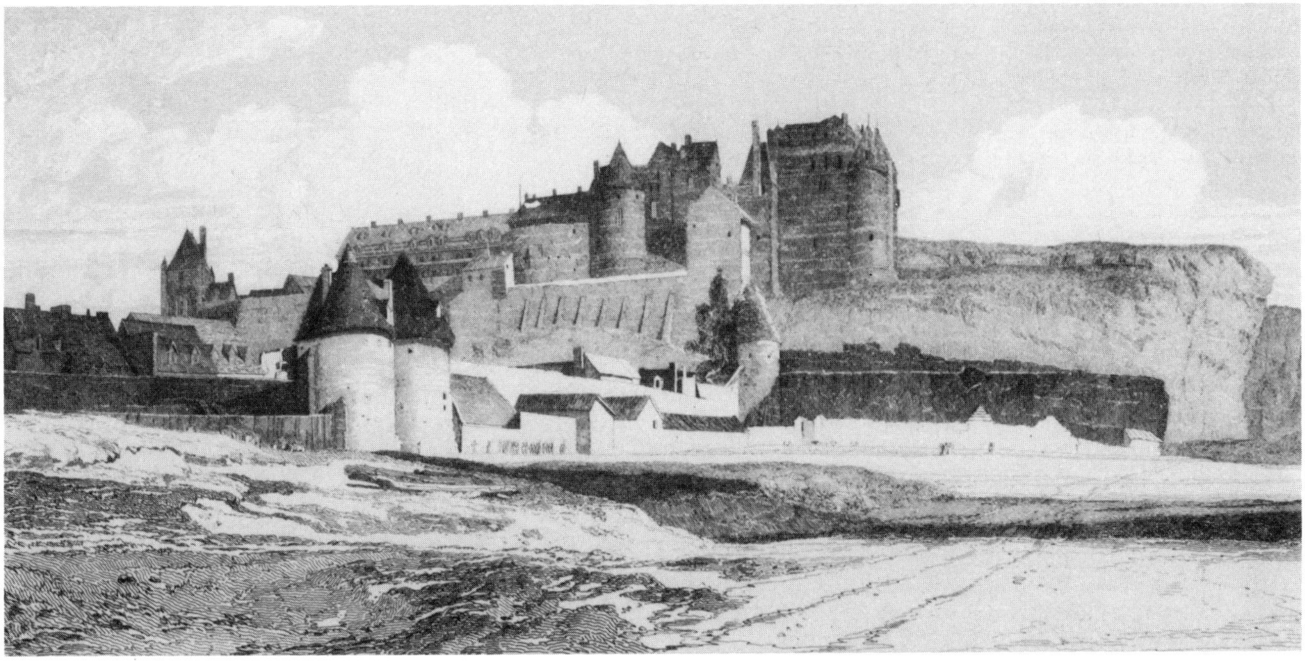

179 Castle at Dieppe, published 1820

as much in the patterns of the foreground and the brick and stonework as in the architectural detail of the large archway.

[1]Pevsner, *North-East Norfolk and Norwich* p. 232. [2]Also etched by JSC, Popham No. 185.

179 Castle at Dieppe, published 1820

Etching on medium white, wove paper, plate cut; 24.8 × 42.3 (9¼ × 16⅝). PROV: Purchased with 15 other Normandy etchings showing early states, three others including an early state of *Norwich Thorp,* from Colnaghi, through the Beecheno Bequest Fund, 1942. (11.135.942). PUB: *Architectural Antiquities of Normandy,* 1822 vol. I pl. 34. REF: Popham No. 234.

Cotman's first sight of Dieppe Castle was on 20 June 1817: 'This castle is fine in every point of view, from its architecture, situation, & Picturesque effect. Oh! Such a Picture!'[1] He returned to draw the fifteenth century castle from two viewpoints on 22 June 1817.[1] At least five drawings resulted, all probably dating from 1817 as his second and last visit in 1818 was only brief. The drawing for this composition was sold in Cotman's 1824 sale, lot 17, as *View of the Castle at Dieppe, and the Military Prison, taken from the shore near the Baths.*[2] A copy by Mary Anne Turner is in her Book of Drawings, No. 40.[3]

No. 179 is an early state, before much new work on the still plain white walls, foreground and the two main cloud masses. The inscription on the final state would read *Castle at Dieppe / London Published 1st April 1820, by J. & A. Arch, Cornhill, & J. S. Cotman, Yarmouth / Drawn & Etched by J. S. Cotman / PL.34.*

[1]JSC to DT and to his wife, 21 and 22 June 1817 (BM). [2]Signed and dated 22 June 1817; with Spink & Son Ltd. *English Watercolour Drawings* Annual Exhibition 1982 No. 51. [3]Dieppe subjects by or after Cotman are fully discussed in Rajnai 1975 No. 21.

180 Cathedral Church of Notre Dame, At Rouen, West Front, published 1821

illustrated on p. 150

Etching on thick buff, wove paper; plate cut, 54.1 × 40.3 (21¼ × 15⅞). INSCR: in plate l.l. *Drawn & Engraved by J. S. Cotman Yarmouth 1821,* l.r. *JSC* (monogram). PUBL: *Architectural Antiquities of Normandy* 1822 Vol. I pl. 51, 52. PROV: Beecheno Bequest (61.116.935). REF: Popham No. 250; Kitson 1937 pp. 197, 234-5, 238.

See the entries for No. 94, *Rouen from Mont Ste. Catherine* and No. 95, *Rouen looking up the Seine, Mont Ste. Catherine in the distance* for a discussion of the circumstances of Cotman's visits to Rouen.[1]

Cotman had some difficulty in sketching the Cathedral, a task he tackled most assiduously in 1817: 'July 5. begun the Cathedral but how finish it? What a thing!!! it is!!.'[2] A week later he wrote to Dawson Turner: 'I did not finish My Cathedral till Wednesday 4 O'clock, & now it is all to redraw,—for it is all on separate pieces of paper & nearly all of it done with y Camera lucida— which I did not know how to manage.'[3]

The etching, developed from these sketches,[4] is the largest of those published by Cotman and is remarkable for the architectural detail of the facade. The day the first proof was complete, Cotman wrote to William Stevenson, the Norwich bookseller: 'The first proof of *Rouen Cathedral* is just off, a work of more than twenty weeks' of hard labor. The chance of its coming off well or ill, from the good or bad qualities of the copper, & no way connected with yourself has been a matter of speculation and anxiety . . . The subject is a magnificent one, and shd it prove a bad plate, disgrace must attach to me for so vile a murder. However, to makes matters smooth with you, I have reserved a ghost-like proof for your folio. Such a state will be [of] interest to you as the ornaments are more distinctly seen than they will be when more finished up.'[5]

No. 180 is the last state before the final addition of the title and publication details added to the final version, published in *The Architectural Antiquities of Normandy,* 1822.

[1]For other drawings of this subject see Rajnai 1975 p. 80. [2]JSC to DT, 6 July 1817 (BM). [3]JSC to DT, 12 July 1817 (BM). [4]The pencil drawing, dated 1817, was formerly in the collection of Norman Newall; Kitson 1937 p. 234. [5]JSC to W. Stevenson, 3 April 1821 (BM).

181 Château Gaillard (South West View), published 1821

illustrated on p. 160

Etching on off-white, wove paper; plate 25.3 × 35.2 (9 15/16 × 13 13/16). PUBL: *Architectural Antiquities of Normandy* 1822 vol. II pl. 81. PROV: see No. 179. (15.135.942). EXH: Munich 1979-80 (178) repro. p. 318. REF: Popham No. 278; Kitson 1937 pp. 205, 239, 283.

Cotman visited Château Gaillard, near les Andelys, twice in 1818; once with the Turner ladies on 24 June, and again ten days later, but this time on his own.[1] Elizabeth noted in her diary that it was 'the finest castle I ever did or I believe I ever shall see,'[2] a sentiment echoed by Cotman who commented that it was 'a most magnificent castle & as magnificently situated.'[3]

Elizabeth Turner describes the circumstances of their visit: 'Thinking to obtain a better view of the castle we walked to the meadows beneath, close to the bank of the river, from which it is really still

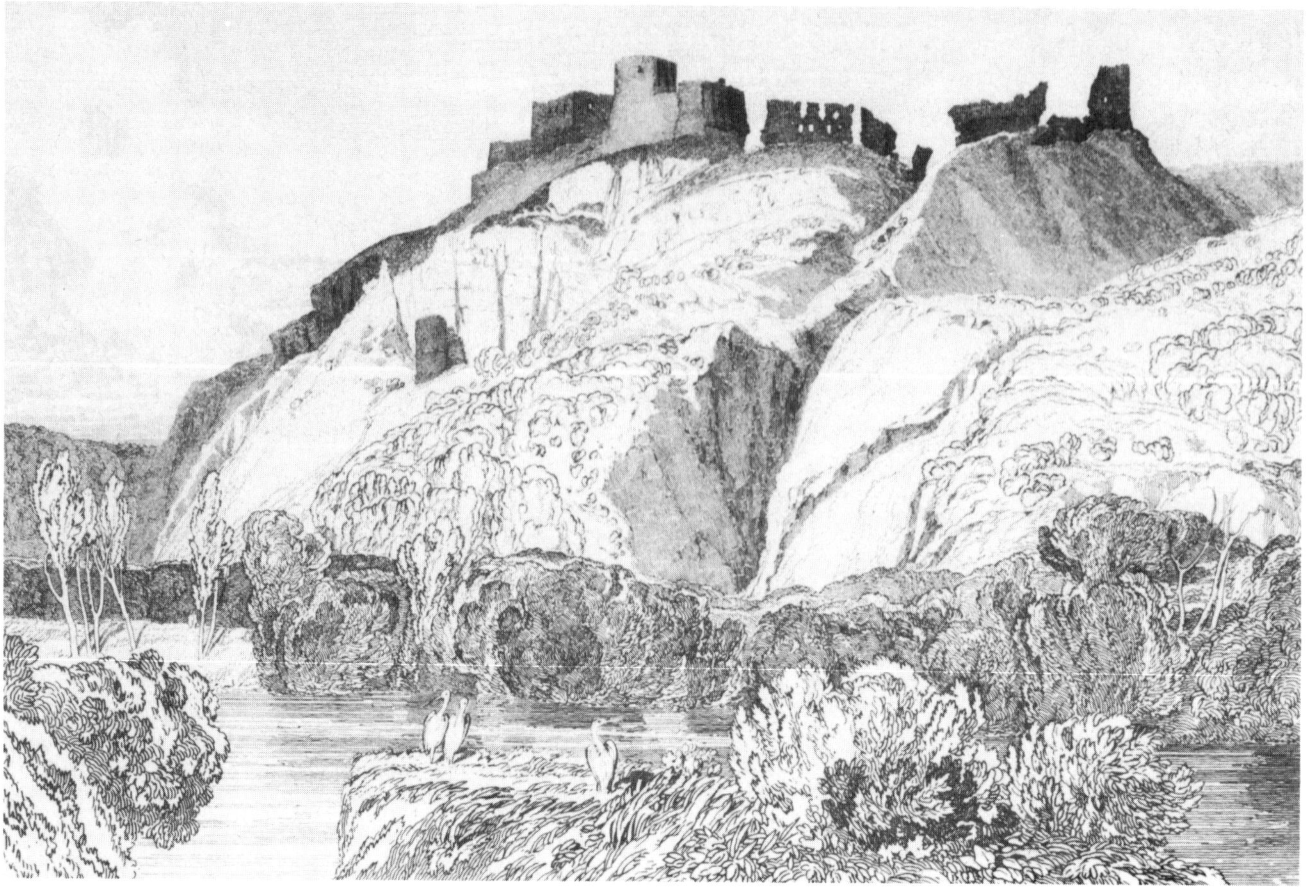

181 Château Gaillard (South West View), published 1821

finer. The cliff here is cut down straight from the walls of the castle so as to give them the effect of being much higher & where that was not strong enough it is built in with stone which is still in fine preservation.'[4]

No. 181 is an early state, prior to additional work in the foreground foliage and the hillside in the middle distance. The sky is almost finished, except for some more work still to be done on the cloud formation to the right of the composition. The work on the castle ruins is complete. The lettering for the final state was to read: 'CHATEAU GAILLARD / South West View / Drawn and Etched by J. S. Cotman / London Published 1st Octr. 1821 by J & A Arch. / Cornhill & J S Cotman Yarmouth. Pl. 81.' The North East View of the Château[5] was published the same day.[6]

[1]The circumstances of Cotman's two visits are fully discussed in Rajnai 1975 No. 3. [2]Elizabeth Turner's Diary, p. 42. [3]JSC to DT, 25 June 1818 (BM). [4]Elizabeth Turner's Diary, p. 45. [5]Popham No. 277. [6]Château Gaillard subjects by or after Cotman are fully discussed in Rajnai 1975 Nos. 3, 4 and 5. Drawings relating to this composition are listed in *Ibid* No. 3, n.7.

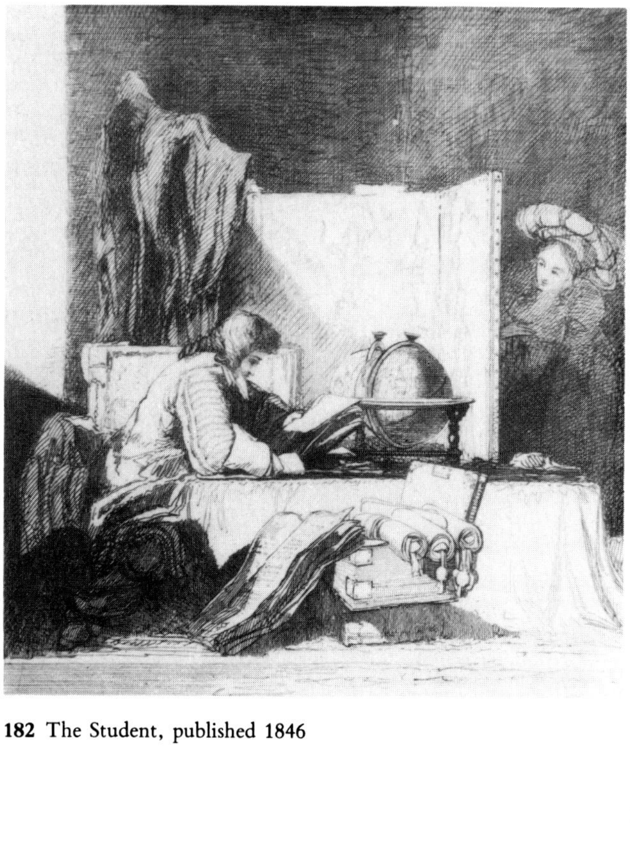

182 The Student, published 1846

182 The Student, published 1846

Etching on india paper laid on thick white, wove paper; plate 20.5 × 18.2 ($8\frac{1}{8}$ × $6\frac{7}{8}$) on full margin. PUBL: *Eight Original Etchings* 1846. PROV: Purchased from Miss E. V. Cole, together with six other etchings from the same series and two others, 1949 (12.29.949). REF: Popham No. 342; Kitson 1937 p. 301, pl. 132.

This is one of eight[1] original etchings by John Sell Cotman which were eventually published by Charles Muskett, a Norwich book-seller, in 1846. Kitson observes that 'According to a note by Dawson Turner in his copy of a book containing eight etchings by Cotman which was published after the latter's death, these plates were executed in 1833.'[2] The compositions all reflect a more personal choice of subject, divorced from the requirements of his various archaeological commissions and publications. *The Student* is comparable to another in the series, *An Ecclesiastic Reading,*[3] but is more assured in its handling. See also the entry for the watercolour of the same title, No. 110.

[1]Popham Nos. 342-349. [2]Kitson 1937 pp. 300-301. [3]Popham No. 345.

183 Scene on the Beach, published 1846
illustrated on p. 153

Etching on india paper laid on thick white, wove paper; plate 15.1 × 22.8 ($5\frac{15}{16}$ × $8\frac{15}{16}$) on full margin. PUBL: *Eight Original Etchings* 1846. PROV: See No. 182. (17.29.949). REF: Popham No. 348; Kitson 1937 p. 301.

Although published in 1846, this composition dates from *c.*1833 (see previous entry). For a discussion of the elements of this composition, see the entries for No. 113, *Storm on Yarmouth Beach* and No. 114, *Stormy Weather.*

184 Norwich, Thorp, published 1838

Soft ground etching with pencil on medium cream, wove paper; plate 10.8 × 8.6 ($4\frac{3}{8}$ × $3\frac{7}{16}$) on full margin. INSCR: in plate, l.l. *Norwich Thorp,* l.r. *J. S. Cotman* u.r. *18.* PUBL: *Liber Studiorum* 1838 pl. 18. PROV: See No. 179 (3.943). REF: Popham No. 312; Kitson 1937 p. 136.

No. 184 derives from a sketch[1] which, although inscribed with the date 1805, is probably later.

This impression is not the final state. Although both the *Liber Studiorum* title and plate number have been added, the background landscape to the right has been blocked in with pencil only, as has the fisherman's rod. This suggests that the impression is an artist's proof which Cotman himself worked on immediately prior to publication.

[1] H. M. Gaskell Collection (Kitson 1937 p. 136).

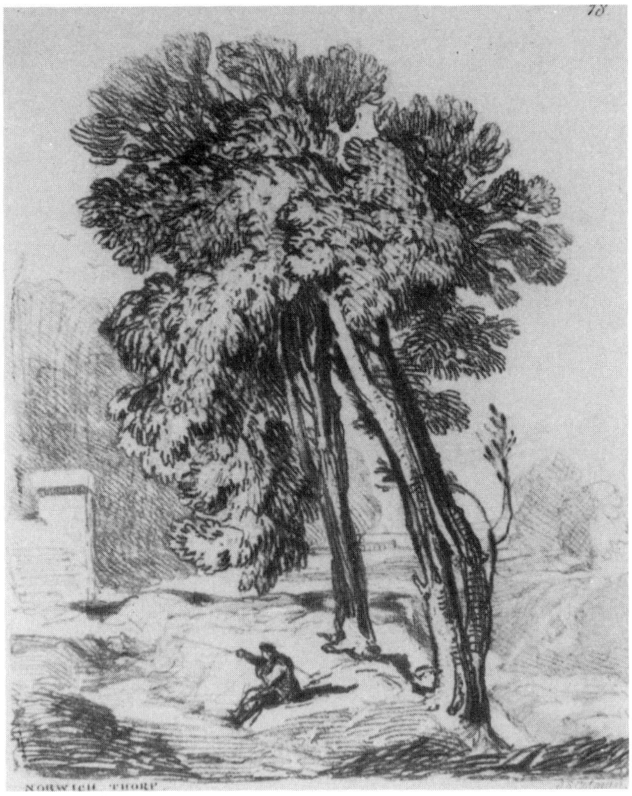

184 Norwich, Thorp, published 1838

185 Kilgarren Castle, N. Wales, published 1838

Soft ground etching on medium cream, wove paper; plate 15.2 × 20.2 ($5\frac{5}{16}$ × 8) margins cut. PUBL: *Liber Studiorum* 1838 pl. 27. PROV: Purchased from Colnaghi through the Beecheno Bequest Fund for £2, 1942 (125.942). REF: Popham No. 320; Kitson 1937 pp. 126, 136.

The drawing[1] from which No. 185 derives is dated 1810.

This impression is an early state, prior to the addition of the title, plate numbers and a considerable amount of reworking in the lighter areas. It presumably shows the penultimate state before publication by H. G. Bohn in 1838. Roulette work may be seen in the rock faces to the left in the Bohn version, in addition to reworking on the tree tops to the left.

This is one of ten castle subjects in the *Liber Studiorum* presumably derived from Cotman's Welsh and Yorkshire tours. These include *Dolbadern Castle, N. Wales,*[2] *Ragland Castle, Monmouthshire,*[3] *Harlech Castle N. Wales,*[4] *Caernarvon Castle,*[5] *Bambro' Castle, Northumberland*[6] and *Conway Castle.*[7] The title, *Kilgarren Castle, N. Wales* was added to the Bohn version. Cilgerran is the northernmost castle in Pembrokeshire, in a commanding position on the south bank of the river Teifi.

[1] V&A E224-1939. [2] Popham No. 307. [3] *Ibid* No. 317. [4] *Ibid* Nos. 318 and 322 (see Nos. 186, 187). [5] *Ibid* Nos. 321 and 325. [6] *Ibid* No. 323. [7] *Ibid* Nos. 324 and 326.

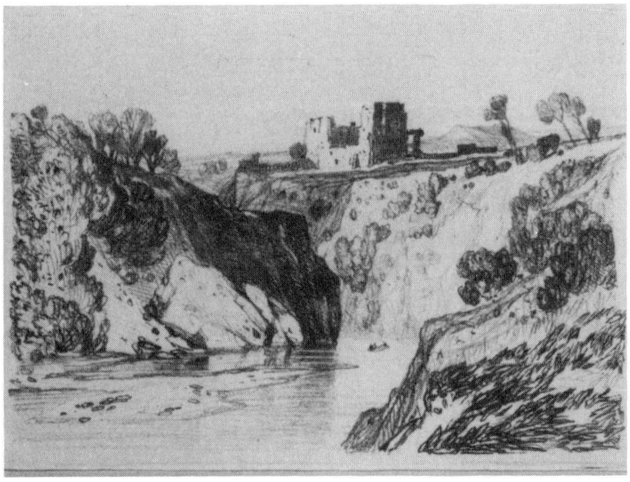

185 Kilgarren Castle, N. Wales, published 1838

186 Harlech Castle, North Wales, *c.*1808-9

Pencil with chalk on tracing paper; 11.9 × 18.7. ($4\frac{1}{16}$ × $7\frac{5}{16}$). INSCR: *Verso,* in pencil l.r. *49.* PROV: Sale, G. H. Murrell, Norwich, 26-27 Nov. 1826, 2nd day, lot 223 *Fourteen of the original drawings for Cotman's Liber Studiorum, by John Sell Cotman,* bt. Thomas Jeckyll 42s.; bt. R. J. Colman with eleven other drawings from the above lot; R. J. Colman Bequest 1946. (492.235.951). REF: Rajnai & Allthorpe no. 7 n.10.

This drawing was instrumental in the production of the plate[1] for Cotman's soft ground etching, finally published by Bohn as plate 25 of the *Liber Studiorum* in 1838. The design is closely related to Cotman's original sketches of Harlech (see Nos. 11 and 12), but probably derives from the period *c.*1808-9, the dates of the preliminary drawings[2] for two similar compositions also published in the *Liber Studiorum.*

The design is in reverse of the final etching. No. 186 is the last preparatory drawing, drawn on the sheet of paper which was stretched

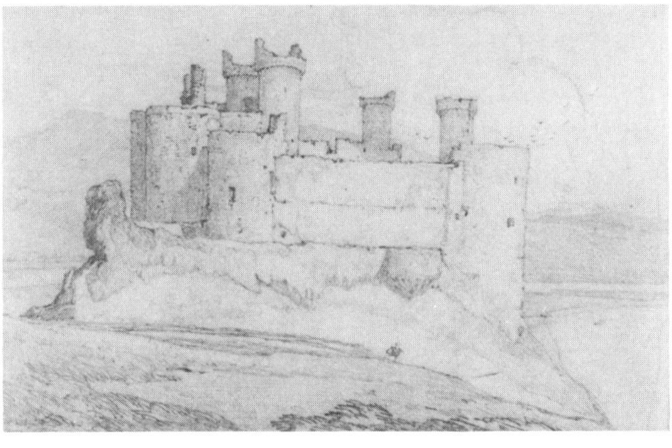

186 Harlech Castle, North Wales, *c.*1808-9

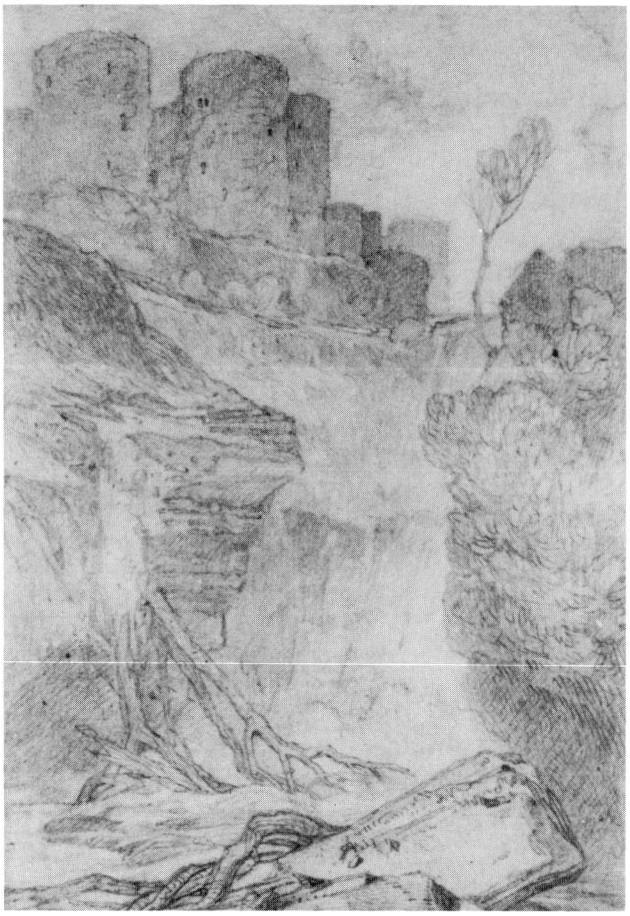

187 Harlech Castle, North Wales, *c.*1808-9

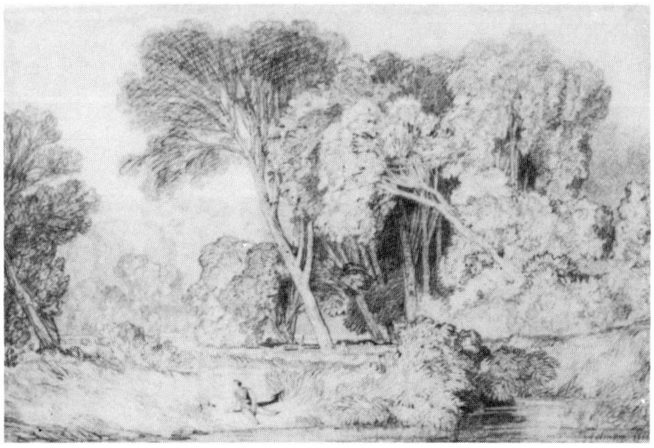

188 Walsingham, Norfolk, 1810

over the grounded plate. Once the sheet was removed, a mirror image of the drawing was left on the plate, which could then be immersed in acid in the normal manner associated with etching. This technique reproduces not only the lines of the composition, but their texture as well. Nos. 187 and 188 also represent this final stage of the preparation of the plate.

A similar pencil drawing[3] at Norwich shows the same composition with two artists sketching in the right foreground. However this is more closely related to a drawing copy,[4] of which a pupil's copy[5] is in the Victoria and Albert Museum.

[1]Popham No. 318. [2]*Bambro' Castle, Northumberland* 1808 (Popham No. 323); *Dolbadern Castle, N. Wales* 1809 (Popham No. 307), see Kitson 1937 p. 136. [3]NCM 491.235.951. [4]No. 2076 (Christie's, 9 Nov. 1976, lot 58). [5]V&A E3213-1948.

187 Harlech Castle, North Wales, *c.*1808-9

Pencil with chalk on tracing paper; 18.2 × 12.5 ($7\frac{3}{8}$ × $4\frac{7}{8}$). INSCR: *Recto,* in pencil l.l. *41.* PROV: See No. 186. (493.235.951). REF: Rajnai & Allthorpe No. 7 n.10.

This drawing was instrumental in the production of the plate[1] for Cotman's soft ground etching, published by Bohn as plate 29 of the *Liber Studiorum* in 1838. Unlike the design for No. 186, there is no known on-the-spot drawing for this composition, which shows the castle gatehouse from the north-east.

The broken branches, rocky outcrop and waterfall recall the design for *The Judgement of Midas,* published as plate 6 in the *Liber Studiorum* (see No. 149). As in the case of a number of the soft ground etchings of this period, Cotman evinces a strong affinity with Gaspar Poussin (see also No. 188).[2]

See Nos. 11, 12 and 186 for other drawings of Harlech Castle by Cotman.

[1]Popham No. 322. [2]Cotman's relationship to Gaspar Poussin in his soft ground etchings in particular is discussed by Anne French, *Gaspar Dughet, called Gaspar Poussin 1615-75,* GLC, 1980, pp. 93, 94.

188 Walsingham, Norfolk, 1810

Pencil on tracing paper; 15.0 × 22.3 ($5\frac{7}{8}$ × $8\frac{3}{4}$). INSCR: *Recto,* signed and dated in pencil l.r. *J. S. Cotman 1810.* PROV: Possibly the same as for No. 186; R. J. Colman Bequest, 1946. (607.235.951). REF: Rajnai & Allthorpe No. 122, n.6.

This drawing represents a stage in the production of the plate for Cotman's soft ground etching, finally published by Bohn, as plate 5[1] of the *Liber Studiorum* in 1838. A comparison between the two versions reveals a degree of additional roulette work on the final plate, particularly in the hatched shading of the trees.[2]

[1]Popham No. 300. [2]For other Cotman drawings of Walsingham subjects see Rajnai & Allthorpe No. 122.

Exhibitions

This index contains details of exhibitions to which drawings in this catalogue were lent. Since 1946, drawings from the Colman Collection have not been lent to exhibitions because of the terms of the Colman Bequest. The abbreviated titles are those used in the text.

RA 1802
London, Royal Academy.

RA 1805
London, Royal Academy.

Norwich Society 1807
Norwich, Sir Benjamin Wrenche's Court, *Third Exhibition by the Norwich Society of Artists, consisting of Paintings and Drawings.*

Norwich Society 1808
Fourth Exhibition (see 1807 above).

Norwich Society 1809
Fifth Exhibition (see 1807 above).

BI 1810
London, British Institution.

Norwich Society 1810
Sixth Exhibition (see 1807 above).

APW 1810
London, 16 Old Bond St., The Associated Painters in Water Colour.

Norwich Society 1812
Eighth Exhibition (see 1807 above).

Norwich Society 1823
Eighteenth Exhibition (see 1807 above).

BI 1823
London, British Institution.

Norwich Society 1824
Nineteenth Exhibition (see 1807 above).

OWCS 1825
London, The Old Water-Colour Society.

OWCS 1826
London, The Old Water-Colour Society.

Norwich Society 1830
Norwich, Exchange Street, *Twenty-third Exhibition of the Norfolk and Suffolk Institution for the promotion of the Fine Arts, consisting of Paintings Drawings and Engravings.*

Norwich Society 1832
Twenty-Fifth Exhibition (see 1830 above).

OWCS 1833
London, The Old Water-Colour Society.

OWCS 1834
London, The Old Water-Colour Society.

Norwich 1839
Norwich, St. Andrew's Broad Street, *The First Exhibition of the Norfolk and Norwich Art-Union.*

Norwich 1856
Norwich, Exhibition Rooms, Broad Street, St. Andrew's, *Exhibition of the Norfolk & Norwich Fine Arts Association and of the Photographic Society.*

Norwich 1860
Norwich, Government School of Art, Norfolk and Norwich Fine Arts Association, *Exhibition of the Works of Deceased Local Artists.*

Norwich 1867
Norwich, St. Andrew's Hall, *Norwich and Eastern Counties Working Classes Industrial Exhibition.*

London, International Exhibition 1874
London, Victoria & Albert Museum, *International Exhibition of Art and Industry.*

Norwich 1874
Norwich, St. Andrew's Hall, British Medical Association, *A Loan Collection of the Works of Norfolk and Suffolk Artists, exhibited at the Soirée.*

RA 1878
London, Royal Academy, *Exhibition of Works by the Old Masters, and by Deceased Masters of the British School, Including a Special Selection from the Works of the Principal Representatives of the Norwich School.*

London, Suffolk Street 1878
London, Suffolk Street Galleries, *Mr. Cox's Exhibition of Pictures by the Old Masters . . . and by Deceased Artists of the British School, including those of the Norwich School.*

Norwich 1878
Norwich, St. Andrew's Hall, *Art Loan Exhibition in aid of the fund for the Restoration of St. Peter Mancroft Church.*

RA 1882
London, Royal Academy, *Winter Exhibition*

London, Conduit Street 1882.

Swaffham 1882
Swaffham, Assembly Rooms, *Fine Art Exhibition.*

Norwich 1883
Norwich, *Fine Art Exhibition in aid of the New Norfolk & Norwich Hospital.*

Norwich 1885
Norwich, St. Andrew's Hall, *Art Loan Exhibition in aid of the fund for the Restoration of St. Peter Mancroft Church.*

Newcastle 1887
Newcastle, *Royal Mining, Engineering and Industrial Exhibition (International and Colonial), Jubilee Year.*

Grosvenor Gallery 1888
London, Grosvenor Gallery, Winter Exhibition, *A Century of British Art.*

Norwich, Art Cirle 1888
Norwich, Old Bank of England Chambers, Queen Street, *Norwich Art Circle Ninth Exhibition, Drawings by the late John Sell Cotman.*

BFAC 1888
London, Burlington Fine Arts Club, *Exhibition of Drawings in Water Colour and in Black and White by John Sell Cotman.*

Gt. Yarmouth 1889
Great Yarmouth, Town Hall, *Art Loan Exhibition in aid of the Book Fund of the Free Library.*

London, Whitechapel, St. Judes 1889.

RA 1891
London, Royal Academy, *Exhibition of Works by the Old Masters.*

RA Winter Exhibition 1892
London, Royal Academy, *Exhibition of works by the Old Masters and by deceased masters of the British School including a collection of watercolour drawings, studies and sketches from nature.*

Norwich 1894
Norwich Agricultural Hall Gallery, *Collection of Pictures and Water-Colour Drawings exhibited . . . during the Grand Oriental Bazaar, Promoted by the CEYMS and the YMCA combined.*

RA Winter Exhibition 1894
London, Royal Academy, *Winter Exhibition.*

London, Guildhall 1896
London, Corporation of London Art Gallery, The Guildhall, *Loan Collection of Watercolour Drawings.*

Earls Court 1897
London, Earls Court, *The Victorian Era.*

Norwich 1902
Norwich, St. Andrew's Hall, *Art Loan Exhibition in Aid of the Funds of St. George's Club for Working Girls.*

Norwich 1903
Norwich, Castle Museum, *Loan Collection of Drawings in the New Picture Gallery.*

Paris 1906
Paris, Galeries Shirleys, 9 Boulevard Malesherbes, *Exposition Rétrospective des Aquarelles et Dessins des Maîtres Anglais des XVIIIe et XIXe siècles,* No lenders are given in the catalogue, whose introduction was written by Percy Moore Turner.

Carfax Gallery 1911
London, Carfax Gallery.

Manchester 1912
Manchester, Whitworth Art Gallery, *Loan Exhibition of Water Colour Drawings by Deceased British Artists, Also of a Collection of Paintings and Drawings by J. Sell Cotman.*

London, Paterson Gallery 1913
London, 5 Old Bond St. Wm. B. Paterson, *Loan Collection of Pictures and Drawings by R. P. Bonington and J. S. Cotman.*

Norwich, Crome Centenary 1921
Norwich, Castle Museum, *Crome Centenary Exhibition.*

Tate 1922
London, National Gallery, Millbank, *Exhibition of Works by John Sell Cotman and some related painters of the Norwich School.*

Wembley 1924 and 1925
London, Wembley, *British Empire Exhibition.*

Norwich 1925
Norwich, Castle Museum, *Centenary of Norwich Museum, Loan Collection of Pictures Illustrative of the Evolution of Painting from the XVIIth century to the Present Day.*

Exhibitions continued

London, Walker's Galleries 1926
London, Walker's Galleries, *John Sell Cotmans from the Bulwer Collection.*

London, Suffolk Street 1927
London, Suffolk Street, Royal Society of British Artists, *Pictures and drawings being the entire Collection of the late W. A. Coates, Esqre.*

Ipswich 1927
Ipswich Museum, *Bicentenary Memorial Exhibition of Thomas Gainsborough, RA.*

London, Olympia 1927 & 1928
London, Olympia, *Daily Telegraph Exhibition of Antiques and Works of Art.*

Brussels 1929
Brussels, Musée Moderne, *Peinture Anglaise,* Retrospective British Art.

Tokyo 1929
Tokyo, Teikoku Bijutsu, *European Painting.*

Norwich 1930-31
Norwich, Castle Museum, R. J. Colman lent nearly 100 oils and drawings from his collection.

RA 1934
London, Royal Academy, *Exhibition of British Art c. 1000-1860.*

Bucharest, British Council 1935-36
Bucharest, *British Art,* British Council.

London, Wildenstein's Galleries 1937
London, Wildenstein's Galleries, Bond Street, *Centenary Memorial Exhibition of John Constable RA, His Origins and Influence.*

London, Agnew 1938
London, Thomas Agnew & Sons Ltd., *The Sixty Fifth Annual Exhibition of Water-Colours and Pencil Drawings.*

Paris 1938
Paris, Louvre, *La Peinture Anglaise XVIII*e *et XIX*e *siècles.*

Norwich 1942
Norwich, Castle Museum, *The Seven Cotmans, Loan Exhibition of Pictures to mark the centenary of the death of John Sell Cotman.*

Norwich 1945
Norwich, Castle Museum, R. J. Colman lent 13 oils and 84 watercolours.

Arts Council, Norwich School of Painting 1947
Arts Council travelling exhibition, *The Norwich School of Painting.*

Arts Council 1947
Arts Council, *English Romantic Art.*

Norwich, Arts Council 1947
Norwich, Castle Museum, *Loan Exhibition of Water Colours by John Sell Cotman from the Colman Collection.*

Lowestoft 1948
Lowestoft, Art Centre, *Loan Exhibition of Watercolours of the Norwich School.*

Cambridge, Arts Council 1948
Cambridge, *Loan Exhibition of Water-Colours of the Norwich School.*

Leeuwarden 1948
Holland, Leeuwarden, Friesch Museum, *Paintings and Watercolours of the Norwich School.*

British Council 1949
Lisbon and Madrid, *One Hundred Years of British Painting 1730-1830,* British Council.

British Council 1949-50
Hamburg, Kunsthalle; Oslo, Kunstnerneshus; Stockholm, Nationalmuseum; Copenhagen, Statens Museum fur Kunst, *British Painting from Hogarth to Turner,* British Council.

Aldeburgh, Third Festival 1950
Aldeburgh, *Third Festival Exhibition,* June.

Kettering 1952
Kettering, Alfred East Art Gallery, *Crome, Cotman and the Norwich Artists.*

Stoke-on-Trent 1953
Stoke-on-Trent, Hanley Museum and Art Gallery, *Norwich School Exhibition.*

Paris 1953
Paris, Orangerie des Tuileries, *Le Paysage Anglais de Gainsborough a Turner.*

Hampstead 1953
Hampstead Artists' Council, *Artists at Work from Sketch to Finish.*

Harrogate 1953
Harrogate Art Gallery, *Exhibition of Norwich School Painting.*

Art Exhibitions Bureau 1953-54
Nottingham, Southsea and Bolton, *The Norwich School of Painting,* Art Exhibitions Bureau.

Kidderminster 1954
Kidderminster Art Gallery, *Water Colours of the Norwich School.*

Rotterdam 1955
Rotterdam, Museum Boymans, *Engelse landschapschilders van Gainsborough tot Turner,* British Council.

Geneva & Zurich 1955-56
Geneva, Le Musée Rath and Zurich, Le Cabinet des Estampes de l'école polytechnique federale, *L'Aquarelle Anglaise 1750-1850.*

Norwich 1956
Norwich, Castle Museum, *Water-Colours by British Landscape Painters (c.1820 to c.1870).*

King's Lynn 1956
King's Lynn, The Guildhall of St. George, *Architectural Drawings and Watercolours by John Sell Cotman.*

Leicester 1956
Leicester Museums and Art Gallery, *A Hundred Years of British Landscape Painting 1750-1850.*

Worthing 1957
Worthing Art Gallery, *Norwich School Painters.*

Agnew 1958
London, Thomas Agnew & Sons Ltd., *Crome and Cotman, Exhibition in aid of the Friends of the Norwich Museums.*

Derby & Nottingham 1959
Derby, Museum and Art Gallery, and Nottingham, University Art Gallery, *Norwich School.*

Council of Europe 1959
London, Tate Gallery, *The Romantic Movement,* Council of Europe.

Bedford 1960
Bedford, Cecil Higgins Museum, *John Sell Cotman.*

Manchester 1961
Manchester, Whitworth Art Gallery, *The Norwich School.*

RA 1961-62
London, Royal Academy, *Primitives to Picasso.*

China & Berlin 1963-64
China: Peking, Shangai, Nanking, Chungking, Sian, Canton and Shenyang, *British watercolour painting during three centuries,* 1963 and Berlin, National Gallery, *English Watercolours, 1964.*

Swansea 1964
Swansea, Glynn Vivian Art Gallery, *Art in Wales,* Arts Council.

Bedford & Cambridge 1966
Bedford, Cecil Higgins Museum, and Cambridge, The Arts Council Gallery *Norwich School Pictures.*

British Council 1966-67
Cologne, Rome, Warsaw and Zurich, *British Painting from Hogarth to Turner,* British Council.

USA 1967
Florida, Tennessee and Louisiana, USA, *Landscapes of the Norwich School.*

Rouen 1967
Rouen, Musée des Beaux-Arts, *Watercolours of the Norwich School.*

Kenwood 1969
London, Kenwood, The Iveagh Bequest, *Drawings of the Norwich School.*

Norwich 1969 and V & A 1970
Norwich, Castle Museum, and London, Victoria & Albert Museum, *A Decade of English Naturalism 1810-1820.*

King's Lynn 1970
King's Lynn Museum and Art Gallery, *King's Lynn 20th Festival Exhibition, The Cotman Family.*

Colnaghi 1970
London, P. & D. Colnaghi & Co. Ltd., *A Loan Exhibition of Drawings and Watercolours by East Anglian Artists of the 18th and 19th Centuries.*

Japan 1970
Tokyo, National Museum of Western Art, and Kyoto, National Museum of Modern Art, *18th — 19th century British Landscape Painting.*

Paris 1972
Paris, Petit Palais, *La peinture romantique anglaise et les préraphaelites.*

Tate 1973
London, Tate Gallery, *Landscape in Britain c.1750-1850.*

Milan 1975
Milan, Palazzo Reale, *Pittura inglese 1660-1840,* British Council.

Hamburg 1976
Hamburger Kunsthalle, *William Turner und die Landschaft seiner Zeit.*

Harlow 1976
Harlow, The Playhouse, *East Anglian Landscape.*

The Hague 1977
Haags Gemeentemuseum, *Romantische Aquarellen de Norwich School.*

Bordeaux 1977
Bordeaux, Galerie des Beaux-Arts, *La peinture britanntique de Gainsborough à Bacon.*

Ipswich 1978
Ipswich, Ipswich Museums, Christchurch Mansion, *Leonard Squirrell Retrospective.*

Sudbury 1978
Sudbury, Gainsborough's House, *Paintings and Drawings by J. S. Cotman.*

Brighton 1979
Brighton Art Gallery & Museum, *Painters of the Sea.*

Munich 1979-80
Munich, Haus der Kunst, *Zwei Jahrhunderte Englische Malerei, Britische Kunst und Europa 1680 bis 1880.*

Norwich 1980
Norwich, Sainsbury Centre for Visual Arts, *Medieval Sculpture from Norwich Cathedral.*

Koblenz 1980
Koblenz, Mittelrhein-Museum, *Watercolours of the Norwich School from the Castle Museum, Norwich.*

Nottingham 1981
Nottingham, Castle Museum, *Great British Watercolours.*

USA 1981-82
New York, Omaha, Los Angeles and Chicago, *Before Photography. Painting and the Invention of Photography.*

China 1982
Peking, Shenyang and Hong Kong, *British Drawings and Watercolours,* British Council.

Important Cotman Sales

1824 Christie's Sat. 1st May 1824
'A highly valuable and interesting collection of two hundred and fifty original drawings in pencil, sepia and colours, by that distinguished artist Mr. J.S. Cotman, consisting of one hundred and fifteen views, of picturesque and remarkable subjects in Normandy, which have never been engraved, a few of the original drawings for the plates published in Mr. Cotman's Norman Antiquities, and many beautiful miscellaneous subjects. Which, it is presumed, will form a delightful treat to the antiquary, and the lover of the arts, and well deserve the attention of publishers. The whole of which will be sold by auction, . . .'

Lugt records only two known copies of this catalogue, one with Christie's which is annotated and another in the Frick Art Reference Library, New York. There is however another annotated copy in the library of the National Gallery of Edinburgh

1834 Norwich, Spelman, at the residence of John Sell Cotman, Esq., St. Martin's, Palace Plain, Wed.-Fri. 10th-12th Sept. 1834.
'The extensive and valuable collection of rare and fine engravings and etchings, a few paintings and drawings, library of books, books of prints, a collection of ancient armour, foreign & miscellaneous curiosities, carvings, models, plaster casts, copperplates, and a few remaining articles of household furniture, which will be sold by auction, . . .'

An annotated copy of the catalogue, with notes and a letter with instructions to the auctioneer from Cotman, is in the Art Dept. Archives, NCM. It was formerly in the collection of James Reeve.

1843 Christie's, Wed. & Thurs. 17th-18th May 1843
'The beautiful original works in oils, and water-colours; of that distinguished and highly esteemed artist, John Sell Cotman, Esq., deceased; which (by order of the executors), will be sold by auction, . . .'

1843 Christie's, Tues. 6th June 1843
'The interesting library of German, French and English books, curious antiquarian works and books of prints, including copies of the Normandy and Norfolk, of John Sell Cotman, Esq. deceased. Which (by order of the executor) will be sold by auction, . . .'

1861 Norwich, Spelman, Thurs. 16th May 1861
'The valuable and genuine Cotman Collection, including 120 water colour drawings, paintings, rare old engravings and etchings, late the property of John Sell Cotman, deceased, . . .'

1862 Norwich, Murrell, Wed.-Thurs. 26th-27th Nov. 1862
'Highly important sale by auction of a rare and valuable collection of works of art, by the following artists: John Sell Cotman, Miles Edmund Cotman, Varley, Sillett, Hobart and Teniers, Pritchett, Hannah, S.D. Colkett, Rev. Nursey, and others.'

Manuscript Sources

This list includes all known Cotman sources, given in alphabetical order of location.

Mr. Christopher Barker Collection
Letters from Cotman to Dawson Turner and Dawson Turner family papers, some containing references to Cotman, including letters from Hudson Gurney to Dawson Turner and Elizabeth Turner's Diary June, July 1814. Also Dawson Turner's Journal of a three weeks tour with Thos. Phillips, Esq., R.A. through Rouen, Vernon and Montes to Paris. Autumn, 1815.

Corpus Christi College, Cambridge
Letters from Cotman to Thomas Kerrich.

Trinity College, Cambridge
Letters from Cotman, Auguste Le Prevost and de Gerville to Dawson Turner in the Collected Correspondence of Dawson Turner.

National Gallery of Scotland, Edinburgh
Letters from Cotman to Dawson Turner.

BM, Print Room, London
Letters from Cotman to Dawson Turner; letters to Cotman from Dawson Turner, the Cholmeley family and others. Reeve Collection.

Letters from Cotman to his wife and Dawson Turner from Normandy (see Bibliography under Isherwood Kay, H.) and Cotman letters subsequent to the Normandy Tours. Presented by Mrs. Rowland Barker, 1936-12-12.

BM, Dept. of Manuscripts, London
Letters to and from Cotman, the Cotman family and others. ADD MSS 37029.
Dawson Turner's grangerised Blomefield's *Norfolk*: 53 vols. of drawings and watercolours by the Turner girls and others, including copies after Cotman; with indexes. ADD MSS 23013-52, 23053-67.

National Portrait Gallery, London
Letters from Cotman to John Britton, John Britton Collection.

RA, Library, London
Letter from Cotman to Dawson Turner, Anderdon Catalogues (see Bibliography under Gage, John).

RIBA, Library, London
Letters to and from Cotman and T.L. Donaldson.

V & A Library, London
Letter from Cotman to Dawson Turner.

NCM, Art Dept. Archives
Letters from Cotman to S. Bignold, Hudson Gurney and Mrs. A.M. Hall. Also Mary Ann Turner's Diary: Journal of a tour from London to Rouen and the Northern parts of Normandy, June and July 1818.

Norfolk and Norwich Record Office
Letters from Cotman to Edward Bell, Rev. C.P. Burney and Messrs. Boydell.

North Riding Record Office
Letters from Cotman to the Cholmeley family and Cholmeley family papers (see Bibliography under Holcomb, Adele M., and Ashcroft, M.Y.).

Bibliography

This bibliography serves also as an index to abbreviations and is therefore arranged under authors' names in alphabetical order (or the title of the periodical when the author is anonymous). It contains only sources, both published and unpublished, to which reference is made in the text. Abbreviations, where appropriate, are appended in parentheses. Letters are listed separately under Manuscript Sources.

The Academy 21 July 1888.

Allthorpe-Guyton, Marjorie, *John Thirtle 1777-1839, Drawings in Norwich Castle Museum,* Norfolk Museums Service, 1977.

Allthorpe-Guyton, Marjorie, *The Norwich School,* Norfolk Museums Service Information Sheet, 1979.
(Allthorpe-Guyton 1979)

Allthorpe-Guyton, Marjorie, with Stevens, John, *A Happy Eye. A School of Art in Norwich,* Norwich, Jarrolds, 1982.
(Allthorpe-Guyton & Stevens 1982)

'Norwich School Pictures for Norwich Art Gallery', *Apollo Magazine,* Nov. 1941.
(*Apollo* Nov. 1941)

'Causerie', *Apollo Magazine*, Jan. 1942.
(*Apollo* Jan. 1942)

The Architect 21 April 1922.

Artwork, Autumn 1930.

Art Union Oct. 1839.

Barnard, G.V., 'The Nation's Treasures: Norwich Castle Museum and Art Gallery'. *The Studio,* Aug. 1947.
(Barnard, *The Studio* Aug. 1947)

Barnard, G.V. *Paintings of the Norwich School,* Norwich, n.d., *c.*1950.
(Barnard)

Batchelor, Arthur, 'John Sell Cotman local exhibits at the Tate'; *Eastern Daily Press* 13 April 1922.
(Batchelor, *EDP* 13 April 1922)

Bell, C.F., 'John Sell Cotman (The Bulwer Collection)', *Walker's Quarterly,* Nos. 19-20, June 1926.

Binyon, Laurence, 'The Art of John Sell Cotman'. *The Portfolio,* April 1897.
(Binyon 1897)

Binyon, Laurence, 'Life and Work of John Sell Cotman', Masters of English Landscape Painting, J.S. Cotman, David Cox, Peter de Wint', ed. Charles Holmes, *The Studio,* 1903. Special Number.
(Binyon 1903)

Binyon, Laurence, 'The Art of John Sell Cotman', *Burlington Magazine* Cotman Number, July 1942.
(Binyon, *Burlington* July 1942)

Blomefield, Francis, . . . *A Topographical History of the County of Norfolk* . . . 2nd edition 11 vols, London 1805-1810. First published 1745.

Brayley, Edward, and Britton, John, *The Beauties of England and Wales or Delineation Topographical, Historical and Descriptive,* London, 15 vols, 1801-?1826

The British Heritage, London, Oldhams Press Ltd, 1948.
(*British Heritage* 1948)

Britton, John, *The Architectural Antiquities of Great Britain,* vol. 2, London, 1809.

Brooks, Vincent, *Five examples of Sepia Drawings after Cotman prepared for the Use of Schools in Connection with the Board of Trade Department of Science and Art* Lithographed by Vincent Brooks, Day & Son, London. Printed and Published for the Department of Science and Art by Vincent Brooks, Day & Son, Gate Street, Lincoln's Inn Fields and Sold by Chapman and Hall 193 Piccadilly. 1st edition 1863, 2nd edition 1870.

Brooks, Vincent, *Nine Examples of Pencil Drawings after Cotman* . . . (as above), published 1873.

Burlington Magazine, Nov. 1936.
(*Burlington* Nov. 1936)

Butlin, Martin, and Joll, Evelyn, *The Paintings of J.M.W. Turner,* pub. for The Paul Mellon Centre for Studies in British Art and The Tate Gallery, New Haven and London, Yale University Press, 1977.
(Butlin & Joll)

Chambers, John, *A General History of the County of Norfolk, intended to convey all the Information of a Norfolk Tour* . . . 2 vols, Norwich and London 1829.

The Christian Science Monitor Oct. 1936.

Churchill, W. A., *Watermarks in Paper in Holland, England, France, etc, in the XVII and XVIII centuries,* Amsterdam, Menno Hertzberger & Co., 1935.

Clifford, Derek, *Watercolours of the Norwich School,* London, Cory, Adams & Mackay, 1965.
(Clifford)

Collins Baker, C. H., and James, Montague R, *British Painting,* London, The Medici Society, 1933.
(Collins Baker & James 1933)

Norwich Castle Museum, *The Colman Collection of Norwich School Pictures, Illustrated Guide,* 1951.
(*Colman Collection Guide* 1951)

'*The Norwich School of Painting* by W. F. Dickes Reviewed', *The Connoisseur,* May 1906.
(*Connoisseur* May 1906)

Conrad, H. E., *England, Ein Führer,* München, Prestel-Verlag, 1977.
(Conrad 1977)

Cordingly, David, *Marine Painting in England 1700-1900,* London, Studio Vista, 1974.
(Cordingly 1974)

Cundall, H. M., 'The Norwich School' ed. Geoffrey Holme, *The Studio,* 1920. Special Number.
(Cundall, *The Studio* 1920)

AMB 'Cotman Honoured. Notable Exhibition of Norwich Artist's Work at Tate Gallery', *Daily Chronicle* 6 April 1922.
(*Daily Chronicle* 6 April 1922)

Davis, Frank, 'Norwich Castle's Treasury of Local Landscape Artists', *Illustrated London News,* 2 Oct. 1965.
(Davis, *ILN* 1965)

Day, Harold A. E. *East Anglian Painters,* vol. III, Eastbourne, Eastbourne Fine Art, 1969.
(Day 1969 vol. III)

Dickes, W. F., *The Norwich School of Painting,* London and Norwich, Jarrold & Sons Ltd., 1905.
(Dickes)

Eastern Daily Press. Specific references made in the text.
(EDP)

Eastern Evening News. Specific references made in the text.
(EEN)

Eurich, Richard 'Paintings that Inspire. The Baggage Wagon by Cotman', *The Artist,* April 1966.
(Eurich 1966)

Excursions in the County of Norfolk, two vols, London, 1818, 1819.

Farmer, Rita L, 'The descent to Yarmouth', *East Anglian Magazine,* Feb 1970.
(Farmer, *East Anglian Magazine* Feb. 1970)

French, Anne, *Gaspard Dughet called Gaspar Poussin 1615-75, A French landscape painter in seventeenth century Rome and his influence on British Art,* Greater London Council, The Iveagh Bequest, Kenwood 1980.

Gage, John, 'Documents of Crome and Cotman', *Burlington Magazine,* April 1969.

Girtin, Thomas, and Loshak, David, *The Art of Thomas Girtin,* London, Adam & Charles Black, 1945.

Goldberg, Norman L., 'America honours the Norwich School', *The Connoisseur,* Feb. 1967.
(Goldberg, *Connoisseur* Feb. 1967)

Goldberg, Norman L., *John Crome the Elder,* New York University Press, 1978.
(Goldberg 1978)

Gordon, Jan ' "Dying" Cotman Pictures, Masterpieces saved', *The Observer,* 20 Sept, 1936.
(Gordon, *Observer* 20 Sept. 1963)

Graves, Algernon, *A Century of Loan Exhibitions 1813-1912,* 5 vols., London, pub. Algernon Graves, 1913-1915.

Guillemard, Dr., 'Girtin's Sketching Club', *The Connoisseur,* Aug. 1922.

Hamilton, Jean, *The Sketching Society 1799-1851,* London, V & A, 1971.

Hardie, Martin, 'Cotman's Water-Colours: The Technical Aspect', *Burlington Magazine* Cotman Number, July 1942.
(Hardie, *Burlington* July 1942)

Hardie, Martin, *Water-colour Painting in Britain,* 3 vols. ed. Dudley Snelgrove, Jonathan Mayne and Basil Taylor, London, B. T. Batsford Ltd., 1966-1968.
(Hardie, vol. 2)

Hawcroft, Francis W., 'The Norwich School', *The Mackintosh Caley Monthly News,* vol. 11, No. 5, May 1959.
(Hawcroft, *MC News* 1959)

Hawcroft, Francis W., 'The Norwich School of Painting', *The RCH Magazine,* vol. 8 no. 2, 1966.
(Hawcroft, *RCH Magazine)*

Hemingway, Andrew, 'Cotman's "Architectural Antiquities of Normandy": Some amendments to Kitson's account', *The Walpole Society,* 46th volume 1978.

Hemingway, Andrew, *The Norwich School of Painters,* Oxford, Phaidon, 1979.
(Hemingway 1979)

Herrmann, Luke, *Il Paesaggio Nella Pittura Inglese dell 'Ottocento,* Milan, Fratelli Fabbri Editori, 1967.
(Herrmann 1967)

Holcomb, Adele M., *John Sell Cotman,* British Museum Prints and Drawing Series, London, British Museum Publications Ltd., 1978.
(Holcomb 1978)

Holcomb, Adele M., and Ashcroft, M. Y., *John Sell Cotman in the Cholmeley Archive,* North Yorkshire County Record Office Publications No. 22, Aug. 1980.

Holmes, C. J., 'John Sell Cotman as a Painter in Oils', *Burlington Magazine,* Jan. 1904.
(Holmes, *Burlington* 1904)

Isherwood Kay, H., 'John Sell Cotman's Letters from Normandy 1817-1820', Parts I and II, *The Walpole Society,* vols. XIV and XV, Oxford University Press 1926-27.

Isherwood Kay, H, 'Moreton Old Hall. A Painting by John Sell Cotman'. *The Connoisseur,* Feb. 1936.
(Isherwood Kay *Connoisseur* Feb. 1936)

Jacobs, Michael, and Warner, Malcolm, *The Phaidon Companion to Art and Artists in the British Isles,* Oxford, Phaidon, 1980.
(Jacobs & Warner 1980)

Kaines Smith, S. C., *Cotman, British Artist Series,* London, Philip Allan & Co, 1926.
(Kaines Smith 1926)

Kennedy North, S. K. *Report on the Treatment of Watercolour drawings by John Sell Cotman and John Crome in the Colman Collection, Norwich, carried out between September 1934 and August 1936,* with photographs, October 1936. Privately printed.

Ketton-Cremer, R. W, *Felbrigg,* London, Rupert Hart-Davis, 1962.

Kitson, Sydney D., 'John Sell Cotman', *The Old Water Colour Society's Club, Seventh Annual Volume,* ed. Randall Davies, 1930.
(Kitson, *OWCS* 1930)

Kitson, Sydney D.,'The Colman Collection of Works by the Norwich Painters', *Country Life,* 7 Nov. 1936.
(Kitson, *Country Life* 7 Nov. 1936)

Kitson, Sydney D., 'More Cotman Discoveries — Sketches as "Backings", *The Illustrated London News,* 23 Jan. 1937.

Kitson, Sydney D., *The Life of John Sell Cotman,* London, Faber & Faber, 1937.
(Kitson 1937)

Kitson, Sydney D., 'The Norwich School of Painting with special reference to the work of John Sell Cotman', *The Colman Collection Catalogue,* privately printed for R. J. Colman, Oxford University Press, 1942.

Maas, Jeremy, *Victorian Painters,* London, Barrie & Rockliff, 1969.
(Maas 1969)

MacColl, D.S., 'Cotman', *The Saturday Review,* 15 April 1922.
(MacColl, *Saturday Review* 15 April 1922)

Mallalieu, Huon, *The Norwich School, Crome, Cotman and their Followers,* London, Academy Editions, & New York, St. Martin's Press, 1974.
(Mallalieu 1974)

Morning Post. Specific references made in the text.

Grundy, Frederick John, *A Catalogue of the Pictures and Drawings in the Collection of Frederick John Nettlefold,* 4 vols., London and Derby, 1933.
(Nettlefold Catalogue)

Norfolk Chronicle. Specific references made in the text.

Catalogue of the Pictures, Drawings, Etchings and Bronzes in the Picture Gallery of the Norwich Castle Museum, no. date (1897. According to Geo.A. Stephen, 'Norfolk Celebrities' II. *Norfolk Artists An Annotated Catalogue of the Books, Pamphlets and Articles Relating to Deceased Norfolk Artists in the Norwich Public Library,* published Norwich 1915 p. 6). Printed Jarrold & Sons, Norwich.
(NCM ?1897)

- 2nd Edition, no date (1899. According to Stephen *op. cit.*). Printed Edward Burgess & Sons Ltd., Norwich.
(NCM ?1899)

- 3rd Edition 1904. Printed Edward Burgess & Sons Ltd., Norwich.
(NCM 1904)

- 4th Edition 1909. Printed 'Norwich Mercury' Co. Ltd., Norwich. Illustrated.
(NCM 1909)

Catalogue of the Norwich School and Other Pictures in the Art Galleries of the Norwich Castle Museum. 1937. Printed A. E. Soman & Co. Ltd., Norwich. Illustrated.
(NCM 1937)

Norwich Mercury. Specific references made in the text.

Oppé, A. P., 'The watercolour drawings of John Sell Cotman', ed. Geoffrey Holme, *The Studio,* 1923. Special Number.

Oppé, A. P. 'Cotman and the Sketching Society', *The Connoisseur,* Dec. 1923.

Oppé, A. P. 'Cotman and his Public', *Burlington Magazine* Cotman Number, July 1942.

Oppé A. P. 'The Colman Exhibition of Cotman at Norwich', *Burlington Magazine,* Aug. 1945.
(Oppé, *Burlington* Aug. 1945)

Hind, C. Lewis, 'Water-Colours: Then and Now. From Cotman to Dodge Mackintosh', *Pall Mall,* 12 April 1922.
(*Pall Mall* 12 April 1922)

Palmer, Charles John, *The Perlustration of Great Yarmouth,* 3 vols., Great Yarmouth, 1872-1875.

Parker, Constance-Anne, 'The Norwich School, or The Death of the Blues', *In Britain,* Oct. 1975.
(Parker, *In Britain* 1975)

Pevsner, Nikolaus, *The Buildings of England, North-East Norfolk and Norwich,* Penguin Books, 1962.

Pevsner, Nikolaus, *The Buildings of England, North-West and South Norfolk,* Penguin Books, 1962.

Pevsner, Nikolaus, *The Buildings of England, Staffordshire,* Penguin Books, 1974.

Pevsner, Nikolaus, *The Buildings of England Yorkshire: The North Riding,* Penguin Books, 1966.

Pidgley, Michael, 'Cornelius Varley, Cotman and the Graphic Telescope', *Burlington Magazine,* Nov, 1972.

Pidgley. Michael, *John Sell Cotman's Patrons and the Romantic Subject Picture in the 1820s and 1830s,* Unpublished Doctoral Thesis, University of East Anglia, 1975.
(Pidgley)

Popham, A. E., 'The Etchings of J. S. Cotman', *The Print Collectors' Quarterly,* London, J. M. Dent & Sons Ltd, Oct. 1922.
(Popham)

Rajnai, Miklós, assisted by Allthorpe-Guyton, Marjorie, *John Sell Cotman Drawings of Normandy in Norwich Castle Museum,* Norfolk Museums Service 1975.
(Rajnai 1975)

Rajnai, Miklós, *The Norwich School of Painters,* Norwich, Jarrold Arts Series, 1978.
(Rajnai 1978)

Bibliography continued

Rajnai, Miklós, and Allthorpe-Guyton, Marjorie, *John Sell Cotman 1782-1842, Early Drawings (1798-1812) in Norwich Castle Museum,* Norfolk Museums Service, 1979.
(Rajnai & Allthorpe)

Rajnai, Miklós, assisted by Stevens, Mary, *The Norwich Society of Artists 1805-1833, A dictionary of contributors and their work,* pub. for the Paul Mellon Centre for Studies of British Art, by the Norfolk Museums Service, 1976.

The RCH Magazine, Magazine of the Reckitt & Colman Holdings Group of Companies, Christmas 1964.
(*RCH Magazine* Christmas 1964)

Rienaecker, Victor, *John Sell Cotman 1782-1842,* Leigh-on-Sea, F. Lewis, 1953.
(Rienaecker)

Robertson, J. Logie, ed. *The Poetical Works of Sir Walter Scott,* Oxford University Press, first pub. 1904.

Roget, John Lewis, *A History of the 'Old Water-Colour' Society now The Royal Society of Painters in Water Colours,* originally published London, Longmans, Green & Co. 1891, reprinted Woodbridge, Antique Collectors Club, 1972.
(Roget vols. i & ii 1891 (1972))

Rushton, Ray, 'John Sell Cotman — The Great Years: Norwich Castle Museum', *The Royal Sociey of Arts Journal,* Aug. 1979.
(*RSA Journal* Aug. 1979)

Rutter, Frank, 'Homage to Cotman. Russell Colman Collection. Anticipating the Surrealists', *Sunday Times,* 20 Sept. 1936.
(Rutter, *Sunday Times* 20 Sept. 1936)

Rutter, Frank, 'Cotman sketches pasted on the back of Cotman Water-Colours: newly found examples of the Great Norwich Landscape Artist's Work', *The Illustrated London News,* 19 Sept. 1936.
(Rutter, *ILN* Sept. 1936)

Stothard, Mrs. Charles, *Letters written during a Tour through Normandy, Britanny, and other parts of France in 1818: including local and historical descriptions; with remarks on the manners and characters of the people. With numerous engravings, after drawings by Charles Stothard, FSA,* London, Longman 1820.

The Times Specific references made in the text.
(Times)

Turner, Dawson, *Account of a Tour in Normandy; undertaken chiefly for the purpose of investigating the Architectural Antiquities of the Duchy, with observations on its History, on the Country, and on its inhabitants. Illustrated with numerous engravings,* 2 vols, London 1820.

Drawings of Architecture and Scenery in Normandy 1822. Volume with 116 pages of pencil and brown wash drawings by Elizabeth and Mary Anne Turner, Collection Christopher Barker. (Dawson Turner's Library sale, Puttick & Simpson, 5th day, Fri. 20 May 1859, lot 1413).

Warren, Geoffrey A., 'The Genius of Water-Colour', *Norfolk Fair,* Sept.-Oct.1968.
(Warren, *Norfolk Fair* 1968)

Wedmore, Frederick, 'John Sell Cotman', *The Magazine of Art,* Oct. 1888.

Wilenski, R. H., *English Painting,* Faber, 1933.
(Wilenski 1933)

Williams, Iolo A., 'Early English Watercolours and some cognate drawings by artists born not later than 1785', London, 1952. Published by *The Connoisseur.*
(Iolo Williams)

Worsley, W. A., *Early English Water-Colours at Hovingham Hall,* 1963 exhibition catalogue.

Vignette from the title page of
A Narrative of the Grand Festival at Great Yarmouth, 1814 (see No. 173)

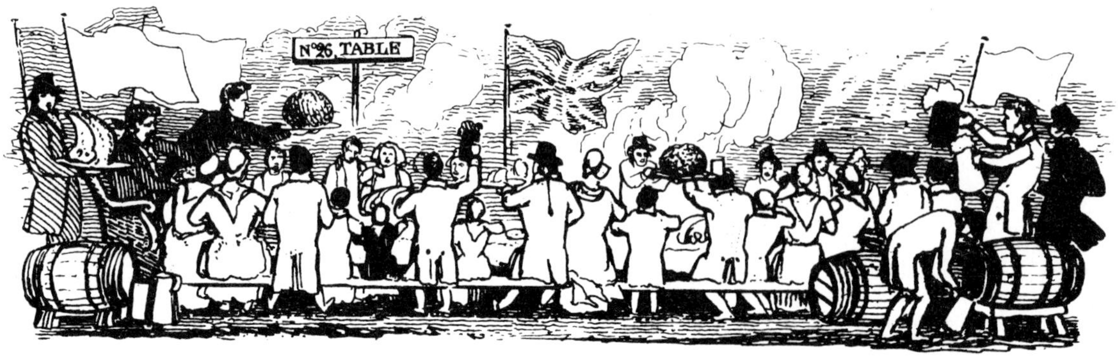